HORACE

HORACE

BY

EDUARD FRAENKEL

CLARENDON PRESS · OXFORD

Oxford University Press, Walton Street, Oxford OX2 6DP

OXFORD LONDON GLASGOW
NEW YORK TORONTO MELBOURNE WELLINGTON
KUALA LUMPUR SINGAPORE HONG KONG TOKYO
DELHI BOMBAY CALCUTTA MADRAS KARACHI
NAIROBI DAR ES SALAAM CAPE TOWN

First published 1957
Reprinted as paperback 1980

British Library Cataloguing in Publication Data
Fraenkel, Eduard
   Horace.
   1. Horace – Criticism and interpretation
   871'.01   80–41456
   ISBN 0–19–814376–1

Printed in Great Britain
at the University Press, Oxford
by Eric Buckley
Printer to the University

TO
CORPUS CHRISTI COLLEGE
OXFORD

PREFACE

THIS book is not meant to be a biography of Horace nor does it deal primarily with such topics as Horace and his age, Horace and Roman history, Horace and Greek poetry, Horace and religion, Horace and women, Horace and politics, Horace and philosophy. These and similar themes have been amply discussed in many books and articles, some of which are useful. My own purpose is a different one. I assume that in approaching a real poet it should be our main concern to try to understand his poetry. This task, in the case of Horace, is far more difficult than might appear at first sight.

Throughout his poetic career Horace showed himself an exacting author. He cared little about pleasing the average reader, but preferred to write for a few highly educated men who would be prepared to give him their undivided attention and who would be awake to the careful structure of a poem and to its minute detail, subtle hints, sometimes elusive transitions. Small wonder, then, that his publication of three books of *carmina* in 23 B.C. proved a failure as far as the general public in Rome was concerned.

But it is not only the intrinsic character of Horace's work but also its later history, in particular the use made of it for the purposes of school teaching, that has caused most of the modern reader's difficulties. Nowadays it has become almost impossible to approach one of Horace's poems with an unprejudiced mind. *Expertus dico.* How often did I think that I had completely disentangled myself from the snares of traditional exegesis, only to discover, after decades of intense study, that at some crucial point I was still interpreting not the words of Horace but the unwarranted opinion of some of his commentators. Even now it will probably happen more than once that the specious fallacy of a *fable convenue* defeats my attempts to free myself and others from certain current prejudices. But I may at least claim that what induced me to write this book was my desire to remove from the poems of Horace some of the crusts with which the industry of many centuries has overlaid them and to enable a sympathetic reader to listen as often as possible to the voice of the poet and as seldom as possible to the voices of his learned patrons.

Lest this confession should sound arrogant, I will at once add that without the great work performed by a long series of scholars I could never have considered writing anything about Horace. In my own interpretations I have always tried not to conceal the extent of my debt to others.

No useful purpose would have been served if I had attempted to touch briefly on all the poems of Horace. A rapid glance over a great number of odes or epistles cannot bring us any nearer to an adequate appreciation of such complex works; what is required is a certain measure of calm and concentration. Here it is indeed true that πλέον ἥμισυ παντός. A selection was therefore necessary. But any selection is bound to be influenced to some degree by personal tastes. I can only hope that my own choice will on balance be considered a fair one and that what I have chosen will be sufficient to bring out at any rate the most significant aspects of Horace's writings. I have deliberately allowed a good deal of space for the interpretation of the poems which seem to be most difficult for a modern reader to appreciate. Moreover, I have tried to give an idea of the artistic unity of some of Horace's books. Finally, I have endeavoured to outline the history of his poetry from his early experiments to his maturest and most perfect works.

Since the book is confined to a selection of poems, it may seem strange that it contains a whole chapter on the *Epodes*. I am aware that most of them are not popular with the English-speaking nations. Yet when Horace was working on them he was already well on his way to writing true lyrics; there is in his *Iambi* a good deal that can help us in our attempt to understand the great achievement of his *Carmina*. It follows that some of my observations on the *Epodes* are fundamental to my interpretation of the *Odes*.

The typescript was handed over to the Delegates of the Press at the end of 1955; therefore no literature published after that date could be taken into account.

My first thanks are due to the Delegates of the Clarendon Press for accepting this book for publication at a difficult moment. During the period of printing I have received the kindest support from the Secretary to the Delegates and from the Staff of the Clarendon Press. They never failed me on the many occasions when I turned to them for advice and they were always most generous in complying with my wishes.

For many years I used to bring to Mr. A. F. Wells sections of this book, uncouth, just as I had produced them, *more ursae pariens*, and with infinite delicacy and patience he took charge of them, *lambendo effingens*. At a later stage I enjoyed the kind assistance of Mr. R. G. M. Nisbet: he advised me on many niceties of English style and also helped me with the correction of the proofs. A third friend, Mr. F. A. Lepper, checked for me some points arising out of the *Vita*.

Without my wife's encouragement and practical help the book could not have been written.

During the last twenty-three years Corpus Christi College, Oxford, has been my second home. And when, some time ago, I was faced with the prospect of having my studies cut short, the College came unhesitatingly to my rescue and provided me with magnificent facilities for the continuation of my work. What I now can offer to Corpus is only a small token of my profound and lasting gratitude.

E. F.

Corpus Christi College
Oxford

15 January 1957

CONTENTS

LIST OF ABBREVIATIONS   xiii

I. VITA HORATI   1

II. THE EPODES
    1. Epode X   24
    2. Some preliminary remarks   36
    3. Epode XVI   42
       The construction of *Epod.* 16. 15–16   53
    4. Other epodes in the iambists' manner   55
    5. Epodes of a different type   65
    6. The two Actium epodes   69

III. BOOK I OF THE SATIRES
    1. Satire II   76
    2. Satire III   86
    3. Satire I   90
       The text of *Sat.* 1. 1. 108   97
    4. Satire VI   101
    5. Satire V   105
    6. Satire IX   112
    7. Satire VII   118
    8. Satire VIII   121
    9. Satire IV   124
   10. Satire X   128
       The meaning of *Sat.* 1. 10. 27–30   133

IV. BOOK II OF THE SATIRES
    1. Preliminary remarks   136
    2. Satire VI   138
    3. This book as a whole   144
    4. Satire I   145

V. ODES, BOOKS I–III
    1. Odes related to Alcaeus   154
    2. Odes related to other Greek poems   179
    3. Odes addressed to Maecenas   214
    4. The Odes to Agrippa and Pollio   233
    5. Odes concerned with Augustus   239
    6. The three epilogues   297

VI. EPISTLES, BOOK I

1. Introduction   308
2. Epistle XIV   310
3. Epistles II and XVIII   314
4. Epistle XVII   321
5. Epistle IV   323
6. Epistle VII   327
7. Epistle XIX   339
8. Epistle XIII   350
9. Epistle XX   356

VII. CARMEN SAECULARE   364

VIII. THE LETTER TO AUGUSTUS   383

IX. ODES, BOOK IV

1. Ode VI   400
2. Ode III   407
3. Ode I   410
4. Odes X and XIII   414
5. Odes XI and XII   416
6. Ode VII   419
7. Ode VIII   421
8. Ode IX   423
9. Odes IV and XIV   426
10. Ode II   432
11. Ode V   440
12. Ode XV   449

INDEXES

GENERAL INDEX   455

POEMS & PASSAGES DISCUSSED   461

WORDS: LATIN & GREEK   464

A SELECT LIST OF ABBREVIATIONS

Baxter. Q. Horatii Flacci *Eclogae*, castigavit et notis illustravit Guilielmus Baxterus, varias ... observationes addidit J. Matthias Gesnerus, London 1809.

D. added to quotations from the iambists and the lyric poets refers to *Anthologia Lyrica Graeca*, ed. E. Diehl.

Dacier. Les œuvres d'Horace, traduites en Francois, avec des notes ... par M. Dacier, 10 vols, Paris 1691.

Dillenburger. Q. Horatii Flacci *Opera omnia* recognovit et commentariis ... instruxit Guil. Dillenburger, 4th ed., Bonn 1860.

F Gr Hist *Die Fragmente der griechischen Historiker*, von F. Jacoby. Berlin–Leiden 1923–.

J. M. Gesner. See Baxter.

Giri. Orazio, *Odi ed Epodi*, commentati da G. Giri, 11th ed., 1951.

Heinze. Kiessling's commentary re-edited by R. Heinze:
Odes and Epodes, 7th ed., 1930;
Satires, 5th ed., 1921;
Epistles, 4th ed., 1914.

Kiessling. Q. Horatius Flaccus erklärt von A. Kiessling:
i, *Oden und Epoden*, 2nd ed., 1890;
ii, *Satiren*, 1886;
iii, *Briefe*, 1889.

L. and P. added to quotations from Sappho and Alcaeus refers to the marginal numeration in *Poetarum Lesbiorum Fragmenta* ed. E. Lobel et D. Page, 1955.

Lambinus. Q. Horatius Flaccus, opera Dionys. Lambini ... emendatus ..., commentariis illustratus, 2nd ed., Paris 1568.

Lejay. Horace, *Satires*, publiées par P. Lejay, Paris 1911 (when referring to *Epistles*, 'Lejay' means his small annotated edition in *Œuvres d'Horace*, Texte latin publ. avec ... des notes explicatives par E. Plessis et P. Lejay, 8th ed., Paris 1919).

Lenchantin. Q. Horati Flacci *Carminum libri IV Epodon liber Carmen Saeculare* rec. M. Lenchantin de Gubernatis, Turin 1945.

Mitscherlich. Q. Horatii Flacci *Opera* illustravit Christ. Guil. Mitscherlich, Lipsiae 1800.

L. Müller. Q. Horatius Flaccus, *Oden und Epoden* erklärt von Lucian Müller, 1900.
Satiren und *Episteln* des Horaz, mit Anmerkungen von Lucian Müller, 1891–3.

Obbarius. Q. Horatii Flacci *Carmina*. Kritisch berichtigt, erklärt ... von Theodor Obbarius, Jena 1848.

Orelli–Baiter. Q. Horatius Flaccus rec. I. G. Orellius, editio tertia, cur. I. G. Baiterus, 1850–2.

Orelli–Baiter–Hirschfelder. 4th ed., 1886, of Orelli–Baiter's edition of *Odes, Carm. Saec., Epodes*.

Orelli–Baiter–Mewes. 4th ed., 1892, of Orelli–Baiter's edition of *Satires* and *Epistles*.

Palmer. *The Satires of Horace*, edited, with notes, by Arthur Palmer, London 1883.

Pasquali, *Or. lir.* G. Pasquali, *Orazio lirico*, Florence 1920.

Plessis. Œuvres d'Horace, *Odes, Épodes et Chant Séculaire* publ. par F. Plessis, 1924.

RE Paulys *Real-Encyclopädie der classischen Altertumswissenschaft*; Neue Bearbeitung von G. Wissowa, W. Kroll und K. Mittelhaus. Stuttgart 1894–.

RGVV *Religionsgeschichtliche Versuche und Vorarbeiten*, ed. A. Dieterich, R. Wünsch, L. Malten, etc. 1903–.

Ritter. Q. Horatius Flaccus, comment. . . . illustr. ed. Franciscus Ritter: vol. i, *Carmina et Epodi*; vol. ii, *Satirae et Epistulae*. Lipsiae 1856–7.

Shorey. Horace, *Odes and Epodes* edited . . . by P. Shorey, Boston [1898].

H. Schütz. Q. Horatius Flaccus, erklärt von Hermann Schütz: i, *Oden und Epoden*, 3rd ed., Berlin 1889; ii, *Satiren*, 1881; iii, *Episteln*, 1883.

Tescari. Quinto Orazio Flacco, *I carmi e gli epodi* commentati da O. Tescari, Turin 1936.

Thes. l. L. *Thesaurus linguae Latinae*, 1900–.

Ussani. *Le liriche di Orazio* commentate da V. Ussani (for *Odes*, Book i, the second edition is used, for the rest the third), reprint, Turin, 1940–2.

Villeneuve. Horace, Tome i, *Odes et Épodes*; Tome ii, *Satires*; Tome iii, *Épîtres*. Texte établi et traduit par F. Villeneuve, Paris, 1927–34.

Wieland. Horazens *Satyren* . . . übersezt und mit Einleitungen . . . versehen von C. M. Wieland, Leipzig 1786.

Horazens *Briefe* . . . übersetzt und mit historischen Einleitungen . . . versehen von C. M. Wieland, Leipzig 1790.

Wickham. The Works of Horace, with a commentary by E. C. Wickham: vol. i, *Odes, Carm. Saec., Epodes*, 3rd ed., 1896; vol. ii, *Satires, Epistles, Ars P.*, 1891.

Wilamowitz, *S. u. S.* U. von Wilamowitz-Moellendorff, *Sappho und Simonides*, 1913.

I

VITA HORATI

HORACE tells us far more about himself, his character, his development, and his way of life (his βίος), than any other great poet in antiquity. Some of the biographical data contained in his writings can be supplemented from the short but valuable Life of Horace that has come down to us in a few manuscripts of his poems.[1] It is anonymous, but as early as the sixteenth century it was seen that it represents in substance the *Vita Horati* which Suetonius wrote as part of the section *De poetis* of his monumental work *De viris illustribus*. A direct proof is provided by Porphyrio's introduction to his commentary on the epistle to Augustus, ii. 1, *Apparet hunc librum, ut supra diximus, hortatu Caesaris scriptum esse. Cuius rei etiam Suetonius auctor est. Nam apud eum epistula invenitur Augusti increpantis in Horatium, quod non ad se quoque plurima ⟨eius modi poemata⟩[2] scribat.* The passage in the *Vita* to which this comment refers contains a verbatim quotation from Augustus' letter to Horace; it will be discussed later on. In the process of being incorporated into an edition of Horace the Suetonian *Vita* was abridged at a few points;[3] the cuts do not, however, seem to have been considerable.[4]

This ancient biography, together with some excerpts from the poems and some additional observations, will here be used to recall certain facts which it will be convenient for the reader to have before him.

The *Vita* begins: *Q. Horatius Flaccus Venusinus.* The three elements of his name are all attested by the poet himself.[5] So is the fact that he was

---

[1] For detailed information on the MSS, some of them now lost, of the *Vita* see *Q.Horati Carminum libri IV . . .* rec. M. Lenchantin de Gubernatis, Turin [1945], pp. xxxiii ff.; a sufficient summary is given in Klingner's second edition (1950) of Horace, p. 1.

[2] My supplement, *exempli gratia*. The phrase used by Augustus, as quoted in the *Vita*, is *in plerisque eius modi scriptis*. Porphyrio, on *Sat*. 1. 4. 138 f., speaks of Horace's writing of satires as *poemata scribere*.

[3] The omission of the list of Horace's genuine works is the most obvious instance; see p. 21 below.

[4] 'L'esposizione, in confronto con quella consacrata a Virgilio, è più arida e più breve: non tanto per effetto di tagli eventualmente operati, in qualche punto, dall' *excerptor*, quanto per la natura stessa delle cose che così suggeriva o imponeva. Su Orazio infatti il lavoro critico ed erudito, e magari anche fantastico, delle generazioni precedenti a Suetonio era stato assai minore che non su Virgilio (e su Terenzio stesso)' (A. Rostagni, *Suetonio De Poetis*, Turin 1944, 108).

[5] See the 'Index nominum' in the Teubner editions of Horace.

Venusinus, born at Venusia. When in his latest satire, a programmatic poem, he wanted to account for the fighting spirit which he had in common with his model Lucilius, he wrote:

> sequor hunc, Lucanus an Apulus anceps:
> nam Venusinus arat finem sub utrumque colonus,
> missus ad hoc, pulsis, vetus est ut fama, Sabellis,
> quo ne per vacuum Romano incurreret hostis,
> sive quod Apula gens seu quod Lucania bellum
> incuteret violenta.[1]

What Horace says here is not irrelevant to the point which he wishes to make in the particular context of the satire; we notice, however, that he also welcomes the opportunity to dwell with pride on the early memories of his birthplace. But whereas the settlement of Latin colonists at Venusia after the end of the third Samnite war was in the days of Horace no more than a piece of antiquarian local history, the effect of a later change in the population of his town was keenly felt by Horace himself when he was a small child. It is not directly recorded that Venusia was among the many Italian towns which had part of their citizens expelled, or deprived of their estates, to make room for Sulla's veterans.[2] But Niebuhr[3] combined what our sources tell us in general terms about Sulla's measures against the Italian towns with Horace's special reference[4] to the *centuriones* at Venusia; he thus came to the convincing conclusion that Venusia, which in the crisis of the Social War had gone over to Rome's enemies, and consequently had to be reconquered by Metellus,[5] suffered after Sulla's final victory a fate similar to that which it suffered in Horace's lifetime at the hands of the triumvirs. Horace lets us catch a glimpse of the role that Sulla's centurions and their families continued to play in the life of Venusia. My father, Horace says, though by no means well off, did not think the local school good enough for my education; he therefore decided on an extraordinary course and took me all the way to Rome to let me have the benefit of the best and most expensive teaching:

> causa fuit pater his, qui macro pauper agello
> noluit in Flavi ludum me mittere, magni

---

[1] *Sat.* 2. 1. 34 ff. This is a good illustration of Cicero's general statement, *Leg. Agr.* 2. 73, (*maiores*) *colonias sic idoneis in locis contra suspicionem periculi collocarunt ut esse non oppida Italiae sed propugnacula imperi viderentur.*

[2] For the evidence see, for example, T. Rice Holmes, *The Roman Republic*, &c., 1923, i. 61 n. 1.

[3] *Vorträge über römische Geschichte*, iii. 132 f., in connexion with an appreciation of Horace which, despite some serious errors, is still worth reading. Kiessling, on *Sat.* 1. 6. 71 f., implicitly adopts Niebuhr's conclusion. Lejay's note on 1. 6. 73, *centurionibus*, 'les colons militaires envoyés à Venouse, II, 1, 35', is unfortunate.

[4] *Sat.* 1. 6. 71 ff.   [5] App. *B.Civ.* 1. 52 f.

quo pueri magnis e centurionibus orti,
laevo suspensi loculos tabulamque lacerto,
ibant octonos referentes idibus aeris. (*Sat.* i. 6. 71 ff.)

If we want to grasp the implications of Horace's words, we must listen *perpurigatis auribus*. His first concern is to make his father's motives plain, and this end he achieves perfectly. But his mode of expression conveys something else besides. The emphatic phrasing of the passage points to a strong emotion:[1] pent-up spite vents itself in the detailed description of those haughty youngsters who, suitably dressed up[2] and inflated with their own importance, could be seen strutting to the schoolmaster's house, *magni . . . pueri magnis e centurionibus orti*. Any painful experience that distressed us in our childhood remains for ever fixed in our memory.[3] After so many years Horace still resents most vividly the behaviour of the centurions' children. When they were playing together, they may have bullied and insulted him: 'and what are *you* doing here, a freedman's son? *My* father, you know, . . .' It is quite likely that it was not only the low educational standard at the elementary school of Flavius that made it undesirable for Horace's father to send his son there.

Horace is justified in saying that he was *longe sonantem natus ad Aufidum*, for the Aufidus (now Ófanto), one of the largest rivers of southern Italy, dominates that part of the country. Venusia (Venosa) itself is not situated on the bank of the river but a good way south of it.[4]

Memories of his home country and visions of the characteristic features of its landscape accompany the poet throughout his life; his mind is so full of them that there always seems to be an overflow, ready to permeate his verse, lyrics as well as *sermones*. Like many eminent Italians in all ages, Horace, in the midst of his successes in Rome and the world at large, remains the devoted son of his native region. At the height of his achievement it is his greatest pride that his bold undertaking, the revival of the old Lesbian songs in the tongue of Italy, will be praised

---

[1] Cf. Kiessling's note on *magnis e centurionibus orti*.

[2] The picturesque line (74) *laevo suspensi loculos tabulamque lacerto* is as indispensable here as it is out of place at *Epist.* i. i. 56. Cf. Jachmann, *Studi in onore di U.E. Paoli*, 1955, 395 f.

[3] It is not, however, only unpleasant experiences that are so faithfully remembered. There is in a late work of Horace an echo of his life as a schoolboy which in its simple directness is truly moving, since no old man ever ceases to feel keenly what is described here: *Epist.* 2. 2. 197 f. *ac potius, puer ut festis Quinquatribus olim / exiguo gratoque fruaris tempore raptim.* The ancient world did not know week-ends and had to make the most of such holidays as there were.

[4] An excellent map of the region will be found at the end of *CIL* ix ('Italiae Regio II'). In the same volume, pp. 44 f., Mommsen has put together the evidence for the history of Venusia. (For Mommsen's clash with the *sindaco*, the burgomaster, of 'la città di Orazio' see Wilamowitz, *Erinnerungen*, 2nd ed., 161, and compare Mommsen's notes on *CIL* ix, no. 445 and especially on 604, where his burning indignation still reverberates.)

qua violens obstrepit Aufidus
et qua pauper aquae Daunus agrestium
regnavit populorum.[1]

In the most majestic of his 'Roman Odes' he mentions not Venusia
itself, but some neighbouring townlets, the names of which will have
meant very little to most of his Roman readers.[2] In the same context[3]
we hear of the *Voltur Apulus*, 'Monte Vulture' (near Melfi), a very
impressive isolated peak of unmistakably volcanic shape; the traveller
who goes by train from Foggia to Bari will see it for a long time on his
right hand, standing out against the skyline: it is, in fact, the main
landmark of the whole district.[4]

When Horace reports how, after a long absence, he could once more
set eyes on the familiar Apulian hills and feel on his skin the burning of
the *scirocco*, which he chooses to call by its local name, there is in his
words a ring of deep satisfaction:

incipit ex illo montis Apulia notos
ostentare mihi, quos torret Atabulus. (*Sat.* 1. 5. 77 f.)

It is a well-known feature of Latin literary history that, as far as we
know, from the beginning to the end not one of its important figures,
whether poets or prose writers, hailed from the city of Rome. Horace,
like Livius Andronicus, Naevius, Ennius, and others, was a Southerner,
by temperament no less than by extraction; in this respect as in most
others he strongly contrasted with his friend, the Mantuan Virgil.

The biographer continues: *patre, ut ipse tradit, libertino et exactionum*[5]
coactore. This clause refers to the satire (i. 6) of which *libertino patre
natum*[6] is the keynote (6 and 45 f.) and where Horace says of his
father (85 f.)

nec timuit sibi ne vitio quis verteret, olim
si praeco parvas aut, ut fuit ipse, coactor
mercedes sequerer.

The word *coactor* can denote various activities, but the scholia on this
passage are clearly right in assuming that Horace is speaking of a

---

[1] For the interpretation of this vexed passage see pp. 304 f. below.
[2] See p. 274 below.   [3] *Odes* 3. 4. 9.
[4] In July 1930 Monte Vulture was the centre of terrible earthquakes; Venosa was
almost completely destroyed.
[5] The old conjecture *auctionum* has been rightly abandoned by recent editors. But the
use of the rather general term *exactio* (cf. *Thes.l.L.* v. 2. 1134) is not very helpful in this
context, and, above all, it seems likely that Suetonius, who clearly refers to *Sat.* 1. 6. 86,
would have been content with quoting Horace's own expression *coactor*. I therefore consider it possible that *exactionum* was added by someone who wanted to have *coactor* explained somehow; that the need for such an explanation was felt by some later readers is
obvious from the scholia.
[6] Cf. also *Epist.* 1. 20. 20.

coactor argentarius. The functions of a *coactor argentarius* were connected with auctions, which, as is shown by the evidence from Plautus onwards, were exceedingly common and important in the business life of the Roman world.[1] It is the *coactor* who, for the purposes of the auction, takes the place of the seller of the goods. The whole business is being transacted not between the seller and the purchaser, but, on the one hand, between the seller and the *coactor* and, on the other, between the *coactor* and the purchaser. The *coactor* receives a small recompense, *merces*.[2] Since immediately after the auction he pays to the seller the money, which he has then to recover from the buyer, he fulfils the function of a banker and is therefore also called *argentarius*. Whereas the *coactor* is concerned with the financial side of the transaction, the *praeco*, whom Horace mentions together with the *coactor*, is in charge of the actual auctioneering and the preceding advertisement. The two occupations are closely connected. Horace's description of the *praeco* Volteius Mena[3] must not be taken as a portrait of his own father, but a good deal of his filial devotion and of his sympathy with the class to which his father belonged seems to have gone into that delightful picture.

No son ever set a finer monument to his father than Horace did in the sixth satire of Book I.[4] There is no need to recapitulate the passage: a reader who cannot afford the time to read it at leisure, and add to it *Sat.* 1. 4. 105 ff., had better leave Horace alone.

The poet knows that he owes more to his father than to anyone else;[5] it would be madness not to be satisfied with being the son of such a man, *nil me paeniteat*[6] *sanum patris huius* (1. 6. 89). Horace's description

---

[1] Mommsen's classic pages on the Roman auction, *Hermes*, xii. 91 ff. (*Ges. Schriften*, iii. 225), were published in 1877, but up to our own time many commentators (some of them throwing in a misinterpretation of Cic. *Rab. Post.* 30), translators, writers of books and articles, persist in making Horace's father a collector of taxes or something like that. Kiessling's and Lejay's notes on *Sat.* 1. 6. 86 are, of course, correct. For further information see *RE* ii. 2270 ff., iv. 126, xxii. 1198 f.

[2] The term *merces* (*Sat.* 1. 6. 87) recurs in the receipts of the Pompeian banker L. Caecilius Iucundus which gave rise to Mommsen's article (see the last footnote).

[3] *Epist.* 1. 7. 50–95.

[4] For the general character and the structure of this satire see pp. 101 ff. below.

[5] We sense a similar gratitude when Cicero says, *De orat.* 2. 1, *si homines non eruditi summam essent prudentiam . . . consecuti, . . . stultum in nobis erudiendis patris nostri, optimi ac prudentissimi viri, studium videretur.*

[6] Readers should be on their guard against such inadequate renderings as 'I ne'er shall need To blush for that dear father' (Conington), or 'I never can be ashamed of such a father' (Palmer; but see his own later note on Plaut. *Amph.* 5. 1. 71), or 'ich möchte es nicht bereuen' (Kiessling), or 'never could I be ashamed' (Fairclough in the Loeb edition), or 'je ne saurais rougir' (Villeneuve). Wickham, L. Müller, and Lejay say nothing on *nil me paeniteat*. The early Latin use of *paenitet me*, 'I am not satisfied', and *me non* (*haud*) *paenitet*, 'I am satisfied', is amply illustrated from Plautus and Terence by P. Langen, *Beiträge zur Kritik und Erklärung des Plautus*, 1880, 247 ff. On *Sat.* 1. 6. 89 the admirable Dacier, nowadays unduly neglected, observes 'Les premiers Latins se sont servis du verbe

of his father is warm-hearted but free from sentimentality or exaggeration. We see before us one of the common people, a hard-working, open-minded, and thoroughly honest man of simple habits and strict convictions, representing some of the best qualities that at the end of the Republic could still be found in the unsophisticated society of the Italian *municipia*.

After the μέν clause,[1] *ut ipse tradit* . . ., there follows in the *Vita* the δέ clause, *ut vero creditum est*,[2] *salsamentario, cum illi quidam in altercatione exprobrasset 'quotiens ego vidi patrem tuum bracchio[3] se emungentem'*. When in the apocryphal traditions of ancient biography the need was felt to let the father of a man of notoriously humble origin practise some particular trade, the occupation of a seller of salt fish, *salsamentarius*, ταριχο- πώλης, was an obvious choice.[4] In the case of Horace there was, moreover, a special reason for bringing into play the *salsamentarius*. In his epistle to Florus (ii. 2) Horace says 'you urge me to take up writing poetry. In my present circumstances I have very good reasons for not doing so.' 'Besides,' he continues (58 ff.), 'what kind of poetry?'

> denique non omnes eadem mirantur amantque:
> carmine tu gaudes, hic delectatur iambis,
> ille Bioneis sermonibus et sale nigro.

The last line points unmistakably to the satires, which in some respects maintain the manner of Bion the Borysthenite. To them the term *sal nigrum* is very properly applied: it had been Horace's ambition, especially at the earlier stages of his writing satires, to follow closely his great forerunner Lucilius, who *sale multo urbem defricuit*.[5] But in the

---

poenitere, pour dire *n'estre pas content*' and quotes Ter. *Haut.* 72. Before him Lambinus, ad loc., had also noticed this meaning (though not its primarily archaic use) and had quoted, besides Ter. *Phorm.* 172, passages from Livy and Cicero, among them *Cael.* 6, again quoted in Heinze's helpful note (I cannot, however, concede to Heinze that 'es spielt doch auch hier [*Sat.* 1. 6. 89] die Bedeutung "bereuen" . . . hinein'). Other instances from Cicero can be found in Meusel's commentary on Caes. *B.Civ.* 2. 32. 12; I would add a particularly striking one, *Rep.* 6. 16, *iam vero ipsa terra ita mihi parva visa est ut me imperii nostri . . . paeniteret*, and a reference to the end of Tac. *Hist.* 2. 19 (archaism?). Plautus uses (*Bacch.* 1182) *me nil paenitet* and (*Mil.* 740) *nihil me paenitet*; did Horace perhaps borrow the whole phrase *nil me paeniteat* from an earlier poet, possibly Lucilius?

[1] Some sixteenth-century editors thought fit to emphasize its preparatory character by reading *ut ipse ⟨quidem⟩*.

[2] Suetonius makes it perfectly clear what, with the poet's own testimony before him, he believes to be facts and what not. He adds the story about the *salsamentarius* not because he is uncritical or a gossip-monger but because, like many ancient biographers, he thinks that the *rumores* that cluster round the figure of a famous man are worth recording. Cf. W. Steidle, 'Sueton und die antike Biographie', *Zetemata*, Heft 1. 59.

[3] Lenchantin, op. cit. (see p. 1 n. 1), p. xxxix and p. 1, accepts the old conjecture *cubito*, regardless of Plut. *Mor.* 631 d and Macrob. *Sat.* 7. 3. 6.

[4] Cf. Suidas, vol. ii, p. 81, 1 ed. Adler, Δίδυμος, Διδύμου ταριχοπώλου, γραμματικὸς Ἀριστάρχειος κτλ.; Juvenal 4. 32 f.

[5] *Sat.* 1. 10. 3 f.

context of the epistle, where *sale nigro* is closely connected with *Bioneis sermonibus*, the 'black salt' also alludes to Bion's personal history: his father, according to the son's explicit testimony, was a ταριχέμπορος. When this allusion was recognized,[1] it was also understood that the story about Horace's father being a *salsamentarius*, who had been seen *bracchio se emungens*, was in fact a reproduction of Bion's much prettier account in his letter to Antigonos Gonatas.[2]

About Horace's education, both at school and at the university, the *Vita* is silent. But we learn something about that period of his life from the poet himself. In a few lines[3] the schoolboy Horace is pictured, making his way, under the eyes of his father, to the expensive school in Rome.[4] These lines contain no indication of any subject of the lessons. But that the *Odyssia* of Livius Andronicus was forcibly crammed into ·the children is stated in a passage which even nowadays is generally known:

> non equidem insector delendave carmina Livi
> esse reor, memini quae plagosum mihi parvo
> Orbilium dictare. (*Epist.* 2. 1. 69 ff.)

However, Horace and his little fellow sufferers 'did' the real Homer as well, presumably somewhat later. From the manner in which Horace, many decades after, speaks of it it appears that the reading of the *Iliad* was a principal item in the curriculum. I cannot bring myself to tear the relevant sentence out of its context, but will rather quote the whole passage at once. This survey of his youth, with special emphasis on his intellectual and moral development, is the only coherent piece of autobiography which we possess from Horace's pen.[5]

> Romae nutriri mihi contigit atque doceri
> iratus Grais quantum nocuisset Achilles.
> adiecere bonae paulo plus artis Athenae,
> scilicet ut vellem curvo dinoscere rectum
> atque inter silvas Academi quaerere verum.   45
> dura sed emovere loco me tempora grato
> civilisque rudem belli tulit aestus in arma
> Caesaris Augusti non responsura lacertis.

[1] First, it seems, by A. T. H. Fritzsche. Cf. Kiessling on *Epist.* 2. 2. 60; R. Heinze, *De Horatio Bionis imitatore* (Diss. Bonn 1889), 6.

[2] Diog. Laert. 4. 7. 46. The king asked Bion the question τίς πόθεν εἰς ἀνδρῶν; πόθι τοι πόλις ἠδὲ τοκῆες; Bion, realizing that he had been maligned by some courtiers, wrote back: ἐμοὶ ὁ πατὴρ μὲν ἦν ἀπελεύθερος, τῷ ἀγκῶνι ἀπομυσσόμενος—διεδήλου δὲ τὸν ταριχέμπορον—γένος Βορυσθενίτης, ἔχων οὐ πρόσωπον, ἀλλὰ συγγραφὴν ἐπὶ τοῦ προσώπου, τῆς τοῦ δεσπότου πικρίας σύμβολον. μήτηρ δὲ οἵαν ὁ τοιοῦτος ἂν γήμαι, ἀπ' οἰκήματος (*ex lupanari*) . . ., and finally, retorting to Homer with Homer, ταύτης τοι γενεῆς τε καὶ αἵματος εὔχομαι εἶναι.

[3] *Sat.* 1. 6. 78 ff.   [4] Cf. p. 104 below.

[5] The end of *Epist.* i. 20, which contains some autobiographical data, is entirely different. See pp. 360 ff. below.

unde simul primum me dimisere Philippi,
decisis humilem pennis inopemque paterni   50
et laris et fundi paupertas impulit audax
ut versus facerem. (*Epist.* 2. 2. 41–52.)

   The section opens with *Romae nutriri mihi contigit*, a succinct yet
weighty clause, headed by the name of the all-powerful city which in
the sphere of cultural life had taken its place beside *Athenae, quae
nutrices Graeciae*. In Horace's words there is pride and also gratitude
(*mihi contigit*). It is perhaps with a twinkle of humour that the poet,
after such a beginning, sums up the benefits of his school lessons,
atque doceri iratus Grais quantum nocuisset Achilles. No matter what the
Iliad meant to him personally, here he merely formulates an accepted
pedagogic view. It was a wide-spread conviction—and Horace, for
a special purpose, conformed to it in one of his letters to Lollius[1]—
that Homer wrote for our moral education and that, in particular, the
Iliad, opening with *MHNIN*, was meant to demonstrate the terrible
consequences of *ira*.

   Before leaving the first two lines, we may for a moment consider their
wider implication. A man born in the south of Italy looks back on his
schooldays in Rome. What he primarily recollects is his reading of the
oldest Greek poem. By the time of Horace's youth the alliance of the
Roman mind with the thought, the poetry, and the art of Greece was
firmly established and had in fact become the foundation on which the
whole moral and intellectual life of educated men rested. The works of
Virgil and Horace were destined to strengthen that foundation still
further.

   After the school there comes the university, *the* university, for there
was in effect only one: *adiecere bonae paulo plus artis Athenae*. An affectionate note is as clearly marked in *bonae . . . Athenae* with its emphatic
hyperbaton as, three lines later, in *loco . . . grato*. The following
two lines (44 f.) give an account of the principal lectures which
Horace attended; the subjects correspond roughly to what we should
call moral philosophy and theory of knowledge. We may assume that
Horace was seriously interested in these and kindred matters and also
that he led a far more industrious and parsimonious life than Cicero's
son, who, born in the same year as Horace, went up to Athens about the
same time as Horace and also professed to study philosophy. But even
so it is hardly possible to imagine young Horace spending all his time
attending lectures and discussing philosophical problems with his
teachers and his fellow students. Strictly personal amusements and
adventures apart, one particular activity is likely to have occupied him

---

[1] Cf. p. 316 below.

in his spare time at Athens. We have no record of it, but at any rate a guess seems permissible.

Horace's *Epodes* show that at the time when he was working at them he was not only familiar with Archilochus and Hipponax, and possibly some other early iambographers, but was also interested in Anacreon,[1] knew Bacchylides,[2] and, we may be sure, several other lyric poets as well. Afterwards, when Alcaeus had become his chief model, he did not confine his recasting activity to him, but also drew upon a large store of other types of Greek lyric poetry, a much larger one than we can hope ever to verify with the help of the scanty fragments left to us. Of Pindar he knew—and probably owned a copy of—the seventeen books of the Alexandrian edition.[3] It cannot be strictly proved but seems very likely that his interest in those early poets was roused in the days when he was an enthusiastic young student at Athens. Part of their work had long ceased to be a living force; only grammarians and other learned specialists would concern themselves with it. Access to the many papyrus rolls in which the productions of *Pindarus novemque lyrici* slumbered must have been considerably easier in Athens than in Rome before there existed the public libraries founded by Asinius Pollio and by Augustus. I like to think that it was at Athens that Horace first came across the bulk of pre-classic and classic Greek lyrics and that in those happy days he now and then may even have dreamed of paying homage to the half-forgotten masters by renewing in his native tongue their forms and some of their themes. He may also have ransacked the Athenian bookshops or, in other cases, ordered copies from a professional scribe, so as to have in his possession the texts he admired so much. The idea of making the writing of poetry his profession would not, of course, have occurred to him at that stage.

The philosophical studies, the reading of poetry, the whole peaceful existence at Athens were brought to a sudden end by the hard times whose inrush the poet depicts as a cataclysm: its floods were to carry him eventually to the battlefield of Philippi (46–48). The bare outlines given in the letter to Florus can be filled in with the help of other sources.

About the end of August 44 B.C. Brutus, after he had failed in his hopes of raising an effective resistance against Antony in Italy, betook himself to Athens. The Athenians had a long experience in bestowing spectacular honours on tyrannicides. In the case of Brutus the programme of the ceremonies was executed with perfect precision. To him

---

[1] From *Epod.* 14. 9 f. there follows an acquaintance with the traditions about Anacreon's life but not necessarily with his poems. But since a few years later he used Anacreon freely, it is probable that he had read him when he wrote those lines.

[2] See p. 66 n. 6 below.   [3] See p. 435 below.

and to Cassius, who joined him at Athens for a short time, splendid
receptions were given and a decree was voted to the effect that bronze
statues of Brutus and Cassius should be erected by the side of the
famous group of Harmodios and Aristogeiton.[1] Brutus in his turn
behaved with equal propriety. He was careful to conceal his very
energetic preparations for the war against the Caesarians. Instead he
ostentatiously attended the lectures, and took part in the discussions, of
the famous heads of the great philosophical schools.[2] It is easy to
imagine what impression the presence of so eminent a guest in the
audience must have made on the young students from Rome, Marcus
Cicero, Horace, and others.[3] They had heard and read a great deal
about the dark evil of tyranny and the glory that in the past had
crowned the heroic champions of liberty. And now there was among
them the man who but a few months ago had slain one of the greatest
tyrants of all time. They could watch him sitting with them in the
same halls, walking with them up and down the squares, sharing in
their own and their masters' disputations. How could they help being
fascinated by him? Brutus would talk to them amiably, pick out of
their number those whose fathers or family connexions were important
and indeed any young man who seemed to him promising,[4] and would
persuade them to join his cause. So Horace, like many of his fellow-
students, found himself in the retinue of Brutus. It is not known when
he was given a definite appointment. Late in 43 or early in 42 we find
him with Brutus in Asia, presumably at Clazomenae or Smyrna.[5]
Finally, perhaps not long before the battles of Philippi, Brutus made
him, a freedman's son, *tribunus militum*, an appointment which was
bound to rouse some annoyance and envy.[6] Under the late Republic
the *tribuni militum* were, as a rule, *nobiles adulescentes*, of senatorial or
equestrian rank, to whom the tribunate served as a stepping-stone to a
career in the army or in the magistrature.[7] They had not served

---

[1] See Dio Cass. 47. 20. 4.

[2] Plut. *Brut.* 24. 1 f. Θεομνήστου . . . ἀκροώμενος τοῦ Ἀκαδημιακοῦ καὶ Κρατίππου τοῦ
Περιπατητικοῦ καὶ συμφιλοσοφῶν, ἐδόκει παντάπασιν ἀργεῖν καὶ σχολάζειν. ἔπραττε δὲ τὰ
πρὸς τὸν πόλεμον ἀνυπόπτως. καὶ γὰρ εἰς Μακεδονίαν ἔπεμψεν Ἡρόστρατον κτλ. The great
Cratippus was at that time the principal teacher, and even a kind of private tutor, of
Cicero's son.

[3] Some of them are listed by R. Syme, *The Roman Revolution*, 198. We may add the
Pompeius (the cognomen *Varus* which we find in the heading of the MSS and in the
scholia probably goes back to the early literature *De personis Horatianis*) to whom *Odes* ii. 7
is addressed.

[4] Plut. *Brut.* 24. 2 f. τοὺς σχολάζοντας ἀπὸ Ῥώμης ἐν ἄστει νέους ἀνελάμβανε καὶ συνεῖχεν.
ὧν ἦν καὶ Κικέρωνος υἱός, ὃν ἐπαινεῖ διαφερόντως καί φησιν . . . θαυμάζειν οὕτω γενναῖον ὄντα
καὶ μισοτύραννον. To the elder Cicero Brutus writes in eulogistic terms about his son, Cic.
ad Brut. 9. 3. 6.

[5] Cf. Lejay on *Sat.* 1. 7. 23.   [6] *Sat.* 1. 6. 47 f.

[7] See Marquardt, *Staatsverw.* ii.[2] 366 f. and Lengle, *RE* vi A. 2443 ff., whose cautious

previously with the rank and file, and some of them had little, if any, military experience. Consequently their usefulness in action may sometimes have been as dubious as it appears in Caesar's brilliant and amusing description of their behaviour when a clash with Ariovistus and his Germans seemed imminent.[1] But such a failure should not be regarded as typical; Caesar's own *commentarii* provide sufficient examples of tribunes discharging their duties with competence and courage.[2] It seems only to have happened in exceptional circumstances that the actual command of the legion in battle lay in the hands of the tribunes (six to each legion).[3] It was obviously an emergency measure when at Philippi one of Brutus' legions fought under the command of its tribunes, of whom Horace was one.[4] At the height of the crisis it may have seemed all-important to put in charge young men whose loyalty could be trusted, even if they were lacking in military experience.

The second battle of Philippi, about the middle of November 42, ended with the rout of the army of Brutus and the suicide of its commander. Horace escaped, as did his otherwise unknown friend Pompeius[5] and Cicero's son. We shall never know in detail what happened to Horace on the battlefield or how he found his way to safety. All he tells us is that he fled. Far too much has been written about *relicta non bene parmula*.[6] In the long process of whitewashing (or, to call it by a loftier name, 'Rettungen') not only common sense but also syntax has fallen a victim.[7] Nowadays there seems to be a tendency to cling to the reality of *relicta parmula* as to a picturesque and venerable relic, which may help to bring Horace's person somewhat nearer to the feelings of a modern reader. The scholars who take Horace's phrase in this literal way[8] discard as irrelevant the fact that some poets with whom Horace was thoroughly familiar and who inspired him in various ways, Archilochus,[9] Alcaeus,[10] and, possibly, Anacreon,[11] had said of themselves

assessment of the scanty evidence for the period that concerns us here is especially valuable.

[1] *B.Gall.* 1. 39. 2 ff.   [2] See Lengle, loc. cit.

[3] See Caes. *B.Gall.* 7. 62. 6. In regard to the Titinius (time of Augustus, cf. Münzer, *RE* vi A. 1547. 36) who was *tr. mil. pro legato* (*CIL* iii. 605; Dessau, *Inscr. sel.* 2678) Lengle, op. cit. 2445. 13, observes 'ausnahmsweise'.

[4] *Sat.* 1. 6. 48 *quod mihi pareret legio Romana tribuno.* Lengle's comment, op. cit. 2444. 59 f., 'wo man die Befehlshaber nahm wie man sie fand', is pertinent.

[5] *Odes* ii. 7.   [6] *Odes* 2. 7. 10.

[7] One scholar has proposed to take *relicta non bene parmula* as explanatory of *celerem fugam*, another to punctuate after *sensi*, i.e. to make *relicta n.b.p.* go with *cum fracta virtus.* . . . These artificialities are refuted by W. H. Alexander, *Proc. and Trans. Roy. Soc. Canada*, third series, vol. 36, 1942, sect. ii, pp. 17–20.

[8] See, for example, Alexander (cf. the last footnote); K. Meister, *EPMHNEIA, Festschrift Otto Regenbogen*, 1952, 131 ff., and the recent literature quoted by him, p. 132 n. 14.

[9] Fr. 6.   [10] Fr. 428 Lobel and Page; cf. D. L. Page, *Sappho and Alcaeus*, 153 ff.
[11] Fr. 51 Diehl.

that in the course of a battle they had thrown away their shield.[1]
Now it is perfectly true that to indicate a 'borrowing' from an earlier
poet is no substitute for a proper interpretation of the later poet's own
thought and intention. It is therefore necessary to ask this question:
why was Horace, in the context of his poem to Pompeius, not content
with speaking in general terms of his escape from Philippi; why did he
insist on such a drastic sign of cowardice? The answer is to be sought
in two directions. First, 'the mode in which he makes his confession is in
accordance with his habitual candour and ironical self-depreciation'.[2]
Secondly,[3] the friend to whom the ode *O saepe mecum* is addressed survived because he took part in the *celeris fuga* from Philippi. That was an
undeniable fact. But the last thing Horace would wish to do was to
hurt his friend's feelings. He therefore speaks of his own soldierly
deficiency in the crudest possible manner. It is characteristic of Horace
that he will always ascribe also to himself any particular weakness with
which a friend has to be charged or against which he is to be warned.
Instances of this tactful expression of his fellow-feeling are to be found
throughout Horace's work; in the *Epistles* they are of special importance.

Now that this point has been cleared up, we should not hesitate to
say what effect *relicta non bene parmula* was meant to have—and must
have had—on the educated and sensitive readers for whom Horace
wrote. They knew enough about Archilochus and Alcaeus to grasp the
allusion, and, if they were the right kind of readers, they also knew
enough about Horace not to be lured into a realistic interpretation of
that particular detail. They must have understood that Horace admitted unmistakably his flight from Philippi, and also that the motif
of the shield was a conventional poetic device, in its relation to the
actual happenings in no way different from the Homeric mist by
means of which a few lines later (13 ff.) an Olympian god whisks the
poet away from the battlefield.[4]

Later in life, and especially when the régime of Augustus was
established and Horace himself had come to be convinced of its
necessity,[5] he might have passed over in silence the days of Philippi and
all they implied for him. In fact, however, he did the very opposite. He
recalls the decisive battle and his own participation in it on the losing

---

[1] We do not know how early ῥίψασπις came to be used 'metaphorically' of any soldier
who fled from the battlefield.

[2] W. Y. Sellar, *Horace and the Elegiac Poets*, 2nd ed., 17.

[3] The following remarks owe much to K. Meister's (see p. 11 n. 8) sympathetic
interpretation.

[4] As long ago as 1879 H. Jordan, *Krit. Beiträge zur Gesch. d. lat. Sprache*, 352, wrote 'es ist
unmöglich aus Horazens *relicta non bene parmula* . . . etwas anderes zu folgern, als daß er die
Flucht des geschlagenen Heeres geteilt hat'.

[5] See pp. 354 ff. below.

side not only in the ode to Pompeius but also, as we have seen, in the much later second epistle to Florus and, most significantly, in the great centre-piece of his cycle of patriotic hymns.[1] Moreover, the sketch of an autobiography at the end of his book of the *Epistles* alludes, unnecessarily as it might seem, but unmistakably, to his share in that campaign.[2] Thus he professed time and again, without idle ostentation, but with unwavering firmness, his loyalty to the men who had kindled his youthful enthusiasm. His admiration for the heroism of the younger Cato is expressed in two of his most majestic *carmina*.[3]

It remains to examine the concluding sentence of the section in the letter to Florus quoted above, *unde simul primum . . . ut versus facerem* (49 ff.). Philippi shattered all his hopes; the proud flight[4] had ended in a crash. It was bad enough that there could be no longer any idea of his making a career in the magistracy. But worse was to come. On returning home Horace, who until then had probably never had to worry about money, found himself suddenly under the necessity of earning a livelihood. He alludes to the catastrophe in his economic situation very briefly: *inopemque paterni et laris et fundi.* The most probable, if not the only possible,[5] meaning of these words is that he lost his father's town-house and farm during the expropriations of land to which Venusia with its territory was subjected either in 43 B.C. or a few months after Philippi.[6] Accepting this interpretation we may say that the estate of Horace in the south of Italy was struck by the same blow that about the same time fell, or threatened to fall, on the estate of Virgil in the north.

The assertion *paupertas impulit audax ut versus facerem* can be properly understood only within the context of the epistle. Florus had blamed Horace for not answering his letters and had, moreover, complained *quod exspectata tibi non mittam carmina mendax* (24 f.). Horace, in reply, produces various reasons because of which, so he says, he does not want, or is not able, to write poetry at present. The argument of the section that concerns us here is this: in my early days after the catastrophe of Philippi *paupertas impulit audax ut versus facerem*; but (52–54) now, having all I need, I should be stark mad *ni melius dormire*

---

[1] 3. 4. 26.   [2] Cf. p. 360 below.   [3] Cf. p. 236 and p. 295 n. 3.

[4] It was noticed in antiquity (see Porphyrio) that *decisis humilem pennis* points back to the phrase he had used in his brief autobiography, *Epist.* 1. 20. 20 f., *in tenui re maiores pennas nido extendisse.*

[5] For a sceptical view see C. G. Zumpt in Wüstemann's re-edition (1843) of Heindorf's commentary on the *Satires*, 9.

[6] App. *B.Civ.* 4. 3, says that in 43 B.C. the triumvirs promised the veterans allotment of land from eighteen of the richest Italian towns, and among the towns which he specially mentions is Venusia. But we do not know to what extent the plan was executed forthwith and how much remained a mere promise until in 41 Octavian had to see the measure through (Suet. *Aug.* 13. 3; Dio Cass. 48. 2. 3; App. *B.Civ.* 5. 3).

putem quam scribere versus. What are we to make of this? In the many passages of self-justification which we find in Horace's writings he never tells a downright lie, but neither does he consider himself obliged under all circumstances to speak the whole truth. His adroitness in evading any unwelcome suggestion must always be taken into account, and no less his propensity to εἰρωνεία and understatement. In the present instance he does not want his reader to infer from his words that it was solely *paupertas audax* that impelled him to write his early poems. But he does mean to say that, had it not been for the ruin of his former expectations and the loss of his property, he would not have become a 'professional' poet although, like many educated Romans, he might have written some verse in his spare time. Finally, it could not occur to any of Horace's contemporaries to take his words as indicating that after Philippi he had hoped to make a living out of the work of his pen. Such a hope would have been absurd. And as for the chance of finding a wealthy patron who might support him, that was, at best, a very remote one.

What saved Horace from penury was not any kind of literary work but something very different. The Suetonian *Vita*, after the passage quoted above (p. 6), continues: *bello Philippensi excitus a M. Bruto imperatore tribunus militum meruit; victisque partibus venia impetrata scriptum quaestorium comparavit.* The first half of this sentence does not tell us anything we have not already learnt from the poet himself, but the second half does. In more than one book on Horace it is said that he became 'a clerk in the Treasury'. That may do as a rough translation of *scriba quaestorius*, but it hardly gives the modern reader an adequate idea of the nature of the office and of the social position of its occupants.[1] The highest rank of the *apparitores*, the assistants of the magistrates, was that of the *scribae quaestorii*.[2] They were, indeed, employed at 'the Treasury' and concerned with the public finances, but since the *aerarium* served also as the equivalent of a 'Public Record Office', they also had other equally important duties to discharge. They were responsible for putting down the resolutions of the Senate and keeping records of them in the *aerarium*. If an interested party wanted to have access to certain official documents, the *scribae* had to produce the volume in question and see to it that authentic copies were made. These duties required not only intelligence and some experience in business but also a certain amount of legal knowledge.[3] The influence of the *scribae* was the greater since they remained in office, as a rule for

[1] A strong protest, supported by the evidence in Cicero, against the usual undervaluation of the *scribae* was made by Zumpt, op. cit. (see the last footnote but one) p. 14 n. 1, a few years before Mommsen published his article *De apparitoribus magistratuum Romanorum.*

[2] Cf. Mommsen, *Staatsrecht*, i.[3] 346 ff.; Kornemann, *RE* ii A. 850 ff.

[3] Cf. A. H. M. Jones, *JRS* xxxix, 1949, 41.

life,[1] whereas the quaestors, who were young men, changed from year
to year. Many of the *scribae quaestorii* belonged to the *ordo equester*. Their
situation was profitable enough to make it worth while to purchase the
post; that happened more than once[2] and happened, according to
Suetonius (*scriptum quaestorium comparavit*), in the case of Horace. The
work involved might be heavy, but was not necessarily so: most of it
could be put on the shoulders of subordinate servants so that the
scriptus quaestorius itself was often little more than a sinecure.[3] The
scribae quaestorii were divided into three *decuriae*.[4] Horace, describing
the troubles that face him when in town, enables us to catch a glimpse
of a meeting of the corporation of his colleagues.[5]

The poet's economic circumstances changed completely when, at
some time before 31 B.C.,[6] presumably not long after the publication of
the first book of his *Satires*, Maecenas presented him with the Sabine
farm which was to mean so much to him. It is likely that, in consequence of this change, he resigned his post as *scriba*, or at any rate
ceased to spend much trouble on it;[7] he could now be expected to
attend a meeting of the corporation only when some extraordinary
matter was under discussion.

The next section of the *Vita*, or rather the common heading of the
two following sections, runs: *ac primo Maecenati, mox Augusto insinuatus
non mediocrem in amborum amicitia locum tenuit*. This exceedingly rough
summary[8] of a long and complex series of events is correct in so far as it
states that Horace's connexion with Maecenas preceded his connexion
with Augustus and that both men valued their friendship with the poet
very highly. But when Suetonius in this context says *insinuatus*,[9] he puts

[1] Cf. Mommsen, op. cit. 339.

[2] Cf. ibid. 340 n. 2; Jones, loc. cit.

[3] This point is emphasized by H. Dessau in *Anatolian Studies presented to Sir W. M.
Ramsay*, 1923, 136, in an article discussing an inscription from Antiochia Pisidiae which
was made known by Ramsay, *JRS* vi, 1916, 90, an epitaph, *L. Pomponio Nigro vet(erano)
leg(ionis) V Gal(licae) scribai q(uaestorio)*. Dessau makes it very probable that this Pom-
ponius Niger was for a time Horace's colleague as *scriba quaestorius*.

[4] For this particular use of *decuria* see Mommsen, op. cit. 342.

[5] *Sat.* 2. 6. 36 f.

[6] Cf. *Epod.* 1. 25–32; *Sat.* 2. 6. 53 ff.

[7] 'Wenn H. damals seinen Posten als *scriba* noch innegehabt hat, so ist das eine Sinekure
gewesen' (Heinze on *Sat.* 2. 6. 36 f.).

[8] It looks as if the sentence was written rather hastily. On such a matter we shall not
judge Suetonius too severely when we consider the enormous bulk of the work *De viris
illustribus* and the amount of scattered evidence he had to collect for it. But when full
allowance is made for such considerations, there still remains the impression that in
writing the Life of Horace he was mainly interested in the extracts he was able to produce
from the correspondence of Augustus; he does not even seem to have gone to the trouble of
re-reading the entire satire i. 6.

[9] This is one of his favourite expressions. In the small portion of his output which we
possess he uses it four times, always—as in the present passage—in the form *insinuatus* and
governing a dative.

on the facts his own interpretation, the interpretation of a man living at the court of Hadrian. That need not worry us since for the history of Horace's friendship with Maecenas and with Augustus we are provided with the most reliable and detailed evidence.

In the sixth satire of Book I Horace gives a painstakingly accurate account of the beginnings of his relationship with Maecenas.[1] He stresses the chronology;[2] from his statements it emerges that Virgil spoke to Maecenas about Horace only a few months after he, Virgil, had been accepted *inter amicos Maecenatis* in consequence of the publication of his *Eclogues*, a book that had an instantaneous and almost unbelievable success. The conclusion to be drawn from these data is obvious. Virgil—and a little later his friend and fellow-poet Varius—could not possibly approach Maecenas and tell him 'I have a friend, a very nice and bright young man, a certain Horace; would you care to see him?' If they were to venture on such an attempt at all, one condition must have been fulfilled: Horace must already have written some poems, epodes or satires, or both, which his well-wishers could show to Maecenas. The rest of the story need not be told here. Whatever the ups and downs in the relations of Horace and Maecenas, there was never in them anything to which the term *insinuatus* could be applied. The same is true of the *amicitia* between Horace and Augustus, about which something will be said later on.[3]

The *Vita* continues: *Maecenas quantopere eum dilexerit satis testatur illo epigrammate:*

> *ni te visceribus meis, Horati,*
> *plus iam diligo, tu tuum sodalem*
> †*nimio*[4] *videas strigosiorem,*

sed multo magis extremis iudiciis tali ad Augustum elogio:[5] '*Horati Flacci ut mei esto memor*'.

It is a good thing that the fame of Maecenas, a very noble figure, does not rest upon his poetry[6] or, for that matter, on his prose style.

---

[1] For the description of their first meeting see pp. 103 f. below.

[2] Cf. also *Sat.* 2. 6. 40 ff.

[3] See pp. 353 ff. below.

[4] The old conjecture *ninnio* (a very slight change) is probable (so also Kappelmacher, *RE* xiv. 227), taking the word not as a name, but as a common noun. Cf. Hesychius, νίννον· τὸν καβάλλην ἵππον and Leo on Plaut. *Poen.* 371. For the usage compare, for example, Liv. 27. 47. 1 *strigosiores equos*.

[5] Christ's interpretation, *Bayer. Sitzgsb.*, Philos. Cl., 1893, 70, which takes *elogium* in its technical sense, 'clausula adiecta testamento' (so also A. Rostagni, *Suetonio De poetis*, 113), seems to me preferable to the compromise in *Thes. l. L.* v. 2, p. 405. 30 ff. Maecenas had made Augustus his heir (Dio Cass. 55. 7. 5).

[6] Mommsen's outburst, who called Maecenas 'den unleidlichsten aller herzvertrockneten und worteverkräuselnden [recalling Tac. *Dial.* 26. 1 *calamistros Maecenatis*] Hofpoeten' (*Röm. Geschichte*, i.⁹ 232) is as exaggerated as are many similar verdicts in that great book.

Even if we allow for a good deal of self-mockery in the few fragments of his verses which have come down to us, it must be said that there is very little in them to enjoy. As a hopeless epigone he keeps on sailing in the wake of the masters whom he admired when he was young. As for the specimen before us, we may assume that this exceedingly lame parody of one of the loveliest poems of Catullus was hastily scribbled on the writing-tablets while the *tabellarius* who was to bring them to Horace was waiting. The full worth of Maecenas appears in the clause of his will, which admits of no comment.

The next section of the *Vita*, about Horace and Augustus, contains some excerpts of great value from the emperor's letters to the poet; another piece is quoted in the following section *de habitu corporis*.[1] Here Suetonius had full scope for scholarly investigation. A large portion of the vast correspondence of Augustus had been published in the decades after his death. But Suetonius did not depend upon the published volumes only. Under Hadrian he was 'secretary', more accurately chief of the Imperial Chancery, *ab epistulis*,[2] that is to say he was in charge of the whole official correspondence of the Empire[3] and presumably had also the custody of the private and the secret letters of the imperial house.[4] Consequently he had access to the originals of Augustus' letters, some of which may have remained unpublished. He mentions more than once that he had inspected the autographs.[5] We now return to the text of the *Vita Horati*.

Augustus epistularum quoque ei officium obtulit, ⟨ut⟩ hoc ad Maecenatem scripto significat: 'ante ipse sufficiebam scribendis epistulis amicorum: nunc occupatissimus et infirmus Horatium nostrum a te cupio abducere. veniet ergo ab ista parasitica mensa ad hanc regiam et nos in epistulis scribendis adiuvabit. The employment which Augustus had in mind for Horace has nothing to do with the post *ab epistulis*, occupied by Suetonius under Hadrian;[6] for this was a later creation. The context makes it clear that what Augustus wanted was a secretary to help him with his private correspondence. The Princeps was a letter-writer of amazing energy and conscientiousness. One comparatively small instance, of which a record is luckily preserved, appears to be typical. Cornelius Nepos, in the

[1] All the fragments of Augustus' correspondence and indeed everything that is preserved of his official and private writings can be conveniently read in the careful edition by H. Malcovati, *Imperatoris Caesaris Augusti Operum Fragmenta*, 3rd ed., Turin 1948.

[2] Recently (cf. *Ann. Épigr.*, 1953, pp. 27 f., no. 73) an inscription was found in the forum of Hippo Regius, from which we learn that Suetonius was not only *ab epistulis Imp. Caes. Traiani Hadriani Aug.* (that had been known before), but also *a studiis* (cf. O. Hirschfeld, *Die kaiserl. Verwaltungsbeamten*, 2nd ed., 332 ff.) and *a bybliothecis* (cf. ibid. 302 ff.).

[3] Cf. ibid. 320 ff.; L. Friedlaender, *Sittengeschichte*, 9th ed., i. 55 ff.

[4] Cf. Hirschfeld, op. cit. 324.   [5] Suet. *Aug.* 71. 2; 87. 1; 87. 3.

[6] The difference is pointed out by Hirschfeld, op. cit. 319 n. 3.

appendix which he added to his *Life of Atticus* after Atticus had died in March 32 B.C., first mentions that Octavian, towards the end of Atticus' life, betrothed the infant granddaughter of Atticus, Vipsania Agrippina, to his own stepson, the boy Tiberius; he then continues (19. 4 ff.) *quae coniunctio necessitudinem eorum sanxit, familiaritatem reddidit frequentiorem. quamvis ante haec sponsalia non solum cum ab urbe abesset* [scil. Octavian] *numquam ad suorum quemquam litteras misit quin Attico mitteret, quid ageret, in primis quid legeret quibusque in locis et quamdiu esset moraturus, sed etiam, cum esset in urbe et propter infinitas suas occupationes minus saepe quam vellet Attico frueretur, nullus dies temere intercessit quo non ad eum scriberet, cum modo aliquid de antiquitate ab eo requireret, modo aliquam quaestionem poeticam ei proponeret, interdum iocans eius verbosiores eliceret epistulas.* The expression *infinitae occupationes* will not seem exaggerated when we consider the tasks which faced Octavian at that time, and yet he made it possible to correspond regularly with the old gentleman to such an extent and in such a manner. But there was bound to come a moment when the mountains of private correspondence proved too heavy even for Augustus; hence the project put forward in his letter to Maecenas.

In that letter the clause *veniet ergo ab ista parasitica mensa ad hanc regiam* has time and again been made the object of appalling distortions. But readers familiar with the ways of Augustus will not find it difficult to recognize here 'quel tono urbanamente scherzoso che il principe spesso assumeva nello scrivere a familiari ed amici'.[1] It goes without saying that Augustus would never have seriously alluded to himself as *rex*. It should also be plain that the joking use of *mensa regia* couples itself in the writer's whimsical mind with *parasitica mensa*, since in Rome, at least from the time of the early *fabula palliata* (of which Augustus was very fond[2]), the man who maintains a parasite, his τρέφων, was called his *rex*;[3] Horace himself uses the word in this sense.[4]

Horace rejected the emperor's offer on the ground of bad health. The thinness of the excuse was patent,[5] but Augustus did not resent it: *ac ne recusanti quidem aut succensuit aut amicitiam suam ingerere desiit. exstant epistulae, e quibus argumenti gratia pauca subieci: 'sume tibi aliquid iuris apud me,[6] tamquam si convictor mihi fueris;[7] recte enim et non temere feceris, quoniam id usus mihi tecum esse volui si per valetudinem tuam fieri posset.' et*

---

[1] E. Malcovati, *Athenaeum*, N.S. xv, 1937, 208.

[2] Cf. p. 396 below.

[3] Cf. my *Plautinisches im Plautus*, 191 ff.

[4] *Epist.* 1. 17. 43 *coram rege suo.* I do not mind joining those who, convicted by Housman (*CR* xxii, 1908, 89), *abeunt carbone notati*

[5] Cf. pp. 327 f. below.

[6] A colloquial phrase; cf. Cic. *Fam.* 13. 29. 6 *tantum tibi sumito pro Capitone apud Caesarem quantum ipsum meminisse senties*; 13. 50. 1 *sumpsi hoc mihi pro tua in me observantia . . . ut . . ..*

[7] Cf. p. 300 below.

rursus: 'tui qualem habeam memoriam, poteris ex Septimio quoque nostro audire;[1] nam incidit ut illo coram fieret a me tui mentio. neque enim si tu super-bus amicitiam nostram sprevisti, ideo nos quoque ἀνθυπερηφανοῦμεν.' There is no need to praise the easy grace and perfect *urbanitas* of these utter-ances. The voluminous Greek compound[2] at the end of the last clause is in fact no less spontaneous and conversational than the rest. Educated Romans had long been in the habit of speaking Greek, and indeed thinking in Greek, whenever there was stirring in their mind some particular shade of thought or feeling with which they, thanks to their Greek education, were perfectly familiar, but which it proved hard, and sometimes impossible, to express adequately in Latin. In this respect the manner of Augustus in ordinary conversation and intimate letters did not differ from that of Cicero and many others. The verb ἀνθυπερηφανεῖν is not, so far, attested anywhere else; that may be a mere accident, but it is equally possible that Augustus, with perfect linguistic correctness, should have coined it on the spur of the moment.[3]

Suetonius—here we may regret his scholarly succinctness—goes on: *praeterea saepe eum inter alios iocos* 'purissimum pene⟨m⟩'[4] *et* 'homuncionem lepidissimum' *appellat.* That is how Augustus would talk and write to people he was fond of. A letter to his grandson C. Caesar[5] begins: *ave, mi Gai, meus asellus iucundissimus.*[6]

Suetonius, after producing his excerpts from the letters of Augustus to Horace, adds: *unaque et altera liberalitate* [scil. *eum*] *locupletavit.* Up to this point the biographer has been discussing the relations of the

---

[1] Septimius is possibly the man to whom Horace addresses *Odes* ii. 6 and *Epist.* i. 9 (but the identity of the addressees of these two poems is not certain: Porphyrio's assertion may be based on a guess); cf., for example, Kiessling, introduction to *Epist.* i. 9; Christ, *Sitzgsber. Bayer. Ak.* 1893, 75 n. 1; Stein, *RE* ii A. 1560.

[2] Here restored with certainty.

[3] The verb ὑπερηφανεῖν is common in Hellenistic Greek, also with a personal object; see Liddell and Scott and add *Pap. Flor.* 367 (iii. 89), a private letter, third century of our era, some expressions of which were compared with the present passage of Augustus' letter to Horace by Vitelli, *Bull. Soc. Royale d'Archéol. d'Alexandrie*, no. 23, 1928, p. 293. The writer begins Ἐγὼ δὲ οὐ μιμήσομαί σε οὐδὲ τὰς ἀπανθρώπους σου ἐπιστολάς, ἀλλὰ κτλ. and says later on (10 ff.) ἀλλὰ δηλονότι πλούτῳ γαυρωθεὶς καὶ πολλῇ χρημάτων περιουσίᾳ ὑπερηφανεῖς τοὺς φίλους.

[4] Lenchantin, op. cit. (see p. 1 n. 1 above) 2, should not have attempted once more to vindicate the MS reading *pene*. The noun *penis*, whatever its original meaning, or mean-ings, had long been used solely in an improper sense (cf. W. Wendt, *Ciceros Brief an Paetus IX 22*, Diss. Giessen 1929, p. 24). Hence it came to serve as an affectionate denotation of a little boy, like πόσθων (Ar. *Peace* 1300) and similar words; cf. Nehring, *Glotta*, xiv, 1925, 163 f. Augustus talks to Horace, who, incidentally, happened to be *corporis exigui*, in the playful and affectionate tone which would be used in addressing a nice boy. The vocative (for in the letter the *appellare* must have been done in the vocative) *homuncio lepidissime* is in the same vein as *purissime penis.*   [5] Gell. 15. 7. 3.

[6] For this use of the nominative see Löfstedt, *Syntactica*, i, 2nd ed., 99 ff.—The Emperor Commodus *habuit et hominem pene prominentem ultra modum* [*animalium*], *quem onon appellabat, sibi carissimum* (Lampr. *Comm.* 10. 9, cf. Housman, *CQ* xxiv, 1930, 13). I am not quite sure that some such *sous-entendu* is absent from the use of *asellus* in Augustus' letter to Gaius.

Princeps with Horace in general. He now goes on to speak of the high
esteem in which Augustus held Horace's poetry. This whole section
will be examined later on in connexion with the *Carmen Saeculare* (p.
364 below) and the epistle to Augustus (p. 383 below).

The next section, in accordance with a fixed biographical pattern,
deals with the poet's physical appearance. *Habitu corporis fuit brevis
atque obesus, qualis et a semet ipso in saturis*[1] *describitur et ab Augusto hac
epistula: 'pertulit ad me Onysius*[2] *libellum tuum, quem ego †ut accusantem†*[3]
*quantuluscumque est boni consulo. vereri autem mihi videris ne maiores libelli
tui sint quam ipse es. sed tibi statura deest, corpusculum non deest. itaque
licebit in sextariolo scribas, quo circuitus voluminis tui sit ὀγκωδέστερος,*[4]
sicut est ventriculi tui. The joke about the pint-pot may to a modern
reader seem somewhat laboured; but that would certainly not have
been the effect it made on Horace and his contemporaries. The manu-
facture of papyrus as writing material was a monopoly of Egypt;
consequently the stuff was expensive, and for ordinary purposes cheaper
substitutes had to be used.[5] Potsherds were common all over the ancient
world, not least in Rome, where there stands to the present day, not
far from the ancient *Emporium*, a conspicuous piece of evidence, Monte
Testaccio. A sufficiently big fragment of a large wine-jar or some
similar earthen vessel provided an excellent surface to write on; it is in
fact to ostraca from Egypt that we owe, among other texts, some
valuable pieces of Greek poetry.[6] Why, then, should not Horace write
a poem, not indeed on a *sextariolus* (that is Augustus' joke), but on a
potsherd?[7] The *libellus* that Augustus has received from him is a τεῦχος,

[1] *Sat.* 2. 3. 308 f., but also *Epist.* 1. 20. 24 and 1. 4. 15. Rostagni, *Suetonio De poetis*, 118,
rightly observes that here *saturis*, used rather loosely, does not exclude the *Epistles*.

[2] It is exceedingly doubtful whether this was the man's name. Hübner, the editor of the
inscriptions from Spain, attempted to vindicate it with the help of an inscription from the
Tarraconensis, *CIL* ii. 3286 ('litteris aevi Antoniniani bonis'), in which, l. 10, a freedman
with the cognomen *Onysianus* appears. J. Bernays, *Rh. Mus.* xvii, 1862, 313 f. (*Ges.
Abh.* ii. 305 f.) identified the Onysius of the letter with Vinnius Asina, the messenger who
was to carry a copy of Horace's *carmina* to Augustus (*Epist.* i. 13); this wild guess ought not
to have been revived by Rostagni, loc. cit. The Greek of the Princeps was proof against
any temptation to combine *Onysius* with ὄνος.

[3] No plausible emendation has been suggested.

[4] ὀγκωδέστατος MSS: -ερος Leo in the margin of his copy of Reifferscheid's Suetonius.
The correction seems to me necessary. The confusion of -τερος and -τατος is very common;
see Cobet, *Nov. Lect.* 119; Gow on Theocr. 12. 32; and cf., for example, A. *Sept.* 568,
598, 657.

[5] Cf. in general W. Schubart, *Einführung in die Papyruskunde*, 39. G. Glotz, 'Le Prix du
papyrus dans l'antiquité grecque', *Annales d'histoire écon. et soc.* i, 1929, 3 ff., shows that
after Alexander's conquest of Egypt papyrus became cheap in the Greek world for a few
decades, but the price soon went up again and remained high for good.

[6] e.g. Sappho, fr. 2, Lobel and Page, and the longest (three complete lines) fragment
(57 Wyss) that we possess of the *Lyde* of Antimachus of Colophon.

[7] For vases or fragments of vases being used as writing material in the Latin-speaking
part of the Empire see R. Cagnat, *Cours d'épigraphie latine*, 4th ed., 350.

a *volumen,* a papyrus roll: its shape has something in common with the shape of a *sextariolus*—and of the poet's *embonpoint.* In a society not very touchy about personal remarks the witticism might be thought not too bad.

There follows a brief section about Horace's sexual habits, *ad res venereas* and so forth. The time is past when scholars could feel justified in obelizing this section. Its theme is a customary item in biographies of this type; its usual place is, as here, after the section *de habitu corporis.* Suetonius says *traditur . . . dicitur;* he thus makes it clear that what he reports in this section is based on nothing but *rumores.*[1] The filthy detail was presumably a *locus communis;* Lessing compared Seneca's very similar report[2] about the rich Hostius Quadra, who lived under Augustus.[3]

The beginning of the next sentence, *vixit plurimum in secessu ruris sui Sabini aut Tiburtini,* does not add anything to the information provided by Horace's poems, and its continuation, *domusque ostenditur circa Tiburni luculum,* merely shows that in antiquity the local guides knew their business as well as their modern successors.

After *Tiburni luculum* the text of the *Vita* runs: *venerunt in manus meas et elegi sub titulo eius et epistula prosa oratione quasi commendantis se Maecenati, sed utraque falsa puto: nam elegi volgares, epistula etiam obscura, quo vitio minime tenebatur.* It would be absurd for any biographer of a poet to discuss some fakes ascribed to him without saying a word about his genuine poems. Otto Jahn saw what had happened. Suetonius, no doubt, began this section with a list of Horace's books, *Iambi, Saturae,* etc., but the man who transferred the *Vita* from the *De poetis* to a copy of Horace's works did not see why he should waste paper to tell the reader something that a glance over the books in front of him would show him anyhow. He therefore omitted the catalogue of the authentic Horatian poems and retained only Suetonius' interesting remarks about the fakes. At least one of the motives that led to the fabrication of these deliberate forgeries can be inferred with a high degree of probability.[4] The published work of the two leading Augustan poets, Virgil and Horace, consisted only of poems written at their mature period, beginning from the time when they were about thirty years of age. After they had been dead for some time, some sections of the public seem to have been obsessed by a fervent desire to know something about the early production, the *elementa poetae,* of each of them and also about their first contacts with the great, Octavian in the case of Virgil

[1] Cf. p. 6 n. 2 above.
[2] *Nat. Quaest.* 1. 16. 2.
[3] For the connexion between the obscene detail in the *Vita Horati* and the story about Cratinus (Ps. Acro on Hor. *Epist.* 1. 19. 1) see Meineke, *Hist. crit. com. Graec.* 46 f.
[4] Cf. *JRS* xlii, 1952, 7 f.

and Maecenas in the case of Horace. To satisfy both this demand and a more subtle ambition of their own, some unknown amateurs set to work and presented the literary world with such products as the *Culex*, dedicated to the boy Octavius, the future Augustus, and the *epistula Horati commendantis se Maecenati*. In dealing with this nonsense Suetonius shows himself a worthy pupil of the great Alexandrian school of γραμματική, which culminated in the κρίσις ποιημάτων, ὃ δὴ κάλλιστόν ἐστι πάντων τῶν ἐν τῇ τέχνῃ. He does not content himself with declaring firmly *utraque falsa puto*, but, in the best tradition of the craft,[1] gives precise reasons for his judgement. It is a fair guess that, if by some mischance the prose epistle and the *elegi* had come down to us, they would be treated with great reverence by many scholars in many lands, and we should enjoy the benefit of a large literature on *Orazio minore*.

The *Vita* concludes with this section: *natus est*[2] *VI Idus Decembris L. Cotta et L. Torquato consulibus,*[3] *decessit V Kal. Decembris C. Marcio Censorino et C. Asinio Gallo consulibus,*[4] *post nonum et quinquagesimum ⟨diem quam Maecenas obierat, aetatis agens septimum et quinquagesimum⟩*[5] *annum, herede Augusto palam nuncupato, cum urgente vi valetudinis non sufficeret ad obsignandas testamenti tabulas. [humatus et] conditus est extremis Esquiliis iuxta Maecenatis tumulum.*

The year and the month of Horace's birth are attested by the poet himself,[6] but information about the day must have come from some

---

[1] Cf., for example, Schol. A Hom. Σ 39, ὁ τῶν Νηρεΐδων χορὸς προηθέτηται (i.e. before Aristarchus) καὶ παρὰ Ζηνοδότῳ ὡς ʿΗσιόδειον ἔχων χαρακτῆρα κτλ. (we are here concerned not with the correctness of the judgement [cf., on the one hand, Wilamowitz, *Ilias und Homer*, 165, on the other Von der Mühll, *Kritisches Hypomnema zur Ilias*, 270], but with the method of argumentation); Hypothesis Eur. *Rhes.* τοῦτο τὸ δρᾶμα ἔνιοι νόθον ὑπενόησαν, Εὐριπίδου δὲ μὴ εἶναι, τὸν γὰρ Σοφόκλειον μᾶλλον ὑποφαίνειν χαρακτῆρα (Wilamowitz, *Kl. Schriften*, i. 9 ff., [cf. also his *Einleit. in die griech. Tragödie*, 155 f.] concluded from the polemics in the scholia that there existed an earlier ὑπόμνημα, probably of the first century B.C., in which observations on detail served to disprove the authorship of Euripides); Schol. Thuc. 3. 84. 1, τὰ ὠβελισμένα οὐδενὶ τῶν ἐξηγητῶν ἔδοξε Θουκυδίδου εἶναι. ἀσαφῆ γὰρ καὶ τῷ τύπῳ τῆς ἑρμηνείας καὶ τοῖς διανοήμασι πολὺν ἐμφαίνοντα τὸν νεωτερισμόν. Asconius in the epilogue of his commentary on Cicero's speech *In toga candida* (72. 18 ff. St.), bluntly says: *feruntur quoque orationes nomine illorum* [i.e. of Catilina and Antonius] *editae, non ab ipsis scriptae, sed ab Ciceronis obtrectatoribus: quas nescio an satius sit ignorare.* The great scholar is so annoyed at the silliness of those products that he cannot bring himself to say more about them.

[2] As a rule Suetonius indicates the date of the birth in one of the first few chapters of a *vita*; for its postponement and its bracketing with the date of the death some non-Suetonian parallels are adduced by F. Leo, *Griech.-röm. Biogr.* 19.

[3] 8 Dec. 65 B.C.   [4] 27 Nov. 8 B.C.

[5] For information on the detection of the lacuna and the authors of the supplements see Klingner's and Rostagni's notes. I have not accepted Rostagni's *Romae*, since where he puts it (after *obierat*) it would be in the wrong place (cf., for example, Suet. *Aug.* 100. 1; *Tib.* 73. 1), and, if it were put in its proper place, after *decessit*, it would be difficult to account for its omission.

[6] *Epist.* 1. 20. 26 f. For the year cf. also *Epod.* 1. 13. 6, *Odes* 3. 21. 1.

other source. In Greece, during the classical (as distinct from the Hellenistic) period, little or nothing was made of a private citizen's birthday;[1] consequently we do not know the birthday of any of the great Attic poets. In Rome religious motives, presumably connected with the importance of an individual's *genius*, led to a different custom. More than one Augustan poem has as its theme *venit natalis ad aras*. One of Horace's late poems[2] was written on the occasion of the birthday of Maecenas. The birthday of any person of any importance would be known to, and celebrated by, the circle of his friends at least; the biographer was therefore able to record it in the case of both Virgil and Horace.

. . . *herede Augusto palam nuncupato, cum urgente vi valetudinis non sufficeret ad obsignandas testamenti tabulas.* The ordinary form of a will was the 'mancipatory' will, *per aes et libram*, that is to say 'a declaration of the testator before seven witnesses (the five witnesses required in every *mancipatio*, the *libripens*, and the *familiae emptor*) that one or more wax tablets contained his will, which he sometimes, but not necessarily, read to them'.[3] Since *caput et fundamentum intellegitur totius testamenti heredis institutio,*[4] the will began with the 'heredis institutio', *Lucius Titius heres esto*. If the testator was incapable of signing a will, an oral *nuncupatio heredis*, if declared *palam*, i.e. in the presence of the required number of witnesses, would be equally valid.[5] We have already seen (pp. 16 f. above) that in Maecenas' will, also, Augustus was instituted heir. The Princeps set great store on being thus honoured in the *suprema iudicia* of his friends.[6]

Horace was laid to rest close to the tomb of Maecenas, in surroundings dear to him: *nunc licet Esquiliis habitare salubribus.*

[1] What Herodotus (1. 133. 1) remarks about the Persians is significant.

[2] *Odes* iv. 11.

[3] F. Schulz, *Classical Roman Law*, Oxford 1951, 243.

[4] Gaius, *Inst.* 2. 229. Cf. Schulz, op. cit. 239.

[5] Ulpian, *Dig.* 28. 1. 21 pr. '*Heredes palam ita ut exaudiri possunt nuncupandi sint*'. *licebit ergo testanti vel nuncupare heredes vel scribere: sed si nuncupat, palam debet. quid est palam? non utique in publicum, sed ut exaudiri possit: exaudiri autem non ab omnibus, sed a testibus: et si plures fuerint testes adhibiti, sufficit sollemnem numerum exaudire.* Cf. P. F. Girard, *Manuel du droit romain*, 4th ed., 1906, 806 n. 2, who quotes the passage in Suetonius' *Life of Horace*.

[6] Suet. *Aug.* 66. 4 *quamvis minime appeteret hereditates, ut qui numquam ex ignoti testamento capere quicquam sustinuerit, amicorum tamen suprema iudicia morosissime pensitavit, neque dolore dissimulato si parcius aut citra honorem verborum, neque gaudio si grate pieque quis se prosecutus fuisset.*

II

THE EPODES

I. EPODE X

WE begin our survey of the book with Epode X, *Mala soluta navis exit alite*. Its content is poor, but it shows a skilful structure, and the ornamentation of its detail is rich. The poem is divided into three sections. A brief introduction (1 f.) outlines the situation that gives rise to the imprecations (3–14) and predictions (15–20) which form the theme of the central part. A sharply separated epilogue, marked as such by *quodsi*,[1] concludes the epode (21–24). The leading figures in the central part as well as in the epilogue are the winds, or rather the storm-deities (24 *Tempestatibus*), who are called upon to assault and wreck the ship. Each of them, Auster, Eurus, and Aquilo, is given a full couplet at the beginning of the main part (3–8). By the omission of the west wind it is implied that its blowing would be to the advantage of the travellers: their route appears to be the common route from Italy to Greece. This inference is confirmed by the mention of the Ionian Sea at l. 19.

In this carefully proportioned architecture the *piano nobile*, exactly in the middle (11–14),[2] is allotted to a mythological *exemplum* taken from the catastrophe of the Locrian Ajax, one of the chief episodes in the old stories about the 'Return from Troy'. This scene of the heroic world serves to ennoble the fierce curses by a fine conclusion; the following six lines (15–20), the last of the main part, contain no longer imprecations but a prophecy of what is in store for the passengers and the crew. This is the liveliest section of the epode: the misery of the voyagers is painted in suggestive colours, and the effect is heightened when the poet suddenly turns to Mevius, who here, and here only, is addressed directly (15 f.). In the lines describing the final catastrophe (19 f.) the south wind appears again, this time under its Greek name, *Notus*. So this couplet harks back to the couplet (3 f.) in which *Auster* was invoked. In other words, the two sentences describing the havoc to be wrought by the south wind are symmetrically placed at either end of the principal

---

[1] As at *Odes* 1. 1. 35; 3. 1. 41; Prop. 1. 1. 37; 2. 14. 31; 2. 32. 61; 3. 6. 41, and elsewhere.

[2] Ten lines precede the mythological παράδειγμα and ten lines follow it. In Epode III, too, the παράδειγμα, taken from the story of Medea, is placed in the centre (9–14), but since so much has to be said about that poison, the *exemplum* fills six instead of four lines so that there is no complete symmetry.

section: they form a kind of frame to this section. At the same time the mention of the wind in the last line (20) of this part facilitates the transition to the vow to the wind-goddesses. These powerful deities, whose sonorous name concludes the epode, will, so the poet hopes, fulfil his unholy wishes.

If we want to illustrate the polish which is characteristic of the whole poem, it will suffice to look at the treatment of the winds. Auster (3 f.) is invoked directly, in the vocative and the imperative, but for Eurus and Aquilo (5–8) the third person is used: here a variation is brought in by the chiastic arrangement, *Eurus . . . differat; insurgat Aquilo*, which also has the effect that the verb *insurgat*, strong in itself, receives still greater emphasis. At the end of the main part (19 f.) the former pattern is abandoned altogether and Notus is kept in a syntactically subordinate position.[1]

To turn to another formal device. In this short poem much is made of sound patterns. In the central section the howling of the winds is suggested first by the frequency of the 'littera canina',[2] 3 f. *horridis utrumque verberes . . . Auster*, and especially 5 f., *niger rudentis Eurus inverso mari fractosque remos differat*, where every word has its *r*, and at the end, 19 f., by the abundance of *u*-sounds, *Ionius udo cum remugiens sinus . . . ruperit.*[3]

So the epode appears, on a first reading, as a product of adroit craftsmanship. But our troubles begin as soon as we ask the question (we hope not an impertinent question): What is it all about? Horace hurls the most terrifying execrations against a man called Mevius, but, as F. Leo puts it,[4] 'ne verbo quidem tam gravis odii causam indicat'.

---

[1] The subtle variation in *fluctibus, mari, aequore, sinus*, and in *navis, ratem, carinam* has been noticed by the commentators.

[2] Both the rhotacism and the accumulation of *u* sounds were noticed by Heinze. For *littera canina* see Lucilius 377 Marx; Persius 1. 109 f. (cf. the scholium). Catullus 42. 16 f., *ruborem ferreo canis exprimamus ore*, plays with it. For the sequence of *r*'s at Virgil, *Ecl.* 7. 41 f. and the harshness expressed by them see Heinze, *Neue Jahrb. f. d. klass. Altert.* 1907, 166.

[3] For *u*-sounds employed by Ennius in the *Achilles* to enliven the description of a rainstorm, see my *Plautinisches im Plautus* 176 n. 1, and cf. Catullus 64. 155, *quod mare conceptum spumantibus exspuit undis*. The possibility of a much older deliberate use of repeated *u*'s is suggested by E. Norden, *Aus altrömischen Priesterbüchern*, Lund 1939, 122. Virgil's clauses (*Georg.* 1. 486) *resonare lupis ululantibus urbes* and (*Aen.* 7. 18) *formae magnorum ululare luporum* always remind me of the sinister sentence in the first French story I read at school, Alfonse Daudet's *La Chèvre de Monsieur Seguin*, 'Hou hou! faisait le loup'. The *u*-sound may, of course, convey quite different impressions. In the last two lines of Virgil's first eclogue, which are among the finest in Latin poetry, the long series of *u*'s helps, so it seems, to picture the darkening of the colours in the rich subalpine landscape that calls to mind backgrounds on paintings of Titian and Giorgione. Claudian 28 (*De sexto consulatu Honorii*) 628 f., *mucronis acutum murmur, et umbonum pulsu modulante resultans*, suggests the ominous rumbling of the weapons and also the hollow sound of the shields.

[4] *De Horatio et Archilocho* (University Programme, 'Ad praemiorum . . . renuntiationem . . . invitant', Göttingen 1900), 8.

There is no hint at the sort of crime which Mevius is supposed to have committed, nor is anything said about the man himself; he remains an entirely shadowy figure. All that we hear of him is that he is *olens Mevius*. That, if true, is certainly unpleasant, but this complaint is far too common, both in the ancient and in the modern world,[1] to justify such a violent outburst. But perhaps we have to assume that Mevius, besides being a general nuisance, had offended Horace in some particular manner and so provoked his hatred? If this suggestion or a similar one be made, it should be rejected without hesitation. Those kind readers who from time to time feel tempted to supplement a Horatian poem by reading into it what in their opinion the poet has failed to say himself are respectfully but firmly asked to shut this book and never to open it again: it could only disappoint and distress them. My interpretations are, without exception, based on the conviction that Horace, throughout his work, shows himself both determined and able to express everything that is relevant to the understanding and the appreciation of a poem, either by saying it in so many words or by implying it through unambiguous hints. If he does not tell us anything about the reasons for his hatred of Mevius, I conclude that he does not want us to concern ourselves with those reasons.

At this point I think I hear indignant protests: 'but we know enough about Mevius; he was a poetaster whom Virgil in the *Eclogues* had treated with scorn and whom consequently Horace attacked in this epode'. This opinion is not unknown to me, and I also know that it is based not on any indication in the poem itself, but on the guess of an ancient commentator or, perhaps, on that of his source, one of the authors *qui de personis Horatianis scripserunt*. In the scholia (Porph.) we read *hic est M[a]evius[2] inportunissimus poeta, quem et Vergilius cum simili contumelia nominat (Ecl.* 3. 90): 'qui Bavium non odit, amet tua carmina, Mevi*', and consequently the heading of the epode in one branch of our manuscripts runs *in Mevium poetam*. The guess was a pretty obvious one. The name Mevius is not very common,[3] and the only Mevius in Horace's time of whom anything is known is the man who in Virgil's scornful line is bracketed with Bavius (it is always a good thing for a Rosencrantz to be in the company of a Guildenstern; hence *Sulcius*

---

[1] F. Skutsch, *Glotta*, ii, 1910, 234 ff. (*Kl. Schriften*, 394 f.), quotes some amusing instances.

[2] For the spelling see the inscriptions (cf. the next footnote) and cf. W. Heraeus in his Teubner edition of Martial, p. xlviii.

[3] The comparative rarity of the name can be safely inferred from its scanty occurrence in the inscriptions. For our purposes it is sufficient to look up Dessau's *Inscr. Lat. Sel.*, vol. iii, p. 100, and to compare the few instances of *Mevius* with the numerous examples of more ordinary names. When in the law texts (at least as early as Gaius, *Inst.*) *Mevius*, used as a symbolic name (like *Titius*, etc.), occurs frequently, this is probably due to the freak of some teacher.

acer ambulat et Caprius).[1] It is therefore unlikely that the Mevius of the tenth epode should be wholly unrelated to the Mevius against whose poetry Virgil inveighed. It is, however, necessary to draw a sharp line between possible implications which may or may not have been noticed by the friends of the poet to whom he first recited his epode and the meaning of the published poem which, without relying on any outside information, should be self-evident to a sensible reader. While admitting the possibility that Virgil and his admirers were delighted at Horace's choice of the name Mevius for the victim of his curses, we must guard against the assumption that the effect, or the understanding, of the epode depends in any way on the reader's being aware that Mevius happens to be a poet. If the man's bad poetry were in the least relevant to the invective, Horace would have said, or implied, that Mevius was a poet. There was nothing to prevent him from doing so, and, as regards possible consequences of a libel, it would surely be the mention of the name, and not of the poetry, which might involve some risk. As the epode stands, the versifying activities of Mevius have no place in it, and they cannot be used to account for the hatred which seems to be the essence of the poem.

So far we have examined the epode itself. It is now time to consider a piece of information which has come to us from outside. No external material can, in the case of a real poem, that is to say of a self-contained poem, supply a clue not contained in the poem itself. This general rule holds good also for the Mevius epode. But the acquaintance with a poem which, in a strictly qualified sense, must be regarded as Horace's 'model' will, perhaps, enable us to see why in this nicely constructed and richly ornamented epode there is so very little of real substance.

Among a mass of papyri which had shortly before been given to the University Library at Strasbourg (most of them containing late documents) R. Reitzenstein discovered in 1899 two fragments of a literary papyrus, which, fully aware of their importance, he published without delay.[2] The two fragments, as has been recently established beyond

---

[1] For the period after the publication of Virgil's *Eclogues* nothing is known about Mevius. Tenney Frank's assertion (*Catullus and Horace*, 165) that 'men like "Bavius" and "Maevius" parodied Vergil's Eclogues and Georgics' is based on a piece of sham evidence; see Wissowa, *RE* iv. 1629. W. Kroll, *RE* xv. 1508, is right in dismissing as mere guesses all that the scholiasts say about Mevius, except Porphyrio on *Sat.* 2. 3. 239 (where the quotation from Mevius has dropped out, as Kiessling, *Index Schol.* Greifswald 1880, 5, saw). The passage in Horace to which this scholium is appended alludes to the scandalous liaison of the younger Aesopus, the son of the famous actor, as to a thing of the past; therefore the poem in which Mevius attacked the same young man may well have been written about the time of Virgil's *Eclogues* or even earlier.

[2] *Sitz. Berlin* 1899, 857 ff. (with a plate). For the extensive literature on these fragments see *Anthol. Lyr. Graeca*, ed. E. Diehl, fasc. 3, 3rd ed., 1952, 34 (on Archil. *frs.* 79, 80),

doubt,[1] belong to two different columns of one and the same roll.
The first fragment alone concerns us for our present purpose, although
for the question of the authorship the second fragment also must be
taken into account. The first fragment consists of the end of a poem,
thirteen fairly well preserved lines; we cannot say how much is missing
at the beginning.[2] This is what we have:[3]

. . . .

κύμασι πλαζόμενος.
κἂν Σαλμυδησσῷ γυμνὸν εὐφρον‒ ∪ ∠
Θρήικες ἀκρόκομοι
λάβοιεν· ἔνθα πόλλ' ἀναπλήσει κακὰ
δούλιον ἄρτον ἔδων·
ῥίγει πεπηγότ' αὐτόν, ἐκ δὲ τοῦ χνόου
φυκία πόλλ' ἐπιχέοι,
κροτέοι δ' ὀδόντας ὡς κύων ἐπὶ στόμα
κείμενος ἀκρασίῃ
ἄκρον παρὰ ῥηγμῖνα κυμαν‒ ∪ ∠.
ταῦτ' ἐθέλοιμ' ἂν ἰδεῖν
ὅς μ' ἠδίκησε, λὰξ δ' ἐφ' ὁρκίοις ἔβη,
τὸ πρὶν ἑταῖρος ἐών.

'. . . drifting, struck by the waves. And at Salmydessos, when he lies naked,
may the topknotted Thracians seize him in a kindly spirit[4]—there he
will have his fill of sufferings, eating the bread of slavery—himself stiff with
cold, and from the scum may piles of seaweed heap over him, and may
he gnash his teeth like a dog lying face downwards in helplessness right at
the edge of the surf, tossed by the waves (?).[5] This I would see him suffer
who wronged me and trampled under foot our oaths, he who was once on
our side.'

In this poem fierce hatred mingled with contempt finds a powerful
voice, and yet, with so much passion, every phrase and every sentence
is kept strictly under the control of a masterly mind. The impact on the

where also a revised text, based on the re-collation of the papyrus by J. Schwartz and O.
Masson, can be found. It is this text which I follow.

[1] By J. Schwartz and O. Masson; see the latter's article in *Rev. Ét. Grec.* lxiv, 1951,
427 ff. Schwartz regards it as very improbable that the two fragments come from neighbouring columns.

[2] Nothing can, so far, be made of the few letters of a second poem which, separated by a
paragraphos, follows in the same column.

[3] For detailed information on missing or illegible letters, etc., see Masson's article and
Diehl's edition. At the beginning of our text it is idle to speculate whether κύμ[ατι] or
κύμ[ασι] is more likely, since we do not know what preceded: there may have been an
epithet. At the last line but one I fail to see that the interlinear gloss ἐπὶ ὁρκίοις justifies us
in giving up the ἐφ' ὁρκίοις of the text. Our knowledge of psilosis in early Ionian is very
flimsy.

[4] The continuation of εὐφρον. . . is uncertain; the expression is likely to be ironical.

[5] The end of the sentence cannot be restored with certainty.

ear, on the eye, and on the sense of smell is strong throughout. Every detail, the surf, the seaweed, the dog, the wretched man's frozen body, is there, life-like, or rather in even sharper outlines than they would appear to us in actual life. Despite the abundance of images there is nothing diffuse or entangled in this piece. One execration after another is hurled out from the depth by a volcanic force. The language retains the vigour and directness of impassioned speech, and the few Homeric reminiscences heighten the pathos without rendering the expression artificial. The clear-cut clauses fill the simple metre in a natural flow, and if at one place an interruption, a 'parenthesis', breaks the continuity of the curses, since the speaker is carried away by the rapture of his revengeful anticipation (ἔνθα πόλλ' ἀναπλήσει κακὰ δούλιον ἄρτον ἔδων), it is as if the very voice of life had for a moment exhausted itself and must take a fresh breath. After gloating upon the appalling pictures of his enemy's hoped-for misery, the poet abruptly concludes with the climax of his curses, ταῦτ' ἐθέλοιμ' ἂν ἰδεῖν.[1]

It is unfortunate that, right at the beginning of our study of Horace's work, we have been forced to look at the epode on the Strasbourg papyrus. A reader who, under the fresh impression of this poem, turns to the Mevius epode may find it difficult to overcome a dislike, if not for Horace, at any rate for the Horace of the epodes. But the Greek poem could not possibly be left aside. When Reitzenstein published the Strasbourg papyrus, he ascribed the poems of both its columns to Archilochus and added the observation that the first epode seemed to have inspired the Mevius epode of Horace. Soon afterwards Leo published his paper *De Horatio et Archilocho*,[2] and since that time the relation of Horace's tenth epode to the Ionic poem has been a stock-in-trade of Horatian scholarship, and rightly so.[3] The true character of

---

[1] Scholars who are fond of labels might speak of a 'Racheformel'. For similar outbursts of fierce hatred and vindictiveness cf., for instance, Hom. Z 284 f. εἰ κεῖνόν γε ἴδοιμι κατελθόντ' Ἄϊδος εἴσω, φαίην κεν φίλον ἦτορ ὀϊζύος ἐκλελαθέσθαι, Aesch. Cho. 267 f. οὓς ἴδοιμ' ἐγώ ποτε θανόντας ἐν κηκῖδι πισσήρει φλογός (L. R. Farnell's excellent interpretation, *CQ* iv, 1910, 185, has been rightly accepted by G. Thomson ad loc.), *Prom.* 972 f. χλιδῶντας ὧδε τοὺς ἐμοὺς ἐγὼ ἐχθροὺς ἴδοιμι, Soph. *Aj.* 384 ἴδοιμί νιν, καίπερ ὧδ' ἀτώμενος (a participle going with νιν would naturally follow, but, before he can utter it, Ajax is interrupted by the chorus warning him μηδὲν μέγ' εἴπῃς), *Trach.* 1039 f. τὰν ὧδ' ἐπίδοιμι πεσοῦσαν αὔτως, ὧδ' αὔτως, ὥς μ' ὤλεσεν, *Phil.* 1043 f. εἰ δ' ἴδοιμ' ὀλωλότας τούτους, δοκοῖμ' ἂν τῆς νόσου πεφευγέναι, 113 f. ἰδοίμαν δέ νιν, τὸν τάδε μησάμενον, τὸν ἴσον χρόνον ἐμὰς λαχόντ' ἀνίας, Eur. *Hec.* 441 f. ὡς τὴν Λάκαιναν . . . Ἑλένην ἴδοιμι, Ar. *Ach.* 1156 ὃν ἔτ' ἐπίδοιμι τευθίδος δεόμενον, Lucian, *Dial. meretr.* 10. 1 ὃν κάκιστα ἐπίδοιμι ἀπολλύμενον, Plaut. *Trin.* 42 *teque ut quam primum possim videam emortuam*, Prop. 2. 16. 45 *haec videam rapidas in vanum ferre procellas*.

[2] See p. 25 n. 4 above.

[3] Theodor Plüsz, *Das Jambenbuch des Horaz*, 1904, 66, did not believe that Horace was in any way influenced by the Strasbourg epode; he even denied that he received from it any 'Anregung'. On purely logical grounds it is hardly possible to refute such extreme scepticism: the points of contact between the two poems could be accounted for without

that relation was at once properly understood.[1] There is no case here
of a thorough reproduction or even of the borrowing of some characteristic detail: all that the two poems have in common is their fundamental theme, the cursing of a hated man who is about to start on a
voyage and the anticipation of his utter ruin. In every other respect
the Greek and the Latin epode are totally different. In the Greek poem
we watch the eruption of an enormous passion; in the Latin poem the
human element is hardly discernible. After reading the Mevius epode
we ask in vain: why all this commotion? The Greek epode culminates
in revealing the full truth: the man cursed, who was in all probability identified in the now lost beginning,[2] had committed what in
the poet's society was considered the most heinous crime: ὅς μ' ἠδίκησε,
λὰξ δ' ἐφ' ὁρκίοις ἔβη, τὸ πρὶν ἑταῖρος ἐών. To the Ionian iambist a
poem such as this was certainly a means of venting his pent-up emotions, but also something more: a very real and formidable weapon
both in his personal fight and in the fight of his party or gang. If the
gods should not fulfil the poet's imprecations and bring misery upon
the traitor, then he would at least be exposed to all men as the contemptible wretch he was. A poem of this kind realized its primary
function in actual life rather than in what we mean by literature.
Horace's *Epodes*, on the other hand, have their being within the sphere
of literature; the effect which they may have on the reader of the book
is all the poet can hope to achieve through them. For reasons which will
become clear as we go on[3] Horace could not possibly think of rivalling
the early poets' attempts to influence life directly and, in particular, to
use poetry as a weapon in a serious attack. If he wanted to adopt a
theme of Archilochus or of another early iambist, he had no choice but
to empty it of its substance of primary life and to turn it into a bare
topic of literature. That is exactly what happened in the metamorphosis by which the theme of κύμασι πλαζόμενος became the theme of
Mala soluta navis.

The reason why Horace wrote the tenth epode was obviously not
hatred of Mevius, or, for that matter, of any other individual, but the

assuming any indebtedness of Horace to the Greek epode. But if we remember that
Horace, according to his own testimony, leant in his *iambi* largely on the Ionian iambists,
Archilochus in the first place, then it appears utterly unlikely that the recurrence of the
fundamental theme of κύμασι πλαζόμενος κτλ. in *Mala soluta navis* should be due to a
mere chance.

[1] Reitzenstein, *Sitz. Berlin* 1899, 861, said cautiously that Horace 'unserem Gedicht
[fr. 79a D.] die Anregung zu einer seiner Epoden entnommen zu haben scheint', and Leo,
De Hor. et Archil. 8, pointed out the great differences between the two poems.

[2] Reitzenstein, loc. cit.: 'Der Gegner mußte im Eingang genannt sein.' Or, if his name
was not mentioned, it is likely that he was, at the beginning, described in unambiguous
terms.

[3] See pp. 42 ff. below.

wish to produce a polished poetic invective reminiscent of Archilochus. This end had to be obtained in the manner which Horace described many years after:

> Parios ego primus iambos
> ostendi Latio, numeros animosque secutus
> Archilochi, non res et agentia verba Lycamben. (*Epist.* 1. 19. 23 ff.)

In the tenth epode it looks as though *animi*, θυμός, *per se*, not *animi* directed against somebody or something, had become the theme of the poem. The target, it is true, has a name, Mevius, but this Mevius is devoid of all individual features; what sort of man he is is as irrelevant to the epode as is the cause of Horace's animosity against him. It is a fair guess that the name Mevius was chosen to give pleasure to Virgil and his friends, who despised the poetaster of that name.[1] But any such associations, if they were encouraged at all, remain outside the orbit of the epode, in which nothing suggests that the man attacked is a poet. However, the fact that he is called Mevius furnishes an approximate date for the poem. The period between the battle of Philippi (42 B.C.) and the battle of Actium (31 B.C.) is known to us as a fast-living age with an extraordinary productivity in many branches of poetry. In such an age a literary quarrel like the quarrel between Virgil and Mevius is soon pushed into the background and an allusion to it, or a *sous-entendu* which depends on its being remembered, becomes stale after a short time. It is therefore safe to conclude that the Mevius epode was written not long after the publication of Virgil's *Eclogues* (about 39 B.C.); in other words this poem belongs in all probability to the earliest in Horace's book of *iambi*. This point may have a bearing on the hotly disputed question of the authorship of the first Strasbourg epode;[2] it ought at any rate to be considered in connexion with it.

---

[1] See pp. 26 f. above.

[2] For a summary of the discussion see the third edition of Diehl's *Anthol. Lyr.* Immediately after Reitzenstein's publication of the papyrus F. Blass, *Rh. Mus.* lv, 1900, 341 ff., attributed both the first and the second epode to Hipponax; some of his arguments are deceptive and none is conclusive. In 1938 Hipponax found a vigorous champion in G. Perotta. The case for Hipponax was much strengthened when the ancient commentary *Pap. Oxy.* xviii. 2176, published in 1941 (*Anthol. Lyr.*[3], Diehl, fasc. 3, pp. 115 ff.), put it beyond doubt that Hipponax did write epodes. The attempts of various scholars to make a compromise and give Epode I to Archilochus and Epode II to Hipponax, which would mean that the papyrus comes from an anthology, have been successfully refuted by Masson, *Rev. Ét. Grec.* lxiv, 1951, 438 ff. This is not the place to deal again with the highly complex controversy. I must not be guided by my strong conviction that the glorious piece, κύμασι πλαζόμενος κτλ., belongs really to Archilochus. But I may be allowed to point to a weakness in the armour of the fighters for Hipponax. Masson, *Rev. Ét. Grec.* lix–lx, 1946–7, 12, says, 'l'élément capital est la présence au vers 3 [of fr. 80 D.] du nom Ἱππῶνα[ξ', and again, *Rev. Ét. Grec.* lxiv, 1951, 433 n. 2, 'le meilleur argument, rappelons-le, est la présence du nom d'Hipponax au v. 3'. I cannot admit that the context in which the name occurs, as far as it can be made out (the preceding sentence is unfortunately

According to Horace's own testimony his *iambi* were primarily an adaptation of the *Parii iambi* of Archilochus. We know, for Horace implies it himself,[1] that he also drew on Hipponax. But it is not likely that he should have done so at a very early stage. His general practice seems to have been first to follow (for the purpose of free adaptation) one favourite poet, the classic of a particular genre, and later, when the need of variation made itself felt, to widen his compass. That happened in his relation to Lucilius and, so far as we can see, to Alcaeus. But, since too many unknown factors are involved, this consideration alone would not provide a decisive argument for the authorship of Archilochus.

In recasting his Greek model Horace, it will be remembered, attempted to make up for the lack of spontaneity by painstaking workmanship. If we direct our attention to the spirit and the manner of execution in *Mala soluta navis*, we see that, so far from being reminiscent of early Greek poetry, they show a definitely Hellenistic character.[2] We noticed already (p. 24 above) the sharp division of the poem into three parts, introduction (1 f.), main section (3–20), and epilogue (21–24). As regards the separation of the epilogue from the preceding section, a seemingly small point ought not to be overlooked. At the end of the first clause of the epilogue,

> opima quodsi praeda curvo litore
> porrecta mergos iuverit,

iuverit alone represents the παράδοσις, the reading which from ancient books was handed down to the Middle Ages. The reading *iuveris* occurs in texts of the humanistic period; it is a conjecture which had been anticipated in the (probably Carolingian) hyparchetype of a few medieval manuscripts.[3] Many a reader, coming from *tuis* and *tibi* at ll. 15 f., must have wished to read at l. 22 *iuveris* instead of *iuverit*; and the conjecture was expressly recommended by Lambinus and Bentley and put in the text, for instance by Dacier and many editors down to

---

irrecoverable), makes it possible to assume that ῾Ιππῶνα[ξ] or ῾Ιππωνα[κτίδης] (P. Maas) is the name of the poet. ῾Ιππωνα . . . and the disgusting Ἀρίφαντος are, in two strictly parallel clauses, put on the same footing. Ariphantos is clearly an enemy of the speaker; how, then, could ῾Ιππωνα . . . be the speaker himself? As Leo said, *De Hor. et Archil.* 7, 'Hipponactis alicuius nomen cum aliis poetae inimicis in altero fragmento commemoratum etiam certius ostendere ei [i.e. to Reitzenstein, who implied by his treatment of the passage what Leo said explicitly] videbatur hos versus non Hipponactis esse'.

[1] *Epod.* 6. 14.

[2] Reitzenstein, op. cit. 861, calls the tenth epode 'ein im Grunde von alexandrinischem Empfinden beeinflußtes Document'.

[3] Cf. O. Keller, *Epilegomena zu Horaz*, 1879, 385, and in the second edition of vol. i of Horace, edited by Keller and Holder (1899), pp. lxxiv ff.; about the futility of most of those conjectures see p. lxxvi.

our own time.[1] On closer inspection, however, it will be seen that the change to *iuveris* destroys not only the architecture of the epode (by running the main part and the epilogue into one), but also the realistic picture which the poet gives of the shipwreck. At least the latter point might have worried the commentators, but apparently it has not. For the other implication of the conjecture, the complete disregard of the incision between l. 20 and l. 21, the defence of one of the champions of *iuveris* will suffice: 'The transition from the second person to the third, without the new subject being indicated, would be in very bad taste'.[2] On the contrary, the fact that the last four lines are no longer addressed directly to Mevius emphasizes, like the *quodsi* at l. 21,[3] the separation of the epilogue from the body of the poem. But it is time to turn to the thought of the passage. What is meant by *opima praeda*? Here scholars are content with ludicrous explanations, and even those who reject the second part of the scholiast's (Porph.) silly comment, 'opimam praedam corpus ipsius Mevii intellegamus, ex quo apparet et pinguem fuisse', follow him in assuming that *opima praeda* refers to Mevius alone.[4] But how on earth is that conceivable? We have heard (15–20) that, if the gods lend an ear to the poet's imprecations (and he feels confident that they will—hence his prophecy), the ship will founder with every one on board.[5] Since violent storms are blowing, no one will be able to swim to safety. So the *mergi* will have the crew and all the passengers to feast upon, truly a *praeda opima* for them.[6] As for Mevius himself, it is naturally taken for granted that he will perish, but, in marked contrast to the Strasbourg epode, no direct reference is made to him at the end of the poem.

A feature similar to the sharp distinction of the three sections of the epode is the neat arrangement of the different winds. A poet of the archaic period might possibly have described the blasts of the hurricane or have singled out Boreas or another wind for special mention,

---

[1] e.g. Keller and Holder (for a defence of *iuveris* see Keller, *Epil.* 385), Lucian Müller, Ramorino (Florence 1911), Plessis, Tescari, A. Y. Campbell. Villeneuve prints *iuverit* but translates 'Si . . . tu régales les plongeons.'

[2] L. Müller.

[3] Cf. p. 24 above.

[4] e.g. Heinze: 'hier ist der Leichnam eine "fette Beute" im Gegensatze zu den Fischen, mit denen die *mergi* sonst vorlieb nehmen müssen'. This is not substantially different from L. Müller's note (who, however, reads *iuveris*): 'er heißt "eine fette Beute", weil die *mergi* sehr gefräßig sind, selbst ekelhafte Speise nicht verschmähen und selten einen so guten Bissen, wie den Leichnam eines Menschen, finden'.

[5] It is well known that, if there is one bad man among the passengers, the gods are prepared to let the whole ship sink. Compare, for example, the passages quoted by Heinze on Hor. *Odes* 3. 2. 27 ff. and by Denniston on Eur. *El.* 1355, and add Petronius 105. 1.

[6] Bentley was quite near to the truth, and yet missed it, when he blamed those who read *iuverit* for not noticing 'tum incertum fore, utrum ipse Maevius, an quivis alius ex *navitis suis*, an simul omnes hic *praeda mergorum* intelligendi sint'.

but it would hardly have occurred to him to summon the unfavourable winds one by one and allot to each of them precisely a complete distich (3–8).[1] A similar device is used in a contemporary work which, like Horace's tenth epode, bears unmistakable, though different, signs of the influence of Hellenistic poetry, the *Dirae*. This poem, to be read in the editions of the 'Appendix Vergiliana', was written, shortly after the publication of Virgil's *Bucolica*, by a gifted, if somewhat rough, poet whose identity is unknown. The poem bears the title *Dirae* because it deals with the curses uttered by a farmer against the estate which had been his own and is now becoming the prize of a usurping 'soldier' (we should say 'ex-soldier'). This theme reflects, of course, the confiscations of land in Italy arranged by the triumvirs for the benefit of their veterans, but its choice was obviously suggested by some of Virgil's *Eclogues* and the extraordinary success which they immediately won. The author manages to blend a national subject with topics derived from a certain type of Hellenistic poetry, *Ἀραί*, 'Curses'. In the central part, where the displaced farmer invokes upon his land thorough destruction by fire and floods, we read these lines (37–39):

> Thraecis tum Boreae spirent immania vires,
> Eurus agat mixtam fulva caligine nubem,
> Africus immineat nimbis minitantibus imbrem.

Here the symmetrical arrangement of the three winds and their doings is very similar to that in the tenth epode. The similarity might be accounted for by the assumption that either Horace borrowed from the *Dirae* or vice versa, but it seems far more likely that both poems are for this detail indebted to some Hellenistic model.

It is perhaps advisable to go a step farther. *Dirae* would not be a bad title for the Mevius epode.[2] But we must not jump to the conclusion that Horace's poem was formed after the model of one of the Hellenistic *Ἀραί*. Of the *Ibis* of Callimachus scarcely anything is known,[3] except that it was a not very long invective in verse, directed against an adversary (according to the ancient grammarians, against Apollonius Rhodius), who was cursed under the disguise of that dirty bird the ibis; the poem was full of recondite stories and enigmatic allusions.[4]

---

[1] For the recurrence of Notus–Auster at the end of the main part (19 f.) see p. 24 above.

[2] In one of the two main branches of our MSS we in fact read the heading *invisum sibi Mevium devovet*, etc.

[3] See Pfeiffer on *fr.* 382.

[4] Heinze, on *Epod.* 10. 12, remarks that this insertion of a mythical *exemplum* is in keeping with the technique of Hellenistic *Ἀραί*, as can be seen especially from Ovid's *Ibis*. The analogy is not very close, for in the *Ibis* the main body of the poem consists entirely of long lists of parallel cases (catalogue-like, obviously after the fashion of the Hesiodic *Ἦ οἵη*, cf. also Euphorion, *Berl. Klassikertexte*, v, 1, p. 58, col. 2 [Page, *Gr. Lit. Pap.* i. 494], l. 6 ἦ ὅσσον . . ., l. 10 ἦ καί νιν . . .). We need not exclude the possibility that the insertion

The 'manner of stringing a series of briefly outlined stories on the thread of an imprecation'[1] can be more clearly recognized in a poem of a follower of Callimachus, Euphorion, a fragment of which has come to light on a piece of a page of an ancient parchment codex from Egypt.[2] It appears that such products of laborious erudition did not exert any direct influence on Horace's epode. Nevertheless, it is possible that the existence of Ἀραί as a genre of Hellenistic poetry has something to do with the manner in which Horace treats his theme, but there is no evidence of that being the case.

The Mevius epode has also been brought into connexion with another genre of Hellenistic poetry: it has been termed a *propempticon*, using this title in an ironical sense, since the wishes here uttered are the reverse of the wishes customary in an ordinary *propempticon* such as Horace's *Sic te diva potens Cypri*. It is not improbable that the particular turn which Horace gives to the curses against Mevius owes something to those προπεμπτικά which seem to have developed in Hellenistic poetry and subsequently became a favourite with the Roman poets from the time of Cinna and Catullus on. In this connexion attention has been drawn to some typical features. In a *propempticon* it was usual to pray for a lull of the contrary winds and for the blowing of the favourable one, as may be seen from Theocritus 7. 57 f., Horace, *Odes* 1. 3. 3 f., Ovid, *Am.* 2. 11. 41 (cf. also 9 f.), Statius, *Silv.* 3. 2. 42 ff. In the Mevius epode the position is necessarily reversed. Moreover, whereas in the context of a *propempticon* it was natural to vow a sacrifice and some celebration should the vessel safely reach port,[3] Horace turns that friendly custom into its opposite by promising a sacrifice to the *Tempestates* if they wreck the ship and drown every one on board.[4]

To sum up. Horace did not attempt to reproduce the true nature of the old Greek *iambus* which had partly suggested to him the theme of his epode. His borrowing was confined to the most general outlines of the subject. As if to make up for the resulting loss, he embroidered his own poem with many elaborate devices, most of them derived from Hellenistic poetry. Consequently what had been a weapon in a serious

---

of the παράδειγμα in *Epod.* 10. 11–14 was stimulated by Hellenistic models, but an influence of classical Greek lyrics seems equally probable. For the connexion by means of the temporal clause (13 f. *cum Pallas*, etc.) compare, for example, Pind. *Pyth.* 8. 41, Bacchyl. 13 (12), 110. What T. Plüsz, *Das Jambenbuch des Horaz*, 67, says about a comparison between Mevius and Ajax is a free invention of his own.

[1] Wilamowitz, *Berl. Klassikertexte*, v. 1, p. 64.
[2] For editions see the last footnote but one.
[3] Theocr. 7. 63 ff.; Ovid, *Am.* 2. 11. 46.
[4] It is to the credit of Dacier that he illustrated this prayer to the *Tempestates* with the help of one of the earliest Latin poems, the epitaph of L. Cornelius Scipio, consul of 259 B.C. (*CIL* i. 2², no. 9). He had come across the text of the inscription not in Sirmond's publication, but in a book of the famous Gassendi.

struggle became in his hands a dexterous display of literary patterns. If we want to understand the necessity which lay behind this startling transformation, we must try to obtain a wider outlook.

2. SOME PRELIMINARY REMARKS

In the modern world it is a familiar idea that a poem has its normal place in a book and that it is primarily to the potential reader of the book that the poem addresses itself. This idea is correct so far as the literature of highly advanced societies is concerned. In the Greek world the conditions under which a poem came into existence were, at least from the fourth century B.C., not fundamentally dissimilar to the conditions prevailing in the Renaissance or in our own time. But we are confronted with an entirely different situation when we turn to the seventh and sixth centuries B.C., the period during which, on the one hand, certain types of recitative poetry, such as elegy and iambics (the latter term covering poems in trochaic tetrameters as well), and, on the other hand, lyrics proper evolved their forms and became for a time the most productive and most significant genres of Greek poetry. If we are to form an idea of the life out of which iambics, elegies, and various types of song grew and of the function which poetry fulfilled within that life, we shall first of all have to cast off some conventional conceptions.

Nowadays it is natural for many educated persons to open a book of verse when they want a rest or a change from the humdrum of their daily occupations, and hope to be diverted or, perhaps, exalted by lofty thoughts and the spell of noble rhythms and sounds. Whatever their motives, these modern readers look on poetry as something clearly separated from any practical activities and from the whole sphere of 'real life'. That, however, was not so during the early period of Greek literature. At that stage poetry, far from belonging to a domain remote from man's practical life, rather formed an integral, and indeed a highly important, part of it. This phenomenon may be illustrated by the position allotted to elegiac and iambic poems in the social life of the seventh and sixth centuries B.C. A work of one of those early elegists and iambists was originally destined not to be read but to be listened to as it was being recited, as a rule probably by the poet himself. Such a recitation could take place wherever the men whom the poet wished to address were likely to be found together. A most suitable opportunity was at hand in the banquet or symposium, which played such a prominent part in the normal life of a Greek and which provided special advantages for the undisturbed delivery of poetry, whether recited (often with the accompaniment of an instrument) or actually sung.[1] From time immemorial some kind of poetical entertainment had been considered an all but indispensable element of a symposium. It would not be sufficient merely to say that the symposium provided an excellent opportunity for the performance of many types of poetry, for the existence of symposia as an established institution was in fact one of the main incentives for the composing of poems.

The banquet, however, was not the only occasion on which an elegist or iambist could hope to find an audience. The male inhabitants of southern cities have always been in the habit of spending a large portion of their time in some open square. There they will stand or sit in groups for hours on end, apparently doing nothing at all, and in fact sometimes without any definite purpose, chatting and listening, while, according to the season, they either bask in the sun or enjoy the shade of a sheltered corner. But often they are not really being idle: they may be waiting for a profitable chance, *una combinazione*, to turn up, or discussing something with their companions, a bit of business, the prospects of the harvest, politics, a journey to foreign lands, in short anything that is of importance to them. An almost unlimited scope of topics presents itself, from a harmless joke to the most dangerous intrigue, from a casual remark to serious deliberations on the nature of the universe and man's precarious fate. As you go past the motley groups, you may, out of the sea of voices, pick up incoherent snatches of arguing, persuading, cheating, and instructing. Anyone familiar with the life of Piazza Signoria in Florence or Piazza Colonna in Rome or the Σύνταγμα in Athens will find it easy to elaborate the picture, especially if he remembers that Greek townspeople always εἰς οὐδὲν ἕτερον ηὐκαίρουν ἢ λέγειν τι ἢ ἀκούειν τι καινότερον. There was always, in the cities of Ionia and of the Greek mainland, an audience for the poet who felt himself capable of catching and holding the attention of a crowd or some smaller group. It was in all probability at such informal gatherings of the citizens that harangues like μέχρις τεῦ κατάκεισθε; or ὦ λιπερνῆτες πολῖται, τἀμὰ δὴ συνίετε ῥήματα and many of Solon's poems were first delivered. Such harangues and manifestoes were different from anything that in the modern world would be likely to be put into verse. Their natural place was not somewhere outside the practical life of the people but in its very centre. There they fulfilled a definite, non-interchangeable, function by communicating

---

[1] Cf. especially the first two chapters of R. Reitzenstein's *Epigramm und Skolion*, a fascinating picture of permanent value, although Reitzenstein went too far in regarding the symposium as the only occasion for such recitals (the same view had been taken by K. O. Müller, *Gesch. d. griech. Lit.* i, 3rd ed., 178 f.). For a more balanced judgement see Wilamowitz, *Aristoteles und Athen*, ii. 304, and *Die griech. Lit. des Altertums* (in P. Hinneberg, *Die Kultur der Gegenwart*, Teil I, Abt. VIII), 3rd ed., 29 ff.

emotions, ideas, and projects which at that period could not have been communicated through any other medium. Wilamowitz is right in stating that many of the early elegies and iambics were primarily an address to the people, arising out of a special occasion and serving practical purposes. And he helps our understanding when he tells us that Solon used those poetical genres for the same end for which later on Pericles used a speech, and Demosthenes either a real speech or a pamphlet couched in the form of a speech.[1] But when in this context the great scholar terms one of Solon's poems a versified harangue,[2] some caution is needed lest the pointed phrase lure us into an over-simplification. We must not forget that the political elegies, iambics, and tetrameters, even those which seem to us least poetic, are still unmistakable poetry and as such fundamentally different from orations and pamphlets.[3] It has been well said of the early elegists that emotion is always essential to their poetry and that 'excited by events or circumstances of the present time and place, the poet in the circle of his friends and countrymen pours forth his heart in a copious description of his experience, in the unreserved expression of his fears and hopes, in censure and advice'.[4] Emotional elements are important also in oratory, but there they are on the whole subservient to the objective of achieving the πιθανόν, of persuading and directing the audience, whereas in poetry they come forth, as it were, in their own right. It would be perfectly legitimate for a poet, without any special purpose in his mind, to give vent in his verse to any passion by which he feels shaken. Nor should we treat as irrelevant the difference in style, imagery, and so forth which separates even the driest and most prose-like product of an elegist or iambist from any political speech or pamphlet. But after making these qualifications, it is important to recognize the fact that in the life of many early Greek communities certain types of poems filled the place which at a later stage would be occupied by prose works. Above all, it must not be forgotten that elegies and iambics came into existence not as literature, but as practical tools for some very real tasks and that they were often used as formidable weapons.

These provisional remarks would perhaps be sufficient to provide a general background for the interpretation of some of Horace's epodes. But what has here been said about the early Greek iambics and elegies is relevant also to the lyrics, both monodic and choric, of the same

---

[1] For the reference to Wilamowitz's comments see the preceding footnote.

[2] 'Eine Volksrede in Versen' (*Arist. u. Athen*, ii. 304).

[3] Cf. Reitzenstein, *Epigramm und Skolion*, 48, 'sie [i.e. Elegy] bereitet die Entwicklung der kunstmäßigen Prosa vor, aber sie ist nie für die Prosa eingetreten'.

[4] K. O. Müller, *Gesch. d. griech. Lit.* i, 3rd ed., 179 f. (i. 145 f. in Donaldson's English translation).

period and of the period which followed it, in other words to poems which exerted a strong influence on Horace's *carmina*. It will therefore be convenient not to disrupt what belongs together, but at this point to consider also the early Greek lyrics in their relation to the life of which they formed a part.

As regards monody, a song performed by a single person, it was again the banquet that furnished the richest opportunities. No proper symposium could be held without songs: they were as indispensable to it as were certain material requisites such as wine, garlands, perfumes, incense, a flute-girl, and so forth. In fifth-century Athens, about which we are best informed, the range of banquet songs was wide. A less educated or less musical member of the company would be content with singing a modest *skolion*, whereas his more skilful neighbour might be able somehow to reproduce an ode of Simonides or Pindar. But the most desirable chance would be that at the banquet a poet should sing some poem of his own, especially composed for the occasion. Many such songs were written by Alcaeus, Anacreon, and others. They were adjusted to the situation of a limited circle and to its experiences, moods, and interests; the connexion of these songs with the life from which they sprang was no less intimate and direct than in the case of the early elegies and iambics. We have to regard this kind of poetry as having its being primarily within a particular banquet hall. Suitable topics will be found in the defeat of a citizen hateful to the party assembled here, in the love affair of one of the guests, in an awkward peculiarity of another, in short in anything that has a bearing on the life of the banqueters present in this room on this particular evening. Such a song owes a great deal to the social background and to the relations between the various individuals; at least part of its charm flows from the intimate atmosphere in which it originated.

Passing on to choric lyrics, we may for a moment dwell on their most important type, hymns and other religious songs. They all fulfil a vital function within an established system of worship. In many a case the absence of a cult-song would render the cult itself incomplete and almost meaningless. What would be the use of our city offering costly sacrifices to Apollo at one of his great shrines or dedicating a new temple to him if we did not make it known to him and to the whole of Hellas what we are doing and also what sort of benefits we are asking the god to bestow on Abdera or Thebes or Athens or whatever our city may be called? The recognized means to that end is παιωνίζειν, the performance of a paean by a choir. If we have a fine poem composed for the purpose and see to its being carefully rehearsed, we may hope not only to please the god but at the same time to enhance the glory of our community. Sometimes paeans were sung at the places where, in

front of a sanctuary or an altar, a procession came to a halt, but sometimes the performance of special procession-songs, προσόδια, would be
more appropriate. Some cults required παρθένεια, hymns delivered by a
chorus of maidens, whereas other cults required different types of song.
We need not go into further detail. In whatever direction we look, we
find the same general conditions. During the period with which we are
here concerned the fundamental character of any sacred song was
dictated by the special requirements of a special ritual. The poem had
its prearranged place in the religious life of the community; it served
an immediate purpose, and the poet, however eminent, was expected
mainly to speak not on his own behalf, but as the mouthpiece of those
who had commissioned him to write the poem.

I will conclude this selection of illustrations, a mere sketch, by saying
a few words on the ἐγκώμια or ἐπινίκια, poems sung by a chorus to
celebrate a victory won at one of the local or one of the Panhellenic
games. Here again it must be realized that such a poem was intended
to be far more than a reflection of a part of actual life in the mirror of
literature or a kind of ornamental addition to the victory, something
which might as well have been omitted. The song was an indispensable
element of the celebrations, it was indeed the crowning piece in a
sequence of events which to many a Greek boy or youth or man was to
be the supreme glory of his life. On the evening after a victory at
Olympia or Delphi or wherever else it might be, it was customary for
the friends of the victor to improvise a gay procession, a κῶμος, and,
preferably with the accompaniment of some instrument, to cheer their
successful companion.[1] But a far more splendid κῶμος awaited the
victor on his coming home. There it could be abundantly demonstrated
that from the achievement of the one individual a lasting fame would
descend upon his family, his ancestors, and his whole city. A series of
traditional topics of eulogy had to be dealt with in the song; otherwise
the victory would have been deprived of an essential part of its fruit.
Some kind of festival song had probably its fixed place in any such
celebration, but it was a matter of chance, and depended in a large
measure on the social and economic situation of the victor and his
family, whether a famous poet could be induced to compose the
ἐπινίκιον. However, whether great works of poetry or products of
simple craftsmanship, the poems written for such an occasion formed
an organic element in the life of the society which gave rise to their
production. The difference between these poems and comparable

---

[1] Schol. Pind. Ol. 9. 1 h (p. 268, 2 ff. Drachm.) ἔθος δὲ ἦν κωμάζειν τὴν νίκην ἑσπέρας
τοῖς νικηφόροις μετ' αὐλητοῦ· μὴ παρόντος δὲ αὐλητοῦ εἰς τῶν ἑταίρων ἀνακρουόμενος ἔλεγε·
τήνελλα καλλίνικε. Cf. (as also for my following remarks on the main celebration and its
ἐπινίκιον) Wilamowitz, Pindaros, 121 f.

works of 'literature' will become clear when, in the last chapter of this book, we examine Horace's Pindarizing epinikia on the victories of Drusus and Tiberius.

A first step towards a new attitude to lyrics was taken when men began to acquire the habit of reading for themselves some of the monodies and choral odes written by the great masters of the past. This habit was firmly established in fifth-century Athens, as is shown by ample evidence. Boys learnt in the course of their musical curriculum, from a copy owned by their teacher, the words and the tunes of many famous songs, and at the symposia some members of the company would be able to render some of those elaborate compositions, which by then had come to represent what we might call classic poetry and music. When a comic playwright chose to borrow, first of all a tune, but also a sentence or two from Alcaeus and Anacreon, or from Stesichorus, Simonides, and Pindar, he could expect that his borrowing would be recognized and appreciated by a substantial section of the audience. We need not assume that during this period texts of the lyric poems (or, for that matter, any other texts) were plentiful, but there was probably a sufficient number of them in circulation, and an enthusiast could acquire a copy or have a fresh one made for him.[1] These readers, then, were already separated by a considerable distance from the conditions out of which the poems had grown and they could not be greatly interested in the immediate purpose for which the songs were originally destined. What must have mattered most to these later readers could only be the more general and, as it were, timeless elements of the poems, those very elements on which the greatness of any work of art or poetry depends in the last resort. So it happened that poems once written for a special occasion and intimately linked up with its particular background and circumstances became subject to a process of emancipation. It was almost inevitable that finally a stage should follow at which poems of every genre, elegies, iambics, and all sorts of lyrics, were no longer produced for a special occasion and addressed to a limited audience, but were from the outset composed to find their place in a roll of papyrus, where any reader, of the present or of some future generation, in any region of the Hellenic or the hellenized world, if he cared for such poems, might pick them up. When the book had become the normal means for the transmission of poems, the emancipation of poetry from the conditions of the life of a definite society was complete.

---

[1] It is very unlikely that the Athenians of the later fifth century should have had to resort to copies of single lyric poems; at that time there must have already existed some collections of at least certain groups of the poems of the most important λυρικοί. Wilamowitz

3. EPODE XVI

The discrepancy between the general conditions of early Greek
poetry and the general conditions of poetry in Horace's own time could
not possibly present itself nearly as distinctly to Horace as it presents
itself to the modern student of literary history. But whether distinctly
perceived or instinctively sensed, the discrepancy was there, and the
serious difficulties ensuing from it were bound to make themselves felt
as soon as Horace endeavoured to walk in the footsteps of Archilochus
and, later on, of Alcaeus and other lyric poets. In the Mevius epode he
managed to avoid too obvious a clash of the two heterogeneous types of
poetry by depriving the poem of the old iambist of all elements of
actuality and reducing it to a mere literary topic, which he then em-
bellished with rich Hellenistic embroidery. Such an expedient might
suffice for a comparatively light work. But as soon as Horace tackled
more ambitious tasks, he could not be unaware of the obstacles which
were in his way when he attempted either to render or to modify his
ancient models. The consequences of this situation appear clearly in a
poem which is probably the noblest among his early works, Epode
XVI, *Altera iam teritur*.

It is not Horace's fault that insufficient attention has been paid to a
feature of this epode which might have led to a better understanding of
the entire poem. Horace purports to be addressing an assembly of
Roman citizens. Since a poet is always at liberty to speak, out of the
pages of his book, to anyone he chooses, it would have been possible
for Horace to confine himself to a purely poetic address, an address to
his contemporaries in general. But far from doing that, he stresses
most explicitly the very peculiar role in which he is communicating his
project to the people. We are led to imagine the poet (l. 66 *me*) in the
act of haranguing a large body of citizens. When we remember the
circumstances of Horace's personal life at the time of the early epodes,
we may feel tempted to assume that what he had here in mind was
some informal gathering where men would talk about their anxieties.
But this subterfuge is barred, since Horace, by various devices, compels us to regard his speech as part of the procedure of a political
assembly. He begins by painting Rome's present situation and her
prospects in the darkest colours (1–14). In this section nothing points

Neue Jahrb. f. d. klass. Altert. xxxiii, 1914, 231 (*Kleine Schriften*, i, 392), with special regard to Alcaeus, speaks of 'die Liedersammlungen, die es natürlich schon vorher [i.e.
before the Alexandrian edition] gab', and A. E. Harvey, *CQ* n.s. v, 1955, 159, rightly
says that 'there is no reason to think that the Alexandrian editions [of the lyric poets] were
the first which had existed' and that 'at some stage [I would say before the last third of the
fifth century] the poems had been collected from very various sources (temples, public
monuments, private archives, etc.)'.

to any particular setting; it might be an introduction to a soliloquy of
the poet, or, which comes to the same thing, to a communication with
the reader. But at ll. 15 f. we discover to our surprise that we are to
think of a formal political assembly,[1] for at this point the poet is
obviously addressing a definite audience in these terms: 'perhaps you,
all in common or at any rate the better-minded section,[2] are looking
for means of freeing yourselves from these disastrous troubles.'[3] He
then goes on to indicate the remedy which he himself considers by far
the best and which, in the form of a motion,[4] he submits to the assembly (23 f.): 'Is this your pleasure? or has anyone a better recommendation to make?'. If we attempted to work out the implied 'stage
direction', we should, after the question *an melius quis habet suadere?*,
have to assume a short pause. No one replies; therefore the motion is
carried unanimously. The speaker continues: 'The omens are favourable; why not go on board ship without delay? But let us bind ourselves
by a solemn oath', and so forth. By staging the action in this particular
manner Horace conveys the impression of a debate on a political
platform. Moreover, we shall see that he deliberately employs certain
technical terms and formulas borrowed from the procedure of a
political body in Rome.

What we here have before us is an extraordinary venture. Was any
contemporary reader to imagine that Horace, a freedman's son and
himself at that time in a rather precarious position and obliged to earn
his livelihood as *scriba quaestorius*, could dare, even if only in the world
of poetic fiction, to usurp something resembling that jealously guarded
prerogative of the higher magistrates, the *ius agendi cum populo*? But even
if we leave aside the difficulties connected with the person of the poet,
there are in this epode some indications of a constitutional background
by which any Roman reader must have been extremely puzzled. The
assembly which the poet purports to address appears to be an assembly
of the Roman People,[5] and yet what we are told is incompatible with

---

[1] Horace builds up a kind of dramatic action, a feature which was in all probability
absent from the political poems of Archilochus and rather points to Hellenistic models (cf.
Klingner, *Die Antike*, v, 1929, 25). It is, perhaps, a sign of a certain immaturity that the
turn taken at ll. 15 f. comes as a surprise and that up to that point the background has not
been made clear. For the full development of this type of dramatic technique compare
Odes i. 27, *Natis in usum*, and my observations on it (pp. 180 f. below). There a dramatic
action is superimposed on a theme of Anacreon as it is here on a theme (broadly speaking)
of the early iambists.   [2] For *melior pars* in this context cf. Livy 42. 46. 5.

[3] For the interpretation of ll. 15 f. see pp. 53 ff. below.

[4] For the force of *sententia* at l. 17 see below.

[5] That is the impression which an unprejudiced reader is bound to receive; see, for
example, the first sentence of C. Giarratano's commentary (Turin 1930) on this epode
(104): 'È un discorso che il poeta immagina di tenere al popolo romano in assemblea.'
Kiessling's idea (on 15–24) of a 'Kriegsrat' is not only without any foundation in the poem
but is incompatible with the whole situation presupposed in it.

any assembly of the *populus* or sections of it. There existed in Rome, broadly speaking, two distinct types of constitutional meetings of the *populus Romanus*: *contiones* and *comitia*. Neither of them, even in its general outlines, corresponds to the kind of assembly hinted at in Horace's poem, for in neither would it be possible that a question such as *an melius quis habet suadere?* should be asked. In both *contiones* and *comitia* it is, as a rule, only the magistrate who speaks.[1] In a *contio* the assembled citizens have merely to listen to the communication of the magistrate who has convoked them, whereas in *comitia*, after the speech of the magistrate, the assembly is asked, not indeed to discuss the proposal or to suggest amendments, but to vote in a strictly regulated form by saying (or writing down) either 'aye' (*uti rogas*) or 'no' (*antiquo*). This is the very opposite of the procedure in the Athenian Assembly, where the 'principle of liberty'[2] is manifested in the regulation that, after prayers have been said and details of the agenda settled, the herald asks the question τίς ἀγορεύειν βούλεται;—which means that any citizen has the right to take part in the debate. It would, of course, be absurd to assume that Horace intended in any way to connect the Roman theme of *Altera iam teritur* with the institutions of a Greek city. What does, however, clearly emerge is the fact that he adopts formulas used in the Roman Senate. In the Senate the presiding magistrate, after explaining the nature of the issue, asks the senators *quid de ea re fieri placet?*[3] Accordingly the senator whose turn it is to state his opinion commonly concludes by saying *placet mihi . . . monumentum fieri quam amplissimum* or *placet mihi in eum severe animadverti* or whatever the case may be. These formulas are alluded to in *sic placet?* at l. 23, as Bentley saw.[4] Nor is this all. In an *oratio* addressed by the Emperor Claudius to the Senate and preserved on a papyrus[5] the concluding section begins with the words *Haec, patres conscripti, si vobis placent, statim significate simpliciter et ex animi vestri sententia; sin displicent, alia reperite . . . remedia.* This has been compared with a passage in which Dio Cassius[6] describes

---

[1] What matters here is the typical features, and therefore we might for the present purpose disregard altogether the exceptional instances in which a magistrate made use of his right to allow a private citizen to speak in the assembly (*producere in contionem*; cf. Mommsen, *Staatsr.* i³. 201; G. W. Botsford, *The Roman Assemblies*, 148 f.). But even if we take such instances into account, there remains the fundamental difference that a private citizen, a *quivis ex populo*, could never take the initiative and make a proposal of his own such as suggested by the words *an melius quis habet suadere?*

[2] Eur. *Suppl.* 438 τὸ ἐλεύθερον ἐκεῖνο.

[3] Cf. Brissonius, *De formulis* ii. 43 (p. 152 of the Leipzig edition of 1731); Mommsen, op. cit. iii. 957. For the reply of the senator *placet mihi . . .* see Brissonius, op. cit. ii. 50 (p. 157); Mommsen, op. cit. 977.

[4] Had his remark been followed up, we might have been spared many errors in the interpretation of the epode.

[5] *BGU* 2, no. 611. For the text and a bibliography see now S. Riccobono, *Fontes Iuris Romani*, Pars prima, *Leges*, 2nd ed., 1941, no. 44, pp. 285 ff.   [6] 55. 4. 1.

Augustus' dealings with the Senate.[1] Dio says that Augustus had the measures which he was going to propose put down on tablets and posted in the Senate House; the senators, as they walked in, could read the proposals so that, if something did not please them or they were able to make a better suggestion, they might say so, ὅπως, ἄν τι μὴ ἀρέσῃ αὐτοῖς ἢ καὶ ἕτερόν τι βέλτιον συμβουλεῦσαι δυνηθῶσιν, εἴπωσιν. From the similarity of this sentence to the passage in the speech of Claudius, *si vobis placent . . .; sin displicent, alia reperite . . . remedia*, it must be inferred that in both cases we hear an echo of the formula with which in the Senate the presiding magistrate used to conclude his recommendation of the proposal in hand. It is probable that long before Augustus the same formula was employed for the same purpose, for in the *Epidicus* of Plautus (263 f.) the slave says *si placebit, utitor; consilium si non placebit, reperitote rectius*, where the implication seems to be that the slave is posing as *senatum consulens*, just as elsewhere in Plautus a slave is posing as *senatum convocans*.[2] But be this as it may, there can be no doubt that in the epode the general form of the question (though not the verb *suadere*) *an melius* (ἕτερόν τι βέλτιον Dio) *quis habet suadere?* recalls the transactions of the Senate as does the preceding question *sic placet?*[3] Finally, it is of the procedure in the Senate that we are reminded by the words (l. 17) *nulla sit hac potior sententia*, for in the Senate 'the *sententia* is the proposal of a decree, the reply of the individual senator to the question of the presiding magistrate.'[4]

And yet the assumption that the poet's imaginary assembly should be thought of as the session of a kind of senate is excluded by the tenor of the whole epode and in particular by ll. 15 f. and ll. 36 f. What is presupposed here is obviously an assembly of the people or of a representative section of it. And it is to the procedure of such a body, but not of the Senate, that *suadere* (23) belongs.[5] It is significant that the poet interpolates the heterogeneous idea of a *suasio* into a sentence which, as we have seen, recalls a formula used by the presiding magistrate in the Senate. This detail makes it clear, as does indeed the whole conception, that Horace, on the one hand, is bent upon producing a semblance of serious political transactions, and, on the other hand, makes it impossible for the Roman reader to connect the parliament of the epode with any real political institution in Rome. The poet borrows his technical or quasi-technical formulas simultaneously from the procedure of the Senate and from the procedure in the Assembly.

[1] See J. Stroux, *Sitz. Bayr. Akad.*, Phil.-hist. Kl., 1929, Heft 8, 74.
[2] See *Philol.* lxxxv, 1930, 355.
[3] In the Athenian Ecclesia, of course, the citizen can at the end of his motion say εἰ δέ τις ἔχει τι τούτων βέλτιον, λεγέτω καὶ συμβουλευέτω (Dem. 9. 76).
[4] Mommsen, op. cit., iii. 977.
[5] For *pro contione suadere* and the like see Mommsen, op. cit. iii. 394.

This apparent inconsistency fulfils an important purpose: while a certain atmosphere of an orderly political debate, leading up to a vital decree, was created, no contemporary reader could for a moment feel tempted to think either of the Senate or of a *contio* or of any other piece of the machinery of the real state.

It is easy to see that the complete unreality of the constitutional conditions under which Horace's assembly appears to transact its business is in harmony with the complete unreality of the poet's proposal. This proposal demands that at least a large portion of Rome's citizens shall emigrate to the Islands of the Blest. It would be fatal to try to shrink from the implications of so astounding an idea. Several scholars have thought that the proposal does not mean what its words say but the very opposite. The epode, so they argue, is ironic; Horace wishes to stamp those citizens who would be willing to emigrate as cowards and deserters.[1] This idea could never occur to a reader sensitive to the tone of the poem; the passage ll. 37–40 alone should be sufficient to refute any such hypothesis.[2] But wrong though the assumption of an ironical sense is, it is at any rate less ingenuous than are the attempts to obtain from the epode some information on actual political trends in contemporary Rome. It has been suggested that the epode 'has a definite occasion; an addressee, the Roman public; and an avowed practical purpose',[3] and that '*melior pars* is, of course, the writer's own party; and their longing to migrate is due to the fact that they are only too obviously beaten'.[4] But it is very hard to believe that the project of emigration was prompted by any tendencies of a political group or that Horace expected to see his poem taken as an instrument of political propaganda. He was no adolescent when he wrote the epode. Nor was he by nature a sentimentalist, remote from the struggles of the world. He was a level-headed man, always on guard against any kind of delusion and long inured to party strife and civil

[1] Cf. for example, Th. Plüsz, *Das Jambenbuch des Horaz*, 1904, 107 ff., and R. C. Kukula, *Römische Säkularpoesie*, 1911, 23 ff. These scholars were not, of course, the first to find in 'amara εἰρωνεία' the clue to the poem; see the protest against that interpretation in Orelli–Baiter's note (3rd ed., 1850, p. 724).

[2] Plüsz was altogether too prone to wriggle out of a difficulty by resorting to that last expedient of a despairing commentator, the assumption of 'sarcastic irony'. Cf. my note on A. *Ag.* 1523 f. (p. 719).

[3] A. Y. Campbell, *Horace*, 1924, 133.

[4] Ibid. 132. A similar view is taken by Rostovtzeff, *Yale Review*, Autumn 1936, 108 f.: 'In this political poem he gave expression to the current opinion of his group, sharply opposed by the supporters of Octavian, whose mouthpiece was Vergil. . . . Is there any place under the sun for its better citizens? . . . Yes, if they decide to break forever with the past. Then a blessed land awaits them somewhere in the romantic twilight of the West', etc. Cf. also R. Syme, *The Roman Revolution*, 218, 'The war of class against class, the dominance of riot and violence . . . engendered feelings of guilt and despair. Men yearned for escape, anywhere, perhaps to some Fortunate Isles beyond the western margin of the world, without labour and war, but innocent and peaceful.'

war. After the catastrophe of Philippi he was prepared to resign whatever high hopes he may until then have nourished both for the Republic and for his own career. Not for a moment could he think that the fantastic project which he recommended in his epode reflected the views of any political group or that it would be taken seriously by such a group. The only persons to whom the poem could hope to appeal would be not politicians but lovers of impassioned poetry. And yet Horace was not content to present this project as a poetic fantasy: he took pains to set it against some kind of political background, which, moreover, he elaborated by means of quasi-constitutional formulas. In doing so he seems to have made a mockery of his own efforts, since his work could fulfil its function only if kept within the sphere of poetry. The reason for this apparent inconsistency is not far to seek.

Horace had taken it upon himself to write *iambi* after the fashion of Archilochus. It was a hazardous enterprise. He could not possibly confine himself to composing invectives against minor figures such as Mevius or against an anonymous upstart or some repulsive old woman. The nature of the poetry of Archilochus, viewed as a whole, demanded that, in any attempt to revive the Ἀρχιλόχειος χαρακτήρ, the life and the struggles of the commonwealth should play a part. To this demand Horace's own frame of mind during the years following Philippi responded eagerly. It would probably be an exaggeration to say that he undertook the writing of Archilochean *iambi* mainly because they provided him with a fine instrument for the expression of political passion in general and of a defeated patriot's bitterness in particular. This view, besides being dangerously modern, does not sufficiently take into account the conditions under which Roman poetry evolved. The evolution of this poetry, *Livi scriptoris ab aevo*, might be broadly described as the gradual conquest of one poetic genre after another through continuous adaptation of such Greek models as had not been latinized before. However, it is probable that the θυμός, the *animus*, of Archilochus, expressed with particular vigour in the poet's pronouncements on the affairs of the πόλις, the *res publica*, was among the major incentives that caused Horace to turn to the Parian knight who called himself a servant of the god of war.[1]

But Horace had still another reason for not leaving aside the political poems of Archilochus, the poems in which their author had displayed his most intense fervour. At an early stage of his poetic activities

---

[1] Leo, 'Die röm. Lit. des Altertums', *Die Kultur der Gegenwart*, i. 8, 3rd ed., 1912, 444, after speaking of the *Satires*, says: 'Schon vorher, in der athenischen Studentenzeit, muß ihn der Geist des Archilochos ergriffen haben, der auch in den politischen Gedichten der älteren Generation wehte.' This guess has a good deal to recommend it.

Horace, like his admired older friend Virgil, had determined to abandon the pretty trifles which had pleased the preceding generation of poets, and to endeavour instead to produce works of a serious and virile character. This he could not hope to achieve if he excluded from his *iambi* the greatest issue of the time, the deadly struggle in which Rome and her war-lords were engaged. *Audax iuventa*, he plunged into an almost unbelievable venture. Undaunted by the complete change in the conditions of life and literature, undaunted also by the gulf between his own precarious position and the unfettered freedom of Archilochus, he pretended to speak from a public platform to his fellow citizens as if he held a place in the body politic comparable to the place held by the Ionian poet six hundred years before. It is true that Horace provides some kind of belated justification for appearing in such a strange role when, at the very end of the epode, he says that he is speaking as an inspired prophet (66 *vate me*). But if his functioning as *vates* may explain the confidence with which he anticipates the success of his plan, it cannot account for the manner in which he makes a proposal to an assembly of Roman citizens. This bold conception, on which the whole poem hinges, is clearly due to the influence of ancient poetic harangues such as ὦ λιπερνῆτες πολῖται, τἀμὰ δὴ συνίετε ῥήματα.[1]

It has been suggested that Horace derived from Archilochus not only the general idea of the political speech but also the nucleus of its subject-matter, the plan of emigrating to secure a better future for the community.[2] But if Archilochus really advanced a similar plan, he probably did so to further some practical purpose. If Horace, on the other hand, had attempted to recommend a measure of practical politics, he would have exposed himself not only to derision but to the risk of serious trouble with the Roman authorities. This was not a time when a nobody, a young man who ought to have been grateful to the victors for allowing him to escape alive from the wreckage of his party, could be suffered to meddle with the affairs of the state and to incite the people to discontent. It was therefore essential for Horace to make it quite clear that the fundamental idea of his poem was not meant to

---

[1] Archil. *fr.* 52 D.

[2] Reitzenstein, *Gött. gel. Anz.* 1904, 952, pointed out the relation between the sixteenth epode and the poems in which Archilochus addressed his fellow citizens. He suggested the possibility that also the subject of Horace's proposal, an emigration to some better place (though not, of course, to the Islands of the Blest), might have been inspired by Archilochus, who (*fr.* 54 D.) seems to have advised the Thasians to leave their island and settle down elsewhere. This ingenious suggestion was anticipated by K. O. Müller, *Gesch. d. griech. Lit.* i³. 226 n. 33 (i. 181 n. 1 of the English translation), quoted in Lucian Müller's commentary. On this no certainty is possible. It is, however, obvious that Horace in this epode drew also on poems of Archilochus which had nothing to do with his main theme. The dependence of l. 39, *muliebrem tollite luctum*, on a passage in the elegy to Pericles (Archil. *fr.* 7. 10), τλῆτε γυναικεῖον πένθος ἀπωσάμενοι, was noticed by Mitscherlich. If we had more of Archilochus, we should probably find other reminiscences as well.

be translated into terms of practical politics of his own day. This he did by widely separating the procedure in his imaginary assembly from any kind of procedure known in a real assembly in Rome, by conflating constitutional formulas incompatible with each other, and, above all, by making his whole proposal Utopian, painting it in colours borrowed partly from mythical tales and partly from old, almost mythical, history.

Following a hint in an ancient commentary,[1] many scholars have assumed that the idea of making the Islands of the Blest the goal of the proposed flight was suggested to Horace by an episode in the life of Sertorius which Sallust had reported in the first book of his *Histories*.[2] Sertorius, at an early stage of his career, once met some sailors just returned from the fabulous 'Atlantic Islands' far away in the western ocean, 'which are called the Islands of the Blest'. When he heard of that remote paradise and of the effortless life it offered, 'he felt an irresistible desire to settle in those islands and live in peace and be rid of tyranny and ceaseless wars'. It is possible, but not provable, that Horace remembered the story of Sertorius. What is more important is that this story, as well as the prophetic vision in the epode, expresses a perennial longing of men condemned to live in what is called a civilized world. Who would not every now and then wish to escape

> unto an isle so long unknown
> and yet far kinder than our own?

Horace's description of that wonderland—no matter from where it was inspired—belongs to the same sphere of mythical tales and poetic fantasies as his whole project. A flight to the Happy Islands is the last thing anyone would dare to propose to an assembly of Roman citizens however disheartened.[3] As for the solemn oaths which the

---

[1] Ps.-Acro on l. 41.

[2] The substance of Sallust's account is preserved in Plutarch, *Sertorius* 8. 2–9. 1.

[3] The fantastic character of this project can be illustrated by a passage in a speech delivered a few years before Horace wrote his epode. Cicero, *Phil.* 13. 49, after reading to the Senate a letter from Antonius to Hirtius and Caesar, concludes by stating that any compromise, any negotiated peace with 'that bad man' is impossible: '*Prius undis flamma*', *ut ait poeta nescio quis, prius denique omnia, quam . . . cum re publica Antonii redeant in gratiam. monstra quaedam ista et portenta sunt et prodigia rei publicae. moveri sedibus huic urbi melius est atque in alias, si fieri possit, terras demigrare . . . quam illos . . . intra haec moenia videre.* Obviously the idea of *moveri sedibus*, etc., though not strictly belonging to the ἀδύνατα (such as *undis flamma*) or τέρατα (*monstra*), borders on the sphere of those inconceivable phenomena. The phrase *si fieri possit*, too, is relevant. (I owe the reference to the passage in Cicero to a marginal note by J. Vahlen in one of his copies of Horace.) The alleged attempts to look for another capital to supplant Rome (cf. p. 267 below) have nothing to do with the theme of the sixteenth epode.—I hope my own interpretation has made it clear why I cannot follow Reitzenstein, *Gött. gel. Anz.* 1904, 952, and Harald Fuchs, *Der geistige Widerstand gegen Rom*, 1938, 10 and 37 f., who believe that Horace was indebted to Oriental religious prophecies for his project of the emigration to the Islands of the Blest.

emigrants must swear, Horace himself indicates his prototype (17 ff.).
He trusts that his readers will recognize Herodotus' account[1] of
the emigration of the Phocaeans.[2] That event, it is true, belonged to
history, but its date was so remote and much of the story so strange
that an ancient reader would probably place it within the region of
myth, a region which anyway in antiquity was never marked off
sharply from the region of history. In the tale of the flight of the
Phocaeans, including the ceremonies by which they bound themselves,
the fabulous element prevails.

Horace, then, has been at pains to detach the proposal made in his
epode from the world of political realities. Both the matter of the
motion and the forms of procedure are rendered wholly imaginary.
And yet, viewed as a whole, *Altera iam teritur*, unlike the Mevius epode,
is anything but an artificial product. No reader can remain unmoved
by the real indignation and sorrow with which the poet watches the
fate of Rome. Rome, after centuries of triumphs, seems now, through
the blindness of her own children, ready for destruction.[3] And as a foil
to all the shame and misery there appears in the distance, dream-like,
the fairy-land where everything is peace and happiness. If this vision
does not appeal to us, it says more for our sophistication than for our
humanity. Horace's attempt to imitate directly the political poetry of
Archilochus was bound to fail, but although he chose a platform which
would break under him, he succeeded in writing a great, if not a
perfect, poem.

Finally, something must be said about the relation of *Altera iam
teritur* to Virgil's fourth eclogue. A formidable mass of literature has
been devoted to this problem. It is a real problem, and cannot therefore be evaded by the apparently easy assumption that both poets

---

[1] 1. 165.
[2] Possibly the same method of confirming an oath was mentioned by Alcaeus; see the
scholium *Pap. Oxy.* xviii, 2166, p. 40, col. 2. 6 ff. (=*Poet. Lesb. Fragm.* ed. Lobel and
Page, 152) with Lobel's note.
[3] The arrangement of ll. 3–10, *quam neque . . . valuerunt . . . nec . . . nec . . . nec . . .
domuit . . ., impia perdemus . . . aetas*, where a negative relative clause (or a series of such
clauses) is followed by a principal clause which contains the positive antithesis, deserves
perhaps a brief comment. I suspect that we have here a traditional pattern, expressing a
particular type of indignation or lament. I quote at random a few instances: Cic. *Pis.* 10
*quas leges . . . potuit . . . nemo convellere, quam potestatem minuere . . . nemo . . . conatus est, haec
sunt . . . sepulta, Phil.* 2. 68 *quam domum aliquamdiu nemo aspicere poterat, nemo sine lacrimis
praeterire, hac te in domo tam diu deversari non pudet?* and in the famous prologue of Laberius
(*Com. Rom. Fragm.* ed. Ribbeck[3], p. 359), ll. 7 ff., *quem nulla ambitio, nulla umquam largitio,
nullus timor, vis nulla, nulla auctoritas movere potuit in iuventa de statu: ecce in senecta ut facile
labefecit loco* and so forth. The contrast is always between the past when certain things
did not happen and the present when they do. We may compare (formally slightly
different and with an ironical sense) the outburst in the Πόλεις of Eupolis (*fr.* 205 K.),
οὒς δ' οὐκ ἂν εἵλεσθ' οὐδ' ἂν οἰνόπτας πρὸ τοῦ, νυνὶ στρατηγοὺς ⟨ἔχομεν⟩. ὦ πόλις, πόλις κτλ.
It may be worth while to look for this pattern elsewhere.

'drew from a common source or rather perhaps from material which had become common coin'.[1] Since most of the arguments put forward in the discussion were far from certain, more than one good scholar felt so baffled that he gave up the whole game. But now the position is different: Bruno Snell has conclusively proved the priority of Virgil.[2] Virgil took over from Theocritus the general idea and a few expressions and placed them in a different context, blending them, moreover, with a phrase which he had already used.[3] Horace had Virgil's poem before him. He inserted the topic of the goats (49 f.) into his description of the Islands of the Blest (emphasizing the idea that it is out of kindness to man that the goats behave in that way), but the other element of the Virgilian passage, *nec magnos metuent armenta leones*, he transferred to the series of ἀδύνατα (33)[4] and so connected two sections of his poem by a subtle link as he did elsewhere in this epode.[5]

[1] W. W. Tarn, *JRS* xxii, 1932, 152. Tarn is not, however, alone in resorting to this explanation. The assumption of a common source could account for a number of similarities in the two poems, but not for the affinity between *Ecl.* 4. 21 f. and *Epod.* 16. 49 f. and 33. This point was rightly emphasized by H. Düntzer, *Jahrb. f. Philol. u. Pädag.* ic (*Fleckeisens Jahrb.* xv), 1869, 316 ff., by Kiessling, *Philol. Unters.* ii, 1881, 112 f., and by F. Skutsch, *Neue Jahrb.* xxiii, 1909, 29 (*Kl. Schriften*, 370).

[2] *Hermes*, lxxiii, 1938, 237 ff. The passages from Theocritus and Virgil on which Snell bases his argumentation had all been adduced in various commentaries on the fourth eclogue and also by Düntzer, op. cit. But Düntzer, following Kirchner, C. Franke, and others, took it for granted that the sixteenth epode was written in 41 B.C., i.e. before Virgil's eclogue; he was therefore forced to beg the question. K. Büchner, *Bursians Jahresb.*, Suppl. cclxvii, 1939, 164 f., does not seem to have fully grasped Snell's arguments. And when he considers it unlikely that Theocr. 11. 12 should have been imitated by Virgil (*Ecl.* 4. 21), 'because the situation in Theocritus is so very different', he ignores the practice, characteristic of Virgil, of gathering a phrase or two from an earlier poet, Greek or Latin, and adapting them, often together with other borrowings of different origin, to a new context. Were it not for the power by which Virgil remoulded and unified everything he touched, one might sometimes be tempted to think of *lexis compostae ut tesserulae omnes arte pavimento atque emblemate vermiculato*. The elaborate hypotheses by which W. Wimmel, *Hermes*, lxxxi, 1953, 317 ff., attempts to refute Snell have not convinced me. For the controversy see also the detailed ἐπίκρισις by H. Fuchs, *Westöstliche Abh. Rudolf Tschudi . . . überreicht*, 1954, 43 n. 12, who reaffirms the priority of Virgil's fourth eclogue. So does, with additional arguments, C. Becker, *Hermes*, lxxxiii, 1955, 341 ff.

[3] *Ecl.* 7. 3, *distentas lacte capellas*. Virgil's seventh eclogue, probably one of the earliest, is doubtless earlier than the fourth.

[4] In the interpretation of this clause, *nec ravos timeant armenta leones*, I cannot agree with Snell, op. cit. 238 f. It is true that the behaviour of the cattle (and, for that matter, of the goats, l. 34) is not, strictly speaking, a result of the *mirus amor* described in ll. 30 f. But it would be wrong to deny the existence of a link of thought between ll. 31 f. and 33. The *mirus amor*, first used in the sexual sense, takes a wider meaning as the thought moves on so as to comprise all kinds of strange likings shown by the animals. There is here some looseness, such as Horace would not, perhaps, have tolerated in his maturest works, but it is a not unnatural looseness. Horace is not, as Snell suggests, swept away by the recollection of Virgil's line, but seizes the opportunity of connecting the ἀδύνατα with the blessings on those islands, typical of the Golden Age.

[5] A detail in the story of the Phocaeans (Hdt. 1. 165. 3: they sank an iron ingot into the sea and ὤμοσαν μὴ πρὶν ἐς Φώκαιαν ἥξειν πρὶν ἢ τὸν μύδρον τοῦτον ἀναφανῆναι) is taken out of its original context and, with a slight variation, is made to function as one of the

The relative chronology of the two poems is now settled, but that, unfortunately, does not enable us to establish the date of the composition of the sixteenth epode. This is partly due to the fact that we do not know at what time between the end of 41 B.C. and the autumn of 40 B.C. Virgil's fourth eclogue was written.[1] Assuming that it was written before the official beginning of Pollio's consulate, January 40, and assuming, moreover, that Horace became acquainted with the eclogue soon after it was written, it would be possible to place the composition of *Altera iam teritur* within the last few months of the Perusine war or in the period of the subsequent campaign which was brought to an end by the *pax Brundisina* (autumn 40 B.C.). If, on the other hand, the second half of the year 40 were to be regarded as the time during which the fourth eclogue was written, the earliest possible date for the composition of the sixteenth epode would be the spring of 38 B.C., when the outbreak of a fresh war between Sextus Pompeius and Octavian marked the end of the short breathing-space gained by the pacts of Brundisium and Puteoli. But an even later date could not, of course, be excluded. Much though we should like to reach a more precise result, I do not think that firm reasoning can be carried much further. It may, however, be permissible to dwell for a moment on a speculation about probabilities, without attaching to it undue importance.

We have seen that a very early date for the sixteenth epode cannot *a priori* be excluded: the poem may have been written during the final stage of the Perusine war or shortly after. That would mean that Horace in the course of a few months had attained not only mastery in handling a very difficult metre but also a remarkable skill in composing

---

ἀδύνατα (25 f. *simul imis saxa renarint vadis levata*). The suggestive picture of l. 10, *ferisque rursus occupabitur solum*, recurs in ll. 19 f., *habitandaque fana apris reliquit et rapacibus lupis*, so that the anticipation of Rome's ruin in the future is illustrated by the ruin of Phocaea in the past.

[1] It had long been assumed that the eclogue refers to the pact of Brundisium. E. Norden, *Die Geburt des Kindes*, 1924, 4 ff., protested against this assumption but did not convince Heinze and other scholars (H. J. Rose, 'The Eclogues of Vergil', *Sather Classical Lectures*, xvi, 1942, 179 f., seems to lean towards Norden's opinion). I myself think that here Norden is right, although his arguments are not certain. It was one of the most important features of a Golden Age—whether thought of as belonging to the past or to the future— that there had been, or would be, no enmity between any living creatures. A poet who wanted to make the expected child appear as the bringer of a Golden Age was therefore bound to connect with him a universal and lasting peace, whatever the particular political and military situation might be at the time when he was writing his poem. Norden, while showing that the end of 41 B.C. must be regarded as a possible date, has not, however, proved that a later date is out of the question (on this point cf. R. Syme, *CQ* xxxi, 1937, 4).—After this section of my book was written, G. Jachmann published his important article, 'Die vierte Ekloge Vergils', *Annali Scuola Norm. Sup. di Pisa*, xxi, 1952, Fasc. I–II, 13 ff. He insists on the close connexion of the eclogue with the *foedus Brundisinum* (53 ff.). I maintain what I have said above. The eclogue may well have been written after the conclusion of the *foedus*, but this assumption is not required to account for the glorification of peace in the poem.

a poem of an exacting genre yet unknown in Roman literature. His personal life at that time must have been far from quiet. The second battle of Philippi, which shattered all his hopes, was fought in November 42 B.C. Soon after he had his estate confiscated and lost all his property. It is not known when he was given the post of *scriba quaestorius*, but it was probably in 41 B.C. Well-educated and intelligent though he was, he cannot at first have found it easy to get used to the routine of his office. It is difficult to imagine that in those circumstances he should have had sufficient leisure and freedom of mind to cope with the training indispensable to a literary achievement such as the sixteenth epode. We need not press his autobiographical statement[1] to the point of assuming that he never wrote verse at all before the events of 42/41 B.C. At Athens he, like most of his fellow students, must have dabbled in poetry. But that was a very different matter from the serious efforts he made afterwards. It is unlikely that so long as his mind was given to quite different ambitions he should have attempted the task of renewing the poetry of Archilochus. These improbabilities disappear if we assume that the sixteenth epode was written in the spring of 38 B.C. or somewhat later. Besides, Virgil's *Eclogues* were by that time published as a book. But, I repeat, what has been said here is only a speculation.

The construction of *Epod.* 16, 15–16

The couplet ll. 15 f., *forte quid expediat communiter aut melior pars malis carere quaeritis laboribus*, has for centuries been disputed. F. Leo's attempt[2] shows to what lengths even an eminent Latinist would go in this case.[3] I am convinced that Lambinus is right (Bentley rejected his interpretation on account of the order of words and based his own text on the worthless reading *quod expediat*). Lambinus paraphrases thus: 'Fortasse quid expediat, vos omnes quaeritis, aut melior pars vestrum: carere, id est, ut careatis laboribus.' That *communiter aut melior pars quaeritis* must be taken together (as it is taken in the scholia) is shown by ll. 36 f., *omnis . . . civitas aut pars . . . melior* (pointed out by Heinze). The syntactic function of the clause *malis carere laboribus* cannot, so far as I see, be made out with certainty. Lambinus suggested two alternative ways: (*a*) to regard the infinitive as consecutive (ὥστε), or (*b*) to take it as in apposition to, or parallel with, *quid expediat*. The former view was followed, for example, by Kiessling, who produced parallels which are not exactly comparable; the latter, which seems preferable, by

---

[1] *Epist.* 2. 2. 49 ff.

[2] *Analecta Plautina*, i (Progr. of the Univ. of Göttingen 1896) 32 n. 1.

[3] Afterwards, *Gött. gel. Anz.* 1904, 850, Leo spoke of 'die längst gefundene Interpretation der überlieferten Worte'.

G. Kirsten, *De infinitivi . . . apud Horatium usu.*[1] It must, however, be admitted that in either case the order of words seems somewhat twisted, but the same thing is true of several passages in the epodes where there is no doubt about the construction. Apparently it was only by degrees that Horace, in the structure of his sentences, attained that *lucidus ordo* which is characteristic of his masterpieces. Heinze felt some uneasiness at the initial position of *forte* (= *fortasse*). But the instances quoted in *Thes. l. L.*[2] are sufficient to show that a non-enclitic use, and also initial position, of *forte* in this sense, though rare, is good Latin.

Some recent discussions make it necessary to add a warning to what I wrote several years ago. Madvig,[3] without knowing that his expedient had been forestalled,[4] disrupted the sentence by punctuating thus: *Forte quid expediat!* and explained 'hoc est, forte aliquod remedium'. The great man's impromptu, deservedly forgotten, was in our days revived by Barwick[5] and by Axelson[6] (the latter translates 'Eine tapfere Tat möge uns retten!'). These scholars do not seem to have sufficiently considered a point of grammar: would Horace—or, for that matter, Virgil—have used *forte quid* in an independent sentence? In other words, would Horace instead of *dic aliquid dignum promissis*[7] ever have said *dignum quid dicas*, or would Virgil ever have said *aut magnum quid* instead of *aut aliquid . . . magnum?*[8] The answer is an uncompromising No. In Virgil indefinite *quis*, *quid*, etc., occur only after *si* (the majority of instances), *seu* and *ne*, *neu*. In Horace the very numerous cases of indefinite *quis*, *quid*, etc., are all confined to secondary clauses, with two—apparent—exceptions, *Sat.* i. 3. 56 f. *probus quis nobiscum vivit* and—slightly different—i. 3. 63 *simplicior quis et est qualem* . . .. These passages in fact confirm the rule, 'da der Gedanke an beiden Stellen hypothetisch zu fassen ist'.[9] At *Sat.* i. 4. 80 *quis* is rightly taken as interrogative by the scholiast and, for instance, Reisig, Wüstemann, and Heinze.

But not only grammar, but also the context makes it necessary to take *forte* = *fortasse*. Up to this point the speaker had given a picture of Rome's decline and of the grim future that awaits her. Now he turns to the assembly: *forte quaeritis quid expediat* . . .. This is a common device in public speeches, in the law courts as well as in *contiones*. It will be sufficient to quote Cic. *Verr.* ii. 3. 40 *sed vos fortasse . . . id in hoc loco*

[1] *Diss.* Leipzig, 1938, 16 n. 1.   [2] vi. 1131. 75 ff.
[3] *Adversaria critica*, ii. 58 f.
[4] See O. Keller, *Epilegomena*, 400.
[5] *Philol.* xcvi, 1944, 44 f.
[6] *Ut Pictura Poesis* (*Studia Latina P. I. Enk . . . oblata*), 1955, 50 ff.
[7] *Sat.* 2. 3. 6.   [8] *Aen.* 9. 186.
[9] L. Müller. Axelson's remark, op. cit. 51, 'Der Gebrauch von nicht enklitischem *quis* = *aliquis* wie sat. i 3, 56 und 63' is inadequate.

quaeritis, num . . . ceperit, ii. 5. 180 *quaeret aliquis fortasse,* '*Tantumne igitur laborem . . . suscepturus es?*', Manil. 22 (beginning of a new section) *requiretur fortasse nunc quem ad modum . . . reliquum possit magnum esse bellum.* Such formulas of transition, beginning with an adverb like *fortasse* and introducing a new section of the speech, follow Greek models. The type in general is so common that only very few examples need be quoted: Dem. 19. 237 Ἴσως τοίνυν ἀδελφὸς αὐτῷ συνερεῖ κτλ., 20. 18 Τάχα τοίνυν ἴσως ἐκεῖνο λέγειν ἂν ἐπιχειρήσειε Λεπτίνης κτλ., 21. 191 Τάχα τοίνυν ἴσως καὶ τὰ τοιαῦτ' ἐρεῖ κτλ. What interests us here is the formula *quaeret aliquis fortasse* or *forte quid expediat . . . quaeritis.* Compare, for instance, Andoc. 1. 117 Φέρε δὴ τοίνυν, ὦ ἄνδρες (τάχα γὰρ ἂν αὐτὸ βούλοισθε πυθέσθαι) ὁ δὲ Καλλίας τί βουλόμενος ἐτίθει τὴν ἱκετηρίαν; Plat. *Apol.* 20 c Ὑπολάβοι ἂν οὖν τις ὑμῶν ἴσως· "Ἀλλ', ὦ Σώκρατες, τὸ σὸν τί ἐστι πρᾶγμα; πόθεν κτλ.", Dem. 23. 187 Ἴσως τοίνυν ἐκεῖν' ἄν τίς μ' ἔροιτο, τί δήποτε κτλ., 9. 63 Τί οὖν ποτ' αἴτιον, θαυμάζετ' ἴσως κτλ., and, in a more elaborate form, 9. 70 Καὶ ἡμεῖς τοίνυν . . . τί ποιῶμεν; πάλαι τις ἡδέως ἂν ἴσως ἐρωτήσας κάθηται. The earliest example which I have found comes from the *Supplices* of Euripides. There (184 f.) Adrastus begins a new section of his oration by anticipating a question in this form: τάχ' οὖν ἂν εἴποις· Πελοπίαν παρεὶς χθόνα πῶς ταῖς Ἀθήναις τόνδε προστάσσεις πόνον; .(For the use in tragedy of formulas of public speeches see my note on A. *Ag.* 1393 and the passages referred to there.) Cf. also Heniochus *fr.* 5. 4 f., vol. ii, p. 433 Kock (Stob. 43. 27, vol. iv. 7 f. Hense), τάχ' ἄν τις ὑποκρούσειεν ὅ τι ποτ' ἐνθάδε νῦν εἰσι, κἂν ἔροιτο (?)· παρ' ἐμοῦ πεύσεται.

4. OTHER EPODES IN THE IAMBISTS' MANNER

When we turn from Epode XVI to Epode VII, *Quo, quo scelesti ruitis?*,[1] we at once notice a difference in volume and vigour, but also some closely similar thoughts and expressions. The period 7. 5–10, *non ut . . . aut . . . ut . . ., sed ut . . . sua urbs haec periret dextera,* though on a much smaller scale, is in form and matter parallel to 16. 2–10, *suis et ipsa Roma viribus ruit: quam neque . . . aut . . . nec . . . nec . . . -que . . . nec . . . domuit . . . -que . . ., . . . perdemus,* etc.[2] In detail the recurrence of the emphatic hyperbaton, 7. 9 f., *ut . . . sua urbs haec periret dextera,* and 16. 2, *suis et ipsa Roma viribus ruit,* is worth noticing. Far more significant,

---

[1] Possibly *scelesti* still retains something of its old force, 'under a curse' (Sonnenschein on Plaut. *Most.* 504; cf. the commentators on Catullus 8. 15).

[2] At the end of 16. 2 we should accept the punctuation of Lambinus, Baxter, Orelli-Baiter, Meineke, Kiessling, Wickham, and others, and put a colon rather than a full stop after *ruit.* Of course, the relative clause, ll. 3–8, depends on the principal clause *impia perdemus,* etc. (9 f.), but there is no completely fresh start at the beginning of l. 3. Tescari rightly observes on ll. 3–10: 'Questi versi sono un' amplificazione epesegetica del v. 2'.

however, is the similar building-up of the dramatic action. In both poems the background is some imaginary assembly of citizens which is being addressed by the poet. In VII we find a direct address right at the beginning (*quo . . . ruitis?*),[1] whereas in XVI it is delayed until l. 16. The fiction by which, as in a dramatic play,[2] it is suggested that the assembled citizens might reply to the questions of the speaker (7. 14 f. *responsum date. tacent*, etc.) is on the whole the same as in XVI, but in VII it is handled with greater discretion: no attempt is here made to invest the procedure with an appearance of reality by means of quasi-constitutional formulas. Since we possess no reliable clue for the date of VII (although it is clear that it cannot have been written many years after XVI),[3] it is impossible to determine whether the greater restraint in VII is the result of growing maturity, or whether, on the contrary, Horace proceeded from a more cautious attempt to the venture of the sixteenth epode. One topic in VII to which nothing in XVI corresponds is of special interest: at the end (17 ff.) the present misery of the Roman people is traced back to a crime committed in the remote past. The same note was struck by Virgil in a passage which seems to belong to the oldest strata of the *Georgics*, 1. 501 f., *satis iam pridem sanguine nostro Laomedonteae luimus periuria Troiae*; this passage was to have a noticeable influence on one of Horace's early odes (i. 2), *Iam satis terris*.[4]

We now pass to a group of epodes (VI, IV, VIII, XII) the theme of which, though varied in detail, is essentially the same, fierce invective. In VI, as in the Mevius epode, it is the adornment of the detail that matters most. The dog which barks at harmless passers-by while dodging any serious danger represents a type of person, the cowardly

---

[1] I am not sure whether the similarity of *Quo, quo scelesti ruitis?* to [Plat.] *Clitoph.* 407 b, ποῖ φέρεσθε ἄνθρωποι; (cf. Reitzenstein, *Gött. gel. Anz.* 1904, 952 n. 1; Heinze, ad loc.; Stroux, *Philol.* xc, 1935, 329) is more than accidental. In any case we may ask whether the form of the beginning does not perhaps go back to a type represented by Callinus, *fr.* 1. 1 Μέχρις τεῦ κατάκεισθε;

[2] See, for example, Ar. *Ach.* 113–16; Eur. *Iph. Aul.* 1245; Plaut. *Truc.* 4–6; and also Plat. *Crat.* 435 b τὴν γὰρ σιγήν σου συγχώρησιν θήσω.

[3] Dillenburger and Kiessling, followed by Heinze and Plessis, thought that Epode VII was written early in 38 B.C., others, e.g. Hirschfelder in the re-edition of Orelli–Baiter, preferred 36 B.C. These scholars started from l. 3, *Neptuno super*, in which they saw an allusion to one of the wars with Sex. Pompeius. This is possibly correct, but *Neptuno super* could also be taken in a more general sense. However, 38 or 37 or, perhaps, even 36 B.C. would, on internal grounds, seem to be suitable dates. Tescari and Giarratano, with some earlier commentators, think of 41 B.C. The dates suggested by A. Y. Campbell, *Horace*, 1924, 144 ('the occasion is the final breach between Octavian and Antony in 32') and Th. Plüsz, *Das Jambenbuch des Horaz*, 46 f. (about the time of the battle of Actium) are much too late: by that time Horace had given up haranguing the people κατὰ τὸν Ἀρχίλοχον.

[4] Cf. p. 243 below.

slanderer.[1] No doubt Horace had come across such persons. He may even have had in mind a particularly unpleasant individual. But if that was so, he has not taken advantage of his experience to furnish the victim of this invective with any individual features. Therefore the attempts, both ancient and modern, to identify the dog start from wrong premises. Horace makes it clear (3 f.) that he has not himself been attacked by the slanderer. He may have been annoyed by the behaviour of a person of that type, but his annoyance can hardly have been strong enough for him to write this epode. His primary motive was probably to produce a menacing poem after the fashion of the Ionian iambists. It is significant that he mentions in this epode (13 f.) two of the most eminent early writers of ἴαμβοι, Archilochus and Hipponax, as his models. There is a faint possibility that the masking of the tiresome man as a barking dog was suggested by Hipponax,[2] but the image was familiar in Greek and Roman common talk as well as in literature. Horace has made the most of it: what merits the epode has are due to the picturesque description of the dogs and their ways. The characterization of the various dogs fulfils a function analogous to that of the description of the various winds in Epode X. Unfortunately the picture is marred when the poet, shortly after being represented as a sheep-dog of good breed, appears in the disguise of a bull (11 f.).[3] We notice here a lack of the discretion and the sense of consistency which distinguish the mature works of Horace.

Epode IV is a finer poem. It presents itself as a spontaneous outburst. The opening couplet gives the impression that there had been a long-standing feud between Horace and his adversary. But this personal hostility provides merely an introduction: in the rest of the poem it seems to be completely forgotten. The dominating theme of the

[1] The keynote of the poem is given in *canis* at the end of l. 1. Unlike most editors, Klingner punctuates after it, rightly, cf. 'Kolon und Satz I', *Nachr. Gött. Ges.*, Phil.-hist. Kl. 1932, 208.

[2] See Reitzenstein, *Neue Jahrb.* xxi, 1908, 87 n. 1. He refers to Leonidas, *Anth. Pal.* 7. 408. 3, where the verb βαΰζειν is used of the θυμός of Hipponax. (A. D. Knox, *Herodas, Cercidas*, etc. [Loeb Library, 1929], p. xiii, ought not to have printed the words in the form given them by W. Headlam, *CR* xv, 1901, 401, ὁ καὶ τοκέωνε βαΰξας, for the dual of nouns denoting parents is, as a rule, avoided; cf. J. Wackernagel, *Sprachl. Unters. zu Homer*, 55, and *Vorles. über Syntax*, i. 83; W. Schulze, *Kl. Schriften*, 322. But Headlam's alternative suggestion, op. cit. 402, τοκέωνα, is worth considering.) If Leonidas alludes to an expression by which Hipponax described his own invectives, Horace may have put the image to a different use.

[3] Giarratano, on l. 12, remarks 'Non è già che Orazio abbia qui sostituito alla metafora del cane quella del bue: qui *tollere cornua* è detto in senso traslato' (a subtle difference between 'metafora' and 'senso traslato'!). In both places there is a metaphor, and the one clashes with the other. Trying to understand a poet is one thing, whitewashing him at all costs is another. Lucian Müller compares with l. 12 accumulations of similes which belong to an entirely different type: they show copiousness, not inconsistency.

epode is neither the poet's own relation to the man attacked nor the individuality of the man, but the typical figure of the upstart.[1] The type, common in all ages,[2] is especially conspicuous at a time of political crisis and social and economic disintegration. About seven years earlier a characteristic Roman pasquinade was posted up on the house-fronts and the pillars of the capital:

> concurrite omnes augures, haruspices.
> portentum inusitatum conflatum est recens:
> nam mulos qui fricabat, consul factus est.[3]

The lampoon, which excited Virgil,[4] was directed against P. Ventidius Bassus, a man of humble origin who, through industry and a genius for organization, had in Caesar's wars made plenty of money. This 'shark', *pesce cane* (as the *Remi nepotes* of to-day call such a man), used his newly acquired wealth to climb up the ladder of the magistracies. No doubt the *liberrima indignatio* of the people of Rome found a similar expression on many similar occasions. Horace picked up the popular subject and treated it in a manner reminiscent of Catullus.[5] With a felicitous stroke he concludes the poem by making us listen to the comments of the populace. Exactly half of the epode is occupied by the talk of this chorus.[6] From the last four lines it has long been inferred, rightly as it seems, that the epode was written during the Sicilian war between Octavian and Sextus Pompeius, 37/36 B.C.

Epodes VIII and XII, with all their polish, are repulsive. The obscenity of both language and matter was probably intended to carry on characteristic traits of a certain type of early Greek *iambi*. In this respect Hipponax has at least as strong a claim to be regarded as Horace's model as has Archilochus.[7] Improper subjects treated in coarse language played also an important part in some branches of Hellenistic poetry. It is not known whether Horace was influenced by

[1] That the victim of this invective represents a type rather than any particular contemporary has been well shown by F. Jacoby, *Hermes*, xlix, 1914, 459 f. I cannot, however, agree with his assumption that the concluding lines are aimed at Octavian and that therefore the whole epode is meant to hit him. Nothing points to such an intention. Besides, the epode was in all probability written when Horace already belonged to the intimate circle of Maecenas.

[2] Anacreon *fr.* 54 D., πρὶν μὲν ἔχων βερβέριον κτλ., was compared as early as Toup.

[3] Gellius 15. 4. 3.

[4] Cf. my paper 'Vergil und Cicero', *Atti e Memorie della R. Accad. Virgiliana di Mantova*, N.S., vol. xix–xx, 1926–7.

[5] Cf. Jacoby, loc. cit.

[6] For the habit of concluding epodes (and later odes) with an *oratio recta* see below, p. 66 and p. 428 n. 1.

[7] For the special type of αἰσχρολογία which dwells on the revolting physical peculiarities of the person attacked compare, for example, the recently discovered fragments of an epodic poem of Hipponax, *fr.* x Diehl[3], p. 115.

Sotades, the amusing poet of the early Hellenistic period, whom Ennius, at any rate partly, imitated in one of his minor works. But it is not unlikely that Horace should have adopted some of the indecencies which, shortly before and during his own time, were fancied by several Greek epigrammatists.[1] Moreover, Catullus, his friend Calvus, and possibly other members of that circle as well, had cultivated the same sort of thing.

Epode XII is more elaborate than VIII. Here again we find the device which we noticed in IV: the last half of the poem[2] is in direct speech. Both in VIII and in XII the vilification of the ageing woman purports to be in reply to an outburst of her jealousy (in XII also in reply to fresh advances which she has made to her former lover). In VIII the woman's role is confined to a mere hint (1 f.), in XII it is fully worked out. We may assume that the quasi-dramatic background and especially the lamentations of the jealous women owe something to Hellenistic erotic poetry.[3]

The four invectives at which we have been glancing, epodes VI and IV, VIII and XII, could be regarded, despite a considerable admixture of Hellenistic elements, as attempts to renew some characteristic themes of Archilochus, Hipponax, and other early iambists. The same could not be said of Epode II, *Beatus ille*, one of the best-known poems of Horace.[4] A good deal of its matter would be suitable for a Latin elegy,[5] and similarities to Virgil's *Georgics*, especially the end of the

---

[1] For contemporary epigrams of that type see Heinze's introduction to Epode VIII. A past master in this genre was the Epicurean philosopher Philodemus, who lived in the household of L. Calpurnius Piso, Cicero's enemy. Horace, in his earliest satire (1. 2. 120 ff.), i.e. about the time of his early epodes, quotes one of the lascivious epigrams of Philodemus. An epigram, written about half a century before the beginning of Horace's production, by Meleager, *Anth. Pal.* 5. 204, has a good deal in common with epodes VIII and XII. It is very likely that Horace was familiar with the Στέφανος of Meleager.

[2] Here, as in IV, the symmetry is complete: the epode consists of twenty-six lines, the concluding speech of thirteen.

[3] The repulsive ugliness of a rich elderly wife and her fierce jealousy are amusingly described in Menander's Πλόκιον. Much coarser colours are used in a play by one of the late writers of New Comedy (Plaut. *Asin.* 871 ff.). What the old lady, mother of a grown-up son, reveals there of the intimacies of her married life comes pretty near to the woman's complaints in Epode XII. But we must not confine our attention to the special topic of the jealousy of an *ugly* woman. Some thoughts in Epode XII are clearly inspired by nobler poetic pictures of jealousy. Here it will suffice to refer to Cynthia's speech at the end of Propertius' elegy i. 3. especially ll. 35–40; it must be borne in mind that a fine Hellenistic epigram lies behind the elegy (cf. Reitzenstein, *Hermes*, xlvii, 1912, 81 n. 1, and my remarks in *Das Problem des Klassischen und die Antike*, ed. by W. Jaeger, Leipzig 1931, 53 ff.).

[4] It seems to have been equally popular in antiquity. The metricians, in order to make it clear to their pupils that all you had to do if you wanted to obtain a regular catalectic trochaic tetrameter was to prefix a cretic to an iambic trimeter, concocted this specimen (Victorinus, *Gramm. Lat.* vi. 134. 17 K.):

Socrates beatus ille qui procul negotiis.

[5] Kiessling calls the theme a 'streng genommen elegischen Stoff'.

second book, have long been noticed. It is, however, very probable
that the setting, if not the subject, of the epode links it up with Archilochus. This was pointed out, more than a hundred years ago, by
Lachmann.[1] He recalled Aristotle's statement[2] that in the poem of
Archilochus[3] which began Οὔ μοι τὰ Γύγεω τοῦ πολυχρύσου μέλει the
speaker was not the poet himself but the carpenter Charon. We do not
know what followed after the first four lines, which are quoted by
Plutarch. It is therefore impossible to say whether the poem of Archilochus also concluded with such a complete surprise as does Horace's
epode. But it is obvious that *some* element of surprise must have been
contained in Οὔ μοι τὰ Γύγεω. In listening to the beginning of the poem,
the audience was led to believe that this lofty disregard for wealth and
political power represented the poet's own outlook on life, and only
later (towards the end?) would it become clear that Archilochus had
spoken in the name of a simple artisan. As for Horace's epode, the idea
of putting the glorification of a farmer's life into the mouth of the
fenerator Alfius was perhaps suggested by that very poem Οὔ μοι τὰ
Γύγεω. It should, however, be remembered that Archilochus used the
same device in other poems as well.

The spirit of Epode II is very different from anything likely to be
found in a work of an early iambist. If we leave for a moment the
mocking conclusion, we may see in this poem a fundamentally true, if
slightly idealizing, expression of Horace's own nostalgic longing for the
life of the country-side, a longing which he shared with many of his
contemporaries: *o rus, quando ego te adspiciam?* A tinge of sentimental
exaggeration is almost inseparable from such a mood. It is right to
judge the epode from the impression which it makes upon us as a
whole and not to allow the balance to be completely upset by what has
been called 'the Heinesque surprise at the close.'[4] On the other hand,
justice must be done to the concluding four lines. It would not be
satisfactory merely to say that the poem ends on this mocking note
because Horace wanted to imitate a certain device of Archilochus. It
would be more adequate to assume that Horace seized upon the final
surprise which he found in Archilochus because this turn enabled him
to mix the strong expression of what he really cared for with a dose of
that self-mockery without which he would not, except in moments of
deepest emotion, feel that he was entirely true to his own mind. As

---

[1] First in an appendix to C. Franke's *Fasti Horatiani* (1839), reprinted in K. Lachmann's
Kleinere Schriften, ii. 78. Lachmann's circumspection shows itself especially in the sentence
'sed nobis, quam bella quamve iocosa fuerit imitatio, vix suspicari licet, cum ne exitum
quidem Archilochii carminis, cuius modi fuerit, divinare possimus'. Cf. also Wilamowitz,
S.u.S. 305 f., and, for the analogous situation in Archil. *fr.* 74, his *Glaube der Hellenen*, ii.
113 f.   [2] *Rhet.* 3. 17, 1418ᵇ 30.   [3] *fr.* 22 D.
[4] By Paul Shorey in his annotated edition of the *Odes* and *Epodes*, Boston, U.S.A., 1898.

Sellar in his fine appreciation of *Beatus ille* puts it: 'it is characteristic of Horace, when he is most in earnest, to check himself and bring himself back to the ordinary mood in which he meets society. . . . So he adds a satiric tag to the Epode, to prevent his being taken too seriously. The systematic enthusiasm with which he is carried away to celebrate the happiness of country life . . . is disclaimed with "town-bred irony".'[1] If Horace wanted somehow to detach himself from sentiments which he in fact shared himself, the unexpected substitution of another speaker was an excellent means to that end. Its effect was increased by the happy idea of introducing this particular character, the *fenerator* wholly incapable of carrying his noble feelings into practice.

The poem is rich in suggestive detail, revealing the poet's familiarity with the Italian country-side and the farmer's life. Perhaps Horace also drew on contemporary poems which extolled that way of life. Moreover, a literary topic of a different kind may have contributed something to this epode. In the diatribes of popular philosophers much was made of the theme περὶ μεμψιμοιρίας, of man's permanent dissatisfaction with his own lot and his incorrigible desire to be in somebody else's shoes. This theme appears in the opening part of the first poem of Horace's *Satires*, Book I,[2] where the inconsistency of the μεμψίμοιρος is illustrated by a pretty 'myth' :

> si quis deus 'en ego' dicat
> 'iam faciam quod voltis: eris tu, qui modo miles,
> mercator; tu, consultus modo, rusticus: hinc vos,
> vos hinc mutatis discedite partibus. eia,
> quid statis?' nolint. atqui licet esse beatis. (15–19.)

This is precisely what happens to the *fenerator Alfius*. The second epode, which, on internal grounds, can hardly be regarded as one of the early pieces of the book, was possibly written about the same time as the first satire of the first book.

The relative chronology of Horace's three poems on Canidia cannot

---

[1] W. Y. Sellar, *Horace and the Elegiac Poets*, 2nd ed., 130. The reader would do well to read the whole section (127 ff.). Sellar's judgement seems to me more balanced than either that of Gaston Boissier (quoted by Sellar) or that of Heinze. I fail to see that traits such as *paterna rura bobus exercet suis . . . adulta vitium propagine altas maritat populos . . . inutilisve falce ramos amputans feliciores inserit . . . aut tondet infirmas ovis* are typical of the outlook of 'ces prôneurs ennuyeux de la belle nature', who will 'admirer à froid la campagne', or how the sound realism of such descriptions could be meant to parody 'die Schwärmerei des Städters für das Bauernleben, das er nur als Sommerfrischler kennen gelernt hat', or that it is fair to speak of the 'Einseitigkeit des Gemäldes, das . . . die Mühen und Sorgen der Landwirtschaft kaum andeutet und alles ins rosigste Licht des Vergnügens und Behagens taucht'.

[2] The affinity of *Beatus ille* (or rather of its final effect) to the first part of the satire was pointed out by Heinze.

be established with any certainty, but it is likely that they were written in this order: Epode V, *Sat.* i. 8, Epode XVII.[1] These poems tempt us to ask whether the sorceress Canidia is to be taken as the mask of a real person. The only piece of evidence that seems to provide an answer is unfortunately the kind which can neither be flatly rejected nor unreservedly trusted. The scholiast (Porph.) on *Epod.* 3. 7 remarks: *sub hoc Canidiae nomine Gratidiam Neapolitanam unguentariam intellegi vult, quam ut veneficam Horatius semper insectatur. sed quia non licet probrosum carmen in quemquam scribere, idcirco fere poetae similia adfingunt. sic et Vergilius in Bucolicis pro Cytheride Lycoridem appellat.* The apparently substantial detail *Neapolitanam unguentariam* is not sufficient to render the identification credible, for it is probably nothing more than an inference from 5. 43, *Neapolis* (where Porphyrio observes *nam, ut supra diximus, Gratidia haec Neapolitana fuit*) and from 5. 59, *nardo perunctum,* etc. (where Porphyrio says *hinc scias illam, ut diximus, unguentariam fuisse*). But the scholiast's assertion that Canidia's real name was Gratidia seems plausible enough, and his reference to Cytheris, who, probably in the poems of Gallus and consequently in Virgil's tenth eclogue, appeared as Lycoris,[2] is to the point. The Latin writers of love poems, at least from Catullus on, used to disguise the name of their lady under a pseudonym which was prosodically equivalent to the real name, so that the reader, if he chose, would find it easy to replace Lesbia by Clodia, Licymnia by Terentia, and so forth, without destroying the metre.[3] This type of pseudonym may sometimes have been used also in non-erotic contexts. On the other hand, the possibility must be admitted that an ancient commentator familiar with these common substitutions invented a Gratidia as prototype of Canidia: the one name points as clearly to attractive youth as the other points to old age. On such an issue we cannot hope to reach certainty.[4] We should, of course, like to know whether there existed a sorceress Gratidia and

[1] For the relation between Epode V and *Sat.* i. 8, see p. 123 below. That Epode XVII is later than V is obvious. Many commentators, from J. M. Gesner on, and C. Franke, *Fasti Horatiani,* 129, think that 17. 58 f. alludes to the eighth satire; that is probable though not certain.

[2] Cf. Serv. Dan. on *Ecl.* 10. 2, *Lycoris pro 'Cytheris'; licet enim poetis alia nomina pro aliis ponere.* Cf. also Serv. on *Aen.* 8. 642.

[3] The principle, well known in antiquity, was illustrated by Bentley in his famous note on Horace, *Odes* 2. 12. 13. An equivalent in rhyming verse is found in the third stanza of Goethe's poem 'Hatem' (*West-östlicher Divan, Buch Suleika*), where the expected rhyme induces the reader to put the poet's name in the place of *Hatem*:

> Du beschämst wie Morgenröthe
> Jener Gipfel ernste Wand,
> Und noch Ein Mal fühlet Hatem
> Frühlingshauch und Sommerbrand.

[4] Huelsen, *Rh. Mus.* lxviii, 1913, 19 n. 1, is right: 'Ob die Nachricht, . . . *Canidia* habe eigentlich Gratidia geheißen und sei eine unguentaria aus Neapel gewesen, mehr ist als eine müßige Scholiastenerfindung, muß dahingestellt bleiben.'

whether Horace had met her or heard of her. But we should not forget that that is a subordinate question. Canidia is certainly not a portrait of one single woman, nor are the three poems in which she appears primarily the result of some actual experience of Horace.[1] The most which any such experience can possibly have done is to lend some additional features to a figure which originated in the realm of fiction.[2] Looking at Horace's invective epodes (an important part of his book) as a whole, we may safely infer that he wrote Epode V, the earliest of the poems about Canidia, not so much because he wanted to attack a living sorceress, or a group of sorceresses, and expose their sinister machinations, as because he felt that a fresh victim was required for the aggressive *iambi* which he was determined to write after the fashion of Archilochus. He could not indefinitely go on exploiting such topics as form the themes of epodes VIII and XII, inveighing against the physical and moral repulsiveness of some old woman devoid of any particular interest. With Canidia he hit on something far better. Horace's Canidia, whether or not she had a prototype in real life, is an exciting figure. The sphere to which she belongs provides ample opportunity for bold invention and impassioned language. Witches and their doings, in ancient as in modern times, are bound to stir the imagination. In the Hellenistic and the Roman world the enlightened might laugh at such crude 'superstition',[3] but its attraction remained strong all the same. Horace has made full use of the fantastic element and has carefully mingled all sorts of gruesome ingredients. The recipes used

[1] I have no wish to spoil the pleasure of the many inquisitive readers who busy themselves with the identification of Canidia. Some of her learned patrons regard her as a member of Rome's aristocracy, others are content to see in her one of Horace's less illustrious lady friends. In our time a Caecilia Metella and either the mother or the daughter mentioned in *Odes* i. 16 have been suggested, but I suspect there are many more candidates. In 1808 Philipp Buttmann, 'Über das Geschichtliche und die Anspielungen im Horaz' (reprinted in his *Mythologus*, i. 304), exclaimed: 'Wenn nur nicht das widersinnige Bestreben, den Dichter als Historiker zu behandeln, das Sachengerippt, das im Gedicht selbst liegt, jedesmal als Realität aufzustellen, und dann noch obendrein durch Kombinationen zu vervollständigen, zugleich den Charakter des edlen Dichters so vielfältig gefährdete.'

[2] Few scholars show the discriminating sense of O. Crusius, who wrote in *Philol.* l, 1891, 99 f., 'die Canidia-Gedichte des Horaz, in denen uns — was noch immer verkannt wird — keinerlei persönliche Erlebnisse des Dichters anvertraut, sondern lediglich Nachtstücke in der Manier der Hellenisten und des Sophron, nur mit breiterem römischem Farbenauftrag, dargeboten werden'. Cf. also P. Lejay's commentary on the *Satires*, 219: 'ces trois œuvres [epodes V and XVII and *Sat.* i. 8] sont un jeu littéraire', etc. Heinze (see his introduction to Epode V), who rightly said that we need not assume a personal enmity between Horace and Canidia, nevertheless believed firmly in the reality of Canidia and went even so far as to find the mainspring of these poems in the poet's desire to fight against certain evils which he saw spreading around him. Horace, according to this view, was shocked by the dangerous practices of sorceresses and therefore pilloried in the fifth epode a prominent member of the guild (of the 'Hexenzunft').

[3] Cf. *Epist.* 2. 2. 208 f. *somnia, terrores magicos, miracula, sagas, nocturnos lemures portentaque Thessala rides?*

by Canidia[1] do not seem to be very different from those we know
so well,

> Eye of newt and toe of frog,
> Wool of bat and tongue of dog,
> Adder's fork and blind-worm's sting,
> Lizard's leg and howlet's wing.

It has been said[2] that the fifth epode was inspired by the Φαρμα-
κεύτριαι of Theocritus, but the relation between the two poems is
rather vague. It seems, however, possible that, besides the magic rituals
actually practised in Horace's own time, some works of Hellenistic
literature should have influenced this epode;[3] if so, we have no means of
demonstrating it. But the spirit of the whole is indubitably Hellenistic.[4]
This does not mean that the poem owes its characteristic qualities to a
definite Hellenistic model. Its structure, the skilful interplay of narrative and direct speech (at the beginning and at the end the boy is
speaking, in the middle Canidia), and the intensity of the dramatic
action with its sustained pathos—all this may very well be Horace's
own work.

One detail at least can perhaps be regarded as a reminiscence from
Archilochus. The beginning of the epode,

> At o deorum quidquid in caelo regit
>   terras et humanum genus,

recalls the prayer[5]

> ὦ Ζεῦ πάτερ Ζεῦ, σὸν μὲν οὐρανοῦ κράτος,
>   σὺ δ' ἔργ' ἐπ' ἀνθρώπων ὁρᾷς.

But the setting and the context in Archilochus are different.

Epode XVII, placed at the end of the book on account of its
metrical form, is an ingenious, if somewhat laboured, product. It was
a lucky thought to deliver, apparently in good earnest, a palinode in
which the speaker in fact confirms the worst things he had said about
Canidia, with the result that the sorceress, in an outburst of rage,
replies and herself boasts of all the crimes with which she had been
charged. The goddess Helen, who was addressed in the first παλινῳδία
ever composed, forgave, and made her brothers forgive, the re-
pentant sinner (42–44), but for the ungodly Canidia it is fitting to remain relentless to the end. Horace's recantation leaves no doubt that

---

[1] See especially *Epod.* 5. 17–24.

[2] By H. Düntzer, *Jahrb. f. Philol. und Pädag.* ic, 1869, 326, and others.

[3] See J. F. D'Alton, *Horace and his Age*, 1917, 220; W. Kroll, *Studien zum Verständnis der
röm. Literatur*, 1924, 212; and especially S. Eitrem, *Symb. Osl.* xxi, 1941, 63 ff.

[4] Cf. Latte, *Philol.* xcvii, 1948, 41, 'Canidia Alexandrinae potius aetatis genium sapit
quam sexti saeculi'.

[5] Archil. *fr.* 94 D.

he is all the time speaking with his tongue in his cheek; one of the features which make that clear is the quotation in l. 40 from the palinode at the end of one of the most graceful poems of Catullus, 42. 24 *pudica et proba, redde codicillos*.[1]

5. EPODES OF A DIFFERENT TYPE

In the ten epodes which we have so far examined certain modes reminiscent of Archilochus and the other early Ionian iambists could be detected either in the themes or in the general lay-out or in both. That is not so in the seven remaining poems of the book. As far as a χαρακτὴρ Ἀρχιλόχειος appears in them at all, it can be found only in the vehemence with which the poet expresses his feelings and in some ornamental detail. The epodic form is maintained throughout (the one poem in pure trimeters, XVII, belongs to the group already discussed), but in the poems to which we now turn this form serves often as a medium for themes which do not seem to be derived from, or inspired by, works of the old iambographers, but rather to have their origin in different regions of ancient poetry.[2] It must not, of course, be forgotten that such conclusions are hazardous. Our knowledge of the early iambists is very fragmentary, and any new papyrus may reveal an entirely unexpected side of their work. However, with some of these poems we can hope to be on fairly firm ground. It emerges from them that when Horace, after his earlier experimental attempts, gained in maturity and began to plan the publication of a whole book of *iambi*, he found it impossible to confine himself to the adaptation of one literary genre only. He therefore decided to adopt and develop themes outside the range of ἴαμβοι and kindred genres. In doing so he went a long way towards composing lyrics proper, *carmina*.

Epode XIII, *Horrida tempestas*, is a perfect poem, the favourite epode of more than one modern reader.[3] Its depth of feeling and beauty of

---

[1] In the subsequent lines of the epode there seem to be two further, perhaps unintentional, reminiscences from Catullus, l. 41 *perambulabis* (cf. [L. Müller] Catullus 29. 7 *perambulabit omnium cubilia*; I should not have thought there was anything in the similarity, if there were not also *Epod.* 5. 69 *omnium cubilibus*) and 42 f. *Castor . . . fraterque magni Castoris* (cf. [Kiessling] Catullus 4. 27 *gemelle Castor et gemelle Castoris*; the metre of Catullus' *Phaselus* does not admit any form of Pollux, whereas in Epode XVII there was no need for a periphrasis. It should, however, be remembered that *geminis fratribus aedes in foro constituta* was commonly called *aedes Castoris* [Suet. *Iul.* 10. 1]).

[2] The two groups into which, for the purpose of coherent interpretation, I have here divided the epodes should not be taken to indicate a chronological order. It goes without saying that some poems of group I are later than some poems of group II.

[3] Cf. Pasquali, *Or. lir.* 300, R. Reitzenstein, 'Das Römische in Cicero und Horaz', *Neue Wege zur Antike*, ii, 1925, 24, and also the brief but pertinent remarks of Wilamowitz,

expression, and the harmonious blending of ideas of very different origin, make this epode superior to *Odes* i. 7, *Laudabunt alii*, a poem which, not only on account of its epodic form, has often been compared with it.[1] The reason why many of us care so much for this epode is not far to seek: it contains a great deal of what we like best in Horace's odes and seems, indeed, to be one of them. If *Horrida tempestas* had come down to us as one of the *carmina* of Books I–III, not even the most searching critic would be able to discover in it anything incongruous with the character of that collection.

The three principal elements of this poem, the dark and stormy winter day, the poet's sombre mood, and the episode in the early life of the great Homeric hero, all merge into a perfect unity. The manner in which the epode opens with a picture of the grim scene outside, *Horrida tempestas caelum contraxit*, etc., recalls the first sentences in some epigrams of the greatest of the early Hellenistic epigrammatists, Asclepiades.[2] The final section, a fairly extensive speech, belongs to the type which we have found in IV and XII and shall find again in several epodes and odes.[3] The same device was sometimes employed in Greek lyric poems of the classical period, for instance at the end of the Ἀντηνορίδαι of Bacchylides and, on a smaller scale, in Pindar's fourth Olympian ode. In Horace's epode the last sentence of Chiron's speech, ll. 17 f., with its verb *levato*, harks back to the introduction of this speech (10 *levare*, etc.). So the speech is expressly linked up with the general sentence which it is intended to illustrate, and the keynote of the poem (*fide Cyllenaea*[4] *levare diris pectora sollicitudinibus* and *omne malum vino cantuque levato*) is strongly emphasized. The bold and suggestive expression at l. 5, *obducta fronte*, connects the paraenetic part of the poem intimately with the picture of the overcast sky at the beginning.

It is not very likely that Horace should have invented the theme of Chiron's speech independently,[5] but we know nothing about the Greek poem which probably inspired him.[6]

S.u.S. 306 n. 1.

[1] As early as Dacier (note on *Epod.* 13. 11).

[2] Cf. *Anth. Pal.* 5. 167 Ὑετὸς ἦν καὶ νὺξ κτλ., 5. 189 Νὺξ μακρὴ καὶ χεῖμα κτλ., and, a scene at day-time as in Horace's Epode XIII, *Anth. Pal.* 5. 64 (the poet addressing Zeus) Νεῖφε, χαλαζοβόλει, ποίει σκότος, αἶθε, κεραύνου, πάντα τὰ πυρφορέοντ' ἐν χθονὶ σεῖε νέφη.

[3] Cf. Wilamowitz, loc. cit.; Pasquali, *Or. lir.* 144 n. 1 and 300.

[4] This is the correct spelling. Housman's warning (*Journ. of Philol.* xxxiii, 1914, 66) seems to be in danger of being forgotten again.

[5] Cf. Reitzenstein, *Gött. gel. Anz.* 1904, 956; Wilamowitz, loc. cit.; Stroux, *Philol.* xc, 1935, 328 f.

[6] It does not look as though Horace were here indebted to Archilochus, as Crusius, *RE* ii. 506. 62 ff., and Stroux, loc. cit., are inclined to believe. Against this opinion see Sellar, *Horace and the Elegiac Poets*, 126, and Reitzenstein, op. laud. 953 ('Epode XIII, für die ich ein archilochisches Vorbild freilich nicht anzugeben weiß und kaum vermute'). Choric lyrics as a model for Chiron's speech cannot *a priori* be ruled out. [This guess, written down

Epode XI, *Petti, nihil me*, is an elegant piece of writing, but there is little real life in it. F. Leo[1] has shown that this epode has a great deal in common with certain Hellenistic epigrams and several elegies of Tibullus and Propertius; he therefore, in his pointed manner, said of it 'est plane elegia iambis concepta'.[2] In the light of F. Jacoby's article on the origin of the Roman elegy[3] it may be preferable to say that Horace has here made full use of themes current in Hellenistic erotic poetry, especially in epigrams. He apparently took no great pains to adjust these themes to the character of the old iambus or, for that matter, of any other kind of early Greek poetry.[4]

Epode XV, *Nox erat*, shows again an unmistakable affinity to several elegies of the Augustan period and to the kind of Hellenistic epigram by which those elegies were influenced. The first distich reminds us once more of the beginnings of the epigrams of Asclepiades which I quoted before;[5] the similarity to them is here still closer than in the case of *Horrida tempestas*. The principal theme of Epode XV is familiar from Elegy, and its dominating note of jealousy would not surprise us in Propertius. There is, however, in this poem an acrimony which may be intended to render the tone somewhat Archilochean.

In the long-drawn temporal sentence ll. 7 ff., *dum pecori lupus et nautis infestus Orion turbaret hibernum mare*[6] *intonsosque agitaret Apollinis aura capillos*, the notion of 'for ever' is expressed by a peculiar juxtaposition of ἀδύνατα, which seems to have been inspired by a passage in the *῎Ιαμβοι* of Callimachus.[7] The compact last clause, *ast ego vicissim risero*, has the true ring of Archilochus. But, taken as a whole, this epode seems to move in the wake of Hellenistic poetry.

Epode XIV, *Mollis inertia*, takes us still farther away from the sphere of the old ἴαμβος. Here we find ourselves in a society where young poets, yielding to the good-humoured provocation of friends, will talk of their literary ambitions, their frustrations and delays, and, needless to say, also of their most recent love affairs. The atmosphere

several years ago, has been unexpectedly confirmed: see the fragment of a poem by Bacchylides, *Pap. Oxy.* 2364, *Addendum*.]

[1] *De Horatio et Archilocho*, 10 ff.

[2] He had coined this formula for Epode XI before, *Plaut. Forsch.*, 1st ed., 130 n. 2, 'eine Elegie in Epodenform'.

[3] *Rh. Mus.* lx, 1905, 38 ff. For the present problems see especially p. 101 n. 1.

[4] The similarity of *nihil me sicut antea iuvat scribere versiculos* to Archil. *fr.* 20 D. (the gist of its context is known) καί μ' οὔτ' ἰάμβων οὔτε τερπωλέων μέλει is, perhaps, accidental. In any case it would be unwise to go beyond Leo's cautious guess, 'iste fortasse versiculus est quo cum Archilochi poesi carmen Horati cohaeret'.

[5] See p. 66 n. 2.

[6] For the 'zeugma' see Housman, *CR* xv, 1901, 404 f. It may be asked whether Horace, in his mature lyrics, would have ventured anything so harsh, so 'Propertian'.

[7] *Fr.* 202. 69 Pf. (see Pfeiffer's 'Addenda', ii. 119), where Apollo says ἔστ' ἐμὸν γένειον ἀγνεύῃ τριχὸς καὶ ἐρίφοις χαίρωσιν ἅρπαγες λύκοι.

appears to be very much the same as the atmosphere in the circle of the friends of Catullus.[1] This epode, obviously one of the later *iambi*, testifies explicitly to the slow progress of the book, a fact which we should in any case have to infer from the interval between epodes XVI and VII on the one hand, and I and IX on the other. From ll. 9 f., *non aliter Samio dicunt arsisse Bathyllo Anacreonta Teium*, etc., it emerges that Horace, at this stage, was already interested in Anacreon, several of whose poems he was afterwards to adapt to his *carmina*. It was natural that he should also take notice of the traditions on the life of the poet, whether he found them in Chamaileon's work περὶ Ἀνακρέοντος or in some other book.[2]

From Epode III, *Parentis olim*, we can learn how Horace casts into an *iambus* a theme which might have furnished a short poem in hendecasyllables or choliambs for the book of Catullus. The difference in treatment is interesting. In *O funde noster*,[3] which is the account of a trifling mishap that befell the poet, the many accessories and amusing sallies are at least as important as the strange 'cold' which is at the bottom of all the trouble.[4] All this detail, which reflects so much of the life of the poet and his companions, is absent from Horace's epode. In its place we find a good deal of mocking pathos and quasi-Archilochean indignation delivered with feigned grandiloquence. In this respect the epode is not unlike the first three stanzas of *Odes* ii. 13, *Ille et nefasto te posuit die*. A series of elaborate comparisons is used to describe the force of the horrible poison which is now raging in the poet's bowels. Pre-eminence is given to the *venena Colcha*: the story of Medea's sorcery (9–14) fills six lines; to make this story still more conspicuous it is placed exactly in the centre of the poem. This reminds us of Epode X, where the centre is occupied by the tale of the storm which destroyed the Greek fleet on its return from Troy. In marked contrast

---

[1] Catullus' poem XXXV, *Poetae tenero*, is obviously prompted in part by his wish to pay a compliment to the lady-friend of his friend Caecilius, a pretty young woman and a bit of a blue-stocking. But there seems to be more in it. Both at the beginning and at the end of the concluding part (13 f. *incohatam Dindymi dominam*, 17 f. *est enim venuste Magna Caecilio incohata Mater*) we hear the ominous word *incohata*. Its repetition within so short a space in such a polished poem must be deliberate. For many years Caecilius, when asked 'and what are *you* doing?', would have answered 'I am working at my poem on the Great Mother'. This went on for so long that eventually none of his friends expected the *magnum opus* ever to get out of its embryonic stage. As regarded *inceptos olim*, *promissum carmen*, *iambos*, Maecenas was probably more optimistic, and although he had to wait a long time he was in the end not disappointed.

[2] The well-informed Dioscorides and other epigrammatists mention Bathyllos as Anacreon's παιδικά: Kiessling, Crusius, *RE* iii. 137, and Wilamowitz, *S.u.S.* 109, rightly conclude that his absence from our scanty fragments is due to mere accident; Heinze disagrees.

[3] Catullus XLIV.

[4] Reitzenstein, *Neue Jahrb.* 1908, 87 n. 1, compares *Parentis olim* with Catullus XIV, *Ni te plus oculis meis amarem*.

to Medea, the witch Canidia has to be content with a passing remark
(7 f.): her main function in this epode seems to be to link it up with V
and XVII and so to strengthen the coherence of the book. It is very
likely that at least V existed already when Horace wrote III. The
pretty anticlimax at the end (21 f.) is in harmony with the mocking
spirit of the poem; the touch is so light that the apparent curse sounds
almost like an affectionate compliment to Maecenas.

6. THE TWO ACTIUM EPODES

It is possible to guess, with some probability, the reason why Horace
placed the epode *Ibis Liburnis* at the beginning of his *iambi*. It is not
likely that this distinction should be solely due to the aesthetic value
of this epode: it is indeed a fine poem, but so are several of the others.
What is peculiar to the first epode is the directness and intensity with
which it expresses Horace's devotion to Maecenas; it was this quality,
above all, that made it suitable to serve as a dedication of the book.

The epode begins with a sentence of succinct force. The picture of
the majestic battle-fleet and the deep emotion at a great crisis are compressed into the narrow compass of the first two couplets:

> Ibis Liburnis inter alta navium,
> amice, propugnacula,
> paratus omne Caesaris periculum
> subire, Maecenas, tuo.

The vocative *amice*, placed by itself in the first distich,[1] provides the
keynote of this poem rich in expressions of devotion. The danger which
Maecenas is about to encounter seems to have released feelings in
Horace which in normal days he would probably have hesitated to
express so strongly. We need not describe the course of the thought in
detail. It will suffice to quote the central part:

> roges, tuum labore quid iuvem meo,
> inbellis ac firmus parum?
> comes minore sum futurus in metu,
> qui maior absentis habet,
> ut adsidens inplumibus pullis avis
> serpentium adlapsus timet,[2]
> magis relictis, non, ut adsit, auxili
> latura plus praesentibus.

---

[1] The assumption of a hyperbaton *amice* . . . *Maecenas*, in a poem of this group, is highly
improbable. See my remarks in 'Kolon und Satz, I', *Nachr. Gött. Ges.*, Phil. hist. Kl., 1932,
209, where I have also compared the manner in which Horace, in several later poems,
addresses Maecenas: he begins with an allusive characterization and, after an interval
(sometimes a long one), lets the name follow.

[2] For the necessity of punctuating after *timet* see my remarks loc. cit.

A man like Horace is not tempted to assume on such an occasion a heroic pose; he remains what he always is, perfectly sincere, and so he says of himself *inbellis ac firmus parum*. After this confession the simile in which the passage culminates, *ut adsidens*, etc., is the more moving. It comes from an old stock of Greek poetry,[1] but its felicitous application and the beauty of the compact language are Horace's own. The style of the simile as well as its content seems to belong to genuine lyrics. From these heights of hellenized poetry the epode descends gently to the level of ordinary life in Horace's own country, with glimpses of the *latifundia* in the south of Italy and the splendid villas in the neighbourhood of Rome (24–30). Only at the very end (33 f.) a note is struck which carries on, though in a mitigated manner, the traditional sallies of the *iambus*. Here a modern reader will perhaps speak of bathos and resent the intrusion of a jocular spirit into so serious a poem, but for Horace it was important to make it clear that the initial epode of his collection was an *iambus* not merely because of its metrical form.

It may help us to appreciate what Horace has achieved in this mature poem if we look back for a moment on his early political epodes. In XVI, *Altera iam teritur*, and in VII, *Quo, quo scelesti ruitis*, the poet represented himself in the act of haranguing his fellow citizens directly from an imaginary platform. That, it will be remembered, was an overbold fiction, incompatible not only with Horace's personal circumstances but also with the conditions of poetry in his time. Horace had a great gift for learning discretion without losing in strength. He did not repeat the experiments of his early period. As his discernment matured, he endeavoured, instead of building his poetry on an utterly unreal plane, to set it firmly on the ground on which he was himself standing. He had come to realize that, if he wanted to express his anxieties and hopes for Rome's fate, his *locus standi* was not the fiction of participating in an imaginary assembly of the people but his actual friendship with Maecenas. This friendship seems to be the dominant theme of the first epode. But a poem which opens with the picture of the battle-fleet and passes on to *omne Caesaris periculum* cannot be said to be confined to the private sphere of the poet's life. Horace is as inseparably bound to Maecenas as Maecenas is bound to Caesar,[2] and the welfare of every Roman depends on the outcome of the great battle in which Caesar's forces are about to engage in the East. The whole epode is proof of the anxiety with which Horace is watching the political and military events. Compared with the early

---

[1] The commentators quote Aesch. *Septem* 291 ff. and [Moschos] *Megara* 21 ff.

[2] The close parallelism of the two relationships is emphasized by a subtle stylistic device: the syntactic pattern of ll. 3 f., *omne Caesaris periculum subire, Maecenas, tuo* (scil. *periculo*), is not mechanically repeated but slightly varied in 15, *tuum* (scil. *laborem*) *labore quid iuvem meo*.

poems the epode *Ibis Liburnis* shows restraint but no weakening of the emotion with which the poet's mind reacts to the struggles of Rome. Speaking merely as the friend of Maecenas he is yet able, without usurping an alien role, to say all that he wants to say as a Roman patriot. In this respect there is no difference between the first epode and the ninth, *Quando repostum Caecubum*; but what in the former poem is but a concomitant theme predominates in the latter.

The broad outlines of the situation implied in the ninth epode were rightly understood by many scholars up to 1878.[1] In that year F. Bücheler, in a section of his 'Coniectanea',[2] published some brilliant impromptus[3] on this epode. He starts from a re-interpretation of ll. 35 f., *vel quod fluentem nauseam coerceat metire nobis Caecubum*, which former scholars had regarded as pointing to an advanced stage of the banquet.[4] That is wrong, Bücheler asserts, 'cum potationis nunc demum fieri initium praecedentes versus doceant. quod vomitum suum Horatius narrat neque erubuit, ideo credendus est eum narrare qui nulli turpis est nec vitabilis, qui proprie nausea vocatur. fuit igitur tum in nave. . . . adfuit cum Maecenate pugnae Actiacae', etc. Bücheler had not, of course, completely forgotten the explicit statements of several ancient authors who report that at the time of the battle of Actium Maecenas was in Rome as Octavian's vicegerent.[5] But he dismissed these statements very briefly.[6] To the very substantial accounts of the ancient

---

[1] See, for example, C. Franke, *Fasti Horatiani*, 131, who states that the epode was written 'cum primus de Actiaca victoria nuntius Romam perlatus esset'.

[2] *Index schol. hib. Bonn.*, 1878/9, p. 13, reprinted in his *Kl. Schriften*, ii. 320 f.

[3] To have to produce twice a year a learned article in Latin for the 'Index lectionum' must often have been a tiresome burden to a hard-working professor of classics in a German university of the nineteenth century. With the printer on his heels, he was sometimes compelled to glance over the margins of his texts or over his lecture notes and then jot down whatever *observatiunculae* came to hand. Therefore not everything in these *lucubrationes* should be scrutinized too severely.

[4] See, for example, Dacier: 'Le Cecube . . . empéchoit les vomissemens, et Horace le demande, parce qu'il se preparoit à boire avec excés'.

[5] They had been duly taken into account by former editors. See, for example, Bentley (on l. 17), who says that the variant *at huc* would be suitable 'si carmen hoc in castris Caesarianis praesens scripsisset Noster: is vero tum Romae erat cum Maecenate urbi praefecto'.

[6] He mentions in passing 'rerum scriptores', but then refers to Dio Cass. [51. 3. 5] only. Velleius, 2. 88. 1, says *M. Lepidus, . . . Lepidi eius qui triumvir fuerat rei publicae constituendae filius, . . . interficiendi, simul in urbem revertisset, Caesaris consilia inierat. ⟨erat⟩ tunc urbis custodiis praepositus* [cf. Mommsen, *Staatsrecht*, ii³. 729 n. 2] *C. Maecenas*, etc., and, in full agreement with this report, App. *B. Civ.* 4. 50, who adds an important detail: Μαικήνας ἐδίωκε τὸν Λεπίδου παῖδα βουλεύσεως ἐπὶ Καίσαρι . . . τὸν μὲν δὴ παῖδα ὁ Μαικήνας ἐς Ἄκτιον ἔπεμπε τῷ Καίσαρι. Giarratano, in the introduction to his commentary on Epode IX, and other scholars assert that the detail ἔπεμπε . . . ἐς Ἄκτιον is contradicted by Livy (*Periocha* 133) and Velleius loc. cit. That is not the case. Velleius begins chapter 88 with the clause *dum ultimam bello Actiaco Alexandrinoque Caesar imponit manum* because this part of his narrative centres in the execution of Lepidus (*male consultorum poenas exsolvit*); his preceding remarks on the earlier stages of that affair go back in time, as the tense indicates (*consilia inierat*). Livy's epitome

historians, Bücheler preferred a piece of eulogistic poetry: the first of the two *Elegiae in Maecenatem*, ll. 45 ff. *cum freta Niliacae texerunt laeta carinae,* | *fortis erat circa, fortis et ante ducem,* | *militis Eoi fugientis terga secutus,* | *territus ad Nili dum fugit ille caput.* We shall not be inclined to put much confidence in this assertion when we realize that it is one of the ornamental details by which the theme announced in ll. 39 f., *erat comes impiger*[1] *idem* | *miles et Augusti fortiter usque pius,* is worked out; starting as he did from that sweeping generalization, the author could not possibly omit the battle of Actium.[2] Something better than such a flourish, one would think, is required to discredit the solid evidence provided by the ancient historians.

The success of Bücheler's *tour de force* has been, and still is, enormous. Whereas few students of Roman history allowed themselves to be swept off their feet,[3] most of the 'classical philologists' succumbed to Bücheler's persuasion and authority.[4] As his view is not only fatal to the ninth epode but is also based on a misconception of Horace's poetic technique in general,[5] we must here make a firm stand. It will suffice to insist on the main points.[6]

shows clearly that he reported after the capture of Alexandria not the detection of Lepidus' conspiracy or his trial, but his execution (*oppressus et occisus est*). It stands to reason that Octavian, before setting out for the East, left Maecenas in charge of Rome and Italy (see, for example, R. Syme, *The Roman Revolution*, 292).

[1] *impiger*, the reading (conjecture?) of the codex Vossianus, is, I think, rightly preferred by Baehrens and by Bickel, *Rh. Mus.* xciii, 1950, 112 f., to the *integer* of the other MSS; cf. Statius, *Silv.* 3. 2. 91.

[2] Propertius, 2. 1. 25–36, carefully avoids speaking of the military activities of Maecenas (see Rothstein on l. 25 and on l. 35) and does not mention Actium at all.

[3] It is significant that Bücheler's treatment of the ninth epode appeared to the historian H. Dessau, a very conscientious and modest scholar, as 'ein übermütiger Einfall des unvergeßlichen Bücheler' (*Geschichte der röm. Kaiserzeit*, i. 490 n. 1). Tenney Frank, *Catullus and Horace*, 1928, 189, indeed says 'Horace, it is now generally agreed, went to the war and was present at the battle of Actium', but this was never generally agreed. For a sober statement of the facts see, for example, Stein, 'Maecenas', *RE* xiv, 210 f., for an appreciation of the background of the epode see, for example, W. W. Tarn, *JRS* xxi, 1931, 176, and the same writer's remarks in *Cambr. Anc. Hist.* x. 105. Unlike most historians Kromayer, in his last comment on the battle of Actium, *Hermes*, lxviii, 1933, 381 n. 3, did not commit himself on the question whether or not Maecenas and Horace were present at Actium. In the ten pages which F. Wurzel, *Hermes*, lxxiii, 1938, 369 ff., devotes to the epode any allusion to the problem of the participation of Maecenas in the battle is carefully avoided.

[4] Among them were such excellent scholars as Leo, R. Reitzenstein, and Heinze. I will at random mention a few recent voices in favour of Bücheler's view: A. Y. Campbell (in his book *Horace*, 1924, 145, and, more fully, in his second edition, 1953, of the *Odes and Epodes*, 166 ff.); W. Wili, *Horaz*, 1948, 51 and 136; Bickel, *Rh. Mus.* xciii, 1950, 114 f. Only a minority remained critical, for instance Sellar, *Horace and the Elegiac Poets*, 26, and, firmly disagreeing with Bücheler, L. Müller, Shorey, Plessis, and Tescari in their commentaries, and also B. L. Ullman, *Class. Philol.* xxvi, 1931, 229, and Hosius, *Philol. Wochenschrift*, li, 1931, 1352 f.

[5] Therefore Alfred Noyes, whose book *Portrait of Horace*, 1947, is 'written primarily from the point of view of poetry', is fully justified in allowing considerable space (p. vi and pp. 126 ff.) to the rejection of Bücheler's hypothesis.

[6] The unity of the epode is so obvious that I need not discuss the attempts to divide it.

Bücheler's chief argument does not bear close examination. He mentions the traditional interpretation of *fluentem nauseam* at l. 35 and rejects it 'cum potationis nunc demum fieri initium praecedentes versus doceant'. But the preceding lines, 33 f., far from supporting Bücheler's view, prove it to be absolutely wrong. They run

> capaciores adfer huc, puer, scyphos
> et Chia vina aut Lesbia.

These words point to a well-known custom of Greek symposia, which was adopted by the Romans.[1] When a banquet had gone on for a while, larger cups were asked for to facilitate more excessive drinking. That was the moment when ἀφαρπάζειν χρεὼν | οἰνηρὰ τεύχη σμικρά, μεγάλα δ' ἐσφέρειν, | ὡς θᾶσσον ἔλθωσ' οἶδ' ἐς ἡδονὰς φρενῶν.[2] Therefore *capaciores adfer . . . scyphos* points to an advanced stage of the banquet, and the suggestion at ll. 35 f., *vel quod fluentem nauseam coerceat metire nobis Caecubum*,[3] is in keeping with the practice illustrated by Pliny's recipe, *Nat. hist.* 23. 43 *merum . . . remedio est . . . contra inflationes rosionesque praecordiorum et quorum stomachus in vomitiones effunditur*; some of our contemporaries, who can still afford it, will use cognac for the same purpose.

But even if the implication of *capaciores adfer . . . scyphos* were less clear than it is, the idea that we should assume a scene on board ship would have to be rejected, for it is incompatible with the manner in which Horace acquaints his reader with the setting or background of a poem. If Bücheler's view were correct, the poet would be letting us drift in uncertainty almost to the end of the epode, only then, at l. 35, through the one word *nauseam*, to give us a hint, a very ambiguous hint, as to how we are to picture the whole situation. That would mean that Horace had concealed the most essential element of his poem in a riddle, a riddle which had to wait for its solution until in the last quarter of the nineteenth century a resourceful classical scholar applied to it his great ingenuity. Let us not deceive ourselves with the easy consolation that what seems a riddle to us may have been obvious to Horace's friends, who knew (they did not, but let us assume that they

---

[1] For the evidence see, besides the commentators (from Lambinus on) on Horace, *Epod.* 9. 35 and *Sat.* 2. 8. 35, my dissertation *De media et nova comoedia quaest. sel.* (Göttingen 1912) 19, and Pasquali, *Or. lir.* 510 n. 1. Heinze quotes in his note on Epode 9. 33 some of the relevant passages, but, instead of drawing the necessary conclusion, he begs the question and says ' "geräumigere" Becher verlangt man sonst, um die Lust des Gelages zu steigern, in Athen . . . wie in Rom . . .; hier um schneller über Sorge und Furcht hinwegzukommen'. [2] Eur. *Ion* 1178 ff.

[3] It is naïve to identify the *Caecubum* of l. 36 with that of l. 1, as if there existed only one brand of Caecuban wine. The *Caecubum* of l. 36 is a good and strong one, but nothing extravagant, whereas that *repostum ad festas dapes* is 'Auslese'. Cf., for example, Galen, x. 831 K. on the difference between Τιβουρτῖνος ὁ εὐγενής and Τιβουρτῖνος ἄτονος.

did) that he and Maecenas had joined Caesar's fleet. Horace's poems, whether 'Gelegenheitsgedichte' or not, are self-contained works of art: they are not written only for a few initiates, but for any reader of his books. He does not play hide-and-seek with the general reader, but, on the contrary, takes great pains to unfold quickly the setting and background of a poem, especially if the circumstances which he pre-supposes are unusual.[1] A setting on board ship would, according to the conventions of ancient lyric and quasi-lyric poetry, be nothing un-heard-of, but it is far less common than the setting amidst a banquet scene. If Horace wanted to suggest such a situation, he would probably have done so in terms as unequivocal as we find them, for instance, in Archilochus, *fr.* 5 D., ἀλλ' ἄγε σὺν κώθωνι θοῆς διὰ σέλματα νηὸς φοίτα κτλ., or in Alcaeus, *fr.* 46 A (326 L. and P.), 3 f. D., ἄμμες δ' ὂν τὸ μέσσον ναΐ φορήμμεθα σὺν μελαίνᾳ κτλ. (allegory or no allegory, 'we' are thought to be on board ship). What Horace does presuppose here is a banquet scene, as in Epode XIII and in many of his odes. On account of the dominating role played by συμποτικά in the history of elegies, *iambi*, songs, and so forth, from Archilochus and Alcaeus down to the Hellenistic epigrammatists and the Roman poets, one might *a priori* be inclined to regard a poem as belonging to that class if nothing definite points to its being of a different type. And in Epode IX the very beginning suggests that this is a συμποτικόν. *Quando repostum Caecubum ad festas dapes . . . tecum . . . bibam . . .?* The idea of a letter to Maecenas is wholly out of place. The poem, then, purports to be the idealized rendering of some part of a conversation. In many poems there is no particular setting indicated for such a conversation. But the question *quando Caecubum tecum bibam* comes far more naturally if it is not being asked out of the blue, but while the two friends are drinking together, somewhere—it does not matter where—perhaps in Horace's house. Their thoughts (how could it be otherwise?) turn to the great battle a first report of which has just reached Maecenas. The situation as it emerges from the report appears to be what our war correspond-ents call 'confused': things on the whole have gone well for Caesar but it is not yet possible to be confident of final victory. At the beginning of the epode the poet's anxiety finds an expression which springs out of the situation in which he is speaking: 'here we are drinking; when at long last will the moment come when you and I can celebrate Caesar's

---

[1] I am inclined to regard it as a sign of a certain immaturity that in the sixteenth epode it is only at ll. 15 f. that the reader realizes whom the poet is addressing, and that in the Archytas ode (i. 28, in epodic form) it is not until ll. 21 ff. that we learn that the whole opening speech belongs not to the poet but to a dead man. However, these instances provide no real analogy to the kind of last-minute surprise which Bücheler assumes in Epode IX. In Epode II the deliberate sarcastic shock at the end is entirely different from anything conceivable in such a serious poem as Epode IX.

great victory with the most precious wine in your cellar?' Reminiscences of a similar celebration a few years before and indignation at the disgrace brought upon Roman soldiers by Cleopatra and her lover mingle with the picture of the opposing armies and fleets at Actium. But again a note of anxiety is struck: *io Triumphe, tu moraris aureos currus et intactas boves?* The triumph which we are expecting will surpass the greatest victories in Rome's history. But the time for it has not yet come. With an abrupt turn the poet tries to shake off the burden of his solicitude (33) : let us have bigger cups and stronger wines; *curam metumque Caesaris rerum iuvat dulci Lyaeo solvere.*

There exist in ancient literature very few, if any, poems in which the emotions at the height of a great historical crisis are expressed with such vigour and directness. There can be little doubt that Horace conceived the idea of this epode on the spur of the moment, before the military and political consequences of the battle of Actium could fully unfold. He then left the poem as he had written it. That applies also to Epode I, where we may admire his indifference to petty criticism, for when the book appeared everyone in Rome knew that the plans had been altered and that Maecenas had not, after all, joined Caesar's fleet.

The stylistic level of *Quando repostum Caecubum* is, on the whole, as high as the level of Horace's patriotic odes. When he wrote this epode he was in fact ready for pure lyrics. He was, however, careful not entirely to give up the χαρακτήρ Ἀρχιλόχειος which seemed to him essential for the stylistic uniformity of his book of *iambi*. Hence at ll. 13 f. the coarseness of *spadonibus . . . rugosis.*[1] A similar touch is noticeable in the crude expression, near the end, *fluentem nauseam*, the misunderstanding of which has caused so much unnecessary trouble.[2]

---

[1] The same notion is expressed in a dignified lyric style at *Odes* 1. 37. 9 f., cf. pp. 159 f. below.

[2] If Bücheler had considered the nature of the *iambus*, he would not have drawn wrong conclusions from the fact 'quod vomitum suum Horatius narrat neque erubuit'.

III

BOOK I OF THE SATIRES

I. SATIRE II

THE second satire of Book I, *Ambubaiarum collegia*, is probably the earliest, or at any rate one of the earliest, of Horace's satires. Like one of his earliest epodes, X, *Mala soluta navis*, it shows a rather unpleasant and, in itself, not very interesting theme skilfully executed and adorned with a wealth of fine detail. It is necessary to analyse this early satire carefully if we want to form a clear idea of the task that Horace set himself, of the spirit in which he approached it, and of the difficulties that lay in his way and that could be overcome only through prolonged efforts.

The satire opens with an extraordinary line:

> Ambubaiarum collegia, pharmacopolae.

Hexameters consisting of only three words are rare in Latin as well as in Greek poetry. In the present passage the unusual form of the verse is meant no doubt to give the impression of pomposity;[1] the effect of the bulky words and of the heavy rhythm is enhanced by the exotic noun at the beginning. Mock-solemnity continues in the next line up to the end of the fourth foot, *mendici, mimae, balatrones*. But with *hoc genus omne* we are suddenly plunged into plain colloquialism. As we go on, the motley company of those oriental pipers, beggars, and gipsies forms itself, as it were, into a kind of funeral procession:

> maestum ac sollicitum est cantoris morte Tigelli.

If, after being told of such deep and universal sorrow, we expect to hear a good deal about the merits of the deceased virtuoso, seen of

---

[1] In Homer *O* 678 the harshness of the line κολλητὸν βλήτροισι, δυωκαιεικοσίπηχυ conveys to the ear the enormous bulk and weight of the 22-cubit spear for sea-fighting (for the object described here see H. L. Lorimer, *Homer and the Monuments*, 145). Similarly, I feel sure that in the late 'Homeric' hymn (2) on Demeter this unusual type of verse is deliberately chosen for the periphrasis of awe-inspiring Hades (31), πατροκασίγνητος πολυσημάντωρ πολυδέγμων (for the effect of the π-alliteration cf. my note on A. *Ag.* 268). On the other hand, it seems to be due to a mere accident that the line Hes. *Op.* 383 Πληιάδων Ἀτλαγενέων ἐπιτελλομενάων consists of three words. In Lucretius the composition of the line 3. 907 *insatiabiliter deflevimus, aeternumque* (*nulla dies nobis maerorem e pectore demet*) 'expresses solemnity' (C. Bailey ad loc.). The hexameter (Ennius, *Ann.* 623 Vahlen) *introducuntur legati Minturnenses* is presumably the product of a metrician (cf. Keil on *Gramm. Lat.* vi. 634. 15, L. Müller, *De re metrica*², 152). Cf. also F. Munari's edition of Marci Valerii *Bucolica* (Florence 1955), 17, where Ovid *Fast.* 2. 43, *Amphiareiades Naupactoo Acheloo*, and later instances are quoted.

course through the eyes of the *mimae, balatrones*, and the rest of them, we shall be disappointed. The next clause, it is true, sounds promising enough: *quippe benignus erat*. But no sooner has the eulogy begun than it comes to an end. Of Tigellius nothing more is heard in the remaining 130 lines of the satire.

If then the opening two sentences (1–4a) are only a façade, we may be inclined to assume that immediately behind them there lies the main body of the satire. But this is not so. The following section (4b–28a), though much longer and delivered in a more leisurely fashion, has again a preparatory function in that it leads up to the proper theme of the satire, the beginning of which is to be fixed either at 28b or at 37.[1] The preparatory section, from ll. 4b to 28a (or to 36 or to 30) inclusively, appears as a diatribe against the unbalanced behaviour of men. Several individual instances of this particular type of folly are described,[2] and the underlying general idea is formulated in these lines (23 f.):

> si quis nunc quaerat 'quo res haec pertinet?', illuc:
> dum vitant stulti vitia, in contraria currunt.

A little later (28) another aspect of the same idea is expressed: *nil medium est*.[3] The μέσον, the mean, is best for men, but most of them are blind to this truth; they run into extremes although all extremes are bad. This idea, however, is by no means prominent in the rest of the satire from l. 31 on. It reappears once more at ll. 47 f. (*tutior at quanto merx est in classe secunda, libertinarum dico*), but after a few sentences it fades completely out of the picture.

The real theme of the main body of the satire, the theme to which the anecdote about Cato (31–36) forms a transition, is announced in a special proem (37 ff.). The importance of this announcement, a close parody of a famous passage from Ennius, is emphasized by its lofty tone:

> audire est operae pretium, procedere recte
> qui moechis non voltis, ut omni parte laborent . . ..

---

[1] Since it is obvious that the passage from 28b (*sunt qui nolint*, etc.) to the end of 36 forms a transition from the general topic illustrated in 4b–28a to the main theme (37 f.) of the satire, it does not matter very much whether we fix the beginning of the discussion περὶ μοιχείας at 28b or at 37 or, to mention still another possibility, at 31, *quidam notus homo*. In other words, the sentences beginning with (28b) *sunt qui nolint tetigisse* could be regarded either as an appendix to the section which formally concludes with the clause *nil medium est*, or as the first section of the main chapter. In any case we shall have to make a sharp incision before 37 (see below).

[2] That l. 13 is an interpolation was seen by several scholars; Jachmann, *Studi in onore di U.E. Paoli*, Florence 1955, 400 ff., has conclusively proved it. The lines 14 ff. make it clear that Fufidius is a *fenerator*, but it is not said explicitly; it was, I presume, in order to provide what the interpolator considered necessary for the information of the reader that he lifted the line *dives agris, dives positis in fenore nummis* from *Ars P.* 421.

[3] Cf. *Epist.* 1. 18. 9 *virtus est medium vitiorum et utrimque reductum*.

So momentous an introduction leads us to expect that the following discourse will be περὶ τοῦ μὴ δεῖν μοιχεύειν, and this is in fact the case.

Generally speaking, we should never read into a poem, or a particular section of it, what we should like to find in it. In the present instance, with the lines 23 ff. fresh in our mind, we may be tempted to postulate that the rest of the satire also should be dominated by a firm recommendation of the μέσον and an equally firm disapproval of extremes. But the temptation must be resisted. The main part of the poem (from 37 on), viewed as a whole, does not insist either on the advisability of pursuing a μέσον, which in this context would be a love-affair with a *libertina*, or on the necessity of avoiding the two extremes, at the one end a liaison with a *matrona* and at the other dealings with some woman of the lowest order. It does, however, insist on the thought announced at its beginning: adulterous liaisons are exceedingly dangerous and are therefore to be avoided.

The theme of the main part is announced at 40: the *saepe pericla*[1] that threaten the adulterer, that is to say the lover of a *matrona*. This theme is taken up and worked out with a good deal of picturesque detail at the end of the satire (127–34). And, that there should be no mistake, we find in the middle of the poem (78 f.) a repetition of the topic of 37–40,

> desine matronas sectarier, unde laboris
> plus haurire mali est quam ex re decerpere fructus.

This is the main theme of 37–134, and the predominance of this theme is in no way impaired by the brief digression of 47–53a,[2] where the idea of the preferability of the mean plays once more a transitory role. Nor is the line of the argument seriously broken by the passing remark on the charms of a *togata* at 82: this remark is, from the point of view of the whole discussion, as casual and subordinate as is the hint at the παῖς καλός (81 f.), which here leads to the comparison with a *togata*.[3] The warning *desine matronas sectarier* had, of course, long been a commonplace; it seems to have played a part also in one of the early

[1] Here *saepe* belongs to *dura pericla* (so rightly H. Schütz; many commentators are silent on this point). If we take it with *cadat* (so L. Müller and Lejay), the nice balance of the clause is upset and the logic (*ut rara voluptas saepe cadat*) seems questionable. We recognize the well-known usage (cf. Kühner–Stegmann, i. 218), which is by no means confined to early Latin (it is strange that at Plaut. *Poen.* 725 *rem adversus populi saepe leges* even Leo should have considered the possibility of *saepe* being corrupt). The Horace passage, where *saepe* is sandwiched between the adjective *dura* and the noun, is far less harsh than, for instance, Cic. *Verr.* ii. 5. 131 *perpetuo sociis atque amicis.* The view commonly held on the construction of Virg. *Aen.* 1. 198, *neque enim ignari sumus ante malorum*, has in vain been challenged by Conington and Henry.

[2] From 53b on (*verum hoc se amplectitur uno*) there is no longer any use made of the idea that a relation with the *libertina* (or *ancilla togata*) represents the preferable mean. At 63 indeed dealings with an *ancilla togata* seem to be just as harmful as those with a *matrona*.

[3] Text and interpretation of this passage will be discussed presently.

satires of Lucilius.[1] Horace himself says[2] 'among the pieces of moral
advice that I was given by my father there was this *ne sequerer moechas*'.
So long as a man keeps clear of adulterous relations with *matronae*, it
does not matter—that at any rate is the doctrine professed here—with
what sort of women he amuses himself.[3]

When we now look back on the whole satire, we see that it is in the
main a diatribe on the hackneyed theme of the grave and quite unnecessary risks involved in adultery with women of society. But this
theme is not approached directly. Horace takes his start from the singer
Tigellius, who had died a short time ago, only to drop this subject
after a few words and to plunge into a demonstration of the foolishness
of running into extremes instead of keeping to a middle line. This
demonstration is supported by a number of examples; one of them
(28–30) is taken from the contrast between those men who will make
love only to *matronae* and those who care only for women from the
brothel. At this point the discussion takes a completely different course:
desine matronas sectarier remains, apart from a short digression, the theme
of the satire up to its very end.[4]

From these observations two things must be deduced. First, Horace,
at this early stage, does not draw on any fresh experience of his own, on
anything that concerns him personally or that he has very much at
heart. On the contrary, he takes for his principal theme a well-worn
topic. Secondly, Horace is at pains to give to his satire an appearance
of spontaneity and therefore, although he is at present not at all
interested in Tigellius, he begins with the stir caused among the scum
of Rome's population by the death of that virtuoso. Why did he choose
such a roundabout way to a simple end? Very likely Horace, walking
in the footsteps of Lucilius, was attracted by the directness with which
at least some, and probably many, of the earlier poet's satires sprang
from a contemporary event. To mention only one famous example, it

---

[1] I have said elsewhere (*Festschrift R. Reitzenstein*, 1931, 122) what I regard as the upshot of the modern discussion on earlier occurrences, including those in Lucilius, of the
topics treated by Horace in this section.

[2] *Sat.* 1. 4. 113.

[3] Since all that matters for the main body of this satire is the negative warning as
summed up in *desine matronas sectarier*, I ought not to have said (*Festschrift R. Reitzenstein*,
122) that the satire from 64 on is solely concerned with the idea that intercourse with a
prostibulum is preferable to a liaison with a *matrona*. On this one point Wolfgang Schmid,
Philol. xcvii, 1948, 182, is right. From what I have now said it may be seen that in my judgement on the main part of the satire (64–134), I wholly agree with A. Cartauld, *Étude
sur les satires d'Horace*, 1899, 101 f., and with F. Jacoby, *Rh. Mus.* lxix, 1914, 427 n. 2.

[4] Dacier's discernment is admirable. He says: 'Le veritable sujet de cette Piece [the
first section of the satire] est compris dans le vingt-quatriéme vers: *Dum vitant stulti*. . . . Et
dans ces mots du vingt-huitiéme: *Nil medium est*. . . .. Mais le principal but d'Horace est de
parler contre ceux qui . . . auroient creu ne prendre aucun plaisir, s'ils n'avoient point
commis d'adultere.'

was the death of L. Cornelius Lentulus Lupus that gave rise to the
justly admired *Concilium deorum*,[1] which either alone made up Book I
(not the earliest) of the collection of the satires of Lucilius or was at any
rate its most important piece. But if Horace at that early stage of his
poetic career wished to vie with Lucilius in making his satire arise out
of something that had recently happened in Rome, he had soon to
realize how very limited his opportunities were. A wide gulf was fixed
between Lucilius, a senator's brother, himself a Roman knight, the
intimate friend of Scipio and other great noblemen, and Horace, a
freedman's son, who at that time, after a narrow escape from the
catastrophe of his patrons, had to pick his steps most carefully and give
as little cause for annoyance as possible. When we were examining the
poet's early epodes, we saw that his attempts to adopt certain Archilochean themes were bound to end in failure. The place allotted to
poetry within the framework of contemporary life and also the poet's
own circumstances were entirely different in the case of Archilochus, on
the one hand, and of Horace, on the other. Consequently what in the
verses of the old Ionian poet had flowed immediately from his personal
experience and was meant to fulfil a very real function in the poet's
own life as well as in the life of the surrounding society became in
Horace's laborious adaptation a mere shadow, a literary motif that
could scarcely have a bearing on anything real. Now it is obvious that
the distance between the world of Horace and the world of Lucilius
was not nearly so great as that which separated the world of Horace
from the world of Archilochus. Nevertheless, as far as the possibility
of writing poetry inspired by contemporary events was concerned,
Horace's difficulties were equally great in the case of the satires. To
hit at living persons of importance was at that time all but impossible
for Horace. To hit at persons of no importance or at the dead was
tiresome and, if at all, any attack must be made in passing and could
not provide matter of sufficient interest for a whole poem. So he
resorted in the satire *Ambubaiarum collegia* to a make-believe and
began with a theme of sham spontaneity, precisely as he did in
the Mevius epode, which probably belongs to the same period. The
nucleus of that epode was a conventional theme of Hellenistic poetry,
curses, ἀραί—the nucleus of this satire is a conventional theme of the
popular diatribe, 'adultery is perilous and therefore to be avoided'.
What Horace has to say is in neither case of great value, but the
manner in which he says it is masterly.

We have already noticed the mock-solemnity with which the satire
opens,

Ambubaiarum collegia, pharmacopolae.

[1] Cf. F. Leo, *Geschichte der röm. Literatur*, 419 ff., and the references there to Marx and
Cichorius.

This beginning, *molto adagio*, has a delightful counterpart in the stormy ending of the poem, a *prestissimo* which somehow recalls (no blasphemy is intended) the typical finale of an act in a Mozart opera. In this finale there is not only a good strong brio and a sustained crescendo, but also some sinister polyphony, the smashing of the door, the barking of the dog, wild noises all over the house, and women screaming at the top of their voices (127–33):

> nec vereor ne dum futuo vir rure recurrat,[1]
> ianua frangatur, latret canis, undique magno
> pulsa domus strepitu resonet, vepallida lecto
> desiliat mulier, miseram se conscia clamet,
> cruribus haec metuat, doti deprensa, egomet mi;
> discincta tunica fugiendum est et pede nudo,
> ne nummi pereant aut puga aut denique fama.

There is in this passage a racy elegance and a perfection of rhythm for which we should look in vain in the work of Lucilius. Not even at this early stage did Horace fall short of the high stylistic standard for the writing of satires on which he insists in a later satire (1. 10. 9 f.):

> est brevitate opus, ut currat sententia neu se
> impediat verbis lassas onerantibus auris.

And when he there continues *et sermone opus est . . . defendente vicem modo rhetoris atque poetae*, that requirement, too, is fulfilled in the present satire. A good instance is provided by the exordium of the main section (37 f.):

> Audire est operae pretium procedere recte
> qui moechis non voltis, ut omni parte laborent . . . .

Thanks to the scholia, we possess the illustrious model of this passage:[2]

> Audire est operae pretium procedere recte
> qui rem Romanam Latiumque augescere voltis.

This is an echo of a very old introductory formula, which in all probability originally belonged to forensic oratory. Compare, for instance, the first line of the Sausage-man's great report,[3] Καὶ μὴν ἀκοῦσαί γ' ἄξιον τῶν πραγμάτων.[4] Further, Andocides 1. 124 (beginning of a new section) Ἀλλὰ . . . σκέψασθε . . . ταῦτα γὰρ καὶ ἄξιον ἀκοῦσαι, Isaeus 6. 35 (beginning of a new section) Ταῦτα μὲν δὴ . . . περὶ δὲ τῶν ὑπολοίπων . . .

---

[1] For the effect of the repeated *r*-sound see Lejay and Heinze, ad loc., and my remarks on *Epod.* 10. 5 f. (p. 25 above).

[2] Ennius, *Ann.* 465 f. Vahlen.

[3] Ar. *Knights* 624.

[4] This pompous exordium contrasts amusingly with the style of the whole speech, the uneducated clumsiness of which I have illustrated in *Eranos*, xlix, 1951, 53.

πρᾶγμα κατεσκεύασαν, ᾧ ἄξιόν ἐστι προσέχειν τὸν νοῦν, Plato, *Symp.*
220 c (beginning of a new section) καὶ ταῦτα μὲν δὴ ταῦτα· οἷον δ' αὖ
τόδ' ἔρεξε . . . ἄξιον ἀκοῦσαι, Plautus, *Cas.* 879 *operam date, dum mea
facta itero: est operae pretium auribus accipere*, Ter. *Andr.* 217 *audireque
eorumst operae pretium audaciam*.[1] The audacity with which Horace drags
the lofty patriotic notes of Ennius (every reader of Horace thinks of
remque Romanam Latiumque felix alterum in lustrum . . . prorogat) into a very
different sphere is brilliant. The respectable verb *procedere* is degrad-
ingly yoked with *moechis*, and the very syntactical construction in
which it here occurs seems to remove it from the careful language of
educated persons, for it is exceedingly rare to find the impersonal
procedit (without the addition of a nominal or pronominal subject)
governing a dative.[2]

Another specimen of the grand style is the impudent speech addressed by the *muto*[3] to its owner (69 f.):

numquid ego a te
magno prognatum deposco consule cunnum . . .?

At the end of the line the ear is struck by the harsh sound of *-co con . . .
cunn . . .*, and at the beginning a different effect is obtained by the
ἡμιεπές with its heavy rhythm and the magnificence of the obsolete
word *prognatum*.[4]

---

[1] Cf. also H. Haffter, *Untersuchungen zur altlat. Dichtersprache*, 1934, 3 n. 1. A kindred
formula is used by Horace for the beginning of a new section at *Sat.* 2. 3. 77 *audire atque
togam iubeo componere . . .*, where *audire iubeo* is equally solemn, as may be seen from the
passage in the *Achilles* of Ennius (*Trag.* 15 Ribb.) quoted by Plautus *Poen.* 4 *audire iubet
vos imperator* (in the tragedy of Aristarchus there may have been a variation of ἀκούετε
λεῴ).

[2] Instances of impersonal *procedit* are not, of course, lacking although H. Schütz (followed by Kiessling and Heinze) says that they are. See, for example, Plaut. *Cas.* 805, Ter.
Andr. 671, *Ad.* 897 (with *bene*, as Cic. *Verr.* ii. 3. 227, *Rab. Post.* 1 [with the subject *quid*];
cf. in the passage of Ennius *procedere recte*). But as for impersonal *procedit* with a dative, the
editors (Orelli–Baiter–Mewes and others) quote only one certain instance, Livy 2. 44. 1,
velut processisset Sp. Licinio, probably an archaic or archaizing construction. In a passage of a
letter by Caelius, Cic. *Fam.* 8. 12. 3 (quoted by Forcellini), *quibus cum parum procederet ut ulla
lege mihi ponerent accusatorem*, the *ut*-clause may be assumed to serve in lieu of a subject. This
construction, too, is possibly archaic or, perhaps more likely, one of the colloquialisms not
uncommon in the language of Caelius.

[3] See Lucilius 307 with Marx's commentary. For the personification cf. Goethe's
'Meister Iste' in the poem *Das Tagebuch*.

[4] It seems likely that at least as early as Plautus *prognatus* had a very solemn ring and was
felt not to be suitable for ordinary speech. Of the fourteen instances in Plautus only one
occurs in senarii, *Capt.* 170, *prognatum genere summo et summis ditiis*, a passage of a very lofty
style. In a context such as at *Amph.* 365 (a slave speaking!) the parodic tone is unmistakable. A final judgement on the history of the word must be postponed until the article in
the *Thesaurus* is published; in the meantime the paper 'Prognatus' by E. Schwyzer,
Kuhn's Zeitschrift, lvi, 1928, 10 ff., in which the materials of the *Thesaurus* are used, provides
a helpful survey. First occurrence in the epitaph of Scipio Barbatus (also in one of the later
epitaphs of the Scipios, *CIL* i.[2] 10), then in early epic and tragedy. Apparently at home in
legal language in a technical sense (e.g. *CIL* i.[2] 589, i. 5, several passages in Gaius'

To illustrate the subtlety with which in this satire the device of *variatio* is used one example must suffice. The lines 105b–108 consist of an all but literal rendering of an epigram (31) of Callimachus, but only the expression *hiscine versiculis* at 109 hints at the borrowing. Philodemus, on the other hand, is expressly mentioned at 121, but only the gist of his epigram is recognizable in Horace's allusion.

To the preceding brief survey of the satire two observations on points of detail may be added. The first concerns the anecdote reported in 31–35:

> quidam notus homo cum exiret fornice, 'macte
> virtute esto' inquit sententia dia Catonis;[1]
> 'nam simul ac venas inflavit taetra libido,
> huc iuvenes aequom est descendere, non alienas
> permolere uxores'.

If we disregard Horace's own embroidery, we have here the simplest form of an ordinary αἶνος, one of those diminutive stories the only purpose of which is to provide the background for the witty or surprising utterance at the end.[2] The form of the beginning, *quidam notus homo*, is typical; compare the examples quoted in my note on A. *Ag.* 719 and add, for instance, Timocreon *fr.* 4 D. Σικελὸς κομψὸς ἀνὴρ ποτὶ τὰν ματέρ' ἔφα and Ar. *Wasps* 1427 ἀνὴρ Συβαρίτης ἐξέπεσεν ἐξ ἅρματος. As regards the substance of the anecdote about Cato, Horace derived it probably from a collection of *Apophthegmata Catonis* (excerpts from such a collection are preserved by Plutarch). As a mere possibility it may be suggested that the anecdote was originally invented for Solon[3] or another Greek lawgiver[4] and then transferred to Cato. From Plutarch[5] we learn that one of Cato's apophthegms belonged really to Themistocles and another to Pisistratus.[6]

Institutiones). At Terence, *Phorm.* 115, *illam civem esse Atticam, bonam bonis prognatam*, it is used presumably to convey the juridical note. Kraner–Dittenberger–Meusel comment on Caes. *B.Gall.* 2. 29. 4 '*prognati* braucht C. noch 6. 18. 1. Das Wort ist dichterisch, in der älteren Prosa nur in einem Briefe des Caelius bei Cic. *Fam.* 8. 15. 2 [i.e. if we accept Piero Vettori's probable conjecture; in that case Caesar would be called, by way of witty παρατραγῳδεῖν, *Venere prognatus*].'

[1] I am inclined to accept Marx's guess (on Lucilius 1316), '*sententia dia ex Ennio videtur esse sumptum ab Horatio et ab Lucilio per iocum adhibitum in re humili et vulgari*'.

[2] In general see my remarks in *Rh. Mus.* lxxiii, 1920, 366 ff.

[3] Philemon (*fr.* 4 K.) praises Solon as a benefactor because he had turned the appetite of the young men away from honest women, πριάμενον . . . γυναῖκας . . . κοινὰς ἅπασι καὶ κατεσκευασμένας—what follows has a good deal in common with the lines 119–26 of Horace's satire.

[4] In Dio Chrys. 7. 132 ff. (i. 214 ff. v. Arnim) there is a long invective against the νομοθέται who invented the expedient with which Solon is credited by Philemon.

[5] *Cat. Ma.* 8. 4 f. and 24. 8.

[6] For the manner in which Greek apophthegms were sometimes applied to great Romans see also O. Gigon, *Westöstliche Abhandlungen R. Tschudi . . . überreicht*, 1954, 20.

Finally, something must be said about l. 81, for this 'locus impli-
catissimus, quemque frustra aggressi sunt viri eruditi' (Bentley) is by
most modern editors (Vahlen and Vollmer are laudable exceptions)
printed in a form which makes it impossible to understand the passage
and to appreciate a peculiarity characteristic of Horace's early satires:

> quare, ne paeniteat te,
> desine matronas sectarier, unde laboris
> plus haurire mali est quam ex re decerpere fructus.
> nec magis huic, inter niveos viridisque lapillos　　　　　　　　80
> sit licet hoc Cerinthe tuum tenerum est femur aut crus
> rectius, atque etiam melius persaepe togatae.

Here one important decision can be made at once: at 81 *hoc*, as was
seen by J. M. Gesner, is ablative, 'idem quod *ideo*, *ob hoc* etc.'[1] As for
the rest, we have only to follow Bentley, that is to say replace at 81 the
tuum of the παράδοσις by the conjecture *tuo*,[2] punctuate *sit licet*, *hoc*,
Cerinthe, *tuo* and paraphrase (with Bentley's 'veteres scholiastae', i.e.
the 'commentator Cruquianus', p. 309 [it ought to be 319], middle of
the left-hand column, in the first edition by Cruquius, Antwerp 1579)
'Nec huic matronae, licet sit inter niveos et virides lapillos, ⟨ideo⟩
femur aut crus magis tenerum est quam [hoc] tuum, o Cerinthe', etc.[3]
Against this rendering Heinze argues 'Der Verbindung *magis tenerum*
widerspricht schon das beispiellose Hyperbaton.' Compare, however,
the following passages:[4] *maxime*: Cic. *Planc.* 37 *eum* maxime *eis hominibus
qui eius tribus essent esse* notum; *Sest.* 41 *Caesar, quem* maxime *homines
ignari veritatis mihi esse* iratum *putabant.*　　　*minus*: Quinct. 87 *idcirco*

---

[1] Kiessling, at the end of a long faltering note, asks the question 'Oder ist *hoc* = *ideo*
zu verstehen?', L. Müller and Heinze accept this interpretation without ado; they are
right. For this use of *hoc* see Ehlers, *Thes. l. L.* vi. 3. 2745. 57 ff. He quotes six instances from
Horace, all of them, which is worth noticing, from *Satires*, Book I. One of these passages is
very similar to the present one, viz. 1. 1. 45 f., *milia frumenti tua triverit area centum: non tuus
hoc capiet venter plus ac meus.*

[2] An original *tuo* next to *tenerum est femur* lived inevitably in mortal danger. Two Paris
MSS, one of the ninth or tenth century and one of the eleventh century, have *tuo*: it seems
impossible to say whether this is a deliberate correction or an accidental mistake. The
humanists wrote *tuo* to emend the text. One of the countless instances of this kind of corruption occurs at Cic. *Caecin.* 75, where editors read with the MSS *non minus diligenter ea
quae a maioribus accepistis publica patrimonia iuris quam privatae rei vestrae retinere debetis.* I now
see from the apparatus of Baiter–Halm that my correction (*Hermes*, lx, 1925, 440) *quam
privata rei vestrae* was already suggested by someone in the re-edition (1584) of Lambin's
text.

[3] I have slightly rearranged the order of the clauses so as to make the paraphrase
correspond more closely to the text of Horace, but I have not altered the words except that
I have inserted *ideo*. The *hoc* before *tuum* was written by the commentator Cruquianus, but
omitted by Bentley since he read *o* for *hoc*.

[4] There must be many more. I did not wish to spend much time on this matter; so
I only skimmed Merguet's *Lexicon* to Cicero's speeches. The one remaining example,
Cic. *Orat.* 175, I owe to Vahlen's note on Arist. *Poet.* 26. 1461[b] 27 (3rd ed., p. 284).

minus *iudicio pati* paratum *fuisse*; *Div. Caec.* 18 minus *aliquanto nunc
quidem* munitam *quam antea*; *Sest.* 58 *nec* minus *et sibi et huic imperio*
gloriosum *putavit.*   nimis: *Pis.* 17 *eius cui* nimis *videtur senatus in con-
servanda patria fuisse* crudelis; *Orat.* 175 *Thrasymachus, cuius omnia* nimis
etiam exstant scripta numerose. It was for a different reason that Housman,
in a juvenile paper,[1] objected to Bentley's interpretation: 'Can one conceive anything more perverse than that Cerinthus, a third term of
comparison, should be introduced at all?' Perverse only so long as one
does not pause to observe a certain peculiarity of Horace's early
satires. The fact that Cerinthus is being dragged in like that, far
from making the authenticity of the text suspect, ought to be regarded
as a clear pointer to what Horace at that stage thought to be an essential ingredient of the literary genre he had chosen. He seems to have
been obsessed by the idea that a writer of satires, if he wanted to do his
job properly, which meant doing it in the spirit of Lucilius as Horace
understood it at that time, was obliged to hit at as many persons as
possible. And since, if only for reasons of space, not all such invectives
could be fully worked out, it was an obvious expedient to strike a
swift blow at this or that individual, in passing as it were, and be done
with it. These strokes come and go like lightning, for a moment's
amusement, nothing more. An elegant example occurs at 94 f.,

> matronae praeter faciem nil cernere possis,
> cetera, ni Catia est, demissa veste tegentis.

Again, at 1. 3. 44 ff. we are really concerned with types and not with
individuals, but the poet does not find it difficult to jump from
generalities to a sharply personal remark:

> > strabonem
> appellat paetum pater, et pullum, male parvus
> si cui filius est, ut abortivus fuit olim
> Sisyphus.

And, very similarly, at 1. 3. 84 ff.

> > paulum deliquit amicus,
> quod nisi concedas, habeare insuavis: acerbus
> odisti et fugis, ut Rusonem debitor aeris,

there follows an acid anecdote about Octavius Ruso. The last two
instances have this in common that the person at whom the transitory
gibe is directed is brought in by means of a comparison (*ut*). Similarly
in the passage from which we started, 1. 2. 80 ff., the link is formed by
a comparison, though of a different type (*huic*, i.e. *matronae, femur non*

---

[1] *Journ. Phil.* xviii, 1890, 2.

est magis tenerum quam tuum femur est, Cerinthe, etc.). The quick shot cannot have missed the mark: to be flattered as a παῖς καλός, with the
emphasis upon *femur* and *crus,* is, in this society, an exceedingly doubtful compliment.

2. SATIRE III

The third satire of the book was written later, though probably not
much later, than the second.[1] Here again it is the recently deceased
Tigellius who provides the point of departure.[2] It is only fair to say
that the dead virtuoso this time is treated less perfunctorily. We are
given, if not a complete portrait of the man, at any rate a lively and
most amusing sketch of his typical behaviour (4–19). Nevertheless, it is
easy to see that here too, as in *Sat.* i. 2, 'the entry is masked'.[3] The
whole description of Tigellius turns on the one trait that is twice expressly indicated, at 9, *nil aequale homini fuit illi,* and, at the very end of
this section, 18 f. *nil fuit umquam sic impar sibi.* This point of view was
familiar to the contemporaries of Horace. That men, in their whole
conduct of life, should aim at consistency, *aequabilitas,* and avoid inconsistency had by the Greeks long been considered a moral duty;
particular stress was laid on it in the teaching of the Stoa.[4] It would
therefore be natural, after Tigellius has merely provided an illustration
of the type of the *inaequalis* and is then dismissed altogether, to expect
that a wider discussion on men's inconsistencies in general would
follow.[5] But what does follow is something totally different, a pleading

[1] On this head I have nothing to add to the last paragraph of Heinze's introduction to
i. 3 (the substance of it comes from Kiessling, whose less reliable arguments are rightly
omitted).

[2] This Sardus Tigellius is not, of course, the same person as the *cantor* (Tigellius)
Hermogenes mentioned at 129. The facts were understood by Dacier (notes on 1. 3. 3 and
1. 3. 129) and the whole intricate problem solved by C. Kirchner in 1834. In our century
not only B. L. Ullman, *Class. Philol.* x, 1915, 270 ff., but also, unfortunately, a master of
prosopography, Münzer, *RE* vi. A. 943 ff. (in an article published in 1937 under the strain
of that period), have tried to reverse the position, an undertaking that could not possibly
succeed. To mention only one decisive point, the context of *Sat.* 1. 10. 90 proves beyond
doubt that the Tigellius (viz. Hermogenes) addressed there was alive at the time of
Horace's writing.

[3] Kirchner's phrase, quoted by A. Cartault, *Étude,* 66 n. 1, whose own observations may
be compared.

[4] There is a vigorous description of the type of the *inaequalis* (the word is used in this sense
by Horace, *Sat.* 2. 7. 10) in Plato, *Resp.* 561 c-d. Socrates was to become the ideal representative of 'aequabilitas': *praeclara . . . est aequabilitas in omni vita et idem semper vultus eademque
frons, ut de Socrate . . . accepimus* (Cic. *Off.* 1. 90). Cf. Pohlenz, 'Antikes Führertum', *Neue
Wege zur Antike,* ii. 3, p. 53, and his book *Die Stoa,* i. 116 ff., ii. 67 (also on the deeper
meaning of Zeno's formula ὁμολογουμένως ζῆν). It is a subtle touch that the Tacitean
portrait of the model Stoic, Helvidius Priscus, culminates in the clause *cunctis vitae officiis
aequabilis.*

[5] To this theme Horace returned briefly in a much later satire, 2. 7. 7–20.

for leniency towards the defects of our friends (from 19, *nunc aliquis dicat mihi*, to the end of 75).

At 76 a new section begins, marked as such by the initial *denique*.[1] It is connected with the preceding section, for, broadly speaking, the discussion on leniency towards other people's shortcomings continues, but the point of view has changed. The former section was concerned with *amicorum vitia* (26, add 33 *est . . . tibi amicus*, 43 f. *amici siquod sit vitium*, 50 *amicis*, 54 *amicos*, and, at the very end of this section, 73 f. *qui ne tuberibus propriis offendat amicum postulat, ignoscet verrucis illius*). In the latter section what matters is the insistence on the difference between serious offences and venial faults.[2] This sensible differentiation, as is well known, reflects in the main the Epicurean reaction against the most rigid Stoic ethics, which profess ἴσα . . . τὰ ἁμαρτήματα,[3] (*omnia*) *peccata esse paria* in the words of Cicero[4] and Horace (96). The coda of the satire (from 123 *si tibi regnum* to the end) grows naturally out of the main theme, which is a rejection of the ultra-rigid standards of the Stoa, based on its ideal of the self-sufficiency of the wise man.[5] This coda is written with great zest; its slightly flippant tone and amusing detail[6] ward off any feeling of uneasiness that might have been roused by prolonged sermonizing.

In one respect *Sat.* i. 3, compared with i. 2, shows a happy advance towards what was to become the proper end of Horace's finest satires. To give an idea of the harsh criticism to which a relatively harmless type of ἀκαιρία[7] is often exposed, Horace says (63–66):

[1] Lejay (his comment is directed against Kiessling) and Heinze (5th ed.) have a good note on *denique*, used here 'in the sense it usually bears in Lucretius, as a synonym of *praeterea*, *porro*, "again" "once more", introducing a new argument' (Munro on Lucr. 1. 17). This important use of *denique* is neglected in Gudeman's article in the *Thesaurus*.

[2] That *mediocria vitia* should be condoned is a principle which Horace, fully aware of his own shortcomings, has very much at heart, cf. 1. 4. 130 f. and 1. 6. 65 ff.

[3] Zeno *fr.* 224, *SVF* i. 54.

[4] *Mur.* 61.

[5] The connexion of the concluding part with the body of the satire is well explained by Lejay, p. 63.

[6] Commenting on ll. 124–8 Heinze observes that 'in the diatribes of Epictetus the σκυτεύς, besides the τέκτων, constantly represents the class of the artisans; a feature which, as is suggested by Horace's words, can perhaps be traced back to Chrysippus'. But for this feature there exists a piece of evidence much earlier than Epictetus. Zeno (*fr.* 273 *SVF* i. 62 f., cf. *Teletis Reliquiae*, ed. Hense, 2nd ed. 46) had told a delightful anecdote about Crates the Cynic. One day Crates, in the workshop of the shoemaker Philiscus, was reading, aloud of course, the *Protrepticus* of Aristotle, which was dedicated to King Themison of Cyprus. The shoemaker, without interrupting his stitching, listened attentively; therefore Crates said (it is for the sake of the apophthegm that the little tale is told): ἐγώ μοι δοκῶ, ὦ Φιλίσκε, γράφειν πρὸς σὲ προτρεπτικόν. πλείω γὰρ ὁρῶ σοι ὑπάρχοντα πρὸς τὸ φιλοσοφῆσαι ἢ ᾧ (ἢ ᾧ Diels: ὦν codd.) ἔγραψεν Ἀριστοτέλης. The shoemaker, on account of his thirst for true wisdom, turns out to be superior to the king.

[7] Theophr. *Char.* 12. 2 ὁ . . . ἄκαιρος τοιοῦτός τις οἷος ἀσχολουμένῳ προσελθὼν ἀνακοινοῦσθαι.

> simplicior quis et est qualem me saepe libenter
> obtulerim tibi, Maecenas, ut forte legentem
> aut tacitum impellat quovis sermone: 'molestus,[1]
> communi sensu plane caret'[2] inquimus.

There is nothing forced or unpleasantly intentional in the device by
which Maecenas here comes into the picture. Horace's behaviour to
him is mentioned in an easy, almost casual manner, by way of ex-
emplification of a certain social type. But no attentive reader can miss
the note of gratitude and happiness that permeates this brief personal
digression. The passage looks like a first tentative step on the road that
was soon to lead the poet to perfect mastery in describing his own way
of life, his βίος.

Viewed as a whole, however, the satire i. 3 does not rise much above
the level of a very skilful effort.[3] No doubt there are in it some fresh
and spontaneous elements, but in the main it seems to be an elegant
embroidery of themes derived from the textbooks of Hellenistic moral
philosophy. The nucleus of the poem is clearly to be seen in the diatribe, or diatribes, on the *vitia* and *peccata*, to which the exordium about
Tigellius is but loosely prefixed. Here, as in i. 2, the start from the
singer, whose recent death was fresh in everybody's memory, is meant
to provide the subsequent general discussion with a semblance of
spontaneity and so to make the satire appear more Lucilian. Equally in
the vein of Lucilius is the repeated ὀνομαστὶ κωμῳδεῖν. But the men at
whom Horace gibes in passing, are not, like those whom Lucilius
multa cum libertate notabat, eminent figures of his own day; they are, at
any rate most of them, mere ghosts, either dead or insignificant per-

---

[1] The two paraphrases in the scholia offer the choice of beginning the comment either
with *molestus* or after it. It may be possible to make a case for the latter interpretation
(taking *impellat sermone molestus* together), but with many editors I feel that the whole
sentence gains in strength and poise if the criticism begins with *molestus*.

[2] The commentators, including Bentley, have written a great deal about the meaning
of *communi sensu* in this context. However, I agree with H. J. Thomson, *CR* xxxiv, 1920, 21:
'one may doubt whether . . . in fact it means more than the feeling or perception which
men in general have; the reader being left, as usual, to understand what the particular
feeling or perception is'. The phrase *communi sensu plane caret* comes very nearly to the same
thing as the slave's remark in Terence's *Eunuchus* (460), *ex homine hunc natum dicas?* An outspoken Italian would say *che animale!*

[3] To illustrate the stylistic polish it will suffice to point to two sets of variations within one
short section, 44–53. In ll. 44–48 there are four grammatical objects (as distinct from the
predicate nouns) of a strictly parallel order, but all are indicated by means of different
nominal or verbal constructions, viz. (1), the simplest, *strabonem*, (2) *male parvus si cui
filius est*, (3) *hunc . . . distortis cruribus*, (4) *illum. . . . pravis fultum male talis*. Moreover, in the
first of these clauses the verb is *appellat*, in the last *balbutit*, whereas in the two middle
clauses the verb is to be understood from the context. Turning to 49–53 we notice that the
four principal verbs, the function of which corresponds in each case, have these forms: (1)
dicatur, (2) *postulat ut videatur*, (3) *habeatur*, (4) *numeretur*. Monotony is avoided at all costs.
A very similar refinement of detail is often found in Virgil; see, for instance, my remarks
JRS xxxv, 1945, 10.

sons. Immediately after Tigellius there follows (21) Maenius, a spend-thrift of noble family, who after his death had been ridiculed by Lucilius.[1] Of Balbinus (40) nothing is known. The poor wretch Sisyphus (47), a dwarf in the household of the triumvir Antonius, could safely be mentioned; besides, he was already dead when Horace wrote this satire. As for the 'mad' Labeo (82), one thing is certain: on chronological grounds he cannot possibly be identified (as was done by Porphyrio) with the great lawyer M. Antistius Labeo. His real identity must necessarily remain uncertain. But the hypothesis that the person who is here alluded to is C. Atinius Labeo, tribunus plebis in 131 B.C., is worth considering.[2] As tribune he had the censor Q. Caecilius Metellus Macedonicus arrested in the street and was about to put him to death when another tribune interceded. This act, of which Cicero *Dom.* 123 speaks as *ille furor tribuni plebis* (Horace, at 83, varies the preceding *insanior* by *furiosus*) falls within the period covered by the earliest books of Lucilius.[3] Metellus, it is true, was more than once bitterly attacked by Lucilius. But that does not exclude the possibility that the poet, always bent on finding fresh butts for his wit, should occasionally have poked fun at Metellus' enemy, the insane tribune. If that was the case, Labeo would have to be added to the list of Lucilian characters who make a transient appearance in Horace's early satires. We now continue our survey. The moneylender Ruso (86 ff.) remains to us a very dim figure;[4] obviously he was a fiend to his debtors, but not a man of great consequence. A more interesting problem arises out of the story about the occupation of *Alfenus vafer*, 130 ff. Here Porphyrio assures us that the man in question is no other than the famous jurist P. Alfenus Varus, consul suffectus in 39 B.C.; many scholars believe this to be true.[5] But, as Wieland, a real poet and a scholar of admirable tact and common sense, says at the beginning of his extensive discussion of this point,[6] 'Mir ist nicht unwahrscheinlich

[1] Cf. Marx on Lucilius 1203, Münzer, *RE* xiv. 248.

[2] This suggestion, made by Lobeck's pupil F. A. W. Spohn early in the nineteenth century, is mentioned by Orelli and many other editors.

[3] Cf. Leo, *Gesch. d. röm. Lit.* 411.   [4] Cf. Münzer, *RE* xvii. 1854.

[5] So most of the editors of Horace and, for instance, E. Klebs, *RE* i. 1472, and *Prosopographia Imperii Romani*, i. 49 (in the re-edition of the *Prosopographia* the article on this Alfenus is omitted), and also W. Kunkel in his excellent book *Herkunft und soziale Stellung der röm. Juristen*, 1952, 29. A subtle, if unconvincing, defence of Porphyrio's tale was attempted by Tenney Frank, *CQ* xiv, 1920, 160. On the other hand, P. Krüger, *Geschichte der Quellen und Litteratur des röm. Rechts*, 2nd ed., 1912, 69 n. 49, after quoting Porphyrio, says 'Ob Horaz an den Juristen gedacht hat, steht dahin', and at least some editors of Horace have firmly denied that Horace's Alfenus was the jurist, e.g. Wieland (see the next footnote), L. Müller, and Heinze, who rightly observes 'dies wäre der einzige Witz, den sich H. über einen so hochgestellten und angesehenen Zeitgenossen erlaubte'. F. Schulz, *History of Roman Legal Science*, 1946, 42, is equally firm in rejecting the scholiast's story.

[6] C. M. Wieland, *Horazens Satyren aus dem Lateinischen übersezt und mit Einleitungen und*

[personally, I would say, 'I am sure'], daß uns dieser Scholiast hier wieder seinen gewöhnlichen Streich gespielt hat.' Generally speaking, we know that those *qui de personis Horatianis scripserunt,* when they came across the mention of a person of whom nothing was known except what Horace says about him, were quick to identify him with some famous namesake belonging to roughly the same period. And in the case of Alfenus, who is supposed to be the jurist, we have only to remember that the Labeo of 82 was identified by Porphyrio with the great lawyer, which is clearly impossible. Let us then not try to raise the *vafer Alfenus* above the humble station to which he belongs. Finally there comes (139) Crispinus, a contemptible man, mentioned here as a miserable follower of some ridiculous Stoic preacher and at 1. 4. 14 as a hasty poetaster (by way of preparation for both these passages he is introduced in the overture of the book, 1. 1. 120).

To sum up. None of these persons was really worth attacking, but within the literary genre which Horace had chosen they served a modest purpose.

3. SATIRE I

This is perhaps a suitable place to say something about the first satire, *Qui fit, Maecenas,* for this satire, though more polished and more comprehensive than II and III, is related to them by the significant fact that only the first three satires of this book have as their principal theme a topic of popular moral philosophy.

The consistency of *Qui fit Maecenas* has for a long time been the subject of an animated controversy.[1] Many scholars, differing only on small points, have held and hold the view which Arthur Palmer, with refreshing directness, formulated thus: 'The avowed subject of the satire is the discontent of men with their lot, and their envy of that of others, 1–20 [he probably means 19]. But this theme is only prefatory to an attack on avarice: this is the real subject, 28 *sqq.,* the *avarus* being selected as the most striking instance of the discontented man. There are in reality two subjects, discontent and avarice, but Horace tries to treat them as one, and the suture is apparent.' The champions of this harsh criticism can indeed produce arguments for their case which, on the face of it, are impressive. First of all, the bulk of the section concerned with φιλοπλουτία seems badly out of proportion in a discussion the avowed theme of which is μεμψιμοιρία. Moreover, Horace himself seems to point to a 'suture' by saying towards the end (108) *illuc unde*

---

erläuternden Anmerkungen versehen, i, Leipzig 1786, 113 ff. He quotes a monograph on Alfenus Varus by the Dutch jurist Everard Otto, who had come to the same conclusion.

[1] A bibliography of stupendous, if rather terrifying, completeness has been incorporated by H. Herter in his extensive article on the first satire, *Rh. Mus.* xciv, 1951, 1 ff.

abii redeo. But a closer inspection should make us pause. Our eagerness to look in a work of literature for traces of stitching and patching ought not to prevent us from paying attention to the connective tissues of a live organism.

A strong link between the two apparently incongruous elements of this satire was pointed out with great lucidity by Moriz Haupt.[1] He stressed the importance of the thought expressed in 29 ff.: the various classes of persons whose μεμψιμοιρία had been described before and who, nevertheless, if a god offered to them the possibility of a change, would prefer to remain what they are—all of them *hac mente laborem sese ferre, senes ut in otia tuta recedant, aiunt, cum sibi sint congesta cibaria.* The real reason why men are never contented with their own lot lies in their πλεονεξία. It is *avaritia* that is at the bottom of the misguided yearning after other men's lot. All those people would not be prepared to have a change; rather will they, out of greed, put up with any toil and danger. Greed impels them to call other people happy, to envy them and try to outdo them. Haupt rightly inferred that in the section beginning with the weighty introduction of 27 (*sed tamen amoto quaeramus seria ludo*) *avaritia* appears as the primary cause from which the poet derives the μεμψιμοιρία. He also saw that this thought is taken up in the concluding part from 108 on.[2] Here it is made perfectly clear that the μεμψίμοιροι are actuated by greed, πλεονεξία: 111 f. *neque se maiori pauperiorum turbae comparet,* 113 *sic festinanti semper locupletior obstat.* A further observation may be added: the idea that the reason why men willingly undergo so much toil and discomfort lies in their greediness

[1] See the publication of extracts of his university lectures by C. Belger, *Moriz Haupt als academischer Lehrer,* 1879, 265 f. Since the book has become rare, it may be convenient for the reader to have the relevant passage before him. 'V. 29 ist der Gedanke ausgesprochen, daß die Leute, die, wenn ihnen der Mühe oder Gefahr zu viel wird, sich an die Stelle anderer wünschen, doch aus Habsucht, die sie unter nichtigen Vorwänden verstecken, die Mühsal ihres Berufes fort und fort ertragen . . . Der wahre Grund, daß die Menschen mit ihrem Loose nicht zufrieden sind, ist, daß sie nie genug haben. Neidisch blicken sie auf den Besitz Anderer, suchen es Andern zuvorzuthun im Erwerben und gelangen so nie zu Zufriedenheit und Glück. Die avaritia ist also der Grund, aus dem überhaupt jene Verkehrtheit der Menschen hergeleitet wird. Denn der Faden, an dem sich die Gedanken dieser Satire aufreihen, ist dieser: "Die Menschen pflegen oft das Loos Anderer als ein glücklicheres zu preisen als das ihre. Nicht aus richtiger Betrachtung und aufrichtiger Gesinnung, sondern in Unmut und Überdruß einzelner Stimmung. Denn tauschen würden sie doch nicht; sie tragen Mühe und Gefahr aus schnöder Habsucht, aus Habsucht preisen sie Andere glücklich, aus Habsucht beneiden sie die Andern und suchen ihnen zuvorzukommen".'

[2] The value of Haupt's appreciation of the intimate connexion between the concluding part, 108 ff., and all that precedes it is not impaired by the fact that his judgement on the reading at 108, and consequently on the meaning of *ut* (he, followed by many of his successors, took *ut avarus = utpote avarus*) is erroneous. A thorough examination of this crucial point cannot be made without going into a good deal of technical detail; I have therefore dealt with it separately, pp. 97 ff. below. But I need hardly say that what I have discussed there forms an essential part of my argumentation.

permeates the whole satire, and the emphasis laid on the toil (*labor*) is as pronounced in the central section on *avaritia* (93 f. *pauperiem metuas minus et finire laborem incipias*) as in the opening and concluding sections on μεμψιμοιρία (5 *multo iam fractus membra labore*, 30 f. *hac mente laborem .sese ferre . . .*, and 112 *hunc atque hunc superare laboret*).

What has been said here is perhaps sufficient to make us sceptical about Heinze's assumption that Horace in this satire contaminated materials which he derived from two different classes of Greek sources, one dealing with φιλοπλουτία and another dealing with μεμψιμοιρία; 'but he did not succeed in wiping out completely the traces of this procedure.'[1] However, we must go further. It is in fact the evidence of those very sources referred to by Heinze, the sources utilized by him in such excellent fashion from his doctoral dissertation on,[2] that is to enable us to deal the death-blow to his theory.

It is now generally recognized that the diatribe περὶ αὐταρκείας by a certain Teles (third century B.C.), large excerpts of which are extant,[3] depends to a considerable extent on some 'sermons' of Bion of Borysthenes, an eminent representative of a whole group[4] of migrating preachers who propagated an unpretentious kind of 'philosophy' in the form of semi-serious 'diatribes', where an ample provision of entertaining anecdotes, fables, examples from everyday life, history, poetry, and so forth, helped to season the dishes of true wisdom. It has also been seen that characteristic elements of that diatribe περὶ αὐταρκείας recur in the first satire of Horace, who at a much later time spoke of his satires as *Bionei sermones*.[5] The ideal of αὐτάρκεια implies necessarily the fight against μεμψιμοιρία (this term occurs near the beginning of our excerpts, p. 6. 5 Hense). What especially interests us here is the close connexion between μεμψιμοιρία and πλεονεξία. It would be idle, so the preacher tells his audience (pp. 9 f. H.), to try to alter circumstances. Man should follow the example of the sailors. Just as they adjust their manœuvres to the conditions of wind and weather, so should he do (p. 10. 6): καὶ σὺ πρὸς τὰ παρόντα χρῶ. γέρων γέγονας· μὴ ζήτει τὰ τοῦ ἰσχυροῦ . . . ἄπορος πάλιν γέγονας· μὴ ζήτει τὴν τοῦ εὐπόρου δίαιταν κτλ. After these strong warnings against μεμψιμοιρία the speaker arrives at the sad conclusion (p. 11. 4 ff.): ἀλλ' ἡμεῖς οὐ δυνάμεθα ἀρκεῖσθαι τοῖς παροῦσιν (harking back to σὺ πρὸς τὰ

---

[1] Heinze in the third paragraph of his introduction to this satire, p. 2, middle (in his last edition, 1921).

[2] *De Horatio Bionis imitatore* (Bonn 1889), a juvenile piece of work and as such inevitably one-sided, but full of fruitful suggestions.

[3] *Teletis reliquiae*, ed. O. Hense (2nd ed., 1909), 5 ff.

[4] See Wilamowitz, 'Die griech. Literatur des Altertums', *Die Kultur der Gegenwart*, i. 8, 3rd ed., 1912, 164.

[5] *Epist.* 2. 2. 60.

παρόντα χρῶ), ὅταν καὶ τρυφῇ πολὺ διδῶμεν κτλ.[1] So this whole section culminates in the idea that πλεονεξία is the cause of all our troubles. The moral of ἀρκεῖσθαι τοῖς παροῦσιν is the same that underlies Horace's lines 59 f. *at qui tantuli eget quanto est opus . . .* and 61 f. *at bona pars hominum decepta cupidine falso 'nil satis est', inquit, 'quia tanti quantum habeas sis'.*

There existed numerous other diatribes on the inconsistency of man and his μεμψιμοιρία. One of them found its way into the collection of faked Hippocratic letters; it is now printed as number seventeen.[2] This diatribe is certainly later than Horace, but scholars are now convinced that the remarkable points of agreement between it and Horace's first satire cannot be explained by assuming a dependence of the Greek writer on Horace, but only by assuming common sources. So this late piece is suitable to represent, at any rate in substance, one type of those treatises that Horace knew and exploited in Satire I. Some of the topics are almost identical. Under the heading δυσαρεστεῦνται πᾶσι[3] we read, *inter alia,*[4] ἡγεμόνες καὶ βασιλέες μακαρίζουσι τὸν ἰδιώτην, ὁ δὲ ἰδιώτης ὀρέγεται βασιλείης, ὁ πολιτευόμενος τὸν χειροτεχνεῦντα ὡς ἀκίνδυνον, ὁ δὲ χειροτέχνης ἐκεῖνον ὡς εὐτονεῦντα κατὰ πάντων. Up to this point the passage was quoted by Heinze.[5] Nine lines farther down[6] we read: κατασκάπτουσιν, εἶτα ἐποικοδομέουσι, χαρίζονται, εἶτα μετανοοῦσι καὶ ἀφαιρεῦνται τὰ φιλίης δίκαια . . . καὶ τουτέων πάντων αἰτίη ἡ φιλαργυρίη. That is to say, the general thesis in which this diatribe against μεμψιμοιρία and inconsistency culminates is identical with what Haupt, without using the 'Hippocratic letter' or considering Horace's sources at all, recognized as the fundamental idea of Horace's first satire: 'Die avaritia ist also der Grund, aus dem überhaupt jene Verkehrtheit der Menschen [i.e. the μεμψιμοιρία] hergeleitet wird.' So far then from having to contaminate treatises about μεμψιμοιρία with treatises about φιλοπλουτία, Horace found in the current discussions of such topics by philosophizing preachers, Cynics and others, the various manifestations of μεμψιμοιρία reduced to their primary cause, φιλαργυρία.[7] In passing we may notice that the author of that treatise, after making the decisive point about φιλαργυρίη, protests that men in the weakness with which they yield to their passions are no better than animals, or, rather, are more unreasonable, τίς γὰρ λέων ἐς γῆν

---

[1] G. C. Fiske, *Lucilius and Horace*, 192, quotes this passage, but, engrossed as he is in his endeavour to reconstruct Lucilius, he does less than justice to its context. Surely πλεονεξία here is something more than 'one of the most striking illustrations' of μεμψιμοιρία.

[2] *Œuvres d'Hippocrate*, ed. Littré, ix. 348 ff.; *Epistolographi Graeci*, ed. Hercher, 298 ff.

[3] p. 368 L., l. 4 from the bottom.   [4] p. 370, ll. 2 ff.

[5] *De Horatio Bionis imitatore*, 15 f.   [6] p. 370 L.

[7] I now see that Herter, *Rh. Mus.* xciv, 1951, 11 f., also stresses the importance of the 'Hippocratic' passage on φιλαργυρίη and justly traces the idea of *avaritia* being regarded as the cause of μεμψιμοιρία to Horace's sources (he says Bion; I would prefer a wider term).

κατέκρυψε χρυσόν; τίς ταῦρος πλεονεξίην ἐκορύσατο; κτλ. One of the symptoms of πλεονεξία, from which the animals are free, is ἐς γῆν κατακρύπτειν χρυσόν. It appears that the topic which occurs in 41 f. of the first satire, *quid iuvat immensum te argenti pondus et auri furtim defossa timidum deponere terra?*, belonged to the traditional illustrations of the theme and was taken over by Horace along with a good deal of the rest.

But to return to our main issue. The result which we have so far reached confronts us with a problem. If Horace, as he obviously did, found in the diatribes at his disposal the doctrine that the different forms of μεμψιμοιρία had one common cause, πλεονεξία, *avaritia*, and if, furthermore, he adopted that doctrine, why did he not demonstrate in unmistakable terms the connexion between cause and effect and so give a straightforward answer to his initial question *qui fit . . . ut nemo . . . illa contentus vivat, laudet diversa sequentis?* Why did he deal with the primary cause in the form of a long digression, explicitly characterized as such by the formula (108) *illuc unde abii redeo*? The answer is not far to seek. The clumsy formula of transition, *illuc unde abii redeo*, cast in a Lucilian mould, is employed on purpose. Not only does it remind the reader that Horace, though in a much more refined style, is still continuing the *satura* of Lucilius; the formula and the device of the digression whose end it marks are also a means of loosening what otherwise might become too tight and systematic an arrangement. Throughout his *sermones* Horace, 'cet ennemi de la rigueur didactique',[1] takes great care never to give the impression of delivering a lecture or preaching a sermon: he wants to talk, as a gentleman will talk in congenial company. In a talk it is perfectly proper to wander, or seem to wander, from the subject under discussion and elaborate some side-issue; after a while you may, with a not wholly original phrase such as *illuc unde abii redeo*, return to your starting-point and finally wind up the argument. Horace is in fact fully aware of the causal nexus between φιλαργυρία and μεμψιμοιρία, but he chooses not to lay it bare and only every now and then lets us catch a glimpse of it through the glittering embroidery of his conversation.

But we cannot do justice to the arrangement and the thought of this satire unless we pay full attention to its concluding part, 108 ff.[2] Apparently Horace, who says *illuc unde abii redeo* and, moreover, by a partially verbatim (*nemo . . . laudet diversa sequentis*) quotation, sends the reader back to the initial lines of the satire, is merely repeating the question he had asked at the beginning. But that is so only in appearance. In fact a momentous shift has occurred between the beginning

---

[1] E. Courbaud, *Horace . . . à l'époque des Épîtres*, 1914, 319.
[2] For the reading at 108 and the punctuation of the following lines see my remarks pp. 97 ff. below.

and l. 108. The long tale of the havoc wrought by *avaritia* in almost every walk of life (28–100) has become so impressive that it is now possible to substitute for the question *qui fit ut nemo . . . illa* (i.e. with the lot that has fallen to him) *contentus vivat* the question *nemon ut avarus se probet*, in other words to replace the subject 'no one' by the subject 'no greedy person'. After what we have heard from l. 28 to l. 100 those who are not in the grip of φιλοπλουτία and πλεονεξία and are therefore free from the vice of μεμψιμοιρία seem to be negligibly few. Nevertheless, there are such men. At the very end of the whole discussion (117 ff.) we are told:

> inde fit, ut raro, qui se vixisse beatum
> dicat et exacto contentus tempore vita
> cedat uti conviva satur, reperire queamus.

So, after the depressing series of frustrated wretches there appears at long last the comforting figure of the *vir sapiens*. Men like him, as the poet expressly says, are rare, but such men do exist. In the concluding section of the satire Horace seems to be correcting his initial question, saying, as it were: 'it was rash of me to deny wisdom to every one (*nemo*); I ought to have denied it to every greedy person'. Horace is no Pharisee; not even in his most secret thoughts could it occur to him to pride himself ὅτι οὐκ εἰμὶ ὥσπερ οἱ λοιποὶ τῶν ἀνθρώπων. But he does know that he belongs to the small community of those who strive to keep clear of greed and to sail towards true peace of mind: *nos ad beatos vela mittimus portus . . . vitamque ab omni vindicabimus cura*. The tactful poet, in a discussion addressed to his sympathetic friend, need not crudely refer to his own ideals: it is sufficient for him to conclude with the general statement *inde fit ut raro qui se vixisse beatum dicat . . . reperire queamus*.

Horace's skill in handling ornamental detail appears very clearly in the way in which the interspersed little tales, αἶνοι, *fabulae* (the term occurs at 70 and 95), vary both in matter and in form. The first (15–19), followed by an ἐπιμύθιον (20–22), represents the kind of myth, well known from Plato, which played an important role in the diatribes of the Hellenistic moralists.[1] The next, 33–38, is taken from the world of animals, as were innumerable αἶνοι since the days of Hesiod, Archilochus, and Aesop. Next comes a story, culminating in an apophthegm, about an anonymous (*quidam*) Athenian miser (64–67); appended to it is a brief mention of the sufferings of Tantalus. Finally there appears a native counterpart of the anonymous from Athens, *Ummidius quidam*; his story (95–100) concludes in truly dramatic fashion: *at hunc liberta securi divisit medium, fortissima Tyndaridarum*.

---

[1] Cf. Heinze on l. 16.

As for the date of this satire, I have nothing to add to Lejay's remark (p. 8), 'Pas d'indice chronologique'.[1] It is tempting to assume that the opening poem was written at a time when the book was drawing to its conclusion. That is in fact the case in the second book of the *Satires*, where ii. 1 is clearly either the latest or one of the latest satires of that book. But i. 1 is essentially different from ii. 1 (or, for that matter, from *Odes* iv. 1) in that it lacks the definite character of a prelude to the whole following book. It contains but few hints at topics of the other satires: 24 f. *quamquam ridentem dicere verum quid vetat?* links up with 1. 10. 14 f. *ridiculum acri fortius et melius magnas plerumque secat res*, and 74 *panis ematur, olus, vini sextarius* is perhaps to be connected with the description of Horace's own modest way of life in the last section of the sixth satire.[2] 1. 1. 104 seems to point to 1. 2. 12, and the whole discussion from 1. 1. 101 on could be given the motto of that section of i. 2, *dum vitant stulti vitia, in contraria currunt*. Only very few among the κωμῳδούμενοι of the other satires of this book appear in the first: at 14 Fabius,[3] at 102 Nomentanus,[4] and at 120 Crispinus.[5]

But if it remains uncertain at what stage Horace planned and executed this satire, we can at least guess with some confidence what induced him to place it at the beginning of his book and to incorporate in it the dedication to Maecenas. Its formal qualities made this poem eminently suitable to represent the new—or renewed—literary genre: it was very polished, had a pleasant variety of tones, and, being neither prolix nor sketchy, was of the right size. But above all, it fully showed Horace's capacity for *ridentem dicere verum*. The truth he was telling here was one that both Maecenas and Horace himself had very much at heart. We know from Horace's later work that he, in agreement with views held by Augustus, regarded *avaritia* as one of the most serious menaces to a healthy life of Roman society. 'The plea for a moderation of men's worldly ambitions was to be the first part of Horace's grand message to the nation.'[6] It is likely that in the hard and sobering period of his life after the catastrophe of Philippi he soon came to realize the political consequences of πλεονεξία and φιλοπλουτία.[7] But in his opinion the humble genre of *satura* was not a suitable medium for the message

---

[1] Precisely the same comment was made by Kiessling at the end of his introduction to this satire. It has often been said that the passage 114 f. points to an acquaintance with the end of *Georgics* I (Palmer's expedient is delightful: 'It is just as likely that Virgil copied Hor.'). But a detailed analysis makes it probable (see *Festschrift R. Reitzenstein*, 125 n. 1) that both Virgil and Horace draw on Ennius.

[2] Compare especially 1. 6. 112 and 115 ff.

[3] Cf. 1. 2. 134.   [4] Cf. 1. 8. 11.

[5] Cf. 1. 3. 139 and 1. 4. 14.

[6] Solmsen, *Am. Journ. Phil.* lxviii, 1947, 340, referring to *Odes* iii. 1.

[7] This is the only point on which I slightly disagree with the excellent last paragraph but one of Heinze's introduction to *Sat.* i. 1.

which he was later on to convey through his paraenetic lyrics. He may, however, have trusted that his friend and patron would understand the wider implications of his picture of *avaritia*. At the same time Maecenas 'would infer from the opening section [and from the conclusion as well] that his friend was content with the lot that had fallen to him, and he would find in this avowal an expression of gratitude as well as the reason for the dedication'.[1] This book of satires was the first book that Horace dedicated to Maecenas.

The text of *Sat.* 1. 1. 108

The views on the text of l. 108 (after *redeo*), which have now been current for more than a hundred years, can be divided into three main groups. The view to be found in the most respectable modern editions and commentaries is that we have to accept the reading of the Blandinius vetustissimus, *qui nemo ut avarus*; about the meaning of these words opinions differ widely. The two other groups of editors accept neither the reading of the Blandinius vetustissimus nor that of all the other manuscripts, *nemon ut avarus*. One of these two groups, by now reduced to very few adherents, advocates *nemo ut avarus*, which was conjectured by Heinrich and became popular in German editions about the middle of the nineteenth century.[2] The third, more numerous, group of scholars substitutes for the *qui* of the Blandinius vetustissimus some other monosyllable: in Klingner's apparatus criticus four such attempts (*cur, nunc, cum, si*) are registered; Herter[3] mentions in addition *quia* (Fritzsche and others), *quod* (F. Marx), and concludes his survey with a conjecture of his own, *quam*.

The suggestions belonging to the last two groups need not be taken into account unless and until it has been proved that neither the reading of the Blandinius vetustissimus nor that of the other manuscripts yields a satisfactory text. We therefore have to examine first of all the reading of the Blandinius vetustissimus, *qui nemo ut avarus*, which nowadays meets with the greatest favour. Its supporters do not seem to find any difficulty in a construction in which the clause *illuc unde abii redeo* is followed by a series of subordinate clauses with an explanatory function. This construction, however, runs counter to the very nature of the clause *illuc unde abii redeo* and of analogous expressions. Such a clause is complete in itself. You may, of course, append to it a fresh thought, for instance indicate your purpose by adding a final clause beginning with *ut*, as does Lucilius (1227), *nunc ad te redeo, ut quae res me*

[1] Heinze.
[2] Keller clung to this reading from his first edition and his *Epilegomena* (1879), 431 f., to his edition of 1925.
[3] Op. cit. 41.

impendet agatur, and Seneca, *Epist.* 16. 6, *illo nunc revertor, ut te moneam*
.... But you must not add a subordinate clause in order to explain more
fully what was the issue at the starting-point to which you are now
returning. With that issue your audience or your readers have been
made familiar before; now it is sufficient to warn them that, after a
digression, you are again taking up the former point. We need not
trouble to inquire whether this restriction in the use of formulas of the
type of *illuc unde abii redeo* is logically inevitable; for our present purpose it is sufficient to state that no sensible member of the Latin-
speaking community would have burdened such formulas with a
subsequent explanatory clause. Horace himself provides two more
instances, characteristically in the first book of the *Satires* (6. 45 and 7.
9); he used these expressions in all probability after the fashion of
Lucilius, in whose scanty fragments only the one example mentioned
above is accidentally preserved (quoted as evidence for the construction *me impendet*). Cicero's writings yield a rich harvest of illustrations;
the formulas under discussion are always complete in themselves and
have a stop after them. See, for instance, *Att.* 1. 16. 10 *redeo ad alterca-
tionem*; 5. 2. 3 *sed redeo ad illud*; 5. 11. 6 *nunc redeo ad ea quae mihi mandas*; 5.
13. 3 *redeo ad urbana*; 5. 20. 8 *redeo ad urbana*; *quae ego . . . ex tuis . . .
litteris . . . cognovi*; 5. 21. 13 *sed ad rem redeo*; *Fam.* 7. 28. 3 *quare ad prima
redeo*; 13. 1. 6 *sed redeo ad prima*; *Pis.* 17 *sed iam redeo ad praeclaram illam
contionem tuam,* and, a little later, *ad misericordiam redeo eius cui nimis
videtur senatus . . . fuisse crudelis*; *Rab. Post.* 20 *redeo igitur ad crimen et
accusationem tuam*; *De orat.* 2. 62 *sed illuc redeo*; *Nat. D.* 3. 60 *sed eo unde
huc digressi sumus revertamur*; *Tusc.* 5. 66 *sed redeat unde aberravit oratio*; 5.
80 *sed adhibeat oratio modum et redeat illuc unde deflexit.* When Tacitus[1]
concluded one of his long digressions with the words *sed ad inceptum
redeo,* he deliberately borrowed the phrase from Sallust.[2] The appal-
lingly dry clause of *Culex* 41 *sed nos ad coepta feramur* deserves a mention
here. A single, but momentous, exception from the general practice
would exist if we allowed the punctuation and interpretation of
Lucretius 5. 780 ff. to be dictated by a careless convention. The lines
are usually punctuated thus:

> nunc redeo ad mundi novitatem et mollia terrae   780
> arva, novo fetu quid primum in luminis oras
> tollere et incertis crerint committere ventis.

But Giussani removed the comma from after *arva* at 781 and put it
after *novitatem* at 780, and his commentary runs: ' "Ora ripiglio
l'argomento dei primi tempi della terra . . .", ma non: *redeo ad mollia*

---

[1] *Ann.* 4. 33. 4.

[2] *Iug.* 4. 9 *nunc ad inceptum redeo*; 42. 5 *quam ob rem ad inceptum redeo*; similar turns are
likely to have occurred in Sallust's *Histories.*

arva etc., chè s'ha a sottintendere "e dirò". Costr. *quid primum mollia terrae arva*, etc.' Accordingly Diels translates: 'Jetzt nun kehr' ich zurück zu der Jugend der Welt und ich schildre, welche Geburten zuerst die noch weichen Gefilde der Erde wollten ins Licht neu heben', etc.[1] So the rule that clauses such as *illuc unde abii redeo* are treated as self-contained units may be considered well established.[2]

What, then, are we to do with the passage in the first satire? The answer is so simple that one almost blushes to put it down. We have merely to cast an eye on the text of our manuscripts. For simplicity's sake I copy here the text of Bentley's edition (I might as well take that of Lambinus or of Dacier or of any other sixteenth- or seventeenth-century editor):

> Illuc unde abii redeo. nemon[3] ut avarus
> se probet, ac potius laudet diversa sequentis?
> quodque aliena capella gerat distentius uber   110
> tabescat? neque se maiori pauperiorum
> turbae comparet? hunc atque hunc superare laboret?
> sic festinanti semper locupletior obstat:
> ut cum carceribus . . ..

The text of 108 as printed here is the text of all our manuscripts (except the Blandinius vetustissimus) and that of the scholiasts as far as can be made out. It speaks for itself, provided we approach it with an unbiased mind.[4] The series of parallel clauses beginning with *nemon ut avarus se probet* belongs to the class of 'repudiating questions' in the subjunctive on which modern grammarians have written a great deal.[5]

---

[1] Cyril Bailey, whose punctuation of the text is the conventional one, translates (i. 473) 'Now I return to the youth of the world, and the soft fields of earth, and what first', etc., but he paraphrases rightly (iii. 1450) 'Now . . . I must return to the youth of the world and show what the land first brought forth into the light of day.' Neither he nor Munro mentions the point in their notes on 780 ff.

[2] These formulas have of course a Greek origin; see, for example, Plat. *Phaed.* 78 b ὅθεν δὲ ἀπελίπομεν ἐπανέλθωμεν, εἴ σοι ἡδομένῳ ἐστίν, *Crat.* 437 d ἐπανέλθωμεν δὲ πάλιν ὅθεν δεῦρο μετέβημεν.

[3] Bentley and the other early editors print *nemon*; the manuscripts have here and *Sat.* 2. 7. 34 *nemon*, correctly, cf., for example, Lindsay, *The Latin Language*, 204, and the ample discussion in Dziatzko–Hauler's edition, 1913, of Terence's *Phormio*, 234 f.

[4] The bias has proved formidable from the first half of the nineteenth century on. An instructive illustration of its strength (I could quote many more) is provided by A. Grabenstein, who in his sober and solid doctoral dissertation, *De interrogationum enuntiativarum usu Horatiano* (Halle 1883), correctly stated (p. 39) that from the point of view of language there is not the slightest objection to the MS reading *nemon ut avarus*, taken in the sense in which I take it; but the young scholar, mesmerized by the kind of textual criticism and interpretation which he found everywhere, instead of following up his grammatical observations, declared that 'illa indignatio a totius satirae ratione . . . prorsus abhorret' (a repetition of C. Kirchner's comment on l. 108) and settled down on *redeo, nemo ut avarus*.

[5] For bibliographical references see, besides the well-known books on Latin grammar, S. A. Handford, *The Latin Subjunctive*, 11 ff., 66 ff., and G. E. Duckworth's commentary on the *Epidicus* of Plautus, 242 f. Morris's articles in *Am. Journ. Phil.* are still worth consulting.

This mode of expression is in keeping with the climate of a somewhat heated conversation;[1] consequently the bulk of our evidence comes from Plautus and Terence. But it is by no means alien to the language of Cicero,[2] and can even be found in speeches in Livy.[3] Horace, as is to be expected, uses it in the epodes and *sermones* (i.e. satires and epistles), but not in the odes. We find such a question beginning with *utne* (with the same force as *-ne ut*[4]) at *Sat.* 2. 5. 18, *utne tegam spurco Damae latus?*, and one put in the third person at *Epist.* 1. 18. 16 f. *scilicet ut non sit mihi prima fides?* At *Sat.* 1. 1. 108 the repudiating question has its full force. 'It sounds absurd: can it be true[5] that no greedy person is content with his own situation, but that (each)[6] rather praises those who follow different lines?' etc. It seems impossible, and yet it is so. The amazement at the absurd behaviour of all greedy men is not merely expressed in a single question, but rushes in violent agitation through a cataract of four interrogative clauses (108–12) or five if at 109 we take *se probet* and *laudet diversa sequentis* as two distinct units. When the flood of questions has exhausted itself, the speaker takes breath and sums up the result of that unceasing chase with its constant frustration: *sic festinanti semper locupletior obstat.* Then, to round off the tale of men's insanity, he adds the grandiose image, painted partly in Ennian colours,[7] of the chariot race.

It only remains to say, and I am not the first to say so, that the reading of the Blandinius vetustissimus, *qui nemo ut avarus*, is a sad interpolation,[8] made by one who, incapable of understanding Horace's subtle and far from obvious progress of thought, wanted this passage to correspond closely, not to say mechanically, with the beginning of the satire. This is not the place to take up the old discussion about the limitations of the value of the Blandinius vetustissimus. I am not foolish enough to deny the genuineness of *campum lusumque trigonem* at *Sat.* 1. 6. 126 or to believe that such a reading could be the result of a

---

[1] Cf. J. B. Hofmann, *Lat. Umgangssprache*, 51 f., 109.

[2] See, for example, *Sest.* 17 *hocine ut ego nomine appellem eversores huius imperi . . .?*, and notice, as in the instances from Livy (next footnote), the beginning with *-ne ut.*

[3] 4. 2. 12 *illine ut impune . . . concitent finitima bella . . .?*, 5. 24. 10 *victamne ut quisquam . . . praeferret . . .?*, both in oratio obliqua. These two passages and the one mentioned in the preceding footnote are quoted by Kühner–Stegmann, ii. 511.

[4] For instances of both see e.g. C. E. Bennett, *Syntax of Early Latin*, i. 190.

[5] I borrow these expressions ('it sounds absurd: can it be true'), which bring out certain undertones of this kind of question, from S. A. Handford, *The Latin Subjunctive*, 72, who very properly uses them to illustrate the analogous question (again put in the third person) Plaut. *Epid.* 225 *utin impluvium induta fuerit?*

[6] I have added 'each' because the negative element of *nemo* is disregarded in the following clauses. This slight looseness, common in Greek (see Kühner–Gerth, ii. 566 f.), is found also in Cicero and other Latin writers, cf. the notes of Orelli–Mewes, Lejay, Heinze on the beginning of this satire.

[7] Cf. p. 96 n. 1 above.

[8] Cf. p. 317 n. 5 below.

lucky conjecture. I confess however, that I am less happy about certain other items in Giorgio Pasquali's optimistic list.[1] But that is
another story.

4. SATIRE VI

The sixth satire seems to stand halfway between the earliest satires,
II and III, with their diatribes on conventional topics and their somewhat mechanical invectives against a number of more or less shadowy
characters, and Horace's free self-representation in the most perfect
poems of the two books of *sermones*.[2]

The beginning of this satire, *Non quia, Maecenas*, is obviously intended to be a counterpart to the beginning of the book, *Qui fit,
Maecenas*. These two passages are different in character from the only
other passages in this book where Maecenas is addressed in the vocative, 1. 3. 64 and 1. 6. 47. In the two latter passages it is within a
strictly limited context and in regard to the intimacy between Maecenas
and Horace that the poet, in a flash of lively imagination, turns to
his friend and addresses him directly. At 1. 1. 1 and 1. 6. 1, on the other
hand, Maecenas is addressed before the theme of the discussion has
even been indicated. Here the vocatives can have only one meaning:
the book as a whole and, by way of reminder, its second half are
dedicated to Maecenas. This repetition of the dedication at the beginning of the second half of a book has, if no precise parallel, at any rate
certain analogies in Augustan poetry. Of the four books of Virgil's
Georgics each is dedicated to Maecenas by having near to the beginning
his name in the vocative, but only in Books I and III is there a full
proem, including an apostrophe of Maecenas. And later on Horace
himself, when he had decided to open the third book of his *carmina*
with the 'Roman Odes', addressed Maecenas in the first ode of the
second half (3. 16. 20) and so made it clear that this book as well as
I and II was dedicated to his friend and patron.

The first section, to the end of 44, turns upon the question whether
or not a man's value depends on noble birth. The opening four lines
show a magnificence far above the average level of a *sermo*;[3] their style
is in harmony with the emphasis that is here laid on Maecenas' rank
as *Tyrrhena regum progenies*, a fact that is stressed, not indeed to flatter

---

[1] *Storia della tradizione*, 382 f.

[2] No chronological conclusions should be drawn from such an observation. The
evolution of the style of a poet (or, for that matter, of any artist) does not, as a rule, proceed in an unbroken straight line.

[3] For the lofty note in *imperitarent* and also for the possibility that l. 4 echoes a line of
Ennius, see p. 191 n. 5 below.

him, but to make his behaviour as described in the following lines the more impressive. The exalted tone of the beginning is deliberately reversed in the almost vulgar expression at l. 5 *naso suspendis adunco*.[1]

The general thesis of this first section is illustrated, in the manner already familiar to us, by a series of attacks upon various individuals, and again we notice that none of the victims is an important person still alive at the time of Horace's writing. First comes a certain Valerius Laevinus (12 ff.) who disgraced his illustrious lineage[2] by disreputable conduct. It is not known to what period he belongs,[3] but Horace makes it perfectly clear that he is speaking of a dead man. He says *unius assis non umquam pretio pluris licuisse*; moreover, this clause is parallel to the preceding *multos saepe viros . . . vixisse*, etc.[4] The case of Laevinus proves that not even the common people, for all their snobbishness, would allow him, on account of his noble birth, to get away with such misbehaviour; 'how much less should we, who have nothing in common with the prejudices of the rabble,[5] put men's pedigree before their merits!' The next person at whom Horace lashes out is one Tillius (24–26), otherwise unknown.[6] There follows Barrus (30), a character probably taken over from Lucilius.[7] Finally there appears in this section a man who is made the object of a disparaging remark on account of his humble origin. His name, Novius (40), is

---

[1] Observed by Kiessling.

[2] The glory of the house of the Valerii finds an admirable expression in the style: *Laevinum, Valeri genus, unde Superbus Tarquinius regno pulsus fuit.* That *Valeri genus* is solemn was noticed by Heinze, and the same thing, for the period of Horace, is true of *unde* in the sense of *a quo* (at *Sat.* 2. 3. 238 *unde* is local or, at any rate, halfway between the local and the personal sense, cf. *qui amant a lenone* in Plautus). This use was once common in Latin, but began to fade out, even from technical language, by the end of the Republic; see my remarks *Sav. Zeitschr.* liv, 1934, 313 ff. (for *quo = ad quem* I ought to have quoted the text of the *lex Iulia repetund.*, Cic. *Rab. Post.* 8 ff., QVO EA PECVNIA PERVENERIT). Its stylistic value in Horace can be assessed from its occurrence in the solemn prayers *Sat.* 2. 6. 21 and *Odes* 1. 12. 17. As for *Odes* 3. 11. 38 f., *ne longus tibi somnus unde non times detur*, I am not convinced that *unde* is 'persönlich'; it seems to be stronger when taken as neutral, 'from where you do not fear it'.

[3] Ritter's guess (ad loc.) that this Laevinus appeared somewhere in Lucilius is ingenious but cannot be proved.

[4] It is therefore not sufficient to say with Heinze 'es ist kaum anzunehmen, daß er noch lebte, als H. dies schrieb'. Volkmann's assertion, *RE* vii. A. 2315 (at the bottom of the page), 'quaest. ca. 715', is naïve.

[5] Klingner, *Philol.* xc, 1935, 461 ff., rightly rejected Kiessling's and Heinze's view on *a volgo longe longeque remotos* and returned to the traditional interpretation, according to which *nos . . . remotos* refers to both Maecenas and Horace (and to men of similar convictions). In this connexion it seems worth while to compare 97 f. *demens iudicio volgi, sanus fortasse tuo.* A kindred thought is expressed *Odes* 2. 2. 17 ff. *Phraaten* dissidens plebi *numero beatorum eximit Virtus populumque falsis dedocet uti vocibus.*

[6] His identification with the brother of Tillius Cimber, one of the murderers of Caesar, rests on unsafe foundations; see Heinze (5th ed., 1921) on l. 25. It is unfortunate that Münzer, *RE* vi. A. 1037 f., used only Heinze's third edition.

[7] For a detailed discussion see *Festschrift R. Reitzenstein*, 130 n. 1.

presumably meant to indicate that he simply represents the type of the *homo novus*.[1]

It is with a sigh of relief that we greet the announcement (45) *nunc ad me redeo libertino patre natum*, by which we are assured that now the parade of dreary characters is over and that we shall at last be allowed to enjoy the company of a far more interesting and pleasant man, Q. Horatius Flaccus. It is indeed Horace at his very best whom we meet here. He himself seems glad to get out of the Lucilian masquerade: with a smiling adaptation of a dry half-line from Lucilius[2] he plunges into a world of his own. And yet it was to a considerable extent the encouragement he received from Lucilius that enabled Horace to produce a faithful, detailed, and lively picture of his own personality and his own world. But of this something more will be said later on.

For Horace, to render a true account of himself and lay open the foundations of his way of life means, first of all, to speak of his father. In doing so he not merely describes him as his son's greatest benefactor: he makes us see the whole man. 'There is scarcely any individual portrait in all ancient literature which leaves on the mind so real an impression of worth, affection, and good sense, as this picture of the poet's father.'[3] But what Horace tells us about himself does not fade beside the portrait of his father. We are shown an abundance of colourful detail, from the schoolboy's early impressions to the grown-up man's daily routine; moreover the decisive event in the poet's life, his first visit to Maecenas, is given its due dimensions. Above all, the whole poem conveys the atmosphere within which the man Horace has his being. To the poet and to his readers the satire is *sermo*, clearly distinct from the more exacting genres of poetry. And yet it would be wrong to regard the main body of this satire as a versified description which might as well have been given in prose. We should have to narrow down the definition of poetry in a wholly arbitrary manner if we wished to call in question the poetic character of a passage like this (56–61):

> ut veni coram, singultim pauca locutus—
> infans namque pudor prohibebat plura profari—
> non ego me claro natum patre, non ego circum
> me Satureiano vectari rura caballo,
> sed quod eram narro. respondes, ut tuus est mos,
> pauca.

This is, on a small scale, a perfect dramatic scene, emotionally strong

---

[1] Cf. Münzer, *RE* xvii. 1215 (so already Wüstemann in the re-edition [1843] of Heindorf's commentary).   [2] Lucilius 1227 *nunc ad te redeo*.

[3] W. Y. Sellar, *Horace and the Elegiac Poets*, 2nd ed. 12. I like the admiration expressed in these words but can accept the judgement only if it be granted that Plato's presentation of Socrates as a character in the dialogues should not be termed a portrait.

and rich in undertones. The stifling embarrassment of the young poet,
the painful reserve of Maecenas, and the sincerity of the two men come
out with forceful directness. The choice of the words is as apt[1] as the
sound is suggestive.[2] The grandeur of the sentence (58 f.) *non ego me
claro natum patre . . . caballo*[3] sets off the simplicity of the following clause,
sed quod eram narro.

Taking full advantage of the freedom granted to the *satura*, Horace
paints every now and then, with a nimble stroke of his brush, an
exquisite still life:

> inde domum me
> ad porri et ciceris refero laganique catinum;[4]   115
> cena ministratur pueris tribus, et lapis albus
> pocula cum cyatho duo sustinet, adstat echinus
> vilis, cum patera guttus, Campana supellex.

No doubt he does relish these small things and all the modest comfort
of his domestic life. But his mind is not immersed in concern for them;
neither here nor anywhere else in his work is there any taint of bour-
geois pettiness or philistinism.

In this satire and in several others not only the life of the poet lies
spread out before our eyes, *votiva veluti descripta tabella*, but a good deal
of the life of the city of Rome as well. There is the schoolboy, but
recently arrived from the remote South and now proudly walking the
streets of the capital, in clothes and with a retinue so expensive that any
passer-by would assume that he was the son of a very rich house
(78–80). We get a glimpse of the terrifying traffic in the centre of the
city (42 f.),

> si plostra ducenta
> concurrantque foro tria funera magna;

---

[1] Most commentators, from Porphyrio on, have seen that at l. 57 *infans* has its 'etymo-
logical' sense. The *Thesaurus*, however, vii. 1. 1347. 45 explains (with H. Schütz) 'qualis
puerorum est'.

[2] I have no quarrel with Kiessling's note on 56, 'er beginnt befangen und stockend, was
die Alliteration *pudor prohibebat plura profari* malt', but I would add that the *p*-alliteration
often expresses great excitement in general; see my note on A. *Ag.* 268.

[3] The bold pomposity of *Satureiano* (Cichorius, *Unters. zù Lucilius*, 26 f., offers the very
attractive hypothesis that the word alludes to some passage in Lucilius, who probably
owned estates near Tarentum) will not escape the reader, nor will its pleasant contrast
with the homely *caballo*. The tmesis (wrongly denied by Lejay) in *circum . . . vectari* is
presumably another element of the exalted style, although it must be remembered (cf.
Wackernagel, *Vorlesungen über Syntax*, ii. 175) that *super, ante, circum, praeter* have a higher
degree of independence than the other 'prepositional' prefixes and sometimes undergo
tmesis even in prose.

[4] Horatian scholars are much indebted to B. L. Ullman, *Class. Phil.* vii, 1912, 442 ff.,
for making it clear that *laganum* is a kind of *minestrone*, ingredients of which are *porrum* and
cicer. But as regards *lasanum* at l. 109, he ought not to have joined those editors who wish to
deprive us of the amusing spectacle of the commode travelling peacefully in the company
of the wine-vessel (for the meaning of *oenophorus* see, as against Lewis and Short and many
translators, Marquardt-Mau, *Privatleben der Römer*, 650, and Marx on Lucilius 139).

after a while we stroll by the side of the poet in front of the green-
grocers' stalls, and in the evening we allow our curiosity to draw us into
quarters which at that hour the respectable citizen would rather
avoid (111–14):

> quacumque libido est,
> incedo solus; percontor quanti holus ac far,
> fallacem circum vespertinumque pererro
> saepe forum; adsisto divinis.

So nowadays a lover of the real Rome might stroll along Via dei
Coronari or through Trastevere; so, in bygone years, the writer of this
book used to explore Piazza Montanara and the crowded little streets
near by, long since things of the past.

5. SATIRE V

In the case of the famous fifth satire of the book, the so-called *Iter
Brundisinum*, we are able to form at least some idea of the relation
between a single satire of Horace and a single satire of Lucilius.
*Lucilio hac satyra aemulatur Horatius iter suum a Roma Brundesium usque
describens, quod et ille in tertio libro fecit, primo a Roma Capuam usque et inde
fretum Siciliense* (Porphyrio on 1. 5. 1). The scholiast's statement is
borne out by the comparatively numerous fragments which we possess
of the *Iter Siculum* of Lucilius; the work done by F. Marx in reas-
sembling, co-ordinating, and illustrating the scattered remnants of this
particular satire is justly admired as a masterpiece of scholarly interpretation.[1] But before examining the detail, we should try to obtain a
right perspective of the complex situation that lies behind the decep-
tively simple formula *Lucilio hac satyra aemulatur Horatius*, etc.

It is well known that the journey described in the *Iter Brundisinum*
was undertaken by Horace in the retinue of Maecenas in the spring of
37 B.C. The poem itself makes it abundantly clear that this journey
furnished plenty of matter which Horace thought worth describing and
enjoyed describing. In other words, what modern critics of literature would call spontaneity must have played an important role in the
making of this satire. If that is so, to what extent is the statement
Lucilio hac satyra aemulatur still valid?

If a modern poet had had certain experiences, partly of an exciting
and partly of an amusing nature, similar to those which Horace had on

[1] Cf. Leo, *Gött. gel. Anz.* 1906, 842.

his journey to Brundisium, and if he felt the urge to make them the theme of a poem, he would be at liberty to do so without first looking round for a model on which he might, at any rate partially, lean or for an established literary mould into which he might cast his own conception. When for instance Clough, in the autumn of 1848, 'composed very rapidly' the 1700 or so hexameters of *The Bothie*, he did not have to ask himself whether or not an English poet had ever treated a similar subject in a similar form. He could, using words and rhythms such as came to him, often imitative and mocking, sometimes entirely his own, speak of everything that was stirring within him, memories of Oxford and the scenery of the Highlands, the world of the classics and doubts about God, the social injustices of the age and the sprawling of ugly gas-lit cities, the search for truth, a young man's delight at bathing, climbing, and shooting; the circle of his friends, his gentle and understanding tutor, his first love. Listening to the meditations of his mind and to the longings of his heart, to any inner voice, he might say *che ditta dentro, vo significando*. In all this his situation would be different from that of any ancient poet after the early period when each of the various genres of Greek poetry had 'attained to its natural form'.

We know that a modern poem may be, and often is, linked with earlier literary works by threads more tight and more numerous than were those that linked many Hellenistic or Latin poems with their models. But what matters for our present inquiry is not the number and strength of such literary links; rather is it the poet's awareness of their existence, or, more precisely, the fact that this leaning on some model or models was quite deliberate and that it influenced from the outset the conception of his work. It would be wholly inadequate to assume that Horace wrote the *Iter Brundisinum* primarily because his mind was full of lively pictures of the journey which he had undertaken in the spring of 37 B.C., that he wished to express this personal experience and that then, secondarily as it were, he adorned his poem with certain features borrowed from Lucilius' *Iter Siculum*. But it would be equally inadequate to assume that Horace was primarily bent upon renewing in some way the satire written by Lucilius about his journey to Sicily and that the experience of his own journey, with which a lucky coincidence provided him, only served to colour and vary the fundamentally Lucilian pattern of his poem. The insistence on a sole primary source of inspiration seems to be due to a widely, though often unconsciously, accepted modern fallacy, which ascribes to all periods of literature an outlook that is in fact a heritage of the Romantic movement.

It may be questioned whether in the study of modern poetry more good than harm has been done by the sharp separation of an immediate personal experience (*Urerlebnis*) from an experience obtained through cultural channels such as philosophy, literature, decorative art, and so forth (*Bildungserlebnis*). There cannot, however, be any doubt that such a rigid dichotomy, when applied to ancient poetry, can do nothing but harm. Certainly in many poems of Horace the 'primary' and the 'literary' type of experience blend with such perfect harmony that it would be idle to try to assign priority to the one or the other. Here a few illustrations will suffice. In the sixteenth epode (see pp. 47 ff. above) the indignation and despondency of the Roman patriot are a genuine and strong motive, and at the same time it is obvious that without the inspiration coming from Archilochus Horace could not have written the poem he wrote. What is apparent in this early work can be equally well demonstrated in a late poem, *Odes* iv. 6, *Dive, quem proles Niobaea*.[1] Behind it there lies unmistakably Horace's exultation at the unhoped-for triumph of his poetry and at the fresh human contacts it brought with it. But if he wanted to voice this exultation in one of his solemn lyrics, he had to transform it into an element of a Pindarizing paean, and the form he had chosen (in fact more than a mere form) had in its turn an inspiring effect on the poem in suggesting the noble picture of the warrior Achilles and of the fate of Troy. To return to the *Iter Brundisinum*. Horace would not have written it without his personal experience in the spring of 37 B.C., but bent as he was at that time upon continuing the satires of Lucilius in a more polished form he would not have written it either had he not been stimulated and encouraged by the existence of the *Iter Siculum*, which proved to him and to his readers that the description of such a journey was a suitable theme for a *satura*. No priority can be assigned to the personal experience in a case where only the joint impact of a personal experience and a literary tradition was capable of bringing forth a particular poem.

It is not unlikely that the fundamental design of the *Iter Siculum* was similar to that of the *Iter Brundisinum*, since in either case an arrangement according to the various stages of the journey was dictated by the nature of the subject. As for the detail, the scantiness of the fragments of Lucilius permits only very rarely a direct comparison. But at least in one case where the theme is the same a considerable difference in its treatment can be observed. In Horace's satire (56 f.) the buffoon Sarmentus provokes his adversary with this sneer:

> 'equi te
> esse feri similem dico'.

[1] See pp. 400 ff. below.

In the corresponding situation of the *Iter Siculum* one of the two champions[1] said:[2]

> dente adverso eminulo hic est
> rinoceros.

No doubt this is much more vigorous and amusing, not only because the rhinoceros is a more exciting creature than the wild horse, but also because the direct identification, μεταφορά,[3] derived from the talk of the common people,[4] is stronger and more suggestive than a mere comparison such as *equi te esse feri similem dico*. Here, then, Lucilius appears superior to Horace in sheer comic force. And so he does in another passage of the *Iter Siculum*, a description which shows his eruptive style to great advantage (110 ff.):

> verum haec ludus ibi, susque omnia deque, fuerunt,
> susque haec[5] deque fuere, inquam, omnia, ludus iocusque:
> illud opus durum, ut Setinum accessimus finem,
> aigilipes montes, Aetnae omnes, asperi Athones.

This groan comes as an amusing surprise to readers acquainted with the low foothills in the vicinity of Sezze. The bombastic expressions are of a piece with the wild exaggeration throughout the description. To Horace, however, such a sally must have seemed ludicrous and lacking in discretion; and what he thought of a particular feature, the interspersion of a Greek epithet (*aigilipes montes*) is known from his lively discussion of this point.[6] Moreover, he demonstrates directly in what manner a polished writer ought to deal with a subject of this kind, for he gives his own variation of the theme of *illud opus durum* in these lines (77 ff.):

> incipit ex illo[7] montis Apulia notos
> ostentare mihi, quos torret Atabulus et quos
> numquam erepsemus, nisi nos vicina Trivici
> villa recepisset . . ..

How slender the motif has become in its rejuvenated form, *quos*

---

[1] Who he was and from where he came is not known. The corrupt *novit lanus* was by Turnebus altered to *Bovillanus*, which Housman, *CQ* i, 1907, 62, Cichorius, *Unters. z. Lucilius* 253 n. 2, and G. C. Fiske, *Lucilius and Horace*, 363 n. 218, regard as very plausible. Terzaghi reads *Novi* (Marx) *nanus* (G. Lafaye, *Revue de Philol.* xxxv, 1911, 23, not Lejay as Terzaghi says), although Housman, loc. cit., had recalled the fact (cf. Lachmann, *Comm. on Lucr.*, p. 326) that 'the first poet to use such forms as a gen. *Nŏui* from a nom. *Nouius* is Propertius'.

[2] Lucil. 117 f.   [3] Arist. *Rhet.* 3. 4, p. 1406[b]20 ff.

[4] Cf. *Plautinisches im Plautus*, 45 ff.

[5] *haec* (F. Dousa: *et* codd.) is rightly accepted by Housman, op. cit. 71, as against Marx.   [6] *Sat.* i. 10. 20–30.

[7] *ex illo*, i.e. *Benevento*. For the topographical problems of this section and the following ones see T. Ashby and R. Gardner, *BSR Papers*, viii, 1916, 108 ff.

numquam erepsemus! There is here, too, an exaggeration, but it is uttered with an ironical smile rather than a broad grin, as if we were passing from Rabelais to Voltaire. The barest minimum of space is allowed to this detail. Once more we are reminded of Horace's own maxim (1. 10. 9 f.),

> est brevitate opus, ut currat sententia neu se
> impediat verbis lassas onerantibus auris.

While he only hints at the toil of the ascent, he finds the room he needs, not indeed to picture an imaginary Alpine scenery with Etnas and Athoses, but to give an idea of a characteristic feature of the Apulian landscape and, above all, of his own emotion on returning

> in montes patrios et ad incunabula nostra,

as Cicero said at one of his rare moments of real poetry. Intense feeling, without the slightest touch of sentimentality, is compressed into the apparently matter-of-fact statement *incipit ex illo montis Apulia notos ostentare mihi, quos torret Atabulus.* Carried away by the memories of his childhood, he does not mind calling the Scirocco by its local name. Should a reader in the city of Rome be puzzled by the oddity, the Venusian poet could not help it.

There is in this satire a passage where Horace's gift for conveying the atmosphere of a particular region shines superbly (14–26):

>   mali culices ranaeque palustres
> avertunt somnos; absentem cantat amicam[1]
> multa prolutus vappa nauta atque viator
> certatim .   . . .
>
> . . . .
> .   .   .   quarta vix demum exponimur hora;
> ora manusque tua lavimus, Feronia, lympha.
> milia tum pransi tria repimus atque subimus
> impositum saxis late candentibus Anxur.

I have known, early in this century, the Pomptine Marshes when they were still infested by malaria, still very lonely and, to modern eyes though not to the eyes of Horace and his contemporaries, very beautiful. Horace has caught the true character of that melancholy stretch of marshland. The travellers' passage on board the trekschuit takes place at night. But not a wink of sleep: the mosquitoes know their business, nor does the terrific orchestra of the frogs neglect its duty.[2]

---

[1] Klingner, *Hermes*, lxx, 1935, 397 n. 2, has carefully examined this passage; result: *ut*, which appears only in one branch of our manuscript tradition (*ut cantat*), is interpolated. I am entirely convinced.

[2] Cicero, *Fam.* 7. 18. 3 (written to Trebatius, who had special connexions with Ulubrae)

And on top of it all (how very Italian!) there is the never-ending contest of *canzonette d'amore* performed by the two drunken *popolani*. After
that appalling night the party can at last get out of the wretched barge:
the calm purity of the morning shines through the simple sentence *ora
manusque tua lavimus, Feronia, lympha*. But the full glory of deliverance
from the night's unpleasantness is kept for the end of this section, when
they reach Terracina, where their friends are to join them:

> subimus
> impositum saxis late candentibus Anxur.

This is not an entry in an itinerary; it is a colourful picture of the
lovely town perched on its bright rocks and greeting from afar the
travellers as they emerge from the swamps below. Perhaps it was
the first time in the history of European poetry that so faithful and so
suggestive a picture of a definite piece of landscape was given in a few
words. The ability to achieve such a thing, though conspicuous in
Horace, is not peculiar to him alone: we should perhaps rather regard it as one of the fresh conquests of the generation of Virgil and
Horace.[1] When we read[2]

> tardis ingens ubi flexibus errat
> Mincius et tenera praetexit harundine ripas,

we have before our eyes the lake-like stretches of water with which the
slow-flowing Mincio surrounds the city of Mantua on three sides so as
to make it look like a peninsula.[3] The glorious lines[4]

> tot congesta manu praeruptis oppida saxis
> fluminaque antiquos subterlabentia muros

irresistibly conjure up the vision of countless Italian townlets. And no
one who, on an early morning, has looked down from the height of
Perugia and seen the blue hilltops arising out of a sea of thick white
mist can fail to recognize that particular landscape in the description of
Propertius.[5]

No less faithful than the portrait of the country is the portrait of the
country-folk. The sketch of the noisy argument that develops between

---

*has litteras scripsi in Pomptino, cum ad villam M. Aemili Philemonis devertissem, ex qua iam
audieram fremitum clientium meorum, quos quidem tu mihi conciliasti; nam Ulubris honoris mei causa
vim maximam ranunculorum se commosse constabat.*

[1] Catullus makes us share his rapture at his return to Lake Garda, but he does not make
us *see* either the lake or the peninsula of Sirmione.
[2] *Georg.* 3. 14 f.
[3] Compare also the conclusion of Virgil's first eclogue (see p. 25 n. 3 above).
[4] *Georg.* 2. 156 f.
[5] 4. 1. 123 ff.

the bargemen and the servants of the party (11–13) is a little master-piece. In passing we may notice that it is precisely as a proem to this specimen of lower-class behaviour[1] that Horace produces a flourish in the hackneyed manner of heroic epic:

> iam nox inducere terris
> umbras et caelo diffundere signa parabat.

Elsewhere in this satire he sets off the very plain subject-matter by employing an order of words that, if not downright artificial, is at any rate *recherché* (71 f.):

> ubi sedulus hospes
> paene macros arsit dum turdos versat in igni,[2]

and shortly afterwards (86):

> quattuor hinc rapimur viginti et milia raedis.[3]

The warmest feeling and the greatest delicacy of touch manifest themselves where Horace relates how he and Heliodorus were met by the other members of the party, among them some of Horace's nearest friends. First, at Anxur (27–33):

> huc venturus erat Maecenas optimus atque
> Cocceius, missi magnis de rebus uterque
> legati, aversos soliti componere amicos.
>
> .   .   .   .
>
> .   .   interea Maecenas advenit atque
> Cocceius Capitoque simul Fonteius, ad unguem
> factus homo, Antoni non ut magis alter amicus.

Maecenas optimus is certainly an affectionate expression; and the compliments paid to the two other diplomats are fine and appropriate.

---

[1] Similarly the duel of the two buffoons is introduced by the invocation of the Muse (51 ff.) *nunc mihi paùcis Sarmenti scurrae pugnam Messique Cicirri, Musa, velim memores* . . . . Heinze says that this invocation consists of a mixture of high poetry and conversational language; according to him the polite form of the request *velim memores* contrasts with the lofty epic style. But when we read in the late poem of Sulpicia, ll. 58 f., *optima, posthac, Musa, velim moneas*, we may consider the possibility that *velim memores* was a conventional formula in such invocations, although direct imitation of Horace cannot be excluded (cf. Sulpicia 48). The parodic tone of the opening *nunc* has been well illustrated by the scholiast and Lejay; see also 2. 3. 224 *nunc age* . . . and compare Virg. *Aen.* 7. 37.

[2] Kiessling (followed by Heinze) and Lejay think that 'le désordre des mots peut servir à peindre l'agitation', etc. I should not call it disorder and would prefer to see in this venture a refinement after the model of certain Hellenistic poets. See, for example, Pfeiffer's notes on Callimachus *fr.* 6 and *fr.* 178. 10; Apoll. Rhod. 4. 475 f.; Catullus 44. 9 with A. Riese's valuable note; Hor. *Sat.* 2. 1. 60; and a passage in a poem of the girl Sulpicia [Tibullus] 3. 16. 5 f. A silly exaggeration: [Virgil] *Catal.* 13. 1 f.

[3] 'Ganz kühn ist die Umstellung von *et* nach bekannter Neigung der augusteischen Dichter bei Horaz *Sat.* 1. 5. 86' (J. Wackernagel, *Festschrift Gustav Binz*, Basel 1935, 34 [*Kl. Schriften*, 237], note).

But a powerful crescendo is to come at the next stage but two (39–44):

> postera lux oritur multo gratissima; namque
> Plotius et Varius Sinuessae Vergiliusque
> occurrunt, animae qualis neque candidiores
> terra tulit neque quis me sit devinctior alter.
> o qui complexus et gaudia quanta fuerunt.
> nil ego contulerim iucundo sanus amico.

To assess the value of this outburst of enthusiasm one has to remember that Horace was not lavish with his superlatives. When we compare the last sentence of this section with 1. 6. 89, *nil me paeniteat sanum patris huius*, we discover that here we are listening to the voice of the poet's heart: he prizes these friendships as he prizes the memory of his father.

It is not necessary to go into further detail. Our glance through the *Iter Brundisinum* will have shown that Horace, while adopting the general pattern of the *Iter Siculum* of Lucilius and also modifying some of its detail, succeeded in producing something new, something that was entirely Horatian.

6. SATIRE IX

It is very likely that Horace, when he had written a number of satires and conceived the plan of publishing them in a book, determined to make the book consist of ten satires. For since Virgil's extraordinarily successful book of ten eclogues had ushered in a new era of Roman poetry, ten, or a multiple of it, seems to have been considered by Horace, and by some contemporary poets as well, the ideal number for the poems of a book.[1] Presumably it is to the plan of bringing the satires up to the sum of ten that the three satires which in Horace's book precede the epilogue, satires VII, VIII, IX, owe, at any rate in part, their existence. To them we now turn, starting with IX.

The very beginning of this satire shows that the poet, while narrating something that had actually happened to him, is not forgetful of Lucilius. In Lucilius (1142) an anecdote about Scipio Aemilianus began *ibat forte domum*.[2] Another αἶνος in Lucilius (534) began *ibat*

---

[1] The reason why Book II of Horace's *Satires* contains only eight poems will be discussed later on. *Odes*: Book II twenty, Book III thirty; in the case of Book I there was an overflow. The book of the *Epistles* consists of twenty letters. The first book of Tibullus contains ten elegies. It is not known whether Virgil, in including ten poems in his first published book, followed some Hellenistic or Roman model. That Book IV of Horace's *Odes* and Books I and III of Ovid's *Amores* contain fifteen poems (ten plus half of ten) may be accidental.

[2] This, no doubt, is the beginning of the αἶνος itself. The preceding three and a half lines contained apparently an introduction to the little story. These lines in the form in which we have them (in Festus) are absolutely unintelligible: Marx's attempt to whitewash the text was briefly criticized by Leo, *Gött. gel. Anz.* 1906, 857, and at great length by

forte aries.[1] It is not improbable that Lucilius once opened a tale about himself with the phrase *ibam forte* . . . . We should not, however, assume that the particular theme of Horace's ninth satire had an analogy in the work of Lucilius.

This satire is nowadays the most popular of all and still read in many classical sixth forms where one otherwise shuns the *sermones*. It is commonly called 'The Bore'. There is no harm in giving it this title, provided it does not suggest a wrong idea about the poem itself. Here as elsewhere in the *Satires* of Horace we must guard against the temptation of looking in them for that attitude of mind which most modern readers customarily, if unconsciously, seek in a Latin satire, the prototype of which for them is the satire of Juvenal.[2] Reading *Ibam forte via sacra* with an unprejudiced mind we can hardly fail to see that Horace's primary object cannot have been to hold up to ridicule and contempt either an individual bore (there is no hint at any particular person) or the bore as a type. Of course, the bore is pictured, and the picture is perfect. To suffer a disagreeable person gladly needs a saint, and Horace was far from being a saint. Being entirely human, he groans. And yet he pictures the nuisance rather good-naturedly. When we consider what a spate of acid certain satirists would have poured out on such an occasion, we once more realize that a Horatian *satura* can be very different from what we generally mean by satire.[3] Whatever might have become of a similar theme in the hands of other writers, in Horace's poem the bore remains a δευτεραγωνιστής. The central figure of the poem is clearly indicated in the first as well as in the last words: *Ibam forte* . . . and *sic me servavit Apollo*: 'I' and 'me'. The subject of this satire is something that happened to Horace on a very ordinary day. It was a fine day (no Italian, of the past or of the present, would go for a walk in the rain), and the poet was at peace with himself and with the world, his mind pleasantly occupied.

Housman, *CQ* i, 1907, 69 ff. For the beginning of an αἶνος with *forte* compare Hor. *Epist.* 1. 7. 29.

[1] This manner of introducing a story goes back to αἶνοι in their oldest and simplest form. Compare Archilochus *fr.* 81 D. Ἐρέω τιν' ὑμῖν αἶνον, ὦ Κηρυκίδη, ἀχνυμένη σκυτάλη. πίθηκος ᾔει θηρίων ἀποκριθεὶς μοῦνος ἀν' ἐσχατίην κτλ. Even in the late transformations by Babrius this type is still recognizable, see 1. 1 ἄνθρωπος ἦλθεν εἰς ὄρος κτλ., 54. 1 εὐνοῦχος ἦλθε πρὸς θύτην κτλ., 61. 1 ᾔει κυνηγὸς ἐξ ὄρους κτλ., 96. 1 λύκος παρῄει θριγκόν κτλ.

[2] See also pp. 144 f. below.

[3] 'With every desire to imitate Horace, he [Pope] cannot touch any of his subjects, or any kindred subjects, without infusing a bitter ingredient. It is not given to the children of men to be philosophers without envy. Lookers-on can hardly bear the spectacle of the great world. If you watch the carriages rolling down to the House of Lords, you will try to depreciate the House of Lords. Idleness is cynical. Both Béranger and Horace are exceptions to this. Both enjoy the roll of the wheels; both love the glitter of the carriages; neither is angry at the sun. Each knows that he is as happy as he can be—that he is all that he can be in his contemplative philosophy' (W. Bagehot, *Literary Studies*, II, 2nd ed. 286).

> Ibam forte via sacra, sicut meus est mos,
> nescio quid meditans nugarum, totus in illis.

Little did he foresee what was soon to befall him. *Accurrit quidam* . . . : the very speed of the onrush, so different from Horace's leisurely pace, bodes ill. And then the little tragedy unfolds, scene by scene, things going from bad to worse for Horace, up to the catastrophe, where he almost breaks down (72–74):

> huncine solem
> tam nigrum surrexe mihi. fugit improbus ac me
> sub cultro linquit.

At this most critical juncture there appears, in good tragic fashion, ἀπὸ μηχανῆς θεός: *sic me servavit Apollo.* It is, besides the wealth of delightful detail, the truly dramatic structure of the whole that gives this satire its unique charm.

To sustain a strong dramatic tension in reporting a trifle that had happened to himself is an achievement of which a great poet of the preceding generation was no less capable. It seems worth while to turn our thoughts for a moment from *Ibam forte via sacra* to Catullus' tenth poem,

> Varus me meus ad suos amores
> visum duxerat e foro otiosum.

The lady welcomes her boy-friend's friend in an engaging manner; she seems to him rather nice, and when it comes to women, he is an expert who can trust his first impression:

> scortillum, ut mihi tum repente visum est,
> non sane illepidum neque invenustum.

They talk of this and that. Catullus, as everybody in Rome knows, is just back from Bithynia; so after some preliminary phrases the young woman, instigated by a healthy curiosity and, perhaps, not wholly uninterested in the resources of a potential customer, inquires

> quid esset
> iam Bithynia, quo modo se haberet,
> et quonam mihi profuisset aere.

The sadly negative answer which Catullus has to give is not enough to put off the clever girl and her companions:

> 'at certe tamen', inquiunt 'quod illic
> natum dicitur esse, comparasti
> ad lecticam homines.'[1]

---

[1] If no other profit at all can be got from staying in a province, the one thing on which a man will pin his hopes is the acquisition of some native slaves. Cf. Cic. *Att.* 4. 16. 7 *etiam*

This temptation proves too strong for Catullus. Disappoint such a charming girl? Not he. *Ego, ut puellae unum me facerem beatiorem,* 'it is true', he replies, 'I hit on a bad province; however, I was able to buy eight strong men'. In fact, he confesses to his reader, he had not a man in the world who could have carried on his shoulders the foot of a broken couch. The girl—by now Catullus is angry and, forgetting the compliments he paid her a few moments ago, calls her *cinaediorem*— the girl immediately catches out the poor braggart. 'Darling', she says, 'be good and let me have them for a short time: you see, I want to attend divine service in the temple of Sarapis and to be carried there.' 'Wait a moment', I told the girl, 'what I have just said about having them, that was a slip. I have a friend, Gaius Cinna; it is he who bought them. But he or I, what difference does it make to me? I use them exactly as if I had bought them myself. But you, you have no manners, you are a nuisance: won't even allow a fellow to be a bit careless.'

There is in the little poem intense drama on a minute scale. A drawing-room Nemesis takes charge of the silly young man and brings him, so very pleased with himself at the beginning, to the deserved downfall. The poet reports the vicissitudes of his own fate with sublime detachment. His terse hendecasyllables present every shade of the scene and every change of temperature without admitting a single superfluous word.

In *Ibam forte via sacra* there is no superfluous feature either, but Horace deliberately paints on a large canvas whereas Catullus chose for his picture a small medallion. The room that Horace has at his disposal does not confine him to a succinct account of a dramatic scene: he is at liberty to include in his satire a considerable section of his world. Again, as in the sixth satire, we are given glimpses of the city of Rome, walking down the Sacra via to its western end and there turning south-west to the *aedes Vestae* (35),[1] near the *tribunal praetoris*, close to

---

illud iam cognitum est neque argenti scrupulum esse ullum in illa insula (i.e. Britannia) *neque ullam spem praedae nisi ex mancipiis, ex quibus nullos puto te litteris aut musicis eruditos exspectare.*

[1] Horace says *ventum erat ad Vestae* although it is clear that only two definite persons had arrived. To justify this use of the 'impersonal passive' Kiessling excogitated a psychological reason, which Heinze but slightly varied ('es ist, als könnte H. sich nicht entschließen in diesem Falle ein "wir" zu gebrauchen'). There is no need to look for special reasons. The use is old and fairly common with verbs such as *ventum est, itur,* and the like. Compare, for example, Plaut. *Curc.* 643 ff. A *nutrix quae fuit?* B *Archestrata; ea me spectatum tulerat per Dionysia. postquam illo ventum est* . . . (subject is only the nurse carrying the baby); *Mil.* 1403 *ultro ventumst ad me* (subject is one woman); Ter. *Phorm.* 1010 *qui mihi, ubi ad uxores ventumst, tum fiunt senes*; Plaut. *Bacch.* 447 *itur illinc iure dicto* (subject is the paedagogus); *Men.* 964 *nimis proventum* (in the non-local, transferred sense) *est nequiter* (he might have said *proveni*). It seems that this use of the passive survived long after the archaic period, especially in certain set phrases. Cf., for example, Cic. *Rab. Post.* 28 *nam ut ventum est Alexandream* . . . (those who arrived at Al. were Gabinius and Postumus); Sall. *Iug.* 91. 1

which the incidents that are reported in the rest of the satire took place.[1] For a moment (18) our thoughts wander to a place at the outskirts of the city, to Caesar's gardens on the other side of the Tiber, south-west of Porta Portese. As for the population, only one section is mentioned in passing (70), the Jews, whose strange customs and 'superstitions' aroused a keen interest in Horace and his contemporaries.

The brightest light in the poem falls on Maecenas and the circle of his friends. Here (48–52) Horace's voice has a very different ring from the cool detachment and the irony of his other replies to the bore:

> 'non isto vivimus illic
> quo tu rere modo; domus hac nec purior ulla est
> nec magis his aliena malis; nil mi officit, inquam,
> ditior hic aut est quia doctior; est locus uni
> cuique suus.'

That the impassioned sentence *domus hac nec purior ulla est nec magis his aliena malis* in its phrasing so closely resembles the sentence by which in the *Iter Brundisinum* his enthusiasm for his friends is voiced (1. 5. 41 f.), *animae qualis neque candidiores terra tulit neque quis me sit devinctior alter*, is in all probability no accident but due to the fact that in either case the same strong sentiment is expressed in the same strong syntactical form, the form of a negative statement which in fact is equivalent to the boldest positive superlative. Should confirmation be wanted, it can be found in a much later Horatian passage on the highest stylistic level. In an imaginary ἐπινίκιον after the fashion of Pindar, Caesar Augustus is to be praised[2] as the one

> quo nihil maius meliusve terris
> fata donavere bonique divi
> nec dabunt, quamvis redeant in aurum
> tempora priscum.

With the firm structure of the dramatic scene and the mellowness of the prevailing mood goes a variety of stylistic shades; none of these qualities is likely to have been conspicuous in the work of Lucilius. The wide range of the style may be illustrated by a few examples. The first short sentences that pass between the bore and Horace (4–8), like the opening lines of many scenes in Terence, have the characteristic colour of the polite, if thoroughly conventional, phraseology favoured

cum ad flumen ventum est (preceded by *pergit* [i.e. Marius] *ad flumen Tanain*, followed by *ibi* . . . *iubet*); Livy 1. 56. 9 f. *is* (Brutus) *tum ab Tarquiniis ductus Delphos* . . . *quo postquam ventum est* . . .; Suet. *Nero* 48 (subject is all the time Nero) *equum inscendit* . . . *audiit* . . . *agnitus est* . . . *et salutatus. ut ad deverticulum ventum est* . . . *evasit.*

[1] Some exceedingly bold speculations about the road followed by Horace have been refuted by F. Castagnoli, *Bull. Comun.* lxxiv, 1954, 52 f.

[2] *Odes* 4. 2. 37 ff.

by the educated classes. Their shallowness and quick pace give us the impression that we are catching snatches of a typical conversation in the street. The rapidity is even greater in the similar passage at ll. 62 f.:

> consistimus. 'unde venis et
> quo tendis?' rogat et respondet.[1]

The prophecy of the old woman (31–34) is a splendid piece of parody:

> hunc neque dira venena nec hosticus auferet ensis
> nec laterum dolor aut tussis nec tarda podagra;
> garrulus hunc quando consumet cumque; loquaces,
> si sapiat, vitet, simul atque adoleverit aetas.

Ὁ ὦτα ἔχων ἀκουέτω: he cannot miss the travesty of awe-inspiring language. A few observations on points of detail will confirm the general impression. In the phrase *hosticus ensis* the epithet must have struck contemporary readers as a lofty archaism.[2] In the next line but one the words *quando consumet cumque* are remarkable both for the archaizing tmesis and for the oracular mystery of the date suggested by *quando cumque*, 'on some day, whenever that will be'.[3] The last sentence with its momentous verb *vitet* contains the traditional culmination of this kind of prophecy; compare, for instance, Pindar, *Pyth.* 4. 75 τὸν μονοκρήπιδα πάντως ἐν φυλακᾷ σχεθέμεν μεγάλᾳ, Herodotus 7. 148. 3 κεφαλὴν πεφύλαξο, Ar. *Eq.* 1039 τὸν σὺ φύλαξαι,[4] 1080 f. ἀλλ᾽ ἔτι τόνδ᾽ ἐπάκουσον, ὃν εἶπέ σοι ἐξαλέασθαι χρησμὸν Λητοΐδης Κυλλήνην μή σε δολώσῃ, and Horace's (*Sat.* 1. 4. 85) *hunc tu, Romane, caveto*, which

---

[1] It seems strange that many editors who quote the parallel 2. 4. 1 'Unde et quo Catius?' (others compare Plat. *Lys.* 203 a ποῖ δὴ πορεύῃ καὶ πόθεν; and the beginning of the *Phaedrus*, ποῖ δὴ καὶ πόθεν;) still punctuate thus: 'unde venis?' et 'quo tendis?'. For the strong, but quite natural, compression in *rogat et respondet* compare Aesch. *Cho.* 677 f. ἀγνὼς πρὸς ἀγνῶτ᾽ εἶπε συμβαλὼν ἀνὴρ ἐξιστορήσας καὶ σαφηνίσας ὁδόν.

[2] The history of the rare word *hosticus* as it emerges from Ehlers's article in the *Thesaurus* is of considerable interest. Like *prognatus* (see p. 82 n. 4 above) and *imperitare* (see p. 191 n. 5 below and cf. p. 101 above) it seems to have had a solemn ring as early as Plautus. There are, including the uncertain conjecture *Mil.* 450 and the not quite certain conjecture *Most.* 357, three Plautine instances, none of them in senarii. In the one Plautine passage where the word is in the MSS, at *Capt.* 246, it occurs in the same prayer-like entreaty at the beginning of which we find *imperitabam*. It also occurs in tragedy (Accius). Its technical use (*ager hosticus*), according to the important testimony of Varro, belonged to the language of the *augures*. It is with this technical use that Livy's phrase *in hostico* is closely connected. In Horace there is only one other instance, *Odes* 3. 2. 6, *ex moenibus hosticis* ('diese τειχοσκοπία hat homerische Färbung' Heinze). Virgil does not use it. Ovid has it once (*Fast.* 4. 893) in a prayer and once (*Pont.* 1. 3. 65) in the phrase *hostica tellus*, a poetic paraphrase of *ager hosticus*; in a third passage, *Trist.* 3. 10. 66 *hostica flamma*, it is used gratuitously, and so by Columella, Silius, and later writers.

[3] See the pertinent remarks by P. Ferrarino, 'Cumque e i composti di que', *Mem. Accad. di Bologna, Classe di Scienze Morali*, serie iv, vol. iv, 1942, 23 f.

[4] For the voice of the verb and the implied ambiguity see R. A. Neil, ad loc.

clearly echoes oracles and presumably a particular oracle reported by
Ennius.[1]

The finale (from 74 *casu venit*), if not quite so brilliant as the prestissimo at the end of the second satire, yet is swift, lively, and amusing.
The very last words, *sic me servavit Apollo*, show Horace putting into
practice one of his own principles. In the tenth satire (20–30) he
attacks Lucilius for interspersing his Latin poems with Greek words.
Lucilius in his sixth book (231) had begun a verse in Latin and concluded it with τὸν δ᾽ ἐξήρπαξεν Ἀπόλλων, quoting Homer (Υ 443)
directly. Horace deliberately recalls Lucilius, but translates the quotation into Latin. It is not, however, only through the Homeric half-line
at the end that memories of a great battle are roused: we have been
prepared for them by the conclusion of the preceding narrative. For in
the detail of *clamor utrimque* and *undique concursus*, which is wholly
appropriate to the scene on the Forum, we recognize at the same time
a typical element of descriptions of battle-scenes. In an account of a
heroic battle, Plaut. *Amph.* 227, we hear: *clamorem utrimque efferunt.*
Cicero in a passage of a letter[2] where he applies to himself the words of
one of those boastful slaves who in *fabulae palliatae* pose as triumphators
speaks of his achievements thus: *sic acriter et vehementer proeliatus sum ut
clamor concursusque maxima cum mea laude fierent.* We may further compare
Sallust, *Cat.* 45. 3 *simul utrimque clamor exortus est*, Virgil, *Georg.* 4. 75–78,
miscentur magnisque vocant clamoribus hostem . . .; concurritur, and Livy
1. 48. 2 (speaking not of a battle, but of a riot in the *curia*), *clamor ab
utriusque fautoribus oritur, et concursus populi fiebat in curiam.* The warlike
note on which Horace concludes his report of a very ordinary incident is a magnificent touch.

7. SATIRE VII

Many scholars believe that Satire VII, *Proscripti Regis Rupili pus*, is
the earliest satire and 'in all probability the earliest of all the extant
compositions of Horace'.[3] This very old belief[4] has often been rejected
but will not die. In matters concerning Horace I know of no *fable convenue* that was ever killed for good. The perfect neatness and easy poise
of *Proscripti Regis* make it all but impossible to see in it a very early

---

[1] See Kiessling and Heinze, ad loc., and add L. Müller's quotation of the oracle in
Livy 5. 16. 9, *Romane, aquam Albanam cave lacu contineri, cave in mare manare suo flumine sinas.*
[2] *Att.* 1. 16. 1.
[3] So Arthur Palmer at the beginning of his notes on i. 7. In his note on l. 18 he goes so
far as to assume 'that the satire was written before the battle of Philippi'; the same view
was held by H. Schütz (p. xiii and p. 94 of his commentary).
[4] In 1839 the clear-headed and courageous Karl Franke (*Fasti Horatiani*, 101) had to
face the unanimous conviction that this satire was Horace's earliest poem.

satire.[1] Moreover, 'it is unlikely that it should have occurred to Horace to report a *bon mot* in hexameters until other larger poems after the fashion of Lucilius had provided a frame, as it were, within which a trifle like this might also find a place' (Heinze). The size of i. 7, which is by far the shortest of all Horatian satires, is about a quarter of the size of the demonstrably early satires i. 2 and i. 3. But, it is argued,[2] 'who will versify such nothings several years after the event?' There we are faced with a characteristic modern point of view. As we shall see, it was precisely for such nothings (*Nichtigkeiten*), or, to say it in Latin, *nugae*, as themes to be embroidered by him, that Horace was looking when he had decided to fill up his book of satires by the insertion of a few additional pieces.

Horace introduces his little tale as something that has become, or so he pretends to believe, the common gossip of the town:

> opinor
> omnibus et lippis notum et tonsoribus esse.

Is it in the least likely that this assertion should be taken at its face value as was done by Bentley and others? We may safely assume that in the months preceding the battle of Philippi far too many events of real importance took place to make it worth while even for an officious busybody to inform the inhabitants of the capital of a trivial incident that had occurred some time ago at one of the many lawsuits before the praetor in remote Asia. But even granting that such a trifle could have aroused some interest at the time, the knowledge of it would in all probability have been confined to the few persons, among them Horace, who happened to be present at that court. Above all, had the story been so well known, Horace could perhaps have alluded to it somewhere, but would certainly not have told it *dedita opera* and at such length. Readers familiar with the ways of Horace should not be deceived by his presentation of the tale. It would not be at all like him to begin by saying 'I am going to tell you a story which, I am confident, you have never heard before'. Instead he starts with a whimsical piece of Horatian εἰρωνεία: *opinor omnibus et lippis notum et tonsoribus esse.*

It is easy to see that the nucleus of this satire is an αἶνος, an αἶνος of that very old and plain type where only a minimum of straightforward narrative is given, just enough to enable the listener to understand the *dictum*[3] at the end.[4] Here the goal of the tale is the *dictum* of Persius,[5]

---

[1] This is the strongest point in Franke's argumentation. His attempt to find in the satire an allusion to Octavian's expedition against Sextus Pompeius is arbitrary.

[2] By F. Skutsch, *Neue Jahrb.* xxiii, 1909, 32 n. 1 (*Kl. Schriften*, 373 n. 1).

[3] In the sense in which Cicero uses the word *De orat.* 2. 222 and elsewhere.

[4] See *Rh. Mus.* lxxiii, 1920, 368 f.

[5] I do not fully understand why he uses in his entreaty the very unusual expression *per magnos deos te oro*. Is it perhaps implied that he, the eastern Greek, who is doing big

which hinges upon the poor pun on *rex* or *Rex*.[1] However, Horace's poem as it stands is anything but a mere αἶνος. To see that clearly we have only to remember how Catullus shaped such an αἶνος. His fifty-third poem is a perfect example:

> Risi nescioquem modo e corona,
> qui, cum mirifice Vatiniana
> meus crimina Calvos explicasset,
> admirans ait haec manusque tollens:
> 'di magni, salaputium disertum'.

In these slender hendecasyllables the style of a matter-of-fact report seems to be carried to extremes. True, there is, right in the centre of the little poem, the warm note of *meus . . . Calvos*, preceded by *mirifice* and followed by *admirans*, but apart from it nothing is said that is not strictly necessary as a clue to the *dictum* that fills the last line. The beginning with *Risi*[2] *. . . modo* gives the impression that this baga-telle had been jotted down immediately after the incident had occurred; that, too, is essential to the nature of this light genre.[3] Horace, on the other hand, transposes a trivial theme into a genre that neither is, nor pretends to be, light. He wants to bring out all the facets of his little gem and he is in no great hurry. So he has time for an exten-sive parenthesis, 10–18, glittering in its epic pomp. The characteriza-tion of the two adversaries goes far beyond the immediate requirements of the anecdote. They are made to represent in two extreme types the two most important groups among the population of the Mediterra-nean world controlled by Rome: on the one hand, Rupilius Rex, a *Praenestinus*, in appearance, manners, and acid wit a typical product of the stout race of Italy, on the other Persius, a *Graeculus*, a capitalist from one of the degenerate eastern cities, exceedingly tough and a vicious slanderer. Rex, likened to a *durus vindemiator*, pours over his adversary floods of the kind of coarse jeering which could be overheard

---

business at *Clazomenae*, invokes the deities of Samothrace, whose cult was wide-spread in that part of the world?

[1] Cicero's retort on Clodius (*Att.* 1. 16. 10), *regem appellas, cum Rex tui mentionem nullam fecerit?* has long been quoted. But a still greater man seems to have resorted to a pun on the same word and name; his joke was meant to save a highly embarrassing situation. When Caesar, on 26 Jan. of 44 B.C., returned to Rome from the celebration of the *feriae Latinae*, some among the populace greeted him as king. He protested with good-natured humour (only afterwards, annoyed by the action of the tribunes, did he lose his temper, οὐκέτι τὴν ὀργὴν κατέσχεν) and οὐκ ἔφη Βασιλεὺς ἀλλὰ Καῖσαρ καλεῖσθαι (Dio Cass. 44. 10. 1, cf. App. *B.Civ.* 2. 108), 'my cognomen is not Rex but Caesar'.

[2] One of Cicero's letters to his brother (2. 12. 1) begins *Risi nivem atram*.

[3] Catullus himself, in a poem (56) which, though not culminating in a *dictum*, has a great deal in common with *Risi nescioquem* (it begins *O rem ridiculam*), says *deprendi modo pupulum . . .*, and a poem of Furius Bibaculus (*Fragm. Poet. Lat.* 81) begins *Catonis modo, Galle, Tusculanum tota creditor urbe venditabat.*

by many a roadside in the country,[1] but this time all his *Italum acetum* is of no avail: the Greek carries the day with one felicitous pun. However, it is pretty obvious that *victrix causa deis placuit, sed victa poetae*, for there is nothing morally wrong with Rex, whereas the fulsomeness of the other man's flattering oratory (23–26) appears utterly contemptible.[2]

This satire, too, has at least some Lucilian touches. The mention in passing of Sisenna and Barrus (8) is, perhaps, reminiscent of Lucilius, and so is almost certainly the deliberately clumsy formula of transition[3] at l. 9, *ad Regem redeo*, which here is not required by the context.[4] But viewed as a whole, this refined poem seems neither in matter nor in form to have any important features in common with Lucilius.

8. SATIRE VIII

The nucleus of the eighth satire can be as easily discerned as that of the seventh. The prototype of *Olim truncus eram* is, broadly speaking, the widespread class of those dedicatory epigrams in which the dedicated object, addressing a passer-by, gives a brief account of its history ('formerly I was such-and-such a thing, but now I have become what you see before you') and sometimes adds some indication of its present circumstances. An epigram by Simias of Rhodes[5] may here represent the type; it is suitable for the purpose just because Simias 'does not particularly shine in his epigrams'.[6]

Πρόσθε μὲν ἀγραύλοιο δασύτριχος ἰξάλου αἰγὸς
δοιὰ κέρα,[7] χλωροῖς ἐστεφόμαν πετάλοις·
νῦν δέ με Νικομάχῳ κεραοξόος ἥρμοσε τέκτων,
ἐντανύσας ἕλικος καρτερὰ νεῦρα βοός.

'Πρόσθε μέν, olim, I was the double horns of a wild goat, under the green leafage of the forest; but now the bowmaker has shaped me and,

---

[1] Horace here, 28–31, unmistakably relishes his own recollections of the jokes about the cuckoo.

[2] The commonplace character of Persius' effusions must have seemed appalling to a man of any taste. Orelli–Baiter and others have compared a passage from the famous hymn of the Athenians in honour of Demetrios Poliorketes, quoted by Duris, *F Gr Hist* 76 F 13 (cf. K. Scott, *Am. Journ. Phil.* xlix, 1928, 231, Immisch, 'Zum antiken Herrscherkult', *Das Erbe der Alten*, ii. 20, 1931, 7 ff.), ll. 9 ff. σεμνόν τι φαίνεθ', οἱ φίλοι πάντες κύκλῳ, | ἐν μέσοισι δ' αὐτός, | ὅμοιον ὥσπερ οἱ φίλοι μὲν ἀστέρες, | ἥλιος δ' ἐκεῖνος. Cf. also Housman on Manilius 1. 385 and 4. 765.

[3] Cf. on 1. 6. 45, p. 103 above.

[4] Lejay's comment, 'gaucherie de composition qui trahit le débutant', is perhaps a little too ingenuous.

[5] *Anth. Pal.* 6. 113. Cf. Hermann Fränkel, *De Simia Rhodio* (Göttingen 1915), 103 f.

[6] Wilamowitz, *Hellenistische Dichtung*, i. 112.

[7] H. Fränkel's emendation is rightly accepted in Diehl's *Anthol. Lyr.*; Waltz does not mention it and prints an inferior conjecture.

adding a taut string, turned me into a bow for Nicomachus.' Here, as in *Olim truncus eram*, the decisive metamorphosis has been brought about by an artisan, a bowmaker here, a carpenter, *faber*, there. The lovely scenery that in bygone days surrounded the speaker is but lightly touched upon, χλωροῖς ἐστεφόμαν πετάλοις. In Catullus' *Phaselus*, grown from the same root of an epigram of the πρόσθε μὲν . . . νῦν δὲ type, the nostalgic note is stronger, since this is no longer an epigram but a semi-lyrical poem:

> ubi iste post phaselus antea fuit
> comata silva: nam Cytorio in iugo
> loquente saepe sibilum edidit coma.

But in the case of *Olim truncus eram* it is not enough to point in general to the type of dedicatory epigrams relating a metamorphosis undergone by the dedicated object. Here a more special model is recognizable: this satire, as has long been seen, develops the theme of poems, whether in epigrammatic form[1] or strongly influenced by epigrams, in which Priapus speaks of himself and of things that happened to him. It is well known that in addition to the Hellenistic poems of that kind countless Latin *Priapea* were written, especially towards the end of the Republic and under the early Empire.[2] The extant collection of *Priapea* provides an instance of the topic that underlies the first sentence of Horace's satire (*Olim truncus . . . maluit esse deum*): *Priap.* 10. 4 f. *lignum rude vilicus dolavit et dixit mihi 'tu Priapus esto'*, to which we have to add two of the 'Virgilian' *Priapea*, 2. 1 f. *Ego haec, ego arte fabricata rustica, ego arida, o viator, ecce populus* and 3. 3 *quercus arida rustica fomitata securi*.[3] Nor is it uncommon in these poems that Priapus, as in Horace's satire, reports certain incidents which he witnessed at night-time; there is, however, the difference that the incidents reported in the *Priapea* concern the god far more directly than do the performances of the two witches in the satire.

However, *Olim truncus eram* is as little a *Priapeum* as *Proscripti Regis*

---

[1] Among the Greek Priapus epigrams listed by H. Herter, 'De Priapo', *RGVV* xxiii, 1932, 16 ff., I have not been able to find an example of the πρόσθε μὲν . . . νῦν δὲ type. But remembering that most of the Hellenistic poetry on Priapus is lost, I am inclined to assume that epigrams on Priapus which followed that pattern did exist.

[2] Cf. Bücheler, *Rh. Mus.* xviii, 1863, 381 ff. (*Kl. Schriften*, i. 328 ff.).

[3] In Hérédia's *Les Trophées* there is a cycle of five sonnets under the title *Hortorum deus*. The first sonnet has as its motto *Olim truncus eram ficulnus*. Leaving aside all Horace's adornment, the poet instinctively recovers the basic epigrammatic theme and brings into prominence the antithesis of πρόσθε μὲν . . ., νῦν δὲ . . . (at the beginning of the second quatrain, 'J'y veille. A coups de serpe, autrefois, un berger M'a taillé dans le tronc d'un dur figuier d'Égine', and at the beginning of the last tercet, 'A présent, vil gardien de fruit et de salades, Contre les maraudeurs je défends cet enclos'). The ancient pattern is enriched by the modern sentiment that breathes in the poem and becomes strongest at the end ('Et je ne verrai plus les riantes Cyclades').

Rupili is a poetic αἶνος of the type of Catullus' *Risi nescioquem*. It is certainly profitable, in dealing with a particular poem, to use our methods of minute analysis and comparison. But after using them we must step back and view the particular poem in its entirety. We then shall not find it difficult to recognize its individual character.

Horace, for the purposes of his Priapus satire, had at his disposal a truly romantic, if somewhat gruesome, stage, a place which, though modernized and made sanitary, was still haunted by memories of its recent past when it served as the poor people's cemetery. On this stage an exciting dramatic play is to be performed. A leading lady was not far to seek: Horace had only to fetch her, as it were from across the street, from one of his own *iambi*.[1] And so that formidable actress, the witch Canidia, puts in another appearance, οὐκ οἴη, for she brings with her, from the fifth epode, her old companion Sagana. The drama takes its course and its conclusion is worthy of such a stage and such actors. It is not even necessary to bring in a god on a machine, for a god is on the premises already. He produces the most wonderful explosion, which the witches, very understandably, ascribe to a miracle and flee in horror, leaving behind valuable trimmings of their anatomy. But Priapus, being an educated Hellenistic god, volunteers a physical explanation as dry as the wood of which he is made.

Maecenas is not mentioned directly, but the locality in which the action takes place clearly refers to him, and the pleasure which this hilarious satire could be expected to give him will have been foremost in Horace's mind when he conceived it. It was Maecenas who was chiefly responsible for the change which turned that district outside the Porta Esquilina[2] from a dreary proletarian burial-place into a splendid residential quarter; his *alta domus*,[3] the *moles propinqua nubibus arduis*, from where the view stretched to the Sabine hills on the one side and to the Alban hills on the other,[4] dominated the plateau at that eastern end of Rome.

> nunc licet Esquiliis habitare salubribus atque
> aggere in aprico spatiari:[5]

[1] Cf. pp. 62 ff. above.

[2] For a discussion of the topographical problems see Platner and Ashby, *Topog. Dict.* 269, and the literature quoted there. A picturesque description of the 'field of death' can be found in R. Lanciani, *The Destruction of Ancient Rome*, 14 f. The numerous *puticuli*, discovered during the rebuilding of Rome after it had become the capital of Italy, are also mentioned in Kiessling's note on l. 8.

[3] *Epod.* 9. 3.

[4] *Odes* 3. 29. 6–10.

[5] Ll. 14 f. I think that at the beginning of the following relative clause Bentley's *qua* must be right. At ll. 10 f. Heinze's (not Kiessling's) and Klingner's punctuation is unfortunate; other considerations apart, it is refuted by what Heinze himself (following Mommsen, *Ges. Schriften*, iii. 202 n. 1) observes on *mille pedes in fronte* . . ..

a pleasant and healthy spot in full sunshine to set off the night-scene in the decaying cemetery. The poet, in describing the happy transformation, pays a handsome compliment to the friend who has brought it about.

A Lucilian touch may be seen in the manner in which at l. 11 the two wretches Pantolabus and Nomentanus are mentioned, primarily to represent the *misera plebs* (10), but also to provide in passing a piece of ὀνομαστὶ κωμῳδεῖν and so to harmonize this satire with a characteristic feature of many of the others. As a whole, however, the eighth satire has as little of Lucilius as has the seventh.

Any attempt to reconstruct the various stages in the composition of an ancient book is bound to be very hazardous. However, in the case of satires VII and VIII, and possibly of IX as well, we are on fairly solid ground. The particular character of these pieces seems to suggest that Horace, after writing a number of satires, looked round for fresh themes which might help him to vary the contents of his book and round it off. Not unnaturally he hit upon some of those unpretentious subjects of which the most influential group of poets of the previous generation, Calvus, Catullus, and the rest of them, would have made short poems in hendecasyllables, choliambs, and so forth. But given his position in the struggle for a new style in poetry, he could not possibly think of writing *nugae* like those poets, *nugae* merely transformed into hexametric poems with an occasional admixture of *Lucilianus character*. Horace, at this stage, wanted to create round the nucleus of some bagatelle, some παίγνιον, a new and many-coloured world of his own. So he produced poems which, if for their basic motifs they owed something to a different literary genre, became in volume and style and also in spirit true Horatian satires.

9. SATIRE IV

Latin poetry, a child of the Hellenistic age, had almost *ab origine* been 'self-conscious' in the primary sense of the word, that is to say given to reflecting upon itself, aware of its own limitations, of the means at its disposal, and of the ends it was aiming at. Theoretical reflection had a considerable share in producing it. The most many-sided and most influential of all early Roman poets, Ennius, is representative in this respect as in others. Behind his spirited writing there lies a great effort of sober thought and selective planning.[1] In the work of Lucilius

---

[1] For this aspect of Ennius' work, which is often concealed by his enthusiastic attitude (*numquam nisi potus ad arma prosiluit dicenda*), see especially Leo, *Gesch. d. röm. Lit.* 209–11, and S. Mariotti, *Lezioni su Ennio*, 1951, 104 ff.

theoretical, and often polemical, discussions on problems of style and on
the classification of various genres of poetry played an important part.[1]
His contemporary, and in certain respects his adversary, Accius combined with his own poetic work literary criticism and a study of literary
history. This intimate connexion between κρίσις ποιημάτων and production of poetry was maintained and intensified as time went on.
The leading poets of the generation immediately before Horace
gathered round P. Valerius Cato, praised as

> Cato grammaticus, Latina Siren,
> qui solus legit ac facit poetas.

It was, then, no novelty in itself when Horace undertook to discuss
themes which we are accustomed to regard as belonging to the theoretical treatment of poetics. What was new, however, was the use he made
of theoretical discussions on such topics and the place which they came
to occupy in his whole work. They cannot be considered mere accessories. We find him given to reflections on the norms of poetry, his
own poetry, and that of his fellow poets, from a very early stage to the
latest period of his production. Some of his final views are laid down in
the greatest of his *sermones*, the letter to Augustus;[2] his early views
are expressed in the fourth satire, *Eupolis atque Cratinus*. But whether
late or early, all his writings on problems of poetics, while drawing
on a large store of theories, served an eminently practical purpose.[3]
As soon as Horace, stirred by his own genius and encouraged by the
example of Virgil, Varius, and perhaps some other poets of the same
generation, had determined to make his fame as a poet, being by temperament a fighter, he wanted to fight against all kinds of prejudice,
amateurish slovenliness, philistinism, reactionary tendencies, in short
to fight for the new and noble type of poetry which he and his friends
were endeavouring to bring about. It was partly on account of that
struggle that Horace wrote those *sermones* in which he deals with
problems of literature: they were meant to be used as weapons of
defence as well as of attack. But it is obvious that he wrote them also
to give to himself and to his readers an account of what he was
attempting to achieve and of the means which he had chosen as
most suitable to his ends. As was natural he began by demonstrating
his convictions and principles in close relation to the matter in hand,
his *saturae*.

---

[1] With the help of Leo's thorough account, op. cit. 415–18, the relevant fragments can
easily be found.

[2] See pp. 383 ff. below.

[3] This fact is often misunderstood, and in particular the *Epistula ad Pisones*, misnamed *De
arte poetica*, has had to suffer from this misunderstanding.

The discussion in the fourth satire is twofold: on the one hand, Horace is examining certain stylistic requirements of the *satura*, on the other hand, its moral justification. But since a *sermo* must not degenerate into a lecture or a treatise, the two points are not kept rigidly separate, but are discussed in such a manner that the thought seems to glide easily to and fro. The satire opens with a sonorous 'tricolon crescendo':

Eupolis | atque Cratinus | Aristophanesque poetae.

These three playwrights *atque alii quorum comoedia prisca virorum est* are introduced in order to emphasize what by the current doctrine[1] was held to be the most significant feature of Old Comedy, the stigmatizing of all sorts of rogues.[2] In Horace's time it was taken for granted, probably on the authority of Varro,[3] that Lucilius with his ὀνομαστὶ κωμῳδεῖν was walking in the footsteps of Old Comedy. It is in fact Lucilius at whom the pithy introductory period of this satire aims, and immediately after reaching this point (6 *hinc omnis pendet Lucilius*) Horace plunges into the discussion of his real theme. A brief acknowledgement of some positive qualities of Lucilius is followed by a sharp attack on his stylistic deficiency, his hasty[4] and slipshod manner of writing. This leads to a general invective, enlivened (at 14 ff. and 21 f.) by two sallies of ὀνομαστὶ κωμῳδεῖν, against the poetasters who take pride in a maximum output or the greatest possible publicity, regardless of the quality of their work. I myself, Horace goes on, shun publicity; and here, while explaining this personal reluctance, he imperceptibly shifts the argument from the artistic point of view to the moral one (23 ff. *volgo recitare timentis ob hanc rem, quod sunt quos genus hoc minime iuvat, utpote pluris culpari dignos*). There follow examples of the various types of persons (with an ὀνομαστὶ κωμῳδεῖν thrown in at 28) who are, and know that they are, *culpari digni*; very naturally *omnes hi metuunt versus, odere poetas* (33). Therefore the writer of satires, who

---

[1] This doctrine, in origin Peripatetic, was propagated through various channels. Cf. Leo, *Hermes*, xxiv, 1889, 73 ff., Kaibel, 'Die Prolegomena περὶ κωμῳδίας', *Abh. Gött. Ges.*, Phil.-hist. Kl., N.F. ii. 4, 1898. For all the relevant texts see *Com. Graec. Fragm.*, ed. G. Kaibel, 1899.

[2] Horace says that the writers of Old Comedy, *si quis erat dignus describi quod malus ac fur, quod moechus foret . . .* , censured him with full παρρησία, *multa cum libertate notabant*. It seems worth while to observe that the idea of interpreting the ὀνομαστὶ κωμῳδεῖν of Athenian comedy in terms of the *nota censoria* was older: Cicero *Rep.* 4. 11 (*comoedia Graeca*) *populares homines improbos, in re publica seditiosos, Cleonem, Cleophontem, Hyperbolum laesit. patiamur, etsi eius modi cives a censore melius est quam a poeta notari*, and *Brut.* 224 *Hyperboli, cuius improbitatem veteres Atticorum comoediae notaverunt*.

[3] Cf. Leo, *Hermes*, xxiv, 1889, 79.

[4] The objection to *scribere multum* (13) is not, of course, new. Compare, for instance, Callim. *Ap.* 108 ff.; *fr.* 1. 23 f. and 398 Pf.; Catullus 22. 3 and 95. 9 f.

attacks whomsoever he pleases and exposes his victims to everyone's scorn, is regarded as a most dangerous animal.[1] To these accusations Horace replies (38) *agedum, pauca accipe contra*. But instead of the expected defence of the *satura* as something morally justifiable we are given a lecture on the particular form and the relative value of this literary genre, which, so we are told, being nearer to ordinary talk, cannot claim to be regarded as true poetry. This whole section (39–63) is clearly marked as a digression;[2] it concludes with *hactenus haec*, and the following sentence (64 f.), *nunc illud tantum quaeram, meritone tibi sit suspectum genus hoc scribendi*, brings us back to the question which was raised in ll. 24–38, that is to say the question whether and under what conditions the satirist's personal attacks are morally defensible. The discussion of this problem fills the remaining eighty lines of the satire. That its treatment does not become too theoretical is due to the insertion of a good deal of ὀνομαστὶ κωμῳδεῖν (65 f.,[3] 69, 72, 109–14), but above all to the role which is here allotted to Horace's personality, his gratitude to his father, his outlook on life, his sincerity (130 f.), and his habit of spending his spare time on some innocent literary amusement (138 f.). The confession that writing satire in the manner in which he does it is part and parcel of his own nature and is for him a moral necessity—this confession, coming from so honest a man, is likely to prove a more effective defence than any theoretical demonstration could be. Horace is still far from achieving the perfect self-portraiture which delights us in his maturest satires, but he is well on his way to it.

We see, then, that of the two aspects under which Horace attempts to vindicate his *satura* it is the moral, and not the artistic, aspect which is given the lion's share. We should not make the mistake of regarding the discussion on metre and style as of secondary importance: the very passion displayed in the criticism of Lucilius makes it clear how seriously Horace takes these literary problems. But for the moment he dwells more extensively on the moral issues involved in his argument. That corresponds to the contents of his demonstrably earliest satires, i. 2 and i. 3, which are entirely concerned with moral topics, and is in harmony with the whole spirit of the opening satire, *Qui fit, Maecenas*. But it also reflects the narrow view which at this initial stage he took of the essential character of the satires of Lucilius. He had not yet

---

[1] The warning (34) *faenum habet in cornu, longe fuge* is rightly compared by Pfeiffer with Callim. *fr.* 191. 78 f. ἀλλ' ἢν ὁρῇ τις, 'οὗτος Ἀλκμέων' φήσει καὶ 'φεῦγε· βάλλει· φεῦγ'' ' ἐρεῖ 'τὸν ἄνθρωπον'.

[2] Cf. Knoche, *Philol.* xc, 1935, 480.

[3] Should not at l. 65 and 70 the reading *Sulgius* and *Sulgi* be accepted? A name *Sulcius* seems to be otherwise unknown. For *Sulgius* in inscriptions see, in addition to W. Schulze, *Z. Gesch. lat. Eigennamen*, 372, Dessau, *ILS* iii. 138.

discovered that ὀνομαστὶ κωμῳδεῖν, though a striking feature, was by no means the most significant or the most valuable feature in the work of Lucilius.[1]

10. SATIRE X

To come from Satire IV to Satire X is not unlike meeting again, after an interval of a few years, one whom we had known as a very young man. The shape and colour of his face are still the same, but its lines are now more firmly drawn and there is in it a determined expression which we had not noticed before.

The beginning of the tenth satire[2] refers explicitly to the first section of the fourth. But whereas in the former poem Lucilius was merely in general terms accused of hasty and slovenly workmanship, we are now given a piece of what our contemporaries like to call constructive criticism. Horace does not deny that in the writer's ability to make the audience grin with amusement there lies a certain *virtus* (8 *et est quaedam tamen hic quoque virtus*),[3] but this is, after all, only one of the many *virtutes*, ἀρεταί, required for the making of a good satura. At this point Horace raises, as it were, his voice[4] and solemnly announces what sounds almost like stylistic commandments for those who venture upon this literary genre (9–15):

> est brevitate opus, ut currat sententia neu se
> impediat verbis lassas onerantibus auris;
> et sermone opus est modo tristi, saepe iocoso,
> defendente vicem modo rhetoris atque poetae,
> interdum urbani, parcentis viribus atque
> extenuantis eas consulto. ridiculum acri
> fortius et melius magnas plerumque secat res.

In formulating these rules Horace sets an exceedingly high standard, a standard of which, despite his *urbanitas*,[5] the amiable and easy-going

---

[1] As regards the date of i. 4, I agree with Heinze that we cannot safely go beyond the two conclusions that must be drawn from the text: later than the second, earlier than the tenth satire. The chronological guesses which are offered, after others, by H. Schütz (and again by Lejay, 108) are arbitrary.

[2] About the origin of the eight lines which in a few manuscripts are prefixed to the tenth satire I have nothing to add to my observations in *Hermes*, lxviii, 1933, 392 ff.

[3] Here *virtus* has at least a strong connotation of its well-known technical sense, the sense intended by Theophrastus when he examined the ἀρεταί of the λέξις and by Caesar when he spoke of *comica virtus* (he did indeed).

[4] It is not at random that he says at l. 9 *est brevitate opus* and two lines later *et sermone opus est modo tristi* . . . . No reader familiar with Horace's economical style and skilful use of *variatio* will miss the emphasis in the phrase repeated after such a short interval. He seems to insist on the conviction that these things, so far from being left to the writer's will and pleasure, are absolute necessities.

[5] Lucilius is called by Cicero (*De orat.* 2. 25) *homo doctus et perurbanus*, and Horace, while criticizing him, acknowledges that he is *comis et urbanus* (1. 10. 65).

Lucilius falls as short as does the sharp and polished Juvenal, for, whatever gods may have bestowed their gifts on that powerful writer, the Grace who dispenses *urbanitas* was certainly not among them, nor was his the faculty *parcentis viribus atque extenuantis eas consulto*. It is only fair to add that Horace himself afterwards betrayed his noble ideal of *satura* in some of the violent efforts of his second book. But in the present context it is, above all, important to realize that these stylistic demands are by no means a mere matter of form. As is clear from the whole section and particularly from its conclusion, *ridiculum acri fortius et melius magnas plerumque secat res*, the dominating interest is in the moral function of this kind of writing or, to put it differently, in the moral conceptions that lie behind it. The stylistic attitude which Horace postulates for the *sermo* is the adequate expression of a definite attitude in actual life, of a definite behaviour in conversing with our fellow men. There should be serious criticism (*sermone opus est modo tristi*), without which healthy life in a community is not possible, sometimes impassioned language should be used (*sermone . . . defendente vicem modo rhetoris atque poetae*), but above all you must preserve *urbanitas*, which is as much as to say you must not behave like a boor or a doctrinaire. If we look for a fuller documentation of these ideas about an educated man's conduct in human society, we instinctively turn to Cicero's books *De officiis*.[1] There (1. 136) the ideal type of the *sermo* to be used in actual life is described, if more fully and warmly, yet essentially in the same terms as those which Horace applies to his literary *sermo*: *maximeque curandum est ut eos quibuscum sermonem conferemus et vereri et diligere videamur. obiurgationes etiam nonnumquam incidunt necessariae, in quibus utendum est fortasse et vocis contentione maiore et verborum gravitate acriore, id agendum etiam ut ea facere videamur irati. sed ut ad urendum et secandum sic ad hoc genus castigandi raro invitique veniemus nec umquam nisi necessario, si nulla reperietur alia medicina; sed tamen ira procul absit, cum qua nihil recte fieri, nihil considerate potest.*

The maxims laid down in ll. 7–15 lead to a reference to the writers of Old Comedy, with (16) an all but verbatim quotation of 1. 4. 2; but this time those ancient playwrights are mentioned not because Lucilius depends on them, but because they fulfil the stylistic demands which have just been formulated; they therefore ought to serve as a model to the writers of the present day. But certain people refuse to learn from them: *quos neque pulcher Hermogenes umquam legit neque simius iste nil praeter Calvum et doctus cantare Catullum*. Here the listener will prick up his ears: this is a battle-cry, a challenge directed against a whole gang of *littérateurs*, very different from the occasional gibing at

---

[1] I followed this obvious track spontaneously, but then saw that Lejay on l. 14 quotes part of the passage of Cicero.

some obscure poetaster which in the long fourth satire was all that was
to be heard of literary criticism of contemporaries. This outburst
prepares the way for the assault upon the poet Alpinus (36 f.)[1] and to
the wholesale condemnation of a group of poets at the end of the
satire (78–80 and 90 f.).

The rather timid defence offered for Lucilius (20 f.) *at magnum fecit
quod verbis Graeca Latinis miscuit* provokes from Horace an angry (*o seri
studiorum*) protest: in poetry—as in dignified prose—only pure Latin,
without any admixture of Greek words, should be used.[2] At l. 31 the
discussion takes a somewhat unexpected turn: *atque ego cum Graecos
facerem, natus mare citra, versiculos, vetuit me tali voce Quirinus . . .*, 'and so[3]
when I, born on this side of the sea, tried to write Greek verses,
Quirinus[4] stopped me . . .'. There was in the preceding discussion no
thought of writing Greek poetry, but only of using Greek words in
Latin poetry. Why, then, this departure? The answer is suggested by
the following section, in which Horace explains why he, unlike many
eminent poets of his day, has chosen as his modest task the revival of
the *satura* of Lucilius. He is going to speak of his own work as a Latin
poet, and it is to this theme that the little story about Quirinus provides
a refined transition. The statement 'Quirinus stopped me from writing
Greek verses' clearly implies 'so I wrote Latin verses instead'.

The heading under which Horace puts his account of his own work
is typical of this master of smiling understatement; he says (37) *haec
ego ludo* precisely as at 1. 4. 139 he had said *inludo chartis*. He does not
wish to write either poetry destined for recitation or poetry to be performed on the stage (38 f.). He does not wish to, for it is not in his
nature; besides, there is no need for it since all the genres belonging to
those two classes of poetry are well provided for. And so he goes on to
pass in review the eminent contemporary writers first of dramatic
poetry and then of the different types of *epos*.[5] With the literary field so

---

[1] The questions concerning the identity of this Alpinus have been settled by Nipperdey,
Opuscula, 499 ff. He shows (*a*) that the Alpinus of whom Horace speaks at 1. 10. 36 and the
Furius mentioned at 2. 5. 41 must be one and the same poet, and (*b*) that that poet cannot
be Furius Bibaculus. Morel, *Fragm. Poet. Lat.* 83, was not justified in assigning *frs.* 15 and
16 to Bibaculus without any comment.

[2] The manner in which ll. 27–30 have been treated by most editors makes it necessary
to discuss them more fully than could be done in a footnote; see pp. 133 ff. below.

[3] Here *atque* signifies the transition from a general principle to its application in a particular case. See for this use Hand, *Tursellinus*, i. 478 f.; Kühner–Stegmann, ii. 21.

[4] Heinze has seen that here Quirinus, the patron of undiluted *Latinitas*, takes the place
which in this vision of a poet belonged primarily to Apollo. The ultimate prototype is the
passage from the beginning of Callimachus' Αἴτια, *fr.* 1. 21 ff., which from Virgil's
Eclogues on so strongly attracted the Augustan poets (cf. Pfeiffer, *Hermes*, lxiii, 1928, 322 f.).

[5] Heinze's comment on *forte* (*Thes. l. L.* vi. 1. 1159. 61 f. depends on Heinze) and *acer* at
l. 43, 'die Epitheta der epischen Helden, auf Gedicht und Dichter übertragen', is insufficient. Lejay is right: '*Forte epos* est à la fois le vers plein et sonore et le vers des héros.' For

crowded by masters of the craft, what was left for him, Horace, but to
modernize, more successfully than Varro Atacinus and some others,
the satura of Lucilius? This brings him back to the criticism of
Lucilius with which this satire began. Lucilius is again charged with
the offence of which in the former satire[1] both he and certain versifiers
of Horace's own day were accused, hasty production of masses of
haphazard stuff.[2] But, taken as a whole, the criticism of Lucilius is now
more mellow and more profound than it was before, not only because
his great qualities of *comitas* and *urbanitas* are generously recognized
(65), but particularly because his work is now judged by the standards
not of Horace's but of Lucilius' time: such as it is, his work marks an
advance over the writings of the earlier, wholly primitive poets;[3] it
would have been still more polished had Lucilius been lucky enough to
live in an age of more refined taste (65–71). The lessons to be learnt
from the partial failure of Lucilius are plain, and Horace is determined
to profit from them in his own endeavours: you cannot be too careful
in pruning what you have written (72 f.), and you should never yield
to the temptation of pleasing the many rather than a few competent
judges (73–75). To the question *an tua demens vilibus in ludis dictari
carmina malis?* the answer is obvious, *non ego*. He strengthens the point
by appending, with exemplary *brevitas*, a pretty anecdote: *nam satis
est equitem mihi plaudere, ut audax, contemptis aliis, explosa Arbuscula dixit.*
And now he takes up the idea of *satis est . . . mihi plaudere* and, by means
of one of his subtle amplifications, makes it the theme of the whole
concluding section of the satire—and of the book. He draws up a
catalogue of those readers for whose judgement he does not care and of
those whose applause he hopes to win. By doing so he is also paying an
elegant compliment to the same Lucilius whose shortcomings he has
just been criticizing. In a section of his earliest published book (the
twenty-sixth in the collection of his works), presumably a kind of

the use of *fortis* to denote a certain style of prose see *Thes. l. L.* vi. 1. 1156. 65 ff., and add,
for example, Cic. *Orat.* 95, Sen. *Controv.* 1, praef. 20; for the corresponding use of *acer* see,
for example, Cic. *Orat.* 99 init. and Hor. *Sat.* 1. 4. 46. The antithesis of ll. 43 ff. of our
satire recurs in Domitius Marsus' famous epigram (*Fragm. Poet. Lat.* 111) on the death of
Virgil and Tibullus, *ne foret aut elegis* molles *qui fleret amores aut caneret* forti *regia bella pede.*
For a full discussion on *molle atque facetum* (with bibliography) see H. J. Rose, 'The Eclogues
of Vergil', *Sather Class. Lectures*, xvi, 1942, 24 ff. and 226.

[1] 1. 4. 9–21.
[2] 50 f. and 67 ff.
[3] On the meaning of l. 66, *quam rudis et Graecis intacti carminis auctor*, a great deal has
been written. I accept Nipperdey's interpretation, *Opusc.* 508, 'concedo Lucilium esse
limatiorem quam eum, qui condiderit (nihil aliud significat *auctor*) carmen aliquod rude, et
in quo nulla Graecae artis vestigia insint: nam hoc est *intactum Graecis*, ut poetice dixit
Horatius pro intactum litteris Graecis. Idem igitur poterat his quoque verbis efferre: non
dico rudem esse Lucilium et Graeca arte Graecisque litteris destitutum'. So also Leo,
Gesch. d. röm. Lit. 424 n. 1, and (only in his last edition) Heinze.

proem to what was to follow, Lucilius had spoken, both in general terms and naming some individual persons, of the readers whom he did not wish to have and of those he would like to have. To that section belonged the line (593) *Persium non curo legere, Laelium Decumum volo*; the gist of a pronouncement made in the same context is preserved in Cicero's well-known paraphrase[1] *neque se ab indoctissimis neque a doctissimis legi velle, quod alteri nihil intellegerent, alteri plus fortasse quam ipse.* Horace borrows from Lucilius the idea of listing desirable and undesirable readers, but he uses it not in a proem but in the epilogue of his book. Lest such an outspoken pronouncement might seem vain or ponderous, Horace makes it arise easily and naturally from a discussion on the risks of hankering after the wrong kind of popularity.

But although the general idea of this catalogue of adversaries and well-wishers was suggested by the proem of Lucilius, its principal function is different and its aim more ambitious. All that Lucilius apparently did was to name the readers, and the type of readers, whom he fancied and to contrast them with those for whom he did not care. This declaration of his choice was, like most of his writing, an entirely personal matter. Horace, on the other hand, takes sides in a struggle between rival literary parties. He ranges himself uncompromisingly with those poets who are endeavouring to overcome the cult of pretty trifles, to outgrow a torpid traditionalism and to produce a poetry treating great and noble themes in a new and purer style. His place is on the side of Virgil, Varius, Asinius Pollio (it is significant that these three poets appear twice, in different contexts, 42–45 and again 81–85),[2] and of all those associated with them. Horace is proud to belong to this circle; without overreaching himself (*haec ego ludo*) he knows that he has contributed and is contributing his proper share to the common

---

[1] *De orat.* 2. 25.

[2] At l. 84 practically all editors, in accordance with the paraphrase of the scholia, begin the new sentence with *ambitione relegata*. Only Heinze removes the full stop after *uterque* (83) and puts it after *relegata*. I think he is right. First, *ambitione relegata* is, among honest people, an all but indispensable qualification when praise (83 *laudet*) is being asked for; there is always a strong suspicion that the praise may be inspired by insincere motives. It is hardly necessary to adduce instances; I will, however, quote Seneca, *Dial.* 10. 15. 2 *habebit . . . a quibus audiat verum sine contumelia, laudetur sine adulatione.* Secondly, and this I regard as decisive, the series of apostrophes from l. 84 on, with the four times repeated pronoun of the second person (as in religious prayers or hymns), becomes far more emphatic if it begins with *te dicere possum.* We are first given the impression that the number of the friends whose approval Horace desires was completed with the list given in ll. 81–83, from Plotius to the two Visci. But then, apparently as an afterthought, he starts afresh: '(in addition, there are many more); you . . . and you . . . and you . . . I can without difficulty name among those whose applause I should like to win'. I have given this clumsy paraphrase to dispose of Reitzenstein's (*Hermes*, lix, 1924, 13) objection to Heinze's punctuation, 'Der Anfang der neuen Reihe mit *te dicere possum* scheint mir zu kahl, das Wort *possum* dabei . . . befremdlich'. At 1. 6. 52 a sentence concludes with (*prava*) *ambitione procul.*

effort. His epilogue goes far beyond a personal confession: it is the manifesto of an advancing force. The new poetry of a new generation has found a voice to express its victorious spirit.

The meaning of *Sat.* 1. 10. 27–30

It would be useless to try to summarize the long and involved dispute about lines 27–30 of this satire. It is a sad story: even scholars of the high rank of Arthur Palmer have gone astray. Heinze's comment ends on a note of despair.[1] Lejay retains, justly, *oblitus*, but remarks on 29 'intermiscere a pour sujet Pedius et Corvinus' although the belief that in a context like this 'facile ad *intermiscere eos* (i.e. Pedium et Corvinum) suppletur' (Orelli–Baiter–Mewes) is not based on fact.[2] I propose to state briefly the points that seem to me to have been settled in the past and then to add a few observations of my own.

By far the most valuable contribution to the interpretation of the passage comes from Bentley. But the giant, as so often, was in a hurry and therefore resorted at one point to a violent expedient when a moment's pause might have enabled him to finish the job.

At 27 Bentley hit the mark by rejecting *latine*. The glorious phrase *oblitus patriaeque patrisque Latini* should really be proof against meddling. If some 'thinking copyist' who (little blame to him!) could not make out the meaning of the following *cum* clause tried to improve things by changing *Latini* into *latine*, that is no reason for us to follow him. As for *pater Latinus*, he is here patently the ἥρως κτίστης of all those who speak Latin.[3] This *pater Latinus* has perhaps more in common with the second partner in the 'Hesiodic' firm of Ἄγριος ἠδὲ Λατῖνος than with the father-in-law of Aeneas.

Bentley has also exposed the nonsense in the paraphrase of the scholia, *an et quando causam durissimam Petilli de furto Capitolino adversus Pedium Publicolam sive adversus Messalam Corvinum peroras?* It was this misinterpretation that induced Heinze to say 'Q. Pedius . . . hat vielleicht gerade durch die Verteidigung des Petillius vorübergehend Aufsehen erregt'. In fact, Pedius and Corvinus have nothing whatsoever to do with the *causa Petilli*, as Bentley saw. He justly insists on the difference between the singular *causa* at 26 and the plural *causas* at 28. The defence in the *cause célèbre* of Petillius is mentioned by way of hypothesis (*cum . . . tibi peragenda . . . sit*) as a first instance of forensic

---

[1] 'aber dabei [i.e. accepting, as he does, Bentley's conjecture *oblitos*] hat der Zwischensatz *cum Pedius* . . . bisher wenigstens eine befriedigende Erklärung nicht gefunden.'

[2] See, for example, the collections in Kühner–Stegmann, i. 700 f.; K. Kühnast, *Die Hauptpunkte der Livianischen Syntax*, 106 ff.; Lebreton, *Études sur la langue et la grammaire de Cicéron*, 376 ff.

[3] J. M. Gesner, following Bentley, paraphrased well 'oblitus originis ab illo rege, cuius et nomen debet commendare linguam' and Kiessling, too, understood this correctly.

oratory; there follows, independently, the example of some unspecified speeches delivered by two of the most famous orators of the time.

But we have not yet solved the problem of the subject of *intermiscere* at 29. Here Bentley spoiled everything by introducing his unfortunate *oblitos* in place of *oblitus*. When we read *patriis intermiscere petita verba foris malis*, both grammar and common sense demand that we should take it to mean 'you would like to mix up . . .'. And 'you' here can be none other than the person with whom Horace is arguing, the man fond of seasoning his mother tongue with Greek phrases. But in what capacity is it that, according to Horace's hypothetical suggestion, his interlocutor might practise the *intermiscere*? Certainly not, as the scholiast in the innocence of his heart assumes, as an opponent of Pedius and Corvinus at the trial of Petillius. That trial is done with at the end of 26. Horace no longer maintains the playful idea that his interlocutor might be thought of as delivering a speech in court, but he still dwells on the problem of the use of Greek words in forensic oratory. He wants to pin down the Græcomaniac and therefore insists: 'so you would prefer, when Pedius and Corvinus toil as counsel, you would prefer to contaminate their native speech with foreign phrases!' You would: as a listener of course. Here as in the whole discussion on Lucilius the function of the interlocutor is that of a critic. Horace pretends to imagine him sitting in the *corona*, when Pedius, and on another occasion Corvinus, deliver their speeches, and at the end observing 'not bad; but I should prefer to have some Greek in it' (that is what the man might say, but Horace, to show the absurdity of such a reaction, uses the word *intermiscere*, which has the connotation of *contaminare*).[1] It is utterly wrong to say that the meaning of the *cum* clause remains obscure unless *exsudet* is supported by *latine*. When the *cum* clause is followed by *patriis intermiscere petita verba foris*, it is inevitable to infer that the *verba* of those two men are *patria*, entirely free from foreign elements. Besides, Messalla Corvinus was famous for his rigid purism, and presumably Pedius, of whom we know nothing, shared that taste. When such men sweat, we may be sure that their perspiration is genuinely Latin and nothing else.

The conclusion which we have reached can be confirmed by an examination of the use of *intermiscere*. The commentators seem to think that it is synonymous with *miscere*, which occurs at the beginning of this section (21). True, *intermiscere* is sometimes used so, but not always. The verb is surprisingly rare.[2] It occurs for the first time in the *Bellum*

---

[1] See below.

[2] When I had realized the bearing of Virg. *Ecl.* 10. 5 on the interpretation of our passage, I asked Dr. Ehlers to let me have all the instances of *intermiscere* contained in the schedules of the *Thesaurus*, and he kindly did so.

Hispaniense, in the description of a battle-scene, 31. 6 *cum clamor esset intermixtus gemitu*. At first one might think it an arbitrary use on the part of this strange and sometimes affected writer,[1] but considering the five passages in which Livy uses the verb in descriptions of battles it does not seem unlikely that some earlier historian should have coined it for such a context (the only other passage in Livy where the verb occurs is the one which I shall quote presently). However that may be, in the passage of the *Bell. Hisp.* the verb is little more than a strong *miscere*. The instance that in time comes next proves particularly interesting, Virg. *Ecl.* 10. 4 f. (addressing Arethusa) *sic tibi cum fluctus subterlabere Sicanos, Doris amara suam non intermisceat undam*. Both the construction and the meaning of the verb correspond exactly to those at *Sat.* 1. 10. 29 f. In either case the *intermiscere* would have the effect that the thing placed in the dative (the sweet waters of Arethusa or the pure *Latinitas*, the *patria verba*, of the speeches) would be contaminated and debased by the thing denoted as the direct object of *intermiscere* (the salt sea or the *verba petita foris*). Similarly we read at Livy 4. 56. 3 *turbam indignorum candidatorum intermiscendo dignis* and at *Dig.* 28. 1. 21. 3 (Ulpian) *nullum actum alienum testamento intermiscere* (in the following sentence, *quod si aliquid pertinens ad testamentum faciat, testamentum non vitiatur*, the verb *vitiare*, 'to make void', is noteworthy in regard to the particular shade of *intermiscere* with which we are concerned).

One final remark. Most scholars are now agreed that at 28 *Poplicola* belongs to *Pedius* and not to *Corvinus*. Münzer, in one of those less fortunate articles of his late period,[2] tried in vain to reverse the position: the ignorant concoction of [Virgil] *Catal.* 9. 40 must not be used as evidence.[3]

---

[1] For a good assessment of his style see A. Klotz in the introduction to his commentary (1927), 7 f.

[2] *RE* xix. 40. 67; cf. p. 86 n. 2 above.

[3] See T. Birt, *Erklärung des Catalepton* (1910), 92 f. Hanslik, *RE* viii. A. 131. 25 f., follows Münzer.

IV

BOOK II OF THE SATIRES

I. PRELIMINARY REMARKS

WE do not know at what date Horace completed the first book of his *sermones* nor is it possible to say how much time elapsed between the publication of Book I and the writing of the earliest of those satires which eventually were published as Book II. It is, however, obvious that Horace, when he started again, had made up his mind on some points of principle. On the one hand he maintained the continuity of his work by still writing satires *Lucili ritu* (2. 1. 29), of course in the more refined style suitable to the new age; on the other hand, he introduced a considerable change by presenting his new satires, all but one, in the form of dialogues. He seems to have felt that to carry on exactly the same form as in the first book might prove tiresome to the reader. The structure of the dialogues shows great skill; the characters of the interlocutors are carefully chosen, and some of the introductory sentences are meant to recall passages in famous dialogues of Plato. At 2. 4. 1 it is not sufficient to compare *Unde et quo Catius?* with phrases used at the beginning of certain Platonic dialogues. The answer of Catius,

> non est mihi tempus, aventi
> ponere signa novis praeceptis, qualia vincent
> Pythagoran Anytique reum doctumque Platona,

should make it clear that this whole passage is an elegant transformation of the beginning of the *Phaedrus*, Ὦ φίλε Φαῖδρε, ποῖ δὴ καὶ πόθεν; . . . (228 b) εἰς περίπατον ᾖει . . . ἐξεπιστάμενος τὸν λόγον . . . ἐπορεύετο δ' ἐκτὸς τείχους ἵνα μελετῴη. ἀπαντήσας δέ τῳ νοσοῦντι περὶ λόγων ἀκοήν κτλ. In the second satire of this book the announcement of the theme in the first line is followed by a parenthesis,

> nec meus hic sermo est, sed quae praecepit Ofellus . . .,

echoing the beginning of Eryximachus' speech in the *Symposion* (177 a), οὐ γὰρ ἐμὸς ὁ μῦθος, ἀλλὰ Φαίδρου τοῦδε, ὃν μέλλω λέγειν.[1] Finally, it

---

[1] Quoted by Heindorf. Several commentators assume that Horace had in mind not the passage in Plato but the lines of Euripides (*fr.* 484 N.²) to which Plato alludes. That seems to me unlikely in this dialogic satire. As far as I can see, it has not been noticed (not even by Reitzenstein, *Nachr. Gött. Ges.*, Phil.-hist. Kl. 1914, 207 f.) that a tactful adaptation of the beginning of the *Symposion* is found in the opening scene of a famous

seems to me very likely that the opening dialogue of the eighth satire is intended to strike Maecenas and other educated readers as a playful adaptation of the beginning of the *Timaeus*. There, of course, yesterday's ἐστίασις of the δαιτυμόνες did not, as in the satire, consist in a material feast, but in a discussion περὶ πολιτείας. But this difference cannot conceal the fundamental similarity of the invention, and Horace's words (4 f.) *da, si grave non est, quae prima iratum ventrem placaverit esca* show a witty παρῳδεῖν of *Tim.* 17 b εἰ μή τί σοι χαλεπόν, ἐξ ἀρχῆς . . . πάλιν ἐπάνελθε αὐτά.

Another formal refinement is to be seen in the unmistakable parallelism between the two sermons jokingly delivered at the Saturnalia, Satires III and VII, and again between the two satires which might be given the motto δεῖπνά μοι ἔννεπε, Μοῦσα, IV and VIII. It is, perhaps, more doubtful whether, as was suggested by Boll,[1] an intentional parallelism exists also between the consultation of Trebatius, I, and the consultation of Tiresias, V, and still more doubtful whether the reader is supposed to look on Satire II as a parallel to VI, in so far as the Ofellus satire might just be taken to be what *Hoc erat in votis* indubitably is, a glorification of the self-sufficient life in the country. Yet even if we reserve judgement on the completeness of the parallelism, we may admit that the division of the book into two roughly symmetrical parts is marked by several corresponding features in the first and in the second half.[2]

But the fact that Satire VII varies the theme of III and Satire VIII varies the theme of IV has still another significance. We can hardly avoid the conclusion that Horace, as he went on writing *sermones*, began to run short of suitable subjects and settings. Possibly it was for the same reason that in this second book he contented himself with eight poems instead of attaining the ideal number of ten.[3] Unlike many writers, satirists and others, Horace was wise enough not to continue his work to the point where it would have to be done *invita Minerva*. But even so the second book of his *sermones*, while containing

Latin work : compare Tacitus *Dial.*, beginning of chapter 2, *nam postero die quam Curiatius Maternus Catonem* (a tragedy) *recitaverat . . . venerunt ad eum M. Aper et Iulius Secundus* with *Symp.* 173 a ὅτε τῇ πρώτῃ τραγῳδίᾳ ἐνίκησεν Ἀγάθων, τῇ ὑστεραίᾳ ᾗ τὰ ἐπινίκια ἔθυεν κτλ., and compare the preceding words παίδων ὄντων ἡμῶν ἔτι with the much discussed expression in *Dial.* 1 *iuvenis admodum audivi*. The action of the *Dial.* takes place in the house of the tragic poet Maternus precisely as the action of the *Symp.* takes place in the house of Agathon.

[1] *Hermes*, xlviii, 1913, 143 ff.

[2] I do not know whether Boll's thesis can be strengthened by the observation that the second half of the book (5. 1) begins with *Hoc quoque* as the second half of the *Georgics* begins with *Te quoque* and the second half of the *Aeneid* with *Tu quoque*, or whether that is purely accidental. The second of the three books of Ovid's *Amores* begins with *Hoc quoque composui*.

[3] See p. 112 above.

some masterpieces and proving throughout a model of resourcefulness
and balanced execution, shows in more than one place signs of strain.

2. SATIRE VI

Within the limits set to a general survey of the work of Horace it is
not possible, nor does it seem necessary, to discuss separately every
satire of Book II. Instead I propose to concentrate on Satires VI and I,
and to add a few observations on the rest.

The beginning of the sixth satire is magnificent without being heavy.
The first few words, *Hoc erat in votis*, are a solemn expression of thanksgiving, as if the poet were saying *hoc modo nunc voti compos factus* (or
damnatus) *sum*.[1] After the initial clause solemnity gives way to a homely
note in the brief account of the typical features of a smallish farm such
as Horace had been praying for:

> modus agri non ita magnus,
> hortus ubi et tecto vicinus iugis aquae fons
> et paulum silvae super his foret.[2]

The fulfilment, he adds with noticeable emphasis, has gone beyond his
wishes: *auctius atque di melius fecere. bene est.* Then, turning to Hermes
$\kappa\epsilon\rho\delta\hat{\omega}os$,[3] he prays, not for further gain, but for an undisturbed and
sensible enjoyment of the blessings he has already been given:

> nil amplius oro,
> Maia nate, nisi ut propria haec mihi munera faxis.

Such a prayer, aiming at $\tau\hat{\omega}\nu\ \check{o}\nu\tau\omega\nu\ \nu\hat{\upsilon}\nu\ \dot{a}\gamma a\theta\hat{\omega}\nu\ \check{o}\nu\eta\sigma\iota\nu$, befits the religious
man and the sage alike. A sketch of its history in Greek and Roman
worship has been given elsewhere;[4] here, in connexion with Horace,
who on another occasion prays to Apollo[5] *frui paratis . . . mihi, Latoe,*

---

[1] Is perhaps *hoc erat in votis* an echo of a set phrase which was used when someone, in
thanking a deity, said that the wishes which he had uttered when making his vow were
now fulfilled? There is a strangely similar passage in Virg. *Aen.* 12. 259, where the augur
Tolumnius says *hoc erat, hoc, votis . . . quod saepe petivi.*

[2] After mentioning field, garden, and house Horace says that 'moreover' (*super his*, for
linguistic illustration see Lejay) he had hoped for 'un po' di bosco' (Pasquali, *Or. lir.* 76).
This is how most scholars have understood the passage. A local meaning of *super his* (so
Kiessling, followed by Heinze) would be out of place here.

[3] Cf. p. 141 below.

[4] See my commentary on A. *Ag.* 350; add Dittenberger, *Sylloge*, 3rd ed., no. 1219 (third
cent. B.C.),20 ff. $\dot{\epsilon}\pi\epsilon\dot{\upsilon}\chi\epsilon\sigma\theta a\iota\ \tau o\hat{\iota}s\ \dot{\epsilon}\mu\mu\dot{\epsilon}\nu o\upsilon\sigma\iota\nu\ \ldots\ \epsilon\hat{\upsilon}\ \epsilon\hat{\iota}\nu a\iota\ \kappa a\dot{\iota}\ \tau\hat{\omega}\nu\ \dot{\upsilon}\pi a\rho\chi\acute{o}\nu\tau\omega\nu\ \dot{a}\gamma a\theta\hat{\omega}\nu\ \check{o}\nu\eta\sigma\iota\nu$,
[Arist.] *Rhet. ad Alexandr.* 3. 1. 1420^{b} 9 $\kappa a\dot{\iota}\ \tau\hat{\omega}\nu\ \dot{\upsilon}\pi a\rho\chi\acute{o}\nu\tau\omega\nu\ \dot{a}\gamma a\theta\hat{\omega}\nu\ \check{o}\nu\eta\sigma\iota\nu\ \check{\epsilon}\sigma\chi o\mu\epsilon\nu$, Hippo-
damus π. $\epsilon\dot{\upsilon}\delta a\iota\mu o\nu\dot{\iota}as$ ap. Stob. 103. 26, vol. v, p. 911, 16 ff. Hense, $o\dot{\upsilon}\ \gamma\dot{a}\rho\ \mu\acute{o}\nu o\nu\ \tau\dot{a}\nu\ \kappa\tau\hat{a}\sigma\iota\nu$
$\check{\epsilon}\chi\epsilon\nu\ \delta\epsilon\hat{\iota}\ \tau\hat{\omega}\nu\ \kappa a\lambda\hat{\omega}\nu,\ \dot{a}\lambda\lambda\dot{a}\ \kappa a\dot{\iota}\ \tau\dot{a}\nu\ \check{o}\nu a\sigma\iota\nu$; Plutarch, *Mor.* 1101 d $\pi\hat{a}\sigma a\nu\ \epsilon\dot{\upsilon}\pi\rho a\xi\dot{\iota}as\ \check{o}\nu\eta\sigma\iota\nu,\ \dot{\omega}s$
$\dot{\epsilon}\kappa\ \theta\epsilon\hat{\omega}\nu\ o\dot{\upsilon}\sigma a\nu,\ \epsilon\dot{\upsilon}\chi\acute{o}\mu\epsilon\nu o\nu\ \kappa a\dot{\iota}\ \delta\epsilon\chi\acute{o}\mu\epsilon\nu o\nu$; Terence, *Eun.* 1048 f. (Menander) *o Iuppiter, serva*
obsecro haec bona nobis; Cic. *Att.* 4. 18. 5 *si etiam sapis ac frui tuis commodis cogitas.*

[5] *Odes* 1. 31. 17 f.

dones and makes several utterances of a similar kind, it will suffice to mention the *ipsa verba* of Augustus,[1] *compos factus votorum meorum, patres conscripti, quid habeo aliud deos immortales precari quam ut hunc consensum vestrum ad ultimum finem vitae mihi perferre liceat ?* From these words we learn also the important fact that in the satire *nil amplius oro* . . . is the organic continuation of *hoc erat in votis* (*compos factus votorum meorum* as Augustus says), and that the statement *modus agri* . . . *bene est* is inserted by way of illustration. The thought of the introductory words of Horace's invocation of Mercury, *nil amplius oro*, is confirmed by the following ten lines of the elaborate prayer (6–15), which, after repeating the initial idea (13 *si quod adest gratum iuvat*), culminates in the sentence *hac prece te oro: pingue pecus domino facias et cetera praeter ingenium*, a sentence neither more nor less serious than the warning given by Apollo to Virgil[2] *pastorem, Tityre, pinguis pascere oportet ovis, deductum dicere carmen.*

The first sentence in which Horace formulates his claim to the god's benevolence deserves a brief comment. He says (6 ff.)

> si neque maiorem feci ratione mala rem
> nec sum facturus vitio culpave minorem
>
> .   .   .   .
>
> .   . si quod adest gratum iuvat . . ..

At 2. 3. 176 ff. a wealthy landowner on his death-bed implores his two sons, one of whom is a spendthrift, the other a miser:

> quare per divos oratus uterque Penatis,
> tu cave ne minuas, tu ne maius facias id
> quod satis esse putat pater et natura coercet.

According to the convictions of a man like Horace, the same behaviour is dictated alike by the rules of sound economy, by moral decency, by the limitations of human nature, and by the wisdom pleasing to the gods whoever they be.

After the conclusion of the prayer to Mercury Horace enters on his proper theme at 16, *ergo ubi me in montes . . . removi*.[3] This section opens with another prayer, adorned by a lofty invocation after the well-known fashion,[4] 20 *Matutine pater, seu Iane libentius audis*.[5] It does not seem to have been noticed that the tone of the question at 17, *quid*

---

[1] Suet. *Aug.* 58. 2, taken from the records of the Senate.

[2] *Ecl.* 6. 4 f.

[3] Editors of ancient poetry are on the whole strangely reluctant to assist the reader in his task by using indentation, which was invented for the purpose. Here at least Wieland, Vollmer, Ramorino, Lejay, and perhaps others as well, have marked the fresh start at 16.

[4] Cf. E. Norden, *Agnostos Theos*, 144 ff.

[5] For the solemn ring of the archaizing *unde* (= *a quo*) at the beginning of the next line see p. 102 n. 2 above.

prius inlustrem saturis musaque pedestri ?, is in harmony with the exalted prayer that follows. In that prayer Heinze observed the unparalleled use of *carmen* (22) when the work in question is one of the *sermones*. It is to this momentary elevating of the present poem to a higher level, the level of a *carmen*, of lyric, that the question *quid prius*[1] *inlustrem ?* forms a prelude. *Pindarus novemque lyrici* were familiar to Horace long before he embarked on writing lyrics himself. He will have remembered the beginning of hymns such as Pindar *fr.* 89 a[2] Τί κάλλιον ἀρχομένοις . . . ἢ βαθύζωνόν τε Λατὼ καὶ θοᾶν ἵππων ἐλάτειραν ἀεῖσαι; It is certainly no mere coincidence that in Horace's strongly Pindarizing ode i. 12 one of the quasi-triads[3] begins (13) *quid prius dicam solitis parentis laudibus.* Up to the clause (22 f.) *tu carminis esto principium* the gravity of religious language is maintained, but immediately afterwards the prayer turns almost imperceptibly into a description of Horace's harassed life in Rome. With a few more words addressed to Matutinus, *Romae sponsorem me rapis*, the god is dismissed.

What is the meaning of these invocations of two deities? We need not trouble about the jocular apostrophe to *Matutinus pater*, the patron of the early morning's business; but what are we to think of the apparently serious prayer to Mercury? Wieland, a sensitive poet and scholar, but not, of course, free from certain tendencies of the eighteenth century, discusses the point in his very fine introduction to this satire. He states in general that 'the noble convictions which make this poem so interesting' are not hypocritical, but express Horace's true feelings and are 'indelible features of his character'. However, as the honest commentator he is he feels bound to make one reservation though he expresses himself with great caution:[4] he finds it hard to believe in the sincerity 'of the devout (*andächtige*) apostrophe to Mercury, 4–15'. Wieland thinks that 'in these professions of traditional Roman orthodoxy Horace's prudence had a greater share than his mind and heart. For the Sabine peasants it was necessary above all to quench the prejudices which people, not without reason, might have conceived against Horace's piety.' We need not dwell on this assumption, which is part and parcel of the strange idea that this satire was written 'to give pleasure to the good people his neighbours [at his Sabine farm]'.[5] But the problem raised by Wieland is a real one. If Horace expected his favourite readers, Maecenas and his other friends, to take this prayer to Mercury as the manifestation of a belief in the god as his personal benefactor, he would indeed be guilty of hypocrisy. It is,

---

[1] In the sense of *potius* (Heinze). Cf., for instance, *Epist.* I. I. 88.
[2] 80 Bowra. [3] Cf. p. 293 n. 2 below.
[4] 'Die einzige Ausnahme, die vielleicht zu machen ist, möchte wohl', etc.
[5] 'Seinen wackern Nachbarn zu gefallen' (first section of Wieland's introduction).

however, safe to assume that he relied on the sympathetic understanding of those enlightened men whom he knew to be capable of
seeing the difference between the feelings that lay behind his prayer
and the form in which he expressed them. With the possession of his
Sabine farm his old wishes had been fulfilled; he felt happy and thank-
ful, and his sense of discretion, strengthened by reflections on human
life, taught him not to desire more, but to enjoy what he had received
in such a manner as befitted a man of his convictions. He knew also
how precarious all such blessings are. Why should he not address the
expression of his gratitude to the god, why not ask the god to help him
to maintain true wisdom and *frui paratis*? If, as an individual, he no
longer believed in a son of Zeus whose business it was to function as
κερδῷος, Horace was poet enough to adopt and transform the hopes,
the fears, and even the prayers of bygone generations. To speak as an
interpreting poet is one thing, to speak as a hypocrite another.[1]
Neither the opening prayer to Mercury nor the manifestation of old-
fashioned religiosity at the centre of the satire should be dismissed as
mere make-believe. The happy tone of the latter lines (65 ff.),

> o noctes cenaeque deum, quibus ipse meique
> ante Larem proprium vescor vernasque procacis
> pasco libatis dapibus,

warrants their sincerity, and the man who joins in the peasants'
homely ritual in such a mood is no liar, whatever his philosophical
convictions may be.

The workaday language, which at once conveys the feeling of the
early morning's rush (23 f.),

> Romae sponsorem me rapis: 'eia,
> ne prior officio quisquam respondeat, urge',

is interrupted by a sentence in an entirely different style. Instead of
simply saying 'whatever the weather and the season', Horace speaks
inflatis buccis, using the hackneyed phraseology of epic poetry,

> sive aquilo radit terras seu bruma nivalem
> interiore diem gyro trahit, ire necesse est,

and thereby mocking his own misery. After this brief ascent into a
higher sphere the language returns to the level of the streets of Rome,
whose conflicting noises and multitudinous chatter will surround us
until Horace's nostalgic imagination removes us to the quiet of his
Sabine farm.

---

[1] Perhaps the reader may care to take these remarks together with those on the Mercury
ode, i. 10, pp. 163 ff. below.

If we want to do full justice to this most accomplished of all Horatian
satires, we must be careful not to upset the perfect balance of its two
halves by regarding the first part, the description of Horace's life in
town, as a mere preparation, or foil, for the second part. No doubt his
heart belongs to his farm and to the people there, but it is with no
less faithfulness and intensity that he describes the routine of his life
in the capital. We hear the deafening noise around him and feel the
heavy pressure of the traffic as he desperately elbows his way to the
height of the Esquiline. We see his face fall when, far too often, there
emerges out of the crowd a person whom he knows or is supposed to
know and who will importune him with some nonsense or with a piece
of tiresome business. The voices bits of which we catch are as varied as
they would be in actual life. There is the acquaintance (at any rate he
knows Horace and knows that he is going to the house of Maecenas),
whom the poet in his hurry has been pushing and who, not unnaturally
annoyed, does not mince his words (29), *quid tibi vis, insane, et quam rem
agis improbus ?* And at the other end of the scale we hear that nuisance,
the cringing sensation-monger, who uses fulsome language (51 ff.), *o
bone, nam te scire, deos quoniam propius contingis, oportet, numquid de Dacis
audisti ?* Anxious though Horace is to hurry on, he is suddenly way-
laid by a slave with a message from his master, who asks Horace to support him in court on the following day (34 f.); a moment later a
colleague, a member of Horace's *decuria scribarum*, reminds him that
to-day his fellow officials are having a meeting of the very greatest
importance, which Horace must attend at all costs (36 f.); no sooner
has he shaken this man off than he is again stopped, this time by an
individual who presses into his hands a document to which he wants
Maecenas to attach his seal (38). So it goes on and on; the whole day
is being squandered away (59).[1] Oh, he groans, when shall I be back
at my farm in the cool valley of the Digentia? (60).

And yet Rome is to Horace by no means all unpleasantness and
worry. While he is sighing so movingly, his face is all the time lit up
by a faint yet unmistakable smile. There is no denying it: Horace does
enjoy being such a well-known figure, watched whenever he is seen in
the company of Maecenas, and pestered by an envious crowd when he
is on his way to the great man. Not in vain does Maecenas occupy such
a large space in this picture of Horace's days in Rome.[2] The poet's life
is indissolubly linked up with the life of his patron. We shall see how
consciously Horace at this stage uses his *sermones* as a means of self-
portraiture, and without the presence of Maecenas the picture of his
own life would be incomplete. But in the context of this satire the

[1] In defence of the much-attacked *perditur* I have nothing to add to Heinze's note.
[2] 31, 38, 41–48.

prominence allotted to Maecenas fulfils still another function. Horace's gratitude for the blessings he had received and his determination to be contented with them were at the beginning of the poem voiced in terms of prayer and were addressed to a deity. There the man who was the immediate cause of those blessings was not even hinted at. But when the poet goes on to describe his daily life, a life which, with all its restlessness and its *aliena negotia centum*, remains a rich and happy one, Maecenas comes into his own. Through Horace's comically exaggerated display of his various discomforts there shines his delight at being so near to the friend whose trust he will not betray by boasting of his privileges to envious fools. But the full measure of Horace's gratitude is not indicated until the second part of the satire (from 60 on). In the picture of his life at his farm nothing points any longer to the person of Maecenas, but Maecenas will have understood that this picture of the simple and self-contained happiness of which he had been the instrument was the deepest manifestation of Horace's thankfulness.

The tale of the two mice with which the satire concludes is one of the best-known and most-admired pieces of Roman poetry; there is therefore no need to praise it again. Suffice it to say that of all the αἶνοι with which the *sermones* of Horace are interspersed[1] this fable is for liveliness of the whole and delicacy of the detail second only to the story of Volteius Mena at the end of the seventh epistle. The prestissimo account of the catastrophe that brings the little feast to a sudden end (111–15) reminds us of the brilliant finale of Horace's earliest satire (1. 2. 127–33), but we notice here, without any loss of energy, the restraint of a mellower art.

Horace does not, as he does in dealing with his routine in town, describe a day of his actual life on his farm. What he does give is a vision of his *Sabinum* as it arises in a day-dream amidst his hectic occupations in Rome. It is therefore the more natural that he should idealize what he is longing for. No sensible reader will be tempted to believe that peasants in the region of Vicovaro, whether *sotto il buono Augusto* or in any other age, would talk as if they had perused Cicero's *De finibus bonorum et malorum* or some similar books (72–76). The poet is no photographer, he remains a poet even in his *sermo pedester*. On the other hand, the convictions and meditations with

---

[1] Cf. Quintilian, *Inst.* 5. 11. 19 f. (he was aware of the use Horace made of αἶνοι). It is rewarding to study the many αἶνοι in *Sat.* ii. 3 (as it seems to me, the best element in it). There is in them an admirable variation of themes as well as of style. Anecdotes from everyday life in Italy, the Roman theatre, society gossip, Greek tragedy, Graeco-Roman comedy, the Lives of the philosophers have contributed to them, and the presentation is always fresh, the introductions and conclusions are witty, sometimes surprising, and never repetitious.

which Horace here credits the countryfolk are not unnatural in the
sense in which the sweet sentimentalities of the Arcadian shepherds in
the poetry of the late Renaissance and after must be called unnatural.
Solid honesty, combined, perhaps, with a good deal of shrewdness, and
steadfast principles are indeed at home in those humble cottages, where
one spurns the sophistication and the idle talk of the townspeople. The
form in which Horace makes his rustic friends talk about the things
which they hold most precious is a form lent to them by the poet, but
the substance of their talk and the scale of values which is manifested in
their meditations are their own.

Finally, it appears that the man who in this late satire laid such
stress on the ideas outlined in a few weighty sentences (72–76) was
ready to write sometime *sermones* of a different kind.

3. THIS BOOK AS A WHOLE

Perhaps it is unfair to judge the rest of the second book by the
standard of the uncommonly happy sixth satire, but if we apply this
standard we shall find that the seven other satires, with the exception of
the quite different introductory one, fall short of it. All of them show
perfect polish and none is devoid of splendid passages, but, viewed as a
whole, they too often betray the writer's effort, worst of all the third,
which, for all its glittering ornament, looks like a prolonged *tour de
force*. However, the eighth satire, though its theme does not provide the
poet with an opportunity of showing himself at his best, is yet a very
pretty divertissement. One has only to read the long excerpts[1] from the
δειπνητικαὶ ἐπιστολαί of the Macedonian Hippolochus (end of the
fourth, beginning of the third century B.C.) to appreciate what Horace
has made of a subject that can be so terribly boring.

The particular character of the fifth satire is easy to discern. It is
significant that the early-nineteenth-century scholar K. G. Zumpt
and the twentieth-century scholar Hugh Last agree almost verbatim
in their description of it. The former calls it 'one of the most vigorous
satires, which corresponds more than all the others to the idea of this
type of poetry',[2] and the latter speaks of it as 'the most satirical of his
[Horace's] *Satires*'.[3] To both these eminent historians the word satirical
has, or ought to have, only one meaning, namely, consistent with the
manner of Juvenal.[4] What they had in mind was distinctly formulated

---

[1] Athenaeus 4. 128 c–130 d.
[2] 'Eine der kräftigsten Satiren, die mehr als alle andern dem Begriffe dieser Dichtungs-
art entspricht, ist II, 5', Zumpt in his article 'Über das Leben des Horaz . . .', published
in Wüstemann's re-edition of Heindorf's commentary on the *Satires*, 1843, 33.
[3] *Cambr. Anc. Hist.* x. 438.
[4] This interpretation of 'satirical' is widely accepted. It underlies, for instance, Matthew

by W. Y. Sellar: 'If Juvenal recognised any affinity between his own invective and the "Venusina lucerna", it must have been with the spirit of this Satire [ii. 5] that he found himself in sympathy.'[1] These judgements are perfectly adequate. Unlike Horace's finest satires, *Hoc quoque, Tiresia* is no mirror of the poet's own βίος, nor does it aim at giving a picture of some part of human life in general. It is a caricature, full of vigour and brilliant wit, but acid and cynical throughout. Its lurid colours are not affected by the sunshine or by Jupiter's clouds; its speaker comes from the nether world, and when he bids us farewell, *sed me imperiosa trahit Proserpina: vive valeque*, we are not sorry to see him go. Had Horace followed this track still farther, he might have been in danger of changing from the pugnacious yet good-natured *Venusinus* into a venomous *Aquinas*. Being Horace, he checked himself, and when he realized that the natural stream of his *sermones* had ceased to flow, he abandoned the writing of such poems.

4. SATIRE I

Among the many Roman jurists whose names figure in the Emperor Justinian's vast compilation,[2] there is only one of whose personality we really know something, C. Trebatius Testa. This exceptional position he owes to the fact that he was on terms of friendship with two of the friendliest of friends, both great artists and capable of conveying an idea of another man's individuality, Cicero and Horace. Cicero's letters to him are perhaps the most enchanting pieces that we possess from the pen of that unsurpassed letter-writer. Their ease and happiness[3] seem to be partly due to the personal charm of the addressee. Most of these letters date from the years 54 and 53 B.C. At that time Trebatius already showed great promise as a lawyer;[4] and altogether he appears as an amiable, if rather temperamental, young man.

Arnold's assertion (*Essays in Criticism*, new ed., 1884, 84) that Pope's 'satirical power was certainly greater' than that of Horace.

[1] *Horace and the Elegiac Poets*, 2nd ed., 70. He adds 'and perhaps the second of Book I', but there the similarity is only on the surface.

[2] The *Digest* informs us about the views held by Trebatius on many controversial problems, but no direct quotation from any of his writings is preserved. Cf. O. Lenel, *Palingenesia iuris civilis*, ii. 343–52.

[3] Only one letter, *Fam.* vii. 17, is written in an entirely different style; to see that, one has only to observe the majestic folds of its sentence structure. On this occasion Cicero finds it necessary seriously to lecture his young friend. Not until the last three sentences (from *hoc, quemadmodum vos scribere soletis in vestris libris*) does he resume his habitual light tone.

[4] I think, however, that, before inferring too much from the passage in the letter by which Cicero recommends Trebatius to Caesar, *Fam.* 7. 5. 3, *accedit etiam quod familiam ducit* (for the meaning of this expression see Sonnet, *RE* vi. A. 2252 f.) *in iure civili singulari memoria, summa scientia*, some allowance should be made for the jocular tone of the letter.

Cicero has often to treat him like a spoilt child, but he never tires in his care for his young friend, who seems to have chosen him as his mentor. 'Avec ce jeune homme obscur, pour lequel il avait une si vive affection, Cicéron se mettait à l'aise. Il osait rire librement, ce qui ne lui arrivait pas avec tout le monde, et il riait d'autant plus volontiers qu'il le savait triste et qu'il désirait le consoler.'[1] Cicero's enthusiasm for Trebatius remained unimpaired; in the summer of 44 B.C., in which he dedicated to him his *Topica*, he wrote to him[2] *amabilior mihi Velia fuit, quod te ab ea sensi amari: sed quid ego dicam te, quem quis non amat?*

The relationship which arose many years after the death of Cicero between Trebatius and the much younger Horace was very different from that between Trebatius and the great consular, more than twenty years his senior. A scholar who has carefully examined the evidence for the life and personality of Trebatius warns us not to conclude from Horace's satire that there existed between the two men an intimate friendship.[3] On the other hand, it is clear that there was between them far more than a nodding acquaintance. Horace, whose discretion in matters of social intercourse we know, would never have invented a talk with Trebatius in such familiar if respectful terms unless he was sure that the famous jurist really cared for him, liked his wit and his writings, and would be very pleased with the compliment of being chosen to usher in Horace's book. There may have come into play also an accessory factor. The birthplace of Trebatius was in all probability Velia in Lucania.[4] Now when Horace says (34 f.) *sequor hunc* (i.e. Lucilius), *Lucanus an Apulus anceps: nam Venusinus arat finem sub utrumque colonus . . .*, it seems not unlikely that one of his motives for stressing this point was his wish to suggest to Trebatius that he, Horace, considered himself his friend's *conterraneus*.[5] Nor is it far-fetched to assume that, when in the house of some friend in Rome Horace was first introduced to the eminent lawyer, not only personal sympathy but also the fact that they both came from the same part of Italy drew the two southerners together. Such regional ties have always been and still are very strong with the people of Italy. But however that may be, Horace must have known Trebatius well and have sincerely liked and trusted him. There is no formality in this satire, no constraint whatsoever. Despite the difference in age and social status, Horace is as much at ease in turning to Trebatius as was Cicero. The σπουδογέλοιον

---

[1] Gaston Boissier, *Cicéron et ses amis*, 16th ed., 1912, 247.

[2] *Fam.* 7. 20. 1.

[3] Sonnet, *RE* vi. A. 2258 f. The difference between the Roman conception of *amicitia* and its counterpart in modern society has also to be borne in mind.

[4] See Sonnet, op. cit. 2254.

[5] For the meaning of this word see not the rendering in the *Thesaurus* but Mommsen, *Hermes* iii, 1869, 61 f. (*Ges. Schriften*, iv. 396).

of the tone, too, is very similar in both cases. Trebatius seems to have belonged to the happy race of profoundly amiable men who, whether actually present or merely thought of, make everybody feel cheerful. Horace pictures Trebatius as a great, and, as befits a *iureconsultus*, slightly terrifying authority in his own profession, but he also slips in a hint, obviously from personal acquaintance, at his passion for swimming in the river.[1]

The dialogue in this latest of Horace's satires owes some of its grace to the blending of two different elements: the advice given by Trebatius stresses at the end the legal point of view (80 ff.) and once or twice uses juridical or quasi-juridical language,[2] but on the whole its substance is common sense and discretion based on a rich experience of human life. A discussion of the moral issues involved in the publication of satires, with an occasional glance at possible legal consequences, suited Horace's purpose to perfection. We have seen[3] that the fourth satire of Book I was a vindication of his *satura* from both the artistic and the moral point of view, but that there the moral aspect prevailed. In the tenth satire the moral problem was not raised at all: there the discussion was solely concerned with the stylistic requirements with which the *satura* as well as any poem worthy of the new age would have to comply. Finally, in ii. 1, Horace deals almost exclusively with the moral justification of his satires, or, to put it differently, with their contents; only in passing (2 ff. *sine nervis*[4] *altera quidquid composui pars esse putat similisque meorum mille die versus deduci posse*) does he mention the unfavourable criticism which their style has met with in certain quarters. The reasons that induced Horace to insist here on the defence of his matter rather than his form cannot be guessed with certainty. Book I may have been criticized because of some of its invectives, although this does not seem very likely since Horace had hardly attacked persons of any consequence. Or perhaps after having firmly established the style of his genre, he may no longer have found it necessary to defend its form. What I myself think most probable is that he was anxious, on abandoning the writing of satires, to give a final account of

---

[1] On 7 f., *ter uncti transnanto Tiberim*, the commentators have duly referred to Cic. *Fam.* 7. 10. 2 *studiosissimus homo natandi* (i.e. Trebatius).

[2] See the commentaries on 6, *aio*, and on the imperatives in -*nto* (8 f.), where the scholia notice the *verba iuris*. (Cf. also in the *edictum* [855] of Ballio, Plaut. *Pseud.* 858 ff., the imperatives *spectato, progredimino, proferto, sinito, teneto*.) In the clause at 7 f., *ter uncti transnanto Tiberim*, Kiessling finds also an allusion to the language of medical prescriptions. That is not unlikely, especially in view of Trebatius' words at 60 f., *o puer, ut sis vitalis metuo*, which seem to echo a phrase used by physicians or midwives. Cf. Varro, *De vita pop. Rom.*, *fr.* 82 b Riposati (Serv. Dan. in Virg. *Aen.* 10. 76) *dum exploretur an vitalis sit qui natus est*. Cf. the corresponding use of ζώσιμος. [3] pp. 126 f. above.

[4] In addition to the parallels quoted in the commentaries compare, for example, Cic. *Orat.* 91 *hoc in genere nervorum vel minimum*; *Brut.* 177 *lenitas eius* (Caesar Strabo Vopiscus) *sine nervis*; Tac. *Dial.* 18. 5 *Ciceronem a Calvo ... male audisse tamquam solutum et enervem*.

what he now regarded as their proper subject and to define the spirit in which he thought they ought to be written. With this important end in mind, he would not divert the reader's attention to formal issues.

In this introductory poem Horace is at pains to make it clear that Book II, despite some changes in the form of its satires, belongs closely together with Book I. So the backbone of this satire, the discussion about Lucilius, is an amplification and, as we shall see, also a correction of what in the fourth and the tenth satire of Book I had been said about that poet. Of details meant to link together the two books I will mention two. At l. 22 the verse *Sat.* 1. 8. 11 is quoted, of course in the usual manner of a free adaptation.[1] At l. 48 Canidia is mentioned. She has no special importance here: any other *venefica* or sorceress would do. The real purpose of the reference to her is to remind the reader of her role in Book I, and it is for the same reason that her name reappears in the very last line of Book II.

Since Horace is consulting a lawyer, he begins

> Sunt quibus in satura videor nimis acer et ultra
> legem tendere opus,

with an ambiguous reference to 'the law', which may be either some part of the common law, especially that against libel, or the *lex saturae*, the sum of rules valid for this particular type of literature.[2] To the poet's polite request, *Trebati, quid faciam praescribe*, the jurist replies curtly *quiescas*.[3] Horace's desperate rejoinder, almost an outcry, *ne faciam, inquis, omnino versus?*, is answered in still sterner fashion: *aio*. Not even the pathetic admission (6 f.) *peream male si non optimum erat: verum nequeo dormire* seems to move the unsentimental lawyer: he merely doles out an ironical prescription against insomnia. But after inflicting these stings Trebatius changes his tone and begins to take his friend's predicament seriously (10 ff.):

> aut si tantus amor scribendi te rapit, aude
> Caesaris invicti res dicere, multa laborum
> praemia laturus.

At first sight this may look like a purely subsidiary topic, an expedient suggested by Trebatius in his attempt to dissuade Horace by all means from writing any more satires. But if that is a reader's impression, he will soon correct it, for the theme of the *laudes Caesaris* is pursued at

---

[1] See Jachmann, *Studi in onore di U. E. Paoli*, Florence 1955, 393.

[2] The commentaries quote *Ars P.* 135 *operis lex*. Compare also Juvenal 7. 102 *operum* (i.e. historiarum) *lex*. R. Hirzel, *Themis, Dike und Verwandtes*, 381, n. 4 and n. 5, quotes passages where νόμος or *lex* is used of metrical laws, and from Josephus and others ὁ τῆς ἱστορίας νόμος and the like.

[3] Cf. Cicero *Qu. Fr.* 2. 13 (12), 1, written in May 54, 'if my work on the *De re publica* does not succeed', *aggrediemur alia, quoniam quiescere non possumus.*

considerable length (10–20), and the extraordinary subtlety in the execution of this section clearly indicates Horace's serious concern. Towards the end of this satire Horace, driven to self-defence by the lawyer's wry implication that his writings belonged to the class of *mala carmina*,[1] reveals that Caesar had made known his approval of some of Horace's satires. Whether by that time the two men had met we do not know. But it was inevitable that, given the sympathetic interest which Rome's first citizen had shown in the work of the promising young poet, some of Horace's well-wishers who were in close contact with Caesar should have suggested to the poet the writing of an epic to glorify Caesar's achievements. About the same time Virgil had to ward off a similar suggestion.[2] The nature of that design and his own connexion with the men who sponsored it will have made it desirable for Horace not simply to ignore it but somehow to react to it in public. He discharges this delicate obligation with great tact and resourcefulness. By making the suggestion of such a poem come from Trebatius he avoids the awkward situation of having spontaneously to announce that he cannot and will not write it. Trebatius is on terms of friendship with Caesar as well as with Horace; for him it is perfectly natural to encourage his young friend to venture upon so rewarding a task (*aude Caesaris invicti res dicere, multa laborum praemia laturus*). Horace's reply is admirable (12–15):

> cupidum, pater optime, vires
> deficiunt: neque enim quivis horrentia pilis
> agmina nec fracta pereuntis cuspide Gallos
> aut labentis equo describat volnera Parthi.

The tone of this refusal could not be more respectful (*pater optime*), and the poet's regret sounds wholly sincere. It is because he is fully aware of the greatness of the theme that he shows himself unwilling *laudes egregii Caesaris . . . culpa deterere ingeni*. In the form of a negative sentence Horace pays a high tribute to Caesar's military achievements, to which only a warlike poet could do justice. But his excuse, adroit though it is, does not succeed in putting off the shrewd Trebatius, who now outlines the other great sphere of Caesar's activities (16 f.):

> attamen et iustum poteras et scribere fortem,
> Scipiadam ut sapiens Lucilius.

Again Horace gives an evasive answer, showing thereby the most tactful consideration for Caesar (17–20). He has managed to praise,

---

[1] ἀεὶ μὲν ἥβᾳ τοῖς γέρουσιν εὐμαθεῖν, but, although I have read a good deal about it since, I see no reason to recant what I have said (*Gnomon*, i, 1925, 194 ff.) on Cicero's quotation from the XII Tables, *si quis occentavisset*, etc., and on Horace's use of *mala carmina* in this passage. Cf. also F. Marx, *Rh. Mus.* lxxviii, 1929, 410 f.

[2] *Georg.* 3. 16–39.

though briefly and, as it were, indirectly, both Caesar the military commander and Caesar the statesman. To this ingenious device he will return in the latest of his *sermones*, the great epistle to Augustus.

But we have not yet done with the last suggestion made by Trebatius. For him as a character in this dialogue it is the obvious thing to refer Horace, the renewer of the Lucilian *satura*, to Lucilius, who in his writings testified to the moral greatness of the younger Scipio Africanus. However, the reader of this satire may also be interested in the way in which Lucilius is here brought in. In the fourth and the tenth satire of Book I it was the criticism of his style that started the discussion about him. That criticism, as we have seen, is irrelevant for the purposes of the present satire, which is concerned with subject-matter and moral values. We notice, and shall bear in mind, that Lucilius as described in this passage, a Lucilius who is called *sapiens* and praised for having given a portrait of one *iustus* and *fortis*, seems rather different from the master of fierce invective as Horace had characterized him in the earlier satires. We also notice that this passing reference to Lucilius, apparently spontaneous, serves in fact as a preparation for the elaborate picture in ll. 29–34. This reference is in its turn preceded by an allusion to Lucilius which will not have escaped Horace's contemporaries. Trebatius' suggestion (10 f.), instead of writing satires *aude Caesaris invicti res dicere, multa laborum praemia laturus*, recalls the advice which in the earliest book published by Lucilius purports to have been given him by a friend (620 f.),

> hunc laborem sumas, laudem qui tibi ac fructum ferat:
> percrepa pugnam Popili, facta Corneli cane.[1]

We have, then, a gradual intensification of the manner in which Lucilius is referred to in this satire: first a veiled allusion (10 f.), then a brief, though laudatory, mention (17), and finally a full appreciation (29–34). This studied arrangement would in itself suggest that Horace set great store by what on this occasion he had to say about Lucilius. That this was in fact the case is made abundantly clear by the memorable lines 30 ff.,

> ille velut fidis arcana sodalibus olim
> credebat libris, neque si male cesserat usquam
> decurrens alio, neque si bene; quo fit ut omnis
> votiva pateat veluti descripta tabella
> vita senis.

---

[1] Corpet's (cf. Marx, vol. i, p. cxv) discovery that the two lines, quoted separately by Nonius, belong together was confirmed by Marx's reference to Horace's Trebatius satire; Terzaghi has thought fit to separate them again. It is, of course, Lucilius himself who is here addressed (so, following Marx, Leo, *Gesch. d. röm. Lit.* 413, Kappelmacher, *RE* xiii, 1627); Cichorius's different hypothesis, *Unters. zu Lucilius*, 114, has as little probability as his whole reconstruction of this section of Book XXVI.

Coming from Book I, the reader will be greatly surprised: it is difficult
to recognize in this portrait of Lucilius the features which one remembers from the descriptions in Horace's earlier satires. And yet it is
here, and only here, that we are given an adequate idea of the true
significance of the work of Horace's great forerunner. As we go on
(63 ff.) we see that the indulgence in personal invective, which seemed
to be the main, almost the only, characteristic in the former picture of
Lucilius, is by no means absent from the new description. But here that
characteristic is seen in perspective and judged as an outcome of a
very high moral standard and as an integral element in the rich and
amiable personality of the man who deserved to be the intimate friend
of the best Romans (65–74). At l. 70 there is an unmistakable hint at
Lucilius' famous definition of *virtus* (1326–38). However, to change
Lucilius into a peace-loving messenger of pure virtue—that would be
a falsification of which Horace could never become guilty. His Lucilius,
though *sapiens*, remains the impassioned fighter he had been in actual
life. But Horace now knows that to speak of the fighting spirit of
Lucilius is not the same thing as to give an idea of the mind of Lucilius
as mirrored in his writings. What appeared in these writings was something immeasurably wider, something that never before had been
expressed in poetry and would remain unique in ancient literature.
His lasting friendship with Scipio and Laelius or a transitory love
affair, the care for his large estates or some quarrel with a learned
fellow poet about certain niceties in Latin grammar, fierce derision of
his and his friends' political enemies or a letter venting his mortifica-
tion because the addressee did not come to see him when he was so
terribly ill, the great struggles within the *res publica* and some trifling
incident which Lucilius happened to watch, problems of rhetoric, of
poetry, of philosophy, all these and a hundred other topics made up his
saturae, and each topic was entitled to a place in these wholly personal
records, not because it was important or distinguished in itself, but
because it formed an organic part in the βίος,[1] the *vita*, the way of life,
of this one man, Lucilius, who, without vanity or arrogance, was so
glad to be himself, and not somebody else, that, at a very early stage
of his career as a writer, he could say (671 f.):

> publicanus vero ut Asiae fiam, ut scripturarius
> pro Lucilio, id ego nolo, et uno hoc non muto omnia.

His extensive writings, as they lay in thirty books spread out before the
reader, provided, not occasional glimpses of one or another detail of
his way of life, but a survey of its whole. That is why Horace, using the

---

[1] For the implications of the word see, for example, F. Leo, *Die griech.-röm. Biographie* 86,
96 f.

emphatic hyperbaton so common in lively speech, Greek or Latin,[1] says without exaggerating:

> quo fit ut *omnis*
> votiva pateat veluti descripta tabella
> *vita senis.*

How, we may ask, did Horace succeed in drawing this picture of the work of Lucilius, in comparison with which his former description of it looks like a caricature or at any rate a fragmentary sketch? To find an answer we must consider human nature. No artist, no writer, no reader will ever be able to recognize in another man's work the true expression of any particular experience, moral or otherwise, unless he has before had an analogous experience himself. Only when Horace in his own work had freed himself from direct imitation of certain obvious features of his model, above all the personal invective, and had begun to use his *satura*, not solely but largely, as an instrument of self-portraiture— only then was he capable of seeing that the work of Lucilius was primarily self-portraiture. And, vice versa, the better he understood Lucilius in his entirety, the less did he find it necessary to borrow details from him and the more did he feel justified in following his own genius and speaking with a new voice. Here, as in his communion with Archilochus, it came to pass that the old master, whose influence at first threatened to enslave his admirer, gradually assisted him to become his own self.

When Goethe, towards the end of his long life, had his collected writings republished, he prefixed to the *Zahme Xenien*, a work of his old age, the whole passage (30–34) *ille velut fidis . . . vita senis.*[2] Probably he would not have chosen this motto if Horace had not concluded his description with the word *senis*. But what above all must have caught his imagination and roused his sympathy was the extraordinary picture of an ancient poet whose conception of his poetry seemed to correspond precisely to the account that Goethe himself used to give of the impulse of his own poetic work. Nowadays no reader needs to be told that Goethe read into Horace's lines his personal conception of his own poetry. Any idea of a 'confession'[3] must be left aside when we are

---

[1] Cf. my *Iktus und Akzent*, 162 ff., Commentary on Aesch. *Ag.*, Index, 837, *s.v.* 'Hyperbaton'; see also p. 265 n. 3 below. For *omnis . . . . vita* cf. Cic. *Fam.* 11.21.3.

[2] In 'Ausgabe letzter Hand', 3. Band, Stuttgart und Tübingen 1828, p. 225. The critical apparatus in the Weimar edition, iii. 1890, 436, informs us that in the MS (there exists no autograph) the prefixed quotation from Horace is 'in Riemers Hand, auf besonderm aufgeklebtem Blättchen; die Worte *omnis* und *Vita senis* doppelt unterstrichen'. It seems unlikely that in this we should have to see an interference of the magisterial Riemer. I am inclined to believe that Goethe roughly remembered the passage, perhaps from the time when he read Wieland's translation, and asked Riemer to see to it that the quotation was given correctly.

[3] The *locus classicus* is the often quoted passage in Book VII of *Dichtung und Wahrheit*: 'Denn bei der großen Beschränktheit meines Zustandes . . . war ich genötigt alles in mir

dealing with either Lucilius or Horace. These ancient poets produce pictures of their own βίος not because they want to unburden their soul and clear their mind, but because they consider their day-to-day life with its many facets highly suited to their capacity for neat and suggestive description and to their bent towards sincere, if not always profound, meditation on human affairs. Lucilius, as seen through Horace's eyes, entrusts all his doings and his secret thoughts to his books as he would entrust them to reliable friends, but he does not put down a confession in the sense which after St. Augustine every one, even Goethe, was bound to connect with the word. And yet Goethe was right when he sensed something congenial in the pictures that Lucilius and Horace in their verses gave of themselves and of the world in which they moved: these pictures, as they emerged from Horace's words about Lucilius and from his own *sermones*, had a good deal in common with analogous pictures in Goethe's work. They were distinguished by qualities which Goethe valued very highly, comprehensiveness and directness, realism, conscientious accuracy in every detail, and a sincere and unflattering, yet not unkind, description of many human beings and, above all, of the poet himself and his reactions to things good and evil.

Horace's final appreciation of Lucilius can help us, perhaps better than anything else, to understand why he decided not to write any more satires. Once he had learned to see the noblest potentialities of this literary genre in its capacity for serving as καλὸν ἀνθρωπίνου βίου (and primarily τοῦ τοῦ ποιητοῦ βίου) κάτοπτρον, it could no longer satisfy him to write invectives against the baseness of legacy-hunters or produce witty descriptions of the refinements of a costly dinner. Instead, obeying the call that had in him become invincibly strong, he gave his whole mind to his lyrics. But he did not entirely forget the ideal of that other kind of writing in which a poet, *velut fidis arcana sodalibus*, entrusts his whole being to his books. When many years after, with a richer experience of human life and also a good deal of resignation, he returned to the writing of *sermones*, they were indeed to contain perfect pictures of his βίος, but not as satires.

selbst zu suchen. Verlangte ich nun zu meinen Gedichten eine wahre Unterlage, Empfindung oder Reflexion, so mußte ich in meinen Busen greifen; forderte ich zu poetischer Darstellung eine unmittelbare Anschauung des Gegenstandes, der Begebenheit, so durfte ich nicht aus dem Kreise heraustreten, der mich zu berühren, mir ein Interesse einzuflößen geeignet war. . . . Und so begann diejenige Richtung, von der ich mein ganzes Leben über nicht abweichen konnte, nämlich dasjenige, was mich erfreute oder quälte, oder sonst beschäftigte, in ein Bild, ein Gedicht zu verwandeln und darüber mit mir selbst abzuschließen, um sowohl meine Begriffe von den äußern Dingen zu berichtigen als mich im Innern deshalb zu beruhigen. . . . Alles, was daher von mir bekannt geworden, sind nur Bruchstücke einer großen Konfession, welche vollständig zu machen dieses Büchlein ein gewagter Versuch ist.'

V

ODES, BOOKS I–III

I. ODES RELATED TO ALCAEUS

FOR the ode i. 14, *O navis referent*, we possess the skeleton of the interpretation current about the middle of the first century of our era. Quintilian's statement[1] on the meaning of this ode is probably a summary of what, as a schoolboy or a young man, he had learned about it, either from the lips of his teacher or from a commentary.[2] To illustrate the common type of ἀλληγορία which *aliud verbis, aliud sensu ostendit*, Quintilian quotes the beginning of this ode, from *O navis* to l. 3 *portum*, and continues *totusque ille Horati locus, quo navem pro re publica, fluctus et tempestates pro bellis civilibus, portum pro pace atque concordia dicit*. But a commentator, however near to Horace's own time, may be wrong; the question whether or no *O navis referent* is to be taken as an allegory must either be answered by the poem itself or cannot be answered at all. From the sixteenth century to our own time there have been some scholars, Bentley among them, who rejected the allegorical interpretation and assumed that Horace's lament is directed to a ship on which he himself (or, according to others, Octavian) had been sailing in circumstances of danger. I am under no obligation to refute this view, since I write for those who are willing not to read into the poems of Horace any facts of which the words of the text say nothing. I will, however, remark that the beginning of the last stanza, *nuper sollicitum quae mihi taedium, nunc desiderium curaque non levis*, is sufficient to show the impossibility of any non-allegorical interpretation.

For Horace's own contemporaries it must have been perfectly natural to refer the ship to the *res publica*. In the Hellenic and the hellenized world it had long been a common habit to speak of a ship when in fact the πόλις, the *res publica*, the State, was meant. The com-

---

[1] *Inst.* 8. 6. 44.

[2] One of the interpretations which we find in the scholia agrees completely with the exegesis in Quintilian (Schol. on 1 *per allegoriam . . . designat . . . rempublicam*, on 3 *portum; pacem*, on 5 *grave bellum intellegi voluit per ventum tempestuosum*). For a detailed analysis of the scholia on this ode see R. Reitzenstein, *Nachr. Gött. Ges.*, Phil.-hist. Kl. 1918, 393 ff. It does not seem to have been noticed that the other interpretation, *in hac ode ad Marcum Brutum loquitur* (so Porph. and the scholia in the Paris MSS φ ψ λ, separately published by H. J. Botschuyver, Amsterdam 1935) is possibly derived from two passages in which the metaphor of the stormy sea is used in connexion with the last struggle of Brutus, *Odes* 2. 7. 15 (*allegoricos significat Pompeium . . . petisse rursum partes Bruti*, Porph.) and *Epist.* 2. 2. 47 f. (*Bruti autem arma significat*, Porph.).

mentaries on *O navis referent* provide some illustrations from Greek poetry, where the elaborate picture of a ship tossed by wild storms represents the distress of the community. Perhaps even more significant than such full-scale similes is the common habit of speaking of the ruler as the helmsman.[1] This Greek conception was adopted in Rome, where Cicero and others used it freely;[2] it is to this adoption that we owe the word 'government'. Cicero shows also that in his time the image had not yet faded into a mere metaphor: it was still possible to realize its original connotations.[3] We may therefore safely conclude that Horace was in no danger of being misunderstood by his readers when he expressed his anxiety at the situation of the commonwealth by addressing himself to a ship in distress.[4]

The ode, then, taken by itself, shows that Horace, whose object was to give a fine picture of a ship's sufferings and perils, was not content with the effect of this picture as such, but expected the reader to refer the fate of the ship to the fate of the *res publica*. The correctness of this 'allegoric' interpretation becomes even more evident as soon as we turn to the Greek poem which Horace had in mind when he conceived the idea of *O navis referent*.

At least as early as Baxter it was noticed that this ode is related to a fragment of Alcaeus,[5] ἀσυννέτημμι τὼν ἀνέμων στάσιν κτλ. There are indeed very considerable differences between the two poems,[6] and apart from the general theme which they have in common, the distress of the ship, their affinity appears mainly in the description of the tattered sails (λαῖφος δὲ πὰν ζάδηλον ἤδη, καὶ λάκιδες μέγαλαι κὰτ αὖτο: *non tibi sunt integra lintea*). But even if we do not consider the fragmentary state of what we have of Alcaeus' poem,[7] the similarity would be close enough to make it all but certain that Horace is here not independent of the Lesbian poet. The free manner in which he uses his model reminds us of the Mevius epode[8] where only the particular kind of curse and, perhaps, a detail or two seem to be derived from the

[1] See, for example, Pindar, *P*. 1. 86 νώμα δικαίῳ πηδαλίῳ στρατόν, Aesch. *Septem* 2 f. ὅστις φυλάσσει πρᾶγος ἐν πρύμνῃ πόλεως οἴακα νωμῶν.
[2] For Cicero's use of *gubernator* and *gubernare* in the political sense see *Thes. l. Lat.* vi. 2. 2348. 37 ff. and 2351. 73 ff.
[3] Cf. Cic. *Att*. 2. 7. 4 *iam pridem gubernare me taedebat, etiam cum licebat; nunc vero, cum cogar exire de navi non abiectis sed ereptis gubernaculis, cupio istorum naufragia e terra intueri.*
[4] Excellent prophet though he was (*Odes* 3. 30. 6 ff.), he could not anticipate that in the twentieth century someone would endeavour to demonstrate that 'the *navis* is Horace and his own life'.   [5] 46A D., 326 L. and P.
[6] This has, from Welcker on, often been observed; see especially Pasquali, *Or. lir.* 36 f.
[7] Lobel's suggestion that the fragment (46B D., 73 L. and P.) beginning with πὰν φόρτιον belongs to ἀσυννέτημμι τὼν ἀνέμων στάσιν is very attractive. It would, however, be wrong to see in the detail *interfusa nitentis vites aequora Cycladas* an echo of l. 6 of that fragment, ἔρματι τυπτομ[έναν]: the matter is different.
[8] See pp. 29 f. above.

Ionian iambist. There is, however, in *O navis referent* a more significant link with Alcaeus than the details which I have mentioned; I mean the sustained ἀλληγορία by which the picture of the struggling ship, lively and suggestive in itself, is meant also to convey the idea of the perils that threaten the *res publica*. The author to whom we owe the quotation of the fragment of Alcaeus,[1] says explicitly that the first impression which the reader receives from the poem ἀσυννέτημμι τὼν ἀνέμων στάσιν is deceptive and that in fact Μυρσίλος ὁ δηλούμενός ἐστι καὶ τυραννικὴ κατὰ Μυτιληναίων ἐγειρομένη σύστασις. The hypercriticism of the nineteenth century brushed this testimony aside, but meanwhile we have come to realize its correctness, partly because we have learned to weigh carefully the words of Pseudo-Heraclitus,[2] and partly because some of his statements have been confirmed by new fragments of Alcaeus.[3] There can be no doubt that in the complete poem which Horace had before him the reference to the πόλις was made as clear as we now know it to have been in the kindred poem quoted together with it.[4] In his own ode Horace preferred not to lift at any point the veil of the allegory. It would be idle to speculate on his reasons for this restraint; they may have been of a purely artistic kind, but it is equally possible that political considerations made too outspoken an utterance undesirable. However, the poet's adroitness enabled him, without any direct reference, to make his meaning perfectly clear. Unlike Alcaeus he turned his whole poem into an apostrophe to the ship and thus obtained an admirable instrument for expressing his profound anxiety, an anxiety which, in the absence of any hint at events concerning the private life of the poet himself or one of his friends, could only be referred to the common cause, the fate of the *res publica*. To enliven his

---

[1] [Heraclit.] *All.* 5, p. 6 f., ed. Bonn.

[2] The different editions of Kiessling–Heinze's commentary show the progress from bold self-assurance to discretion. Of the interpretation of Pseudo-Heraclitus Kiessling said 'alberner Weise allegorisch', Heinze, 6th ed., 'die Deutung trifft schwerlich zu' (cf. Wilamowitz, *Kl. Schriften*, i. 396); Heinze, 7th ed., gives, instead of a mutilated excerpt, the comment of the ancient author in full (from τίς οὐκ ἂν εὐθὺς κτλ. on) and adds the pertinent remark 'das besagt doch wohl, daß der erste Eindruck des Lesers durch den Fortgang des Gedichts berichtigt wurde'.

[3] Considerable fragments of the poem which Ps.-Heraclitus discusses together with ἀσυννέτημμι κτλ., because in both the storm that befalls the ship means the political crisis in Mytilene, have been found on *Pap. Oxy.* 1789 (*frs.* 119 ff. D., 6 L. and P.). There we read at l. 27 μοναρχίαν. So the author's statement on the one poem has been confirmed, and it would be hazardous to doubt what he says in the same context about the other. Cf. also C. Theander, *Eranos*, xli, 1943, 156 ff. A scholion in the lower margin of the papyrus, of which only Μυρσίλου can be made out, refers possibly to a third poem.

[4] See the last footnote. From what has been said it follows that we need not assume that for the allegorical interpretation Horace had to rely on a commentary on Alcaeus (so Pasquali, *Or. lir.* 21), although on general grounds it is highly probable that he did not read Alcaeus (or, for that matter, Pindar and other difficult poets) without a commentary.

apostrophe Horace uses a sustained and consistent personification, with the result that his warnings as well as the expressions of his grief and fear seem to be addressed to a living being. Most of the modern commentators have not paid sufficient attention to this device,[1] probably because they were too busy trying to find the answer to a question which nothing in the poem leads us to ask. Riddles are the delight of many Horatian scholars, and if the text itself does not provide a sufficient supply, they will invent some of their own. Here they ask 'where is Horace, on board ship or ashore?', and a heated contest has been fought over the issue.[2] We leave this phantom alone and return to the study of the actual poem.

O navis referent is certainly not one of Horace's masterpieces; but, without any illusion about its merits as a whole, we should strive to keep an open mind and appreciate the felicitous touches in the detail. The phrases are chosen with admirable skill in such a way as to intensify the idea that it is to a living being that the poet is speaking.[3] All the verbs lead our imagination in the same direction. *O quid agis?*, at the beginning of an urgent exhortation, has, perhaps, a more emphatic sound to Roman ears than to ours.[4] There follows *fortiter occupa*, then *nonne vides ut . . .*, then *gemant* and *vix durare possint*, then *voces* and *iactes*, then *tu nisi ventis debes ludibrium, cave*, where the impatient warning seems almost to descend to the level of excited everyday language, and at last *vites*. Moreover, by *nudum latus* and *saucius* we are reminded of a human body. Finally, the ship, whose boasting of her *genus et nomen* will be of no avail, comes from a very noble stock: *Pontica pinus, silvae filia nobilis.*[5]

In treating the ship as a woman Horace follows a very old Greek tradition. To the Greeks ships were female as they are to the English; accordingly the Athenian triremes all bore women's names. The poets

---

[1] Kiessling, at the end of the second paragraph of his introduction to this ode, remarked 'Zum Ersatz [i.e. of the features in Alcaeus which Horace had to sacrifice] ist die Personifikation des Schiffes bis ins Einzelnste durchgeführt — wie ja auch heutzutage seemännische Redeweise das Schiff gern als lebendiges Wesen auffaßt', but this sound observation is omitted in Heinze's later editions.

[2] In this case even Wilamowitz, who usually maintained an independent attitude, joined in the popular game: *S. u.S.* 312. For a more recent contribution see G. Carlsson, *Eranos*, xlii, 1944, 4 f.

[3] Perhaps it is not merely due to a coincidence that the same kind of intentional ambiguity seems to have been noticeable in at least one poem of Alcaeus. Lobel, *Pap. Oxy.* xxi. 120, in his note on a commentary on Alcaeus (now Lobel and Page, *Poet. Lesb. Fragm.* p. 248, col. 2. 8) observes 'αὐτῆς I suppose, "the ship". But many of the words and expressions following seem more applicable to a πόρνη than to a ship. The same kind of mixture seems to occur in Ἀμ. 61 [*Poet. Lesb. Fragm.* 166], 20 seqq.'

[4] Cf. Cic. *Catil.* 1. 27 *si mecum patria . . . si cuncta Italia, si omnis res publica loquatur:* 'M. Tulli, quid agis? . . .'.

[5] The name of the renowned birthplace forms an essential element of the pedigree (for the tone of the passage cf., for instance, 3. 9. 14 *Thurini Calais filius Ornyti*).

took advantage of this long-established personification; hence the delightful invention in the second parabasis of Aristophanes' *Knights* (1300), where the τριήρεις have arranged a protest meeting and one of them, an elderly lady, is haranguing the others: ὦ παρθένοι.[1] In the Hellenistic period we find, for instance, the ships of Paris called αἱ ἰουλόπεζοι . . . εὐῶπες . . . πελαργόχρωτες, αἱ Φαλακραῖαι κόραι,[2] and Virgil, presumably stimulated by some Hellenistic model,[3] narrates how the ships of Aeneas were turned into sea-nymphs.[4] Horace's use of the inherited idea is a happy one; by the refinement which he applies to it he compensates, up to a point, for what his ode lacks in vigour and directness. Up to a point, for let us not forget that a reader who comes fresh from ἀσυννέτημμι τὼν ἀνέμων στάσιν is bound to be chilled by *O navis referent*. The song of Alcaeus, even if we know it to be an allegory, gives us the feeling as if we ourselves, amidst the raging seas, were exposed to all the *dura navis mala*, whereas Horace's ode fills us rather with admiration for a fine piece of art. On a higher level we find here something of the difference between κύματι πλαζόμενος κτλ. and *Mala soluta navis exit alite*.[5] There is, however, one passage in the ode where the *vox humana* dominates over the rich instrumentation and makes us stir:

> nuper sollicitum quae mihi taedium,
> nunc desiderium curaque non levis.

We should very much like to know when it was that Horace felt impelled to raise his voice with such passion. But no reliable dating of the ode appears to be possible. It would be quite wrong to assume that in the poet's opinion Rome and her empire were out of all danger after the defeat of Antony and Cleopatra. Nevertheless, weighing the full heaviness of the words *nuper sollicitum . . .*, we are probably justified in agreeing with the many scholars who believe that this poem was written several years before the battle of Actium. In that case it would have to be regarded as one of Horace's earliest experiments, perhaps the earliest of all, in writing after the manner of Alcaeus.

The ode i. 37 dates itself: it was written in the first excitement at the news of Cleopatra's death a few weeks after the capture of Alexandria (1 August 30 B.C.). The jubilant note on which it begins, *Nunc est bibendum*, would be readily echoed in the hearts of the common people, but to a reader who was *sermones utriusque linguae doctus* the opening

---

[1] The second parabasis was written not by Eupolis, but by Aristophanes: see Pohlenz, *Nachr. Gött. Akad.*, Phil.-hist. Kl., 1952, 120 ff.

[2] Lycophron, *Alex.* 22 ff.

[3] See E. Norden's commentary on *Aen.* VI, 3rd ed., p. 169.

[4] *Aen.* 9. 77 ff.

[5] Cf. p. 30 above.

words would mean more, since they invest the celebration of the present day with the dignity of early Greek poetry. One of the songs of Alcaeus began:

νῦν χρῆ μεθύσθην καί τινα πὲρ βίαν[1]
πώνην, ἐπεὶ δὴ κάτθανε Μύρσιλος.

What caused the jubilation of the aristocratic party in Mytilene and of Alcaeus, who spoke in their name, was the downfall of the tyrant Myrsilus. What gave rise to Horace's exultant ode was the downfall of his nation's most dreaded enemy, the Egyptian queen. But there the similarity ends: the two poems move in widely separate spheres. In Horace's second line the epithet *Saliaribus* takes us at once to Rome and thus preludes the momentous subject of the next stanza,

dum Capitolio
regina dementis ruinas
funus et imperio parabat.

After the first clause, *nunc est bibendum*, there is in the ode no further reminiscence of Alcaeus. This type of adoption, where only the opening words of a Greek poem are taken over, has, by a useful term, been called the borrowing of a motto.[2]

The beginning of the second stanza,

antehac nefas depromere Caecubum
cellis avitis,

seems to allude to the sentence with which the ninth epode began, as if the poet were saying 'the anxious question which we asked when the first news of the battle of Actium reached us has at last been answered; only now, after the fall of Alexandria and the death of Cleopatra, is it right for us to speak of full victory and celebrate it in the most solemn manner'. The third stanza, too, is linked up with the Actium epode:

contaminato cum grege turpium
morbo virorum.

A comparison with the analogous passage in the epode (13 f.) *spadoni-bus . . . rugosis*, provides an excellent opportunity to learn that in any polished piece of ancient poetry the rules (Horace would say the *leges*)

---

[1] *Fr.* 39 D., 332 L. and P. I have accepted Lobel's correction πὲρ βίαν for πρὸς βίαν; on the improvement of the sense thus obtained see Lobel, Σαπφοῦς μέλη, p. xlv; R. Pfeiffer, *Gnomon*, vi, 1930, 318 f.

[2] This term probably occurred to several scholars independently. Pasquali, *Or. lir.* 9 n. 1, refers for it to E. Norden (1909), but it had already been used by R. Reitzenstein, *Gött. gel. Anz.* 1904, 959, and *Neue Jahrb.* xxi, 1908, 87. This sort of limited adoption will often be found when a classicistic school of poetry insists on its connexion with some admired forerunners. Speaking of those poems of Ben Jonson's in which he uses ancient models, Sir Ernest Barker once said (*The Spectator*, 1936, 890): 'There are times when he simply takes his cue from the Latin or Greek original, and then lets his own Muse soar', etc.

of the different literary genres and especially the difference in their stylistic level are strictly observed. The coarse directness suitable to the character of the Archilochean *iambus* proved impossible in the style of dignified lyrics: here the poet had to resort to allusive paraphrase.

In depicting some dramatic moment of the battle of Actium the tone of the ode rises to the level of great epic, or Pindaric, poetry (12–20, notice especially the similes at 17 ff.). This section ends with a concise clause describing Caesar's aim (20 f.), *daret ut catenis fatale monstrum*. Here *monstrum*, in this case a *monstrum* brought about by Rome's *fata*, probably contains less of what we hear in monster and more of what a Greek heard in τέρας, a Roman in *portentum* or *prodigium*,[1] something outside the norm of nature,[2] something at which we look with wonder and often with horror. To *fatale monstrum* there is appended a long relative period: it fills the last three stanzas of the ode. The feeling of horror recedes, and admiration takes its place. At the end of the poem written to celebrate Cleopatra's defeat her greatness dominates over everything else. The architecture of this concluding section is worthy of the subject:[3] its flanks are formed by participial clauses (22 *quaerens*, 30 *invidens*) so as to stress the symmetry of the whole. Within that frame we find first two *nec* clauses (22–24), then, in symmetrical contrast to them, two *et* clauses (25–27), the latter of which is enlarged by an *ut* clause (27 f.), and finally, with a happy change from the preceding clauses which centre round a verb, a monumental attribute (29), *deliberata morte ferocior*.

The magnanimity with which the defeated queen is extolled[4] should not be taken as an isolated phenomenon. It springs from that deep respect for dignity in man's behaviour which the Greeks, though they did not, of course, always practise it, at any rate held up to themselves as an ideal. And as an ideal it took root in the Roman mind, whose hardy, if somewhat dry, nature proved fertile for the growth of some of the finest plants from the garden of Greek ethics. The rulers of the *orbis terrarum* came to recognize that you ought not to humiliate your defeated enemy, and that by trying to degrade him you will in fact degrade yourself.

We read in the Old Testament such passages as Joshua x. 24, 'Joshua said unto the captains of the men of war which went with him,

---

[1] Cf., for example, Cic. *Cluent.* 188 (of Sassia) *quod hoc portentum, di immortales! quod tantum monstrum in ullis locis . . . dicamus?*; *Catil.* 2. 1 *a monstro illo atque prodigio*; *Phil.* 13. 49 *monstra quaedam ista et portenta sunt et prodigia rei publicae.*

[2] Cf., for example, Cic. *S. Rosc.* 63 *reclamitat istius modi suspicionibus ipsa natura; portentum atque monstrum certissimum est esse aliquem humana specie et figura qui*, etc.

[3] The following analysis is taken over from Pasquali, *Or. lir.* 57.

[4] W. H. Alexander, 'Horace's Odes and Carmen saeculare', *Univ. of California Publications in Class. Philol.*, xiii, No. 7, 1947, 194, comments on *Odes* i. 37: 'Horace, super-heated with Roman patriotism throughout this unpleasantly vindictive ode.'

Come near, put your feet upon the necks of these kings. And they came near, and put their feet upon the necks of them', or, Psalm cx. 1, 'The Lord said unto my Lord, Sit thou at my right hand, until I make thine enemies thy footstool.' The conception found here and also, for instance, in some hymns to Egyptian kings, underlies numerous representations in works of decorative art from the ancient Orient, Egypt as well as western Asia, where we see the enemy lying beneath the foot of the victor or the hoof of his horse. It has been pointed out[1] that representations of that kind are completely absent from the world of Greek and Roman art so long as it maintained its own traditions; the first rare instances of the new and more brutal type, intruders from the east, do not appear until the second century of our era. Horace's praise of Cleopatra shows that the Rome of Augustus, despite its very different outlook on life, had still some moral ideals in common with the Athens of the Persian wars. It cannot be assumed that all fellow-citizens of either Aeschylus or Horace shared the noble feelings expressed by the poets. But it is a fact, and a very important fact indeed, that the poets, voicing what was in the minds of the best men, could, without fear of disapproval, treat the defeated enemy in such a manner at the moment when a life-and-death struggle had been decided. In the later history of mankind it may not often have happened that a victory of similar magnitude was glorified in a poem so jubilant and at the same time so profoundly humane as the ode *Nunc est bibendum*.

A relation of some sort between the ode i. 10, *Mercuri, facunde nepos Atlantis*, and a hymn of Alcaeus is indicated in our scholia (Porph.) by two notes, mutilated and barbarized remnants of a learned commentary. At the beginning we find, by way of title, a general remark, *hymnus est in Mercurium, ab Alcaeo lyrico poeta*, and appended to l. 9 a special note on the story alluded to in the third stanza, *fabula haec autem ab Alcaeo ficta*. The latter statement is confirmed by Pausanias 7. 20. 4 βουσὶ γὰρ χαίρειν μάλιστα Ἀπόλλωνα Ἀλκαῖος . . . ἐδήλωσεν ἐν ὕμνῳ τῷ ἐς Ἑρμῆν, γράψας ὡς ὁ Ἑρμῆς βοῦς ὑφέλοιτο τοῦ Ἀπόλλωνος. The beginning of the hymn in question,[2]

> χαῖρε, Κυλλάνας ὁ μέδεις, σὲ γάρ μοι
> θῦμος ὕμνην κτλ.,

is quoted by the metrician Hephaestion, and from the scholia on Hephaestion we learn that this hymn was the second poem in the first book of the Alexandrian edition of Alcaeus. Its conspicuous position

---

[1] See the articles quoted in my note on A. *Ag.* 907.
[2] *fr.* 2 D., 308 L. and P.

was perhaps one of the reasons which induced Horace to turn to this hymn.[1] In taking up the theme of Alcaeus he thoroughly recast the Greek poem.[2] We have here a perfect illustration of the difference between a typical Horatian ode shaped after a Greek model and the sort of classicistic poetry familiar to us from other periods in literary history.

A very noticeable feature of this ode is the neatness of its structure. The first two stanzas contain an announcement of the theme of the hymn;[3] here the abilities of the god, his ἀρεταί, as well as his main achievements are broadly surveyed. The remaining three stanzas are each separated from one another by a full stop, and in thought, too, each of them is complete and self-contained. First we are reminded of two sharply contrasted scenes in the life of the god (9–12 and 13–16), and then, in deeper and more mysterious notes, he is praised as a mediator between this world and the next (17–20). This arrangement certainly shows a carefully devised plan and a symmetry different from what we might expect in early Greek lyrics, but I cannot admit that, as Wilamowitz put it, 'it savours of the Stoic compendium'. It does not seem difficult to guess the poet's intentions without having recourse either to some Hellenistic compendium of theology or, as other scholars have done, to prescriptions current in the textbooks of rhetoric. Horace placed in the centre of his ode the master stroke of the new-born divine thief, which formed part of the poem of Alcaeus and which we know best from the Homeric hymn to Hermes. Horace does not attempt to outline the old story as such, but merely touches on its salient points. We often have reason to admire his adroitness in compressing a maximum of matter into a minimum of space, but nowhere more so than in this stanza. The main elements of the story are all there, although it may take the reader a few moments to disentangle the closely-knit period and rearrange the events in their chronological order.

After the farce taken from the babyhood of Mercury there follows in the next stanza a generous action of the grown-up god. The poem is concluded by the figure of the ψυχοπομπός, gentle and graceful as we

---

[1] Wilamowitz (*S.u.S.* 311) rightly says that it was Alcaeus' hymn which impelled Horace to write in the same metre *Mercuri facunde nepos Atlantis*. 'Er hatte keine Veranlassung einen Hymnus auf einen mythischen Gott zu machen und hätte es sonst auch unterlassen.'

[2] This has been shown especially by R. Reitzenstein, *Zwei religionsgeschichtliche Fragen*, Strassburg 1901, 69 n. 1 ('Der Hymnus des Alkaios ist dem Dichter natürlich bekannt, aber er ist trotz der ausdrücklichen Angabe der Scholiasten im wesentlichen nicht nachgebildet. Der Geist des Liedes ist alexandrinisch'); cf. also Wilamowitz, loc. cit., and Pasquali, *Or. lir.* 64 ff.

[3] *te canam* recalls the ἀείσομαι or ἄρχομ' ἀείδειν in hexametric hymns (cf. E. Norden, *Agnostos Theos*, 153), nor is it very distant from σὲ γάρ μοι θῦμος ὕμνην in Horace's immediate model.

see him on the famous Orpheus relief or on the sculptured drum of a column from the temple of the Ephesian Artemis in the British Museum.

Some scholars have inquired what was Horace's real interest in writing the Mercury ode. Such an attempt to get behind the actual poem and peep into the poet's motives is often gratuitous and always hazardous, for there can be no certain answer to questions of that kind. However, in the present instance a useful purpose may be served by taking up the challenge in order to clarify our conception of a fundamental factor in the poetry of Horace.

Wickham says 'the Ode is a study', and Plessis in his commentary, after mentioning the old[1] but wholly unwarranted hypothesis that the ode was written for a festival, observes 'plus probablement simple exercice poétique'. This assumption left Heinze dissatisfied; he rightly insists on the ode being more than 'poetische Stilübung'. He then goes on to give his own view: 'Horace, the *vir Mercurialis* (2. 17. 29), feels that there is a particularly intimate relation between himself and the god who once protected him at Philippi,[2] and whom he worships as his *custos maximus*,[3] and as the giver of the country estate in which he delights.[4] We are meant to find expressed in the opening words of the solemn last stanza the poet's hope that the god will some day bring his *pia anima* also to the *sedes laetae*.' This extraordinary piece of reconstruction shows that even a good Horatian scholar may sometimes miss the sense of a whole poem if he is not on his guard against the temptation of reading into the text certain ideas and sentiments which someone born in the nineteenth century may perhaps take for granted but of which there is no trace in the poem. If the relationship between Horace and his supposed patron Mercury had any relevance to this ode, Horace would have made it clear through the ode itself;[5] as it is, there is in the poem not the faintest allusion to a special allegiance of the poet to the god. Surely Horace did not expect the reader of his hymn to search the volumes of *Q. Horati Flacci opera* on the chance of discovering some passages from which it could be inferred that the poet looked on Mercury as his special patron. This objection would be valid even if the passages on which the commentator has hit proved his point; but they do not. The first item in Heinze's list, *Odes* 2. 17. 29 f., where the poet speaks of himself as one of the *Mercuriales viri*, belongs to a poem in which Horace carries his sympathy with the self-tormenting melancholy of Maecenas so far as to adopt for once his friend's belief in the

[1] Cf. Dacier.
[2] *me per hostes Mercurius . . . sustulit*, 2. 7. 13.
[3] *Sat.* 2. 6. 15.   [4] Ibid. 5.
[5] It should suffice to recall the general principle underlying Horace's poetic technique. However, if the reader wants a special illustration to show how the poet establishes in a hymn a close relationship between a god and himself, the ode iv. 6 will provide it.

truth of astrology; it is in this connexion that he asserts that his own life is controlled by the 'influence' of the planet Mercury.[1] From this idea it is a far cry to the description of the god's various activities in *Mercuri, facunde nepos Atlantis*. As regards the prayer to Mercury at the beginning of *Sat.* ii. 6 (5–15),[2] it has its roots in the particular theme of that satire. Horace is describing his happiness in the possession of his farm in the Sabine hills; he reflects on the kind of profit he hopes to derive from it, and it is therefore natural that he should, in a playful manner, turn to Mercury, the finder of profit, *lucri repertor*.[3] When, on an inscription set up probably at the end of the second century of our era, Mercury is called *lucrorum potens et conservator*,[4] the idea in *lucrorum conservator* is the same as that which in Horace's satire is expressed by the words (15) *utque soles, custos mihi maximus adsis*: the *custodia* here clearly refers to the safeguarding of the poet's possessions and has nothing to do with his being rescued by the god in the battle of Philippi.[5] That brings us to the *pièce de résistance* of the view according to which Horace worshipped Mercury as his personal patron and saviour,[6]

> sed me per hostis Mercurius celer
> denso paventem sustulit aere.

Here it must be firmly stated that Horace, the son of an ageing civilization, the pupil of refined and sceptical philosophers, did not write for people who would credit him with the belief that in the autumn of the year 42 B.C. an Olympian god went to the trouble of producing, on the battle-field of Philippi, a special cloud or mist to wrap round an unknown young man and so remove him out of harm's way. What Horace does expect his reader to do is to remember Homer[7] (precisely as in the preceding stanza *relicta non bene parmula* would be wasted on those who could not recognize the allusion to Archilochus and Alcaeus). A very similar passage in the *Iliad* is 20. 443 f. τὸν (i.e. Hector) δ᾽ ἐξήρπαξεν Ἀπόλλων ῥεῖα μάλ᾽ ὥς τε θεός, ἐκάλυψε δ᾽ ἄρ᾽ ἠέρι πολλῇ. When Horace uses features of a heroic tale to describe what happened to him at Philippi, he does it in a playful spirit,[8] and it is in

---

[1] Cf. pp. 218 f. below.

[2] For a detailed examination of that prayer see pp. 138 ff. above.

[3] Dessau, *Inscr. Lat. sel.* 3200 (= *Carm. Lat. epigr.* 1528); in general cf. Wissowa, *Rel. u. Kultus*, 2nd ed. 305 n. 6; W. Kroll, *RE* xv. 978.

[4] Dessau, op. cit. 3199.

[5] Our commentaries are influenced by the comment (preserved in a badly confused form) in the 'Ps. Acro' scholia on *Sat.* 2. 6. 15, where the explanation *quia in Philippis eum liberavit* is put forward as an alternative and *Odes* 2. 7. 13 f. is quoted in support.

[6] *Odes* 2. 7. 13 f.

[7] The commentators, from Lambinus on, have referred to the Homeric passages which Horace had in mind.

[8] He strikes a more solemn note when, in *Odes* 3. 4. 25–28, his escape from death on three occasions, at Philippi, when the tree nearly fell upon him, and when he was nearly drowned

this spirit that the role assigned to Mercury must be understood. Most unexpectedly Horace found himself snatched away from the turmoil of the battle; surely that was a god's doing, ἐξέκλεψεν . . . θεός τις, οὐκ ἄνθρωπος, and for such a performance no god was as suitable as Hermes, the master thief. The scholiast's (Porph.) comment is not at all bad: *iucunde autem a Mercurio se sublatum de illa caede dicit, significans clam et quasi furto quodam se inde fugisse.* The poet's intention is not difficult to understand, and the theory which makes Mercury Horace's special and permanent protector receives no support from the ode ii. 7.

Heinze's re-interpretation of the Mercury ode, i. 10, ends in a downright *interpolatio Christiana*: 'we are meant to find expressed . . . the poet's hope that the god will some day bring his *pia anima* also to the *sedes laetae*.' This is far more reminiscent of a hymn sung in the Lutheran Church, 'Wenn ich einmal soll scheiden, So scheide nicht von mir', than of anything Horace could ever have felt or thought. Let us give up the unpromising attempts to extort from this ode some information on Horace's private religion and try rather to look on it as a piece of poetry.

We need not here concern ourselves with the vexed question of the definition of poetry. But it will be helpful to remember a point on which a fair amount of agreement seems to exist. A poet may invest with a second, though different, life beliefs which in the actual history of mankind have perished long ago. Horace read the hymn to Hermes at a prominent place in the book of Alcaeus, but he would not have taken up the theme unless he felt that he himself had something to say about the god, something that was not in the Greek poem. What inspired him was not a personal religion of his own, nor, for that matter, a religion of any of his contemporaries, but beliefs of a remote past, ennobled and perpetuated in works of poetry and in monuments of decorative art. The tale of the god's first theft was ready for him in the hymn of Alcaeus; he condensed and polished it and set it in the centre of his ode. This comic episode had to be matched by a serious one, and for this he chose the scene in which Hermes protects Priam on his way to the tent of Achilles. We may regard it as certain that Horace did not find his conception of 'the divine' adequately represented either in the cattle-stealing babe or in the kind-hearted youth who in the dead of night guides the distressed old king safely through the enemy's camp. But it is equally certain that when Horace read in an old poem of the tricks played by the infant god upon his elder brother he was as delighted by the story as we are, and also that he was no less moved than we are by the last book of the *Iliad*. Whatever he thought

at sea, is ascribed to the protection of the Muses which a poet enjoys wherever he may be. But there too no confession of a personal religion is to be looked for.

himself of the power which he may have called τὸ θεῖον, those wonderful
tales captivated his imagination, not only as perfect poetry but also as
manifestations of a belief which once had arisen from human hearts
and which now, in a changed world, was echoed by the heart of a true
poet.

Finally, a word about the last stanza. Horace was hardly the man to
comfort himself with the thought that on the other side of the grave a
friendly ψυχοπομπός would be waiting for him, but he was fully aware
of the depth and beauty of that conception and therefore felt called
upon to bring it back, together with other creations of a bygone age,
to a new life in the sphere of poetry.

It is not only the Mercury ode that has had to suffer from the
critics' incapacity to grasp its poetical intention and from the desire to
read into it religious sentiments incongruous with its spirit: a similar
treatment has been applied to the ode ii 13, *Ille et nefasto te posuit die*.
No special familiarity with Horace's lyrics is needed to see that in this
poem the emphasis lies on the second half (21–40). To this second half,
the scenes in Hades, the first half leads up by investing the description
of the *regna Proserpinae* with some semblance of spontaneity, as if the
poet's narrow escape from being killed by the falling tree had set him
speculating on what he would find in the nether world. However,
Horace does not confine himself to the bare minimum required for his
immediate purpose. Instead of saying merely 'that cursed tree almost
finished me; *quam paene furvae regna Proserpinae et iudicantem vidimus
Aeacum*', and so forth, he elaborates his description of the wicked man
who planted the tree by crediting him with all kinds of abominable
crime (4–10), and then, after returning to the case in hand, appends a
general maxim (13 f.), *quid quisque vitet, numquam homini satis cautum est in
horas*, which in its turn is illustrated by some examples. As a result of
these enlargements the preparatory section of the poem reaches exactly
the length of the second part, the scenes in Hades. No less important
than the symmetry thus achieved is the colour which the hypothetical
crimes in ll. 5–10 add to the affair of the tree. It was in all probability
just a rotten tree, but Horace does not hesitate to ascribe diabolical
intentions to the unknown farmer who planted it: he puts him on the
same level with the most horrible monsters of the human race. These
wild exaggerations are delivered in a tone of light mockery;[1] nevertheless, they have become a victim of the tendency of scholars to find unqualified seriousness almost everywhere in Horace and, moreover, to
regard every Horatian poem as inspired in the main by some particular

---

[1] The same tone can be observed in an analogous context, *Odes* 1. 22. 13 ff. *quale
portentum*, etc.

personal experience.[1] This tendency has marred the interpretation of the whole ode and obscured the true significance of the scenes in Hades. We are asked to believe that Horace wrote this ode because, after being miraculously saved from death, his mind was still filled with terror to such a degree that he could not tear himself away from the vision of the other world into which he had been well-nigh carried. What appears in the ode itself is different: a Nekyia on a small scale as an impressive setting for the glorification of Alcaeus, the power of whose song is so great that it holds spell-bound not only the hosts of the dead and the great tormented sinners but even the monsters of Hell.

Following a hint put forward by Lachmann[2] and adding some further arguments, Orelli-Baiter, Kiessling, and other commentators have rightly assigned this ode to the early period of Horace's Aeolic lyrics. It was 'born out of the enthusiasm which he felt when he had first mastered the new forms',[3] and, I would add, when his intense study of Alcaeus was enhancing his admiration for him. In this ode Horace does not speak of the role he has marked out for himself as the renewer of Lesbian lyric,[4] but is content with praising the old master whom he has chosen as his principal model. By the side of Alcaeus there appears in a moving attitude Sappho, whom Horace was wise enough never to imitate,[5] for the very reason that he understood her so well and admired her so much. In the two lines which are given her in this ode there is a real breath of her poetry, though not yet the mellow beauty which Horace was to reach when speaking of her in one of his latest poems (4. 9. 10 ff.).

Poetry, then, with all its glory, is the mainspring of the ode *Ille et nefasto te posuit die*. As for the tree, there is no reason to doubt that it did crash one day when Horace was near by.[6] At the time the accident

---

[1] See Heinze in the last edition (1930) of his commentary: 'Schreck und Empörung sucht nach einem Schuldigen, sich gegen ihn zu entladen: "Welch verruchter Frevler wars, der dich gepflanzt hat! (1–12)." Das Grauen zittert noch nach in der tiefernsten Betrachtung: "wie wenig ahnt doch der Mensch, von woher der Tod ihn Stunde um Stunde bedroht! (13–20)." Und nun verfolgt er, in seiner Stimmung immer gefestigter, den Weg, den er beinah hätte gehen müssen', etc.

[2] In his 'Epistula' in C. Franke's *Fasti Horatiani*, 238 (reprinted in K. Lachmann, *Kl. Schriften zur class. Philol.* 79 f.).

[3] This sound remark of Kiessling's was reprinted by Heinze as late as the sixth edition (1917) of the commentary, but after it, when the over-serious interpretation had gained full control, it was cancelled.

[4] On this point Heinze (7th ed.) is right against R. Reitzenstein, *Hermes*, lvii, 1922, 358. But the two scholars, who, in matters concerning Horace, seldom saw eye to eye, agreed in regarding the ode as an expression of a very serious emotion and a religious 'Innerlichkeit'.

[5] So Wilamowitz, *S.u.S.* 308 f. It is a pity that he added the comment (309 n. 1) 'Horaz hatte auch schwerlich für die Innerlichkeit und Weiblichkeit der sapphischen Poesie Verständnis.' This judgement is disproved by *Odes* 2. 13. 24 f. and 4. 9. 10 ff. alike.

[6] It may be useful to compare the interpretation of *Odes* i. 34, *Parcus deorum*, p. 256 below. For the 'semblance of spontaneity' cf. also p. 193, on the Europa ode.

may well have given him a shock, but, being a poet, he soon turned it to the best account. First he used it as a spring-board from which his imagination could dive into Hades,[1] and later he referred to the fall of the tree to demonstrate to Maecenas that the fate of both of them followed an astoundingly similar course.[2] The all but fatal accident is again adduced, together with some similar events in Horace's life, to prove that the poet is under the permanent protection of the Camenae[3]; another time[4] he mentions the same accident as the cause of the vow in fulfilment of which he is performing a simple but picturesque ceremony. In Horace's external life, after the troubled years of his early career, very few exciting things happened; those that did happen the poet had to make the most of.

As we go through Horace's *carmina* and, by the way, attempt to trace their literary pedigree, we see time and again that, apart from banquet songs and invitations to banquets, no inherited pattern has left a deeper mark on them and produced in them a greater wealth of happy variations than the pattern of prayers and prayerlike hymns and invocations which had originally been shaped in the actual worship of the gods and then enriched and refined by many Greek poets. Horace adapted this pattern sometimes to the praise of a subject other than a deity. Eduard Norden, in a famous chapter of his *Agnostos Theos*[5] has shown that both the general design of the Messalla ode, iii. 21, *O nata mecum consule Manlio*, and much of its detail can be properly understood only if the extent of its borrowing from the language of prayers is realized.[6] In *Odes* i. 32 we find nothing of the sophisticated playfulness of the Messalla ode—of course not, for i. 32 is a serious poem—but we do find in it the same degree of dependence on forms of prayers. The ode is a prayer to Horace's lyre[7] or, more precisely, the lyre of the Lesbian lyrics. About the opening sentence and its characteristic borrowing from the thought and language of prayers, something will be said presently. The aim of the invocation is expressed in the clause *age*

---

[1] Dacier, at the beginning of his notes on this ode, says 'La chûte de l'arbre qui avoit pensé écraser Horace n'est pas le veritable sujet de cette Ode. Horace employe seulement cette circonstance pour parler de Sapho et d'Alcée, sans qu'il paroisse qu'il en ait cherché l'occasion, et il le fait avec une adresse merveilleuse.' It seems that modern scholars have still something to learn from the seventeenth-century Frenchman, whose commonsense and tact were not impeded by his considerable knowledge.

[2] *Odes* 2. 17. 27 ff.   [3] *Odes* 3. 4. 25–28.
[4] *Odes* 3. 8. 6–8.   [5] 1913, 143 ff.

[6] Norden's main results are incorporated in Heinze's commentary. Again Dacier proved his remarkable flair: on l. 4, *pia testa*, he observes 'Il parle à sa Bouteille comme si c'estoit une divinité. Mais je n'ay pas dû conserver cela dans la traduction', and on l. 6, *moveri*, '*Moveri* est un mot de religion'.

[7] There cannot, of course, be any thought of a real lyre either here or in the many similar passages in Horace; see on *Odes* 4. 6. 35 f., p. 404 below.

dic Latinum, barbite, carmen. The appended participial clause, *Lesbio primum modulate civi qui ferox bello,* etc., contains the equivalent of one of the commonest elements in ordinary prayers and hymns, the account of the birth and childhood of the god.[1] This theme is not completed until the end of the third stanza. The fourth and last stanza begins with a fresh invocation in a very solemn tone,[2] *o decus Phoebi* . . ., which is taken up by a parallel clause, *o laborum dulce lenimen*:

> O decus Phoebi et dapibus supremi
> grata testudo Iovis, o laborum
> dulce lenimen, mihi cumque salve
> rite vocanti.

The concluding words, *mihi . . . salve . . . vocanti,* recall as clearly as the rest of the ode a topic of religious invocations: a similar greeting, χαῖρε, addressed to a god or goddess, forms the end of many Greek hymns. But Horace has changed this topic rather freely. Whereas in the Greek hymns the χαῖρε of the concluding section bids the deity farewell, Horace's *salve* (the expression used to greet someone on meeting him, 'hail', 'welcome') corresponds indeed to a Greek χαῖρε, but in the sense in which we find it at the beginning, and not at the end, of a prayer or hymn.[3] This initial, welcoming χαῖρε has a μοι added to it at the beginning of several hymns, as it has sometimes in ordinary speech;[4] in the farewell at the end of a hymn the pronoun occurs but rarely.[5] Apparently it was after the model of χαῖρέ μοι that

---

[1] Cf. Ar. *Eccl.* 3 γονάς τε γὰρ σὰς καὶ τύχας δηλώσομεν and my remarks on it, *Plautinisches im Plautus,* 102 n. 1.

[2] For *o* in such context see E. Norden, *Agnostos Theos,* 144.

[3] Cf., for example, Alc. *fr.* 2 D., 308 L. and P. χαῖρε, Κυλλάνας ὁ μέδεις, σὲ γάρ μοι θῦμος ὕμνην κτλ.; Cratinus, *fr.* 321 K. χαῖρ', ὦ χρυσόκερως βαβάκτα κήλων, | Πάν, Πελαργικὸν ἀργὸν ἐμβατεύων; Ar. *Thesm.* 972 χαῖρ', ὦ 'Εκάεργε; further (applied to the island of Delos) Pind. *fr.* 87 Schr. (156 Turyn) χαῖρ', ὦ θεοδμάτα κτλ.

[4] Cf., for example, Eur. *Hipp.* 64 (abridged hymn), the beginning of the Cretan 'hymn of the Kouretes' (text in Wilamowitz, *Verskunst,* 499, and Diehl, *Anthol. lyr.* ii, first ed. 279) ἰὼ μέγιστε κοῦρε, χαῖρέ μοι, Κρόνειε, and, belonging to a period probably not very remote from Horace's time, Melinno's hymn on Rome (Stob. 3. 7. 12; iii. 312 Hense) χαῖρέ μοι 'Ρώμα, θυγάτηρ Ἄρηος κτλ.—For the pronoun added to the formula of welcoming in ordinary life cf., for example, Ar. *Lys.* 1074 ἄνδρες Λάκωνες, πρῶτα μέν μοι χαίρετε κτλ.; Soph. *Oed. C.* 1137 (Oedipus to Theseus, whom he is meeting for the first time) σὺ δ' αὐτόθεν μοι χαῖρε. For the pronoun added to the formula of bidding farewell see, perhaps, Homer ψ 19 χαῖρέ μοι, ὦ Πάτροκλε, καὶ εἰν Ἀΐδαο δόμοισι, although there the expression does not yet seem to have become a formula, and Eur. *Hec.* 426 χαῖρ', ὦ τεκοῦσα, χαῖρε Κασσάνδρα τ' ἐμοί.

[5] See the end of the epilogue of the hymn to Asklepios in the copy from Ptolemais in Egypt, written down in A.D. 100, χαῖρέ μοι, ὦ Παιάν, ἐπ' ἐμαῖς εὔφροσι ταῖσδ' ἀοιδαῖς. χαῖρ', ὦ Πύθι' Ἄπολλον. This formula, according to Wilamowitz, 'Nordionische Steine', *Abh. Preuß. Akad.* 1909, 43 n., must be traced back to early hieratic poetry. In the Erythrae copy of the same hymn (Wil., op. cit. 43 f.), first half of the fourth century B.C., the last stanza begins χαῖρέ μοι, ἴλαος δ' ἐπινίσεο τὰν ἀμὰν πόλιν κτλ., where χαῖρέ μοι has perhaps more of *salve mihi* than of *vale.*

Horace, against the common usage, added *mihi* to *salve*.[1] To conclude the remarks on this small point: the formula of greeting at the end of the ode shows an unmistakable, if free, adaptation of a topic of hymnic poetry. This observation alone should be sufficient to protect the text of the final clause from wanton alterations.[2] Even if the conjectures which have been made were less improbable than they are,[3] it should be recognized that *mihi cumque* is what Horace wrote. The well-known stumbling-block is *cumque* used in a manner for which there exists no real parallel. Its exact function in this passage must therefore remain a matter of conjecture. But one thing seems fairly certain: when we find *cumque . . . rite vocanti* in a prayer-like context, we are all but forced to connect this expression in some way with the formulas of prayers which have often been discussed, especially by E. Norden,[4] such as ὅστις δήποτε χαίρεις ὀνομαζόμενος, or, *quoquo nomine, quoquo ritu, quaqua facie te fas est invocare*[5] and the like.[6]

Most of those commentators who do not regard *cumque* as corrupt take it, with the scholiast (Porph.), to be equivalent to *quandocumque*.[7] Perhaps they are right. But is it not equally possible and, considering the religious thought and comparing *quocumque nomine* and similar formulas, even more likely that Horace intended the sense to be '*utcumque rite te voco*, in whatever manner, provided it is done *rite*, I invoke thee'? If he wanted his words to express that, he probably

[1] Heinze says 'die Verbindung von *salve* mit dem Dativ ist eine horazische Kühnheit'. That may be so; we should not, however, forget Virgil *Aen.* 11. 97 f. *salve aeternum mihi, maxime Palla, aeternumque vale*.

[2] It is not my purpose to discuss the vast literature on *mihi cumque*.

[3] Lachmann's *medicumque*, which was put in the text of all editions of Kiessling–Heinze's commentary, does not only deprive us of the indispensable *mihi* but is bad in itself: Horace, most fastidious in his ἐκλογὴ ὀνομάτων, would never make *medicumque* follow close upon *lenimen*.

[4] *Agnostos Theos*, 144 f.

[5] Apul. *Met.* 11. 2. 3.

[6] On the point of principle, viz. the necessity of making use of those formulas for the interpretation of *mihi cumque salve rite vocanti*, I agree with P. Ferrarino, *Athenaeum*, N.S xiii, 1935, 233 f. I cannot, however, follow him when he (cf. also his extensive monograph 'Cumque e i composti di *que*', *Memorie della R. Accad. . . . di Bologna*, Classe di Scienze Morali, serie IV, vol. iv, 1942, 27) connects *cumque* closely with *mihi* and takes it to mean 'qualunque io mi sia'. The same interpretation was given in 1840 by Düntzer, who was followed by Ritter and others, and recently by Ussani ('*mihi cumque*: "a me qual che io mi sia", cioè "per picciolo che io mi sia" '). This view is not commended by the linguistic facts, for from *quicumque, utcumque*, etc., it is a far cry to *mihicumque* (see Lenchantin's sound criticism, *Rendiconti dell' Istituto Lombardo*, Cl. di Lettere, lxxvii, 1943–4, 327 f.), and as regards the sense, Ferrarino's idea that the words express an 'umile e religioso abbandonarsi del poeta alla pura preghiera rituale' seems to me at variance with the spirit of this ode and, generally speaking, an un-Horatian conception.

[7] So, to mention only one of the greatest grammarians, J. Wackernagel, *Vorlesungen über Syntax*, ii. 120. The interpretation put forward by Autenrieth (quoted by O. Keller, *Epilegomena*, 108), F. Skutsch, *Kl. Schriften*, 163, and J. B. Hofmann (in Stolz-Schmalz, *Lat. Gramm.*, 5th ed. 486), 'jederzeit', '*semper*', differs but slightly.

strained the language very considerably and not only gave to *cumque* a meaning which it hardly ever had, but, moreover, increased the obscurity by the position in which he placed *cumque*. These, however, are in this case not fatal objections. Everything drives us to the conclusion that in this clause Horace's starting-point was not a living usage but rather a fossilized formula found in some antiquated relics of hieratic language. In digging it up and introducing it into this solemn prayer he allowed himself the kind of artificiality and indeed linguistic violence which it is difficult to avoid in attempting to revive a phrase that has long been obsolete.[1]

We are now in a position to tackle the beginning of the ode. As regards the first word, the παράδοσις is divided between *poscimur* and *poscimus*, and the external evidence (including the ancient quotations) in favour of either variant is equally strong. It is therefore on internal grounds that the issue must be decided. On this point Bentley's critical genius shows itself in all its power. In his note he first gives a thorough and absolutely fair examination of every argument that could be adduced to support the reading *poscimur* and then explains why he does not hesitate to prefer *poscimus*. Here it will suffice to quote the beginning of his paraphrase, 'Rogamus, inquit; oramus te, Barbite, si quid umquam . . .', and to mention that he recognized and fully illustrated the hieratic character of both *poscimus*[2] and the clause beginning with *siquid*. Bentley's arguments in favour of *poscimus* are greatly strengthened by what has been said about the whole ode being conceived in terms of prayer.[3] *Poscimur* has no natural place in a prayer-like poem; *poscimus*, on the other hand, is most suitable to open the invocation of a deity.[4]

In discussing *poscimus* Bentley, against the former editors, insisted on the necessity of connecting the relative clause *quod et hunc in annum vivat et pluris* not with the preceding *siquid* but with the following *Latinum carmen*.[5] This interpretation has been accepted by numerous scholars,[6]

---

[1] I had long come to the conclusion that Horace's bold use of *cumque* in this passage was, at any rate partially, suggested to him by some archaic, or archaizing, *carmen*. I now see that O. Keller, app. crit. of his second edition, arrived at the same conclusion.

[2] For the meaning of *poscimus* see, for instance, Heinze's note on *Odes* 1. 31. 1 and Norden's commentary on Virg. *Aen.* 6. 45 (p. 136). It is gratifying that Klingner, too, has come round to *poscimus* (see his second edition of *Horace*, 1950, p. xxii).

[3] Ferrarino, *Athenaeum*, N.S. xiii, 1935, 231, is right in calling the ode 'una vera e propria preghiera del poeta alla lirica eolica'.

[4] In addition to the initial λίσσομαι at Pind. *Nem.* 3. 1 (Bentley) and *Ol.* 12. 1 (Heinze) compare, for example, Anacreon, *fr.* 1 γουνοῦμαί σ' ἐλαφηβόλε; Pind. *Pyth.* 12. 1 αἰτέω σε, φιλάγλαε.

[5] Bentley's later treatment of the passage, however, showed the truth of the saying αἱ δεύτεραί πως φροντίδες σοφώτεραι. See below, p. 172 n. 3.

[6] Of its recent champions I mention G. Carlsson, *Eranos*, xlii, 1944, 10 n. 3. The argument which he derives from *lusimus* will be answered presently in the text.

among them several who reject the reading *poscimus*, and in the majority of the commentaries we find it stated as a fact that *quod et . . . pluris* goes with *Latinum carmen*. It must be admitted that Bentley's way of construing the period is exceedingly tempting. At first sight it cannot but appeal to our imagination when it is pointed out to us that here are two stages in the poet's production, an earlier one of παίγνια, and a later one of serious poetry, contrasted in very much the same way as, for instance, in the proem of the *Culex* (*lusimus . . .; posterius graviore sono tibi musa loquetur nostra*).[1] But on closer examination Bentley's view appears to be improbable on grounds of sentence-structure and even more so when we consider the thought implied in it.

Let us take the syntactical point first. A relative clause, as a rule, follows the part of the sentence to which it relates. If it is to precede it, a careful writer will avoid ambiguity. No ambiguity can arise if the relative clause is placed at the beginning of a sentence. But to write *siquid . . . lusimus tecum quod . . . vivat . . . age dic . . . carmen* and expect the reader, against the common order,[2] to connect *quod vivat* not with *siquid* but with *carmen* would amount almost to setting a trap. Horace does not do this sort of thing. I have searched all his epodes and odes without finding anything even remotely comparable. In no passage of these poems can there be any doubt about the connexion of a relative clause.[3] From this point of view it proves utterly unlikely that *quod vivat* should go with *Latinum carmen*.

We now have to examine the criterion provided by the thought.

---

[1] Horace himself, contrasting his own *sermones* with the turgid poems of certain contemporaries, says (*Sat.* 1. 10. 37) *haec ego ludo*.

[2] R. Reitzenstein, *Rh. Mus.* lxviii, 1913, 253, rightly says 'gegen die natürliche Anordnung der Sätze'.

[3] There exists in fact one passage where several editors have done what Bentley did in the case of *Odes* 1. 32. 2 f., viz. made a relative clause look to what follows rather than to what precedes. The passage in question is *Carm. Saec.* 25 ff. *vosque veraces cecinisse, Parcae, quod semel dictum est stabilisque rerum terminus servet, bona iam peractis iungite fata.* Here Lambinus made the clause *quod . . . servet* depend upon *bona . . . fata*; he was followed by, for example, Peerlkamp, Wickham, Kiessling (but not, so far as can be gathered from his paraphrase, Heinze), Vahlen, *Sitz. Berl. Akad.* 1892, 1009 f. (*Gesammelte Schriften*, ii. 374). I regard this as wholly artificial; moreover 'sic verba *veraces cecinisse* nimis abrupta sunt et prope manca; quid tandem, quaeso, *cecinisse?*' (Orelli–Baiter). The objections which Bentley, and others after him, took to the MS reading of the passage have been thoroughly refuted by Lenchantin, *Rendic. Istituto Lombardo*, Cl. di Lettere, lxxvii, 1943–4, 363 f.; he rightly takes *quod semel . . . servet* as the object of *cecinisse*. So did Bentley, but he altered the text. His note on *Carm. Saec.* 26 provides our interpretation of *quod et hunc in annum vivat et pluris* with a powerful, if unexpected, ally. He says 'Latini sermonis ratio poscit . . . ut post *cecinisse quod* verba modi subiunctivi, non indicativi, sequantur . . . Ita Carm. i. 32. 3 "*Lusimus tecum, quod et hunc in annum* Vivat *et plures*".' In other words, when the great man discussed the *Carmen Saeculare*, he had completely forgotten his violent treatment of *Odes* 1. 32. 2 f. and returned to the natural interpretation. Wilamowitz's writings are full of this kind of *felix incuriositas* in regard to his own former assertions; his *Pindaros* 285 (last paragraph), as compared with *Berl. Sitz.* 1901, 1310, provides a typical example.

Here the decisive point was briefly made in Orelli–Baiter's 'Excursus' to this ode[1] and worked out with great precision by Reitzenstein.[2] It is indeed almost inconceivable that in a poem which is so consistently reminiscent of the formulas of prayer, a protasis of the type αἴ ποτα κάτέρωτα . . . ἔκλυες, or εἴ ποτε καὶ προτέρας ἄτας ὕπερ . . . ἠνύσατε, and the like—that such a protasis should be followed by an apodosis which, instead of stressing the parallelism between the present emergency and the case which is adduced as a precedent, would express the very opposite thought and emphasize the difference between the benefit received in the past and that asked for now. Such a differentiation, from the point of view of any praying worshipper, would be madness, for it must be his main concern to make the analogy between the hoped-for action of the god and his action in the past as close as possible: by insisting on the precedent, by telling the god 'you have done for me precisely the same thing before' and, sometimes, by adding 'you are perfectly capable of doing it (δύνασαι γάρ)', he hopes to compel him to comply with his wishes, reluctant though he may be to do so. Horace's general practice in his borrowings from the topics of prayer gives us no right in this case to ascribe to him an absurd deviation from the norm.

Thus far we have in the main followed the arguments put forward by those few among the modern scholars who saw that it is necessary not to detach the clause *quod et hunc in annum*, etc., from *siquid lusimus*. But now we must take a further step. It is not only on account of the origin and customary use of the εἴ ποτε formula that we have to avoid assuming an antithesis of *siquid . . . lusimus* and *age dic Latinum, barbite, carmen*: the principal thought of this very ode warns us not to do so.[3] But this warning will be lost on us if we persist in reading into the poem what we should like to find in it and glossing over what does not agree with our preconceived idea. The current interpretation of this ode shows that by means of one or two slight and apparently harmless retouches it is possible to give the impression that Horace is contrasting some former lyrics of his, written in a light vein and independently

---

[1] 'quam mirum foret hoc enthymema: "Barbite, si quid ludibundi iam ante cecinimus, propter hoc ipsum nunc iam serium ac longe gravius dic carmen Latinum".'

[2] Op. cit. 254: 'Die Formelsprache des Gebetes ist in i. 32 noch treuer [than in iii. 21] gewahrt: paßt in sie der Gedanke "göttliche Leier, *wenn* ich bisher auf dir Vergängliches (Minderwertiges) gespielt habe, so laß mir jetzt ein unvergängliches Lied gelingen"? Der in diesen Formeln immer beschwörende und erinnernde Vordersatz nähme dabei eine für mich weder durch Beispiele zu belegende noch psychologisch faßliche Bedeutung an. Gleichartiges muß genannt werden', etc.

[3] But so strong is the influence of a traditional prejudice that even Lenchantin, op. cit. (p. 172, n. 3) 326, after rightly declining to make *quod et hunc in annum*, etc., depend on *carmen*, continues 'Orazio che nei suoi carmi . . . aveva preso a modello autori di minor impegno, volge ora lo sguardo a poeti di grande ala. Il *latinum carmen* è messo così in opposizione al *lesbium carmen*', etc.

of Alcaeus, with the songs of a higher strain which, inspired by the Lesbian poet, he now intends to produce.[1] The commentators who take this line are forced to assume that the *barbitos* addressed in the first stanza is not yet the instrument once used by Alcaeus but some non-specified lyre belonging to the early period of Horace's lyrics. This assumption is at variance with the whole structure of the ode and, in particular, with the way in which the lines 5 ff. are linked up with the first stanza. If we want to do justice to the closely-knit texture of the poem, we have to conclude that the lyre of Alcaeus is the instrument not only of the *Latinum carmen* but of Horace's former *ludere* as well, in other words that the lyrics denoted in ll. 1 ff. were also of a kind which Horace could claim to be Lesbian, Alcaean. But in drawing this conclusion are we not neglecting the meaning of *lusimus*? I do not think so. It will indeed be necessary to discard the idea that Horace is concerned here with a special type of poetry, with παίγνια, *nugae, ludi*. But it does not follow that we have to deprive *lusimus* of its proper meaning. A reliable way to the understanding of *lusimus tecum* is shown by the preceding words *vacui sub umbra*. Bentley took exception to *sub umbra* and therefore altered it, but this detail is very significant in the present context. If we wish to substantiate the idea we may compare *Odes* 1. 1. 30 ff.,

> me gelidum nemus
> Nympharumque leves cum Satyris chori
> secernunt populo, si neque tibias
> Euterpe cohibet nec Polyhymnia
> Lesboum refugit tendere barbiton.

The life that Horace desires for himself is neither that of the victor in a chariot race at Olympia nor that of a successful Roman magistrate or of a big land-owner or of a modest *colonus* or of a rich merchant or of a man given to simple pleasures or of a warrior or of a huntsman. The poet keeps away from that motley crowd; their pursuits and pleasures mean nothing to him. He seeks a cool grove (*gelidum nemus*); there, *Pieria . . . in umbra*, he enjoys the company of the Muses and watches

---

[1] See, for example, Wickham, 'Come, my lyre, I have drawn strains from thee before which, light though they be, will not soon die: answer now with such music for Roman ears as thou yieldedst of old to Alcaeus'; F. Skutsch, *Kl. Schriften*, 164, 'Bisher hat Horaz . . . für sich allein mit der Leier getändelt, jetzt soll zum ersten Male ein dauerbares lateinisches Lied auf des Alcäus Laute entstehen'; Heinze (who has here retained Kiessling's paraphrase with but a few minor changes), 'So manchmal hast du dich mir, göttliche Leier, zu leichter Tändelei freundlich gesellt; so erhöre mich denn auch jetzt, und schenke mir ein minder vergängliches lateinisches Lied, wie du einst zu griechischen Sängen dem Alkaios erklungen bist', etc. It will be noticed, first, that Horace does not say 'my lyre' or 'göttliche Leier', but *barbite . . . Lesbio primum modulate civi*, and, secondly, that the paraphrase 'such music as thou yieldedst to Alcaeus', 'wie du einst dem Alkaios erklungen bist', is not warranted by the text.

the Nymphs and Satyrs engaged in their παίζειν τε καὶ χορεύειν. In these congenial surroundings there comes to him the sound of the *Lesbous barbitos*. Surely, he will not merely listen to it but do what in the other poem he calls *ludere cum barbito*. Horace, if he wants to give himself to poetry, has to be *vacuus*, to leave behind *fumum et opes strepitumque Romae* and the humdrum of his daily life.[1] Alcaeus, the child of a harder age, a stout warrior and sailor, possessed the strength of mind that enabled him, even amidst the horrors of war or the perils of a sea voyage, to cast off the load of his troubles and write pure poetry, drinking songs and love songs. The two poets are very different men, but, Horace likes to think, they have this in common that it is in poetry that both of them find *laborum dulce lenimen*. This idea pervades the ode i. 32 from the beginning to the end. If Horace speaks of some of his early 'Lesbian' poems as products of his *ludere*, he does so not because he wishes to describe them as pieces of light, unpretentious poetry as distinct from more exacting works,[2] but probably because he wishes to set his playing with the *barbitos* against the background of *labores* and everything that an ordinary Roman would regard as *res seria*.

The fundamental idea of this ode seems to be that the writing of lyrics, in particular the writing of Alcaean lyrics as Horace understands it, has the power to lift the poet above the care and toil of his life. This idea accounts for the incompleteness of what Horace, in the two central stanzas, says about the poetry of Alcaeus: certain serious themes which are prominent in the work of Alcaeus and accordingly emphasized in Horace's Hades ode (ii. 13) are here pushed into the background. Alcaeus is described as the man

> qui ferox bello tamen inter arma,
> sive iactatam religarat udo
> litore navim,

> Liberum et Musas Veneremque et illi
> semper haerentem puerum canebat
> et Lycum nigris oculis nigroque
> crine decorum.

Nothing is here said of the στασιωτικά. This omission serves to intensify the contrast between the Lesbian poet's harassed life and the triumphant freedom of his art; his drinking songs and love songs show his

---

[1] See his lively complaint *Epist.* 2. 2. 65–80 (77 *scriptorum chorus omnis amat nemus et fugit urbem* is reminiscent of the end of *Odes* i. 1, l. 78 *umbra* of the beginning of i. 32). Cf. also *Epist.* 1. 7. 44 f. *mihi iam non regia Roma, sed vacuum Tibur placet aut imbelle Tarentum.*

[2] On this point I agree with Wilamowitz, *S.u.S.* 310 n. 2, 'Was will er nun haben? Man denkt an erhabene Gegenstände wie er sie später behandelt, im Gegensatz zu der Erotik. Dann hat er aber die Vergleichung mit Alkaios schlecht durchgeführt: der machte ja gerade Liebeslieder *inter arma*', etc.

mind unruffled by all he had to endure and prove by their very ease
that to him poetry was *laborum lenimen*.

It is not difficult to guess what induced Horace to write this poem.
The more he studied Alcaeus, the more he came to admire not only
his art but also his manly spirit. His enthusiasm for 'the Lesbian citizen' is expressed no less strongly, though differently, in this ode than in
Ille et nefasto te posuit die. Moreover, this ode bears witness to Horace's
delight in following his great model and also to his hope that in doing
so he too might be able to produce something that will last. He sees his
way clear before him. *Age dic Latinum, barbite, carmen*: he wants to
bring forth Latin poems, but his instrument shall be the *barbitos* (a
rarer and more solemn name than either *lyra* or *cithara*) of the old
Greek poet. His own works shall blend the language and thought of a
Roman with the *spiritus Graiae Camenae*. The unification of these two
elements was to remain his most cherished aim; in one of his latest
lyrics he gratefully accepts the praise of being *Romanae fidicen lyrae*, the
κιθαρῳδός of the Roman lyre.

If our interpretation of the ode is in the main sound, that is to say
if no fundamental contrast is intended between some earlier poems of
Horace and the new poems which he hopes to write, then nothing can
be guessed about the kind of poem or poems indicated by *Latinum
carmen*. For some time Horace had been writing Latin lyrics in 'Lesbian' style; he was determined to go on with it. But he does not give
us any clue as to the theme or themes he has in mind.[1] The freshness
of his enthusiasm for the Lesbian poet points, perhaps, to an early
stage in Horace's writing of Alcaean lyrics, but not even that is certain.
Since he did not care to specify the meaning of *Latinum carmen* in this
context, we must not try to extract from the phrase something definite. Generally speaking, our satisfaction at being able to affix a date to
one more poem should never be bought at the price of misrepresenting
the thought of the poet.

Odes i. 9, *Vides ut alta stet nive candidum Soracte*, is dear to many of us
primarily because it reminds us of the days when, either from a *ter-
razzo* on the roof of one of the tall and weathered houses off the Corso
or from the height of the Gianicolo, we gazed at the queer sil-
houette which the isolated sharp peak of Monte Soratte forms against
the northern horizon. We also like the ode because it contains several
passages of great beauty, among them some happy adaptations of

---

[1] It is very instructive, by way of contrast, to compare *Odes* iii. 25, *Quo me, Bacche, rapis*
(on it see pp. 257 ff. below). There the enthusiasm is even stronger and ecstatic language
is used throughout, and yet it is made perfectly clear what the theme will be of the songs
that are to be brought forth by the poet's inspiration.

Alcean motifs. But we have to admit that as a whole the poem falls short of the perfection reached by Horace in many of his odes. Its heterogeneous elements have not merged into a harmonious unit. Line 18 *nunc et campus et areae* and what follows suggest a season wholly different from the severe winter at the beginning. This incongruity cannot be removed by any device of apologetic interpretation.[1] To put it somewhat crudely: the 'Hellenistic' ending of the ode and its 'Alcaean' beginning have not really coalesced. Horace, when he had reached the stage of perfect mastery, considered it all-important that a poem, like any work of art, *sit quodvis, simplex dumtaxat et unum*.[2] It is not unlikely that at the time when he published the collection of the first three books of his *carmina* he was aware of the imperfect structure of the Soracte ode but nevertheless deemed it, and rightly, a poem fine enough to stand as he had written it.[3]

Odes i. 18, *Nullam, Vare, sacra vite prius severis arborem*, like the Alexandria ode, i. 37, takes from Alcaeus the 'motto' at its beginning[4] and the metre:[5] μηδ' ἐν ἄλλο φυτεύσῃς πρότερον δένδριον ἀμπέλω. The continuation, *circa mite solum Tiburis et moenia Catili*, brings us immediately to the neighbourhood of Rome, just as the mention of *Saliares dapes* in the second line of the Alexandria ode produces a Roman atmosphere. But even the 'motto' is not left unchanged. Apart from the name of the addressee, Horace adds to the name of the vine the epithet *sacra*, which was, perhaps, suggested to him, as Orelli assumed, by a passage in the *Athamas* of Ennius.[6] Be this as it may, it is obvious that the epithet gives a solemn tone to a sentence which in the words of Alcaeus sounds like a matter-of-fact piece of advice. And a solemn tone is characteristic of the whole ode.[7] Its centre is occupied by a serious warning (7-11), the emphasis of which is strengthened by two *exempla*. A variety of sonorous names of Bacchus and the picture of his thiasus with its instruments add to the grandeur of the poem. The refinement of these details as well as of the general structure of the ode

---

[1] See on this point Kiessling, *Philol. Untersuchungen* (ed. Kiessling and Wilamowitz), ii, 1881, 63, whose criticism as well as his positive appreciation of the ode are still worth reading. The kind of excuses which he rejected were renewed by A. Y. Campbell, *Horace*, 1924, 225, 'the third stanza itself implies a transition from winter to spring; the advice thereafter becomes general'. Even if we accept, as many commentators do, a mitigating interpretation of *nunc* at l. 18, there remains the fact that the picture of the season at the end of the ode is not compatible with the beginning, where *Soracte alta nive candidum* suggests a very severe winter.

[2] *Ars P.* 23.

[3] I have been brief on this ode, since its analysis by Pasquali, *Or. lir.* 75 ff., is particularly helpful.

[4] Cf. above, p. 159 n. 2.

[5] Alc. *fr.* 97 D., 342 L. and P.

[6] Scaen. 124 Vahlen.

[7] Cf. Pasquali, *Or. lir.* 8 f.

points to influences other than that of Alcaeus. It is quite likely that the poem μηδ᾽ ἔν ἄλλο φυτεύσῃς also contained a παραίνεσις to the effect that man should enjoy the gift of Dionysus, but it was probably a παραίνεσις of a very different, and much simpler, kind.[1]

In *Odes* iii. 12, *Miserarum est neque amori*, it is not merely, as in i. 37 or i. 18, the metre and a 'motto' at the beginning that are derived from Alcaeus, but the metre and the theme and setting of the whole ode. Both the metre, pure ionics, and the theme and setting, a soliloquy of a love-stricken girl, are unique in Horace.[2] What little is preserved of the poem of Alcaeus is not nearly sufficient for a comparison with Horace or an estimate of the latter's independence. But even so an interesting difference can be observed. The poem of Alcaeus began[3]

῎Εμε δείλαν, ἔμε παίσαν κακοτάτων πεδέχοισαν,

that is to say, there was no formal preparation or introduction; the girl burst at once into an impassioned lamentation, singing, as it were, with the voice of nature. Horace's Neobule begins with a γνώμη, *Miserarum est*, etc. This γνώμη is also applicable to Neobule's own situation, but as a general sentence it has the effect of rendering the opening of the poem more ornate and probably, according to the taste of the Augustan period, more momentous. A similar device is found at the beginning of several Horatian odes.

From the tattered pieces which are all that is left of the poem of Alcaeus, a coherent thought, apart from the first line, can be recovered only at l. 5, where the scholia on Sophocles have preserved the fine simile of the deer.[4] To this thought nothing in *Miserarum est* corresponds. The topics as well as the sentiments of this ode are partly Roman, partly Hellenistic. 'Il carme della vergine sospirosa non è imitazione di Alceo se non nell' idea generale e nel principio; tutto il resto è oraziano e romano.'[5]

---

[1] In his survey of the pieces of Alcaeus which were first published in volume X of the *Pap. Oxy.* Wilamowitz (*Kl. Schriften*, i. 393) stated that those Horatian odes the principal theme of which is a moral παραίνεσις have their parallels in what we now possess of Alcaeus, but he wisely added 'nur hat Horaz den Inhalt seiner Paränese oft anderswoher, seiner Neigung gemäß selbst aus der Popularphilosophie genommen'.

[2] For the uniqueness of the beginning of ῎Εμε δείλαν see Snell, *Philol.* xcvi, 1944, 289 n. 3. Wilamowitz, *Hellenist. Dichtung*, ii. 114, observes that Hellenistic epigrams put in the mouth of a girl are very rare.

[3] *Fr.* 123. 1 D., 10 L. and P.

[4] It is unfortunate that at the end of the line both Diehl and Page, *Sappho and Alcaeus*, 291 ff., accept Lobel's conjecture φοβέροισιν, without mentioning that H. Fränkel, *Gött. gel. Anz.* 1928, 272 f., and R. Pfeiffer, *Gnomon*, vi, 1930, 317, have shown it to be wrong and correctly interpreted the παράδοσις.

[5] Pasquali, *Or. lir.* 103.

2. ODES RELATED TO OTHER GREEK POEMS

We now leave those odes in which Horace is to a greater or lesser degree indebted to Alcaeus (probably many more poems than we can make out belong to this group) and look at some others in which a marked influence either of a particular piece of Greek lyrics or of Greek poetry in general can be detected.

For *Odes* i. 27, *Natis in usum laetitiae scyphis*, we receive some guidance from the scholiast (Porph.) : *cuius sensus sumptus est ab Anacreonte ex libro tertio*. Of the poem of Anacreon to which this statement refers two fragments are preserved,[1] one

> ἄγε δή, φέρ' ἡμίν, ὦ παῖ,
> κελέβην, ὅκως ἄμυστιν
> προπίω, τὰ μὲν δέκ' ἐγχέας
> ὕδατος, τὰ πέντε δ' οἴνου
> κυάθους, ὡς ἀνυβρίστως
> ἀνὰ δηὖτε βασσαρήσω,

and then, after a gap,

> ἄγε δηὖτε μηκέθ' οὕτω
> πατάγῳ τε κἀλαλητῷ
> Σκυθικὴν πόσιν παρ' οἴνῳ
> μελετῶμεν, ἀλλὰ καλοῖς
> ὑποπίνοντες ἐν ὕμνοις.[2]

The first thing that we are bound to notice as we compare the Greek and the Latin poem is that the metre of Horace's ode is 'not Anacreontic but Lesbian'.[3] It seems an obvious conclusion that at the time when Horace wrote *Natis in usum* he had already made up his mind to use as the instrument of his new lyrics the *Lesbous barbitos* or, in plain language, to adopt in the main the metrical forms of Alcaeus, even where the matter of an ode was derived from a different source. We do not know what induced him to take this course nor whether at an earlier experimental stage he followed the model of Anacreon more closely.[4]

---

[1] *Fr.* 43 D.

[2] P. Von der Mühll, *Hermes*, lxxv, 1940, 422 ff., denies that the two pieces belong to one and the same poem, but he has not proved his case. Leaving everything else aside, the expression by which Athenaeus, to whom we owe the two fragments, introduces the second one, 10. 427 a, καὶ προελθὼν τὴν ἀκρατοποσίαν Σκυθικὴν καλεῖ πόσιν, shows clearly that he is quoting a piece of the same song. προελθὼν in such a context has a fixed meaning and cannot refer to a different poem. Cf., for instance, Plat. *Prot.* 339 c προϊόντος τοῦ ᾄσματος, 339 d ὀλίγον δὲ τοῦ ποιήματος εἰς τὸ πρόσθεν προελθὼν κτλ., Athen. 10. 430 b (Alc., *fr.* 98 D., 367 L. and P.) καὶ προελθών, 13. 559 b Εὔβουλος δ' ἐν Χρυσίλλα ... καὶ προελθών φησιν . . .. Cf. also Wilamowitz, *Pindaros*, 498, who reaffirms Bergk's statement (in regard to [Plut.] *Consol. ad Apoll.* 35. 120 c) that the words καὶ μικρὸν προελθών must refer to a passage of the same poem which had been quoted before.

[3] Wilamowitz, *S.u.S.* 307.

[4] Wilamowitz, loc. cit., has some ingenious speculations on these points.

What we see when we turn from the metrical form of this ode to its content makes it unlikely that the dependence upon Anacreon should go beyond one topic, the dislike for riotous carousing and the warning given to the banqueters not to indulge in such a barbarous habit.[1] We do not know in what manner the poem of Anacreon began[2] nor how it proceeded, but we may be sure that it contained nothing of the dramatic structure which is one of the attractions of this Horatian ode.

The poet joins a banquet at a late hour: heads are far from cool, arguments threaten to lead to blows, and drinking cups are being used as missiles. The poet's appearance on the scene gives the signal for an even wilder tumult. While some of the young men continue their private fights, most of them jump up from their couches and gather round the newcomer, wildly shouting and gesticulating. Horace, with some effort, manages to raise his voice above the din and to persuade the banqueters to go back to their places and lie down in an orderly fashion (6–8). But now they all start pressing him: 'Horace, join us; the Falernian here is good strong stuff, try it; Horace, come, lie down here, no here, no, Horace, here with me.' 'Well', Horace replies, 'I will join you, but only on my own terms. Here is my condition:

> dicat Opuntiae
> frater Megillae,[3] quo beatus
> volnere, qua pereat sagitta.'

This proposal immediately stops the turmoil: everybody is staring at the luckless young man, almost a boy (20 *puer*), à μειράκιον, the victim of so unexpected and indiscreet an attack. He blushes—and says nothing. But the poet insists without mercy: *cessat voluntas? non alia bibam mercede*. Again silence, a very long one. Horace changes his tone to a gentle persuasiveness: I am sure in your affair there is nothing to be ashamed of, and, whoever she is, as you love her she must be all

---

[1] What we now read in Porphyrio's introductory note on this ode, *cuius sensus sumptus est ab Anacreonte ex libro tertio*, is obviously a very mutilated remainder of a learned commentary, where, perhaps, only the thought of the first two stanzas of the ode was traced back to Anacreon (cf., for example, Porph. on *Odes* I. 12. 1, where the note *hoc a Pindaro sumpsit* is correctly appended to the opening words of the ode and followed by the general remark *continet autem haec ode*, etc.).

[2] In all editions of Kiessling-Heinze's commentary we read that the words ἄγε δή, φέρ' ἡμῖν κτλ. were the beginning of Anacreon's song; the same view is held by Pasquali, *Or. lir.* 512 ('il carme anacreonteo comincia con un lieto comando al coppiere') and by Diehl. The possibility that that was so cannot be denied, but there is no proof.

[3] It does not seem possible to make out whether Horace called the girl *Megilla* or *Megylla*. For both forms of the name there seems to be good Greek evidence, cf. Fick and Bechtel, *Die griech. Personennamen*, 198; for the two forms of the suffix see E. Schwyzer, *Griech. Gramm.* i. 485. On such a point the MSS provide no safe guidance: at Virg. *Aen.* 11. 640 the Mediceus and the Bernensis 165 (saec. IX) have *Cat(t)hyllus*.

right; you would not dally with one who is no lady:

> quae te cumque domat Venus,
> non erubescendis adurit
> ignibus, ingenuoque semper
> amore peccas.

Another long pause. 'Come come, you know you can trust me, I am discretion itself' (17 f.). Now at last the boy, flushing, whispers something into the poet's ear. Horace is startled: 'Good gracious![1] My poor boy! That monster? a hopeless case!'

To bring into relief the dramatic character of the ode, I have inserted into my summary, as it were, stage directions.[2] I have not, however, invented anything but only made explicit what is implied in the text itself. Although the ode contains nothing but the words addressed by the poet partly to the *sodales* in general and partly to the brother of Megilla, Horace's consummate skill enables him to make us see what is going on round the speaker and even to hear some of the utterances of the others. This subtle and consistent building up of a dramatic structure in a lyric poem is certainly not in the manner of Anacreon or, for that matter, any archaic poet, but bears the stamp of a later age.

Some of the best Horatian scholars are of the opinion that *Natis in usum* belongs to a group of Hellenistic and Roman poems of which it is characteristic that the poet, assuming the part of a herald, or, in other cases, of one of the spectators, announces or describes an action, especially the performance of a religious ceremony, by reporting its various stages as they unfold one after another.[3] I myself cannot accept this view, for I think that a very important difference lies in the fact that in the ode *Natis in usum* the role of the poet is not that of a neutral observer who conveys his impressions to the reader, but that of a principal actor who either talks to his fellow actors or responds to their actions and utterances.

---

[1] Most commentators say nothing on *a miser*. L. Müller compares *Odes* 2. 17. 5; that passage and *Epod.* 5. 71 are the only other places in Horace where the interjection *a* occurs. In all three passages a strong emotion is indicated. The elegiac poets are very fond of *a*; Virgil has it nine times in the *Bucolics*, twice in the *Georgics*, never in the *Aeneid*. It is characteristic of the style of Ovid's epic speeches that *a* is found nine times in the *Metamorphoses*. For *a miser* cf. *Thes. l. L.* i. 1442. 49 ff.

[2] Long after writing this I saw that Arthur L. Wheeler, 'Catullus and the Traditions of Ancient Poetry', *Sather Classical Lectures*, ix, 1934, 204 f., in his discussion of *Natis in usum* uses the same device, which he, too, calls stage directions. Neither of us is guilty of interpolating: we have merely worked out the clear indications of the poet.

[3] The common features of this group were recognized by R. Reitzenstein (*Hellenistische Wundererzählungen*, 156 ff. and *Neue Jahrb.* xxi, 1908, 84 f., 97 f., 365), who included *Natis in usum* in the group. This classification was accepted by Heinze and by Pasquali, *Or. lir.* 195 f. and 520 (cf. also his *Quaestiones Callimacheae*, Gottingae 1913, 154 f.). For the first part of *Odes* iii. 14, *Herculis ritu*, which has with better right been brought into association with that group, see p. 289 below.

We do not know what model, if any, Horace was following when in this ode he incorporated the essential elements of a complex action into the words addressed by the central figure, the poet himself, to his companions.[1] There are, however, in his own early work certain passages which seem to show him on the way to the type of dramatic technique which he handles to perfection in *Natis in usum*. I am referring to *Epod.* 16. 23 ff. *sic placet? an melius quis habet suadere? . . . sed iuremus in haec*, etc., 7. 13 ff. *furorne caecus an rapit vis acrior an culpa? responsum date. tacent*, etc.; cf. also 5. 3 f. (here the speaker is not the poet but the boy, the victim of the sorceresses) *quid iste fert tumultus? aut quid omnium voltus in unum me truces?* But it is perhaps no accident that these passages come from poems which to Horace and his contemporaries were not lyrics. In another non-lyric poem,[2] *Adeste, hendeca-syllabi*, we find the same technique which we admire in *Natis in usum* employed with equal mastery. There, too, the poet is the principal actor and the whole poem is addressed by him to the 'persons', the *hendecasyllabi*, whom he has summoned, and there, too, the gradual evolution of the action and the reactions of the others to the poet's words are made perfectly clear without any interruption of the *oratio recta*. No reader can doubt that between 6, *persequamur eam et reflagitemus*, and 7, *quae sit, quaeritis*, there is a pause, during which the little poems which Catullus has just addressed have arrived; they are now clustering around him, pressing impatiently for an answer to their question. Line 10, *circumsistite eam et reflagitate*, is by implication as precise a stage direction as any in the dialogue of Greek drama. Between 12, *redde, putida moecha, codicillos*, and 13, *non assis facis?*, there is another pause, and between 20, *redde, putida moecha, codicillos*, and 21, *sed nil proficimus, nihil movetur*, a third. It is certain that Horace[3] remembered the poem *Adeste, hendecasyllabi*, and not unlikely that he was attracted by its refined arrangement and especially by the combination of easy grace and firmness of purpose which has the effect of making the reader witness by stages the progress of a lively action. Perhaps it was from these Catullan hendecasyllables that Horace derived some of the devices he employed so happily in *Natis in usum*.

The central topic of the ode, the teasing of the young man on account of his love affair, betrays unmistakably its dependence on Hellenistic poetry.[4] In fact the general atmosphere of this banquet poem

---

[1] We must not, of course, compare the common type of Hellenistic epigrams in the form of a dialogue.

[2] Catullus 42.   [3] Cf. *Epod.* 17. 40.

[4] See especially Pasquali, *Or. lir.* 514 ff. For an appreciation of the two relevant epigrams, Asclepiades, *Anth. Pal.* 12. 135, and Callimachus 43 Wil., see also Wilamowitz, *Hellenist. Dichtung*, ii. 127 f. (Both epigrams seem to have been in Horace's mind when he wrote *Epod.* 11. 9 f., *in quis amantem languor et silentium arguit et latere petitus imo spiritus*: the

is also Hellenistic. But for all that the importance of its 'Alcaean' form should not be underrated. It is presumably due, at any rate partially, to this form that the stylistic level of the ode is higher than would be compatible with the ἀφέλεια of either a drinking song of Anacreon or a polished Hellenistic epigram. The style, as is not seldom the case in Horace's odes, is loftiest at the beginning and at the end. The poem opens with a general maxim, a γνώμη, the thought of which, though not its form, is taken from Anacreon,

> Natis in usum laetitiae scyphis
> pugnare Thracum est.

Here an indubitable truth, something that is based on the nature of things, is affirmed in an authoritative tone, and the solemn ring of this comprehensive sentence has its effect although we suspect that the poet is pronouncing it 'with his tongue in his cheek'.[1] We enter the ode through the wide arch of a richly ornamented gate, clearly set off against the narrower issue of the situation which then presents itself (*tollite barbarum morem*, etc.). Anacreon's drinking song had in all probability no formal introduction at all but emerged immediately from the background of the occasion, an actual banquet of a given circle of companions, for which it was composed.[2] As regards Horace's finale, it seems to revel in grandeur; its rolling sounds and awe-inspiring images render the mockery of its thought the more delightful:

> quae saga, quis te solvere Thessalis
> magus venenis, quis poterit deus?
> vix inligatum te triformi
> Pegasus expediet Chimaera.

With *Natis in usum* the ode i. 23, *Vitas inuleo me similis, Chloe*, has this in common that it begins with a reminiscence from Anacreon,[3] and that its metrical form is that of Lesbian stanzas. Again we notice a style far more ornate than is likely to have been employed in a poem of Anacreon.[4] This stylistic character of the little poem as a whole should not be left out of account in dealing with the much-vexed beginning of the second stanza,

> nam seu mobilibus veris inhorruit
> adventus foliis,

---

last clause follows Callimachus, but what precedes it is influenced by Asclepiades' ἔρωτος ἔλεγχος and ἐνύστασε.) Cf. also Antiphanes, *fr.* 235 Kock, κρύψαι, Φειδία, | ἅπαντα τἄλλά τις δύναιτ' ἂν πλὴν δυοῖν, | οἰνόν τε πίνων εἰς ἐρωτά τ' ἐμπεσών. | ἀμφότερα μηνύει γὰρ ἀπὸ τῶν βλεμμάτων | καὶ τῶν λόγων ταῦθ'· ὥστε τοὺς ἀρνουμένους κτλ.

[1] 'Il carme oraziano comincia con una massima grave almeno in apparenza' (Pasquali, *Or. lir.* 512).   [2] Cf. p. 39 above.

[3] *Fr.* 39 D., ἀγανῶς οἷά τε νεβρὸν κτλ.   [4] See Pasquali, *Or. lir.* 134 f.

the boldness of which is undeniable.[1] This boldness could be the more easily understood if it were to be regarded as a piece of juvenile audacity.[2] But whether or not *Vitas inuleo* is one of Horace's very early odes, we shall hardly be inclined to see in it much more than a pretty little artefact.

i. 22, *Integer vitae*, is one of the best-known Horatian odes. Not very long ago it was the custom at many German schools to have the first stanza[3] sung at the funeral services in Hall, to a tune not distinguishable from that of an ordinary church hymn; the tempo, needless to say, was *molto adagio*, with a *sostenuto* on the adoneus. But the idea that the beginning of this ode is a serious declaration of high moral principles

---

[1] I am not, however, prepared to follow Porphyrio, Heinze, and other commentators in assuming here a very involved ὑπαλλαγή, nor do I believe, with Wickham, that *veris adventus* is said for 'animae veris comites'. I take the words as they stand: 'For whether the arrival of Spring has shivered among the quivering leaves'. One may, if one likes, call it διθυραμβῶδες, but that seems to be the sense intended by Horace. Perhaps *adventus* was meant to suggest the appearance, the ἐπιφάνεια, of a god, for which the word is so often used (cf. Lucretius 1. 6 and, for other instances, *Thes. l. L.* i. 838. 22 ff.) and to recall the approach of Apollo, announced by the quivering of his sacred trees (Callim. *hymn* 2. 1 ff. οἷον ὁ τὠπόλλωνος ἐσείσατο δάφνινος ὅρπηξ, . . . ἐπένευσεν ὁ Δήλιος ἡδύ τι φοῖνιξ . . . ὁ γὰρ θεὸς οὐκέτι μακρήν; cf. Virg. *Aen.* 3. 90 f.; Seneca, *Oed.* 228; Lucan 5. 154 f.).

[2] There does not seem to exist any certain evidence for an early date of the ode, although some peculiarities suggest it. Kiessling said 'Die frühe Abfassungszeit, etwa gleichzeitig mit ep. 13, verrät sich darin, daß noch nicht wie in den andern Oden dieses Metrums der Pherekrateus mit dem Glykoneus durch Synaphie gebunden ist, sondern den Hiatus zuläßt: v. 3 und 7. Dafür spricht auch die Vokalisierung des *v* in *silvae* (ebenso ep. 13, 2), sowie die Häufigkeit der epitheta perpetua: *pavidam m., m. aviis, mobilibus f., virides l.,* [*aspera t.* Heinze].' It was not until his last edition that Heinze cancelled this passage and substituted the following: 'Metrisch unterscheidet sich diese Ode von den übrigen der gleichen Strophenform, wie Kiessling beobachtet hat, dadurch daß [at the end of l. 3 and l. 7] . . . keine Synaphie besteht; auf frühe Abfassungszeit ist aber daraus schwerlich zu schließen. Man könnte sogar in den beiden Hiaten an dieser Stelle gerade sehr berechnende Kunst finden.' I would not absolutely exclude the latter possibility although it seems more likely that, as time went on and Horace steadily refined his technique, his ear grew increasingly sensitive to the break of συνάφεια: in the many Sapphic and Alcaic stanzas of Book IV there is never a hiatus between two lines, except after 4. 15. 10 (overlooked by Kiessling, who observed the general phenomenon, p. 10 of the 2nd edition of his commentary [p. 11 in Heinze's 6th ed.]), whereas such hiatuses occur often in the earlier Sapphic and Alcaic stanzas. It seems noteworthy that the long *Carmen Saeculare* agrees in this respect with Book IV. But even if we dismiss Kiessling's metrical argument, there still remain the two others. What he says about trisyllabic *siluae* (presumably an artificial, not an archaic, prosody, cf. F. Sommer, *Lat. Laut- und Formenlehre*, 3rd ed. 131; Vollmer, 'Röm. Metrik' in Gercke and Norden, *Einleit. in d. Altertumsw.* i. 8, 3rd ed. 18) is impressive: against its occurrence here and *Epod.* 13. 2 we must set the twenty-eight instances of bisyllabic forms of *silva* in Horace. To Kiessling's third observation, the stylistic one, I would add that the manner in which in ll. 9 f., *atqui non ego te tigris ut aspera Gaetulusve leo frangere persequor*, the enemy (or supposed enemy) is pictured recalls *Epod.* 6. 5 ff. nam *qualis aut Molossus aut fulvus Lacon . . . agam . . . quaecumque praecedet fera.*

[3] Regardless of *Fusce*, which on such occasions very much puzzled me when I was a small boy. Wilamowitz, *Süddeutsche Monatshefte*, xxviii, Heft 1, Oktober 1930, 45, remarks dryly '*Integer vitae* kann an einem Grabe nur singen wer es nicht versteht'.

cannot be dismissed as a schoolmasters' freak: it has its adherents among eminent scholars. Are they right?

An answer to this question can be found in the very clear structure of the ode. The lines 17–22,

> pone me pigris ubi nulla campis
> arbor aestiva recreatur aura,
> quod latus mundi nebulae malusque
> Iuppiter urget,

> pone sub curru nimium propinqui
> solis, in terra domibus negata,

are parallel to the lines 5–8,

> sive per Syrtis iter aestuosas
> sive facturus per inhospitalem
> Caucasum vel quae loca fabulosus
> lambit Hydaspes.

But the two passages are not only parallel, they also supplement one another. Taken together they give a complete picture of the uninhabitable parts of the world, where no human being, unless specially protected, can hope to survive. Moreover, these two passages are arranged symmetrically: they enclose, like a kind of frame, the picture that occupies exactly the centre of the ode, the third and fourth stanzas.[1] This central part fulfils the function which in a paraenetic poem of Alcaeus or another Greek lyric, and in several odes of Horace, falls to a παράδειγμα, an *exemplum*, taken from mythology or history. Its beginning, *namque*, made that function perfectly clear to an ancient reader. The double particle καὶ γάρ (*namque*), when it followed a general maxim or a piece of advice, a παραίνεσις, served from the earliest period of Greek literature to introduce a precedent that was to prove the validity of the maxim or to strengthen the advice. Achilles speaks to Priam thus: νῦν δὲ μνησώμεθα δόρπου. | καὶ γάρ τ' ἠΰκομος Νιόβη ἐμνήσατο σίτου | . . . ἡ δ' ἄρα σίτου μνήσατ', ἐπεὶ κάμε δάκρυ χέουσα. | . . . ἀλλ' ἄγε δὴ καὶ νῶϊ μεδώμεθα, δῖε γεραιέ, | σίτου.[2] Precisely the same arrangement occurs in a drinking-song of Alcaeus addressed to Melanippus,[3] ll. 4 ff., ἀλλ' ἄγι μὴ μεγάλων . . . καὶ γὰρ Σίσυφος

---

[1] For the central position of a mythological παράδειγμα cf., for example, Epode X (see p. 24 above); there the arrangement of the winds (3–8 supplemented by 19 f.) corresponds broadly to the arrangement of the severe zones in *Integer vitae*.

[2] *Iliad* 24. 601 ff. Cf. also *Iliad* 6. 129 ff. οὐκ ἂν ἐγώ γε θεοῖσιν ἐπουρανίοισι μαχοίμην. | οὐδὲ γὰρ οὐδὲ Δρύαντος υἱὸς κρατερὸς Λυκόοργος | δὴν ἦν . . ., (139 ff.) οὐδ' ἄρ' ἔτι δὴν | ἦν, ἐπεὶ ἀθανάτοισιν ἀπήχθετο πᾶσι θεοῖσιν. | οὐδ' ἂν ἐγὼ μακάρεσσι θεοῖς ἐθέλοιμι μάχεσθαι; 18. 115–21 and 19. 90–136; Pindar, *Ol.* 7. 24 ff.; A. *Ag.* 1035–41.

[3] *Fr.* 73 D., 38 L. and P.

Αἰολίδαις βασιλεύς ... ἀλλ' ἄγι μή .... The root of this thought-pattern lay presumably in homely folk-songs. Thus the women of Lesbos, while grinding corn, regulated the rhythm of their movements, and at the same time comforted themselves, by singing of the great ruler who was once engaged in the same dreary work:[1]

> ἄλει μύλα ἄλει·
> καὶ γὰρ Πιττακὸς ἄλει
> μεγάλας Μυτιλάνας βασιλεύων.

Songs of a similar type, referring to famous precedents (καὶ γὰρ . . .), were probably at least as old as the Homeric age.

To return to Horace's ode. Here the tale of the poet's miraculous escape after his encounter with the wolf occupies the place which in Greek poetry would often be occupied by the account of some adventure of a hero.[2] The implication of such a substitution could not be hidden to an ancient reader. It meant that the central part of the ode contained an element of parody, and this element is further emphasized by the style employed in the description of the wolf,

> quale portentum neque militaris
> Daunias latis alit aesculetis
> nec Iubae tellus generat, leonum
> arida nutrix.

It is by no means improbable that Horace on one of his walks in the Sabine hills should have seen a wolf[3]—we are not told at what distance—but, whatever happened in reality, in his poem he mockingly magnifies the monstrosity of the beast. By his treatment of the subject he seems to warn the reader not to take the accident too seriously. What is true of the central part applies to the whole ode. Its lofty thoughts, bold images, and sonorous phrases should not prevent us from appreciating the playful spirit that permeates it. The γνώμη with which the poem begins sounds solemn enough—as does for instance the opening sentence of *Odes* i. 27, *Natis in usum laetitiae scyphis pugnare Thracum est*—but here as there we soon realize the semi-seriousness of the τηλαυγὲς πρόσωπον. And if any reader (though not Fuscus or

---

[1] Plutarch, *Mor.* 157 d, *Carm. popul.* 30 D.

[2] Similarly Propertius, 4. 7. 1 ff., proves the truth of a general sentence with the help, not of a mythological precedent, but of a startling experience of his own, which he introduces by *namque: Sunt aliquid Manes: letum non omnia finit. . . . Cynthia namque meo visa est incumbere fulcro*, etc.

[3] Not long ago in a very cold winter wolves were seen near the railway-line Rome–Monte Cassino–Naples. Higher up, in the mountains of the Abruzzi, a soldier was recently killed by a wolf (report of the Rome correspondent of *The Times* in the issue of 25 Oct. 1950). [I can now add that during the exceptional cold spell of February 1956 a postman was attacked and eaten by wolves near the village of Mandela, in the immediate neighbourhood of Horace's farm.]

Maecenas) was for a moment in danger of making too much of *integer vitae scelerisque purus*, he would think better of it when he came to the last two lines of the poem. The symmetrical arrangement of this ode makes it necessary to connect the end closely with the beginning; thus Horace implies that the *integritas vitae* manifests itself, if not solely, at any rate primarily, in his being in love with Lalage and writing poems in her praise.[1]

We must, however, in our reaction to the over-serious interpretation, be careful not to go too far in the opposite direction.[2] From the easy grace of the ode and the mock-solemnity in some of its expressions it does not follow that there is no deeper feeling behind it. Horace, as he so often does, takes his cue from a topic which, presumably derived from Hellenistic poems, found favour with the Roman elegists,

> quisquis amore tenetur, eat tutusque sacerque
> qualibet: insidias non timuisse decet,[3]

and, as he so often does, he breathes fresh life into a conventional thought. In *Integer vitae* it is the lover and writer of love-poems who will be safe wherever he goes; elsewhere[4] Horace widens and deepens this idea: the poet (not only the writer of love-poems) will everywhere and in every danger enjoy the protection of his divine guardians, the Muses, and of the gods in general:

> di me tuentur, dis pietas mea
> et musa cordi est,

and

> vester, Camenae, vester in arduos
> tollor Sabinos . . . .
> . . . .
> vestris amicum fontibus et choris
> non me Philippis versa acies retro,
>   devota non extinxit arbor
>   nec Sicula Palinurus unda.

Here a feeling known to many poets and artists is expressed in terms of religious language; it is the same feeling that in *Integer vitae* finds a more sophisticated expression. But this sophistication does not conceal the genuine impulse from which the poem springs. The calm happiness

---

[1] Despite the clear structure of the ode Heinze (7th edition, 1930) remarked on the last stanza 'der Ausgangspunkt des Gedichts ist vergessen'. In his former editions he had followed Kiessling, who rightly appreciated the humorous touch in the poem but went much too far when he, like others, regarded it as 'ein durchaus scherzhaft gehaltenes Gelegenheitsgedicht'.

[2] Kiessling (see the preceding footnote) is a typical representative of this exaggeration.

[3] Tibullus 1. 2. 27 f. The commentators also compare Prop. 3. 16. 11 ff. Pasquali, *Or. lir.* 472, adds a reference to the epigram *Anth. Pal.* 5. 25 'Οσσάκι Κυδίλλης κτλ., but there nothing is said of the lover being specially protected.

[4] *Odes* 1. 17. 13 f. and 3. 4. 21 ff.

of Horace the poet gives to this graceful ode its unity and raises it above the level of a mere playing with traditional literary forms.

Odes i. 15, *Pastor cum traheret*, though in itself not a difficult poem, has had to suffer a great deal from the combination of two destructive forces. The first is the tendency, by no means confined to the interpretation of lyrics, to treat any ancient poem, if possible, as a kind of riddle, the solution of which should be the primary concern of a commentator. The other force is the belief in that mysterious working of uniformity which in German is called *Systemzwang*. Applied to the works of Horace it means that no form or setting of a poem can be tolerated if there exists only one instance of it. If in such a case a scholar is afraid of resorting to the most radical cure, the obelizing of the obnoxious poem,[1] he should at least extort from it such a meaning as to make it conform to a common type. Now *Pastor cum traheret* appears to be a piece of epic narrative, without any recognizable reference either to Horace himself or to a contemporary person or event. Such a thing is unparalleled in the *Odes*. Therefore many commentators have been driven to the conclusion that this ode, like the rest, must contain some reference to a contemporary event, in other words that it is an allegory. From this assumption there arises naturally the question 'who are the real persons disguised under the masks of Paris and Helen?'. We have not to go far to find the answer, provided we are prepared to overlook some disturbing details in the tale of Troy and to boil it down to something like this: a guilty couple of royal rank, enjoying, somewhere in the east, across the sea, the fruit of their crime until disaster overcomes not only themselves but also their realm. Once we have gone so far it seems obvious that no others can be meant than Antony and Cleopatra. This is considered a fact by a large body of opinion.[2] On the other hand, several scholars, among them some of great eminence,

---

[1] The whole ode i. 15 was obelized by Lehrs, large chunks of it by Peerlkamp and others. More subtle, though equally wrong, is Becher's assertion, *Suspiciones Horatianae*, 1822, 17 (quoted in Obbarius's commentary), that the ode is a mere fragment; consequently the reader would be at liberty to supply in his imagination whatever he chose.

[2] In recent times above all by Heinze. Of modern scholars who share his opinion I mention at random A. Y. Campbell, *Horace*, 1924, 110 f.; S. Eitrem, *Mélanges Émile Boisacq*, 1937, 353; W. Wili, *Horaz*, 1948, 119 f. There is no need to quote the many earlier commentators who held the same view, but it is perhaps worth while to trace this invention back to its origin. I have not been able to see Charles Vanderbourg's translation of the *Odes* (Paris 1812), from whose notes Obbarius and Orelli–Baiter ('Excursus') quote a 'glossator' (he survives as 'a scholiast' in the notes of Wickham and of Villeneuve) who takes the ode as referring to Antony and Cleopatra, but I am convinced that that glossator is no other than Cristoforo Landino. His edition of Horace ('opera omnia') with a commentary, dedicated to Guidobaldo, the son of Federico di Montefeltro, was printed by Antonio Miscomini at Florence in 1482 (cf. L. Hain, *Repert.* no. 8881). In his introduction

firmly reject the allegorical interpretation and hold that the ode is in fact what it appears to be, a piece of epic narrative in the form of lyrics.[1] That the latter view is correct is confirmed by the information given in the scholia (Porph.), *hac ode Bacchylidem imitatur; nam ut ille Casandram facit vaticinari futura belli Troiani,*[2] *ita hic Proteum.*[3] The lost poem of Bacchylides referred to by the scholiast belonged in all probability to the group which the ancient εἰδογράφοι, i.e. the scholars responsible for the classification in the Alexandrian editions of the poems of Pindar, Bacchylides, and so forth, labelled διθύραμβοι. Thanks to the large Bacchylides papyrus in the British Museum we can form a clear idea of the character of those 'dithyrambs'. Meant to be sung by a choir, they often have as their subject an episode taken from a larger epic context; speech and dialogue play an important part in them. In some respects they are not unlike what we should call ballads.[4] Among the extant διθύραμβοι of Bacchylides there is at least one which in its form has a good deal in common with *Pastor cum traheret*. The poem, 15 (14) in our editions, with the title Ἀντηνορίδαι ἢ Ἑλένης ἀπαίτησις, begins with a narrative, in which first the situation is briefly outlined and then certain details are more fully described, and ends with a direct speech; it has neither a proem nor an epilogue.[5] Of its apparently abrupt

to *Odes* i. 15 he first mentions Porphyrio's statement that the ode was inspired by Bacchylides and then goes on: *Ego autem puto poetam nostrum ut in superiori ode* [i. 14] *per allegoriam Sextum pompeium admonuerat: sic et hac admonere M. antonium ne cleopatrae amore ductus aduersetur octauiano,* etc. Landino, 'imbevuto di neoplatonismo, concepì sempre la poesia come velo avvolgente "arcani e divini sensi" ' (*Enciclopedia Italiana*, xx, 493). He applied to Horace the allegorical interpretation which he had already practised in his commentaries on Dante and Virgil. How pleased this 'rispettabile maestro di scuola' (E. Garin, *Medioevo e rinascimento*, Bari 1954, 212 f.) would be if he could see what a lasting success he has had with his distortion of *Pastor cum traheret*!—A fairly long, if uncritical, eulogy of Landino's work on Horace can be found in G. Curcio, *Q. Orazio Flacco studiato in Italia dal secolo XIII al XVIII*, Catania 1913, 61 ff.

[1] For this view it will suffice to quote Kiessling (see also his discussion in his and Wilamowitz's *Philol. Untersuchungen*, ii, 1881, 78); P. Shorey; R. Reitzenstein, *Gött. gel. Anz.* 1904, 957; Wilamowitz, *S.u.S.* 314; Villeneuve; Helm, *Philol.* xc, 1935, 365.

[2] Cf. Bacchyl. *fr.* 8a Snell, with the editor's notes. For the expression *hac ode Bacchylidem imitatur* compare, for instance, Porph. on *Sat.* 1. 5. 1 *Lucilio hac satyra aemulatur Horatius,* etc., where we can verify the correctness of the statement with the help of the extant fragments of Lucilius.

[3] Is *Proteum* perhaps not a mistake or a corruption but rather a vestige of a fuller comment? Schol. Eur. *Or.* 364, commenting on Νηρέως προφήτης Γλαῦκος, observes μαντεύεται δὲ ὡς ὁ παρ' Ὁμήρῳ Πρωτεὺς καὶ παρὰ Πινδάρῳ Τρίτων τοῖς Ἀργοναύταις.

[4] See Wilamowitz, *Bakchylides* (1898) 29 f., *Textgeschichte der griech. Lyriker*, 43.

[5] Cf. Snell, 6th edition of Blass's *Bacchylides*, 1949, Preface, p. 42* and p. 54 bottom; he rightly agrees with H. Fränkel in regarding l. 63 as the original ending. Wilamowitz, *Textgeschichte der griech. Lyriker*, 42 n. 2, reached the same conclusion, recanting his former opinion (*Gött. gel. Anz.* 1898, 135). The abruptness of the Ἀντηνορίδαι is harmless compared with the perfunctory manner in which Alcaeus sometimes treated an epic episode, as in the case of *fr.* 76 D., 44 L. and P., where the whole poem apparently consisted of eight lines; cf. H. Fränkel, *Gött. gel. Anz.* 1928, 272.

conclusion it has been properly said that the reason for it is not difficult to understand, since 'in the words of Menelaus there is anticipated, as far as the moral issue is concerned, the further course of events, with which the audience was familiar'.[1] Now in the speech of Nereus in *Pastor cum traheret* the destruction of Troy is not merely implied but is prophesied in so many words. To end a poem with an *oratio recta*, it will be remembered, is a device often employed in Horace's epodes and odes.[2] It would be unreasonable to assume that his inclination to use this type of conclusion was due to the particular influence of Bacchylides, for such speeches at the end occurred in other lyrics as well and also in Hellenistic poems. It is, however, worth noticing that, as the concluding speech in the Ἀντηνορίδαι culminates in a veiled prophecy and, for instance, the concluding speech in Pindar's first Nemean ode (this time in indirect form) culminates in an open prophecy, so in Horace, from his early to his late work, several final speeches culminate in a prophecy or some similar anticipation of events to come and thus, by carrying the story into the future, counterbalance the formal abruptness of the poem. That is the case in the fifth, the thirteenth, and the seventeenth epodes, in *Odes* i. 7, iii. 3 (the addition of one stanza in a lighter tone does not change the fundamental character of the structure), further, and most important, in the two mythological tales which will be discussed presently, iii. 11 and iii. 27, and, finally, in iv. 4.

To return to the problem from which we started. We know on good authority that in *Pastor cum traheret* Horace followed the model of Bacchylides, and, moreover, we see that an episode from a larger epic tale could form the sole theme of a dithyramb of Bacchylides exactly as it forms the sole theme of this Horatian ode. That being so, it would be hazardous to seek the reason for the singularity of *Pastor cum traheret* not in Horace's wish to give, like Bacchylides, though in a modernized form, a lyric version of an epic theme, but in a desire to vent his feelings about the great political struggle of his own time under the disguise of a mythological tale. We shall be the less inclined to resort to such an hypothesis when we remember that in certain other Horatian odes the emphasis lies on a myth in which events of uncommon magnitude take place and strong emotions come into play. In *Odes* iii. 27 and iii. 11, to which we shall turn presently, what really matters is the presentation of the long and elaborate mythological scenes and not the apparently personal introduction which is prefixed to each of them, only to be forgotten as soon as the reader's imagination is filled with the great old stories told in the new style of Horace's lyrics.[3] But classical

---

[1] So H. Fränkel, *Nachr. Gött. Ges.*, Phil.-hist. Kl., 1924, 114 n. 3.

[2] Cf. p. 66 above.

[3] In Orelli–Baiter ('Excursus' to *Odes* i. 15) excellent guidance is given; 'Quid, quod

scholars, at any rate many of them, are very punctilious: the mythological odes iii. 11 and iii. 27, thanks to their introductions, fall into line with a common type and are therefore allowed to pass; the mythological ode i. 15 is in its form *sui generis* and therefore objectionable unless we manage to see in it something different from what it appears to be. These rigid critics will not be satisfied with what they have before them, not even when it can be pleaded that *Pastor cum traheret* is an early experiment of a kind which Horace did not care to repeat in his mature period.

About the early date of *Odes* i. 15 there seems to be a fairly general agreement. Disregarding such criteria as might be thought subjective (the 'poor quality' of the poem), we should do well to remember Lachmann's acute observation[1] that in the last line of the ode, *ignis Iliacas domos*, the beginning of a glyconic with a trochee, unique in Horace, is 'nondum perfectae artis documentum',[2] from which he concluded that this poem was 'inter prima quae poeta tentavit'. Two observations of a different kind seem to point in the same direction.

First, *Pastor cum traheret* contains two phrases which sound almost like echoes of one of the earliest epodes, the tenth. That epode begins *mala soluta navis exit alite*; the speech of Nereus begins *mala ducis avi domum*, etc. In the epode the future fate of the victim and his companions is described thus (15:) *o quantus instat navitis sudor tuis*, etc. In *Odes* i. 15 the third stanza begins *heu, heu, quantus equis, quantus adest viris sudor*, etc. (this is the only place in the *Odes* where *sudor* occurs). This sounds very much as though Horace, when composing *Pastor cum traheret*, had snatches of the Mevius epode still floating in his memory, a thing less likely to have happened if the ode was written a very long time after the epode.[3]

Secondly, we find in *Pastor cum traheret* two words which Horace used in his satires but, apart from this ode, nowhere else. The one is *ecce*[4] at l. 27 (three times in the *Satires*), the other *imperitare*[5] at l. 25 (three

amabat huiusmodi, ut ita dicam, picturas mythologicas, ut sunt Hypermestra (iii. 11) et Europa (iii. 27)? in quibus nulla sane est allegoria.'

[1] In his appendix to C. Franke's *Fasti Horatiani*, 238.

[2] It would, of course, be more adequate to say that Horace at an early stage was probably less inclined than later to insist on strict normalization and therefore once admitted the old Greek freedom of variation at the beginning of a glyconic. Kiessling, in his introduction to the ode, justly referred to Lachmann's observation, and so did Heinze as late as 1917, but in his last edition (1930) he omitted the reference.

[3] We shall see (cf. p. 250 below) that the recurrences of certain phrases of some epodes in *Odes* i. 2 are among the arguments that point to a very early date for that ode.

[4] Cf. Lejay on *Sat.* 1. 4. 13.

[5] The history of *imperitare* is interesting. In Plautus we find seventy-eight instances of *imperare*, but only two of *imperitare*, viz. *Pseud.* 703, in a passage the style of which is described by Plautus himself as *paratragoedare*, and in a no less solemn context (after the fashion of prayers) at *Capt.* 244. (Between *imperitare* and *imperare* there is no difference of meaning;

times in the *Satires*). It appears that the poet, as his taste grew more fastidious, did not any longer regard such words as suitable for the style of his *carmina*.[1]

Personally, I consider it possible that *Pastor cum traheret* should be even earlier than the thirteenth epode, a much more accomplished poem not only in the prophecy with which it ends but as a whole. But it would be fatal to erect a system of relative chronology on the foundation of hypothetical data derived from what seems to be the progress in the poet's skill. There are many other possibilities. One could easily imagine that Horace first wrote the thirteenth epode, in which, using a theme of Bacchylides,[2] he followed the typical arrangement of early paraenetic poems, and that, later, in *Odes* i. 15, he attempted to adopt the rarer type of those Greek songs in which an epic episode was given for its own sake, without an introduction or any reference to the poet's own circumstances. This experiment he never repeated, perhaps because he realized that such a 'ballad' would be too little in harmony with the rest of his lyrics. Instead, in the two later odes which culminate in a mythological narrative, he started with a prelude that produces the semblance of erotic lyrics of a common type.

The introductory section, 1–24, of the Europa ode, iii. 27, is a pleasing piece. The elaborate description of the various omens, delivered in a spirit of light mockery and with plenty of picturesque detail, is delightful, and so is the apparent seriousness with which the warning against crossing the treacherous Adriatic Sea (17–20) leads to a prayer, or curse, intended to 'send off' (ἀποπέμπειν) the disaster so that it may plague the enemy's wives and children (21–24).[3] This section is followed by a long mythological story, the apparent purpose of which is, after the manner customary in paraenetic lyrics,[4] to exemplify and

cf., for example, *Men.* 1033.) We must therefore conclude that *imperitare* had a lofty ring as early as Plautus (in Terence it does not occur). It is absent from classical prose, but was probably used by some historians before Sallust, in whom we find it, as in Livy, the Elder Pliny, abundantly in Tacitus, then in Apuleius and so forth (for this stylistic trend in general see *JRS* xli, 1951, 193). It is accidentally preserved in a fragment of Accius and occurs in Lucretius 3. 1028, *magnis qui gentibus imperitarunt*. Heinze, in his commentary on Book III of Lucretius, considered it possible that here as well as at Horace, *Sat.* 1. 6. 4, *olim qui magnis legionibus imperitarent*, there was an echo of some line of Ennius. This suggestion is attractive. If Ennius did use the verb, that might account for its occurrence in the *Aeneid* (only once) and, perhaps, also for the strict limits within which Plautus admits it. One thing, at any rate, is clear: unlike the frequentative (or intensive) derivatives of many other verbs, *imperitare* was never a plain word and never at home in the sphere of ordinary colloquial language. Horace may have taken it from Ennius or from Lucilius or from both.

[1] This applies also to *sudor* (see the text above).   [2] Cf. p. 66 n. 6 above.
[3] For the prayer known as ἀποπομπή and, especially, the passing on of a curse to 'the enemy' see pp. 410 f. below.
[4] See pp. 185 f. above.

to strengthen the moral of the preceding stanzas.[1] In fact, however, it is not the exemplifying function of the story that leaves its impression upon the reader's mind but rather the story in itself. My own experience at any rate is that when I have reached Aphrodite's serene speech at the conclusion of the poem I seem to have forgotten all about the girl Galatea. And I feel confident that what induced Horace to write this ode was not his wish to dissuade a young lady from a voyage, but his intention to recast the old tale of Europa in the new style of his lyrics. His pretended feelings for Galatea provided a suitable pretext for giving the poem a semblance of spontaneity and making it conform to the majority of his odes.[2]

That Galatea and her voyage play but a subordinate role can be seen not only from the size and weight of the part assigned to Europa but also from the loose connexion between the story and the theme which it is meant to illustrate. Horace's warning to Galatea could be boiled down to a simple 'beware of the coming storm'. But did Europa, after being tempted to cross the sea, experience any bad weather? We do not hear of it, and it is in itself utterly improbable.[3] When one of the immortals makes his appearance in a friendly mood—and how much more when the highest god is carrying the girl he loves across the sea[4]— then the divine order demands that the universe shall enjoy undisturbed peace:

$$\text{ἐχέτω δὲ πνοὰς νήνεμος αἰθήρ,}$$
$$\text{κῦμα δὲ πόντου μὴ κελαδείτω.}$$

The storm anticipated for Galatea's voyage does not fit in well with the circumstances of Europa's voyage on the back of Zeus in the shape of a bull. Therefore we should admit that Horace did not take much trouble when he invented a situation which might serve as a prelude to

[1] The transition to the story is made by *sic* (l. 25). The use of this word in introducing the illustrating paradeigma goes back to a very old practice of Greek folk tales; see my note on A. *Ag.* 718.

[2] I agree with Kiessling, who in *Philologische Untersuchungen*, Zweites Heft, 1881, 106 ff., gave an excellent appreciation of i. 15, iii. 11, and iii. 27, and later said in his commentary on iii. 27, 'diesem mythischen . . . Hauptteil ist eine Einleitung voraufgesandt, welche wie in III 11 den mythischen Stoff an ein individuelle Situation anzuknüpfen und ihn so als Erzeugnis lyrisch angeregter Stimmung glaubhaft zu machen sucht. So fingiert er denn ein römisches Mädchen, welches sich anschickt über das Meer zu ziehen', etc. Heinze cancelled all this; instead he gives us this clue to the understanding of the ode: 'Wir aber erkennen erst am Schlusse, daß der Rabe, den Horaz krächzen lassen wollte, in diesem Falle er selbst ist.'

[3] The difficulty has not escaped the commentators; their embarrassment is remarkable. Lambinus observes on l. 25 'Europae exemplo Galateam deterret, ne se mari, quantumvis in praesentia tranquillo, committat'. That would make sense only if Europa were afterwards caught in a storm. The many words with which Dacier (on l. 25) endeavours to cover up the inconsistency are of no avail, nor were later commentators more successful.

[4] ἡ δὲ τότ' ἐρχομένοιο γαληνιάασκε θάλασσα (Moschus, *Europe* 115) is what you would expect in these circumstances.

his fine story. The loose connexion between the two elements was probably in Horace's opinion no serious flaw, for a similar looseness was not uncommon in Greek lyrics, for instance in Pindar.

The mythological part which dominates the whole ode is executed in a grand style. It is in the main a sequence of two dramatic scenes, a long and a short one, each of which is introduced by a succinct narrative to make the background clear. The outstanding piece is Europa's soliloquy. In its form no less than in its thought it is highly dramatic. Its very beginning (34 ff.) adopts a pattern known from Attic tragedy:[1] a passionate utterance is after the first phrase interrupted by the speaker himself, who is carried away by the feeling that what he has been saying is wrong because it is not true or only partially true and in any case does not go to the root of his grief. So here:

> 'pater—o relictum
> filiae nomen pietasque' dixit
> 'victa furore!
> unde quo veni?'

Unmitigated seriousness is maintained throughout this monologue, which reaches its climax when the heroine finds herself on the verge of suicide.[2] At this point Aphrodite enters the stage and delivers the concluding speech as a true θεὸς ἀπὸ μηχανῆς.

Horace has made a great effort to invest his tale of Europa with dignity. In doing so he reacted strongly against a tendency which, if not absolutely predominant, was at any rate very noticeable in the treatment of many an old myth by the poets and artists of the Hellenistic period. There the seriousness of the saga had often to give way to a playful, sometimes even frivolous, spirit. The hymns of Callimachus provide ample illustration.[3] As for the story of Europa,[4] we possess

---

[1] Cf., for example, Soph. Trach. 536 f. κόρην γάρ· οἶμαι δ' οὐκέτ', ἀλλ' ἐζευγμένην· παρεσδέδεγμαι, Eur. Hel. 860 φεῦγ'· ἀτὰρ τί φευκτέον; Or. 579 f. πρὸς θεῶν· ἐν οὐ καλῷ μὲν ἐμνήσθην θεῶν, φόνον δικάζων, Iph. Α. 460 ff. τὴν δ' αὖ τάλαιναν παρθένον· τί παρθένον; Ἅιδης νιν, ὡς ἔοικε, νυμφεύσει τάχα· ὡς ᾤκτισα. In Ter. Haut. 93 ff. filium unicum adulescentulum habeo. ah quid dixi habere me? immo habui, Chreme; nunc habeam necne incertumst the translator has possibly preserved one of the traits which show the influence of the dialogue style of Euripides on Menander.

[2] Robertello on A. Suppl. 457 ff. ἔχω στρόφους ζώνας τε, συλλαβὰς πέπλων κτλ. considered the possibility that that passage was the model of the sentence potes hac ab orno pendulum zona bene te secuta laedere collum. What is certain is the affinity of Europa's soliloquy with tragic scenes. For the detail that the heroine is deliberating which of several methods of suicide she is to choose see Philol. lxxxvii, 1932, 472.

[3] Wilamowitz, Hellenist. Dichtung, i. 183, concludes his brief survey of these hymns with the words: 'Den Eindruck, den ich von den Gedichten empfange, möchte ich mit dem vergleichen, den heilige Geschichten machen, wenn sie Sodoma uns vorführt oder auch Correggio, denn beide nehmen sie innerlich nicht ernst und lassen es durchfühlen.'

[4] It is very instructive to watch the changes in the treatment of this great theme in works of decorative art, from the majestic metope of one of the sixth-century temples at

a Hellenistic version of it, the Εὐρώπη of Moschus, who wrote about the middle of the second century B.C.[1] This hexametric poem had probably no direct influence on Horace, but it can help us to see that in his approach to the old story Horace differs widely from a typical Hellenistic poet. For the present purpose it will suffice to compare Europa's speech in the Greek poem (135–52) with her speech in Horace's ode. The Europa of Moschus vents her feelings while crossing the sea, which may seem more natural than that she should wait until she has safely reached the shore of Crete (*simul centum tetigit potentem oppidis Creten*). What she delivers is not really a monologue, for she is addressing the extraordinary bull on whose back she is riding. The young lady seems as calm as the sea around her; no tempests of passion are raging through her mind, and all that can be noticed on the surface is some glittering ripples. She starts on a note of mild surprise, πῇ με φέρεις θοὲ ταῦρε,[2] τίς ἔπλεο; and goes on 'How walkest thou upon paths so ill for shambling hooves to tread, and fearest not the sea?' Then she turns to lecturing him out of her book of natural history: 'For it is for swift ships to range the sea, but bulls shrink from the paths of the brine. What water for thy liking, what food canst thou find in the salt sea? Dolphins of the deep fare not upon the land, nor yet bulls upon the ocean, but thou dost speed unfaltering over land and ocean too, and thy hooves are as oars for thee.' I should not be surprised, she adds rather frivolously, if soon you became airborne,

ἦ τάχα καὶ γλαυκῆς ὑπὲρ ἠέρος ὑψόσ' ἀερθεὶς
εἴκελος αἰψηροῖσι πετήσεαι οἰωνοῖσιν.

But the bull cannot be drawn by such provoking remarks: he maintains a dignified silence and swims on. So, after a prolonged pause, Europa begins to talk to herself (for talk she must): ὤμοι ἐγὼ μέγα δή τι δυσάμμορος, 'alas! how sad is my lot, that I have left my father's home and followed this bull for so strange a voyaging, and wander all alone'. She has completely forgotten her breeding; what she is doing now is, to put it mildly, not lady-like. How often had she been told never to follow a stranger, and yet she has followed a stranger, and a bull at that. But the worst Europa leaves to the end of her sentence, οἴη. Many a time does Homer remind us that if a young woman had to leave the inner rooms of the house she did so οὐκ οἴη, and that rule was the more binding under the stricter code of later Greek life. The

Selinus (see Gisela M. A. Richter, *Archaic Greek Art*, 125 f.) down to the playful representations belonging to the period of the Empire. Some useful illustrations can be found in A. B. Cook, *Zeus*, iii. 616–28; the reconstruction of the mosaic at Aquileia in his plate XLVIII should, however, be checked by the sober phototypes in G. Brusin's guidebook *Aquileia*, 1929, 112 f.
  [1] Texts of it will be found in the editions of the *Bucolici Graeci*.
  [2] I gladly accept P. Maas's emendation (θεόταυρε codd.), *Glotta*, xxxii, 1953, 311.

least Europa should have done was to take a chaperon with her. But what is the good now of piling reproaches on her own pretty head? The important thing is to find a sympathetic soul, a kind old gentleman ready to get a poor girl out of her predicament. Fortunately there is one at hand, Poseidon. 'Thou that rulest the grey sea, Earth-shaker, come with thy gracious help to me: for I seem to see thee at hand, guiding my journey onward, and surely it is not without heaven's will that I pass through these watery ways.'[1] She feels perfectly confident that in the end all will be well.

Here we have pure gay rococo. This Europa is no heroine; we almost seem to see her in a hoop-petticoat, and above in the sky a swarm of Amoretti floating down from a silvery cloud. There is a light and sure touch throughout and a wealth of gentle mockery. No doubt the poem of Moschus is far more accomplished and enjoyable than Horace's heavy ode.[2] The ode as a whole lacks unity, and its detail too often betrays the effort without that happiness of execution which Horace commands where he is at his best. After admitting this much we should not, however, blind ourselves to the noble devotion which induced the poet to pursue a high ideal. He did care for the great mythological figures and did admire their stature as he found it in many old poems; he wanted to free them from the frivolous tinsel which the taste of later generations had strewn over them and to reinvest them with something like their original majesty. If he failed, his poem must be judged on its merits, but of the poet himself we still should like to say 'den lieb ich, der Unmögliches begehrt'.

The affinity between the Europa ode and the Hypermestra ode (iii. 11) has long been noticed. Precisely as in the one poem the story of Europa purports to be told as a warning to Galatea, so in the other (25 ff.) *audiat Lyde scelus atque notas virginum poenas*, etc. But the setting of iii. 11 is more complex: its introductory part, though substantially a παραίνεσις for the benefit of Lyde, has the form of a κλητικὸς ὕμνος to the lyre invented by Hermes. This device makes it possible to prelude the story of the Danaids with sketches of other mythological scenes, to render the transition from the first to the second part very smooth (22 ff.), and to couch the introduction in the same lofty style as the concluding myth. This myth, like its longer counterpart in iii. 27, is given in a highly dramatic form: a condensed account in emotional language[3]

---

[1] I owe the translation of Europa's speech to the kindness of Mr. F. C. Geary.

[2] I am not, however, prepared to subscribe to Wilamowitz's harsh verdict (*Text-geschichte der griech. Bukoliker*, 101), 'es [Horace's ode] ist wirklich im ganzen und in jedem Zuge geschmacklos und absurd; er selber hätte sich's nicht verzeihen dürfen'. For Wilamowitz's criticism of the kindred Hypermestra ode see his *Aischylos, Interpretationen*, 20 n. 1.

[3] See especially ll. 30–32.

prepares the way to the ῥῆσις of Hypermestra which forms the finale of the poem. In the speech of the heroine a dignity of thought and expression, worthy of tragedy, is maintained throughout, and its grandeur is not impaired by the gentle diminuendo with which this ode, like many others, concludes,

> i secundo
> omine et nostri memorem sepulcro
> scalpe querelam.

We have seen how Horace when he is dealing with a piece of Greek saga strives to get away from the prettiness favoured by many Hellenistic poets and to renew in his own manner the serious spirit that once permeated the old stories. A similar phenomenon can be observed in a poem which, both in its theme and in its size, is entirely different, *Odes* i. 30:

> O Venus regina Cnidi Paphique,
> sperne dilectam Cypron et vocantis
> ture te multo Glycerae decoram
> transfer in aedem.
>
> fervidus tecum puer et solutis
> Gratiae zonis properentque Nymphae
> et parum comis sine te Iuventas
> Mercuriusque.

This ode was compared by R. Reitzenstein[1] with an epigram by Poseidippus,[2] which was probably known to Horace:

> ʽΗ Κύπρον ἥ τε Κύθηρα καὶ ἣ Μίλητον ἐποιχνεῖς
> καὶ τὸ καλὸν Συρίης ἱπποκρότου δάπεδον,
> ἔλθοις ἵλαος Καλλιστίῳ, ἣ τὸν ἐραστὴν
> οὐδέποτ' οἰκείων ὦσεν ἀπὸ προθύρων.

The first couplet, with its enumeration of famous seats of the cult of Aphrodite, follows, in a manner which in this context is, perhaps, not entirely serious, a common pattern of prayers and hymns. Its slowly moving grandeur serves as a foil to the swift directness and simplicity of the second distich that contains the prayer itself and the motive for it. Formally the epigram is addressed to the goddess, but it is really written for the young woman, Καλλίστιον. She is 'no lady', but she

---

[1] *Neue Jahrb.* xxi, 1908, 90 f. He might have quoted the ancient comment (Porph.) *quasi epigramma est hoc in dedicationem Veneris scriptum.*

[2] *Anth. Pal.* xii. 131 (*Posidippi epigrammata*, ed. P. Schott [Diss. Berlin 1905], 64 ff.). He wrote in the first third of the third century B.C.

has always been very kind to the poet, and he shows himself a grateful lover by paying her this handsome tribute. In Horace's ode, on the other hand, Glycera remains completely in the background; it does not matter who she is or what the poet may feel for her.[1] His interest is entirely concentrated on the goddess, and the ode culminates in a description of the manner in which Venus is to visit her shrine in Glycera's house, οὐκ οἴη, ἅμα τῇ γε . . . :

> Nimmer, das glaubt mir, erscheinen die Götter,
> Nimmer allein,
> Kaum daß ich Bacchus den lustigen habe,
> Kommt auch schon Amor der lächelnde Knabe,
> Phoebus der herrliche findet sich ein.
> Sie nahen, sie kommen, die Himmlischen alle,
> Mit Göttern erfüllt sich die irdische Halle.

This first stanza of Schiller's 'Dithyrambe', familiar to many English readers from one of Schubert's greatest songs, has something in common with Horace's ode. But the keynote of the German poem is enthusiasm and, more precisely, the ecstasy of the inspired poet. This emotion was intimately known to Horace—witness, above all, the ode (iii. 25) *Quo me, Bacche, rapis*—but there is no trace of it in this prayer, *O Venus regina Cnidi Paphique*. With a calm detachment, which may be mistaken for coldness, Horace pictures the gods and goddesses as, in the retinue of Aphrodite, they rush into the mortal woman's house, Eros, the Charites, the Nymphs, Hebe, and Hermes.[2] Here we have to use the Greek names, for the particular κῶμος of immortals that unfolds before our eyes takes us away from the Rome of Caesar Augustus and back to many representations in Greek paintings and reliefs and to early Greek songs. To one who had learnt *inter silvas Academi quaerere verum* Hebe, the Charites, and their whole company were no longer living beings, no longer formed part of a religious belief; but Horace the poet understood and enjoyed the beauty of a scene in which the Olympians grant to a mortal the blessing of their presence, their παρουσία. Long centuries in which men turned to sceptical meditation or to artistic play had altered the shapes of the old gods out of recognition, but Horace was still able to forget all those changes, and to

---

[1] In *Odes* i. 19, which is in more than one way related to i. 30, Glycera and Horace's love for her are given their full share.

[2] It should not be overlooked that in the second stanza as well as in the first a topic of very old prayers is used: the goddess is asked to come to the worshipper bringing with her her companion or companions. Cf. Ar. *Knights* 586 ff. (prayer to Athena) δεῦρ᾽ ἀφικοῦ λαβοῦσα . . . Νίκην, ἢ κτλ., *Thesm.* 1146 f. (also to Athena) ἔχουσα δέ μοι μόλοις Εἰρήνην φιλέορτον. The form is parodied in the prayer to the Μοῦσα Ἀχαρνική, who is asked (*Ach.* 672 ff.) σοβαρὸν ἐλθὲ μέλος . . . λαβοῦσα, where the μέλος functions as a companion of the Muse.

make his reader forget them, in the vision of one happy moment. That is why he wrote this little poem, a perfect creation.

The epiphany of an immortal to man also provides the initial theme of *Odes* ii. 19, *Bacchum in remotis carmina rupibus vidi docentem*, but the epiphany described there is as different from the epiphany requested in *Odes* i. 30 as is the one ode from the other. The transformed epigram *O Venus regina Cnidi* gives us a very attractive glimpse, but only a glimpse, of the manner in which, if the prayer be granted, the goddess with her κῶμος may make her appearance; in the lofty ode ii. 19 the theophany, witnessed fully and directly by the poet himself, leads up to a hymn embracing the whole power of Dionysus. In the one poem the goddess is invited to civilized surroundings, *Glycerae decoram . . . in aedem*; in the other the god and his followers are seen in a far-off wilderness, *in remotis . . . rupibus*. The difference of locality is essential: Aphrodite is asked to show herself friendly to Glycera by 'calling on her'; Dionysus admits the poet to his presence outside the paths of men to fill him with divine enthusiasm.[1] The god plays here an unusual role: he functions as χοροδιδάσκαλος of his retinue: *Bacchum . . . carmina . . . vidi docentem . . . Nymphasque discentes et auris . . . Satyrorum acutas*.[2] The poet himself becomes one of the *discentes*, for he has been allowed to watch Bacchus and his thiasus and sing of what he has seen,

> fas pervicaces est mihi Thyiadas
> vinique fontem lactis et uberes
> cantare rivos atque truncis
> lapsa cavis iterare mella.[3]

In the very first sentence of the poem Horace declares emphatically (*vidi . . . credite posteri*) that he is relating a personal experience. On the other hand, we notice that this ode does not go outside the god's proper sphere; it remains a eulogy of Dionysus and his achievements. We may therefore say that, as far as the part played by the poet as an individual is concerned, *Odes* ii. 19 seems to stand half-way between the hymn to Hermes, i. 10, where the working of the god is described in an

---

[1] The expression (6) *pleno . . . Bacchi pectore* has always been compared with that in the other ode on Bacchus, 3. 25. 1 f., *tui plenum*. Heinze rightly adds a reference to the puzzling Virgilian phrase (quoted by the elder Seneca, *Suas.* 3. 5) *plena deo* (for detail see F. Leo, *Senecae tragoediae*, i. 166 n. 8, and E. Norden on Virgil, *Aen.* 6. 77–80). There could be no better rendering of ἔνθεος than *plenus deo*. One would like to know which of the two poets, Virgil or Horace, was the first to hit on the happy translation.

[2] For Dionysus as god of poetry and his connexion with the Muses see especially E. Maass, *Hermes*, xxxi, 1896, 375 ff., who rightly points out the role which these ideas play in Augustan poetry; see also Rothstein on Propertius 2. 30. 37.

[3] It has long been seen (Lambinus) that this stanza is modelled after the *Bacchae* of Euripides. A scene of the *Bacchae* is recalled at the end of *Epist.* i. 16; several reminiscences of the same play are found in *Aen.* VII.

entirely impersonal strain, and the other hymn to Dionysus, iii. 25, where the poet's Bacchic enthusiasm inspires him to venture upon new tasks of his own choosing and to treat themes that have nothing in common with the traditional conception of Dionysus.[1]

The keynote of the third stanza, *fas est mihi cantare*, is continued in the fourth, *fas et beatae coniugis additum stellis honorem*, etc. Here the subject of the poet's singing is·no longer something he has witnessed himself, but three stories which he knows as part of the tradition about Dionysus, the shining fate of Ariadne, and the dark fate of Pentheus and Lycurgus. To recall significant episodes of a god's career was customary in Greek hymns. And a hymnic note is unmistakable also in the next stanza (17 ff.), in which, with the typical repetition *tu . . . tu . . . tu . . .*, the ἀρεταὶ τοῦ θεοῦ are glorified. There follows, introduced by another *tu*, praise of his great warlike achievement in the Gigantomachy, a surprising feat for this particular god and therefore deserving two full stanzas. The concluding four lines of the ode accompany Dionysus on his κατάβασις into Hades:[2]

> te vidit insons Cerberus aureo
> cornu decorum, leniter atterens
> caudam et recedentis trilingui
> ore pedes tetigitque crura.

After the grim fight against the Giants this peaceful picture with its delicate detail comes to the reader as an unqualified delight, and the very sound of the stanza contributes to the effect of a perfect diminuendo.

But no beauty of detail should divert us from the strangeness of this ode as a whole or make us forget the bold conception from which the poem apparently springs, *Bacchum in remotis carmina rupibus vidi docentem.* 'Are we to believe that Horace has experienced the epiphany of the god, that he seriously requires us to believe that?'[3] I think Horace means what he says. He did see Dionysus. Many a time he had read of him and his thiasus, not only in hymns but in all sorts of poems, epic, lyric, dramatic. He had only to close his eyes to see the god before him, not as a dim figure, but life-like in his beauty and strength, and with him nymphs, satyrs,[4] and a large host of revelling followers, demigods, men, women, and animals. But what most deeply excited the poet was

---

[1] See pp. 257 ff. below.

[2] For possible models of this concluding part see Wilamowitz, *Glaube der Hellenen*, ii. 377 n. 2 (implicitly recanting his own former guess, *Griech. Tragödien*, xiii [transl. of Eur. *Bacch.*], 1923, 12 n. 2).

[3] Wilamowitz, *Glaube der Hellenen*, ii. 437.

[4] The lines 3 f. in their context make it clear why Horace, where he introduces his own vocation as the poet of new lyrics, can say (*Odes* 1. 1. 30 ff.) *me gelidum nemus Nympharumque leves cum Satyris chori secernunt populo.*

not nymphs and satyrs; it was the mysterious power that emanated from the god himself, shaking a mortal out of his balance, and filling his breast with contrary emotions by mingling deadly fear with inexpressible joy so that he would wish to escape and at the same time feel happy at being near:

> euhoe, recenti mens trepidat metu
> plenoque Bacchi pectore turbidum
> laetatur, euhoe, parce Liber,
> parce gravi metuende thyrso.[1]

Such emotions were not unfamiliar to Horace. He knew the state of ἔνθεοι φρένες, out of which there might be born, amidst despair and exaltation, some work worth creating. In the ode *Bacchum in remotis* we see how the visions of an old religion, renewed in the enthusiasm of a poet, obtain a fresh life.

In discussing *Odes* i. 30, *O Venus regina Cnidi*,[2] our attention was concentrated on Horace's attitude to the gods of an older tradition. But that prayer to Venus provided also an instance of the manner in which a Horatian ode evolves from the theme of a Hellenistic epigram. The same process will now be illustrated by a few select examples.[3] We begin with iii. 22.

> Montium custos nemorumque virgo,
> quae laborantis utero puellas
> ter vocata audis adimisque leto,
> diva triformis,
>
> imminens villae tua pinus esto,
> quam per exactos ego laetus annos
> verris obliquum meditantis ictum
> sanguine donem.

This ode is not, as has been said,[4] a votive inscription, although it unmistakably owes something to the form of dedicatory epigrams. Any such epigram has as its starting-point the idea of a dedication already made, whereas the second stanza of this ode speaks of the dedication

---

[1] For *parce* in prayers cf. p. 411 n. 1 below.

[2] pp. 198 f. above.

[3] More than to any other scholar it is due to R. Reitzenstein (see especially his article 'Horaz und die hellenistische Lyrik', *Neue Jahrb.* xxi, 1908, 81 ff.) that we can form a clear idea of the links between Horace's odes and certain Hellenistic epigrams. For the appreciation of *Odes* iii. 22, iii. 13, and i 17 see also Wilamowitz, *S.u.S.* 312 n. 1.

[4] See Orelli–Baiter, 'Inscriptio tabulae, qua Dianae consecratur pinus', etc., repeated by, for example, Plessis, 'Cette Ode brève est une épigramme votive', etc.

of the pine-tree as being intended.[1] Neither should we be justified, despite the hymnic character of the first stanza,[2] in speaking of 'hymnus in Dianam' as was done by the systematizing ancient editor who is responsible for the classification in our manuscripts.[3] Horace, here as elsewhere, uses more than one conventional form and uses them with perfect freedom. In this case the influence of epigrams is stronger than that of hymns. That accounts also for the extreme conciseness (two stanzas only), which reminds us of the transformed epigram *Odes* i. 30. Here strict symmetry of the two stanzas is achieved by means of the relative clauses which start at the beginning of the second line of each stanza and fill the rest of them. Short though the ode is, it would be possible to reduce it still further if we wanted to do such a barbarous thing and extract from the poem some kind of fundamental theme. As it stands, it is precisely the care given to certain apparently minor details which, together with the solemnity of the beginning and the implied feeling for the beauty of the tree and its surroundings, produces an effect of great richness. It is not unlikely that the response to such a poem on the part of Horace's most sensitive contemporaries differed considerably from that of a modern reader. And yet, however much we allow for the freaks of our own sentimentality, we may be sure that it has something to do with the nature of this poetry if the simple words *imminens villae tua pinus esto* cause a surge of delight and nostalgia in the heart of everyone who is as fond of the Italian countryside as he is fond of Horace.

Odes iii. 13, *O fons Bandusiae,* has deservedly 'been a general favourite'.[4] One would like to think, though there is no proof, that it was written later than iii. 22, with which it has a good deal in common. The two poems are equal in beauty, but the happy expansion of certain details in the Bandusia ode contrasts with the succinctness of *Montium custos*; the colours are deeper, and the note of exaltation in the last stanza lifts us up to a higher plane. The position of the 'hymnic' and the 'epigrammatic' part is here the reverse of that in *Montium custos*: there some hymn-like predications are followed by the promise of the dedication, *imminens villae tua pinus esto, quam . . . donem*; here the first stanza centres in the promise *cras donaberis haedo,* and it is only in the

---

[1] Heinze cancelled Kiessling's remark that the transformation of the epigram into lyrics 'hat zur Folge daß statt der durch das Epigramm gebotenen Aussage der vollzogenen Weihung die lyrische Verheißung des bevorstehenden Aktes eintritt'.

[2] Including the reminiscences from Catullus XXXIV, which have long been noticed.

[3] For the character and origin of these notes see Klingner, *Hermes*, lxx, 1935, 252 ff.; for the fact that the full form of the original heading is often, as in the present case, preserved in the group Ψ only see ibid. 262.

[4] P. Shorey, *Horace, Odes and Epodes*, 348.

second half of the ode (9 ff.) that we hear, after the fashion of many hymns, an ἀρεταλογία, *te . . . nescit tangere, tu . . . praebes . . . .*. The traditional, partly modified, forms which are blended here are the same as in *Montium custos*, and we see once again that they matter far less than the new spirit with which Horace fills them and the poetic directness that comes from the close contact with tree and fountain, rocks and hilly woodlands. No doubt the commentators are right who localize the *fons Bandusiae* in or near Horace's Sabine farm[1] and refer ll. 10–12 to his own cattle and flock.

The description of the kid (3–8) is parallel to that of the young boar in *Montium custos* (7 f.), but it is not only much longer but also much more intensely felt. It is, perhaps, characteristic of Horace, the *ruris amator*, the deeply humane poet, that he cannot merely think of such a victim as a thing required for a sacrifice but must see it before him, and, as it were, feel it, a living being, warm, pretty, and amusing in its youthful pranks, which only too soon will come to an end:

> cui frons turgida cornibus

> primis et venerem et proelia destinat,
> frustra, nam gelidos inficiet tibi
>   rubro sanguine rivos:

the delicacy of this *frustra* is not easily forgotten. In one of his late poems[2] Horace moves us again by the loving care with which he pictures the little calf he is going to sacrifice on the day of the festival.

In the first three stanzas we see the farm-owner enjoying his land and what lives on it; in the last stanza the poet comes to the fore. Through the poet's song Bandusia, hitherto unknown, will be admitted into the circle of those fountains which the great old singers had once immortalized, Castalia, Hippocrene, Peirene, and all the rest of them. Never before had Horace made such a claim. Time will come when he can venture to grant to his fellow men the gift which he here bestows on the spring in the Sabine hills.[3] But in this poem it is Bandusia, and not the poet, that dominates to the end. And what an end it is!

---

[1] I follow C. G. Zumpt (in Wüstemann's re-edition [1843] of Heindorf's commentary on Horace's *Satires*, 17 n. 1) and others in assuming that Horace transferred the name of a spring near Venusia to a spring in the neighbourhood of his Sabinum. For the document of the year 1103 (used in connexion with Horace by Capmartin de Chaupy in the eighteenth century, see Zumpt, loc. cit.) in which *Bandusinus fons prope Venusiam* is mentioned, see Jaffè, *Regesta pontificum*, 2nd ed. 714, no. 5945.

[2] *Odes* 4. 2. 54–60.

[3] Cf. p. 423 below.

Listening to the swift rhythm of these lines we seem to lose ourselves in
the sounds and glitters of an enchanting scenery,

> cavis impositam ilicem
> saxis, unde loquaces
> lymphae desiliunt tuae.

Odes i. 17, *Velox amoenum saepe Lucretilem,* like iii. 22 and iii. 13, shows
the fusion of two different themes, one common in Hellenistic epigrams—and also in earlier lyrics—another derived from religious
poetry. But the structure of this ode is more complex than the structure of the two others. It will therefore be convenient, if only as a
provisional approach, to try to anatomize the poem. Its second half,
from 14 f. *hic tibi copia manabit,* has as its subject the invitation to a
banquet. This theme, not unnaturally, had long been a favourite in
symposiac lyrics; traces of it appear, for instance, in the fragments of
Alcaeus. The same theme, or a slight variation of it, the description of
the preparations for a banquet, plays a prominent role in Hellenistic
epigrams;[1] it recurs in Catullus' hendecasyllables.[2] In Horace's odes
we often find an invitation to, or a description of the preparations for,
either a normal indoor banquet or a modest *fête champêtre* to be held
somewhere in the garden or the *bosco*.[3] The unpretentious dinner party
to which Horace invites Tyndaris in *Odes* i. 17 is to take place in the
bosco adjacent to his Sabine farm.

The theme of the first half of the ode, taken by itself, has nothing to
do with banquet topics; it belongs to the sphere of religious poetry.
This theme seems to have developed from those prayers (familiar to us
from Horace as well as from Greek poetry) in which a god is requested
to appear to his worshipper. The appearance of the god, anticipated
in the prayer, is often described in detail.[4] In *Velox amoenum* the theo-

---

[1] Cf. Reitzenstein, *Neue Jahrb.* xxi, 1908, 94 ff.

[2] Catullus XIII, *Cenabis bene, mi Fabulle, apud me.*

[3] For the latter type see *Odes* 2. 3. 9–16; 2. 11. 13–17. *Odes* i. 38 does not strictly belong
to this group, for ll. 7 f., *sub arta vite bibentem,* probably refers to a 'pergola' at the house.
An invitation to a simple open-air banquet is the theme of the fine epigram (ap. Athen.
15. 673 b) by Nikainetos of Samos (third century B.C.) which Reitzenstein quotes, op. cit. 97.

[4] *Odes* iii. 18, in more than one respect related to i. 17, shows how the prayer for the
appearance of a god leads naturally to a description of the circumstances in which he is
wont to appear and the effects which his appearance has. For the ritual formulas in this
prayer see Heinze's good observations; he has, however, done less than justice to *lenis
incedas*. From very old times (possibly from a period when men prayed to divert a
daemon from doing harm) it was the custom to prescribe in detail the manner in which
a daemon or god was to make his entrance. Special attention was paid to his gait (*incessus*)
and sometimes also to the manner in which he was to set his feet on the ground and to his
footwear. Compare, in the very old prayer of the women of Elis to Dionysus (Plutarch,
Aet. Gr. 36, 299 b), the clause τῷ βοέῳ ποδὶ θύων; further the prayer to Dionysus, Soph.
Ant. 1144 μολεῖν καθαρσίῳ ποδί; Ar. *Frogs* 330 f. (Ἴακχε, ἐλθὲ . . .) θρασεῖ δ᾽ ἐγκατακρούων
ποδὶ τὰν . . . τιμάν; A. *Pers.* 659 f. (invocation of the ghost of Dareios, formed after the

phany does not lie in the future: we are given typical details of the appearance of Pan which Horace has often experienced[1] and hopes to experience again. He has not indeed seen the god face to face, but the blessings bestowed on his estate, his flocks, and on the poet himself cannot be anything but a result of the divine patron's presence.[2]

About the central stanza, ll. 13–16, something will be said presently. The three stanzas that precede and the three that follow it have themes which, though of very different origin, are linked together by a common thought. The symmetry of the whole structure is emphasized by the fact that the first three and the last three stanzas are complementary to each other and that the selection and arrangement of their detail is strictly parallel.[3] The first three stanzas deal with some of the animals on the farm, the last three with some of the human beings. In the burning heat of the summer day both the goats and their masters seek and enjoy shelter (5 f.; 17 f.; 22) and refreshing food and drink (5 f.; 21); neither of them need have fear lest their enemies should attack them (8 f.; 24 ff.).

We may wonder why, despite the difference in subject and literary origin, the two parts of the ode, the praise of Pan's presence and the invitation to a banquet, do not break asunder. The answer is not far to seek. The ode is held together by the part which the person of the poet plays in it. The beginning, with its emphatic mention of *Lucretilis*,[4] points to the neighbourhood of Horace's Sabine farm; the following clause (*et igneam . . . ventos*) brings us to the farm itself with its flocks. In the phrase *capellis . . . meis* there is a note of happy ownership; moreover, it is this pronoun of the first person that provides the key to the whole stanza: were it not for the sake of Horace, the god would not trouble to come all the way from Arcadia to the Sabine hills. In visiting him, Pan honours Horace, gives him and all he owns a share in the *pax deorum*, and lets him enjoy freedom from fear (*impune tutum per nemus . . . quaerunt . . . nec viridis metuunt colubras*, etc.).

model of prayers and also meant to prepare the spectators for what they are going to see) κροκόβαπτον ποδὸς εὔμαριν ἀείρων; Catullus 61. 9 f. (to Hymenaeus) *huc veni, niveo gerens luteum pede soccum*, and the subtle variation at Virg. *Georg.* 2. 7 f., *huc, pater o Lenaee, veni nudataque musto tingue novo mecum dereptis crura cothurnis*. We may compare also Catullus 68. 70 f., where the apparition of a godlike woman is described, *quo mea se molli candida diva pede intulit*, etc. With *lenis incedas* compare *Odes* 1. 19. 16 (Venus) *mactata veniet lenior hostia*.

[1] Horace insists on the frequency of the god's visits: 1 *saepe*, 4 *usque*, 10 *utcumque*.

[2] iii. 18, *Faune, Nympharum fugientum amator*, a little masterpiece, differs from i. 17 in that it is of refined simplicity. Its structure is straightforward, and it contains no external elements (erotic topics, Greek mythology) such as we find in i. 17. Instead there prevails a strong Italic note (*nonae Decembres, pagus*, and the *tripudiare* at the end).

[3] For some of the devices by which the symmetry is brought out in detail see Heinze's introduction.

[4] In this context it does not matter that a precise identification of Lucretilis has not been possible, cf. Nissen, *Italische Landeskunde*, ii. 616 f.; G. Lugli, *Horace's Sabine Farm* (Rome 1930), 24 f.

In the central stanza, ll. 13 ff., it is the poet and his poetry that dominate:

> di me tuentur, dis pietas mea
> et musa cordi est.

A *fortissimo*! Horace is not a writer to use anaphora idly. Wherever he uses it he does so to stress something which he has very much at heart. It is no accident that the same form serves to express the same thought in one of his most majestic odes, 3. 4. 21,

> vester, Camenae, vester in arduos
> tollor Sabinos,

and again, with only a slight variation, in the proud hymn contemporary to the *Carmen Saeculare*, *Odes* 4. 6. 29 f.:

> spiritum Phoebus mihi, Phoebus artem
> carminis nomenque dedit poetae.

With the words *di me tuentur*, etc., Horace reaches the summit of the ode. To make the ascent perfectly smooth he has prepared it carefully. Already in the preceding stanza we have heard of *res musica*:

> utcumque dulci, Tyndari, fistula
> valles et Usticae cubantis
> levia personuere saxa.

There it seems in the first place to be Tyndaris who is to take delight in the sound of Pan's pipe, for the vocative, embedded as it is in the clause *utcumque dulci . . . fistula valles . . . personuere*, must not be severed from it.[1] It is as if Horace said, 'My dear young lady, you are a good musician yourself;[2] I am sure it will give you pleasure to listen to your divine colleague's sweet tune and to its echo from all the rocks in the valley.' But this pleasing side-issue will not tempt the reader, or Tyndaris, to forget that it is Horace who is being honoured by the god's visit and his musical performance. *Di me tuentur . . .*; it is *his* field, *his* garden, *his* vineyard, and *his* orchard that bear everything in plenty.[3]

---

[1] In many cases it is important to consider the particular context in which Horace puts the name of the person whom he is addressing; see my 'Pindargedicht des Horaz', *Heidelberger Sitz.*, Phil.-hist. Kl. 1932/3, 2. Abh., 13 ff., and cf. p. 215 and p. 433 n. 5 below. In the ode before us, *Tyndari*, placed in the third stanza, serves also to bind together the theophany (1–12) with the invitation to the banquet (17–28).

[2] Tyndaris is in all probability a ψάλτρια (18 ff.); there are no grounds for thinking of a lady like Sempronia as described by Sallust, *Catil.* 25. 2.

[3] In ll. 14–16, *hic tibi copia manabit ad plenum benigno ruris honorum opulenta cornu*, the abundant fruit of the soil is depicted by a rich cluster of phrases expressing in ever new shades the idea of abundance. There is great deftness in this arrangement and especially in the word-order. In a passage of the other Faunus ode, 3. 18. 11 f., *festus in pratis vacat otioso cum bove pagus*, the three words *festus, vacat, otioso* emphasize the happiness of leisure on the holiday, quite simply and with great charm.

As the connexion of thought in the fourth stanza shows (see especially the transition in 14), the poet acknowledges the origin of his prosperity in a spirit kindred to the spirit in which an Italian calls the bread 'la grazia di Dio'. It is for the sake of Horace that the Arcadian god blows his pipe in this part of the world, and when we hear *dis . . . mea . . . musa cordi est* we conclude that in this poem Pan is not merely one of the *agrestum praesentia numina* but also represents the gods in general.

The poet, then, and the bliss he enjoys through the divine protection and through his own craft, occupy the centre of the ode and give unity to the whole poem. The conventional themes of a theophany and an invitation to a banquet are subordinated to a fresh and entirely personal conception. The *pax deorum*, too, which is explicitly described as such in the first part and shows itself in its consequences in the second, has here a special application: the poet and all that belongs to him will be safe from conflict and destruction.[1] But with all that there is no pomposity in this ode;[2] a graceful manner is maintained throughout. We notice a slightly mocking tone in the heavy clause (22 ff.) *nec Semeleius cum Marte confundet Thyoneus proelia*, contrasting with the surroundings in which the simple banquet is to take place. At the end, as a foil to the calm that awaits Tyndaris at the Sabinum, a lively little scene is pictured with the loving intensity which Horace likes to apply to his finales:

> nec metues protervum
>
> suspecta Cyrum, ne male dispari
> incontinentis iniciat manus
> et scindat haerentem coronam
> crinibus immeritamque vestem.[3]

It is only because ever since antiquity many commentators have tried to establish an artificial connexion between *Odes* i. 17 and the ode which precedes it that I find it necessary, by way of digression, to say something here on i. 16. In this playful poem Horace appears to be very anxious not to lift the veil of anonymity that shrouds the lady in question: *o matre pulchra filia pulchrior*. She herself, if she existed at all, would know who was meant, and so probably would a few close friends. That was good enough for Horace, but not for his commenta-

---

[1] It is a related, though different, thought that the lover and writer of love poems enjoys the protection of the gods; cf. on *Integer vitae*, p. 187 above.

[2] Nowadays scholars are apt to become pontifical as soon as they talk about a *vates*.

[3] The phrase *scindat . . . immeritam vestem* provides a good example of the manner in which this elegant poetry sometimes draws on everyday language and merely gives it a slightly nobler turn: Cicero writes to Trebatius (*Fam.* 7. 18. 4) *epistulam tuam . . . conscidi innocentem*.

tors of the riddle-seeking type. In our scholia (Porph.) we read *hac ode*
παλινῳδίαν *repromittit* . . . *Tyndaridi cuidam amicae suae*, and in accordance with this assertion the ode is headed in one group of our manuscripts *ad Tyndaridem* and in another *palinodia Gratidiae*[1] *vel Tyndaridi*.
This queer piece of information has seemed palatable even to scholars
who might be expected to be proof against such things.[2] If Tyndaris
had anything to do with this ode, how, we should like to ask, was the
reader to find it out? Was he perhaps supposed to look round until he
discovered in another poem a woman who could, at a pinch, serve as
matre pulchra filia pulchrior? The reader who forgets that every Horatian
ode is self-contained[3] is in danger of being lured into a quagmire by any
will-o'-the-wisp. That this should still happen in the present case is
the more distressing since the underlying fallacy had been exposed,
nearly a century and a half ago, with special reference to *O matre
pulchra*, by Philipp Buttmann.[4] More than one attentive reader must
have seen that Horace's odes are complete in themselves and consequently never rely on any additional information, whether a superscription (*ad Tyndaridem* and the like) or a gloss or anything else.
Nevertheless, it is still well worth reading Buttmann's pages, where the
principle and its consequences for the interpretation are set forth with
great lucidity and with an admirable insight into the nature of ancient
poetry.[5] Everything that Horace wants to convey to his reader is put
into the text of the poems. It was alien to the poet's intentions, and in
many cases harmful to them, that his editors prefixed to the odes such
headings as *ad Maecenatem*, *ad Tyndaridem*, etc., a practice continued, for
instance, in Mr. Gladstone's translation. As Buttmann points out,[6] it is
characteristic of modern as distinct from ancient poetry that in many

---

[1] This wretched guess, evolved from ll. 24 f., had to provide some badly-needed detail
for the romance of Gratidia–Canidia; see Tenney Frank in *Class. Studies presented to Edward
Capps*, Princeton 1936, 159, and cf. p. 63 n. 1 above.

[2] Heinze, who as late as 1917 had reproduced Kiessling's very sensible introduction
to i. 16, made in his last edition (1930) an astounding volte-face. His argument culminates
in the contention that 'die Einordnung dieses Gedichts an dieser Stelle kann nicht Zufall
sein [even if it is not 'Zufall', does it follow that we should be able to discover the reason
why the poet put it in this place?]; Horaz muß beabsichtigt haben daß der Leser die
Identität der Angeredeten mit Tyndaris ahne'.

[3] This principle is valid even in the extreme—and unique— case of several odes making
up a cycle (iii. 1–6).

[4] The paper in question, 'Über das Geschichtliche und die Anspielungen im Horaz',
printed as an appendix to *Mythologus*, vol. i, was first read in 1808 to the *Akademie der
Wissenschaften* in Berlin.

[5] Buttmann's main title to lasting fame rests of course on his work on the Greek language and its history; for its eminence see J. Wackernagel in 'Die griechische und lateini-
sche Literatur und Sprache', *Die Kultur der Gegenwart*, Teil I, Abt. VIII, 3rd ed., 1912,
396, and the same scholar's *Vorlesungen über Syntax*, i. 26. A grammarian of the first rank,
but by no means a mere grammarian!

[6] See especially his footnote to p. 299.

modern poems the superscription is an indispensable element;[1] we must therefore be careful not to allow our own habits to influence our conception of ancient poetry. On the other hand, as Buttmann again did not fail to observe, it is easy to understand what induced an ancient editor or commentator, who liked uniformity in the superscriptions, to look for a definite addressee of *O matre pulchra* and to settle upon the Tyndaris of the next ode.

Finally, Stesichorus. The existence of his Παλινῳδία was, of course, well known to Horace, who once alluded to a legend connected with it,[2] and it is not unlikely that he had read the poem itself. But the ode *O matre pulchra* owes nothing to Stesichorus, except for the fact that at its end something is said of a παλινῳδία. This simple truth, too, was stated by Buttmann.[3] In this context it may be permissible to dwell for a moment on the phrase *recantatis opprobriis*. Cicero, in his correspondence with Atticus, speaks more than once[4] of a παλινῳδία. This untranslated term was appropriate to a letter or to informal talk, but would have been out of place in Horace's lyrics. Therefore the poet, never shy of coining, within certain limits, new words when he needed them, wrote boldly *recantatis opprobriis*. In so doing he had the support of παλιν-ῳδία. This was a case, if there ever was one, where he could feel confident that *et nova fictaque nuper habebunt verba fidem si Graeco fonte cadent parce detorta*. In English literature the verb 'to recant', according to the *Oxford English Dictionary*, occurs for the first time, at the period of the New Learning, in 1535, and a few years later (1538) we find in Sir Thomas Elyot's Latin Dictionary the gloss '*Palinodia* . . ., nowe of some men called a recantynge'. So we see that the name given, we do not know by whom, to a very old Greek poem came, through the mediation of Horace, to furnish the language of the English-speaking nations with a useful and now very common word.

In discussing *Odes* iii. 22, *Montium custos*, I mentioned[5] the few reminiscences from Catullus' hymn (XXXIV) to Diana which are found in that poem. Another Horatian ode, i. 21, *Dianam tenerae dicite virgines*, owes something more to the same hymn *Dianae sumus in fide*.[6]

---

[1] For instance Keats's *Ode on a Grecian Urn* would be obscure without the clue in the superscription.

[2] *Epodes* 17. 42–44. Cf. Wilamowitz, *S.u.S.* 235; W. Ferrari, *Athenaeum*, 1937, 243.

[3] Buttmann, op. cit. 301.   [4] 2. 9. 1; 4. 5. 1; 7. 7. 1.   [5] p. 202 n. 2 above.

[6] The affinity between Horace's ode i. 21 and Catullus' hymn to Diana was recognized by Bentley, Praefatio to his *Horace*, p. xxvi (p. xx in Zangemeister's reprint, Berlin 1869). Kiessling regarded it as likely that the idea of the ode was suggested to Horace by the poem of Catullus; Wilamowitz, *Hellenist. Dichtung*, ii. 290 f., has shown that Horace is indebted to Catullus not only for the lay-out of his poem but also for some important detail. Ussani ('coincidenze dovute alla somiglianza degli argomenti') and Heinze ('inhaltlich nahestehend') are non-committal.

Like the poem of Catullus, Horace's ode begins with Diana, but unlike Catullus' poem and unlike Horace's own ode iii. 22 this ode does not centre in the goddess. In the opening stanza it is not Diana alone to whom the hymn is directed but the divine triad of which she is a member.[1] True, in the second stanza, where the maidens have their role allotted to them, only Diana is praised, but the rest of the poem, that is to say half of the whole, is entirely devoted to Apollo, who thus appears as the dominating figure. In the concluding part, (which is a promise of the fulfilment of a prayer rather than a prayer),[2]

> hic bellum lacrimosum, hic miseram famem
> pestemque a populo et principe Caesare in
>   Persas atque Britannos
>   vestra motus aget prece,

we recognize an adaptation of the widespread type of prayer in which the worshipper attempts to divert the harmful power of a god in such a manner as to combine wishes for his own and his people's prosperity with a curse upon the enemy.[3] This prayer especially befits Apollo who, as we remember from the beginning of the *Iliad*, is the great sender of *pestis* and any blight, and also the great ἀποτρόπαιος. But in the present instance the effect of the last sentence reaches farther. After hearing of the Roman people and the *Princeps* Caesar, of the Parthians and the Britons, we have all but forgotten Leto and Artemis and their cult-places. Our mind is now filled with the perils that have threatened, and in part are still threatening, the frontiers of the Empire: only one man can ward them off, Caesar. Pasquali, describing the transformation to which Horace subjected certain themes of Alcaeus, says 'gli στασιωτικά divengono carmi civili';[4] similarly, one is tempted to say that here the hymn, or prayer, becomes a patriotic song. The combination of the two themes is the more harmonious since Apollo, even before the victory of Actium, and more definitely after it, was recognized as the special patron of Caesar.[5] A nucleus of the idea of Horace's concluding stanza may be seen in the final prayer to Diana in Catullus' hymn, *Romuli . . . bona sospites ope gentem*. But it is, at best, no more than a nucleus. If we read the two passages side by side we cannot fail to notice in Horace's sentence the greater breadth, intensity, and seriousness which, perhaps at the expense of easy grace, make his ode a typical work of Augustan poetry.

---

[1] For the arrangement of the three objects in the form of a 'tricolon crescendo' (C longer than B, B longer than A, of the type ἢ Αἴας ἢ Ἰδομενεὺς ἢ δῖος Ὀδυσσεύς), *Dianam, intonsum . . . Cynthium, Latonamque supremo dilectam penitus Iovi*, see E. Lindholm, *Stilistische Studien* (Lund 1931), 184, where a selection of other instances from Horace can also be found.   [2] Cf. Pasquali, *Or. lir.* 173 n. 1.

[3] Cf. p. 411 below and also E. Norden, *Aus altrömischen Priesterbüchern*, 1939, 202.

[4] *Or. lir.* 127.   [5] Cf. p. 248 below.

Among the readers who seriously care for the odes of Horace there may be more than one who would place in the first rank ii. 16, *Otium divos*,[1] and would see in its concluding sentence the quintessence of the man's discretion and the poet's modesty and pride:

> mihi parva rura et
> spiritum Graiae tenuem Camenae
> Parca non mendax dedit et malignum
> spernere volgus.

But it is the beginning of the ode which in our present context requires special attention.

> Otium divos rogat in patenti
> prensus Aegaeo, simul atra nubes
> condidit lunam neque certa fulgent
> sidera nautis,
>
> otium bello furiosa Thrace,
> otium Medi pharetra decori

. . . .

The 'solemn introduction, which is linked together by the threefold anaphora of *otium*',[2] will not be lost on a sensitive ear. This emphatic *otium* at the beginning of each of three lines points also to something else, which seems to have received but little attention.[3] At the end of the famous Sapphic poem of Catullus (LI), *Ille mi par esse deo videtur*, we read this stanza:[4]

> otium, Catulle, tibi molestum est,
> otio exultas nimiumque gestis;
> otium et reges prius et beatas
> perdidit urbes.

---

[1] Wilamowitz in a short article, one of the last he published (*Süddeutsche Monatshefte*, xxviii, Heft 1, Oktober 1930, 43 ff.), selected this ode to show Horace at his best; his translation (which rightly includes 21–24) is followed by some pertinent remarks. A thorough analysis of the ode was given by Latte, *Philol.* xc, 1935, 294 ff.; his appreciation of the last two stanzas is particularly helpful. With regard to Latte's discussion (299 n. 7) of the 'difficult' phrase at ll. 26 f., *lento risu*, one might consider the possibility that here and in some other passages of classical Latin *lentus* contains already a tinge, and perhaps more than a tinge, of the meaning 'soft', 'gentle', and the like, which Löfstedt, *Coniectanea*, i, 1950, 81 ff., in the course of an examination of the affinity between *lenis* and *lentus*, illustrates from late Latin texts. It will be remembered that in the passage before us Bentley conjectured *leni . . . risu* and compared Cic. *Rep.* 6. 12 *leniter adridens*.

[2] Latte, op. cit. 294.

[3] Long after I had noticed the relation between the beginning of *Odes* ii. 16 and the end of Catullus LI and had drawn my inferences from it, I found in Mendell's paper 'Catullan Echoes in the "Odes" of Horace', *Class. Philol.* xxx, 1935, 297, the casual remark that most of Horace's contemporaries 'must have recognized that the repeated use of *otium* at the beginning of the line in ii. 16 came from Catullus LI'. The same observation was made by S. Mariotti, *Paideia*, ii, 1947, 303.

[4] As regards the vexed question whether or not the stanza *otium, Catulle* etc. belongs to

It is not surprising that Catullus, like many a lover, makes *otium* responsible for his misery. Ordinary acquaintance with human life is sufficient to understand that. When we hear that Θεόφραστος ὁ φιλό-σοφος ἐρωτηθεὶς ὑπό τινος τί ἐστιν ἔρως, 'πάθος' ἔφη 'ψυχῆς σχολαζού-σης',[1] we are aware that what is uncommon in this anecdote is the neatly shaped apophthegm but not the experience behind it. The verb σχολάζειν, 'to have nothing to do', is derived from σχολή, to which the Latin equivalent is *otium*. 'Idle life' is a very common meaning of *otium*, and it is in this sense that Catullus uses the word in the first two lines *otium . . . tibi molestum est, otio exultas*, etc. But when he continues *otium et reges prius et beatas perdidit urbes*, the modern reader may well wonder what exactly is meant here and how such a thought fits in.[2] A way to the right answer was shown by two Italian scholars.[3] They pointed to a theory which, based on the views of earlier political thinkers, developed during the Hellenistic period and became a favourite with philosophizing, or moralizing, historiographers. According-ing to that theory enjoyment of full peace and prolonged freedom from fear were apt to weaken the energy of a city or a nation, to ac-custom the citizens to a life of luxury (τρυφή) and so to bring them to moral and political decline and finally to ruin.[4] This topic played an important role in the work of the great Poseidonius, an older contem-porary of Catullus. Poseidonius applied it to new subjects,[5] but the

Ille mi par esse, I have found myself changing sides so often that I now feel despondent and inclined, however reluctantly, to agree with Bickel, *Rh. Mus.* lxxxix, 1940, 205 ff., who recommends ἐπέχειν on this point.

[1] Stobaeus, *Flor.* 64. 66 (iv. 468 Hense), quoted, in connexion with Catullus 51. 13 ff. and some similar passages, by E. Rohde, *Griech. Roman*, 3rd ed. 76 n. 1. For other instances of the same topic in New Comedy and Hellenistic poetry see, for example, F. Leo, *Plautin. Forsch.*, 2nd ed. 145; W. Kroll on Catullus 51. 13; and Ferrari in the article quoted below (next footnote but one), 69.

[2] Few readers will be content with a reference (Kroll ad loc.) to Sardanapalus and Sybaris.

[3] Passerini, *Stud. Ital.* n.s. xi, 1934, 52 f., and W. Ferrari, 'Il carme 51 di Catullo', *Annali della R. Scuola Normale Superiore di Pisa*, serie ii, vol. vii, fasc. i, 1938, 67 ff. Tietze's exaggerating criticism, *Rh. Mus.* lxxxviii, 1939, 362 n. 56, underrates the usefulness of the new approach in these two articles; he unnecessarily clings to subordinate points ('Staats-formen'). But Tietze is right in rejecting Passerini's identification (accepted by Ferrari) of *otium* with τρυφή. *Otium* can never mean τρυφή; what it does mean is the state of affairs, or behaviour, or mental disposition, that breeds τρυφή, i.e. *luxuria* and the like. The relation between the dissolute life and *otium* is made perfectly clear for instance by Sall. *Iug.* 41. 1 *mos . . . omnium malarum artium . . . ortus est otio atque abundantia earum rerum quae prima mortales ducunt* (cf. *Hist.* 1, fr. 11 M. *discordia et avaritia atque ambitio et cetera secundis rebus oriri sueta mala*).

[4] According to Polybius the deterioration in Rome's moral standards, which was a consequence of her wide conquests, began early in the second century B.C. See C. O. Brink and F. W. Walbank, *CQ* n.s. iv, 1954, 106.

[5] Cf. F. Jacoby's commentary, *F Gr Hist* vol. ii C, p. 159, ll. 13 ff., ll. 44 ff., p. 160 *passim*; Klingner, *Hermes*, lxiii, 1928, 182 ff. A good example is provided by Diodorus'

topic itself had been formulated so often that we may safely assume
that by then it had come to form part of the conglomerate of ideas
which, with frequent changes of its elements, keeps floating in the
intellectual atmosphere of any educated society. So Catullus could
become acquainted with it without having to consult any book of
a philosopher or historian. From the *otium* in his personal life he passes
by an easy transition to the *otium* in the life of peoples, kings, and
cities, the calm, quiet peace in political and military affairs.[1] The
concluding thought, *otium et reges prius et beatas perdidit urbes*, is not
dragged in but evolves naturally from the statement *otium . . . tibi
molestum est, otio . . . gestis*; this statement is confirmed by means of an
authoritative παράδειγμα, an *exemplum*.[2] The magnitude of the *exemplum*,
which does not point to this or that particular case but to a general rule
established in history, serves to intensify the heaviness of the preceding
self-reproach and to invest it with greater seriousness than it would
have if it were expressed merely in the conventional terms of a lover's
complaint and remorse.

If we now return from the Sapphic stanza of Catullus to the beginning of Horace's ode ii. 16, which is in the same metre, and listen to its
threefold praise of *otium*, we hear in it a delicate, yet clearly perceptible,
undertone. I do not want to exaggerate by saying that there is a
polemic against Catullus in *Otium divos rogat*, etc., but I consider it
likely that Horace hoped his reader would notice the echo and grasp
its implications. No doubt the ode is self-contained, and the unity of its
thought from the beginning to the end is complete. But by recalling
memories of *otium, Catulle, tibi molestum est . . . otium et reges prius et
beatas perdidit urbes* Horace also points to the difference between his own
valuation of *otium* and that voiced by Catullus. He knows, as every
reader of Catullus must know, that in the young poet's outburst of
passion and despondency one possible aspect of *otium* is over-emphasized. But he also knows that his, Horace's, own generation has come to
learn a truer appreciation of *otium*, calm and peace, than was given to
most contemporaries of Caesar and Pompey.[3] And, above all, Horace's
personal creed has its centre in the mellow wisdom, the resignation

adaptation of Poseidonius' account of the Etruscans, *F Gr Hist* 87 F 119, οὗτοι γὰρ τὸ μὲν
παλαιὸν ἀνδρείᾳ διενεγκόντες . . . καθόλου δὲ τὴν μὲν ἐκ παλαιῶν χρόνων παρ' αὐτοῖς ζηλου-
μένην ἀλκὴν ἀποβεβλήκασιν, ἐν πότοις δὲ καὶ ῥαθυμίαις ἀνάνδροις βιοῦντες κτλ. In the next
sentence we find the keyword τρυφή.

[1] Instances of this meaning can be found in any dictionary, see, for example, Lewis and
Short, s.v. *otium* II C. Special attention should be paid to the observations of H. Fuchs,
'Augustin und der antike Friedensgedanke', *Neue philol. Untersuchungen*, 3. Heft, 1926, 185.

[2] An element of the typical παράδειγμα appears also in *prius* (15), which is kindred to the
common ποτέ (*olim*) in παραδείγματα; cf. my note on A. *Ag.* 1040.

[3] For the topical character of the *otium* sentences at the beginning of the ode see Latte,
Philol. xc, 1935, 294.

without bitterness, of which the whole ode is a perfect expression. This attitude, combining the σωφροσύνη of the private individual with the σοφία of a poet who is moved by the *tenuis spiritus Graiae Camenae*, is inseparable from a deep longing for *otium*.[1]

3. ODES ADDRESSED TO MAECENAS

The odes from Books I–III so far discussed have been arranged, though without rigidity, partly according to the Greek models that can be traced in them and partly according to the recurrence of certain themes or, in other cases, certain structural elements. But now it will be more convenient to use a different arrangement and to take together first the odes addressed to Maecenas (to which a few odes addressed to other eminent contemporaries will be appended) and then those poems which are either addressed to or primarily concerned with Augustus. Any such arrangement is bound to be somewhat arbitrary and inadequate, but there seems to be no other way open to a writer who does not want to give a running commentary on all the poems. However, no great harm will be done so long as the reader can be expected to put this book aside as often as possible and read instead a long series of odes in the order in which Horace has arranged them.

It seems fitting to begin our survey of the odes addressed to Maecenas with a short and graceful poem, i. 20, *Vile potabis*. Its subject is as simple as can be, a variation, in a very much reduced form, of a theme common to many epigrams and many Horatian poems, the invitation to a banquet. This ode is not, strictly speaking, an invitation, and the note of an ancient commentator, *Maecenatem ad cenam invitat*, is only approximately true.[2] In the poem it is taken for granted that Maecenas is going to dine with Horace. How that came about and whether Maecenas announced his visit or was invited by Horace is wholly irrelevant: circumstances which the poet leaves out must not become an

---

[1] For other reminiscences from Catullus in Horace's poems see p. 58 and p. 65 n. 1 above and p. 420 n. 2 below.

[2] We should resist the temptation of taking *potabis* at l. 1 as 'futuro dell' invito' (Ussani) or translating 'Come, drink with me' (C. E. Bennett, Loeb edition). Ussani adduces Catullus 13. 1, *Cenabis bene . . . apud me*, without saying that it is followed by *si tecum attuleris*, etc. Rubenbauer, *Bursians Jahresb*. ccxii, 1927, 199 and Hofmann in Stolz–Schmalz, *Lat. Gramm.* 5th ed. 555, are equally wrong; the former refers to Martial 11. 52. 1, ignoring the next line, and Hor. *Epist.* 1. 5. 4, where *vina bibes* is preceded by *Si potes . . . manebo*. It would have been more to the point to quote *Epist.* 1. 7. 71 *post nonam venies*. This phrase and phrases such as *apud me cenabis* (Plaut. *Curc.* 728) do represent a formula of invitation, but *vile potabis Sabinum* does not.

object of his reader's curiosity.[1] Unlike certain similar odes, this poem says nothing of the preparations for the banquet in general; one detail only is singled out, the sort of wine the guest is to expect. The modest quality of that wine and the contrast between it and the wines which Maecenas is in the habit of drinking appear, on the surface of it, to provide the primary topic of this short ode: the opening sentence *vile potabis . . . Sabinum . . .* is worked out in the last stanza. But this appearance is deceptive, for it is with the secondary clause, *Graeca quod ego ipse testa conditum levi*, etc., that the poem takes its decisive turn. A strong emphasis is laid on *ego ipse*, 'I with my own hands',[2] and even stronger emphasis on the date that follows, *datus in theatro cum tibi plausus*, etc. The entire second stanza, the centre of the ode, recalls the splendid spectacle of a day which was probably one of the brightest in the life of a man so prone to melancholy. 'Le principal but d'Horace dans cette Ode, est de faire souvenir Mecene des battemens de mains, des cris de joye, et des acclamations avec lesquelles il fut receu du peuple, lorsqu'il entra pour la premiere fois dans le Theatre, aprés une grande maladie dont il avoit pensé mourir.'[3] The vocative at the beginning of the central stanza, *clare*[4] *Maecenas eques*, placed immediately after the clause *datus in theatro cum tibi plausus*, suggests Maecenas, amidst the thundering applause of the innumerable crowd, making for his seat in one of the front rows reserved for the knights.[5]

[1] C. Franke, *Fasti Horatiani*, 157, remarks with admirable precision: 'Horatius Maecenati, quem noverat apud se in praedio Sabino coenaturum vel potius bibiturum esse, potandum pollicetur *vile Sabinum*', etc. Those who feel inclined to go beyond this statement would do well to listen to Philipp Buttmann, who wrote in 1808 (see his *Mythologus*, i. 317) 'man muß nicht am Ende selbst glauben, den wahren Verlauf in Horazens Kabinet und in Maecenas' Vorzimmer erklügelt zu haben.'

[2] The active can, of course, be used when a person has something done by somebody else (cf. A. C. Pearson on Soph. *fr.* 620, my note on A. *Ag.* 1595, p. 750 top; for Latin instances see Kühner–Stegmann, i. 100, and add, for example, Plaut. *Persa* 315 *metuo ne immaturam secem*, in reply to *secari iubeas* [by a *medicus*]), but I think that a fine detail is ruined in Heinze's note 'H. hat dies Abfüllen . . . bei sich zu Hause (*ipse*), nicht vom Weinhändler besorgen lassen'. How much more sensitive is Dacier's note, 'Horace dit qu'il le fit luy-mesme, pour fair voir à Mecene la joye qu'il avoit euë de mettre sur ses vaisseaux la marque d'un jour si heureux'!

[3] Dacier.

[4] Klingner, in the revised edition (1950) of his text of Horace, rightly joins the many editors who, following Lambinus (not in his text, but in the note on 2. 20. 7, *dilecte Maecenas*) and Bentley, read *clare* (*care codd.*).

[5] *Maecenas, equitum decus* is, in a different sense, made subservient to the context at 3. 16. 20, where the implication was recognized by the scholiast (Ps.-Acro), cf. also Orelli–Baiter and Kiessling ad loc.; Stein, *RE* xiv. 211. For the functional use to which Horace often puts the name of the addressed person cf. p. 206 n. 1 above. It is amusing that in the nineteenth century *Maecenas eques* had to furnish one of the arguments for the assumption of a non-Horatian origin of *Odes* i. 20 (as late as Kiessling). Another argument, based on an alleged error in topography, has been removed by Elter's correct localization of *mons Vaticanus* (*Rh. Mus.* xlvi, 1891, 112 ff.).

Descending from the height of the excitement in the theatre the last stanza returns to the domestic scene with which the ode began; at the end the thought of *vile potabis . . . Sabinum* is taken up, and thus the poem is rounded off. But the last stanza is not a mere echo of the first sentence; it adds a contrast:

> Caecubum et prelo domitam Caleno
> tu bibes uvam: mea nec Falernae
> temperant vites neque Formiani
>   pocula colles.[1]

This contrast, no doubt, is fully justified by the theme of the ode,[2] but it seems also to point to something more important than the difference between the vintages at the disposal of Maecenas and the simple wine at the disposal of Horace. The sentence *mea nec Falernae temperant vites neque Formiani pocula colles*, as it stands, is a mere statement of fact, but he would be a dull reader who could not perceive in it an undertone of happiness and even pride, suggesting something like this: so it is, and it is well that it is so. The implication is less obvious here than, for instance, at the end of *Odes* ii. 16, *te greges centum . . . mihi parva rura*, but here, too, Horace's ideal of *frui paratis, desiderantem quod satis est* and *deorum muneribus sapienter uti* is clearly expressed. The starting-point of the ode was the immediate occasion, and so *vile potabis Sabinum* refers to one particular banquet, but at the end the idea expressed in the words *mea nec Falernae temperant vites*, etc., becomes a symbol of Horace's way of life. It is correct to call the ode a *Gelegenheitsgedicht*, a poem suggested by and written for a special occasion, but it is not enough. Primarily Horace wanted to cheer his friend by reminding him of the scene in the theatre, but in doing so he produced a lasting picture of his own affectionate care; primarily he wanted to prepare Maecenas for the modest drink he should expect at the Sabine farm, but in doing so he made the different brands of wine serve a nobler purpose. Like any good poem this ode goes far beyond the reproduction of a fragment of actual life.

The reader who is familiar with the work of Horace will naturally

---

[1] The concessive element (probably derived from the potential use of the future) in *tu bibes* was recognized long ago by Mitscherlich, who compared *Odes* 1. 6. 1 and 1. 7. 1, to which Dillenburger added 2. 12. 9 f., Orelli–Baiter 3. 23. 13 and Virg. *Aen.* 6. 847 ff. E. Flinck, *Commentationes philol. in honorem I. A. Heikel*, 1926, 31, whom Klingner quotes in his app. crit., has not contributed anything fresh. I have discussed the problem in my article on *Epist.* i. 7, in *250 Jahre Weidmannsche Buchhandlung*, Beilage zu Heft 4 der Monatschrift für höhere Schulen, Berlin 1930, 16 n. 1.

[2] In setting the refinements to which his guest is accustomed against his own homely hospitality Horace apparently takes up a traditional topic: R. Reitzenstein, *Neue Jahrb.* xxi, 1908, 96, compared *Odes* i. 20 and Catullus XIII with Philodemus' invitation to Piso, *Anth. Pal.* xi. 44.

combine *Vile potabis* with the other ode (ii. 17) in which the poet recalls the day when Maecenas was enthusiastically welcomed by the Roman people on his first appearance in the theatre after his narrow escape from death,[1]

> te Iovis impio
> tutela Saturno refulgens
> eripuit volucrisque Fati
>
> tardavit alas, cum populus frequens
> laetum theatris ter crepuit sonum.

The poem begins on a note of gentle reproach, in which there can be heard, perhaps, a slight impatience: *Cur me querelis exanimas tuis?* But this note fades out at once; the voice becomes deep and urgent, anxious to conjure away the friend's dark thoughts: *nec dis amicum est nec mihi te prius obire, Maecenas*—and then, throwing in the full weight of his devotion, *mearum grande decus columenque rerum.*[2] At this point the poet's excitement has become so strong that he bursts into an ejaculation which he allows himself very rarely:[3] *a, te meae si partem animae rapit maturior vis, quid moror altera, nec carus aeque nec superstes integer?*[4] The following three brief sentences (only the last of them is enlarged by a participial clause) express emphatically the speaker's determination, and in the third, *ibimus, ibimus utcumque praecedes*, the emotional ring is particularly noticeable.[5]

The fourth stanza, *me nec Chimaerae*, etc., is one of those passages where a wrong criticism may pave the way to a right appreciation. Meineke said 'Quartae strophae tam ridiculum πάθος est, ut Horatio

---

[1] The grave illness is not expressly mentioned but clearly understood.

[2] Of the various expressions which Horace puts in apposition to the vocative *Maecenas* the present one is the grandest, weightier than even *o et praesidium et dulce decus meum* in the dedicatory ode. *columen* (to Leo, *Hermes*, xviii, 1883, 583, and *Thes. l. L.* iii, 1735 ff., I add Vetter, *Glotta*, ii, 1910, 248 ff., without, however, accepting his rendering 'Grundpfeiler') deserves a word. Leaving aside the technical use (Cato, *Agr.* 15 etc.) and the set phrase *sub divo columine*, we may state that the word in its metaphorical use has, in keeping with the idea it expresses, a lofty ring as early as Plautus (*senati columen, audaciai columen*, etc., cf. also Ter. *Phorm.* 287 *columen familiae*); in Catullus 64. 26 *Thessaliae columen Peleu* we hear possibly an echo of Ennius. Cicero uses it several times mockingly, παρατραγῳδῶν. In Virgil and the elegists it does not occur, in Horace only in the present passage.

[3] For the use of the interjection *a* see p. 181 n. 1 above.

[4] Heinze (7th ed.), on l. 5, assumes, perhaps rightly, that the unusual break (a fresh sentence beginning after the first dactyl of the decasyllable) is meant to picture emotion. The same break occurs at 1. 35. 36 and 2. 13. 8.

[5] The 'emphatic gemination', as E. Wölfflin termed it (*Sitz. Bayr. Akad.* 1882, iii. 427 ff., reprinted in his *Ausgewählte Schriften*, 288 ff.; on p. 294 *Odes* 2. 17. 10 is duly registered), is rare in Horace; for the very old formula *Odes* 1. 35. 15 *ad arma . . . ad arma*, see *JRS* xxxv, 1945, 6 n. 9. The full meaning of *utcumque praecedes* must not be weakened: it means that, *whenever* Maecenas may set out on his last journey, Horace will be ready *immediately* to follow him (see P. Ferrarino, '*cumque* e i composti di *que*', Bologna 1942, 204).

prorsus indignam esse existimem'.[1] It is easy to smile at the great scholar's fierce subjectivity. But in this case there lies behind the sweeping condemnation an admirable feeling for what is normally to be expected of Horace. Horace does not easily indulge in this kind of grandiloquence; he regards as the best gift Fate has bestowed upon him *spiritum Graiae tenuem Camenae*. But it is one thing to discern a poet's characteristic style, another not to allow him any deviation from it. Let us freely admit that in the stanza before us there is a peculiar 'pathos' and then try to understand its implications. Here Horace seems to be bent upon producing something heavy, deliberately, and, I venture to think, with his tongue in his cheek. He does not believe in the reality of those mythological monsters, nor, for that matter, does Maecenas. However, Chimaera and the like[2] are wonderfully suited to give weight to the formidable oath (9 f. *non ego perfidum dixi sacramentum*) and at the same time to make his friend smile at the pretended frightfulness. But that, pleasant though it is, would not suffice to set the tormented mind of the hypochondriac at ease. To console him effectively, Horace ventures into the strange sphere of Maecenas' own creed, astrology.[3] It is well known that in Augustan Rome astrology was vigorously in the ascendant. But if there lived any man in that period whose nature, education, and deepest convictions would lead him to dislike the doctrine τῶν ἐξ ἀστρολογίας πρὸς τοὺς Χαλδαΐζοντας τὴν κακότεχνον ταύτην γοητείαν ὡς ἐν μέρει μαθήματος ἐπαγγελλομένων,[4] it was Horace. And yet he speaks of it here, and only here, in a serious vein.[5] Only by showing his respect for the dogma in which his friend believes can he hope to comfort him.[6] Horace is tactful enough not to parade crude technicalities or to pose as an expert.[7] What he does give has a true poetical value, easy to grasp in *te Iovis impio tutela Saturno refulgens eripuit* with its fine contrast emphasized by

---

[1] *Praefatio*, p. xv. Before him Peerlkamp had obelized the last five stanzas, ll. 13–32.

[2] For the mocking spirit of the end of *Odes* i. 27, *vix inligatum te triformi Pegasus expediet Chimaera*, see p. 183 above.

[3] The astrological section of the ode has been thoroughly illustrated by F. Boll, *Philol.* lxix 1910, 165 ff., *Z. für das Gymnasialwesen*, lxv, 1911, 765, and especially *Sokrates*, v, 1917, 1 ff. (reprinted in Boll's *Kl. Schriften zur Sternkunde des Altertums*, 1950, 115 ff.).

[4] Eusebius, *Praep. ev.* 6. 9. 32.

[5] I am not convinced by Boll, *Philol.* lxix, 1910, 166 f. (re-emphasized *Z. f. d. Gymnasialw.* lxv, 1911, 765) that in the last four stanzas there is 'Humor' meant 'dem Maecenas ein Lächeln abzugewinnen'. If you take your religion seriously (and to its adepts astrology *is* a religion), you do not care to have it treated in a jocular manner. The position is quite different in regard to ll. 13–16 (*me nec Chimaerae*, etc.). I am aware of the subjective element that enters in here. However, it may be safely said that it is easy enough to miss the 'Humor' of a passage, but still easier to read it into a passage where it has no business.

[6] Boll gave in a lecture (excerpts printed in *Kl. Schriften z. Sternkunde*, 388) the neat description 'der nicht sternengläubige Horaz schreibt an den sternfürchtigen Maecenas'.

[7] 'Ohne daß Horaz die Miene des Fachmanns aufsetzte', Boll, *Philol.* lxix, 1910, 165.

the suggestive antithetic order of words, and above all in *utrumque nostrum incredibili modo consentit astrum*, the warmth and splendour of which will be felt by any reader, whether he cares for astrology or not.[1] The sincerity of his friendship and the limpid nature of his poetry enabled Horace to gain beauty even from the sphere of those ideas which he himself may often have regarded as pieces of dark superstition.

The sympathetic understanding of Maecenas' feelings, which is the mainspring of *Vile potabis* and *Cur me querelis*, is noticeable also in *Odes* ii. 12, *Nolis longa ferae bella Numantiae*. This ode culminates in the praise of the perfections of Maecenas' wife Terentia (Licymnia in the poem) and of her and her husband's mutual love. Though rich in delicate touches,[2] the poem as a whole will probably leave most readers cold or, at any rate, not move them to the same extent as *Cur me querelis*. The reason is not far to seek: this is one of the cases in which Horace falls short of his own maxim, *denique sit quodvis, simplex dumtaxat et unum*. The ode is both artificial and overladen. The tribute to Licymnia is here appended to, and appears as a side-issue of, a wholly hetero-geneous theme, a typical *recusatio*, whereby Horace declines the task of making the military triumphs of Augustus a subject of his poetry.[3] This duplicity of theme entails a certain lack of perspicuity in the arrange-ment of the first part of the ode. Before examining the section as a whole, we shall do well to consider an apparently small detail, the function of the particle at l. 9, *tuque pedestribus dices historiis . . ..* Here *tuque* is ob-viously not easy. Whilst several commentators pass it over in silence, others have tackled it, without, however, reaching a satisfactory solu-tion.[4] We shall not get out of the difficulty unless we realize that *tu . . . dices . . . proelia Caesaris* is related to the subsequent *me . . . Musa Licym-*

---

[1] The astrological background of this sentence which centres in *consentit astrum* is the main object of Boll's third article (see p. 218 n. 3) on this ode, with the title 'Sternen-freundschaft'.

[2] Note, for instance, ll. 17–20, where Licymnia is pictured devoting her accomplished dancing to the service of the gods: no one should think of her as a woman who is accus-tomed *psallere saltare elegantius quam necesse est probae*.

[3] For the *recusatio* and for the analysis of the ode in general see Kiessling–Heinze, whose comments are here particularly apposite.

[4] See, for example, the notes of Dacier, Mitscherlich, and Obbarius. According to Dillen-burger's opinion, which was accepted by Wickham, Kiessling, L. Müller, Shorey, Ussani, and others, the present passage is to be classed with several others where *-que*, continuing a negative clause, seems to have a tinge of an adversative meaning, such as appears not seldom in other copulative particles as well, both Greek and Latin. It would be crude and misleading in such cases to speak 'de copulativa particula pro adversativa adhibita'; all we might safely state is that the copulative particle 'erhält im Zusammen-hang leicht einen Anflug adversativer Bedeutung' (F. Leo, *Nachr. Gött. Ges.*, Phil.-hist. Kl. 1895, 423) although it is sufficient to recognize that in a copulative clause very often 'das adversative Verhältnis unbezeichnet gelassen wird' (J. B. Hofmann in Stolz–Schmalz, 5th ed. 660). But I cannot accept Dillenburger's view, for the passages quoted by him and his followers do not in fact support it: *Odes* i. 27. 16; 2. 20. 4; 3. 30. 6. In these

niae cantus, me voluit dicere . . . *oculos* in the same way in which *Caecubum*
. . . *tu bibes* is related to *mea nec Falernae temperant vites neque Formiani*
pocula colles (1. 20. 9–12), or *Laudabunt alii claram Rhodon* . . .*; plurimus* . . .
aptum dicet equis Argos . . . is related to *me nec tam* . . . *Lacedaemon nec tam*
Larisae percussit campus . . . *quam*, etc. (1. 7. 1–14).[1] The connexion of
thought in the first part of the poem could then be summarized thus:
you would not wish[2] the Punic wars, nor the tales of Greek mythology,
to be sung in lyrics, and whilst you, Maecenas, may in prose recount
Caesar's triumphs,[3] my Muse . . . .[4]

But now we must say something more about the beginning. The
content of the bipartite negative period with which the ode opens
(down to 9 *Saturni veteris*) would in ordinary language be subordinated
to the principal thought, for instance like this: 'as you would not wish
to have the Punic wars or the Greek myths treated in lyrics so you
would not want me to sing Caesar's feats of war'. In the place of such
a straightforward arrangement we find what is known as 'comparatio
paratactica'.[5] This form is common in, though not confined to, early
Greek poetry. Pindar especially is very fond of it, and Horace probably
used it after the model of some Greek lyric poets. However, in its
original form a preamble of this kind would lead in a direct line to the
theme in hand: 'you would not wish subject *A*, nor subject *B*, to be
treated in lyrics, nor would you expect me, the lyric poet, to sing
Caesar's deeds'. In the present instance the direct line is broken by the
sentence (9 ff.) *tuque pedestribus dices historiis proelia Caesaris*, etc. The
intrusion of this sentence is due to the requirements of the fully
developed *recusatio*. When the demand for a eulogy of Augustus from

---

three passages the -*que* clause has the same grammatical or 'logical' subject as the one that
immediately precedes it and with the thought of which it is closely connected, and,
moreover, there is in them but a shade of an adversative colour, whereas at 2. 12. 9 we have
an entirely fresh start and, according to those commentators, a most emphatic antithesis.
Heinze, on l. 9, has cancelled Kiessling's note on *tuque* and replaced it by a comment
which, up to a point, describes the progress of thought but does not do justice to *tuque*, for
Heinze, like the others, was not aware of the precise nature of the relation between *tuque*
. . . *dices* and *me* . . . *Musa* . . . *voluit dicere*.   [1] Cf. p. 216 n. 1 above.

[2] Cruquius' note, 'nolis est modi potentialis', is perfectly correct. 'Ob *nolis* je für *noli*,
also prohibitiv gebraucht ist, läßt sich bezweifeln' (H. Schütz). *nolis* in independent
clauses is altogether not very common; where it does occur, it seems to be potential, as in
the only other instance in Horace, *Epist.* 1. 1. 31, and, for example, Plaut. *Bacch.* 914, Cic.
Nat. deor. 1. 78.

[3] When at l. 11 *melius*, emphatically added to the clause *tu* . . . *pedestribus dices historiis*
proelia Caesaris, follows immediately after *Maecenas*, the implication is obvious: your prose
work, Maecenas, will be better suited than any lyrics of mine could be to do justice
to Caesar's deeds.

[4] It follows that after l. 12 (*minacium*) we should not put, as the editors do, a full stop
but a semicolon or, perhaps better, a comma.

[5] For a selection of books and articles in which it is discussed see my note on A. *Ag.*
76 ff., and add Wilamowitz, *Pindaros*, 491.

Horace's pen was made as urgently as Maecenas apparently had made it, it would not suffice for Horace to give the reply he had once given to Trebatius,[1] 'to my great regret I am not fit worthily to do what you want me, *Caesaris invicti res dicere*', but he had to make a counter-proposal and name another candidate for the task he would not undertake himself. This device Horace employs also in *Odes* i. 6, *Scriberis Vario*, and in the much later poem iv. 2, *Pindarum quisquis studet aemulari*. With the latter ode the present one has this in common that the suggestion, boomerang-like, returns to the person from whom it came: 'you will (or may) do yourself what you ask me to do'. In the case of Iullus Antonius Horace did not feel any qualms in suggesting, at any rate as a possibility, that the young man should compose a Pindarizing ἐπινίκιον, but in the case of Maecenas he could not, without being downright ironical, propose a lyric poem; he therefore resorted to the idea of a historical work in prose. I do not think that we need to take this suggestion very seriously; in this context a gentle playfulness would not be out of place, 'why should you not yourself become the historian of Caesar's wars?'[2]

The interplay of themes in the ode would be complicated enough if it reached its centre with a turn like this: whilst you may write the history of Caesar's wars, my Muse bids me sing of love. That would normally be the poet's own love.[3] But as the ode stands its crowning theme is the love of Maecenas and Licymnia. This unexpected climax of a poem that begins as a typical *recusatio* will doubtless have pleased Maecenas, but one would hesitate to say that the fusion of heterogeneous elements has produced here, as it does elsewhere in Horace's work, a harmonious whole.

We saw[4] that the short and unassuming ode i. 20, *Vile potabis*, although no invitation is directly expressed in it, is to be classed with the

---

[1] *Sat.* 2. 1. 12 ff.

[2] It is extremely doubtful whether Maecenas ever planned such a work, and all but certain that if he did plan it, nothing came of it. See, for example, Kappelmacher, *RE* xiv. 226; Schanz–Hosius, *Gesch. d. röm. Lit.* ii. 4. 21.

[3] So Propertius, in the overture of his second book, after asserting that his voice is not strong enough to praise Caesar and that everybody must write about the things he really knows, goes on to say that his love for one woman shall be the sole theme of his poetry (2. 1. 39–48). Despite the wealth of detail and ornament, this elegy, unlike *Nolis longa ferae bella Numantiae*, shows a simple and natural progress of thought. Considering some remarkable similarities, even in detail, between these two poems addressed to Maecenas, it is tempting to assume that Horace had Propertius ii. 1 before him, but we do not know enough of the conventional topics and the conventional arrangement of thought which both poets may have found ready-made for the purpose of a *recusatio*. In certain other cases where similarities between Horatian and Propertian passages are noticeable we should perhaps pause before speaking of 'Propertius' plagiarisms'; see F. Solmsen's warning, *Class. Phil.* xliii, 1948, 106 n. 9.   [4] Cf. p. 214 above.

many poems inviting a friend to a banquet. The two far more elaborate
odes iii. 8 and iii. 29, both, like i. 20, addressed to Maecenas, are invitations in the strict sense of the word. In iii. 8, *Martiis caelebs quid
agam Kalendis*, the unusual occasion which Horace is about to celebrate
gives colour to the poem and much is made of Maecenas' surprise at
the strange preparations made by his friend. Here again[1] we notice
Horace's skill in putting the vocative *Maecenas* in the most effective
place and enriching it with an ornament especially suited to the present context. You are astonished (*miraris*)—and well you may be—for
with all your knowledge of learned discussions both Greek and Latin,
docte sermones utriusque linguae,[2] you will never have heard of a bachelor
solemnly celebrating the *Matronalia*. From this humorous characterization at the beginning of the second stanza the name itself, *Maecenas*, is
widely separated: it supports the imperative at the beginning of the
fourth stanza. To begin with a characterizing invocation and postpone
the vocative of the proper name is a device well known from early
Greek hymns;[3] Pindar uses it often. In Horace we find it, for instance,
in the opening stanza of *Odes* iii. 29 and, in a very solemn form, at the
beginning of *Epist.* i. 1; both these poems are addressed to Maecenas.

In the explanation which Horace gives to his friend (6 ff.) there
appears as the primary reason for the unusual celebration that accident
of the falling tree from which the poet's Muse more than once derived
handsome profit. But in this ode the main emphasis lies on the anticipation of the carefully prepared banquet. Give yourself up to the
pleasures of the present hour and forget your worries—this thought,
one of the oldest topics of symposiac poetry, is here given a characteristic Roman turn, *mitte civilis super urbe curas*, etc. This modification of
the commonplace is particularly appropriate when addressed to one
who shares to such an extent the political cares of the ruler. To
strengthen his advice Horace surveys the situation at the danger-points
of the Empire, where all is now quiet:

> Occidit Daci Cotisonis agmen,
> Medus infestus sibi luctuosis
>   dissidet armis,

---

[1] Cf. p. 215 above.

[2] I regard Bentley's explanation (followed, for example, by Wickham) as sufficient;
Heinze's suggestion that the expression possibly alludes to the *Dialogi* of Maecenas does
not seem to me necessary. For *sermones* = λόγοι Bentley quotes *Odes* 3. 21. 9 f. *Socraticis
sermonibus*: Σωκρατικοῖς λόγοις. Cf., for instance, Cic. *Orat.* 151 *Plato . . . in iis sermonibus
qui* διάλογοι *dicuntur* and *Tusc.* 1. 21 *Dicaearchus . . . in eo sermone quem Corinthi habitum tribus
libris exponit*. Perhaps in all these instances the idea of a discussion in dialogue form is
implied as it is in Cicero's *Tusculanae disputationes*, but if so, it is hardly of primary importance. Besides, it would not be surprising if several of the Greek and Latin books which
Horace had in mind were composed as dialogues, cf. Leo, *Nachr. Gött. Ges.*, Phil.-hist. Kl.
1912, 274.   [3] Cf. O. Regenbogen, 'Lukrez', *Neue Wege zur Antike*, ii. 1, 1932, 65.

> servit Hispanae vetus hostis orae
> Cantaber sera domitus catena,
> iam Scythae laxo meditantur arcu
> cedere campis.[1]

So the convivial poem grows imperceptibly into a *carmen civile* and, while setting Maecenas' mind at ease, it extols the *pax Augusta*. Then, as in many odes, the last stanza strikes a lighter note and brings in a harmless pleasantry,[2] in keeping with the maxim *linque severa*.

We now come to a masterpiece, iii. 29, *Tyrrhena regum progenies*. It is one of the longest Horatian odes and by far the longest of those which have as their subject a banquet or an invitation to it. This uncommon length is but the most conspicuous sign of the grandeur and sublimity which distinguish this poem from the rest of Horace's symposiac lyrics. The bulk of the ode, ll. 5–64, provides the most elaborate example of a class of reflections which is one of the oldest features of drinking songs. They naturally centre in the idea of *carpe diem*. Horace's own contribution to the treatment of the traditional maxims, in the banquet odes and elsewhere, consists in his harmonious blending of topics ultimately derived from very old poetry, convivial and other, with ideas and illustrations developed in popular philosophy, especially during the Hellenistic period. In the present case a sublime character is imparted to the centre of the poem (33–41) by the happy symbolism which pictures the changeability of man's fortune by describing the extreme changes in the appearance and behaviour of the great river:

> cetera fluminis
> ritu feruntur, nunc medio alveo
> cum pace delabentis Etruscum
> in mare, nunc lapides adesos

> stirpisque raptas et pecus et domos
> volventis una, non sine montium

---

[1] The four independent clauses, following one another ἀσυνδέτως with almost strict parallelism (*occidit . . . Cotisonis agmen, Medus . . . sibi . . . dissidet . . ., servit . . . Cantaber . . ., iam Scythae . . . meditantur . . . cedere campis*), give the impression of a long chain of successes. Stylistically very similar are the last two stanzas of iii. 18, where the bounty of the god's peace is pictured in many details, and the same pattern is used 4. 11. 6–12, to suggest the festal glamour and the rushing to and fro in the excited household. In all three passages the first clause begins with a verb (in iii. 8 also the third, in iii. 18 also the fourth and fifth). The three poems are in the same metre.

[2] Horace could never tell Maecenas in earnest *ne qua populus laboret parce privatus nimium cavere*. The idea, deeply rooted in Roman life, that a *homo privatus* must not meddle with affairs of the *res publica*, lends itself readily to jokes; cf. Plautus, *Capt.* 165 f., *Persa* 75 f.

clamore vicinaeque silvae,
    cum fera diluvies quietos

inritat amnis.[1]

This imagery to Horace was eminently poetic; otherwise he would not
have used it, or rather one aspect of it, to give an idea of the style of the
greatest lyric poet (*Odes* 4. 2. 5 ff.):[2]

monte decurrens velut amnis, imbres
quem super notas aluere ripas,
fervet immensusque ruit profundo
    Pindarus ore

and, carrying on the image (10 ff.),

seu per audacis nova dithyrambos
verba devolvit[3] numerisque fertur
    lege solutis.

In the description of the river in iii. 29, as always in Horace's most
accomplished descriptions, vision and sound work together. The third
line of the Alcaic stanza provides an ideal rhythm for the peaceful
flow of the waters:

cum pace delabentis Etruscum
    in mare.

There follows, in a different tempo, the contrast,

nunc lapides adesos

stirpisque raptas et pecus et domos
    volventis una,

where the polysyndeton enhances the effect of a devastating rush.

---

[1] The subject-matter is well illustrated by Pliny, *Epist.* 8. 17. 2 (quoted by Dacier),
*Tiberis alveum excessit et demissioribus ripis alte superfunditur; . . . inde quae solet flumina accipere
et permixta devehere velut obvius retro cogit atque ita alienis aquis operit agros quos ipse non tangit.*
As regards Horace's bold use of *irritat*, I believe that it was suggested by ὀρόθυνον in *Iliad*
21. 311 f. (Scamander speaking to Simoïs), ἀλλ' ἐπάμυνε τάχιστα, καὶ ἐμπίπληθι ῥέεθρα |
ὕδατος ἐκ πηγέων, πάντας δ' ὀρόθυνον ἐναύλους.

[2] It is irrelevant to Horace's appreciation of the topic that it had been applied to a
description of style by earlier writers; cf., for example, Cic. *Orat.* 39 *alter enim* (Herodotus)
*sine ullis salebris quasi sedatus amnis fluit, alter incitatior fertur et de bellicis rebus canit etiam
quodammodo bellicum.* The comparison is, however, much older than the Hellenistic age.
Orelli–Baiter, on 4. 2. 5, quote Pind. *Ol.* 10. 9 f. νῦν ψᾶφον ἑλισσομέναν ὁπᾷ κῦμα κατακλύσσει
ῥέον, Heinze quotes the famous fragment (186 K.) from the Πυτίνη of Cratinus, but much
closer to Horace is the description of Cratinus' poetry in Ar. *Knights* 526 ff. ὃς πολλῷ
ῥεύσας ποτ' ἐπαίνῳ | διὰ τῶν ἀφελῶν πεδίων ἔρρει, καὶ τῆς στάσεως παρασύρων | ἐφόρει τὰς
δρῦς καὶ τὰς πλατάνους καὶ τοὺς ἐχθροὺς προθελύμνους, a piece which may well contain some
elements borrowed from poetry in a higher style (cf. Neil on 527).

[3] *Devolvit* is to be taken together with 3. 29. 38 *volventis una*; the next verb, *fertur*,
belongs to the same image (cf. Cic. *Orat.* 39, quoted in the preceding footnote).

There can be no doubt what river is meant here, *cum pace delabens in mare Etruscum*. The picture of the Tiber, king of Etruria's rivers, is singularly appropriate to form the finest ornament of the poem that begins *Tyrrhena regum progenies*. To this beginning we must now turn. In calling Maecenas *Tyrrhena regum progenies*[1] Horace seems to be speaking with a smile. Maecenas, however proud he was of his descent, would have been startled if Horace, when inviting him to a simple dinner at his place in the country, had seriously referred to his guest's royal ancestors.[2] The pomp of the opening phrase is of a piece with the slightly mocking tone of the third and fourth stanzas[3] and especially with the exaggerated contrast between the *mundae parvo sub lare pauperum*[4] *cenae* and the luxury of the rich.[5] The playful undertone fades out when we come to the description of the midsummer heat and the lovely landscape (17–24); in the rest of the poem a note of mild seriousness, not to be confused with sermonizing, is maintained to the end.[6] Here the sheer power of poetry transforms what otherwise might remain a piece of hackneyed diatribe:

> ille potens sui
> laetusque deget, cui licet in diem
> dixisse 'vixi: cras vel atra
> nube polum pater occupato

[1] For the device of beginning with a descriptive phrase put in apposition to the vocative of the name, which follows later, see p. 222 above.

[2] The context in which Propertius, 3. 9. 1. says *Maecenas eques Etrusco de sanguine regum* is entirely different, and so is the younger poet's relation to Maecenas in general: he addresses him only in the two programme poems ii. 1 and iii. 9.

[3] On l. 10, *molem propinquam nubibus arduis*, the commentators say nothing, except that they recall *Epod.* 9. 3 and the *turris Maecenatiana* (Suet. *Nero* 38. 2). The hyperbolical expression does not seem to have been invented by Horace. Pollux 9. 20, in a section which apparently draws to a certain extent on conventional ἔπαινοι πόλεων (cf. Menander, *Rhet. Graec.* iii. 346 ff. Spengel, and especially p. 349. 21 ὥσπερ ἀκρόπολις κτλ.), gives this list: ἀκροπόλει ἐοικυῖαν, μικροῦ ὑπερνέφελον, ... ὀλίγου ψαύουσαν τῶν νεφελῶν, ἐγγυτάτω τῶν νεφῶν κτλ. These encomiastic phrases may have been used by rhetoricians, but were presumably coined, at any rate some of them, by poets praising Hellenistic cities or buildings. The fuller versions of the topic are lost, but an echo may be recognized in an epigram of Antipater of Sidon, *Anth. Pal.* 9. 58, who (6) calls the temple of Artemis at Ephesus Ἀρτέμιδος νεφέων ἄχρι θέοντα δόμον (the last line of the epigram by the same poet, *Anth. Pal.* 7. 748 [cf. Wilamowitz, *S.u.S.* 243 n. 1], seems to point in the same direction, but the text is uncertain). Passages such as Virg. *Aen.* 8. 98 ff. *domorum tecta . . . quae nunc Romana potentia caelo aequavit* and 4. 89 (of the building of the city-walls) *aequataque machina caelo* are probably variations of the same topic. The idea recurs, with bombastic exaggeration, in Martial 8. 36. 7 f.

[4] *pauperum* is of course to be taken in the Roman sense.

[5] Similarly, at the beginning of *Sat.* i. 6 the pomp with which the noble lineage of Maecenas is described serves as a foil to his treatment of the *libertino patre natus*. Cf. above pp. 101 f.

[6] It is instructive to compare the tone of ll. 25–28 with the slight pleasantry in the treatment of the same topic at 3. 8. 25 f. (cf. p. 223 n. 2 above).

vel sole puro; non tamen inritum
quodcumque retro est efficiet neque
diffinget infectumque reddet
quod fugiens semel hora vexit'.

The subject-matter of this sentence (41–48) contains nothing that had
not been said many times before, but the lines themselves, contrasting
sharply with the preceding picture of devastation, shine with a sublime serenity. The next stanza too, describing the ways of Fortuna,
draws from conventional conceptions;[1] its merit lies in the powerful
phrasing. In the subsequent stanza, still dealing with Fortuna,[2] we
notice a descent to a somewhat lower stylistic level. The expression
resigno quae dedit is deliberately business-like, and *mea virtute me involvo* is
only in part serious: to say such a thing without a smile would not be
like Horace. While asserting his own independence he good-humouredly
parodies the boasting of the rigid satellites of virtue. The last clause of
the stanza, *probamque pauperiem sine dote quaero*, is simple and sincere.
After watching Fortuna's flight the reader, not only Maecenas, is
meant to enjoy the steadiness and unpretentious wisdom of Horace's
way of life. In the ideal which is here pictured there is, again, nothing
novel; men from time immemorial have praised happiness thus:

εὐδαίμων μὲν ὃς ἐκ θαλάσσας
ἔφυγε χεῖμα, λιμένα δ' ἔκιχεν,
εὐδαίμων δ' ὃς ὕπερθε μόχθων
ἐγένετο,

or, in the words of an enthusiastic young follower of the doctrine of
Epicurus:

nos ad beatos vela mittimus portus
vitamque ab omni vindicabimus cura.

---

[1] With l. 50 *ludum insolentem ludere pertinax* compare Seneca, *Dial.* 9. 11. 5 *fortuna illa,
quae ludos sibi facit*, etc., and with ll. 53 ff. compare ibid. section 2, *quandoque autem reddere
iubebitur, non queretur cum fortuna, sed dicet 'gratias ago pro eo quod possedi habuique . . . si quid habere
me tui volueris etiamnunc, servabo; si aliud placet, ego vero . . . argentum, domum familiamque meam
reddo, restituo'*, and Epictetus 2. 16. 28 μὴ διδόμενα δὲ μὴ ποθεῖν, ἀφαιρουμένου δέ τινος
ἀποδιδόναι εὐλύτως καὶ αὐτόθεν, χάριν εἰδότα οὗ ἐχρήσατο χρόνου κτλ. It is obvious that
Seneca does not depend on Horace. Boethius, on the other hand, *Consol.* 2. 2 (p. 180 of
Stewart's text in the Loeb Library), *haec nostra vis est, hunc continuum ludum ludimus; . . .
infima summis, summa infimis mutare gaudemus*, has clearly not only *Odes* 3. 29. 50 in mind but
also 1. 34. 12 f. and 16 (*hic posuisse gaudet*). For the role that this passage of Boethius played
in the medieval and Renaissance conception of Fortuna see A. Doren, *Vorträge der Biblio-
thek Warburg*, 1922–3, 79.

[2] With regard to 53 *laudo manentem* Dacier and other commentators recall the coins of
the Emperor Commodus with the legend FORTVNAE MANENTI (see. H. Mattingly, *Coins of
the Rom. Empire in the Brit. Mus.* iv. 922 and *Introd.* p. clxv); cf. also W. Otto, *RE* vii. 31.
1 ff., and add Plutarch, *Fort. Rom.*, *Mor.* 318 A (ἡ Τύχη) οὕτως εἰσῆλθεν εἰς Ῥώμην ὡς
μενοῦσα.

In substance, Horace has nothing to add, but his eye for the picturesque detail, his ear for the suggestive sound, and his skill in letting a strong pathos gradually fade out, work harmoniously together and leave us with a feeling of perfect calm and happiness:

> tunc me biremis praesidio scaphae
> tutum per Aegaeos tumultus
> aura feret geminusque Pollux.

It is easy to enjoy this rich poem but not quite so easy to recognize in it the various themes which have contributed to its making. That is in itself a remarkable testimony to the poet's gift for blending different elements. However, anyone who, equipped with sufficient knowledge of Horace's lyrics, attempts to analyse the ode *Tyrrhena regum progenies* will see that it combines several topics, each of which could form the principal theme of a separate poem.

The first six stanzas (1–24) contain, broadly speaking, an invitation to a rural banquet,[1] contrasted in the usual way with the refinements in the town houses of the rich. This is the only theme of the short ode i. 20[2] and the chief theme of the not very long odes ii. 3 and iii. 8, in both of which it leads to a paraenetic thought very similar to that in the present poem. A similar transition from the planning of a banquet to a παραίνεσις is found in early Greek symposiac poetry and for instance, in Epode XIII and *Odes* ii. 11 (here the intended banquet is again a rural one). The thought which occupies the exact centre of *Tyrrhena regum progenies*, ll. 29 ff.,

> prudens futuri temporis exitum
> caliginosa nocte premit deus
> ridetque si mortalis ultra
> fas trepidat; quod adest memento

> componere aequus,

---

[1] Heinze labels iii. 29 correctly 'Einladung an Maecenas', but thinks it necessary to qualify this label: 'aber getreu seiner in der ersten Sammlung festgehaltenen Fiktion, daß die Oden an den Anwesenden gesprochen seien [this *petitio principii* is worked out in Heinze's article 'Die horazische Ode', *Neue Jahrb.* li, 1923, 153 ff., reprinted in his book *Vom Geist des Römertums* 185 ff.], vermeidet H. jeden ausdrücklichen Hinweis auf die räumliche Trennung'. Here we have an unmistakable product of *Systemzwang*. Besides, the assertion is not true. The lovely lines *ne semper udum Tibur et Aefulae declive contempleris arvum et Telegoni iuga parricidae* immediately picture to anyone familiar with Rome and its surroundings the skyline as it appears from the *alta domus* of Maecenas or, for that matter, from any elevated point in Rome: east-north-east the Sabine hills with Tivoli and several other *castelli*, and south-east the slopes and ridges above Frascati. Maecenas is wistfully gazing at all that distant beauty but cannot tear himself away from the city to visit Horace.

[2] See pp. 214 ff. above.

is combined with the advice *vina liques* in the brief ode i. 11, *Tu ne quaesieris*. The important role assigned to Fortuna brings to mind *Odes* i. 35 and the end of i. 34, but in the present poem the topic (49 ff.) grows organically out of the thought of the preceding stanzas (from 29 on).

If, despite the variety of motifs, *Tyrrhena regum progenies* does not give the impression of a mosaic-like composition, this is partly due to the unifying effect of a truly lyrical treatment. The lyrical character is perhaps most obvious in the pictures of the great river both in calm and in tumult, but it can be detected in the whole poem. This may be best realized by observing some other sections, which, like the description of the river, are rounded off to form perfect units, as for instance the scene of the burning midsummer day (17–24), or the account of Fortuna's behaviour (49–52), or the sea-piece at the end with the two contrasting types of voyagers (57–64). The lyrical character is produced not so much by the matter as by the treatment, especially by the selection and intensification of moments appealing to our feeling. The reader who wants to obtain a clear idea of this lyrical character should compare, in some detail, the presentation of the Fortuna topic in this ode with its presentation in certain epistles, i. 1. 68 f.; i. 4. 12–14; i. 6 *passim*; i. 11. 22 ff. (very close to 41 ff. of our ode). These passages are not inferior to the ode in dignity and vigour, but they demonstrate and teach, they do not sing. With great intensity, yet in purely rational terms, they expound the doctrine of mature wisdom; there is nothing in them of the almost religious fervour that breathes in the ode.[1]

But it is not the style alone that binds the different elements together. The poem derives its essential unity from the individuality of the poet behind it. At the beginning (1–24) we are shown the simple pleasures which he enjoys at his *villa rustica*, and at the end we see him sovereign master of his destiny whatever evil wind may blow. He knows what to desire and what to avoid. Calm and warmhearted, he attempts to disentangle his ever-worrying friend from some of his many cares and at the same time outlines, without the slightest ostentation, his personal ideal of a life worth living. Because this ode was a perfect monument both of his devotion to Maecenas and of his own outlook on life,[2] and also because he regarded it as very good poetry,

---

[1] Nothing shows this difference better than the change which the reflection on *otium* and *curae* undergoes in its transition from the *sermo* (*Sat.* 2. 7. 111–15) to the *carmen* (*Odes* ii. 16). The main elements of the thought are almost all contained in the former passage, but what is not to be found there is exactly the quality which makes *Otium divos* a real poem.

[2] This was rightly pointed out by Heinze.

Horace deemed it worthy to conclude the collection of his *carmina*—
the epilogue, iii. 30, is, as it were, set apart.

When we turn from the great and glowing poem *Tyrrhena regum
progenies* to iii. 16, *Inclusam Danaen*, we cannot but feel rather chilled.
This ode, despite some happy poetic colouring, has more of the character of a *sermo* than of a *carmen*. The way in which a moral diatribe, not
connected with any particular occasion, seems here to be delivered for
its own sake, has disturbed some commentators and induced them to go
outside the poem and try to find in Horace's life an event which might
have given rise to this ode.[1] Such attempts are doomed to failure; the
popular short cut, marked by the sign-post pointing to 'das Erlebnis
und die Dichtung', does not get us anywhere. And yet it would be
wrong to conclude that this ode is primarily a piece of fine writing.
Horace's gratitude to Maecenas for what he has received from him and
also his unwillingness to receive more are sincere and find strong and
dignified expression. He firmly believes in the ideal of life which he
professes, but we may doubt whether in this ode he has succeeded in
shaping his convictions and ideals into poetry, poetry not, of course,
judged by the standards of modern Romanticism but by the standards
of Horace's own lyrics at their best. Even the tale of Danae, one of the
speciosa miracula of Greek myth, has here degenerated into a frigid
allegory. It is no excuse for Horace that Hellenistic poets had apparently
employed the tale in a similar spirit:[2] on other occasions he shows himself perfectly capable of filling worn-out stories with intense and fresh
life. *Inclusam Danaen* is a very polished poem,[3] and its thoughts are not
unworthy of Horace, but it has no wings.

Finally a word must be said about the function assigned to this ode
within the book. Placed at the beginning of the second half of Book III,
it serves as the dedication of this book to Maecenas. In Book I the same
purpose is allotted to the first poem, in Book II to the last.[4] Neither
place was available in Book III, since Horace would not encroach upon

---

[1] The idea that Horace wrote the ode to justify his refusal of the post of private secretary which had been offered him by Augustus was rightly rejected by C. Franke, *Fast.
Hor.* 195, in 1839, but is still in recent commentaries mentioned as worth considering.
Heinze produced a variation ('Maecenas scheint gewünscht zu haben, sein Dichter
möge, um in den Kreisen der Hauptstadt die ihm gebührende Rolle spielen zu können,
die Mittel zu vornehmerer Lebensführung aus seiner Hand annehmen'), which seems to
me not less arbitrary. Common sense recommends Kiessling's view, 'Ein Glaubensbekenntnis gegenüber dem die Zeit beherrschenden Streben nach Reichtum'.

[2] I cannot quote any instance prior to Horace, but the epigrams by Antipater of
Thessalonice, *Anth. Pal.* 5. 31 (5 f.), and by Parmenion, 5. 33 and 34, probably take this
topic from earlier poetry, and so certainly does Paulus Silentiarius, 5. 217, where the
affinity to Horace is very close.

[3] See Heinze's introduction and especially his remarks on the variation in *pretium,
aurum, lucrum, munera*, etc.   [4] Cf. p. 300 below.

the solid block of the Roman Odes at the beginning nor sacrifice the idea of addressing in the epilogue of his three books the Muse that had inspired all these new lyrics. Besides, a change in the place to be occupied by the dedicatory poem may have been welcome to Horace. That the beginning of the second half of a book was considered a place distinguished enough for a tribute to Maecenas may be seen from the somewhat analogous instance of the first book of the *Satires*, where the opening clause of the sixth satire is addressed to Maecenas as is the opening clause of the first. Within a dedicatory poem a profession of Horace's own ideal in life, such as we find in *Odes* iii. 16, is especially appropriate. The reader will also notice the close analogy between the principal thought in the second half of this ode and the topic at the end of Epode I, the poem which dedicates the book of the *iambi* to Maecenas.

The prefatory ode, i. 1, *Maecenas atavis edite regibus*, is probably one of the latest poems in the collection of the three books: a poet will hardly compose a proem until his work is near its completion. It is therefore not unlikely that most of the passages in this ode which remind us of passages in other odes are in fact deliberate echoes or variations of them and that *Maecenas atavis* is, in this respect too, a real 'overture' to the three books. A list of the main analogies, in form or thought or both, may be useful.

Line 1 *Maecenas atavis edite regibus*:[1] 3. 29. 1 *Tyrrhena regum progenies* 2 *o et praesidium et dulce decus meum*: 2. 17. 3 f. *mearum grande decus columenque rerum* 9 f. *illum, si proprio condidit horreo quidquid de Libycis verritur areis*: 3. 16. 26 f. *quam si quidquid arat impiger Apulus occultare meis dicerer horreis* 12 *Attalicis condicionibus*: 2. 18. 5 f. *neque Attali ignotus heres regiam occupavi* 13 f. *ut trabe Cypria Myrtoum pavidus nauta secet mare*: 3. 29. 58 ff. *ad miseras preces decurrere et votis pacisci, ne Cypriae Tyriaeque merces addant avaro divitias mari* 18 *indocilis pauperiem pati*: 3. 2. 1–3 *pauperiem pati . . . condiscat* 27 f. *seu visa est catulis cerva fidelibus, seu rupit teretes Marsus aper plagas*: 3. 12. 10 ff. *catus idem . . . cervos iaculari et celer . . . excipere aprum* 30–32 *me gelidum nemus Nympharumque leves cum Satyris chori secernunt populo*: ii. 19, first stanza[2] 34 *Lesboum . . . barbiton*: 1. 32. 4 f. *barbite . . . Lesbio primum modulate civi*.

When we look at the structure of this ode we easily recognize in it the familiar pattern of a 'priamel' (*praeambulum*).[3] In Greek poetry, as elsewhere, it was a very old custom to lead up to the point at which the speaker or singer was really aiming by a preparatory chain like

---

[1] For the bold use of *edite* see Heinze's note and cf. *Thes. l. L.* v. 2. 84. 33; *atavis* in this sense is archaizing and solemn.   [2] Cf. p. 200 n. 4 above.

[3] Cf. my note on A. *Ag.* 899–902 (pp. 407 f.).

this: 'To one man *this* thing is the finest, another prizes *that* above all, another *that*, but to me it seems best to have (or be) . . . .' So, for instance, Sappho:[1]

οἱ μὲν ἱππήων στρότον οἱ δὲ πέσδων
οἱ δὲ νάων φαῖσ' ἐπὶ γᾶν μέλαιναν
ἔμμεναι κάλλιστον, ἔγω δὲ κῆν' ὅτ-
τω τις ἔραται.

In Horace we find a similar sequence in *Odes* i. 7, *Laudabunt alii claram Rhodon aut Mytilenen . . .; sunt quibus unum opus est intactae Palladis urbem . . . celebrare . . .; plurimus . . . dicet . . . Argos ditisque Mycenas: me nec tam patiens Lacedaemon nec tam Larisae percussit campus opimae quam domus Albuneae resonantis et praeceps Anio*, etc. Here the structure is more complex than in the example I have quoted from Sappho, for the section in which the speaker professes his own predilection, 10 ff., *me nec tam patiens Lacedaemon*, etc., includes in a negative form (*nec tam . . . nec tam . . .*) a mention of the tastes of several others, and the object of *laudabunt alii* at the beginning is not one place in the Greek world but seven. Nevertheless, the arrangement is fundamentally the same as in οἱ μὲν ἱππήων στρότον.[2]

In the priamel of *Odes* i. 1 the pursuits of various types of men serve as a foil to the poet's own manner of life and his scale of values. The survey of the different βίοι recalls similar passages in Greek poetry, for instance Pindar, *fr.* 221 Schr. (260 Turyn), ἀελλοπόδων μέν τιν' εὐφραίνοισιν ἵππων τιμαὶ καὶ στέφανοι, τοὺς δὲ κτλ. (adduced by Bentley); Solon, *fr.* 1 D. (13 Bergk), ll. 43 ff. σπεύδει δ' ἄλλοθεν ἄλλος κτλ.; Eurip. *fr.* 659 N.² (from the *Rhadamanthys*), ἔρωτες ἡμῖν εἰσὶ παντοῖοι βίου κτλ. (the passages of Solon and Euripides were quoted by Mitscherlich); Bacchylides 10 (9), 38 ff. μυρίαι δ' ἀνδρῶν ἐπίσταμαι πέλονται κτλ. (compared with Horace by Wilamowitz, *S.u.S.* 190 f.). Several kindred passages may have been known to Horace. If a Latin poet wanted to begin with a Greek equivalent to the *honores* bestowed by the vote of the *populus Romanus* (7 f.), the choice of the τιμή ensuing from victory with the chariot in the Olympic games must have been fairly obvious. I will not deny the possibility that Horace had in mind Pindar's passage ἀελλοπόδων μέν τιν' εὐφραίνοισιν ἵππων τιμαὶ καὶ στέφανοι κτλ., but I do not think it necessary to assume that he did.[3] Nor do I see any need to regard Horace's ode as an echo of the epinikion of Bacchylides with which Wilamowitz connected it.[4] Horace probably remembered many

[1] *fr.* 27a D., 16 L. and P.   [2] Cf. my *Plautinisches im Plautus*, 1922, 175 n. 1.
[3] On this point I agree with Dag Norberg, 'L'olympionique, le poète et leur renom éternel', *Uppsala Universitets Årsskrift*, 1945, 6. 7 f. But the main thesis of his article, viz. that Horace is bent upon emphasizing a close analogy between the victor in the Olympic games and the lyric poet, has been well refuted by G. Carlsson, *Eranos*, xliv, 1946, 404 ff.
[4] Wilamowitz, *S.u.S.* 190, discards Pindar as a possible model of Horace because the

Greek passages similar in matter and form, and used them freely. Nor
was he influenced by poetry alone. The discussion of the various types
of βίοι and their relative merits played a great part in the treatises of
Hellenistic popular philosophy with which Horace was familiar.[1]

In the greater part of the ode Horace does not say anything especially original. What he wanted to put forward in this proem to his new
songs was a bold, though not arrogant, statement of his own hopes and,
preparatory to it, an elaborate variation of a theme that had often been
treated before. The weightiest part of the ode, however, is its last
sentence,

> quodsi me lyricis vatibus inseres,
> sublimi feriam sidera vertice.

It is instructive to compare it with the end of the dedicatory poem of
Catullus,

> quare habe tibi quidquid hoc libelli,
> qualecumque; quod, o patrona virgo,
> plus uno maneat perenne saeclo.

It would be wrong to say that Catullus speaks with less confidence or
more modesty than Horace. What does make a difference is the range
of his thought and, moreover, the relation between the conclusion and
the rest of the poem. To take the latter point first. In Catullus the final
prayer to the Muse is loosely attached to the dedication to Cornelius
Nepos; in Horace the words *quodsi me lyricis vatibus inseres*, by being
addressed to Maecenas, are intimately linked up with the beginning.
Secondly, Catullus says merely 'may my book survive through many
ages', a topic common in his and his contemporaries' poetry.[2] Horace,
on the other hand, confronts his reader with a bold poetic picture:
sublimi feriam sidera vertice. And, finally, Catullus looks on his book as an
isolated achievement, whereas Horace's proudest hope is that, thanks
to these *carmina*, his name may be added to the names of the admired

---

Pindaric passage 'is concerned, not with professions, but with the pleasures of life'.
Against this unfortunate differentiation see Pasquali, *Or. lir.* 746. It should not be overlooked that Pindar says τέρπεται, and Horace says (4) *iuvat* and (11) *gaudentem . . . findere
. . . agros*. As regards the supposed models of *Odes* i. 1, Elsbeth Harms, *Horaz und seine
Beziehungen zu Pindar*, Diss. Marburg 1936, 31, shows sound judgement.

   [1] See Heinze's introduction to this ode (p. 2 of his edition of 1930). This aspect has
been somewhat over-emphasized, at the cost of the poetic element, in a learned article by
A. La Penna, *Annali della Scuola Normale Superiore di Pisa*, serie ii, vol. xxiv, 1955, fasc. iii–iv.
In the concluding words *sublimi feriam sidera vertice* La Penna (17) sees a 'scherzosa iper-
bole'. His antithesis (18), 'on the one hand 'l'Orazio pindarico, il vate, il poeta-sacerdote
delle odi romane', on the other 'il vero Orazio, cioè il poeta di Leuconoe e di Taliarco,
della gioia intima e della velata tristezza', presents in a sharp formula the widely accepted
fallacy which the present book is trying to refute.

   [2] Catullus 95. 6, *Zmyrnam cana diu saecula pervoluent*; Helvius Cinna *fr.* 14 Morel, *saecula
permaneat nostri Dictynna Catonis.*

old poets, *Pindarus novemque lyrici.* To be accepted as a worthy heir of their poetry, to be read by those readers who still cared for the classic lyrics of Greece, that would be the crown of his life.

4. THE ODES TO AGRIPPA AND POLLIO

From the odes to Maecenas[1] we pass on to the two poems addressed to two no less eminent contemporaries, Agrippa and Asinius Pollio. The ode to Agrippa (i. 6) is one of those Horatian poems which, either as a whole or in part, have proved so difficult to some scholars that they have resorted to acts of open violence. What we have to do in such a case is not to slur over the difficulty but to tackle it firmly.

Odes i. 6, *Scriberis Vario,* is based on the assumption that the *laudes egregii Caesaris* (which in this case include the *laudes Agrippae*) could successfully be made a theme of poetry only in the grand Homerizing style. We saw[2] that the same idea underlies *Odes* ii. 12, *Nolis longa ferae bella Numantiae.* And also the device of the 'comparatio paratactica' which we found there recurs here, though in a simpler form. So all might be well were it not for the fourth stanza, *quis Martem tunica tectum adamantina digne scripserit,* etc. This stanza proved a stumbling-block to several editors in the nineteenth century. Following Peerlkamp's example, in a slightly milder form (for Peerlkamp himself obelized both the fourth and the fifth stanza), Meineke, M. Haupt,[3] Lehrs, and L. Müller declared ll. 13–16 to be spurious. Housman, impressed by that verdict, did not indeed cut out the objectionable stanza, but adopted even more violent measures: he placed ll. 13–16 after l. 4, substituting at l. 13 *qui* for *quis.*[4] In so doing he not only missed the particular function of the stanza *quis Martem,* etc., within this ode, but also robbed the subsequent *nos convivia . . . cantamus* of its force: this sentence, with the pronoun placed emphatically at the beginning, forms as strict an antithesis to *quis Martem . . . digne scripserit,* etc., as does the beginning of the second stanza, *nos Agrippa, neque haec dicere* [scil. *conamur*], to the preceding *scriberis Vario,* etc. Housman was a victim of the same misconception which had deceived Peerlkamp and his followers. He argued: '*Who is worthy to record the deeds of Mars Meriones and Diomed?* To a question cast in this form the only answer is *No one.*' This conclusion goes much too far. If we applied it rigidly, what, for instance, would become of the proem of the sixth book of the *Annals* of Ennius, *Quis*

---

[1] The one ode which is left out in the preceding section, ii. 20, will be discussed together with the epilogues of the two other books, pp. 299 ff. below.

[2] Cf. pp. 219 ff. above.

[3] Cf. his *Opuscula,* iii. 50.

[4] *Journ. Philol.* xvii, 1888, 303 ff. It should not, however, be forgotten that at that time Housman was a very young man, *audax iuventa.*

potis ingentis oras evolvere belli . . .? Generally speaking, we should say that, whereas the commonest answer to such a *quis* question would be *No one*, in certain cases an answer such as *No ordinary person* is all that is required, and here the context points to something like *No ordinary poet, and certainly not I.* For it is on the intimate connexion between the fourth stanza and the fifth (*nos convivia . . . cantamus*) that the understand- of *quis Martem*, etc., depends.[1] But it would be less than honest to minimize the fact that the form of the question *quis Martem . . . digne scripserit*, etc., lays an extremely strong emphasis on the difficulty, though not the impossibility, of making Τρωϊκά and similar themes a subject of poetry in Horace's day. The task is here described in such a way as to be put almost beyond any man's reach. The point which most of the commentators seem to have missed is that Horace, after the initial stanza, is far less concerned with what Varius might be able or unable to achieve than with what he, Horace, feels absolutely unable to undertake. In a poetic *recusatio*, if it is not to be wholly offensive, it seems desirable that some one else should be suggested who might, perhaps, shoulder the burden which proves intolerably heavy to the poet himself.[2] This entails a certain inconsistency. The poet, anxious to get out of his own predicament, does not want the reader to pay too much attention to the other man's possible chances. If the reader happens to be obstinate, he will be incapable of seeing the point and consequently either query the text of the poem or distort its meaning. In *Odes* iv. 2, *Pindarum quisquis studet aemulari*, we are faced with the apparent paradox that the writing of a Pindarizing poem seems to be expected of the poet Iullus Antonius and that it is at the same time regarded as a task impossible for the poet Horace. In i. 6 an analogous paradox is contained in the suggestion that Varius might undertake a work which Horace, by implication, declares to be one of insurmount-able difficulty.[3]

The ode to Asinius Pollio is the τηλαυγὲς πρόσωπον of the second book.

> Motum ex Metello consule civicum
> bellique causas et vitia et modos
> ludumque Fortunae gravisque
> principum amicitias et arma
>
> nondum expiatis uncta cruoribus,
> periculosae plenum opus aleae,
> tractas et incedis per ignis
> suppositos cineri doloso.

---

[1] It will be seen that on this point I agree in the main with Heinze.
[2] Cf. p. 221 above. [3] For *Odes* iv. 2 see pp. 434 ff. below.

As we enter the poem, a complex scene is disclosed. We have before us the vicissitudes of a past generation's civil war, but we do not as yet learn of any living person to whom these happenings are related: not until we reach the seventh line is the voluminous object followed by its verb *tractas*. Even before the reader is able to penetrate the meaning of the detail he is impressed by the largeness of the picture before him. This effect is brought about by that careful handling of the polysyndeton which we sometimes find in Horace:[1] here it consists of a chain of three -*que*'s and three *et*'s. To render all this still more momentous, there is inserted, between the object proper and its verb, the appositional clause *periculosae plenum opus aleae*. The man who feels called to undertake a great new work has no choice but 'to follow the god', *sequi deum*, even though he knows that the task before him involves peril and that one false step may mean destruction. That this is so and must be so is the firm belief of the artist Horace, who has expressed it in different ways on different occasions.[2] In the present passage the poet makes much of this idea; he does not content himself with the abstract expression *periculosae plenum opus aleae*, but adds a proverbial simile,[3] which he adorns with some picturesque detail, *et incedis per ignis suppositos cineri doloso*.

It is with a comprehensive view that the ode begins. Of the vast material to be treated by Pollio only those topics are mentioned which are fundamental in the account of a civil war. In the opening line the main theme of Pollio's *Historiae* is not called *bellum civile* (*belli* follows after) but, with a choicer phrase, *motum civicum*.[4] It is clear that what Horace means by *belli . . . vitia* is the deterioration and indeed perversion of moral standards ensuing from civil war,[5] those evils which ἐπέπεσε πολλὰ καὶ χαλεπὰ κατὰ στάσιν ταῖς πόλεσι, γιγνόμενα μὲν καὶ αἰεὶ ἐσόμενα, ἕως ἂν ἡ αὐτὴ φύσις ἀνθρώπων ᾖ.[6] This notion is preceded by *belli . . . causas*, an all but indispensable item in the proem of a Hellenistic, or Roman, history of a war.[7] The last item in this triad,

---

[1] Cf. p. 224 above and p. 450 below.   [2] Cf. p. 258 and pp. 435 f. below.

[3] For its proverbial character see the Greek and Latin parallels quoted by the earlier commentators and Orelli–Baiter.

[4] Cicero speaks of *rei publicae motus* and the like, e.g. *Att.* 3. 8. 3, *Pis.* 10, *Rep.* 1. 14; he several times uses the plural *motus* along with *perturbationes*, e.g. *Nat. D.* 3. 16, *Off.* 1. 136, *Tusc.* 3. 7 and 4. 81. The adjective *civicus* seems to have been very rare when Horace wrote; had he perhaps found it in archaic poetry?

[5] Kiessling, following many earlier commentators, glossed *vitia* by 'die namentlich von Pompeius begangenen Fehler' (as if it were *vitia ducum*, used in a similar context by Cornelius Nepos, *Att.* 16. 4). Heinze retained this explanation and put beside it, rather inconsistently, the correct one. It is refreshing to read Dacier's note, 'Ce n'est pas *Imperatorum vitia* . . . comme les Interpretes l'ont expliqué, mais *ipsius belli vitia*, les vices de la guerre civile, c'est à dire les maux qu' elle avoit causés'.

[6] Thuc. 3. 82. 2. Arist. *Pol.* 2. 3. 7, 1265b12 brackets together στάσιν καὶ κακουργίαν.

[7] See *JRS* xxxv, 1945, 3 n. 5, and the article by Pohlenz quoted there.

belli modos, cannot mean 'vicissitudes', as Dacier saw, who pointed out that if it did it would anticipate *ludum Fortunae.* It is a vague term, which probably includes 'et singulas rationes, quibus utraque pars usa erat in his contentionibus civilibus, et totius belli tenorem'.[1]

After paying tribute to Pollio's activity as a tragedian (9–12), to his eminence in the law-courts and in the Senate, and to his successful generalship (13–16),[2] Horace returns to his historical work, but this time he approaches it from a different angle:

> iam nunc minaci murmure cornuum
> perstringis auris, iam litui strepunt,
>   iam fulgor armorum fugacis
>   terret equos equitumque voltus;

> audire magnos iam videor duces
> non indecoro pulvere sordidos
>   et cuncta terrarum subacta
>   praeter atrocem animum Catonis.

The calm and objective *tractas* of the opening stanzas is given up: the work of the historian seems, in the anticipation of his enthusiastic friend, to have sprung into full reality, and now all the mighty things he is going to describe resound in our ears and dazzle our eyes. Is it really asking too much when we expect a reader of Horace to feel how beautifully *iam nunc . . . perstringis auris . . .* is taken up by *audire . . . iam videor* and to let his senses as well as his mind respond to the appeal? Ordinary readers would probably not have stumbled if they had not been impressed by the cleverness of some ancient schoolmaster. We owe it to that unknown wiseacre that we find in the scholia on l. 21 not only the comment required by our feeling for poetry, *Pollionem de ducibus narrantem,* but an alternative, *ipsos duces contionantes.* Bentley was not deceived,[3] but the absurdity will not die.[4]

The two stanzas which we are here examining give the impression of a gigantic thunderstorm spreading across the whole *orbis terrarum.* Out of the struggle of the nameless multitudes there emerges a single human figure, the man of unconquerable mind, Cato. His memory was never betrayed by the poet, who in his youth had adhered to his cause.[5]

---

[1] Orelli–Baiter.

[2] It is perhaps significant that these traditional *virtutes* of a Roman nobleman, and not the literary distinctions, however brilliant, are chosen to serve as a frame for the vocative *Pollio.*

[3] What matters is his admirable discussion of the main point, not the horrible *videre* which he put in the place of *audire.*

[4] Heinze, following Kiessling, adhered to it to the end. I was glad to find in Leo's copy his marginal note, written against the words *non indecoro pulvere sordidos,* 'certe non contionantes (Porph., schol., Kiessl.)'. I do not see any need for dragging in (with Gessner and many others) the idea of a *recitatio* of Pollio's work.

[5] Cf. pp. 12 f. above. On *praeter atrocem animum Catonis* Zieliński, *Horace et la société romaine*

The surprising appearance of Juno (25–28) is probably due to something more than a flight of poetic imagination. The words *Iuno et deorum quisquis amicior Afris inulta cesserat impotens tellure* seem to point to a tradition with which the poet and at any rate some of his readers will have been familiar. We catch an echo of it in the comment of Servius on *Aen.* 12. 841, *constat bello Punico secundo exoratam Iunonem, tertio vero bello a Scipione sacris quibusdam etiam Romam esse translatam.* As regards the religious ceremonies performed after the fall of Carthage at the end of the Third Punic War, the scholiast's brief statement can be supplemented by another valuable piece of evidence. It is preserved by Macrobius,[1] and comes from a writer of the late second and early third century of our era, Serenus Sammonicus, more precisely from his rendering of what he had found *in cuiusdam Furii vetustissimo libro.* Dealing with one of the innumerable 'quaestiones Vergilianae',[2] Macrobius wants to prove that the ceremony of the *evocatio* of the gods of a besieged town is different from that of its *devotio.* He therefore copies from the excerpt of the book of Furius two different *carmina*, one by which *di evocantur, cum oppugnatione civitas cingitur*, and another by which *urbes . . . devoventur iam numinibus evocatis.* Only the former *carmen* concerns us here; it runs: *si deus, si dea est, cui populus civitasque Carthaginiensis est in tutela, teque maxime ille[3] qui urbis huius populique tutelam recepisti, precor venerorque veniamque a vobis peto, ut vos populum civitatemque Carthaginiensem deseratis, loca templa sacra urbemque eorum relinquatis, absque his abeatis, eique populo civitatique[4] metum formidinem oblivionem iniciatis, propitiique[5] Romam ad me meosque veniatis, nostraque vobis loca templa sacra urbs acceptior probatiorque sit, mihique populoque Romano militibusque meis propitii[6] sitis. si ⟨haec⟩ ita feceritis ut sciamus intellegamusque,[7] voveo vobis templa ludosque facturum.*

---

du temps d'Auguste (Paris 1938), 8 f., observes 'les paroles . . . font non moins honneur à Horace et à Pollion qu'à l'empereur lui-même, sous lequel on pouvait se permettre impunément un tel acte de justice posthume pour ses ennemis politiques'.

[1] *Sat.* 3. 9. 6 ff.

[2] That the material on which Macrobius here draws was also used by the commentators on Virgil can be seen from Servius on *Aen.* 2. 244 (with which the comment on 2. 351 must be taken).

[3] *Ille* indicates, of course, a provisional blank in the form, later on to be replaced by the name, as we should use 'X'. Cf. J. Wackernagel, *Vorlesungen über Syntax*, ii. 108.

[4] *civitatique* Serv. on *Aen.* 2. 244: *civitati* Macr.

[5] *propitiique* Huschke: *proditique* codd. I am sure that *proditique* is wrong but not quite so sure that *propitiique* is right. Engelbrecht, *Wiener Stud.* xxiv, 1902, 481, tries to defend *proditi* (in the sense of 'betrayed'); in this he is as unhappy as in his assertion that in the preceding clause *oblivionem* is to be understood of the *oblivio deorum.*

[6] *propitii* Bergk: *propositi* codd. Here again Engelbrecht, loc. cit., practises 'conservative' criticism and asserts that *propositi* means 'vor die Augen gestellt, sichtbar waltend' and that *propositi sitis* is an intensification of *adsitis.*

[7] I have added *haec* and transposed the clause *ut sciamus intellegamusque*, which in the MSS follows after *propositi sitis.* I saw that this transposition was required by the sense

Nowadays most scholars, following M. Hertz,[1] are inclined to assume that the *Furius quidam*, from whose book the author on whom Macrobius depends excerpted the text of the two *carmina*, was L. Furius Philus, consul 136 B.C., the friend of the conqueror of Carthage, Scipio Aemilianus. This is not unlikely. But even if the assumption were not justified, it would make no difference to the present argument. For whoever it was who first thought these two interesting prayers worth preserving, there can be no doubt that the *carmen* with which we are here concerned was composed, or rather adapted,[2] for the occasion mentioned in the scholion on *Aen.* 12. 841, where we are told that at the end of the Third Punic War not only an *exoratio* of the Carthaginian Juno took place but *Iunonem . . . a Scipione sacris quibusdam etiam Romam esse translatam.* So it was with great solemnity that the divine patroness of Carthage was besought to leave her ancient seat and be pleased with a new and worthy home across the sea, in Rome. The only fairly full account of the capture and destruction of Carthage that has come down to us[3] mentions the *devotio* of the city and its territory but says nothing of the *evocatio* of the gods. We ought to be the more grateful for the piece of additional information which is preserved by a stroke of luck. There is no good reason for seeing in the tradition about the *evocatio* of the Carthaginian Juno and her resettlement in Rome an invention of the Severan period.[4]

The goddess complied with the prayer addressed to her on behalf of Scipio, and on her arrival at Rome she was received with the honours due to her. But the story does not end there. About six years after the death of Scipio Aemilianus, C. Gracchus had a bill enacted, the Lex Rubria, to the effect that *complures coloniae in Italia deducerentur et una in solo dirutae Carthaginis.*[5] The site of the latter colony was afterwards visited by Gracchus himself. The new foundation was called Iunonia.[6] This name, I believe, can have one meaning only. It symbolized the

before I noticed that the second *carmen* contains the same formula (section 11) *si haec ita faxitis ut ego sciam sentiam intellegamque.* V. Basanoff, *Evocatio* (Paris 1947), 31 ff., has nothing to say about the text of the *carmen*, which he prints as he found it in the Teubner edition. He even retains *proditique Romam . . . veniatis.*

[1] *Fleckeisens Jahrb.* lxxxv, 1862, 54.
[2] The groundwork of the text was probably much older. At the end of the Republic several instances of similar *evocationes* were known; cf. Pliny, *Nat. hist.* 28. 18, *Verrius Flaccus auctores ponit, quibus credat in obpugnationibus ante omnia solitum a Romanis sacerdotibus evocari deum, cuius in tutela id oppidum esset, promittique illi eundem aut ampliorem apud Romanos cultum.*
[3] App. *Pun.* 135.
[4] So Wissowa, *Religion und Kultus,* 2nd ed. 374, and *RE* vi. 1153. It is not necessary to assume that the Juno whom Scipio removed to Rome was there worshipped as *Caelestis,* in accordance with what is known of the cult at the time of the later Empire.
[5] Livy, *Epit.* LX.
[6] See Plutarch, *C. Gracchus* 11. 1, Solinus 27. 11.

fact that the whole measure was calculated to reverse the policy which
Gracchus' great kinsman and adversary, Scipio Aemilianus, had, however reluctantly, pursued towards Carthage. Scipio had made the soil
of the Punic capital the object of a solemn *devotio* and laid a curse on
anyone who might try to settle there; C. Gracchus chose this very
place for a colony. Scipio had, by means of an *evocatio* and subsequent
acts of worship, induced the Carthaginian Juno to leave her city and
accept new quarters in Rome; C. Gracchus intended to bring the goddess back to her native soil and to present her with a new town, which
was to bear her name.[1]

Horace had no reason to concern himself with the abortive foundation of Iunonia. But it is very understandable that, in his attempt to
anticipate, through free poetic imagination, some of the more colourful
episodes in Pollio's *Historiae*, he should have seized upon the tradition
about Juno's emigration from Carthage.[2] However, he uses the theme
of Juno in an independent spirit: the idea that the catastrophe of
Thapsus was the means by which the goddess visited upon a late
generation of Romans the grim actions of their forefathers—this idea
savours of heroic epic and its mythological apparatus rather than of
historiography dealing with the recent past. In the next two stanzas
(29–36), a series of impassioned questions lays bare the frightfulness of
the civil war. Here, both thought and tone recall some of the earliest
epodes and the early ode i. 2, *Iam satis terris*. After reaching the climax
of his poem Horace breaks off (37 ff.), in a manner which may be influenced by similar turns in Pindar, as, for instance, θυμέ, τίνα πρὸς
ἀλλοδαπὰν ἄκραν ἐμὸν πλόον παραμείβεαι;[3] The horrors of the past seem
to have faded away; in the gentle finale we are watching a scene of
sheltered peace,

> mecum Dionaeo sub antro
> quaere modos leviore plectro.

5. ODES CONCERNED WITH AUGUSTUS

We now must try to find a way through the odes which, to a greater
or lesser extent, are concerned with Augustus. In this group of poems,

---

[1] What Cumont, *RE* iii. 1248, says about the re-erection of the temple of Caelestis in
the Colonia Iunonia is based on insufficient evidence and seems in itself wholly improbable
when we consider the fate of the short-lived colony.

[2] Baxter, in his note on *Odes* 2. 1. 26, *cesserat*, observed 'a Scipione Africano evocata';
more material was added by Mitscherlich, and the reference held its place in the commentaries on Horace up to Orelli–Baiter and Kiessling. Heinze omitted it. In V. Basanoff's
book *Evocatio* the passage of Horace is not mentioned.

[3] *Nem.* 3. 26 f. For other 'Abbruchsformeln' in Pindar see W. Schadewaldt, 'Der Aufbau
des Pindarischen Epinikion', *Schriften der Königsberger Gelehrten Ges.*, G. Kl. v. 3, 1928, 311 f.
The parallelism between Horace, *Odes* 2. 1. 37 ff. and 3. 3. 69 ff. has often been noticed.

the sympathetic understanding of a modern reader is, on the whole, taxed more severely than anywhere else in Horace, and yet it is precisely on the appreciation of some of these poems that our judgement about Horace's achievement as a lyric poet must largely depend. In view of the importance as well as the difficulty of this issue a preliminary warning may not be out of place. This book does not aim at converting those who know beforehand all about the way in which Horace, the author of several entertaining satires and epistles and of such lovely poems as *Donec gratus eram tibi*, was lured, *invita Minerva*, into composing patriotic lyrics. Our sole purpose is to recover, as best we can, the meaning of the poems before us, although most readers may prefer to have these poems treated as part of a clever organization of opinion.[1]

We begin with iii. 24, *Intactis opulentior*. This ode may safely be regarded as an early one.[2] Its general structure and the execution of much of its detail are somewhat clumsy and so fall short of the perfection to which we are accustomed from Horace's maturest poetry. But it is distinguished by noble thoughts and sincerity of feeling. The theme of this 'diatriba poetica',[3] though it had by the time of Horace become a commonplace, was one he had very much at heart.[4] It is significant that this ode contains several topics, and occasionally also expressions, which recur in some of the poet's most momentous poems. In this connexion special attention must be paid to the points of contact between *Intactis opulentior* and some of the Roman Odes.[5] When we compare the

---

[1] The critical historian need not necessarily take a cynical view of great poetry. 'Darf man den richtig fühlenden und heiter gearteten Dichter glücklich preisen, daß er aus den trüben Wolken entsetzlichen Haders eine reinere und bessere Staatsordnung hat hervorgehen sehen, so hat es auch Augustus wohl verdient in so feiner, so aufrichtiger und so würdiger Weise gefeiert zu werden. Die Produkte der Schmeichelliteratur pflegen zu den Werken zu gehören, die noch vor ihrem Urheber vergehen. Die Lieder des Horaz lesen wir heute noch und wenn die Barbarisierung nicht allzu rasch vorschreitet, werden sie noch manches Geschlecht erfreuen; denn im großen und ganzen ruhen sie auf rechter und echter Empfindung' (Mommsen, *Reden und Aufsätze*, 182, from an address delivered in 1889).

[2] On this head I agree on the whole with Heinze's observations, but I find it difficult to accept his argument that 'auch den Sprachstil beherrscht der Dichter noch nicht völlig, wie manche eher der Umgangssprache angemessene Ausdrücke . . . verraten'. Even the brief sketch in chapter iv of B. Axelson's book *Unpoetische Wörter* (Lund 1945), 'Zur Wortwahl des Odendichters Horaz', 98 ff., is sufficient to warn us against drawing chronological conclusions from the occurrence of such expressions. The fact that in this ode no individual person is addressed could perhaps be taken as a further indication of an early date; this fact would, however, be sufficiently accounted for by the particular character of the poem, which appears to be a first step towards the poet's attitude in the Roman Odes, iii. 1–6; the same explanation holds good for ii. 15.

[3] Pasquali, *Or. lir.* 428.

[4] For the 'money-madness' of Horace's age see Last, *Cambr. Anc. Hist.* x. 436 f.

[5] Cf. Kiessling's introductions to iii. 1 and iii. 24 and especially F. Solmsen, *Am. Journ. Phil.* lxviii, 1947, 343 ff.

beginning of the present ode (1–8) with 3. 1. 33–40, we see that the two different topics which make up each of the two passages are the same in both cases,[1] and, what is more remarkable, that also the manner in which the second, the Fear topic, seems to grow naturally out of the first, the Greed topic, is the same. On the other hand, we notice a considerable difference in style: in iii. 24 a matter-of-fact statement in juridical terms,

> caementis licet occupes
> terrenum omne tuis et mare publicum,

in iii. 1 a description that carries picturesqueness almost to the point of euphuism,

> contracta pisces aequora sentiunt
> iactis in altum molibus: huc frequens
> caementa demittit redemptor
> cum famulis dominusque terrae

> fastidiosus.

The topic of 22 f., *metuens alterius viri certo foedere castitas*, recurs at 3. 6. 17 f., and that of 52 ff., *et tenerae nimis mentes asperioribus formandae studiis: nescit equo rudis haerere ingenuus puer venarique timet*, etc., at 3. 2. 1–6. This whole section (9–24) centres in an idea current in the popular philosophy of the time,[2] glorification of the moral standards in primitive societies. Here Horace has retained the traditional application of that idea to barbarian nations, especially those of the far north, whereas elsewhere—and that is perhaps characteristic of him and of Augustan poets in general—he prefers to apply it to the Roman race itself either at an early stage of its history or in environments remote from the demoralizing influences of city life. Examples of the latter application are found in the second epode (41 ff.) and, above all, in the earliest of the Roman Odes, 3. 6. 33–44.

But turns of thought and expressions that recall passages of *Intactis opulentior* are not confined to the odes belonging approximately to the same period but recur in some of Horace's latest works. So we find the juxtaposition, of course a natural one, of *leges* and *mores*, ll. 35 f., *quid leges sine moribus vanae proficiunt*, again in the latest of all epistles, 2. 1. 2 f., *cum . . . res Italas . . . moribus ornes, legibus emendes*, and in an ode

---

[1] Compare, besides the passages quoted in the text, 3. 24. 7 f. *non animum metu, non mortis laqueis expedies caput* with 3. 1. 37 ff. *sed Timor et Minae scandunt eodem quo dominus*, etc. At 3. 24. 3 f. it should be noticed that the emphatic hyperbaton *caementis . . . tuis* stresses the idea of private ownership (cf., for example, *Epod*. 1. 25 f. *non ut iuvencis inligata pluribus aratra nitantur* meis; Virg. *Ecl*. 9. 2 ff. *advena* nostri (*quod numquam veriti sumus*) *ut possessor agelli diceret*), in contrast with *mare publicum*. The verb *occupes* belongs to the same sphere.

[2] See particularly Heinze's notes.

written about the same time, 4. 5. 22, *mos et lex maculosum edomuit nefas.*
The same epistle to Augustus (2. 1. 12–14) refers to the experience of
many a hero who *comperit invidiam supremo fine domari; urit enim fulgore
suo qui praegravat artis infra se positas; exstinctus amabitur idem.* To Augustus,
so the thought proceeds, fate has been kinder: *praesenti tibi maturos
largimur honores*, etc. The connexion in Horace's mind of this general
thought with reflections about Rome's Princeps is much older: in the
ode with which we are here concerned he says (30 ff.) of the man who
is to rescue Rome from her moral decay and end her intestine wars
that he will be *clarus postgenitis, quatenus, heu nefas, virtutem incolumem
odimus, sublatam ex oculis quaerimus invidi.*

The figure of this man is here veiled in generalizing terms (25 ff.):

> o[1] quisquis volet impias
>   caedis et rabiem tollere civicam,
> si quaeret pater urbium
>   subscribi statuis, indomitam audeat

> refrenare licentiam,
>   clarus postgenitis.

But there can be no doubt that Caesar, the future Augustus, is meant.
The thin disguise of the ruler's identity may be due to political considerations, but reasons of poetic discretion would sufficiently account
for it. However that may be, the general, non-individual, expression
provides an additional argument for an early date for the ode; it is not
likely that if the ode had been written a long time after the return of
Octavian from the east in 29 B.C., Horace, in alluding to him, could
have chosen words such as *quisquis volet . . . rabiem tollere civicam.*

Odes i. 2, *Iam satis terris*, too, is an early poem, though probably later

---

[1] Scholars have rightly refused to take the sentence, with Bentley, as a question, *O quis,
quis volet impias caedes et rabiem tollere civicam?*, but they might have heeded his objection to *o
quisquis*. In the commentaries there is, as far as I can see, no helpful remark on the function
of this *o*; Hand, *Tursellinus*, iv. 353, followed by Orelli–Baiter, assumes for the passage a
use which is without parallel. In the early Latin playwrights we find expressions such as Pl.
Men. 1132 *o salve, Trin.* 1163 *o salvete*, Ter. *Andr.* 846 *o salve*, etc., which correspond exactly
to ὦ χαῖρε, etc. (cf. my note on A. *Ag.* 22, where it is also shown that the use of ὦ with the
imperative and of ὦ with the vocative are part of one and the same phenomenon). At
Virg. *Georg.* 2. 35 f., *quare agite o proprios generatim discite cultus, agricolae . . .*, the *o* clearly
belongs to *discite*; the punctuation of many editors (comma after *o*) is artificial. It seems
that not until Virgil was this use extended to optative subjunctives such as *Ecl.* 2. 28 f. *o
tantum libeat . . . habitare, Georg.* 2. 488 f. *o qui me gelidis convallibus Haemi sistat, Aen.* 8. 560
o mihi praeteritos referat si Iuppiter annos, Hor. *Sat.* 2. 6. 8 f. *o si angulus ille proximus accedat,* etc.
In all these cases the wish is very emphatic; the function of *o* approaches that of *utinam*
(Hand, *Tursellinus*, iv. 354). It is important that in the present instance (*Odes* 3. 24. 25–
28), where the distance between *o* and *audeat* is uncommonly wide, the exceedingly strong
emphasis should be perceived.

than iii. 24. It is distinguished by its conspicuous position immediately after the dedicatory ode. From this position we have to infer that Horace thought that among the poems of the three books none contained better praise of the Princeps or did fuller justice to the blessings of his régime. The next ode, i 3, *Sic te diva potens Cypri*, was written for Virgil. But also in i. 2—and this is perhaps one of Horace's subtle links—a signal tribute is paid to Virgil.[1] The very beginning, *Iam satis*, was bound to remind contemporaries of the fervent prayer which, towards the end of the first book of the *Georgics* (498 ff.), crowns the description of the *prodigia* by which the world had been terrified after the murder of Caesar, *Di patrii . . . hunc saltem everso iuvenem succurrere saeclo ne prohibete*. *satis iam pridem sanguine nostro Laomedonteae luimus periuria Troiae*. In every-day language *iam satis* or *satis iam* (with or without *est*) and its stronger variant *ohe iam satis* (with or without *est*) was an ejaculation, sometimes almost a groan, of impatience, 'basta!', 'assez!', 'enough of it!', 'no more of it!', 'stop it!'.[2] This use corresponds exactly to that of ἅλις:[3] *satis iam verborumst*[4] corresponds to ἅλις λόγων and so forth. Virgil lifted the common phrase to a high stylistic level by the context in which he placed it[5] and also by adding *pridem* to *iam* and thus modifying the temporal element. When Horace conceived his early ode on the Princeps he seems to have been deeply stirred by the finale of the first book of the *Georgics* with its picture of the Roman people on the way to self-destruction and haunted by gruesome *prodigia*, and he seems to have felt the beauty of the prayer that implores the gods to spare the *iuvenis* and allow him to become the rescuer of a tormented world. As Horace's mind was at the time full of that great piece of poetry, Virgil's impassioned *satis iam . . . luimus* helped him to give his own ode a forceful beginning. Here, as in the passage of the *Georgics*, the original note of *iam satis* is not lost but

---

[1] The influence of *Georgics* I on this ode has long been noticed by the commentators; see also, for example, Barwick, *Philol.* xc, 1935, 267 ff.; Gallavotti, *La Parola del Passato*, xii, 1949, 220 ff.

[2] For instances of *iam satis, satis iam*, etc., see J. B. Hofmann, *Thes. l. Lat.* vii. 1. 117. I select only a few passages in which the implication of something like 'stop it' is particularly clear: Plaut. *Cas.* 248 *ohe, iam satis, uxor, comprime te*; *Stich.* 734 *ohe, iam satis, nolo obtaedescat; alium ludum nunc volo*; Hor. *Sat.* 1. 5. 12 f. *ohe, iam satis est*; Martial 4. 89. 7 ff. *iam lector queriturque deficitque, iam librarius hoc et ipse dicit 'ohe, iam satis est, ohe, libelle'*. Even in the solemn language of Tacitus the note of impatience is unmistakable when Tiberius writes to Germanicus (*Ann.* 2. 26. 2) *rediret ad decretum triumphum: satis iam eventuum, satis casuum*. At *Odes* 1. 2. 1 *satis* is rightly paraphrased by, for example, Doering, 'nimis multum, satis superque'.

[3] For further detail see my note on A. *Ag.* 1659.

[4] e.g. Ter. *Phorm.* 436.

[5] It should, however, be noticed that a full verb (here *luimus*) may be added also to the colloquial formula in the sense of 'enough of it!'; cf. Plaut. *Capt.* 928 ff. *satis iam dolui . . . satis iam audivi tuas aerumnas . . . hoc agamus* (for the last clause in this context cf. Ter. *Phorm.* 435 f. *hoc age: satis iam verborumst*).

deepened, betraying anxiety rather than impatience: θεοὺς μὲν αἰτῶ
τῶνδ' ἀπαλλαγὴν πόνων.

In the next two lines (*pater . . . rubente dextera sacras iaculatus arcis*)
the boldness of *rubente dextera* has provoked many comments. It seems
very probable that this expression also was stimulated by a passage in
the first book of the *Georgics*, 328 f.,

ipse pater media nimborum in nocte corusca
fulmina molitur dextra.

When Virgil, in 29 B.C., at Atella, recited his poem to Octavian (the
first book, no doubt, he recited himself, for at that stage his voice
would not yet have failed him so that Maecenas had to take over), he
must, by his pronunciation, have made the case and gender of *corusca*
absolutely clear. But on paper the reference of the epithet is ambiguous
and has therefore puzzled many an attentive reader.[1] The commentary
of Servius, it is true, says peremptorily '*corusca fulmina*': *coruscantia*, but
Seneca seems to have wavered: in the variation of Virgil's sentence
which we find at *Oed.* 1029 (*si . . . divum sator*) *corusca saeva tela iaculetur
manu,* he gives *manu* its epithet in *saeva* and makes *corusca* go with *tela*,[2]
whereas the line *Phaedra* 156, *vibrans corusca fulmen Aetnaeum manu*, shows
that when he wrote it he took Virgil's *corusca* to be the epithet of *dextra*.
The latter interpretation is that of Prudentius, who wrote[3] *deus dextram
quatiens coruscam*. And this, to return to our earliest witness, was apparently also Horace's view: *rubente dextera* seems to be a fine variation
of Virgil's *corusca dextra*.[4] No doubt Horace understood his friend's intention rightly, for in Virgil's sentence *fulmina*, weighty in itself, needs
no epithet; on the other hand, a bare *dextra* would sound poor after
molitur; finally, *corusca dextra* produces a picture of great beauty.

Another detail in which Horace follows Virgil is of greater importance since it concerns the man who dominates the ode. At the point
where the poem turns to Rome's leader we read (41 ff.)

sive mutata iuvenem figura
ales in terris imitaris almae
filius Maiae . . .,[5]

---

[1] We need not here register the partly arbitrary, partly compromising opinions about
the syntactic position of *corusca* which have been put forward from the Renaissance on.
Lambinus (note on *Odes* 1. 2. 2) referred to *Georg.* 1. 328 f., but added 'ubi tamen corusca
cohaerere debet cum voce *fulmina* potius quam cum *dextra*'.

[2] In *Thes. l. L.* iv. 1076. 60 the metre is neglected and the passage misunderstood.

[3] *Perist.* 4. 9.

[4] As can be seen from the article *coruscus* in the *Thesaurus*, *rutilus* is occasionally used by
ancient grammarians to interpret *coruscus*, and there occur connexions such as Silius 16.
119 ff. *subitus rutilante coruscum vertice fulsit apex*.

[5] For *filius Maiae* instead of the vocative see J. Wackernagel, *Über einige antike Anredeformen*,
Göttingen 1912 (*Kl. Schriften*, 984).

and it is only at the very end that the *iuvenis* is addressed by name, *Caesar*. This device is clearly modelled after the prayer in the *Georgics*,[1] *hunc saltem everso iuvenem succurrere saeclo ne prohibete*, with its sequence, *iam pridem nobis caeli te regia, Caesar, invidet*, etc. Several years before, at a time when no one, not even an inspired poet, could have anticipated that it was Caesar the son who, from the contest for supreme power, would emerge the winner, Virgil's Tityrus had alluded to him by saying[2] *hic illum vidi iuvenem*. This was a happy disguise and one that was likely to please the man whose name it concealed.[3] So Virgil took it up in the prayer of the *Georgics*; but this time anonymity could soon be dropped and Caesar be addressed overtly. Horace wove the Virgilian thread into his own web and gained a particular effect by concluding his ode with *te duce, Caesar*.

There is still another feature common to *Iam satis terris* and the finale of *Georgics* I. Virgil describes several *prodigia* which occurred after Julius Caesar's death and then continues (471 ff):

> quotiens Cyclopum effervere in agros
> vidimus undantem ruptis fornacibus Aetnam,
> flammarumque globos liquefactaque volvere saxa.

In Horace's reflections on the thunderstorms which had terrified mankind a prominent place is given to the inundation of the Tiber, of which he says:

> vidimus flavum Tiberim retortis
> litore Etrusco violenter undis
> ire . . . .

Thus Horace, like Virgil, attaches with *vidimus* a new thought to the preceding sentences, but, unlike Virgil, he does not use this form to introduce another type of portent but only to elaborate one particular consequence of the disaster he has been describing before.[4] This

---

[1] I. 500 ff.

[2] *Ecl.* 1. 42.

[3] Horace adopted it in a poem earlier than the ode, *Sat.* 2. 5. 62.

[4] Kiessling's analysis, '*Jetzt* ist's genug . . . *Vordem* sah unser Geschlecht . . . und *künftig* werden noch . . . unsere Kinder hören . . .', was in this crude form abandoned by Heinze, who nevertheless still depended on his predecessor for his own interpretation of *vidimus*. His paraphrase (Introd., cf. also his note on 13–16) which fixes a chronological gulf between the third and the fourth stanza, 'Sah doch unser Geschlecht schon einmal . . .', is wholly unwarranted; so is his remark that in *vidimus* 'die Berufung auf eigene Erfahrung . . . entspricht der Art wie die Elegiker mit *vidi* . . . einen selbsterlebten Fall zur Begründung einer allgemeinen Behauptung oder Lehre einführen'. That well-known use of *vidi*, introducing an example to illustrate a general statement or maxim (cf. εἶδον Soph. *El.* 62 and elsewhere), has nothing to do with *Odes* 1. 2. 13, where no such general maxim precedes. The true analogy to Horace's *vidimus*, as has been shown above, is to be found in *Georg.* 1. 472; its position in the sentence, however, is different: *vidimus flavum Tiberim*, etc., is a case of asyndeton explicativum.

observation points to a general difference between the Virgilian passage
and the ode. Virgil, starting from the omens provided by the sun,[1]
gradually widens the scope of his account to include all the horrible
signs which after Caesar's murder manifested themselves in every element and throughout the world. Horace, on the other hand, confines
himself strictly to the phenomena connected with the thunderstorms
from which the poem takes its start. Some of these, it is true, could, and
perhaps should, be regarded as *prodigia*,[2] but they are still on the
borderline between natural, though terrifying, happenings and events
which are definitely παρὰ φύσιν : there is no trace here of the gruesome
signs which are so magnificently described in the *Georgics* and which
caught the imagination of Shakespeare, 'dews of blood, disasters in the
sun', and so forth. There is in fact nothing in this ode that makes it
necessary to think of the portents which could be seen and heard
exstincto Caesare, although a reference to them was taken for granted by
the scholiast and consequently by most of the commentators. That the
ideas in the first part of the ode were, to some extent, stimulated by
the recollection of the *prodigia* after Caesar's death and especially by
the use that Virgil had made of them is very likely, but it must not be
overlooked that Horace preserves a high degree of independence. As
the initial *iam satis* clearly shows, snow, hail, thunderstorms, and the
devastations they caused, have lasted up to the time when the poet is
speaking, nor is it possible to refer to a different period the inundation
of the Tiber described in the fourth stanza, *vidimus flavum Tiberim*, etc.[3]

A reader who is content to follow the poet's guidance without asking
the questions which are suggested by something outside the poem will
not inquire about the particular moment at which the disasters
described in the ode began to make their appearance. He will feel that
the precise date of those events is of little consequence in this poem.[4]

---

[1] 463 ff. *solem quis dicere falsum | audeat? ille etiam caecos instare tumultus | saepe monet . . . |
ille etiam exstincto miseratus Caesare Romam*, etc.

[2] Heinze (on 1 ff.) rightly says that the fact that the Capitol was struck by lightning
implies a *prodigium* (but his inference from *dirae* at l. 1 is hardly cogent: *crescit indulgens
sibi dirus hydrops*).

[3] For *iam satis* and *vidimus* see my remarks above. Barwick's attempt, *Philol.* xc, 1935,
258 ff., to demonstrate that 'die in Vers 13–20 geschilderte Überschwemmung zu den
Prodigien gehört, die bald nach Caesars Tod die römische Welt erschreckten' is without
any foundation in the text of the poem; it has been rejected by Norberg, *Eranos Rudbergianus*,
1946, 403 n. 2, and especially by Gallavotti, op. cit. (see p. 243 n. 1) 218 ff.

[4] Like many earlier scholars (see, for example, the survey in C. Franke, *Fasti Horatiani*,
140 f. and his own sound criticism 146 f.) Gallavotti, op. cit., 227 ff., refers Horace's
description, ll. 13 ff., to the inundation of the Tiber in January, 27 B.C., of which Dio
Cass. 53. 20. 1 speaks. But inundations of the Tiber which flooded or threatened to flood
(that is what Horace says), the area of the Forum Romanum were not uncommon up to
the modern regulation of the embankments (a fine photograph of the Forum flooded by
the Tiber in 1898 is reproduced in R. Lanciani, *The Destruction of Ancient Rome*, 1901, 140),
and we cannot expect to find them all mentioned in our fragmentary records of the Augus-

What does matter is the progress of thought from the first part of the ode to the second (25 ff. *quem vocet divum populus ruentis imperi rebus?* etc.). Rome is terrified by a long sequence of catastrophes which seem to portend her destruction. Who will be the heaven-sent saviour capable of rescuing her at the eleventh hour? In Horace's ode as in the finale of *Georgics* I the series of sinister events forms a dark background against which the figure of the *iuvenis* Caesar is set. It is, however, in a highly uncommon and indeed startling shape that Caesar makes his entry into the ode. After enumerating various deities[1] who might be given the task of saving the Roman world from perdition the poet goes on (41 ff.):

> sive mutata iuvenem figura
> ales in terris imitaris almae
> filius Maiae patiens vocari
> Caesaris ultor.

It is only natural that this extraordinary sentence should have arrested the commentators, but the space allotted to it in the modern discussion of the ode seems out of proportion, and much that has been said about it misses the mark. Here we need not penetrate into the thicket of the studies devoted to Ancient Ruler-cult in general and to the worship of the Roman emperors in particular, subjects on which many scholars of the twentieth century have eagerly seized. As regards Mercury, it has often been said that at the time when Horace wrote *Iam satis terris* it was customary to worship Octavian as the incarnation of that god; but there exists no reliable evidence to support this

---

tan period. In consequence of his identification Gallavotti assumes that the ode was written immediately after the constitutional settlement and the conferment of the name *Augustus* on the Princeps in January, 27 B.C. I find this as hard to believe as Franke did more than a century ago. Heinze's expression, 'die verzweifelte Stimmung des Liedes', certainly contains an exaggeration, but Gallavotti's own description (229), 'quest' ode della fiducia e dell' augurio', is even less appropriate. If Horace, in order to celebrate the constitutional settlement of January 27 B.C., and the extraordinary honours simultaneously bestowed upon Augustus, wrote an ode beginning with *Iam satis . . . nivis atque dirae grandinis*, he would have shown deplorable lack of tact and produced something that was *pessimi ominis*, precisely like the poet who greets the new city of the birds with the hymn κλῆσον, ὦ χρυσόθρονε, τὰν τρομεράν, κρυεράν· νιφόβολα πεδία πολύπορά τ' ἤλυθον. Moreover, the tone of the whole poem, especially in its second part, seems to exclude a date after that settlement. With Franke and the majority of scholars I regard the year 27 B.C. as a *terminus ante quem* for this ode. Gallavotti's conception of 'poesia d'occasione', which he shares with many writers on Horace, is inadequate to explain poems such as *Iam satis terris*.

[1] For this type of 'Reihengebet' cf. E. Norden, *Aus altrömischen Priesterbüchern*, 130, 148 f., and for Greek instances see *Philol*. lxxxvi, 1931, 4 ff. Among the pieces discussed there is A. *Sept*. 86 ff., where near the beginning we read τίς ἄρα ῥύσεται, τίς ἄρ' ἐπαρκέσει θεῶν ἢ θεᾶν;—a remarkable parallel to *quem vocet divum populus*, etc.: the pattern is obviously an old one.

assertion.[1] It is far more likely that the idea expressed in the stanza *sive mutata iuvenem figura*, etc., is due, not to the influence of some actual cult, but to a fancy of the poet.[2] It may be permissible, though merely as a guess, to try to reconstruct some of the reasons which may have induced Horace to choose Mercury, or rather Hermes, for the conspicuous role assigned to him in this ode.[3] From the outset it was clear that only one of the great gods was eligible, and that he had to be young and engaging. Of the limited number thus left Dionysus could not be considered: his character and habits were not suitable for the ruler of Rome; besides, he had been claimed by Antony as his divine counterpart.[4] Apollo, on the other hand, had been regarded, and especially after the battle of Actium, as the Olympian patron of the Princeps; it was not compatible with this important function that his walking *in terris* in the shape of his devoted worshipper should be contemplated even as a possibility.[5] In the case of Hermes no such objection arose. Moreover, Hermes was not so hopelessly aloof as most of the great gods,[6] and could therefore, in the world of poetry, easily be thought of as dwelling temporarily among mortals. He did not have the terrifying beauty of some of the other Olympians, and yet was exceedingly handsome. He, the *facundus nepos Atlantis*, the λόγιος, the ἀγοραῖος, the great civilizer *qui feros cultus hominum recentum voce formavit catus et decorae more palaestrae*, might seem to be the ideal counterpart in Heaven of the statesman, then in the prime of life, who wanted to be the bringer of peace and order, the renewer of economic welfare and high moral

---

[1] The field has been cleared by the careful article of K. Scott, *Hermes*, lxiii, 1928, 15 ff. Conclusion: from Rome or Italy we have no unambiguous testimony for an identification of Mercury and Augustus; in the eastern part of the Empire the private inscription of the *scrutarii* at Cos constitutes a special case. In a later article, *Röm. Mitt.* l, 1935, 225 ff., Scott shows, in my opinion conclusively, that the relief on the altar in the Museo Civico at Bologna has no bearing on our problem (judging from the photograph it seems doubtful whether the face of Mercury is meant to recall the features of Augustus). On the other hand, O. Brendel, ibid. 231 ff., is right in seeing in the Mercury of the stucco fragment from the ceiling of the Farnesina a striking likeness to Augustus. But the decorations of that building are considerably later than Horace's ode (see Brendel, op. cit. 239 n. 4); whether the idea of a Mercury-Augustus was stimulated by the stanza of the poet no one can say.

[2] So, for example, Heinze on ll. 41–52; Scott, *Hermes* lxiii, 1928, 33; A. D. Nock, *Cambr. Anc. Hist.* x. 487; and Wilamowitz, *Glaube der Hellenen*, ii. 429, 'Augustus hat die Versuche unterdrückt in ihm einen νέος Ἑρμῆς oder einen andern Gott inkarniert zu sehen, ein Gedanke, mit dem Horaz gespielt hatte.'

[3] I know of the excursions into Egypt undertaken from the starting-point of the Mercury passage, but I think we can do without them.

[4] See especially O. Immisch, 'Zum antiken Herrscherkult', *Das Erbe der Alten*, ii. 20, 1931, 13 ff.

[5] Cf. Immisch, op. cit. 29, 'Schirmherr ist Apollon dem Princeps, apollinisch ist sein Ideal, nicht aber soll es die eigene Person sein'.

[6] Speaking of the Hermes of the early period Wilamowitz, *Gl. d. Hell.* i. 164, says 'Er ist eigentlich auch gar nicht auf den Olymp gekommen, weil all sein Wirken auf die Menschenerde gehört.'

standards. Finally, I like to think, though I can offer no proof, that there was still something else that turned Horace's thoughts to Hermes. In the scene of the last book of the *Iliad* which he used in *Odes* i. 10. 13 ff. he read of Hermes (347 f.) :

βῆ δ' ἰέναι κούρῳ αἰσυμνητῆρι ἐοικώς,
πρῶτον ὑπηνήτῃ, τοῦ περ χαριεστάτη ἥβη.

When Horace wrote *Iam satis terris* the new αἰσυμνήτης of Rome was no longer πρῶτον ὑπηνήτης but still *iuvenis*, still very good-looking; and Horace, with that fine Homeric comparison in his mind, may well have wished to follow the analogy up. No divine being could represent the *Romulae custos gentis* so adequately as the gentle helper from Olympus who in the shape of a handsome youth sees the heart-broken old king through all the surrounding perils safely to his destination.

If we want to assess the religious relevance of the approximation of Mercury to Augustus as we find it in this ode, we should be careful not to overlook the limitations to which Horace has subjected this idea. So far from stating that the god has borrowed or is going to borrow the shape of the Princeps, Horace merely points to the possibility of such a change as one of several desirable acts of divine mercy; his suggestion belongs to the guesswork of someone who tries to pierce the veil of the future.[1] But even so Horace's conception strikes us as an astounding venture. It is true that, compared with the documents of the worship of Augustus which we possess from the Greek section of the ancient world,[2] Horace even here shows the restraint suitable for a man of Italian breed and for the Roman outlook on life, but it must be admitted that in the last three stanzas of this ode he has carried the approach to certain conceptions of the East farther than anywhere else.[3]

---

[1] F. Altheim, *A History of Roman Religion*, 365, says 'Horace speaks of Mercury as having descended to earth and having entered into the person of Octavian'; Gallavotti, *La Parola del Passato*, xii, 1949, 222, 'Ottaviano è già dio: è stato Mercurio stesso ad assumere il suo aspetto sulla terra'. There is a serious difference between the poet's guarded presentation of his idea and such inaccurate reports. A protest against exaggerations of that kind was made by J. Elmore, *Class. Philol.* xxvi, 1931, 261 f., who goes, however, too far in the opposite direction and underrates the boldness of Horace's invention. Immisch, op. cit. 27, is wholly correct: 'Horazens Worte, die übrigens nur von einer *möglichen* Erscheinungsform reden, geben einen persönlichen Gedanken des Dichters wieder.'

[2] Texts of them can be found in V. Ehrenberg and A. H. M. Jones, *Documents illustrating the Reigns of Augustus and Tiberius*, 74 ff., and a selection also in P. Wendland, 'Die hellenistisch-römische Kultur', etc., *Handbuch z. Neuen Test.* i. 2. 3, 2nd ed., 1912, 408 ff., with a tactful appreciation ibid. 146 ff.

[3] It is outside my task to discuss the religious policy of Augustus himself, but the precariousness of Horace's attitude in this ode will be better understood when I add a reference to the pertinent remarks by Hugh Last, *Cambr. Anc. Hist.* x. 456, 'in religion Augustus aimed above all at a revival of the national cults, and even when he was compelled to compromise with ideas (like some about the relation of his own position in the scale of being to that of ordinary humanity) which had their origin in the Hellenistic East, the

The view that *Iam satis terris* is to be regarded as an early ode has rightly won general acceptance.[1] In this connexion it seems worth noting that the poem at more than one point shows some remarkable points of contact with the epodes concerned with Rome and her fate. At l. 11 f., *et superiecto pavidae natarunt aequore dammae*, we find, represented as a feature of Deucalion's flood, something very similar to what in *Epod.* 16. 34, *ametque salsa levis hircus aequora*, forms part of the ἀδύνατα. At ll. 16 ff., *Iliae dum se nimium querenti iactat ultorem*, etc., the present disasters are viewed as the outcome of some grave offences committed during the earliest period in the history of Rome or what was to become Rome; the same kind of causal nexus is familiar to us from the end of the seventh epode (17–20). The thought of the next stanza, too, recalls the seventh epode (*audiet civis acuisse ferrum, quo graves Persae melius perirent*: *Epod.* 7. 1 ff. *cur dexteris aptantur enses conditi ? . . . non ut superbas invidae Karthaginis Romanus arces ureret intactus aut Britannus ut descenderet . . ., sed ut . . . sua urbs haec periret dextera?*). The dominating part of this stanza, where the emphasis on the verb is stressed by its repetition, *audiet civis . . ., audiet pugnas*, etc., varies a thought of the ninth epode (11 *posteri negabitis*). At the beginning of the next stanza the expression *ruentis imperi rebus* recalls the beginning both of the sixteenth epode (*suis et ipsa Roma viribus ruit*) and of the seventh (*quo, quo scelesti ruitis?*). But of the features which *Odes* i. 2 has in common with the earliest political epode, the sixteenth, one is the most revealing: the use made of the plural of the pronoun of the first person. This use signifies that the poet claims to speak on behalf of the whole people, 13 *vidimus*, 30 *precamur*, 47 *nostris vitiis*.[2] The pronoun *nos*, etc., fulfilling the same function as it does here, seems to be almost completely absent from the first three books of the odes. An instance which, with some qualification, could be adduced occurs, significantly, in the poem which we discussed before the present one, 3. 24. 45 ff., *vel nos in Capitolium . . . vel nos in mare proximum gemmas et lapides aurum et inutile . . . mittamus, scelerum si bene paenitet.*[3] At the end of the sixth Roman Ode, which in all probability is the earliest of the cycle, we read[4] *aetas*

---

alien conceptions were so deftly transmuted that they could be taken up unnoticed into a whole which was unmistakably Italian'.

[1] See, for example, Heinze's commentary and, with some different arguments, Norberg, *Eranos*, xliv, 1946, 398 ff.

[2] Cf. *Epod.* 16. 9 *perdemus*, 24 *moramur*, 25 *iuremus*, 36 *eamus*, 41 *nos*, 42 *petamus*, 53 *mirabimur*.

[3] Here *nos* undoubtedly includes the meaning 'we, the Roman people of the present time', but this sense is tinged with the wider one 'we human beings, such as we generally are', and this latter notion is clearly intended at ll. 31 f. *virtutem incolumem odimus, sublatam ex oculis quaerimus invidi* and also at 3. 5. 1 *Caelo tonantem credidimus Iovem regnare*. It is inevitable that the first person of the plural should sometimes be used ambiguously, meaning, both 'we human beings' and 'we, the Roman people'. For an instance in a different literary genre see Plaut. *Men.* 571 f., with my remarks, *Plautinisches im Plautus*, 160.

[4] 3. 6. 46 ff.

parentum peior avis tulit nos nequiores, mox daturos progeniem vitiosiorem.
There, and at l. 10 f. of the same ode, *impetus nostros*, the prevalent sense
is 'we, the present generation' although the idea of the Roman people
may be included; and the same thing is true of 1. 35. 34 ff. *quid nos dura
refugimus aetas? quid intactum nefasti liquimus?*[1] None of these passages
provides a real analogy to the use of *nos* in the sixteenth epode and in
Iam satis terris, since in both these poems Horace speaks as the mouthpiece of the community. This role of the poet belongs to the strange
fiction which we met in the sixteenth epode.[2] There Horace, in pre-
tending to harangue the people from an imaginary platform, committed a kind of usurpation, a venture which he did not repeat in the
mature patriotic epodes written about the time of the battle of Actium.[3]
The early ode i. 2 shows, though on a minor scale and in a less startling
form, in its use of *nos*, etc., a certain lack of restraint. This phenomenon
has to be taken together with the boldness by which here typical
Hellenistic ideas about the incarnation of a god in the body of a ruler
are, though not directly taken over, yet employed in a mitigated form.

When Horace, many years after, wrote sentences such as *'longas o
utinam, dux bone, ferias praestes Hesperiae'* dicimus and *nosque et profestis
lucibus et sacris ... virtute functos more patrum duces ... canemus*, he did so in
an entirely new spirit, not as the privileged speaker on behalf of the
community, but as one of the humble folk in whom he merged his own
person.[4]

It is in a prayer for the welfare of Augustus, then expected to set out
to conquer Britain,[5] and of the Roman armies ready for a campaign in
the East, that the hymn to Fortuna, i. 35, *O diva gratum quae regis Antium*,
culminates (29 ff.). The bulk of this ode consists of two of the commonest elements of prayers and hymns, a list of the ἀρεταί of the goddess[6]

[1] We leave, of course, out of account the instances of the *pluralis maiestatis* or *auctoris*
such as 1. 6. 5 ff. and 17 ff.; 2. 13. 22, etc.
[2] See pp. 43 ff. above.　　　　　　　　　　　[3] See p. 70 and p. 74 above.
[4] See p. 448 and pp. 452 f., below.
[5] This expedition, whether or not it was ever seriously planned, did not come off; see
Collingwood, *Cambr. Anc. Hist.* x. 793 f.
[6] Ll. 5 f. require a word of comment. Since I was once trapped myself, I would warn the
reader against the temptation of following Markland (in the appendix to his edition of
Eur. *Suppl.*, London 1763, 254), L. Müller, Housman (*CR* xvi, 1902, 445 and on Manilius
5. 568), Tescari, and others in making *ruris* depend on *dominam*. Whatever 'every Roman
child felt in the marrow of his bones', the mature poet of the *Odes* was in the habit of
producing unambiguous constructions. 3. 1. 5 f. (compared by Housman), *regum timen-
dorum in proprios greges, reges in ipsos imperium est Iovis*, is unambiguous and so is *Carm. Saec.*
75 f. *doctus et Phoebi chorus et Dianae dicere laudes*: the 'figurae orationis', epanaphora in
the one case, *et...et...* in the other, prevent any possible doubt. No such safeguard exists
at 1. 35. 6. Moreover, it is in the nature of the ' "Du"-Stil der Praedication' (E. Norden,
Agnostos Theos, 143 ff.), of which this ode to Fortuna is a perfect example, that the single
'membra', *tu . . ., tu . . ., tibi .. .*, and the like, follow one another without an external

and a description of her retinue.[1] An unobtrusive, yet not unimportant, link between the initial part of the ode and the prayer for Caesar towards the end is furnished by ll. 9 ff., *te Dacus asper, te profugi Scythae urbesque gentesque et Latium ferox*, etc., a sentence which is bound to turn the reader's thoughts to the troublesome northern frontier of the Roman world as well as to its centre, recalling in a flash how much everything has changed under the guardianship of Caesar. The political note, with its implications for the present time, is maintained in the next stanza,

> iniurioso ne pede proruas
> stantem columnam[2] neu populus frequens
> ad arma cessantis ad arma[3]
> concitet imperiumque frangat.

Here revolution and civil war are thought of as a dreaded possibility; in the two concluding stanzas of the ode they are represented in horrifying detail, as they live in the memory of a generation which had experienced them to the full:

> eheu cicatricum et sceleris pudet
> fratrumque. quid nos dura refugimus
> aetas? quid intactum nefasti
> liquimus? unde manum iuventus

> metu deorum continuit? quibus
> pepercit aris? o utinam nova
> incude diffingas retusum in
> Massagetas Arabasque ferrum.[4]

connexion and that each forms a self-contained unit. An elaborate syntactic intertwining such as is assumed by Markland and his followers (*te ruris dominam colonus, te aequoris dominam quicumque*, etc.) would be against the style of these simple prayers. That the verb *ambit*, placed near the beginning of the whole sentence, governs also the following clause is, of course, an entirely different matter.

[1] At 17 the implication of *anteit* should not be missed: she walks in front of Fortuna as the lictors walk in front of the magistrate (so Dacier, ·ho, like Lambinus and Bentley, reads *saeva*, rightly); *anteire* and *antecedere* are commonly used of the lictors. Ἀνάγκη here executes the order of Τύχη: what chance has allotted us can never be altered. This idea could well occur to Horace spontaneously, or it may have been suggested by a Greek model, cf., for example, Philemon, *fr.* 10 K., μετὰ τῶν σωμάτων | ἡμῶν, ὅταν γινώμεθ', εὐθὺς χὴ τύχη | προσγίνεθ' ἡμῖν συγγενὴς τῷ σώματι· | κοὐκ ἔστιν ἕτερον παρ' ἑτέρου λαβεῖν τύχην, and, in the epitaph of a Roman woman and her son from Paros, under the Empire, *IG* xii. 5. 302 (quoted by Ruhl, Roscher's *Mythol. Lex.* v. 1331), ἀλλὰ Τύχης οὐκ ἔστι φυγεῖν ἀμετάτροπα δῶρα.

[2] Heinze's comment, 'die hochragende Säule als Symbol der Herrschaft', does not seem to be wholly appropriate: in the image of the pillar it is the solidity of the support that matters most. Clytemnestra (A. *Ag.* 897 f.) calls the king σωτῆρα ναὸς πρότονον, ὑψηλῆς στέγης στῦλον ποδήρη.

[3] For *ad arma . . . ad arma* see, besides the commentaries, Wilhelm Schulze, *Sitz. Berlin* 1918, 484 (*Kl. Schriften*, 163 f.) and add A. *fr.* 140 N.[2] (*Myrmidons*), ὅπλων ὅπλων δεῖ.

[4] The points of contact between these two stanzas and epodes XVI and VII are un-

It is from these dark recollections that the prayer for Caesar's safety derives its force.[1] Men possessed of true insight into the nature of human affairs and the moods of Fortune would not venture to assert, not even in the year 26 B.C., when this ode was written, that the calamity of fratricidal war could never recur; what they could do was to strive to avoid it by remaining conscious of their own guilt and to pray for the support of Heaven.

Odes i. 34, *Parcus deorum cultor*, is, like every Horatian ode, a self-contained poem, but, placed as it is before *O diva gratum quae regis Antium* and ending with a description of the ways of Fortuna, it also serves as a preparation for the prayer to Fortuna that follows it. This connexion between the two odes may justify us in touching here upon *Parcus deorum cultor* although this poem has nothing to do with Augustus.

A particular link between *Odes* i. 34 and i. 35 is furnished by a detail: towards the end of i. 34 we read (12 ff.) *valet ima summis mutare et insignem attenuat deus obscura promens*, and in the first stanza of the next poem *praesens vel imo tollere de gradu mortale corpus vel superbos vertere funeribus triumphos*. In the former passage, it is true, the subject is not *Fortuna* but *deus* (referring back to *Diespiter* at l. 5 and also meaning 'God' without any individualization),[2] but, guided by the parallelism in form and thought, the reader will not be slow to see that the next sentence, *hinc*[3] *apicem rapax Fortuna . . . sustulit, hic posuisse gaudet*, indicates the same kind of action and the same agent as the preceding sentence, in other words that Ζεύς and Τύχη are here regarded as one and the same all-governing Power. This conception was probably familiar to educated persons in Horace's time. Hesiod's famous praise of Zeus, ῥέα μὲν γὰρ βριάει, ῥέα δὲ βριάοντα χαλέπτει, | ῥεῖα δ' ἀρί-ζηλον μινύθει καὶ ἄδηλον ἀέξει,[4] lent itself easily to a description of the

mistakable. The last sentence, *o utinam . . . ferrum*, varies a thought of the earlier ode i. 2 (21 f. *audiet civis acuisse ferrum, quo graves Persae melius perirent*).

[1] A fine appreciation of the function of the last two stanzas and of the structure of the whole ode is given by F. Jacoby, *Hermes*, lvi, 1921, 47 n. 1.

[2] In fact *Diespiter* is here as much or as little a product of 'monotheism' as in the epilogue of a noble prayer, *Epist*. 1. 18. 111 f., *sed satis est orare Iovem quae ponit et aufert* (this describes to perfection the action of Τύχη as well): *det vitam, det opes; aequum mi animum ipse parabo*. In the letter Jupiter naturally appears without his mythological trappings.

[3] *hinc* corresponds to the following *hic* and cannot refer back to *deus*. Wilamowitz's remark, *Glaube der Hell*. ii. 438 n. 1, 'in dem *hinc* ist ausgesprochen daß Fortuna dem Gotte gehorcht', must be due to a slip.

[4] That Horace alludes to it was seen as early as Muretus. The adoption of this topic, applied to Fortuna, into Latin poetry is perhaps older. Varro *Men*. 1, *ita sublimis* (acc. plur.) *speribus iactato homines, at volitantis altos nitens trudito*, is taken by Haffter, *Glotta*, xxiii, 1935, 259, to be addressed to Fortuna, which seems very likely and is certainly more convincing than Buecheler's idea, *Rh. Mus*. xx, 1865, 403 (*Kl. Schriften* i. 536) that *Cura*, or Ribbeck's, *Gesch. d. röm. Dichtung*, i². 253, that 'der Genius der Menschen' is spoken to.

working of Τύχη, no matter whether this application goes back to the
Stoics[1] or to others.[2]

The nature of Τύχη–Fortuna does not appear as fundamentally
different in the two odes, especially when allowance is made for the
necessary consequences of the difference in scope between the elaborate
prayer to the goddess (i. 35) and the brief mention of her ways at the
end of the preceding poem. What the ode *Parcus deorum cultor* lacks in
fullness is amply compensated for by the close connexion into which
Fortuna is brought with the supreme god. There is in this poem a note of
true religious dignity. Are we, then, by recognizing this note, driven
to the conclusion that the ode testifies to a religious conversion which
Horace had undergone? It would be possible to write an amusing and,
perhaps, useful book on 'The Scholiasts' Tyranny over the Reading of
the Classics'. The ode *Parcus deorum cultor* is a case in point. The classifying mind of some ancient schoolmaster excogitated for it the label
'hac ode significat se paenitentiam agere quod Epicuream sectam
secutus inreligiosus extiterit' (Porph.), and so we still read in the most
influential modern commentary that 'the poem is meant to be taken
absolutely seriously as a confession of a religious conversion',[3] despite
all that has been said to discredit this view.[4] If a conversion did take

---

[1] See Werner Jaeger, *Hermes*, xlviii, 1913, 449, and Pasquali, *Or. lir.* 601.

[2] The passage of Hesiod quoted above is applied to Τύχη (or Αἶσα) in several passages of
the literature of the Empire, none of them dependent on Horace. The author (Favorinus?
—for a recent discussion of the problem see Mary G. Goggin, *Yale Class. Studies*, xii, 1951,
150 f., 191 f., 201) of the speech (the second) περὶ Τύχης which found its way into the
collection of the works of Dio of Prusa, *oratio* LXIV (ii. 147 ff. v. Arnim), gives (section 8)
instances of Τύχη (or τύχη) being worshipped under the name of various gods. After
saying that farmers called her Demeter, herdsmen Pan, sailors Leukothea, and helmsmen
Dioscuri, he quotes, without marking the transition, the two Hesiodic lines ῥεῖα δ᾽
ἀρίζηλον . . . ἀγήνορα κάρφει. (There follows the sentence τοῦτο ἄρα ἦν ὁ Ζεὺς ἡ τύχη,
κατέχων μὲν ἐπὶ τῆς δεξιᾶς τὸ ὅπλον κτλ. It seems to me that the passage as it stands in the
MSS has been badly tampered with. The context requires the thought that some people
gave τύχη the name of Zeus, and that that was suitable because Hesiod's words about Zeus
apply to τύχη as well. But τοῦτο ἄρα ἦν ὁ Ζεὺς ἡ τύχη is not sufficient to express this thought,
and what follows, κατέχων μὲν κτλ., seems altogether out of place here and looks as if it
belonged to one of the passages in which the genuine Dio discusses the relationship between
kings and Zeus.) The same lines of Hesiod are paraphrased in a late hymn to Τύχη (Diehl,
Anth. lyr. ii. 313 f., D. L. Page, *Greek Lit. Pap.* i. 432), ll. 4–7; and Quintus Smyrnaeus 13.
474 f. says of Αἶσα: καὶ τὰ μὲν ἀκλέα πολλὰ καὶ οὐκ ἀρίδηλα γεγῶτα | κυδήεντα τίθησι, τὰ δ᾽
ὑψόθι μεῖον᾽ ἔθηκε.

[3] Heinze; cf. also the beginning of his introduction to the ode in the seventh edition of
the commentary (as regards the relevance of *Sat.* 1. 5. 101 ff., the judgement of Lejay
seems to me much sounder) and his discussion in *Neue Jahrb.* 1929, 680 (reprinted in
Vom Geist des Römertums, 222). On the same lines is W. Wili, *Horaz*, 122 f. Even A. D. Nock
(*Cambr. Anc. Hist.* x. 504 and *Conversion*, 1933, 11) takes it for granted that the ode is
evidence of a conversion. This is also the opinion of F. Altheim, *A History of Roman Religion*,
372 and 532 n. 2, who differs from Heinze in some detail, and of Zieliński: see the chapter
'Conversion religieuse d'Horace' (43 ff.) in his book *Horace et la société romaine du temps
d'Auguste*, 1938.

[4] Dacier's argumentation against the traditional view is remarkable although he spoils

place at all, if in this ode 'Horace has treasured up one decisive event of his own life' (Altheim), it should at least be admitted that the effect of this event was anything but permanent. Even if we leave aside the joke in the letter to Tibullus,[1] *Epicuri de grege porcum*, there remains the programmatic declaration,[2]

> ac ne forte roges, quo me duce, quo lare tuter:
> nullius addictus iurare in verba magistri,
> quo me cumque rapit tempestas, deferor hospes.

This frank statement is in harmony with all that we know about Horace's behaviour and general outlook during the period, approximately twenty-five years, for which we have the evidence of his own writings. The statement is unambiguous; it ought not to be disregarded in any discussion on 'the philosophy' or 'the religion' of the poet. Nor should we forget that the very serious culmination (96–103) of *Epist.* i. 18 and also the last sentence in that letter show full adherence to the Epicurean creed.

The doctrine of Epicurus[3] 'explained thunder as caused by the clashing of two clouds. But Horace hears thunder in a clear sky: therefore, he reflects, Epicureanism is false. But does that mean that he abandons Epicureanism? Hardly. Horace is no zealot, who must accept a given creed in its entirety or reject it. As a matter of fact he had no interest in Epicurean science, whether for its own sake or for its application to the question of death; he was no Lucretius. Ethics alone engaged his attention. Nor on the other hand are we to interpret the ode as playful. . . . In saying that Jupiter threw his thunderbolt Horace is serious but not literal, poetic but not playful. . . . The significant part of the poem comes at the end. . . . After depicting the power

his case by resorting to the panacea of irony (he uses this very word in his note on l. 5) and assuming that the ode 'n'est qu'une raillerie continuelle contre les Stoïciens'. Lessing, at the end of his 'Rettungen des Horaz', rejected Dacier's interpretation but agreed with him in abandoning the idea of a conversion; he should not, however, have denied that there is at the beginning of the ode an allusion to Epicureanism. Dr. Johnson's comment as reported by Boswell (29 Apr. 1783, Boswell's *Life of Johnson*, ed. G. B. Hill, iv. 215), 'Sir, he was not in earnest: this was merely poetical', shows that he was as critical of the conventional misinterpretation as were Dacier and Lessing, but we are not told what he thought about the true meaning of the ode. We find a fresh approach to poetry when we come to Herder, *Briefe über das Lesen des Horaz*, 5. Brief 'Übrigens ist sein verrufenes Glaubensbekenntnis, "Der Götter karger, seltner Verehrer—" über das man viel Ungehöriges gesagt hat, ebenso verständig als schön eingekleidet. Was macht uns auf eine höhere Haushaltung aufmerksam, als unvermutet große Veränderungen in der Welt, der Blitzstrahl Zeus am wolkenlos heitern Himmel? Auch in Gegenständen dieser Art kam dem Horaz eine hohe Grazie zu Hülfe.' Of more recent critics who refuse to read into the poem a real conversion I will mention besides Ullman (see the text), only Kiessling (see his commentary), Sellar, *Horace*, 160 f., G. Giri (see his commentary), and L. P. Wilkinson, *Horace and His Lyric Poetry*, 1944, 27 f.

[1] *Epist.* 1. 4. 16.   [2] *Epist.* 1. 1. 13 ff.
[3] Cf. Epic. *Ep.* 2. 100 ff.; Lucretius 6. 400 ff.

of Jupiter, he says that the god makes the mighty to fall and the humble
to rise. Thus the chance observation of a natural phenomenon leads
. . . to a reflection on the uncertainties of life. . . . Nor is it without
significance that Horace passes from Jupiter to the more generalized
deus and finally to Fortune and that the poem which follows is addressed
to the same goddess.'[1] One need not agree with every word of this
careful interpretation, but it seems to me that it comes much nearer
to the true spirit of the poem than the crude simplification of the
scholiast and of those who share his view.

The dogmas of the philosophers and their metaphysical and theo-
logical systems were of but subordinate interest to Horace; what did
excite him throughout his life was the spectacle of Fortune's ruthless
sport and the lesson a wise man should draw from it:

> Fortuna saevo laeta negotio et
> ludum insolentem ludere pertinax
> transmutat incertos honores,
>   nunc mihi nunc alii benigna.

> laudo manentem: si celeris quatit
> pinnas, resigno quae dedit et mea
> virtute me involvo . . ..

The ceaseless and ever-varied ups and downs in the lives of individuals
and peoples not only engaged the thought of Horace as a human being
and a citizen, they also stirred the imagination of the poet. In the
mood in which he wrote *Parcus deorum cultor* he was inclined, freely
adapting a conception of Greek thinkers, to identify the force that
manifested itself in those changes with the supreme power in control of
the world. The excitement which he feels at this conception is genuine;
hence the forcible imagery and the bold language. For a Horatian ode
it was desirable, if not indispensable, to have at least the semblance of
a spontaneous cause; therefore Horace placed in the centre of this
short poem an account of the lightning from a cloudless sky, introducing it by *namque* and thus investing a personal experience with the
dignity of a παράδειγμα of the traditional type.[2] There is no more
reason to doubt that Horace once witnessed a flash of unexpected
lightning than there is reason to doubt that he once escaped being in-
jured by a falling tree. But our primary concern is not the reality of
the accidents but the meaning of the poetry. Neither in the case of *Ille
et nefasto te posuit die*[3] nor in that of *Parcus deorum cultor* is it in the least

---

[1] B. L. Ullman, *Class. J.* xxxi, 1936, 411 f.
[2] Cf. *Odes* 1. 22. 9, *namque me silva*, etc., and my remarks on it, above, pp. 185 f. Wickham
shows himself alive to the importance of this parallel.
[3] Cf. pp. 166 ff. above.

likely that the mainspring of a fine and sincere poem should be seen simply in the emotions produced by those accidents.[1]

We now resume our survey of the odes related to Augustus and turn to iii. 25, *Quo me, Bacche, rapis*. If we succeed in some measure in our attempt to understand this apparently very puzzling poem, we shall find it easier to do justice to the difficult Roman Odes (iii. 1–6) and indeed to all the 'patriotic' lyrics of Horace and perhaps be able to see what position they occupy in the whole of his work.

Quo me, Bacche, rapis naturally turns our thoughts to the other Dionysus ode, ii. 19, *Bacchum in remotis carmina rupibus vidi docentem*.[2] A first quick comparison of the two poems will probably lead the reader to stress their common features rather than their fundamental difference. Both describe, the one as past, the other as present, the poet's participation in the ecstatic rites of Dionysus and his retinue. Both, drawing on the *Bacchae* of Euripides and other works of Greek poetry, convey forcibly the emotions roused by the presence of the god. Both show the effect of Bacchic enthusiasm on the poet in his being inspired with the power to conceive and write lofty poetry. But it is only when we go beyond these elements common to both odes that we become aware of the features which make *Quo me, Bacche, rapis* the more personal document and the more beautiful poem.

The first brief sentence, wrung from the poet's lips by his profound amazement, gives the keynote of the whole ode: *Quo me, Bacche, rapis tui plenum?* Unlike ii. 19, this poem lays the main emphasis not on the god and his achievements but on his mortal follower, moving in Bacchic ecstasy, possessed by the god, *plenus deo*.[3] So intense is the poet's vision of what is happening to the Maenad that he almost identifies himself with her:

> non secus in iugis
> exsomnis[4] stupet Euhias
> Hebrum prospiciens et nive candidam
> Thracen ac pede barbaro

---

[1] The words of the opening sentence, *dum . . . erro, nunc retrorsum vela dare atque iterare cursus cogor relictos*, were turned into an expression of bitter irony by Leopardi, *Palinodia* (1 f. *Errai, candido Gino; assai gran tempo, E di gran lunga errai*, and 244 f., *Or torno addietro, ed al passato un corso Contrario imprendo*).

[2] See pp. 199 ff. above.

[3] For this expression see p. 199 n. 1 above. The kindred phrase which follows at 3. 25. 3, *mente nova*, might have been included by R. Reitzenstein, *Die hellenistischen Mysterienreligionen*, 3rd ed., 1927, 262 ff., in his list of 'die Bezeichnungen für die Verwandlung'. St. Paul, *Ep. Rom.* 12. 2, which he quotes, μεταμορφοῦσθε τῇ ἀνακαινώσει τοῦ νοός, provides a close parallel.

[4] In a modern critical edition Bentley's *Edonis* should not even be mentioned. As if *exsomnis* were not perfect and *in iugis* not sufficiently illustrated by ll. 10–12!

lustratam Rhodopen, ut mihi devio
ripas et vacuum nemus
mirari libet.

The movements of the Maenad and those of the poet are no longer of
their own choosing: an irresistible force draws them on. And although
the god whom they are following fills them with superhuman strength
(*o . . . potens Baccharum . . . valentium proceras manibus vertere fraxinos*), all
the time danger awaits them. It is towards the ends of the world, away
from the paths of civilized men, that Bacchus leads his train, across
mountain-tops and treacherous snowfields, farther and farther into the
unknown. One unguarded step, and the god's ecstatic worshipper will
fall down the precipice. And yet he can neither pause nor turn back;
on he must go wherever the god leads, and in the face of threatening
destruction he will still be jubilant: *dulce periculum est, o Lenaee, sequi deum.*

The idea of mortal danger being inseparable from a great creative
effort is more than once expressed in Horace's poems. It appears in the
ode to Asinius Pollio, ii. 1,[1] and we shall find it again when we come to
iv. 2, *Pindarum quisquis studet aemulari,*[2] but it is in *Quo me, Bacche, rapis*
that it is worked out to its greatest depth. The picture of Bacchic
enthusiasm that Horace had received from the old poets is here transformed into a perfect picture of the enthusiasm of the creative artist.
Horace's own task, the task of producing solemn Latin lyrics of an
unprecedented kind (*dicam insigne, recens, adhuc indictum ore alio . . . nil
parvum aut humili modo, nil mortale loquar*) has become his fate: he cannot
escape it. But inspired and guided by a mysterious force, he feels
capable of an endeavour that seems far beyond the reach of mortal
men, just as the Bacchant's frail body is filled with the power to uproot
tall ash-trees. And yet he is all the time aware of what awaits him if
he fails: ridicule, disgrace, perdition. He can already hear the sneering
of his rivals, *quid dignum tanto feret hic promissor hiatu?* If he does not
succeed in the end, there will be no mercy for him. And Horace is not
the man to comfort himself with the thought that *si deficiant vires
audacia certe laus erit: in magnis et voluisse sat est.* The danger before him is
formidable, but *dulce periculum est . . . sequi deum.*

The poets of the German Romantic School were on the whole un-
sympathetic, and sometimes directly hostile, to Horace. They had no
use for his clear 'realistic' outlook and for the conception of poetry
which underlies his work. It is the more remarkable that the most
romantic of them, Novalis, should once have written a translation of a
Horatian ode. His rendering of the greater part of *Quo me, Bacche, rapis*
(it breaks off after l. 14 *mirari libet*)[3] is of exquisite beauty and also, on

---

[1] See p. 235 above.   [2] See pp. 435 f. below.
[3] Novalis apparently left it without a title; in the edition of 'Novalis Schriften' by

the whole, surprisingly faithful;[1] moreover, the note of mystery, clearly perceptible in the original, is brought out with suggestive force. It is not difficult to guess why this poem exerted its spell on Novalis: it must have appeared to him a perfect picture of his own ideal of the inspired poet, moving, as if in a trance, through the loneliness, 'Einsamkeit',[2] of a far-off gigantic mountain world. And yet Horace's ode is anything but a romantic poem, nor are we at liberty to isolate it from the body of his *carmina*. Up to this point we have, in our survey of the ode, omitted one important sentence, but only when we take this sentence into account and face its implications can we hope to grasp the real meaning of the whole poem.

A modern reader would not be greatly puzzled by this ode if Horace spoke merely in general terms of his being called to write poetry, or lyric poetry. But that is not so. He says most definitely that he is thinking of one theme only (3 ff.):

> quibus
> antris egregii Caesaris audiar
> aeternum meditans decus
> stellis inserere et consilio Iovis?

The edge of this sentence must not be blunted. The goal towards which Horace feels driven by a force stronger than himself is the task of praising the rule of Augustus; it is this task that mysteriously increases his powers and fills him in advance with an almost religious fervour. From the sentence *quibus antris . . . consilio Iovis?* we must not separate the sentence which immediately follows it, *dicam insigne, recens, adhuc indictum ore alio*. These words link up with the opening stanza of the cycle of the Roman Odes (3. 1. 2 ff.), *carmina non prius audita Musarum sacerdos virginibus puerisque canto*. It is impossible not to see the intimate connexion of the two passages: the songs which are anticipated in iii. 25 are in iii. 1 described as being actually recited. It matters little whether Horace wrote *Quo me, Bacche, rapis* when he was planning some great songs in honour of the new régime or when he was already engaged in composing such songs. What is certain is that poems of the type of the Roman Odes had begun to shape themselves in his mind when he conceived the enthusiastic hymn iii. 25.

Tieck and v. Bülow, III. Teil, Berlin 1846, 108, it is headed 'Fragment'; in P. Kluckhohn's edition of Novalis in 'Meyers Klassiker-Ausgaben', i. 395, the editor has added the heading '[Bruchstück einer Horaz-Nachdichtung]'.

[1] The only serious divergence occurs at the beginning, 'Wohin ziehst du mich, Fülle meines Herzens, Gott des Rausches'. This is certainly an ingenious way of recasting *Bacche, tui plenum*, but it completely alters the emphasis and also gives the poem a characteristic romantic complexion, for 'Fülle des Herzens' is a favourite phrase of the German 'Genieperiode' from Goethe's *Werther* on.

[2] At l. 13 *vacuum nemus* is translated by 'der einsame Wald'.

The issue before us must decide our approach to the whole group of Horace's patriotic lyrics. Horace, a past master in εἰρωνεία and understatement, never lies and never pretends. In *Quo me, Bacche, rapis* he speaks of the urge which forces him to immortalize the *decus Caesaris* in tones of an overwhelming emotion and of the most genuine sincerity. From what I know of Horace I refuse to consider the possibility that in this poem he is lying or not being serious. He implies that what he is setting out to do will, if he succeeds, be the crowning triumph of his life. I believe him. I must therefore part company with those scholars who say that the Roman Odes and kindred poems are to be regarded as products of a subtle propaganda, suggested to the poet and all but forced upon him by Maecenas or somebody else.

On the Roman Odes mountains of literature have been piled. It cannot be my object, and here even less than in other sections of this book, to provide a substitute for a full commentary, nor do I wish to dwell on these odes at a disproportionate length. But I must at least attempt to assign to them the place in the work of Horace which by right belongs to them.

The habit of attaching the label 'Roman Odes' to *Odes* iii. 1–6 may be open to criticism. However, this name has been current for a considerable time[1] so that it would not be advisable to look for a different one, and the usefulness of some comprehensive title for the six odes is obvious.

These six odes are bound together by their common metre, their solemn style, by the fact that none of them is addressed to an individual, by the affinity of their main themes, and by the central position which Augustus and his rule occupy in them. From these facts the conclusion has been drawn, and is now generally accepted, that the six odes are intended to form a cycle, the only one in the collection of Horace's *carmina*. Therefore the question arises whether the poet composed the six odes one after another in their present order at a time when the plan of the cycle was already fixed in his mind. Some scholars answer this question in the affirmative, but most of those who have discussed the problem hold the view that at least one or two of the six odes were written earlier than the rest and are probably prior to the conception of the cycle as a whole.[2] It will be best to examine first the chronological problem with which the sixth ode presents us.

---

[1] T. Plüss, *Horazstudien*, 1882, 185 ff., seems to use the term 'die Römeroden' as a matter of course. When Verrall, in 1884, published his *Studies in the Odes of Horace*, he knew Plüss's book (Verrall, 8 n. 2); he himself says p. 106 'the "Römer-Oden" as they are sometimes called'.

[2] See, for example, Plüss, op. cit. 280 ff., 'Ob Horaz die sechs ersten Lieder des dritten

The ode begins

> Delicta maiorum immeritus lues
> Romane, donec templa refeceris
> aedisque labentis deorum et
> foeda nigro simulacra fumo.

This passage had long been regarded as an allusion to Octavian's wholesale restoration of the many ruined or decaying temples,[1] an operation the date of which, 28 B.C., was, even before the discovery of the 'Monumentum Ancyranum', known from Dio Cass. 53. 2. 4. The date was then confirmed by the best possible authority, Augustus himself. This is what he says:[2] *duo et octoginta templa deum in urbe consul sextum* (28 B.C.) *ex auctoritate senatus refeci, nullo praetermisso quod eo tempore refici debebat.* It follows that the ode *Delicta maiorum* cannot have been written later than 28 B.C. It would be difficult to twist the meaning of the strong expressions in Horace's first sentence so as to make them suitable to a time when the restoration of the temples was already far advanced.[3] But neither does there seem to be any need to assign to the ode a date prior to 28 B.C.[4] If, then, iii. 6 was written in or shortly before 28 B.C., it must be earlier than iii. 3 and iii. 5, the date of which, since the name *Augustus* occurs in them, cannot be earlier than 27 B.C.

A more delicate problem is raised by the relation of the first ode to the whole cycle. The days are long past when editors endeavoured to separate the first stanza of iii. 1 from the rest of the ode. But it is still

Buches von vornherein als Cyklus gedichtet hat, also nach einer einzigen ursprünglichen Gesamtidee, in welche schon sechs schön geordnete Teilideen eingefaßt waren? Ich glaube es nicht', etc.; Kiessling, introduction to iii. 1–6; Heinze (cf. also his paper, *Neue Jahrb.* 1929, 675 ff., reprinted in *Vom Geist des Römertums*, 213 ff.); Pasquali, *Or. lir.* 651; W. Warde Fowler, *Roman Essays and Interpretations*, 210 f. There is no need to quote the more recent writers who hold the same view. It should not be assumed that Mommsen ever ascribed a common date to all the six odes; when in his famous Academy address of 1889 (*Reden und Aufsätze*, 168 ff.) he said (181) 'sie werden alle *ungefähr* [my italics] gleichzeitig geschrieben sein' and 'sie schließen wohl zusammen', surely he did not mean to recant his former statement (*Res gestae divi Augusti*, 2nd ed. 86) that iii. 6 was written in 28 B.C. In that public lecture he had to content himself with mere outlines, 'da ich keine Abhandlung schreibe' (letter to Wilamowitz of 14 Jan. 1889).

[1] Cf. F. W. Shipley, 'Building Operations in Rome', etc., *Mem. Amer. Acad. in Rome*, ix, 1931, 32.

[2] *Res Gestae* 20. 4.

[3] H. Silomon, *Philol.* xcii, 1937, 444 ff., by making *petitio principii* serve in the place of interpretation, brings the date of iii. 6 down to 27 B.C.

[4] I cannot agree with Heinze who, on the same lines as P. Jörs, 'Die Ehegesetze des Augustus', *Festschrift für Th. Mommsen*, Marburg 1893, 9 n. 4, postulates (*Neue Jahrb.* 1929, 678 = *Vom Geist des Römertums*, 218) 'das muß geschrieben sein, bevor der Entschluß Octavians ausgeführt, ja bevor er gefaßt war'. It seems the far more natural inference that at the time of the poet's writing the plan of restoring the temples was settled and its execution, perhaps, begun. '. . . è un destino che i pareri de' poeti non siano ascoltati: e se nella storia trovate de' fatti conformi a qualche loro suggerimento, dite pur francamente ch' eran cose risolute prima' (Manzoni, *I Promessi Sposi*, chapter 28. 67).

a widely held opinion that the first four, or the first eight, lines are not internally connected with the body of the ode, and that they were probably prefixed to it only when a poem, written previously and with no regard to the cycle, was incorporated into it.[1] There is something attractive in this hypothesis. For it is quite true that the beginning four (or eight) lines can be fully appreciated only when they are regarded as a proem to the whole cycle, and it is equally true that the rest of the ode, which does not contain a single explicit reference to the commonwealth or to the Princeps, seems to be concerned solely with the morals and the behaviour of individual persons; this 'private' character of the poem appears to be strongly emphasized in the concluding sentence *cur valle permutem Sabina divitias operosiores?* And yet this hypothesis is based on a fallacy. In an article which may be called a model of careful interpretation[2] F. Solmsen has shown that the first ode was planned and executed as an organic part of the cycle. By analysing, along with *Odes* iii. 1, some kindred Horatian poems such as ii. 15, *Iam pauca aratro iugera,* and especially iii. 24,[3] Solmsen makes it clear that the conventional dichotomy of *res privata* and *res publica* is in this case inadequate. Horace regarded 'greed and luxury as a blight on the political life of the nation and as running counter to the best traditions of Roman history'. In harmony with this general outlook 'the poem that opens the cycle of political odes and sets the tone for the whole group proclaims in effect that the moral recovery of Rome is predicated on the same approach to life through which the poet has found his own individual happiness and which he has so frequently expounded in relation to his private existence'.[4] Therefore the idea that the first ode was originally conceived as a 'private' poem and only afterwards adjusted to the cycle must be given up. This conclusion is confirmed by the style, for 'among the poems recommending Moderation III 1 is unique owing to its severe dignity and a certain stern remoteness. . . . There is no warmth or intimacy in this ode. Horace is this time not speaking as friend. He speaks as authority, and the authoritative tone indicates

---

[1] So, for example, Kiessling in the introduction to his commentary on iii. 1–6; W. Warde Fowler, *Roman Essays,* 211, 'It may be that this curious little preface [3. 1. 1–4] was placed where it is when the six odes were *collected*. This first one might begin quite naturally and after Horace's familiar manner with the fifth line'; L. Amundsen, 'The "Roman Odes" of Horace', *Serta Eitremiana,* Oslo 1942, 8 f., 'It must be confessed that there is a distance between strophe 1–2 and the rest of the ode . . . Either an older poem has been placed in the cycle to serve as a more general ethical introduction—or the ode has been composed later on for the same purpose. At any rate we must insist that strophes 1–2 stand by themselves, without any particularly close connection with the ten strophes that follow.'

[2] 'Horace's First Roman Ode', *Am. Journ. Phil.* lxviii, 1947, 337 ff.

[3] See pp. 240 ff. above.

[4] In this connexion the agreement between iii. 1 and 3. 3. 49 ff. (cf. ii. 2) is noteworthy.

that more is involved than the right approach to matters that are of purely personal concern.'[1]

Although so much has been written on *Odi profanum volgus*, few commentators have anything to say on the first word, and its implications do not seem to have been fully grasped. First of all those who have been brought up in certain modern languages must beware of a schoolboy's stock translation (for instance 'ich hasse', in the common German versions, 'Je hais', Villeneuve in the Budé edition).[2] Baxter's note, *Odi, non possum ferre*, came pretty near the mark; Heinze's paraphrase, 'I will have nothing to do with . . .', hits it.[3] Of course the words *odium, odisse* very often, in Horace as elsewhere, mean 'hatred', 'to hate' in the sense of German 'hassen', but often they mean something far less strong. Expressions such as *odio mihi es*, common in Plautus, come much to the same thing as 'tu m'ennuies',[4] 'mi dai noia', 'you make me tired' (described in the *Shorter Oxford English Dictionary* as 'U.S. slang'), and the like. Other set phrases containing *odium* point in the same direction; it would be entirely wrong to find in them the notion of 'hatred'.[5] The same is true of many passages in which the verb *odisse* is used. F. Skutsch[6] examines Plautus *Capt.* 541–6, where *fugitare* and *aspernari* are taken up, with no more than a shade of variation, by *te odit*. This juxtaposition is significant. I quote, at random, Cicero, *Fin.* 1. 4, where *qui Ennii Medeam aut Antiopam Pacuvii spernat aut reiciat* is answered by *Latinas litteras oderit*; 1. 32 *nemo enim ipsam voluptatem, quia voluptas sit, aspernatur aut odit aut fugit?*[7] *Lael.* 47 *virtus . . . quae necesse est . . . res sibi contrarias aspernetur atque oderit.* Just as Plautus and Cicero put *aspernari* or *spernere* beside the verb which comes close to it in meaning, viz. *odisse*, so also does Horace at *Epist.* 1. 7. 20, *prodigus et stultus donat quae spernit et odit.* The same, as it were, reduced, force of *odisse* will be noticed, for instance, at *Odes* 1. 38. 1, *Persicos odi . . . apparatus*, further in the famous but not always correctly understood line *Ars. P.* 188, *quodcumque ostendis mihi sic, incredulus odi*, and also in the passage from which we started.

Odi profanum volgus et arceo is a remarkable transformation of a sacred

[1] Solmsen, op. cit. 350, 352; his detailed stylistic analysis should also be consulted.
[2] The English rendering by 'I hate' is less objectionable (the initial paraphrase of the verb in the *Oxford English Dictionary* is 'to hold in very strong dislike').
[3] For sensible comments to the same effect see, for example, Orelli–Baiter–Hirschfelder on *Odes* 2. 16. 26, Heinze on *Odes* 1. 8. 4 and 1. 38. 1.
[4] Cf. Lindsay on Plaut. *Capt.* 1035.
[5] For all this see F. Skutsch's article 'Odium und Verwandtes', *Glotta*, ii, 1910, 230 ff. (*Kl. Schriften*, 389 ff.). The value of his interpretations depends in no way on the question whether his etymology is the true one.
[6] *Glotta*, ii. 237 f. (*Kl. Schriften*, 396 f.).
[7] Cf. *Att.* 3. 7. 1 *odi enim celebritatem, fugio homines.*

formula. In this clause, as in the following *favete linguis*, Horace adapts
to his proem words customary at the beginning of religious ceremonies.
The presence of βέβηλοι, *profani*,[1] would defile any sacrifice or other act
of a cult and thus render it invalid, *vitiosum* as the Romans call it. To
prevent this happening, the worshipper has to banish in advance those
potentially noxious persons. All this is well known and has often been
recalled in connexion with the beginning of this ode. But the fact that
the initial word uses the singular of the first person (as also does *arceo*)
and that it expresses a personal feeling has not been given the attention
it deserves. '*I* will have nothing to do with . . . *I* keep off.' In antiquity
no one, whether a priest or not, performing a sacrifice or any other
ritual, was ever in a position to speak in his own person, let alone express
personal likes or dislikes. All he was expected and permitted to do was
to function as the instrument and mouthpiece of a community, his
household, an army, an assembly of the people, and so forth. The intensely personal beginning of Horace's ode brings it home from the
outset that what we are going to hear will not be a religious cult but a
transposition of such a cult to a different plane, a 'secularization'.
We are to understand that Horace does not act as a real priest but as
Musarum sacerdos, and we expect that the emphasizing of the 'I', of the
individuality of the poet, will be of great importance to the message of
the *carmina non prius audita*. The last point will become clear in the interpretation of the fourth ode, but the first ode, too, is more easily appreciated if its first word and its implications are considered. '*I* will
have nothing to do with . . .': it was due to the life and nature of this
one man with his particular inclinations and his particular moral and
artistic convictions that a poetry which its author knew to be *insigne*,
recens, indictum ore alio, could come into being. That is the fundamental
reason why there is no real disharmony between the bulk of the first
ode, which concludes with the extremely personal sentence *cur valle
permutem Sabina divitias operosiores?*, and its exordium *Odi profanum volgus
et arceo*.

Before leaving the first ode, a word must be said about its second
stanza in relation both to the rest of the ode and to some other passages
in the cycle. To take the latter aspect first: the expression (3. 1. 6 f.)
Iovis clari Giganteo triumpho clearly points to the Gigantomachy of the
ode in which the cycle culminates, 3. 4. 42–76.[2] The whole sentence, 3.
1. 6–8, has to be taken together with the stanza 3. 4. 45–48; moreover,

---

[1] To the passages quoted by the commentators Juvenal 2. 89, *ite profanae*, might be
added.

[2] Cf. Wilamowitz in his letter to Mommsen of 8 Jan. 1889 (*Briefwechsel*, 360), 'carm.
I hat nichts von Augustus. Nur die Gigantomachie deutet auf das folgende Gedicht' [he
means the fourth ode, discussed in the preceding part of the letter], and Solmsen, op. cit.
350.

this sentence strikes the same note as 3. 6. 5 *dis te minorem quod geris, imperas.*[1] It is, perhaps, less easy to see what exactly is the connexion between the second stanza and the following part of the ode. But I feel sure that we are not in danger of interpolating an alien element if we illustrate the thought which links ll. 9 ff., *est ut viro vir*, etc., to the sentence about the supreme power of Jupiter by quoting, as one of many similar passages, Pindar, *Isthm.* 5. 14 ff., μὴ μάτευε Ζεὺς γενέσθαι . . . θνατὰ θνατοῖσι πρέπει. This thought, again and again modified and modernized in popular philosophy, still meant a great deal to Horace. In the first of the Roman Odes he contents himself with merely implying it. The abruptness of the fresh start at l. 9 might, but need not, be regarded as a Pindarizing touch.

The cultural world in which the mind of an educated Roman moved was composed of a Greek and a Roman sphere. No picture of man's experience was complete unless both spheres were viewed together. This fundamental situation found a natural expression in a number of passages of the Augustan poets, where it produced both variation and comprehensiveness in an arrangement sometimes distinguished by a pleasing symmetry. A fine instance on a small scale occurs in the first sentence of *Georgics* III:

> Te quoque magna Pales et te memorande canemus
> pastor ab Amphryso,[2]

a more elaborate one in the same book, ll. 202–4, where the concluding line recalls in a general way Caesar's Gallic wars:

> hinc vel ad Elei metas et maxima campi
> sudabit spatia et spumas aget ore cruentas,
> Belgica vel molli melius feret esseda collo.

It is significant that here the Greek sphere is represented by the great national games and the Roman sphere by warfare. On a higher level we find the same complementary topics merged into one conception in *Georg.* 3. 17–20, where two lines are given to the Roman triumph and two to the Greek *agones*:

> illi victor ego et Tyrio conspectus in ostro
> centum quadriiugos agitabo ad flumina currus;
> cuncta mihi Alpheum linquens lucosque Molorchi
> cursibus et crudo decernet Graecia caestu.[3]

---

[1] Cf. Heinze on 3. 1. 5.

[2] Cf. 2. 37 f. *iuvat Ismara Baccho conserere atque olea magnum vestire Taburnum.*

[3] The wide hyperbaton *cuncta . . . Graecia* (cf., for instance, Cic. *Att.* 1. 16. 8, *omnem omnibus studiosis ac fautoribus illius victoriae* παρρησίαν *eripui* and p. 152 n. 1 above), expressing enormous emphasis, has the same effect as in Bach's 'Magnificat' the repetition (many times) of *omnes, omnes generationes.*

The panhellenic victory and the triumph on the Capitol, the greatest heights which men could reach, join together as if by nature, and Horace need not have remembered Virgil when he wrote in one of his maturest odes (4. 3. 3 ff.) :

> illum non labor Isthmius
> clarabit pugilem, non equus impiger

> curru ducet Achaico
> victorem, neque res bellica Deliis
> ornatum foliis ducem,
> quod regum tumidas contuderit minas,

> ostendet Capitolio.

In a still later ode the endurance of the Roman race is illustrated by two different comparisons, each filling a whole stanza, the one formed of a picture localized in the landscape of Latium,[1] the other of miraculous happenings in Greek mythical tales (4. 4. 57–64) :

> duris ut ilex tonsa bipennibus
> nigrae feraci frondis in Algido,
> per damna, per caedis ab ipso
> ducit opes animumque ferro.

> non hydra secto corpore firmior
> vinci dolentem crevit in Herculem
> monstrumve submisere Colchi
> maius Echioniaeve Thebae.

But the natural and most suggestive counterpart to figures and scenes of Greek mythology is provided by figures and scenes of Roman history. In *Odes* iv. 7 a nice balance is maintained between the early rulers of pre-Rome and Rome on the one side, Aeneas, Tullus, Ancus (15), and on the other side the heroes of Greek saga, Hippolytus and Pirithous (25–29). And when it is a question of great epic poetry, the warlike achievements of the Roman Republic are as worthy a subject for it as are the battles of the mythical age of Greece (*Odes* 2. 12. 1–9),

> Nolis longa ferae bella Numantiae
> nec durum Hannibalem nec Siculum mare
> Poeno purpureum sanguine mollibus
> aptari citharae modis,

> nec saevos Lapithas et nimium mero
> Hylaeum domitosque Herculea manu

---

[1] The motif, however, is Pindaric, see p. 430 n. 3 below.

Telluris iuvenes, unde periculum
fulgens contremuit domus

Saturni veteris.

But the most majestic example of a parallel representation of the two
spheres is found in the cycle of the Roman Odes. No attentive reader
will fail to notice how intimately the structure of *Odes* iii. 5 corresponds
to that of iii. 3: the dominating part of the one ode is the speech of
Juno, that of the other the speech of Regulus. Horace was, of course,
too careful an artist to repeat his arrangement mechanically: in iii. 3
the speech occupies nearly[1] thirteen out of eighteen stanzas, in iii. 5
nearly six out of fourteen; moreover, in iii. 3 the poem concludes
practically with the speech (the epilogue of the last stanza is clearly
separated), whereas in iii. 5 the speech is placed in the middle of the
ode. But these variations in detail cannot obscure the parallelism in
the structure of the two poems: in both the centre of interest lies in
the weighty speeches. Both are concerned with momentous decisions
in Rome's life. The setting, however, is different. In the third ode Juno's
address to the assembly of the Olympian gods carries on the Homeric
tradition as modified by Ennius,[2] in the fifth ode the narrative purports
to be an account of a famous event of the First Punic War. Taken together, the two scenes show the streams of Greek myth and of Roman
history flowing into a common bed. The parallelism in the structure of
Odes iii. 3 and iii. 5 has the effect that these two poems appear as a
frame in which Horace has set the principal piece of his cycle, iii. 4,
Descende caelo.

In Juno's speech in the third ode it is particularly the warning
against a resettlement of Troy (37–42, 57–68), that has exercised the
ingenuity of the commentators. It occurred to Tanaquil Faber to combine this topic with certain rumours about Caesar the dictator which,
according to Suetonius, *Iul.* 79. 3, circulated shortly before he was
murdered, *quin etiam varia fama percrebruit migraturum Alexandream vel
Ilium, translatis simul opibus imperii exhaustaque Italia dilectibus et pro-
curatione urbis amicis permissa*.[3] Faber, and, following him, many others,
assumed that Augustus was believed to fancy the same project, a
transfer of the capital to the east, with which the Roman gossip had

---

[1] Nearly, for it begins in the middle of the second line of a stanza (l. 18). It is no doubt
intentional that the speech of Regulus also begins precisely in the middle of l. 18.

[2] For the *concilium deorum* in Book I of Ennius' *Annales* (60–66 Vahlen), in which the
deification of Romulus was decreed, see Bentley on Hor. *Carm. Saec.* 16; Marx on Lucilius
3; C. Cichorius, *Untersuchungen zu Lucilius*, 222.

[3] R. Syme, *Pap. Brit. School Rome*, xiv, 1938, 2 n. 6, rightly observes: 'There is no indication that Suetonius believed what he retails as rumour.' This applies also to many similar
reports in Suetonius; cf. p. 6 n. 2 above.

credited Julius Caesar and that the purpose of Horace's ode was to discourage any such plan. Faber's hypothesis was divested of a good deal of its crudity by Orelli and, in a different way, by Mommsen,[1] but even in this mitigated form it proves unacceptable. It is still adhered to by a few scholars;[2] the majority, however, no longer attempt to read a political allegory into the text of the ode.[3]

The speech of Juno, when properly taken in its own setting, refuses to be turned into a piece of Augustan propaganda, and so does the passage of the *Aeneid* which has long been compared with it,[4] ending with *occidit, occideritque sinas cum nomine Troia*.[5] When a proud goddess makes an important concession, she must at least be permitted to score a modest point. That is what happens in the case of Virgil's and

---

[1] *Reden und Aufsätze*, 175: 'Der Dichter spricht nur aus, was die unvollkommene geschichtliche Überlieferung dieser Epoche zu melden versäumt hat. . . . es ist unzweifelhaft, daß . . . gleich mit den Anfängen der Monarchie die Frage in Rom ihren Einzug gehalten hat, ob für den lateinisch-griechischen Großstaat . . . die italische Kontinentalstadt der rechte Mittelpunkt sei', etc. Then Mommsen develops an idea suggested to him by Wilamowitz (see *Briefwechsel*, 359 and 361), viz. that the speech of Camillus in Livy v. 51–54 reflects the same discussions which lie behind the warnings of Horace's Juno 'Horaz wie Livius sprechen im Sinne des neuen Augustus': Rome is to remain the capital of the Empire. (As regards Livy, Warde Fowler, *Roman Essays*, 218 f., follows Mommsen.) It should, however, be noticed that, though the speech of Camillus is Livy's own work, the topic which forms its theme, viz. the project of abandoning the ruins of Rome and emigrating to Veii, belongs to an earlier author, as a comparison with Plutarch, *Camillus* 31 f., puts beyond doubt; cf. A. Klotz, *Rh. Mus.* xc, 1941, 301 f. A warning against underrating the conventional nature of that topic may also be derived from the following passages: Cic. *Leg. Agr.* 1. 18 *Capuam deduci colonos volunt, illam urbem huic urbi rursus opponere, illuc opes suas deferre et imperii nomen transferre cogitant*, 2. 86 *tunc illud vexillum Campanae coloniae vehementer huic imperio timendum Capuam a decemviris inferetur, tunc contra hanc Romam communem patriam omnium nostrum illa altera Roma quaeretur. in id oppidum homines nefarii rem publicam vestram transferre conantur*, etc.

[2] For example by Harald Fuchs, *Der geistige Widerstand gegen Rom*, 1938, 12 and 39 n. 34.

[3] Among the first, as far as I can see, to state the simple truth were Paul Shorey, *Horace, Odes and Epodes*, 1898, 313, on ll. 17–68, who also observes that 'the treatment of myth gives the ode a Pindaric cast', and Lucian Müller, *Q. Horatius Flaccus, Oden und Epoden*, i, 1900, 218 f., who, in summing up his re-examination of the problem, says: 'Es erscheint also für die vorliegende, wie für die übrigen Digressionen des III. Buches, ein poetisches, nicht ein politisches oder sonst praktisches Motiv maßgebend.' Substantially the same view is held by, for example, Reitzenstein, *Gött. gel. Anz.* 1904, 957 f.; Heinze; Amundsen, *Serta Eitremiana*, 1942, 14 f.

[4] 12. 819–28. See, for example, C. G. Heyne on *Aen.* 12. 827; L. Müller, *Horatius, Oden und Epoden*, i, 217 bottom.

[5] E. Norden, *Neue Jahrb.* 1901, i. 323, reproduces Mommsen's view in a somewhat crude form, 'Augustus ließ, wie besonders Mommsen durch Interpretation der dritten Römerode des Horaz gezeigt hat, diesen Plan offiziell desavouieren', and adds the footnote 'Vergil XII 819–837 spricht denselben Gedanken in gleicher äußerer Szenerie aus'; and R. Syme, *Roman Revolution*, 305 (cf. also *JRS* xxxiv, 1944, 101) says 'When the Triumvir Antonius abode for long years in the East men might fear . . . lest the capital of empire be transferred to other lands. The propaganda of Octavianus had skilfully worked upon such apprehensions. Once aroused they would be difficult to allay: their echo could still be heard. Horace produces a divine decree, forbidding Troy ever to be rebuilt (*Odes* 3. 3. 57 ff.); Virgil is quite explicit (*Aen.* 12. 828); and Livy duly demonstrates how the patriot Camillus', etc.

of Horace's Juno. The condition under which the goddess agrees to an appeasement is a matter of ordinary human feeling and therefore of poetry, with no political implication whatever. There is nothing to indicate that under the early principate a transfer of the capital to the east was ever ventilated or that any propaganda was directed against such an idea.

No hypothesis about a hidden political or moral message should divert our attention from the most remarkable fact in the poem itself, the preponderance of the long speech of the goddess. Let us not, however, go too far and treat the first four stanzas as a mere prelude to the Olympian scene. The endless talk of some of our contemporaries about the 'Roman virtues' is certainly tiresome, but it must not make us forget that a just and brave man's steadfastness was to Horace something essential and noble, something he was glad to praise. Nowhere did he praise it with greater dignity than in these stanzas which culminate in a vision of Michelangelesque force,

> si fractus inlabatur orbis,
> impavidum ferient ruinae.

He then goes on to show this ideal embodied in the ancient ἀλεξίκακοι, the saviours of mankind, who through their ἀρετή have won Heaven, and among whom Augustus is to take his place.[1] These ideas meant a great deal to Horace, but they alone would not have given sufficient scope to a poem which was destined to form part of the monumental cycle. The mythical scene proved the means not only of increasing the size of the ode but also of making a stronger appeal to the imagination. In constructing this scene Horace availed himself of a device which he was fond of using: he condensed the main points of the action into a direct speech of a leading character and added to it only the minimum of narrative indispensable to the understanding. This type of arrangement is found on a small scale in Epode XIII and Odes i. 7 and on a larger scale in Odes i. 15, iii. 11, and iii. 27; the latter group shows a structure reminiscent of Pindar and especially of Bacchylides.

We may now, with the necessary modification, apply to Odes iii. 3 and iii. 5 what we have learnt from our analysis of iii. 11 and iii. 27.[2] The ideas expressed at the beginning of Iustum et tenacem and of Caelo tonantem are doubtless of far greater dignity than the love affairs of the girls who, mere προτατικὰ πρόσωπα, stand on the threshold of the Hypermestra ode and the Europa ode. Consequently the opening sections of iii. 3 and iii. 5, compared with those of iii. 11 and iii. 27, appear richer and deeper and also more intimately connected with the later parts of the poems. Odes iii. 3 and, let us add at once, iii. 5 are

---

[1] Of course bibet at l. 12.   [2] See pp. 192 ff. above.

more harmonious compositions than iii. 11 and iii. 27. Nevertheless, these two Roman Odes give the impression that the real interest of the poet was in the speeches of Juno and of Regulus. It seems to me very likely that these speeches began to shape themselves in Horace's mind as soon as he conceived the idea of having the hymn *Descende caelo* surrounded by two broadly symmetrical odes in the grand manner. It follows, then, that due consideration should be given to the autonomous rights of the two speeches with their background in myth and history, and that their dependence on the opening parts of the odes should not be pressed. A certain degree of independence was, in the opinion of Horace, justified also by the model of Greek choric lyrics.

The speech of Juno contains, interwoven with the main theme of the goddess's solemn promise and her warning against greed,[1] a great deal of magnificent detail, starting from the tragic fate of Troy and passing on to a glorification of Rome and her present régime. In the latter section there is one passage of particular significance (53–56),

> quicumque mundo terminus obstitit,
> hunc tanget armis, visere gestiens,
> qua parte debacchentur ignes,
> qua nebulae pluviique rores.

A surprising motive for the warlike enterprise of the Roman soldier![2] From what we read here, we might believe him to be under the patronage of Pallas Athene rather than of Father Mars. The tendency expressed in the clause *visere gestiens*, etc. is in fact a continuation and a revival of that ceaseless striving for ἱστορίη which was the greatest achievement of old Ionia and was bequeathed by her to Athens and to the Hellenistic world. At an early period, long before the age of science dawned, the experiences of certain daring Ionian sailors, who ventured to distant coasts and saw strange peoples, played a part in forming the figure of Odysseus,[3] and thousands of years later, when Greece had become a dim saga, the genius of Dante created in his *Ulisse* the eternal prototype of the man to whom it is an axiom that πάντες ἄνθρωποι τοῦ εἰδέναι ὀρέγονται φύσει[4] and who pays with his life for *l'ardore ch' i' ebbi a*

---

[1] This thought, important in itself, forms also a link with the whole cycle; cf. especially the first and the sixth poem. However, Reitzenstein's summary, *Gött. gel. Anz.* 1904, 958, 'die Göttin verheißt Rom Weltherrschaft und Sieg über alle Feinde, freilich unter der Bedingung daß es *avaritia* und *luxuria* in sich überwindet; das scheint mir der Kern des Gedichtes', seems to me one-sided. One of the greatest obstacles to an understanding of many Horatian odes is perhaps our readiness to substitute for *Orazio lirico* an *Orazio politico* or *Orazio moralista* or both.

[2] Markland *was* surprised and therefore changed *visere* to *vincere* (in the appendix to his edition of Eur. *Suppl.*, p. 256).

[3] See Eduard Schwartz, *Vorträge über den griechischen Roman*, 15 ff., *Die Odyssee*, 197.

[4] *Considerate la vostra semenza:* | *fatti non foste a viver come bruti,* | *ma per seguir virtute e canoscenza* (*Inf.* 26. 118–20).

divenir del mondo esperto. A classic formulation of what lies behind Horace's *visere gestiens* is given in the words which Herodotus makes Croesus speak to Solon (1. 30. 2) φιλοσοφέων γῆν πολλὴν θεωρίης εἵνεκεν ἐπελήλυθας.[1] That this Greek passion for θεωρίη worked as an incitement to long journeys, not only in the case of uncommon men like Solon, is for the later sixth century shown by Herodotus, 3. 139. 1, Καμβύσεω τοῦ Κύρου στρατευομένου ἐπ' Αἴγυπτον ἄλλοι τε συχνοὶ ἐς τὴν Αἴγυπτον ἀπίκοντο Ἑλλήνων, οἱ μέν, ὡς οἰκός, κατ' ἐμπορίην, οἱ δὲ στρατευόμενοι, οἱ δέ τινες καὶ αὐτῆς χώρης θεηταί. The same passion would also induce men to join in a dangerous campaign: Thucydides, describing the reactions of the Athenians to the plan of the Sicilian expedition, says (6. 24. 3): καὶ ἔρως ἐνέπεσε τοῖς πᾶσιν ὁμοίως ἐκπλεῦσαι· τοῖς μὲν γὰρ πρεσβυτέροις . . . τοῖς δ' ἐν τῇ ἡλικίᾳ τῆς τε ἀπούσης πόθῳ ὄψεως καὶ θεωρίας, καὶ εὐέλπιδες ὄντες σωθήσεσθαι. In the present context we are more concerned with the attitude of the common soldier and the ordinary officer than with the activities of the 'professional' scientists such as those who, from the time of Alexander the Great,[2] were attached to the staff of many military·expeditions, Greek and Roman;[3] but there is no sharp dividing line between the interests of the two classes. In the last centuries of the Roman Republic it will have happened more than once that not only the commander-in-chief and his learned companions[4] but also some of the rank and file felt the urge to see and explore the remote parts of the earth, *more humanae cupidinis ignara visendi.*[5] But no matter how often it happened in actual life,[6] the

---

[1] Cf. Arist. *Ath.* 11. 1 (Solon) ἀποδημίαν ἐποιήσατο κατ' ἐμπορίαν ἅμα καὶ θεωρίαν εἰς Αἴγυπτον.

[2] Of Alexander himself our sources often say that πόθος λαμβάνει αὐτόν (ʋr something similar) to see this or that place or sanctuary. This topic and the unmistakable influence it has had on the reports which the Roman historians give about several generals has been a favourite subject of modern discussion. That does not, however, justify Franz Christ, 'Die römische Weltherrschaft in der antiken Dichtung', *Tübinger Beiträge zur Altertumswissenschaft*, 31. Heft, 1938, 58, in saying '*visere gestiens* . . . das ist gar nichts anderes als das innere Moment, das die Alexanderhistoriker für viele Handlungen ihres Helden als Motiv angeben: der πόθος der nun auf den anonymen "Romanus" übertragen wird', etc. That this is much too narrow will appear from what has been said above. The πόθος occurs also in Thuc. 6. 24. 3.

[3] The contribution which the reports of men who took part in military expeditions made to knowledge in geography and ethnology in the Hellenistic and Roman world is well illustrated by E. Norden in several places in his book *Die germanische Urgeschichte in Tacitus Germania*, 1920; on 434 n. 3 he collects passages in which Strabo traces geographical information to some στρατεύσαντες. On a detail however, namely the exploration of the coasts of Africa supposed to have been undertaken by Polybius and Panaetius, the view put forward by Cichorius and accepted by Norden (32) is based on insufficient evidence; see Pohlenz, 'Panaitios', *RE* xviii. 2. H. 422.

[4] Cicero writes to Trebatius (*Fam.* 7. 16, 1) *quod in Britannia non nimis* φιλοθέωρον *te praebuisti, plane non reprehendo.*

[5] Sallust, *Hist.* i, *fr.* 103 Maur.

[6] Military expeditions were not, of course, the only occasions on which the motive of θεωρία came into play. In connexion with the famous embassy to the East undertaken at

poet was entitled to say of the Roman soldier (for it is he who is primarily thought of although the grammatical subject in 53 ff. remains *Roma*) that he sets out to conquer the ends of the world, *visere gestiens, qua parte debacchentur ignes, qua nebulae pluviique rores*. The Roman whom Horace has in mind, while being true to the character and to the past of his own nation, shall not be averse to the zeal for θεωρία, but shall, in this as in every other respect, be also the heir and preserver of what is noblest in the Greek tradition.[1]

The structure of *Odes* iii. 5 and that of iii. 3 show a marked parallelism.[2] Both poems, written probably about the same time, in 27 B.C., clearly originate in a common plan.[3]

With a sound instinct Horace chose as counterpart to the scene of Juno the story of Regulus, 'a myth from Roman history'.[4] The merit of this choice is not impaired by the fact that the story was probably a good deal more hackneyed to the poet's contemporaries than it is to us.[5] From the point of view of the modern historian it may deserve to be called a silly story, but to Horace it afforded an opportunity for a great oration against a tragic background. The end of the hero is not

the order of the Senate by the younger Scipio Africanus the collector of the *Apopthegmata regum*, 'optimis fontibus usus' (F. Marx, *Lucilii Reliquiae*, ii. 172), reports ([Plut.] *Mor.* 200 E) ἐκπεμφθέντα . . . ὑπὸ τῆς βουλῆς . . . πόλεων ἐθνῶν βασιλέων ἐπίσκοπον κτλ. Here, however, there is clearly a political purpose involved.

[1] The important *visere gestiens* is suppressed, or watered down, by several scholars. Conington translates, 'Whate'er the bound to earth ordain'd, There let her reach the arm of power, Travelling, where raves the fire unrein'd, And where the storm-cloud and the shower', and J. Lonsdale and S. Lee ('The Globe Edition of the Works of Horace'), whose rendering is on the whole accurate, give 'Whatever boundary . . . of the world, it she shall reach with her hosts, *exulting* [my italics] to visit the region where,' etc. Similarly Wickham paraphrases '. . . she shall reach them with her arms, and *rejoice* [my italics] to see with her own eyes', etc., and Ussani glosses *gestiens* by 'esultando'. It is well known that *exsultare* comes very near the 'original' meaning of *gestire*, and that *gestire* is fairly often used in this sense, in Early Latin and after. But when it has this meaning it never, before St. Augustine, governs an infinitive. Of *gestire* = *vehementer cupere* with the infinitive there are seven instances in Horace, correctly listed in *Thes. l. Lat.* vi. 2. 1961. 60 ff. Were the scholars whom I have quoted perhaps shocked by the un-Roman appearance of the thought in *visere gestiens*?

[2] See p. 267 above.

[3] See especially Haffter, *Philol.* xciii, 1938, 132 f., 155 f.

[4] 'Ein Mythus aus der römischen Geschichte', Haffter, op. cit. 149.

[5] The legend of Regulus' embassy to Rome and of his subsequent horrible death is unknown to Polybius; the first to speak of it, as far as we can see, is C. Sempronius Tuditanus, cos. 129 B.C.; cf. Klebs, *RE* ii. 2088 ff., De Sanctis, *Storia dei Romani*, iii. 1. 154 ff. From Cicero, *De orat.* 3. 109 (Orelli–Baiter on *Odes* 3. 5. 13 did well to refer to it) as well as *Att.* 16. 11. 4, it is clear that at Cicero's time (and probably earlier) the *causa Reguli* was a famous theme in the schools of the rhetoricians. The relevance of Cic. *Off.* 1. 39 for the version of the Regulus story which Horace follows was pointed out as early as Lambinus. For a thorough examination of the tradition see now H. Kornhardt, *Hermes*, lxxxii, 1954, 101 ff.

narrated but only hinted at;[1] in the way it veils what happened after
the speech this poem is very similar to the Hypermestra ode, iii. 11.

The link between the first three stanzas of *Caelo tonantem* and the
'myth' which fills the rest of the ode is certainly close. And yet the
reader, unless he is of the dogmatizing sort, will feel that it is not
because Horace wants to illustrate the case of the prisoners of Carrhae
that he tells the story of Regulus, but that he dwells on the disgrace of
the prisoners because he wants to pave his way to the story of Regulus.
There were, after all, other possibilities of elaborating the thought that
the shameful defeat of Crassus must be avenged; above all, the sur-
render of the captured standards might have been mentioned. But
Horace produced for the second and the third stanzas of his ode a topic
which would directly lead up to the central theme of the Regulus scene.
This scene owes its place in the ode to the artistic potentialities which
the poet found in it and not to its usefulness in a political debate.
Mommsen regarded the fifth ode as a reply to the clamour of public
opinion for the release of the Roman prisoners in Parthian hands. So
he made it appear as a brilliant piece of versified politics; but the
critics soon learnt not to be dazzled.[2] A survey of the more recent discussion might almost encourage the hope that some readers, and even
some professional scholars, will in course of time again get used to the
idea that Horace was primarily a poet.

We have seen that *Odes* iii. 3 and iii. 5, important in themselves,
serve also as a frame for iii. 4, *Descende caelo*. This arrangement emphasizes the high significance of the fourth ode.[3] Another formal element
points in the same direction: *Descende caelo* with its twenty stanzas is the
longest of these six poems and indeed the longest of all Horatian odes.
This is not a matter of mere size: the extension beyond the normal

---

[1] A fine appreciation of the conclusion of the ode is given by A. Y. Camp bell, *Horace*
1924, 226.

[2] Almost immediately after the publication of Mommsen's lecture Kiessling, in the
second edition of his commentary (1890), protested against the great man's interpretation
of the fifth ode. Later it was rejected by Reitzenstein, *Gött. gel. Anz.* 1904, 957; Heinze
became increasingly sceptical of it (in this regard the difference between the sixth edition
of his commentary and the seventh is instructive, see also his remarks *Neue Jahrb.* 1929, 685
f.); Haffter, op. cit., held much the same view, and an opinion such as Amundsen's
(*Serta Eitremiana*, 1942, 22), 'the myth of Regulus lives its own life', is no longer heretical.
Warde Fowler, *Roman Essays*, 223 f., in 1920 still maintained allegiance to Mommsen.

[3] I find it, not impossible, but hard to believe that iii. 4 was not planned and executed
about the same time as iii. 3 and iii. 5, i.e. in 27 B.C. It seems to me that the objections to
this date have been refuted by W. Theiler, 'Das Musengedicht des Horaz', *Schriften der
Königsberger Gelehrten Ges.*, G. Kl. xii. 4, 1935, 263 f., who in this connexion does full
justice to the tenth stanza (37–40, the settlement of the veterans) and its bearing on the
chronological problem. His arguments, however, have failed to convince Klingner,
Gnomon, xiii, 1937, 41, and Haffter, *Philol.* xciii, 1938, 155.

helps to bring out the greatness and dignity of a subject which in itself
μέγεθος ἔχει καὶ ἀξίωμα.

The first stanza,[1] an exordium not inferior to the proem of the whole
cycle, is bound to raise high expectations. Its lofty note is maintained
in the next stanza, which shows the poet seized by the rapture of θεία
μανία.[2] But then a new thought sets in, and the manner in which it is
presented is apt to disappoint the reader. 'What have Horace's youthful ramblings to do with Augustus' victory over Antony?' This question, asked by an American scholar,[3] represents a typical reaction of
the unprejudiced modern mind.[4] And, in all probability, not of the
modern mind only. We may safely assume that the average reader in
the city of Rome was even more startled than we are when he found
that the solemn invocation of the first stanza and the inspired vision of
the second are followed by a scene in which not only the very ordinary
name of Horace's nurse[5] appears but also the names of three townlets
in the district of Venusia,[6] the existence of which was presumably unknown to anyone who had not lived in that far-off part of Italy.[7] So the
oddity is not an imaginary one. In such a case no good can come from
trying to silence the voice of our discomfort by telling ourselves: 'these
things *are* strange, but this is the work of a classic, and therefore, whatever my own reactions, everything must be all right'. It is more sincere
and more profitable to register the difficulty as it appears to us, and

---

[1] Its hymnic topics, derived from Greek poetry, are well illustrated in the commentaries.
[2] This stanza shares some characteristic features with *Odes* iii. 25. For the force of the
epithet in *amabilis insania* see below, p. 408 n. 3.
[3] Tenney Frank, *Am. Journ. Phil.* xlii, 1921, 171. The thesis of this article, that *Descende caelo* must be regarded as an artistic failure, since it has not been blended into a real
unity, is repeated in Frank's book *Catullus and Horace*, 1928, 225 f.
[4] I recently read the ode with a keen and intelligent 'Upper Bench' at Rugby. These
young men, blissfully ignorant of all the learned discussion about it, immediately put their
finger on the difficulty which we are examining and showed themselves unhappy about
the various ups and downs in the poem and its apparent jumble of heterogeneous matter.
Of printed opinions which show the same attitude I will, in addition to T. Frank's article,
quote only A. Palmer's indignant question (published posthumously in *Hermathena*, lx,
1942, 101), 'But is it to be supposed that Horace could think his readers would care to
know his nurse's name?' and the assertion in Valentina Capocci's booklet *Difesa di
Orazio*, Bari 1951, 65, that this ode 'si frantuma negli elementi più disparati, autobiografia,
attualità, mito, che non riescono a fondersi e restano quasi meccanicamente accozzati
insieme'. Peerlkamp's reaction was the same, and so he excised the 'autobiografia' of
ll. 9–20 and a good deal besides.
[5] 'nutricis extra limina Pulliae . . . . Der Name ist gewöhnlich und die Nennung der
Amme hier ebenso berechtigt wie die der drei apulischen Städtchen', Mommsen, *Reden
und Aufsätze*, 177 n. 1. For instances of *Pullius* and *Pullia* see, for example, the index to
Dessau's *Inscr. lat. sel.* iii. 1. 122.
[6] Cf. H. Nissen, *Ital. Landeskunde*, ii. 831, 907 f.
[7] Far-off even nowadays, for 'Cristo si è fermato a Eboli'. If the name of Bantia is more
familiar to modern scholars than it presumably was to the Romans in Horace's time, it is
on account of the famous bronze tablet, the 'tabula Bantina', with its Oscan and Latin
texts.

then to wait and see whether perhaps, as the poem unfolds, some convincing solution offers itself. If, unfortunately, this should not happen, we must in no circumstances resort to violent remedies or merely argue our perplexity away. Just as an honest editor of a text will dagger the phrase he is forced to consider corrupt but feels unable to emend, so an honest reader should put a mental dagger against the passage which, either in itself or in its context, defeats his understanding.

It was a bold venture when Horace transferred to his own childhood the kind of miracle with which the biographical tradition had adorned the early life of several great Greek poets.[1] The boldness is increased by the insertion of some realistic detail such as the name of Horace's nurse and the list of obscure towns in the neighbourhood of Venusia. The manner in which the fabulous happenings are worked out compels us to view them against a real background and under a glaring sunshine while we, brought up in conventions of romantic poetry, might prefer such miracles to take place in the twilight between the land of fairy-story and the world of every-day life. Nor is the strain on our imagination very much eased in the following stanza (21–24). We should not regard it as impossible that some privileged individuals should manage to write tolerable poetry even during the summer season at Brighton or Bournemouth. But from what we know about life at Baiae during the Augustan period we may be mildly surprised to learn that the Muses, wanting to pay a visit to their old friend, should have chosen the time when he was staying at that fashionable seaside resort. The next stanza (25–28), too, continues in what seems to be an autobiographical strain: on three occasions Horace's life was miraculously saved. Then the prospect widens (29, *utcumque mecum vos eritis . . .*), and through one of the poet's delicate transitions we are led to remote corners of the inhabited world,[2] where the appearance of such menacing tribes as the Britanni, the Concani, the Geloni, and the Scythians on the banks of the Don inevitably calls to mind the man who is now expected to keep them all in submission and peace, Caesar. After this preparation a fresh start, l. 37, *vos Caesarem altum*, carries the poem in a few majestic sentences up to its summit. Looking back from this height at the plainness of the stanzas III–VII (9–28), where a great deal of homely detail diverted our attention and where the poet seemed to be wrapped in egocentric recollections, we feel the same uneasiness as when we

[1] In Pindar's tale, *Ol.* 6. 45 ff. (I do not know why Heinze in his last edition, 1930, cut out Kiessling's reference to this poem), the infant Iamos is nurtured by two snakes with honey (for ἀμεμφεῖ ἰῷ μελισσᾶν see Wilamowitz, *Isyllos von Epidauros*, 165 n. 13), to indicate that he is to be a sweet-voiced seer (hence the snakes).

[2] The topic of ll. 29–36 is fundamentally the same as in *Odes* I. 22. 5–8 and 17–22, where, however, political implications are completely absent.

entered that part of the poem after leaving the magnificent first two stanzas. Was Horace really insensitive to what strikes us, at any rate so far, as a disharmony? Or is there perhaps a particular reason for this admixture of 'formidable realism' in one of his most exalted poems? We shall return to this question. But first the ode must be approached from a different angle.

It has long been observed[1] that ll. 61–64,

> qui rore puro Castaliae lavit
> crinis solutos, qui Lyciae tenet
> dumeta natalemque silvam,
>   Delius et Patareus Apollo,[2]

derive from Pindar,[3] Λύκιε καὶ Δάλοι' ἀνάσσων Φοῖβε, Παρνασσοῦ τε κράναν Κασταλίαν φιλέων. It seems strange that the commentators should not have followed up this trace to find out whether the influence of Pindar's first Pythian ode on *Descende caelo* is limited to the one stanza. The only two 'professional' scholars who seem to have grasped the extent to which the very conception of this ode depends, not on Pindar's poems in general, but on his first Pythian ode, are, so far as I can see, Wilamowitz and Reitzenstein.[4] Before I noticed their brief remarks, I had made a detailed comparison of *Pythian* I and *Odes* iii. 4 and reached the conclusions which I am here trying to summarize. It is

[1] Mitscherlich, whose commentary was published in 1800, says 'observarunt iam alii'.

[2] It was this stanza that floated through Clough's mind when he was repeopling the niches of the Pantheon 'with the mightier forms of an older, austerer worship' (*Amours de Voyage*, viii). He was probably unaware that what he had conjured up was a piece of Pindar.

[3] *Pyth.* 1. 39 ff.

[4] Wilamowitz: see his letter of 8 Jan. 1889 in *Mommsen und Wilamowitz, Briefwechsel*, 360; Reitzenstein, *Gött. gel. Anz.* 1904, 958 n. 1 and *Neue Jahrb.* 1922, 34. Cf. also Kling-ner's brief remark, *Die Antike*, xiii, 1937, 226 (reprinted in his *Römische Geisteswelt*, 3rd. ed., 371). Long ago part of the truth was seen by R. Rauchenstein, *Zur Einleitung in Pindar's Siegeslieder*, 1843, 148, who, after analysing Pythian I, says, 'Es ist ein ähnlicher Gedanke, wie ihn Horaz Od. III, 4. von der Mitte des Liedes an durchführt.' Here it is fitting to pay homage to the scholarship and penetrating mind of Macaulay. In a letter from Calcutta, Feb. 1835 (*The Life and Letters of Lord Macaulay* by . . . Sir George Otto Trevelyan, i. 399 of the edition in 'The World's Classics') he writes: 'I have read Pindar. . . . I was always puzzled to understand the reason for the extremely abrupt transitions in those Odes of Horace which are meant to be particularly fine. The "justum et tenacem" [*Odes* iii. 3] is an instance. All at once you find yourself in heaven, Heaven knows how. What the firmness of just men in times of tyranny, or of tumult, has to do with Juno's oration about Troy it is hardly possible to conceive. Then, again, how strangely the fight between the Gods and the Giants is tacked on to the fine hymn to the Muses in that noble ode, "Descende caelo et dic age tibiâ"! This always struck me as a great fault. . . . My explanation of it is this. The Odes of Pindar', etc. Macaulay, writing at that time, could not, of course, be expected to have formed a true idea of Horace's intentions and of the quality of his Roman Odes, but his sincere and courageous θαυμάζειν led him to see what remained hidden to most Horatian scholars. My attention was drawn to this letter by the Registrar of the University of Oxford, Sir Douglas Veale; afterwards I saw that W. Kroll, *Studien zum Verständnis der röm. Lit.* 246 n., briefly refers to it.

a recognized fact, and the evidence can be found in the commentaries,[1] that *Descende caelo* is interspersed with reminiscences from various Pindaric poems.[2] But it is even more important to realize that only the first Pythian ode influenced Horace's poem in a deeper sense, since it not merely suggested some detail but inspired the general plan of this great ode.

Within the limits of this book it is neither possible nor necessary to give an idea of the overwhelming beauty and the organic structure of Pindar's first Pythian ode, which has been called 'the most sublime of all lyrical poems.'[3] All that is required for the present purpose is a bare outline, not of the whole poem, but of some parts of it.

It is no accident nor is it due to an error or an arbitrary decision of some classifying ancient grammarian that Χρυσέα φόρμιγξ has found its place among the Pythian epinikia. It celebrates indeed a victory won by Hiero in the chariot-race in a Pythian contest, and we may be sure that it was performed in the manner customary for epinikia.[4] But far more important than that success at Delphi was the extraordinary event which Pindar had been asked to extol in the same poem. Hiero, 'the eminent statesman who ruled in Syracuse and practically controlled the destinies of Sicily',[5] wanted his son Deinomenes to be a king in his own right, and for this end, enlarging the town of Katana at the foot of Mount Etna, he founded the city of Aitna, of which Deinomenes was to be the first king.[6]

Χρυσέα φόρμιγξ . . . : the opening part of the poem is perhaps the greatest praise of music ever written. Music, the lyre's work, comes from heaven, or, as Pindar conceives it, the lyre belongs by right to Apollo and the Muses. The music that is meant here may seem to be merely the music to which Pindar's audience is listening here and now, produced by the lyre (or perhaps the cithara) playing a few bars by

---

[1] See also W. Theiler, *Das Musengedicht des Horaz, passim,* and Elsbeth Harms, *Horaz in seinen Beziehungen zu Pindar* (Diss. Marburg 1936), 12 ff.

[2] Special attention should here be paid to Pindar's latest epinikion, one of his most moving poems, Pythian VIII, with its contrast between 'Ησυχία, the daughter of Dike, through whom cities prosper, and the Giants Porphyrio and Typhos (cf. Wade-Gery, *JHS* lii, 1932, 214 f.).

[3] G. Norwood, 'Pindar', *Sather Classical Lectures,* xix, Berkeley 1945, 101.

[4] If Pindar had really intended to write a 'Festchoral' for the celebration of the foundation of Aitna, he would probably have given it the form of a hymn to Ζεὺς Αἰτναῖος. What he did do was to write an epinikion, different from any other, and yet unmistakably a Pythian epinikion: the prayer to Apollo, 39–40b, would alone be sufficient proof (see especially the crowning piece of the τρίκωλον which makes up the vocative, Παρνασσοῦ τε κράναν Κασταλίαν φιλέων). The context (from 35, or rather from 30, on) in which this invocation is set makes it clear that what Apollo is implored to grant to the new city is, not solely, yet primarily a sequence of agonistic victories as glorious as the one which Hiero's chariot recently won at Kirrha.

[5] Ed. Schwartz, *Charakterköpfe,* i. 17.

[6] Cf. also my remarks, *Eranos,* lii, 1954, 68 ff.

way of prelude, and then also by the choir as they join in with their voices and their strictly regulated movements. In the text, however, there is nothing confining the thought to a 'here and now'. The first period of the poem applies indeed to the present performance, but it applies no less to any similar celebration wherever it takes place. In the following sentences (from 5 καὶ τὸν αἰχματὰν κεραυνόν) the orbit of the thought widens greatly. The power of music, this present music and music in general, is effective throughout the world: it puts out the fire of that warrior thunderbolt, it lulls the eagle on the sceptre of Zeus into slumber; even the violent Ares leaves the battle and lets his heart enjoy profound sleep, and the darts of the music strike with a spell the souls of the gods, through the craft of Apollo and the Muses. At this point, after the conclusion of the first pair of stanzas, the epode begins with a powerful contrast: ὅσσα δὲ μὴ πεφίληκε Ζεύς. 'But all those with whom Zeus is not in friendship . . .'[1]—they all are alarmed when they hear the voice of the Muses, all that live on the earth and in the sea, and he who lies in Tartarus, the foe of the gods, Typhos of the hundred heads, who was once reared in the Cilician cave, but now the ridges beyond Cumae and the land of Sicily press upon his shaggy breast, and heaven's pillar holds him down, snow-clad Etna (13–20). The whole of the next stanza and the beginning of the next but one are filled with the description of an eruption of Mount Etna, caused by Typhos, who, bound on a couch of sharp stone under the volcano, tries to change the position of his tortured body and thereby shakes and cleaves the mountain, out of which there burst with a thundering noise streams of fire and smoke and huge pieces of rock.

It is natural that the mountain, the beautiful and terrifying Etna, should play so prominent a role in the poem which was to glorify the foundation of the city lying at its foot. Nor is there anything far-fetched in bringing in Typhos, who provides an eminent example of the general statement (13 f.) about those to whom Zeus is no friend and who also suggests Mount Etna and so leads up to the centre of the poem. In the story which Pindar followed (as did afterwards Aeschylus), Typhos, after the failure of his attempt to commit high treason, was sentenced to penal servitude for life (life in his case being eternity); his prison was situated beneath Sicily's great volcano. Since he was a gigantic monster, it would be unfair to grudge him for his enormous limbs the space of some dozen extra square miles under the surface of the earth. But it seems rather excessive to allow his body to stretch all

---

[1] πεφίληκε is a typical 'Resultativperfektum': in the past Zeus did not extend his φιλεῖν to them, and consequently they are not now among his φίλοι. For other 'Resultativperfekta' in Pindar see J. Wackernagel, *Studien zum griechischen Perfektum* (Göttingen 1904) 9 (*Kl. Schriften*, 1006).

the way from the root of Mount Etna to the northern end of the gulf of Naples. This geographical extravagance did not form part of the traditional story: Pindar invented it himself for the purpose of this particular poem. Cumae, surprisingly mentioned in the first triad, points to the climax of the ode, the praise of the great victories recently won by the Deinomenids, Gelon and his younger brother and successor Hiero (71–80). To any western Greek, at the time when Pindar's poem was performed, in 470 B.C., the name of Cumae carried powerful associations. In 474/3 the people of Cumae, threatened by an Etruscan fleet, had appealed to Hiero, who sent a squadron to their rescue, which inflicted a decisive defeat on the Etruscans and thus prevented them from becoming the masters of southern Italy.[1] Pindar justly connects this event with the still more momentous battle of Himera in which Gelon, together with Theron of Akragas, had defeated a large Carthaginian army. Pindar knew, and pronounced in mighty sentences, what was probably hidden to many intelligent men in the old lands of Hellas, that the overthrow of the two great barbarian powers in the west, the Carthaginians and the Etruscans, was not less important to the survival of the freedom and the very life of the Greek world than was the overthrow of the Persians at Salamis and Plataea, which was achieved at the same time by Athens and Sparta. It is not on account of the splendour commonly attached to such successes that Pindar, who abhorred war,[2] glorifies the military victories of the rulers of Syracuse: he does so because only through these victories was it possible to secure peace. The passage in which the great battles are extolled forms part of a prayer to Zeus of Aitna. Zeus shall enable Hiero and his son, the young king of the new city, to direct the people towards harmonious peace, δᾶμον . . . τράποι σύμφωνον ἐς ἡσυχίαν, by which primarily internal peace is meant. After these words the prayer continues 'grant, I implore thee, son of Kronos, that the Phoenician and the battle-cry of the Etruscans may stay at home in peace and quiet' and so forth.[3]

---

[1] A memorial of this victory is extant, the famous bronze helmet dedicated by Hiero to Zeus at Olympia, where it was discovered in 1817. Shortly afterwards, when the helmet was not yet in the British Museum, Boeckh used it to illustrate the background of Pindar's poem. The inscription on it runs: Ἰάρων ὁ Δεινομένεος | καὶ τοὶ Συρακόσιοι | τῶι Δὶ Τυράν' (= Τυρρανὰ) ἀπὸ Κύμας.

[2] Fr. 110 Schroeder, Snell (99 Bowra, 120 Turyn) γλυκὺ δὲ πόλεμος ἀπείροισιν· ἐμπείρων δέ τις ταρβεῖ προσιόντα νιν καρδίᾳ περισσῶς (adapted, as Lambinus saw, by Horace, Epist. I. 18. 86 f.).

[3] The construction ὄφρα κατ' οἶκον ἔχῃ (intrans.) should not be questioned on the ground that 'intransitive ἔχω does not occur in Pindar'. Christ, ad loc., rightly refers to Hdt. 6. 39. 2 Μιλτιάδης . . . εἶχε κατ' οἴκους. Cf. also Hdt. 6. 42. 2 κατὰ χώρην . . . ἔχοντες, Ar. Frogs 793 ἕξειν κατὰ χώραν. It appears, then, that ἔχειν κατ' οἶκον, ἔχειν κατὰ χώραν, and the like, were set phrases in the ordinary Greek of the fifth century; Pindar must not be forbidden to use them. In the following part of the sentence the epexegesis of ναυσίστονον ὕβριν by means of οἷα . . . πάθον is perfect.

This sentence and the following section are connected with what we might call Hiero's foreign policy, but the wish that the enemy should stay at home in peace and quiet is the necessary complement to, and another aspect of, the prayer that the rulers of Aitna may turn their people σύμφωνον ἐς ἡσυχίαν. Here the noun denoting calm and peace is given the attribute 'harmonious', σύμφωνος. In Pindar's time this word had not yet frozen into a mere metaphor: it still retained its full meaning and its close association with the skill and wisdom of Apollo and the Muses, Λατοΐδα σοφία βαθυκόλπων τε Μοισᾶν (12).[1] The manner in which, through the idea of συμφωνία, the climax of the ode is linked up with its beginning[2] will not have escaped Pindar's audience, the less so since Cumae also appears first in connexion with the defeat of Typhos (see above) and later as the scene of the defeat of the Etruscans. But it is not merely in detail that the two sections of the poem correspond to one another: their parallelism goes much farther. In the first triad the invocation of the golden lyre starts from its function at the present celebration, but, as the praise of the divine instrument continues, the sphere in which its spell works is enlarged more and more until its voice appears as the voice of a power that controls the whole world. 'Zeus and the other gods are proclaimed lovers of the Lyre, his enemies as its enemies—creatures of disharmony and chaos: at once it has grown into all that Plato meant by μουσική, and more—the spirit of serenity, order, concord throughout the Universe opposing and holding in subjection whatever makes for turbulence, jarring discord, the disruption of all.'[3] For Pindar, an aristocrat, a Greek of the great age, there was no need to 'rub in' what was so clearly implied: just as the monsters whom Zeus defeated threatened the world with chaos, so did the barbarians whom Hiero defeated. Out of such a defeat may there again, as in the old days, grow a rule of order and harmony![4]

When we return now to Horace, we shall be in a better position to see how deeply he was impressed by Pindar's ode and how boldly and

---

[1] The implications of σύμφωνον ἐς ἡσυχίαν both in the context in which it is placed and in relation to the beginning of the ode are well brought out in another poem written for a king, *Pyth.* 5. 65 ff. Ἀπόλλων ... πόρεν τε κίθαριν, δίδωσί τε Μοῖσαν οἷς ἂν ἐθέλῃ, ἀπόλεμον ἀγαγὼν ἐς πραπίδας εὐνομίαν.

[2] The closely-knit texture of Pythian I was after Boeckh (see note 4 below), fully recognized by Rauchenstein, op. cit. (see p. 276 n. 4), 147 f., 'Die Harmonie, die schöne Ruhe der Ordnung in der Natur, im sittlichen Leben und im Staate ist dem Zeus lieb und steht unter seinem Schutze; die rohe und wilde, der Ordnung widerstrebende Gewalt schlägt er.'

[3] Norwood, op. cit. (see p. 277 n. 3), 102.

[4] Boeckh's appreciation of the unity of Pythian I (at the end of his commentary on the ode) is worth recalling: 'tranquillitatem sese [i.e. poetam] optare et bella deprecari (vs. 70 sqq.): quiescendum igitur, ut Mars quiescat cithara sonante, qua solus Typhon et qui saevitia et atrocitate pares sint, non deleniantur. Quae quidem poeta eximia arte in unum et integrum coniunxit corpus.'

thoroughly he recast it. Horace's poem, too, starts from music, produced by the Muse,[1] music which, like the voice of the golden lyre in
Pindar's ode, is being heard here and now. For there can be no doubt
that when the first stanza, in which the Muse is called upon to sing and
play her instrument, is immediately followed by *auditis?* and *audire
videor*, we are to understand that by now the music has become audible,
if only to the inspired mind. Later on (21–36) the Muses are invoked as
the poet's guardians who are with him wherever he goes and, in war
and peace, save him from all perils. This power of the goddesses is a
natural concomitant of their being the creators and protectors of
music and poetry, but here it also prepares our mind for the still
wider function which they are to perform as champions of order and
peace against the forces of violence and destruction. This universal
aspect of the power of the Muses is reserved for the point (41) where
the ode, precisely in its middle, reaches its highest level, after turning
to the person of *Caesar altus*. But not even there are we rushed into a
comprehensive view of the μουσικόν: in Caesar's company, too, the
Muses first appear as those who, with their customary arts, entertain
and refresh the tired warrior and statesman (37–40), and only after
this preparation are they praised as the givers of *lene consilium* and all
the blessings of φιλόφρων ἡσυχία.

Horace and a few readers, among them, perhaps, Augustus himself,
will probably have felt what a happy inspiration it was to apply to the
rule of the Princeps some of the fundamental ideas of Pindar's first
Pythian ode, a poem written primarily to celebrate the birth of the
new city founded by the man whom the poet on another occasion
addressed thus: πάτερ, κτίστορ Αἴτνας. It is likely that by the time when
Horace composed his poem many Romans had come to look on Augustus *quasi et ipsum conditorem urbis*.[2] The enemies from whose assaults this
ruler had rescued the civilized world were not only, like the Carthaginians and the Etruscans whom the Deinomenids defeated at Himera
and Cumae, 'barbarians' threatening the peace from without, but
also the far more formidable powers which threatened to undermine

---

[1] The one Muse, Calliope, represents them all, so that the invocation in the plural,
Camenae, which dominates the whole section from 21 to 42, attaches smoothly to the beginning of the ode. The Roman poets, though on purely artistic grounds, follow their Greek
models in varying freely between one Muse and several. This apparent insensitiveness to
the difference between a goddess in the singular and a group of goddesses in the plural is in
Greek poetry, at any rate at its early stage, the product of certain very old beliefs and
forms of worship, where it must never be forgotten 'wie wenig auf Einheit und Vielheit
der göttlichen Personen ankommt' (Wilamowitz, *Griech. Tragödien*, ii. 217). 'Early Greek
poets, following Hesiod, every now and then take the liberty of singling out the name of a
particular Muse, Erato, Kleio, Kalliope, to represent the whole choir: that means hardly
more than if they speak of "the Muse" ' (Wilamowitz, *Die Ilias und Homer*, 474 n. 1).

[2] Suet. *Aug.* 7. 2.

the whole fabric of the Roman State from within. These destructive forces, hostile to the *lene consilium* of the Muses and to the realm of light, reason, and harmony, are in the poem symbolized by the old enemies of the Olympian gods. They attempt to invade heaven and to upset the order of Nature, *tendentes opaco Pelion imposuisse Olympo*. Their story exemplifies, by way of mythological παράδειγμα,[1] the maxim that mild and wise counsel is superior to brutal force. At l. 65 the concise sentence *vis consili expers mole ruit sua*, which harks back to the *lene consilium* at l. 41, emphasizes the lesson to be learnt from the catastrophe of the gigantic rebels. Typhos could not, of course, play nearly as important a role in a poem written for Rome as in the song for the festival of Aitna.[2] Instead, he now appears in the unholy company of the Titans, the Giants, and the Aloadae. We cannot say whether here Horace was inspired merely by Pindar's and other poets' accounts of the battles of those monsters against the gods or whether some famous works of decorative art were also in his mind.[3] I like to think that in the happy days when Horace lived as a student at Athens he would every now and then walk up to the Acropolis, enter the Parthenon, and gaze at Pheidias' statue of the goddess, whose shield 'was decorated inside with a gigantomachy, outside with an amazonomachy, and the sandals with Lapiths fighting Centaurs, all three symbolic of the triumph of the higher over the lower breed'.[4] Then, after coming out of the temple, he may have glanced at some of the metopes on the east side, where again he could see scenes of a gigantomachy. It is less likely, though not impossible, that, when he was on the staff of Brutus in Asia Minor, he should have been able, or should have wished, to visit Pergamon and look at the Great Altar of Zeus with its enormous gigantomachy celebrating the triumph of Attalus I over the invading Celts.[5] Besides, the contest of the gods with the gigantic sons of Earth and other primeval rebels was represented on many works of Greek decorative art, some

[1] The special expression by which the transition to the myth is made at l. 42, *scimus ut . . .*, was possibly suggested by some model in choric lyrics. See Theiler, op. cit. 267 n. 2, who compares Soph. *El.* 837 οἶδα γὰρ ἄνακτ' Ἀμφιάρεων κτλ. and *Phil.* 680 f. (cf. also A. *Cho.* 602 ἴστω δὲ . . . τὰν ἁ παιδολυμὰς τάλαινα Θεστιὰς μήσατο κτλ.).

[2] In Horace's ode Typhoeus (53) figures merely as one of the rebelling giants, and no special reference to him is made at ll. 75 f. *nec peredit impositam celer ignis Aetnen* (this clause was connected by Orelli–Baiter with the Callimachean expression πυρὶ δεῖπνον, but that is unsafe; see Pfeiffer on Callim. *fr.* 590).

[3] The latter possibility is rightly taken into account by Archibald Y. Campbell, *Horace*, 1924, 104, 106, 109.

[4] Beazley in Beazley and Ashmole, *Greek Sculpture and Painting*, 48. Cf. also Wilamowitz, *Glaube der Hellenen*, ii. 95.

[5] Theoretically the possibility that Horace went to Pergamon cannot be excluded: in the autumn of 43 B.C. Brutus spent some time at Smyrna (Plutarch, *Brutus* 28. 6–30; for further evidence of Brutus' stay in Asia see D. Magie, *Roman Rule in Asia Minor*, ii. 1274 n. 53).

of which may have been known to Horace. However, the use which he makes of this topic in *Descende caelo* was primarily inspired by Pindar. For it is as an illustration of the sentence *vos* (i.e. the Muses) *lene consilium et datis et dato gaudetis* that at l. 42 the fate of the Titans, the Giants, and the rest of them is introduced into the poem, and this conflict between the power of the μουσικόν, the σύμφωνος ἡσυχία, on the one side and on the other side the brutal violence employed by the enemies of Zeus is Pindar's conception.

The points at which there is a close analogy between Χρυσέα φόρμιγξ and *Descende caelo* stand out clearly. In both poems we perceive the extension of the idea of music, which at first is merely the music to be heard in the present *melos* and then gradually gains in depth and width until it becomes a universal principle of order and harmony, in conformity to which the whole world is ruled in fairness and justice (*imperio aequo*), the physical world and the political world, the sphere of the living and the sphere of the dead (45–48).[1] For obvious reasons Horace is silent about the enemies who in his own time, like the ancient Titans and Giants, attempted to upset order and peace and therefore had to be subjugated by force. This difference from Pindar is certainly important, but it cannot obscure the affinity in thought and structure.

But we have not yet paid any attention to the feature which most clearly shows the fundamental difference between Pindar's and Horace's approach to their theme. Both begin with the music, the gift of the Muses, which is being heard here and now. But what is the source of this music in each case? In Pindar's poem it is something established in the customs and the cults of a society to which both the poet and those for whom he wrote belonged.[2] The athletic and other competitions at the festivals at Olympia, Delphi, and elsewhere, and the celebrations by which the victor and his city were honoured, first at the sanctuary itself, then, in a more elaborate form, on his coming home, were all an organic part of the life of the community. The games at the festivals were only one of the many occasions which called for musical celebrations. The return of a victorious warrior required, besides other forms of thanksgiving and welcome, the immediate arrangement of singing and dancing choirs: this is the first thing that comes to the Watchman's mind when he sees the beacon sign from Troy.[3] The old

---

[1] The fact that the παράδειγμα of ll. 42 f., *scimus ut*, etc., with Jupiter as its centre and grammatical subject, serves as evidence of the truth of the preceding statement, *vos lene consilium*, etc., makes it inevitable to conclude that Jupiter's rule (45 ff) is to be considered as a manifestation of the same harmony from which the *lene consilium* springs.

[2] With the following section compare the general remarks, pp. 39 ff. above. Some repetition was inevitable.

[3] Aesch. *Ag.* 23 f.

men of Thebes, on hearing that their enemy is slain, cry in jubilation: χοροὶ χοροὶ καὶ θαλίαι μέλουσι Θήβας ἱερὸν κατ' ἄστυ.[1] In the Greek cities choirs were ready for the many different types of songs which were to be offered to the gods or to an individual god or goddess on different occasions. There may also have been traditional forms suitable for the hymns to be performed when a new city was founded: in the case of Aitna the prayers for the new community are merged in the epinikion for the victory of Hiero's chariot. But whatever the occasion, the musical performance had its fixed place in the celebration, and some means for its execution in solemn form was always at hand or easily prepared: its existence could be taken for granted before the poet commissioned had written a single line of the song. The institution of these performances was deeply rooted in the very life, religious and civic, of the society: like the whole of that life it came from the gods. That is why Pindar can start from premisses of unchallenged validity and, without an effort, make the transition from the μουσικόν that is operative in the present performance to the power of harmony that governs the world. Horace had no such ground to stand upon, and he was fully conscious of it: the time was long past when in the boldness of his youthful experiments he imagined that he could disregard the gulf between his own world and the world of an ancient Greek poet. He now faced bravely, and indeed proudly, the limitations of his real position. His poetry, his 'music' was not the joint product of an effort of his individuality and of something that was there before he was born, that existed independently of him and had its roots in a supra-personal sphere. His poetry, though inspired by the Muses, was entirely the work of himself alone. Pindar undertakes a task which is to be done, whether or not he, Pindar, discharges it: had he declined to write the poem for Hiero's festival, someone else would have written it. Horace's *carmina non prius audita* could never have come into existence except by his own effort. Pindar says πείθονται δ' ἀοιδοὶ σάμασιν. For Horace there exist no singers, no festival ceremonies, no tradition which he can follow. He is alone, left to his experience as an individual and to his personal inspiration. This, and not some vain delight in the display of pieces of his own biography, is the reason why he tells us so much about his early childhood and those out-of-the-way places which at that time nourished his imagination and strengthened his mind, why he speaks of dangers overcome and of those favourite retreats where he is allowed to forget the *sescenta negotia* of his life in the noisy capital and is able to listen to the voices of the Camenae. He does not pretend or even wish to be the mouthpiece of a community such as no longer exists; he is determined to remain the man he is, born in a late and distracted age,

[1] Eur. *Her.* 763 f.

walking alone, full of simple strength, with a glad heart and an immense capacity for enthusiasm, and, above all, in continual communion
with the μουσικόν which lifts him up and protects him. He knows the
origin of the power which fills him: he knows that this power does not
come to him from where it came to Pindar. The bold verb in the first
person singular with which the cycle of the Roman Odes begins has its
complement in the extensive personal passages of *Descende caelo*. In these
passages there is nothing Pindaric: they describe the experience which
in Horace's own life was the equivalent of Pindar's creed. So great was
his admiration for the old master, so sympathetic his understanding of
his intentions that, instead of copying him slavishly, he created something quite different, something which resembled the opening sections
of the first Pythian ode only in that it was an equally true image of the
poet's vocation.

The last sentence of the ode shows the gentleness of Horace's mind as
well as the musical power of his verse:

> amatorem trecentae
> Pirithoum cohibent catenae.

This concluding diminuendo reminds us of the peaceful scene at the
end of *Odes* iii. 29, after the description of the raging storms, and of the
last stanza in the Bacchus ode ii. 19. By the happiest inspiration Pirithous is made to bring up the rear of those who have sinned against
the gods. He too has sinned; on him too a severe punishment is inflicted. But how venial seems his sin: *amatorem . . . .* We find it impossible
to connect him with the *immanis turba* of which we heard before. The
unfortunate young lover forms a perfect contrast to those monsters.
Pirithous and his fate appeal to the poet's imagination. One of the
finest of his late odes again ends with Pirithous (4. 7. 27 f.):

> nec Lethaea valet Theseus abrumpere caro
> vincula Pirithoo.

It will be remembered[1] that *Odes* iii. 6, *Delicta maiorum*, was written
in 28 B.C., that is to say before iii. 3 and iii. 5, and probably before all
the other Roman Odes. The poem contains several passages which are
remarkably similar to certain passages in the *Epodes*. Some of the
similarities are confined to merely ornamental detail or to a single,
though significant, trait. The picturesque topic of ll. 30 f., *seu vocat
institor seu navis Hispanae magister*, which recalls *Epod.* 17. 20, *amata
nautis multum et institoribus*, could be easily replaced by another one. Of
greater significance is the romanticizing description of the *mater familias*

[1] p. 261.

and her frugal household in the good old days (37 ff.):

> sed rusticorum mascula militum
> proles, Sabellis docta ligonibus
>   versare glaebas et severae
>   matris ad arbitrium recisos

> portare fustis, sol ubi montium
> mutaret umbras et iuga demeret
>   bubus fatigatis,

where we catch echoes of the second epode (39 ff.),

> quodsi pudica mulier in partem iuvet
>   domum atque dulcis liberos,
> Sabina qualis aut perusta solibus
>   pernicis uxor Apuli,
> sacrum vetustis exstruat lignis focum
>   lassi sub adventum viri
> claudensque textis cratibus laetum pecus
>   distenta siccet ubera,

and (63 f.)

> videre fessos vomerem inversum boves
>   collo trahentis languido.

But it is only when we turn from *Delicta maiorum* to the early political epodes, XVI, *Altera iam teritur*, and VII, *Quo, quo scelesti ruitis*, that we find a similarity, not in one or another point of detail, but in the fundamental attitude of the poems.[1] *Delicta maiorum . . . lues*: the seventh epode, taking up the *scelesti* of its beginning, ends *acerba fata Romanos agunt scelusque fraternae necis, ut immerentis fluxit in terram Remi sacer nepotibus cruor.* And the last sentence of the ode,

> aetas parentum peior avis tulit
>   nos nequiores, mox daturos
>   progeniem vitiosiorem,

describes the continual decline from good to bad, from bad to worse, the same decline which, in its Hesiodic form, appears at the end of the sixteenth epode:

> Iuppiter illa piae secrevit litora genti,
>   ut inquinavit aere tempus aureum,
> aere, dehinc ferro duravit saecula . . ..

There is here an unmistakable difference in scope. Whereas the concluding stanza of the ode confines its view to the last few generations of the Roman people, the thought at the end of the epode, in accordance

---

[1] W. Warde Fowler, *Roman Essays*, 226 f., noticed in *Odes* iii. 6 'the same mood of serious depression as in the sixteenth epode and in ode 24 of this book'.

with the semi-mythical elements of that poem, covers the long periods which make up the whole life of mankind. But the real theme of the epode, maintained to the end, *altera iam teritur bellis civilibus aetas*, is not more comprehensive than the theme of *Delicta maiorum*. In the latter poem the gradual moral deterioration of the people, which was alluded to at the end of the epode, is made the central theme. We are reminded of the doctrine, professed by Posidonius, Sallust, and other historians, that the breakdown of the institutions of the Roman Republic was caused by the increasing moral corruption. Nor is it peculiar to the poets, Virgil[1] and Horace, to express the belief that the gods, by inflicting civil war and self-destruction on the people, avenge some ancient crime. In 46 B.C., Cicero said[2] *di immortales, etiam si poenas a populo Romano ob aliquod delictum expetiverunt, qui civile bellum tantum et tam luctuosum excitaverunt . . ..* It is, however, remarkable that Horace, about three years after the battle of Actium, should have taken, at any rate at times, such a gloomy view of Rome's situation that he was driven to write a poem which began *Delicta maiorum immeritus lues, Romane* and ended on a note of unmitigated pessimism. It is still more remarkable that he should have chosen this very poem for the conclusion of his solemn cycle and should have left it in this conspicuous place when he published his collection in 23 B.C. This calls for an explanation.

First of all we have to remember something of which, although it is very common and natural, classical scholars do not always seem to be sufficiently aware. The Augustan poets—and, probably, other poets in other ages—when they published a book did not trouble to bring every detail in it 'up to date' or to eliminate from it everything that had been appropriate at the time of writing but proved less appropriate at the moment of publication. 'Topicality' is not among the criteria by which great poetry is to be judged. Horace let his book of *iambi* go into the world with these two initial couplets:

> Ibis Liburnis inter alta navium,
> amice, propugnacula,
> paratus omne Caesaris periculum
> subire, Maecenas, tuo.

And yet by then everybody knew that the plan had been changed and that Maecenas had not joined Caesar's fleet but remained in Rome. Virgil, in the epilogue of the *Georgics*,[3] indicates the end of the year 30 B.C. (or the beginning of 29), when Caesar had been successful in Syria and was beginning to rule over a pacified world, as the date of the completion of his poem, and the events of the years 31 and 30 form the background of the *laudes Italiae* in Book II (see 171 f.) and of the

---

[1] *Georg.* 1. 501 f.   [2] *Marcell.* 18.   [3] 4. 560 ff.

proem of Book III (26–33) ; but the magnificent finale of the first book, clearly written before the battle of Actium, betrays deep anxiety for the safety of Caesar and shows in its concluding lines hardly a glimpse of hope:

> frustra retinacula tendens
> fertur equis auriga, neque audit currus habenas.

Why did Virgil not attempt to harmonize this discrepancy? He would certainly not have wished to spoil a masterpiece by touching it up. But this explanation would not suffice when the subject-matter of the passage, the fate of Rome, was of such gravity and when the poet was a man with such a sense of responsibility. It is likely that Virgil, and probably Caesar and Maecenas as well, were convinced that easy-going optimism was dangerous and that, when peace and order seemed to be restored, the terrifying picture of civil war with all its misery and degradation should once more, in the poet's powerful vision, be brought before the nation. In the case of Horace we may be sure that this was his conviction. He was no pessimist, but a shrewd observer and sober judge of human nature. He knew how easily men discard uncomfortable memories and slip back into complacent indolence. He may also have thought that even after several years of peace and after the constitutional reconstruction early in 27 B.C. the poise of Rome's moral and political welfare was still precarious. A clear indication of his view on these matters is contained in the last two stanzas of *Odes* i. 35, *O diva gratum quae regis Antium*.[1] But the testimony of *Delicta maiorum* is far more impressive. For here it is the whole picture that is painted in dark colours, and this picture is the concluding piece of the great patriotic cycle with the figure of *Caesar altus* in its centre.

Odes iii. 14, *Herculis ritu*, was written about three years after the completion of the Roman Odes. Any reader of this poem will notice how different the tone of its first four stanzas is from that of the rest: 'les quatre premiers quatrains de cette Ode sont graves et serieux, et les trois derniers sont badins et enjoués.'[2] It is a far cry from this sensible observation to the sort of criticism which Lehrs practised when he declared that Horace's ode was completed with l. 16, and that what follows in the manuscripts is the product of an interpolator. But even this exaggeration is based on something which is really there, the discrepancy between the first four stanzas and the last three. The stylistic level is different, the setting is different, and the vocatives at the beginnings of the two parts are different. The person addressed in the first line

---

[1] See pp. 252 f. above.   [2] Dacier.

of the second part, *i pete unguentum, puer*, is a young servant, as we find him in many private drinking songs, φέρ' ὕδωρ, φέρ' οἶνον, ὦ παῖ, *Persicos odi, puer, apparatus*, and the like. The vocative at the beginning of the whole ode, *o plebs*, is unique.[1] It has a solemn ring, in harmony with the serious tone of the opening stanza, in which gratitude and relief at the long-delayed return of the victorious Augustus take the form of a comparison of his perilous expedition in Spain with what Hercules, mankind's undaunted servant,[2] once achieved in the same far-off country at the risk of his life. In the following two stanzas we seem to be watching a procession of thanksgivers, including Livia and Octavia, as it gradually forms itself. But what the poet gives us is not a description of the actual ceremony but rather orders for its performance, pronounced, we may imagine, by some person in charge of it. In such a case it will not be misleading to say that the poet takes on the role of a herald. A fiction of this kind was not uncommon in Hellenistic poems, and from there it found its way into Latin poetry.[3] This literary topic implies a somewhat elaborate setting. The very opposite is true of the kind of poems from which the last part of the ode (*i pete unguentum, puer* to the end) is derived, poems the theme of which is the invitation to, or the description of preparations for, some banquet. Such poems, whether in the form of lyrics or in the form of an epigram, are often brief and have the simplest setting and a bare minimum of ornamentation. It remains to consider whether Horace was successful in blending the two heterogeneous elements.

No doubt he might have concluded his ode, as Lehrs wanted him to

---

[1] Peerlkamp was a wild critic but no fool (cf. *JRS* xxxv, 1945, 1 n. 2). As he was determined to obelize the whole ode, he had to find fault with as many expressions as possible. Nevertheless, his note on *o plebs* is excellent: 'Non credo simile in omni Latinitate reperiri exemplum. Iam inusitatum accidisset *o popule*. Quanto magis *o plebs*.' The problem at which this remark hints was fully discussed in J. Wackernagel's admirable paper *Über einige antike Anredeformen*, Göttingen 1912, 13 ff. (*Kl. Schriften*, 980 ff.), where Horace's *o plebs* is taken into account (16). An assembly of the Roman people could not be addressed by *popule Romane*, any more than an Athenian assembly could be addressed by ὦ δῆμε. The vocative *popule* does not occur until the artificial prose of the Empire. Greek Tragedy, in the place of a vocative of λαός or λεώς, uses the nominative, χαῖρε . . . πολισσοῦχος λεώς, χαίρετ' ἀστικὸς λεώς, ἰὼ πᾶς λεώς and the like. It was probably after the model of Greek poetry that, in the context of a solemn apostrophe, Horace ventured *o plebs*, and Ovid, *Fast.* 4. 731, *i, pete virginea, populus, suffimen ab ara*. Wackernagel adds 'a stranger instance is Livy's (1. 24. 7) *audi tu, populus Albanus*'. This phrase can be claimed as the invention either of Livy himself or of an historian who wrote not long before him: it is the twin of *audiat fas* (1. 32. 6, from the same body of formulas of the *fetiales*), to which K. Latte, *Sav. Z.* lxvii, 1950, 56, has applied Wackernagel's remarks on *fas* and *nefas*, *Vorl. üb. Syntax*, i. 297 f., and has thus shown that it cannot belong to the language of the earlier Republic.

[2] The manner in which the conception of Herakles as the hero who μοχθήσας ἀκύμον' ἔθηκεν βίοτον βροτοῖς and so became a saviour of mankind was further developed in the Hellenistic age is illustrated in the commentaries on the beginning of Horace's ode.

[3] See p. 181 n. 3 above. For the connexion of *Herculis ritu* with this type of poetry see especially R. Reitzenstein, *Neue Jahrb.* xxi, 1908, 98 and 365.

do, with *tenente Caesare terras*, and no doubt this would have been a
sonorous and dignified close. But our concern is not what the poem
might have been but what it actually is. Moreover the attempt to cut
the ode into two parts, of which the first would extend to the end of
l. 16, does not really work. For the fourth stanza, *hic dies vere mihi festus*,
etc., could not be conceived, as the first three could, as spoken by 'a
herald' or some such anonymous character: with *mihi* in the first line
and *ego* in the next the person of the poet steps into the foreground.
Horace's skill in shaping smooth transitions makes it equally impossible either to connect stanza IV solely with I–III or to connect it
solely with V–VII. The central stanza is as closely joined with the first
three stanzas as with the last three:

> hic dies vere mihi festus atras
> exiget curas: ego nec tumultum
> nec mori per vim metuam tenente
>   Caesare terras.

The thought, while still dwelling on the *res publica populi Romani*, is
gliding into the sphere of the *res privata* of the poet. And what follows,
the pretty detail familiar from comedy, epigram, and elegy, belongs
entirely to the sphere of private life—or almost entirely. For there are
in these concluding stanzas some ominous traits, strangely contrasting
with the harmless pleasures of the banquet, traits which can only
conjure up visions of the past calamities of the Roman people. The
thunderstorm is over, *tenente Caesare terras*, but you still see here and
there the horizon kindled by lightning. The poet had just said *ego nec
tumultum nec mori per vim metuam*. When he then, apparently to indicate
the impressive age of a noble vintage, speaks in terms like these:

> et cadum Marsi memorem duelli,
> Spartacum siqua potuit vagantem
>   fallere testa,

Marsum duellum and *Spartacus vagans* strike us as a terrible echo of *vis*
and *tumultus* in Italy, and once more we remember the man who has
brought about the change.

The last clause of the ode runs:

> non ego hoc ferrem calidus iuventa
>   consule Planco.

A modern reader might skip over it ('just some year or other of the
period when Horace was a young man'). But few of Horace's contemporaries were likely to have forgotten the year of the battle of Philippi.
It is with a turning-point in the recent history of the *res publica* that the
'private' part of the ode concludes.

We now see that the two parts of the poem, however different the origin of their themes, are woven into one closely knit texture. And yet it must be admitted that the reasons for which the unity of the ode has been questioned are not entirely empty. For all Horace's skill there remains here a faint disharmony. It is difficult to speak of it without overdoing the point. Perhaps we may put it like this. The transition from the thanksgiving and rejoicing of the Roman people to the private celebration of the poet is not in itself objectionable. What does jar is the clash between the role played by Horace in the first part and the role played by him in the second part. In the first three (or four) stanzas the poet, whether we think of him as a kind of herald or as a member of the crowd, appears as a nondescript figure. What he says there could be said by any Roman. But at the end of the poem he induces us to think of the individual Q. Horatius Flaccus, a man who is now grey-haired and was young at the time when Plancus was consul. Perhaps we also dislike, after so majestic a beginning, the all-too-private style in which the description of Neaera, charming in itself, is presented. A critic who voices such misgivings is sure to be denounced as completely devoid of a sense of humour. I am not afraid of that. But I must make it clear that my objections to certain features of this lovely poem would be impertinent if it were not that I am attempting to measure Horace by the highest standard in his own work. About ten years after *Herculis ritu* he wrote the deepest and most harmonious of all odes relating to Augustus, iv. 5, *Divis orte bonis*. There he showed that a transition from the great patriotic theme to the celebrations of humble citizens and of the poet himself can be made, not only without producing the faintest disharmony, but in such a manner that the poem, in turning to that modest subject, reaches the very height of its perfection.

On approaching the great fabric of i. 12, *Quem virum*, we notice above its portal a Pindaric 'motto',[1] *Quem virum aut heroa . . . quem deum?*: τίνα θεόν, τίν᾽ ἥρωα, τίνα δ᾽ ἄνδρα (*Ol.* 2. 2). But on closer inspection we see that, in addition to this echo in the opening sentence, the arrangement of the whole poem is reminiscent of Pindar's second Olympic ode. As W. Christ[2] pointed out, the ode *Quem virum aut heroa*, in free adaptation of the five triads of Ἀναξιφόρμιγγες ὕμνοι, is composed of five quasi-triads.[3] The contents of each of these quasi-triads represent a distinct unit of sense. This arrangement will be illustrated

---

[1] For the use of the term 'motto' see p. 159 above.

[2] *Metrik der Griechen und Römer*, 2nd ed., 1879, 654.

[3] Christ's observation was deservedly taken over by Hirschfelder in his re-edition of Orelli and Baiter's commentary, and at any rate its substance appeared in Kiessling's summary.

by the following summary, in which the implications of Christ's analysis are freely worked out.

Triad I (1–12), Exordium, announcement of the general theme, 'I will sing of man, hero, god'; praise of the power of music. Triad II (13–24), 'gods'; the beginning of the triad is marked by *dicam* (13). Triad III (25–36), 'heroes' (*a potiori*);[1] again beginning with *dicam* (25). Triad IV (37–48), 'men'; the governing verb of the first stanza is *referam* (39). Triad V (49–60), Conclusion, prayer to Jupiter, including the praise of Augustus.

Such a quasi-triadic arrangement was the closest approximation to Pindar's genuine triadic system which was open to Horace, since he could not possibly consider destroying the uniformity of his mono-strophic *carmina*, even if anyhow a direct application of the triadic order (strophe, antistrophe, epode) to non-choric poetry had not been inconceivable in antiquity. The Horatian ode as the poet had shaped it had to remain monostrophic. On the only occasion when, many years after, his task was to compose a song for a choir, he used, as he had done in *Quem virum aut heroa*, the Sapphic stanza and again arranged the song, the Carmen Saeculare, in quasi-triads, thus symbolizing its connexion with the choric forms of the Greeks.

With ancient writers it was a fairly common practice to announce the sections of their subject in terms such as 'I propose to deal with *A* and *B*' and then, in the execution, to let *B* come first. The arrangement of the ode *Quem virum* is a case in point.[2] The announcement in the proem runs *Quem virum aut heroa . . . quem deum?*:[3] in the execution the gods come first (triad II), then the heroes (triad III), and finally the men (triad IV). In the Pindaric poem which Horace deliberately recalls, the threefold question of the beginning, τίνα θεόν, τίν' ἥρωα, τίνα δ' ἄνδρα κελαδήσομεν; receives immediately a threefold answer, ἤτοι Πίσα μὲν Διός· Ὀλυμπιάδα δ' ἔστασεν Ἡρακλέης ἀκρόθινα πολέμου· Θήρωνα δὲ τετραορίας ἕνεκα νικαφόρου γεγωνητέον. It has sometimes been said that in this poem Pindar is bent only upon praising Theron, as though the mention of Zeus and of Herakles were a mere cloak. But this view proves inadequate when the outlook of Pindar and of the society for which he wrote is taken into account: Theron's victory in the chariot race was an ἄγαλμα not only to him but to Zeus and

---

[1] On the special character of ll. 33–36 see below.

[2] A large-scale instance of *ABC* being taken up by *CBA* occurs in *Aen.* VII, where the Fury first incites *matres* (392), then Turnus (445–74), and finally the herdsmen (483–510), but the description of the ensuing warlike action begins with the herdsmen (574), passes on to Turnus (577), and ends with the sons of those *matres* (580 ff.).

[3] Tycho Mommsen, *Annot. crit. supplem. ad Pindari Olympias*, 1864, 14, observes on *quem deum?*: 'climax est, non anticlimax [as in Pindar], ideoque fortius asyndeton tertio loco aptissimum.'

Herakles as well. This connexion between the present and the past is familiar; so the poet need not elaborate it. Horace treats Pindar's tripartite question, τίνα θεόν, τίν' ἥρωα, τίνα δ' ἄνδρα as if it required an answer in which each of the three categories should be represented, not by an individual, but by a group.[1] To each group equal space is apportioned. This arrangement, while producing a symmetrical structure, also makes it possible to glorify a number of gods, heroes, and men, to glorify them for their own sake and yet in such a way that the praise of each group contains symbolic references to Augustus. Augustus himself receives his full share of glory in the last triad, but nowhere in this ode, which in this regard differs completely from Pindar's epinikion for Theron, is he made the direct object of the poet's *celebrare, dicere, referre*. The apparently obvious answer to the opening question *Quem virum . . .?* is avoided or, at any rate, is given only in an indirect form. Had Horace been the courtier into whom many modern critics attempt to turn him, he would have felt obliged to write a very different poem.

The group of the gods (13–24), as is natural, is headed by Jupiter, who here appears not only as πατὴρ ἀνδρῶν τε θεῶν τε and as the ruler of men and gods (13 ff. *parentis . . . qui res hominum ac deorum . . . temperat*) but also as the supreme being who maintains the universe in an established order (15 f.).[2] The praise of his power and perfection culminates in a mighty sentence:

> unde nil maius generatur ipso,[3]
> nec viget quicquam simile aut secundum.[4]

[1] That is the way in which Pindar himself, at the beginning of *Isthm.* 7, works out such a question, Τίνι τῶν πάρος, ὦ μάκαιρα Θήβα, καλῶν ἐπιχωρίων μάλιστα θυμὸν τεὸν εὔφρανας; ἦρα . . . ἀνίκ' . . . ἄντειλας Διόνυσον, 'or at the birth of Herakles, or at the wise counsel of Teiresias, or at the horseman Iolaos', and so forth. A similar pattern for a catalogue of possible objects of praise, out of which the poet has to choose one, is found at the beginning of Pindar's first hymn (for Thebes), *fr.* 29 Schr. (19 Turyn), 'Shall we sing Hismenos or Melia or Cadmus or the Spartoi or Thebes or . . .?' Wilamowitz, *Pindaros*, 192, compares this with *Isthm.* 7 and infers 'da wird wohl Pindar bei sich selbst eine Anleihe gemacht haben'. I think it more likely that this form had its origin in questions which preluded a prayer addressed to a number of gods, as at A. *Sept.* 92 f., τίς ἄρα ῥύσεται, τίς ἄρ' ἐπαρκέσει θεῶν ἢ θεᾶν; (see p. 247 n. 1 above). Cf. also Ar. *Thesm.* 104 τίνι δαιμόνων ὁ κῶμος; followed by invocations of Apollo, Artemis, Leto.

[2] For the beginning of this section with a question of 'Pindaric' form, *quid prius dicam*, see my remarks on *Sat.* 2. 6. 17 *quid prius inlustrem*, p. 140 above.

[3] *unde nil maius*: the sound-pattern sank into Horace's musical memory, and much later, in a poem in the same metre, he praised Augustus himself (4. 2. 37 f.) *quo nihil maius*, etc. For the use of *unde* (for *a quo*) in Horace see p. 102 n. 2 above. The word *generatur*, too, is solemn: from the article in the *Thesaurus* it can be seen that this verb, apart from its technical use (in the language of farmers and the like), occurs, before the period of the archaizing writers, only in elevated style. It is alien to Plautus and Terence, but the author of the 'argumentum' of the *Cistellaria* says *gnatam generat*.

[4] The thought in this line is reminiscent, though probably independent, of the Aeschylean οὐκ ἔχω προσεικάσαι πάντ' ἐπισταθμώμενος πλὴν Διός.

There follow Athena and Dionysus, who distinguished themselves on the side of Zeus in his fight against the Giants, then Artemis, who, *saevis inimica beluis*, protects civilized life, and finally Apollo, 'the slayer of Python and Caesar's champion at Actium'.[1] All these deities stand for peace and order against the forces of destruction; they symbolize, though here only by implication, the ideals of the Augustan régime as clearly as do the fighting gods in the fuller picture of the ode iii. 4, *Descende caelo*.

The next two stanzas (25–32) contain a brief mention of Herakles and an extensive eulogy of two other heroes who like him are ἀλεξίκακοι, the Dioscuri, celebrated here as the rescuers of sailors, the bringers of calm after violent storms (again the symbolic reference to the rule of the Princeps is important).[2] Up to this point the poet has in every case made his choice firmly and finally: 'I shall speak of this god and then of that goddess, I shall not pass over in silence that god nor that nor that; I shall speak of these heroes. . .'. But now (33–36) he seems to hesitate about the order of merit; moreover, he does not, as in the preceding and the following stanzas, promise (*dicam, referam*) to speak of this and that man but merely names possibilities:

> Romulum post hos prius an quietum
> Pompili regnum memorem an superbos
> Tarquini fasces dubito an Catonis
>   nobile letum.

This stanza is one of the most bewildering passages in Horace's odes. I cannot claim to have found a clear solution of its riddles, and when I speak of it at all I do so tentatively. Right at the beginning we are confronted with a very puzzling feature. Why should the poet feel (or pretend to feel) uncertain whether the place immediately after the Greek ἥρωες ἀλεξίκακοι should be given, not to Romulus, but to the reign of Numa or the *fasces* of Tarquinius and so forth? The idea that to the Dioscuri and Herakles there corresponded on the Roman side Romulus was firmly rooted in Horace's mind: there is evidence of it in *Odes* iii. 3 (9–16), a poem earlier than i. 12, and in the much later epistle to Augustus (2. 1. 5–12) as well. Especially in a poem which, in substance if not in form, centred in Augustus, on whom many contemporaries looked as Rome's second founder, it was almost inevitable

---

[1] So Kiessling, whose fine comment on this whole passage was rightly taken over by Heinze.

[2] For Herakles and the Dioscuri as counterparts of Augustus cf. *Odes* 3. 3. 9–12 and 4. 5. 33–36, *Epist.* 2. 1. 5–17. But the connexion which in these passages is overtly established will not be realized in *Odes* i. 12 unless the links between the descriptions of the various gods, heroes, and men and the subservience of all of them to a dominating idea are appreciated.

that the Greek σωτῆρες and φύλακες should be immediately followed by that Roman of whom it had been said *qualem te patriae custodem di genuerunt*. In this connexion another point can be settled. It seems to me impossible to accept the view[1] that the series of the *viri* begins with l. 33 *Romulum*. If anyone was to be classed with the *heroes*, it was Romulus, the son of Mars, who after a glorious career on earth was received into the circle of the immortal gods. Undoubtedly Horace wants us to understand that the list of his *viri* really begins with l. 37, *Regulum et Scauros*, i.e. with the beginning of the fourth triad, so that the function of *referam* at l. 39 is strictly parallel to that of *dicam* at l. 13 and at l. 25. But, on the other hand, we must not neglect the peculiar manner (*dubito memorem*) in which the mention of Romulus is introduced, when he might have simply been added to the Greek heroes by a connective particle. We cannot say what induced Horace to give up the plain sequence at this point. He may have wished to mark sharply the transition from the Greek to the Roman sphere. He may also have wished to touch, in the form of a hesitating deliberation, upon subjects which are, perhaps, to be regarded as being half-way between the heroic world and the world of Roman history. One of these subjects is the person of Romulus, but the others are not persons, but *Pompili regnum, Tarquini fasces, Catonis letum*. There may be more in this than stylistic variation.[2] What is mentioned here, a reign blessed with peace and prosperity, the visible signs of despotic power, a suicide worthy of the hero in a tragedy,[3] seems to have a tinge of the legendary and yet belongs to

---

[1] Put forward by, for example, L. Müller and Heinze.

[2] The form of the expression *superbos Tarquini fasces* and the context in which it is set should not be overlooked in the excitement of the hunt for the particular Tarquinius who keeps hiding under the cover of this ambiguous phrase. The hunt has been going on ever since antiquity (Porph., Ps.-Acro), with little success. The scholia seem to be in the main right in thinking of Tarquinius Priscus, under whom, according to one branch of our tradition (Dion. Hal. 3. 61. 2 and others; see Schwegler, *Röm. Geschichte*, i. 671 n. 5, Schachermeyr, *RE* iv. A. 2377), the *fasces* came from Etruria to Rome. But it seems unlikely that Horace should have chosen *superbos* of all epithets unless he wanted to remind the reader also of the later Tarquinius and of the fate which was brought upon his house by the *fasces*, then truly an instrument of *superbia* (cf. Livy 3. 36. 3 *fasces . . . hoc insigne regium*). The part played by the *fasces* in the *coup d'état* of Tarquinius Superbus may be seen, for example, from Dion. Hal. 4. 38. 2 f.; for their transformation into *insignia* of the consuls see ibid. 4. 74. 1; 4. 75. 2; 5. 2. 1. The whole point of Horace's allusive phrase is lost if we make the *person* of a Tarquinius the object of *memorem*; what Horace does mention as a possible theme is *superbos Tarquini fasces*. We should have to recognize a closely similar ambiguity (although in Virgil it would surprise us less) if at *Aen.* 6. 817 *Tarquinios reges animamque superbam* must be taken together as was assumed by Leo and Norden, who were followed by G. Albini in his careful translation and in the editions by Janell, Sabbadini, and Funaioli. I am inclined to believe that their interpretation is all but inevitable.

[3] To eliminate *Catonis nobile letum* (pace Bentleii Bentleiique adsecularum dictum sit) is a crime against Horace's character. More than once he seized an opportunity of manifesting his unchanged loyalty to the heroes of his youth, the champions of a lost cause. Cf. p. 236 n. 5 above and p. 360 below.

Roman history. So this strange stanza, while rounding off, as a kind of appendix, the two stanzas devoted to the heroes and thus completing the triad, forms at the same time a bridge to the catalogue of the Roman *viri*, Regulus, the Scauri, Aemilius Paullus, and so forth.

The names of the four Roman commanders mentioned at ll. 37 f. 'all recall defeats of Rome: it was in misfortune that Rome's greatness proved its full worth'.[1] There follow (39-44) examples of the gallant austerity which, according to the idealizing historiography and rhetoric of the late Republic, was characteristic of the great Romans of the old days. In the third stanza of this triad the praise of Rome's nobility reaches its climax with the unmistakable allusion to the marriage of Marcellus and Augustus' daughter Julia. Here *Iulium sidus* (47) is the first direct reference to Augustus in this ode, and now we might expect a eulogy of the Princeps to follow immediately. But Horace has something greater in store. Surprisingly the poem returns to Jupiter, but this time he is approached, not as in the second triad with praise only, but with prayer:

> gentis humanae pater atque custos,
> orte Saturno, tibi cura magni
> Caesaris fatis data: tu secundo
> Caesare regnes.

The vocative *pater* harks back to *parentis laudibus* (13 f.), while *custos* is singularly appropriate here where we are to think simultaneously of the highest god and of the ruler on earth. From time immemorial it had been the pride of a good king to be regarded as the φύλαξ, the *custos*, of his flock, his people, and this ideal was revived during the reign of the man to whom it was the most welcome praise that *custode rerum Caesare* the world was allowed to live in peace and without fear.[2] Horace did not find it difficult to identify Zeus with the supreme world-governing principle in which his philosophical training had taught him to believe.[3] So it is proper for him to follow the example of those who had said ἐκ Διὸς ἀρχώμεσθα καὶ ἐς Δία λήγετε Μοῖσαι and to let the ode which, after the proem, began with praise of Jupiter have its conclusion also in a prayer to him. But the chief value of this device is that it enables the poet to touch upon the ruler's greatness in dignified terms without eulogizing him directly. He places Augustus below

---

[1] Kiessling.

[2] *Odes* 4. 15. 17 ff. For φύλαξ in this connexion see W. Schulze's article quoted in my note on A. *Ag.* 1452. The idea of the good ruler being a good shepherd (cf. on A. *Ag.* 795) arises from a similar conception. A. Oxé, 'Σωτήρ bei den Römern', *Wiener Studien*, xlviii, 1930, 38 ff., has done well to examine the use made by Horace and others of *custos*, but, neglecting φύλαξ, he attempts in vain to prove that *custos* is a rendering of σωτήρ. His misconception of *Odes* i. 12 need not concern us.

[3] Cf. on *Odes* i. 34, p. 253 above.

Jupiter, using expressions reminiscent of Roman constitutional life, *tibi cura Caesaris data*[1] and *tu secundo Caesare regnes* and *te minor reget orbem* (as if he were thinking of a *minor* and a *maior magistratus*). It is in no grudging language that Horace extols Augustus, but the religious setting here has a restraining effect and limits the glorification of the mortal. In the early ode i. 2, *Iam satis terris*, Horace had ventured towards a compromise with certain religious conceptions of the Hellenistic East. In *Quem virum aut heroa* he does nothing of the kind. Not only is there in this ode not the faintest hint at a possible deification of the ruler, but all that is said about him is kept within the bounds of strictest Roman propriety. We may assume that in the interval between the writing of *Odes* i. 2 and i. 12 Horace, both as man and artist, had gained in discretion. But it is also likely that, as time went on, he came to form a more adequate idea of the manner in which Augustus himself, no less prudent than tactful, liked to have his person and his achievements celebrated.

6. THE THREE EPILOGUES

It is fitting to conclude our survey of the first collection of Horace's *carmina* with the epilogues of the three books.

I. 38. The first thing we notice is that this short poem is *simplex mundetiis* to an uncommon degree: a sequence of asyndetic, brief, and straightforward sentences.[2] The effect of this deliberate simplicity is the more striking since *Persicos odi, puer, apparatus* comes immediately after *Nunc est bibendum*, which consists almost entirely (i.e. from 5 on) of one long and very elaborate period.[3] The simplicity of the form is a faithful mirror of the thought: the sentence *simplici myrto nihil adlabores sedulus curo*[4] could be regarded as the essence of the poem. Everything

---

[1] Virg. *Georg.* 1. 26 suggests that Caesar the son, on being deified, might accept the *cura terrarum*, a superlative, as it were, of any *cura* which could be the care of a Roman magistrate.

[2] The ode 'besteht aus ganz kurzen selbständigen Sätzchen' (Heinze, *Neue Jahrb.* xix, 1907, 165).

[3] For the structure of its latter part see p. 160 above.

[4] It might be possible to follow Dillenburger, who explains '*nihil allabores sedulus curo* dictum est pro *non curo quidquam sedulus allabores*' (the same interpretation was given by, for example, Meineke, T. E. Page, Wickham, Ussani, L. Müller). But I prefer to regard *nihil* as the emphatic form of the negation and to take *adlabores* as intransitive. The phrase *nihil* (= *prorsus non*) *curo*, with the addition of an object in the accusative, seems to have belonged to colloquial language (Plaut. *Most.* 526 *nil me curassis*, *Capt.* 989 *nihil curavi ceterum*), but it found its way even into dactylic poetry (Catullus 64. 148; Virg. *Ecl.* 2. 6 and 8. 103). The verb *adlaborare* was possibly coined by Horace for *Epod.* 8. 20, where again it is intransitive. The only other instance quoted in the *Thesaurus* comes from Tertullian. The separation of *nihil* from *curo* need not worry us; it is mild compared with the separation of *non* at *Odes* 4. 6. 13 ff. (cf. also 2. 20. 5 ff.); for this word-order see my note on A. *Ag.* 1312 and the comments by Housman which I have quoted there. At *Odes* 1. 38. 6 no comma should be put before *curo*.

here is light and happy, and the picture of the poet whom we see *sub arta vite bibentem* brings back the hours when we too enjoyed good ordinary wine and cheerful company under the foliage of some Italian pergola.

The ode belongs to the class of poems, epigrammatic and other, which have as their theme the preparations for a simple banquet.[1] It is a very graceful little piece. If it were found in any ordinary place in the collection, no one would look for a special meaning underneath its surface. But it is not found in an ordinary place: it concludes a book of lyrics the like of which no Roman reader had ever seen before, a book which represented one of the most daring experiments in the history of ancient poetry. So we must assume that Horace intended the ode, besides its surface value, to refer in some way to the new kind of poetry contained in this book. This inference would be necessary even if it were not strengthened by the analogous function of the concluding poems in the two following books; its consequences, however, are surprising. Here is a book containing such lofty odes as *Iam satis terris* or *Quem virum aut heroa* or, immediately before the end, *Nunc est bibendum*, and yet in its epilogue we are asked to regard *simplici myrto nihil adlabores sedulus curo* as the poet's artistic creed. We have to recognize that εἰρωνεία, the attitude of a man who is habitually *dissimulator opis propriae*, is here carried to the extreme. No more here than elsewhere is Horace telling lies about himself. But he is indulging in an enormous understatement. Why does he do so? Out of modesty? A more convincing explanation has to be sought. The unassuming tone and the simple ideals of this epilogue are certainly meant to be taken together—and to be contrasted—with the proud confidence and the high claims in the final odes of Book II and Book III.[2] But this alone would not account for the restraint in *Persicos odi, puer, apparatus*. Horace would not have concluded his book with this poem if he did not regard the artistic ideal which is symbolized in it as essential to his lyrics. He was convinced that, although it needs art to produce good poetry, no art would be of any avail if it were not supported by nature, the poet's nature which had grown with him from his early childhood, giving him an inner life of his own. On this conviction he insists throughout: *at fides et ingeni benigna vena est* (*Odes* 2. 18. 9 f.); *mihi parva rura et spiritum Graiae tenuem Camenae Parca non mendax dedit* (2. 16. 37 ff.); *quem tu, Melpomene, semel nascentem placido lumine videris, illum . . . quae Tibur*

---

[1] The fine epigram of Nikainetos ap. Athen. 15. 673b (compared by Reitzenstein, *Neue Jahrb.* xxi, 1908, 97) gives a better idea of the kind of poetry which is likely to have influenced Horace than the stilted product of Philodemus, *Anth. Pal.* 11. 34 (compared by Reitzenstein, 95).

[2] 'Dies Gedichtchen stellte er an den Schluß von Buch I, damit es mit *non usitata nec tenui ferar* und *exegi monumentum* contrastire' (Wilamowitz, *S.u.S.* 312 n. 1).

aquae fertile praefluunt et spissae nemorum comae fingent Aeolio carmine nobilem (4. 3. 1–12); *ego nec studium sine divite vena nec rude quid prosit video ingenium* (*Ars P.* 409 f.). So, if the symbol of his poetry which he chose for the end of the first book does not express the whole truth, it does at all events express nothing but the truth.

The epilogue of Book II, *Non usitata nec tenui ferar penna*, is a less happy product. It contains one perfect clause, the one in which there is also a true personal ring, *ego quem vocas, dilecte Maecenas*. Here Horace is innocent of the trouble which his commentators have stirred up. It started with a remark in one branch of our scholia (Ps.-Acro), *ordo est: Maecenas, non obibo ego, quem vocas dilecte*, etc. This *tour de force* can nowadays safely be left to itself,[1] but the feeling by which it was apparently prompted, that *quem vocas* is odd, still disturbs many scholars. The prejudice against admitting here the ordinary meaning of *vocare*, 'to invite (to one's house)', a prejudice at least as old as Dacier,[2] has received blows which ought to have been fatal,[3] but, with marvellous resilience, it has kept alive. We are told that 'the attempts to make it [i.e. *vocas*] = 'ad te vocas', as used of the living, always end in bathos'.[4] But rather than regard our modern standards of high and low as absolute and use them as a criterion for decisions in the text of the poet, we should first try to learn something about the scale of values which was valid for Horace and the men with whom he lived. The

---

[1] As can its progeny, A. Y. Campbell's *quem vocas tu 'docte'*, *Maecenas* (1945; in the edition of 1953 the text is the same, but the inverted commas and the following comma have disappeared).

[2] 'Quelques savans interpretes . . . veulent que *vocas* soit icy un terme de Festin, et qu'il signifie *vocare ad coenam*, prier à souper, comme cette signification luy est assez ordinaire dans les Auteurs Latins; Mais ce sens-là me paroist insuportable dans cette Ode, et je trouve la pensée plus digne d'un parasite que d'un galant homme.' It would not occur to Dacier (with whom Bentley agrees to the letter: 'haec interpretatio parasiti potius gulam quam gratum clientis animum exprimit', quoted with approval by Carlsson, *Eranos*, xliv, 1946, 417 n. 1) to consider possible differences between the code of behaviour valid for a 'galant homme' in the society of Louis XIV and the *urbanitas* of such men as Horace, Maecenas, and Augustus, but scholars of the nineteenth and twentieth centuries might be expected to have a more discerning eye.

[3] See, for example, the perfectly sound interpretation given in Orelli and Baiter's third edition (1850) and by Kiessling, followed, for example, by Plessis, Villeneuve, Tescari. Bücheler's authority, *Rh. Mus.* xxxvii, 1882, 238 (*Kl. Schriften* ii. 442), misled Hirschfelder (*Orelli–Baiter*, 4th ed.), Pasquali, *Or. lir.* 264 (who does not, however, go all the way with Bücheler), and Klingner, app. crit. Plüss, *Horazstudien*, 179, excogitated this: 'Der Dichter ist tot; . . . der liebste Freund ruft die Seele des Abgeschiedenen zum letzten Mal nach Brauch.' This was accepted by Ussani and, with a slight variation (Maecenas addresses, not the dead Horace, but the dying Horace), by Heinze. To say nothing of the tense of *vocas*, how can such a thought be reconciled with the strict parallelism between *non ego pauperum sanguis parentum* and *non ego quem vocas*? The assertion in Heinze's introduction, 'bei ihm weilt der Herzensfreund Maecen, dem seine letzten Worte auf dieser Erde gelten sollen', is wholly unwarranted.

[4] Wickham, ad loc.

information which Horace provides is clear enough. His position had not changed since, many years before the ode *Non usitata*, he wrote:[1]

> quem rodunt omnes libertino patre natum,
> nunc quia sim tibi, Maecenas, convictor, at olim
> quod mihi pareret legio Romana tribuno.
> dissimile hoc illi est, quia non, ut forsit honorem
> iure mihi invideat quivis, ita te quoque amicum,
> praesertim cautum dignos adsumere, prava
> ambitione procul.

'I am now', he says, 'an object of general envy *quia sim tibi, Maecenas, convictor.*' There is no substantial difference between *ego qui sum tibi, Maecenas, convictor* and *ego quem vocas, Maecenas*, just as there is no substantial difference between what is contrasted to it in either case, *libertino patre natus* and *pauperum sanguis parentum*. The passage of the satire enables us to assess the value of the position in which Horace was placed by Maecenas. To state that Horace is *Maecenati convictor* implies, not only in the eyes of the envious multitude, but in Horace's own opinion, that Maecenas is his friend; for the phrase *te . . . amicum* would in this context be pointless if its sense did not strictly correspond to that of *quia sim tibi convictor*. That this expression denotes a close relationship must have been obvious to any contemporary. Augustus writes to the poet:[2] *sume tibi aliquid iuris apud me, tamquam si convictor mihi fueris.* Horace thoroughly enjoys his position as one whom *Maecenas vocat*:

> 'quid tibi vis, insane?' et 'quam rem agis?' improbus urget
> iratis precibus, 'tu pulses omne quod obstat,
> ad Maecenatem memori si mente recurras.'
> hoc iuvat et melli est, non mentiar.[3]

But his pride in this intimacy is in the ode combined with an affectionate consideration for Maecenas: 'the friendship with which you have honoured a man of humble origin shall not be wasted: I, your friend, shall be immortal'. His devotion expresses itself in the epithet which, from the lips of this unsentimental poet, is touching, *dilecte Maecenas*. With this delicate turn he dedicates the book, like the two others, to his friend. The epilogue was the obvious place for this veiled dedication, since he had decided to open Book II with a tribute to Asinius Pollio. Probably it was also for the sake of variation that Horace fancied a plan according to which the dedication was to be placed in Book I at the beginning, in II at the end, and in III in the middle of the book.[4]

The rest of the ode is disappointing. It shows very little of Horace's

---

[1] *Sat.* 1. 6. 46 ff.   [2] Cf. p. 18 above.   [3] *Sat.* 2. 6. 29–32.
[4] Cf. pp. 229 f. above.

usual gift for filling traditional literary devices with a fresh and independent life. The variation of Ennius' famous epigram, of which the
last stanza consists, is skilful but nothing more. The history of the
motifs which make up the first half of the ode need not be re-told here;
the commentaries give sufficient material to trace it.[1] Here, too, we
may admire the poet's dexterity in entwining the various threads, but
he does not carry us with him.[2]

However, the real stumbling-block is the third stanza:

> iam iam residunt cruribus asperae
> pelles et album mutor in alitem
> superne nascunturque leves
> per digitos umerosque plumae.

This detailed description, appropriate to the kind of tale which we
know from Ovid's *Metamorphoses*, is in the context of this ode repulsive
or ridiculous, or both: repulsive, because the lofty idea of the transfigured *vates* leaves no room for the crude zoological precision in
residunt cruribus asperae pelles; ridiculous, because the person who undergoes this metamorphosis is not some poet or a typical poet but a definite
individual, represented in the reality of his personal life, *pauperum
sanguis parentum* and *quem vocas, Maecenas*; he is Q. Horatius Flaccus,
whom the people of Rome knew so well, *corporis exigui, praecanum,
solibus aptum*. Picture this plump and bald little man turning into a
swan, complete with *asperae pelles* and all: *spectatum admissi risum teneatis,
amici?* When we hear an old poet singing βάλε δή, βάλε κηρύλος εἴην
or a chorus of old men ὑπόροφα μέλαθρα . . . ἐστάλην ἰηλέμων γέρων
ἀοιδὸς ὥστε πολιὸς ὄρνις, we follow gladly; but when, two lines after
quem vocas, dilecte Maecenas, we read *iam iam residunt cruribus asperae
pelles, et album mutor in alitem superne*, we resist. *Du sublime au ridicule ce
n'est qu'un pas*: here Horace, for once, forgot to respect the slender line
that separates the two spheres. We have to leave it at that; the days are

---

[1] The fragment of Euripides, 911 N.[2] (cf. Wilamowitz, *Kl. Schriften*, i. 204), which was
compared with *Non usitata* as long ago as Mitscherlich, is now known also from Satyros,
Vit. Eur., col. 17. 29 ff. (v. Arnim, *Suppl. Eurip.* 8); cf. Cataudella, *Atene e Roma*, xli, 1939,
41 ff. It is obvious that the Euripidean chorus spoke of the ascent into heaven in the same
allegorical sense as Horace. Heinze's note (on 13) wants correction, and the fragment
must no longer be quoted with Gomperz's changes as it was printed by Nauck.

[2] I can, of course, only speak for myself. Reitzenstein, no doubt, felt what he said about
this ode (*Neue Jahrb.* xxi, 1908, 100 f.), 'Todesgedanken und Todessehnsucht, die Über-
zeugung daß in ihm, weil er das πνεῦμα empfangen hat, ein Unvergängliches wohnt, das
in neuer, freierer Gestalt weiter leben und wirken wird—das ist es, was Horaz ausspricht'.
But to me it seems that the great scholar read into the poem a modern 'Innerlichkeit' and
a religiosity which is, perhaps, Neoplatonic or gnostic, but certainly un-Horatian. However, Reitzenstein (cf. also his book *Die hellenistischen Mysterienreligionen*, 3rd ed. 321) has
given a valuable interpretation of *biformis* at l. 2, 'one who after his first shape is given a
second shape, a second life'.

past when scholars could expurgate their Horace by obelizing an un-pleasant stanza.[1]

The epilogue of Book III, *Exegi monumentum*, is a poem of a very high order. By its metre—though not by its metre alone—it is closely linked with i. 1, *Maecenas atavis*: in no other ode of Books I–III does the stanza consist of the asclepiadeus minor four times repeated.[2]

To read the ode aloud, one must take a fairly deep breath before starting, for the first sentence continues to the end of l. 5; in between one cannot pause, and the many sonorous expressions have to be given their proper weight. At l. 6 the voice is allowed a rest: the two brief and simple clauses, *non omnis moriar*[3] and *multaque pars mei vitabit Libitinam*, require no effort. But the breathing space is short. After the staccato of these two clauses there follows a legato passage, *usque ego postera crescam laude recens, dum Capitolium scandet cum tacita virgine pontifex*, and then another one, which stretches from the beginning of l. 10 to the middle of l. 14, from where a shorter sentence, a prayer to the Muse, carries the poem to its close.

The magnificent opening period, down to 5 *et fuga temporum*, revives thoughts familiar from Greek poetry, especially choric lyrics; in it there is nothing that might not have been said by a Greek poet. The following sentence is a good example of Horace's almost imperceptible transitions. The name of Libitina (7) is sufficient to bring us from the imagery of Greek poetry to Roman ritual, thus preparing the way for the Capitol, the Vestal virgin, and the *pontifex*, and further for Aufidus, Daunia, and the *Itali modi*. The last sentence (*sume superbiam . . . comam*), thoroughly Horatian in its mood and thought, strikes again a Greek note with *Delphica lauro* and Melpomene.

Polybius, in a famous passage now only indirectly preserved,[4] re-

---

[1] But Peerlkamp's criticism is still worth reading. For a recent attempt to whitewash the passage see G. L. Hendrickson, *Class. Philol.* xliv, 1949, 30 ff. On l. 9 he rightly remarks (as did, for example, Obbarius and Dillenburger) that *iam iam* here, as often elsewhere, refers to something future, but imminent (his collection of examples ignores the existence of *Thes. l. Lat.* vii. 1. 119 f., published in 1934). He then asks 'have we gained anything beyond a possible clarification of Latin idiom in the use of *iam iam . . .?* Is Horace any the less unpleasantly realistic for our pains?' The answer, I am afraid, is in the negative.

[2] On the intimate connexion between i. 1 and iii. 30 see Kiessling, *Philol. Unters.* ii, 1881, 51 n. 6. In Book IV the same metre recurs only in the eighth ode, *Donarem pateras*, which takes up the themes of i. 1 and iii. 30; cf. Heinze in his introduction to iv. 8 and in his article 'Die lyrischen Verse des Horaz', *Berichte der Sächs. Ges. d. Wiss.*, Phil.-hist. Kl. lxx, 1918, 4. Heft, 29 n. 2. Terentianus Maurus, 2693–5, *Gramm. Lat.* vi. 405, puts the first lines of i. 1, iii. 30, and iv. 8 together.

[3] Bergk, on Sappho *fr.* 10, quoted Aristides 28. 51 (ii. 158 Keil), οἶμαι δέ σε καὶ Σαπφοῦς ἀκηκοέναι . . . μεγαλαυχουμένης καὶ λεγούσης ὡς αὐτὴν αἱ Μοῦσαι τῷ ὄντι ὀλβίαν τε καὶ ζηλωτὴν ἐποίησαν καὶ ὡς οὐδ' ἀποθανούσης ἔσται λήθη. I do not know whether the similarity is purely accidental.

[4] 38. 22.

ported that the younger Scipio Africanus, when he saw Carthage, which he had conquered, being razed to the ground, burst into tears. Deep in thought, he was for a long while silent, 'and then, whether deliberately or because it escaped his lips, he quoted this passage of the *Iliad*:

ἔσσεται ἦμαρ ὅταν ποτ' ὀλώλῃ Ἴλιος ἱρὴ
καὶ Πρίαμος καὶ λαὸς ἐυμμελίω Πριάμοιο.

And Polybius asked him outright (for he was his friend and also his teacher) what he meant by saying that. And Scipio, without reserve, said "Rome, for when I consider the fortunes of men, I feel fear for her". And this Polybius put down as he had heard it himself.'[1]

We do not know whether Horace was ever obsessed by similar forebodings of Rome's fall. There is, at any rate, no such undertone in the present poem. Here the long period denoted by *usque . . . dum Capitolium scandet . . . pontifex* cannot be different from *innumerabilis annorum series et fuga temporum*. The future life of Rome with its unalterable ceremonies is taken for granted, if not to the end of all time, yet for so immense a period that no one needs to cast his thought beyond it.

It seems impossible not to be moved by the words

dum Capitolium
scandet cum tacita virgine pontifex.[2]

It takes, however, a moment's thought to realize how time has proved modest that apparently over-bold prophecy, *usque ego postera crescam laude recens, dum Capitolium*, etc. Unless we are careful, we find ourselves lured into the vision of the Vestal, demurely walking beside the *pontifex*, up the gentle flight of stairs, 'la cordonata', which, following the general plan of Michelangelo and designed by Giacomo della Porta, takes us nowadays so comfortably from Piazza Aracoeli up to Piazza del Campidoglio. But in the Vestal's time there was no straight and gentle staircase; she had to pick her steps across the uneven polygonal flagstones of the *clivus Capitolinus*, which from the west side of the Forum Romanum led in a rather steep curve up to the temple of Iuppiter Optimus Maximus.[3] The change in the approach to the Capitol is but one symptom of the gigantic revolution in Rome's history

[1] Is Polybius always 'einer der unerträglichsten antiken Historiker' (F. Jacoby, *F Gr Hist* iii[b] 537)?

[2] Friedrich Theodor Vischer, a man constitutionally out of touch with the spirit of Horace's poetry, could not refrain, when he was in Rome, from quoting *dum Capitolium*, etc., and remarking, with a kind of naïve impudence: 'Horaz hat doch große Momente!' Zieliński, *Horace et la société romaine du temps d'Auguste*, 1938, 225, after quoting *usque ego postera . . . pontifex*, says 'Cette image lui a conquis les cœurs les plus récalcitrants; impossible, en effet, de trouver une expression plus monumentale pour cette religion, monumentale entre toutes, du peuple maître du monde'.

[3] Thanks to the recent excavations we can now form a far better idea of the *clivus Capitolinus*; see G. Lugli, *JRS* xxxvi, 1946, 3, and plate II. 1.

which has affected not only the topography of the city but its whole character. When Horace had been in his grave for many centuries the places around which the life of the ancient Romans had circled were being deserted one after another, and what was left of the dwindling population lived on different hills. There was still a *pontifex*, but he would reside on the Lateran or the Quirinal or the Vatican, and would not care to sacrifice to Iuppiter Optimus Maximus. There was still a city of Rome, but filled with new gods, new rituals, and new ideas. And yet it remained true, and remains true to the present day, that *usque ego postera crescam laude recens*. Horace's boast turns out to be an enormous understatement.

It is a strange coincidence that in the epilogue of Book III as well as in that of Book II[1] the majority of scholars have been misled by the arbitrary assertion in a scholium concerning the manner in which certain parts of a sentence ought to be connected with each other. In the present case an ancient schoolmaster once dictated:[2] *ordo est: ego potens ex humili princeps dicar duxisse Aeolium carmen ad Italos modos, qua obstrepit violens Aufidus et qua Daunus*, etc., and for centuries many good boys have preferred to listen to the schoolmaster rather than to the poet. Not all of them, it is true, accepted the scholiast's paraphrase without any qualification,[3] but they agreed with him on the fundamental point that it is out of the question to take *dicar qua . . . obstrepit Aufidus*, etc., together so that it would mean 'there where Aufidus . . ., there it shall be said of me that I, from humble origin grown powerful, was the first . . .'. And yet this is the simplest and the only natural way of connecting the double clause *qua . . . et qua . . .*.[4] But here, as in the case of 2. 20. 6, *quem vocas*, a conventional feeling is against the natural interpretation, and to its command everybody, or nearly everybody,[5]

---

[1] See p. 299 above.   [2] Ps.-Acro on ll. 10 ff.

[3] Here a small selection of interpretations will suffice. Lambinus: 'Dicar ego, qui ex humili potens et clarus exstiti, qua parte labitur Aufidus . . . princeps deduxisse', etc.; Doering: 'Sensus: Ego oriundus ex ea regione, qua . . . devolvitur Aufidus', etc.; Dillenburger: 'Noli . . . haec [*qua violens*] cum *dicar* artius coniungere; nam nomen Horatii et gloria tam angustis finibus non est circumscribenda'. Orelli–Baiter praise 'Acron' for his arrangement; Kiessling: '*qua . . . populorum* giebt die nähere Bestimmung zu *ex humili potens*' (I have not been able to make out how Heinze construes the passage, and I am particularly puzzled by this comment, 'daß die Ortsbestimmung für das *deduxisse* genau genommen nicht zutrifft', etc.); Ussani: 'Dirà la fama di me che io seguendo il corso dell' Aufido . . . io, da umili origini potente signore', etc.; Plessis: 'Ne pas entendre: On dira dans le pays de Daunus que je fus le premier . . .',

[4] L. Müller felt this but brushed it aside.

[5] Dacier translated calmly 'Par tout dans les lieux où Daunus regna . . . on dira de moy', etc. So did Mr. Gladstone more than two centuries later: 'Where bellows headstrong Aufidus . . . of me it shall be told', etc., whereas Conington had followed the beaten track (' "Born", men will say, "where Aufidus is loud . . ." '). Besides Dacier, very few commentators adhered to the natural interpretation, e.g. G. Giri and Tescari. For Knapp's article see p. 305 n. 3.

submits. 'He is claiming world-wide fame, not merely [of 'merely' Horace says nothing] to be remembered in his birthplace.'[1] I am surprised that Englishmen should find it difficult to think of a man from Penzance or Carlisle who, after achieving fame in London or New York, would be proudest of what the people of Cornwall or Cumberland might say of him at their firesides. As regards ancient Italy, the facts are clear.[2] We know the interest with which the inhabitants of some *municipium* used to follow the careers of their fellow citizens in Rome and to talk about them. Cicero, in his speech *pro Plancio* (19–23), gives us a charming account of the manner in which that particular form of local patriotism was operative in Arpinum, Atina, and other *municipia* of that region.[3] Of the citizens of his own birthplace Cicero says :[4] *in quemcumque Arpinatem incideris, etiam si nolis, erit tamen tibi fortasse etiam de nobis aliquid, sed certe de C. Mario audiendum.* Propertius, in the overture of his last book,[5] says:

> ut nostris tumefacta superbiat Umbria libris,
> Umbria Romani patria Callimachi,

and Ovid, in the epilogue to his *Amores*:[6]

> Mantua Vergilio, gaudet Verona Catullo;
> Paelignae dicar gloria gentis ego.

Following in the footsteps of Ovid, Martial writes:[7]

> Verona docti syllabas amat vatis,
> Marone felix Mantua est,

and goes on to apply the same idea to a number of towns and those of their sons who became famous as writers or poets as, for instance (5–8):

> Apollodoro plaudit imbrifer Nilus,
> Nasone Paeligni sonant,
> duosque Senecas unicumque Lucanum
> facunda loquitur Corduba.

In the magnitude of its claim the epilogue of Book II, *Non usitata,* is

---

[1] Wickham.

[2] Nor have these affections very much changed since. See G. Pasquali, *Storia dello spirito tedesco nelle memorie d'un contemporaneo*, 1953, 127, 'In Italia, paese arcaico, l'*immortalitas gloriae* è ancora ideale altrettanto vivo quanto al tempo di Cicerone. È antico (e questa può essere una costante della natura italiana) che il campanilismo e l'orgoglio provinciale siano ancor oggi forze più attive che in ogni altra nazione europea.'

[3] I had for many years had a reference to the passage of the *Pro Plancio* (with which the opening sections of the first two books of the *De legibus* must be taken together) in the margin of my Horace, when I came across the excellent short article on *Odes* 3. 30. 10–14 by Charles Knapp, *CR* xvii, 1903, 156 ff., an article to which more attention ought to have been paid. Knapp supports his sound view on *dicar qua violens*, etc., by quoting Cic. *Planc.* 19–22 and also Martial i. 61.

[4] Ibid. 20.   [5] 4. 1. 63 f.   [6] 3. 15. 7 f.   [7] 1. 61. 1 f.

certainly not inferior to *Exegi monumentum*, but in this ode the claim is given a special turn. In the former epilogue it was stated in general terms that Horace was certain of immortality because he was a *vates*. That might have been said of many a Greek or Roman poet. But what Horace now pronounces to be the basis of his fame,

> princeps Aeolium carmen ad Italos
> deduxisse modos,

belongs to him alone. With this proud claim, and with the following prayer[1] to the Muse, he recalls the end of the exordium of his collection, where (i. i. 34) the *Lesbous barbitos* plays a prominent part and where the final sentence,

> quodsi me lyricis vatibus inseres,
> sublimi feriam sidera vertice,

makes supreme glory depend upon his being classed with οἱ λυρικοί. At the close of his work he looks back at what he has achieved. In his words there is indeed *superbia*, but, he is confident, *superbia meritis quaesita*. This *superbia* he now hands over to the Muse, the Greek Muse of his *Latinum carmen*, Melpomene.[2] Let us not make the mistake of

---

[1] At. 1. 16 *volens* (*volens propitius* is more common), like its model θέλων, belongs to the set formulas of prayers; cf. my note on A. *Ag.* 664.

[2] It is not because Plessis in his commentary on the *Odes*, 1924, pp. xx ff., was completely deceived by A. W. Verrall, *Studies in the Odes of Horace*, 1 ff., but because some scholars are still haunted by the ghost of Verrall's, not Horace's, Melpomene that I here deal with the fallacy. (I) Verrall applies the term 'tragic' to the odes of Books I–III in a sense which would seem perfectly normal to a newspaper man but could not have occurred to a Greek or Roman, since to them the connexion of the word with τραγῳδία and all it stands for was essential. (II) There is nothing to show that Horace regarded Melpomene as the Muse of tragedy. It was only in late antiquity that each Muse was put in charge of a special department (cf. p. 281 n. 1 above). As regards Melpomene, she remained for a long time the one who μέλπεται. In Apollodorus' Περὶ θεῶν (*F Gr Hist* 244 F 146) Melpomene was the mother of Thamyris, which implies a close connexion with citharody. This is in keeping with what is said of her in the epigram *Anth. Pal.* 9. 504 (where, incidentally, the Muse of tragedy is Euterpe); in *Anth. Pal.* 9. 505. 15 f. her task is χαλκεόφωνος ἀοιδή. That under the (early?) Empire she had not yet been fixed as the tragic Muse is clear from the epigram of Honestus (for the discussion about his date see *RE* viii. 2270) on the monument at Thespiae, published by Jamot, *Bull. Corr. Hell.* xxvi, 1902, 129 ff.,

> Με[λπο]μένα.
> Σύνφθογγόν με λύρης χορδῆι κεράσασαν ἀοιδὴν
> λεύσσεις ἐν δισσοῖς Μελπομένην μέλεσιν.
> 'Ονέστου.

Jamot, 148 f., observes that 'pendant longtemps, Melpomène fut seulement la divinité du chant et de l'harmonie musicale'. (For this epigram and the monument to which it belongs see now W. Peek, Γέρας Κεραμοπούλλου, Athens 1953, 622 f. He infers from certain traces that on the monument Melpomene did actually play the lyre. His suggestion ἐν δισσοῖς does not convince me.) It is arbitrary to find an allusion to the Muse of tragedy in Hor. *Odes* 1. 24. 2 ff. *praecipe lugubris cantus, Melpomene, cui liquidam pater vocem cum cithara dedit.* Here *Melpomene* means 'Muse of my lyrics'. *Odes* iv. 3 refers back to iii. 30 (and to i. 1), and it is for this reason that Melpomene is there invoked.

regarding the prayer at the end as a mere poetic convention. No doubt the figure of Melpomene or any other Muse was to Horace one of the πλάσματα τῶν προτέρων. But he felt that the inspiration which enabled him to write great poetry could not be accounted for in terms of ordinary human skill; he was convinced that it came from heaven. At his maturest stage he was to find a still deeper expression for this conviction and to thank the Muse thus:

> totum muneris hoc tui est
>
> . . . .
>
> quod spiro et placeo, si placeo, tuum est.

EPISTLES, BOOK I

I. INTRODUCTION

Nᴏᴛ all the considerations that led Horace in the years 23–20 B.C. to compose his book of *Epistles* are known, but some lie open before us. He had now made up his mind not to go on writing lyrics. The unsympathetic reception given to his *carmina* by the majority of the public hurt him greatly. The nineteenth epistle reveals the depth of his resentment. He therefore pledged himself to abandon once and for all the thankless task of thrusting upon Roman readers poems which they obviously were unable or unwilling to appreciate. On several occasions he made it clear that his decision to withdraw from writing poetry, which for him meant writing lyrics, was unalterable. Two of these pronouncements belong to the period after the publication of the book of *Epistles*; the first of them is the famous passage in the letter to the sons of Piso[1] *fungar vice cotis, acutum | reddere quae ferrum valet exsors ipsa secandi; | munus et officium, nil scribens ipse, docebo . . .*, the second is contained in a large section of the letter to Florus.[2] The programmatic statement,[3] *nunc itaque et versus et cetera ludicra pono; | quid verum atque decens, curo et rogo et omnis in hoc sum*, must be carefully weighed: Horace does indeed mean what he says, but at the same time there is here a tinge of his characteristic εἰρωνεία (*versus et cetera ludicra*) and, perhaps, also an attempt to make the best of a bad job. Not to write poetry any more must have been a hard decision after he had devoted himself to this task for so many years. Nevertheless, it would be wrong to regard his retiring into philosophical thought and into the writing of philosophizing epistles as a mere *pis aller*. Quite apart from the unfriendly criticism with which his odes had met, Horace may himself have had the impression that the stream of his lyric productivity no longer flowed quite so freely as it used to do. But that is a matter of guesswork. What is certain is that he felt an urgent need to give his time and thought to clearing his mind about the central problems of our conduct of life and the attainment of that wisdom which he had once[4] defined as *quod magis ad nos pertinet et nescire malum est* and which he now[5] defines as *quod aeque pauperibus prodest, locupletibus aeque*.

---

[1] *Ars P.* 304 ff.   [2] *Epist.* ii. 2.   [3] *Epist.* I. 1. 10 f.
[4] *Sat.* 2. 6. 72 f.   [5] *Epist.* I. 1. 24 f.

Together with these trends of thought there worked upon him certain artistic impulses. Many years before he had, through long and patient effort, developed an accomplished manner of presenting a variety of *sermones*. But in the course of his work on the second book of his *Satires* it had already become manifest that the *satira* such as Horace, inspired by Lucilius but gradually freeing himself from direct imitation of his model, had evolved it could no longer serve as a medium for what the mature poet had most at heart. The ideas that now engrossed him were too serious for that genre. Nor was he any longer satisfied with the setting he had chosen. The novelty introduced in Book II, the form of dialogue, produced some amusing effects, but in the long run it proved tiresome; it is significant that in his most perfect satire, ii. 6, *Hoc erat in votis*, he abandoned this form. But though the potentialities of the Horatian *satira* were exhausted, the potentialities of the Horatian *sermo* were not. The fine and flexible style which the poet had shaped for his satires could be adapted to different themes and express a different frame of mind.

It happened more than once at a critical juncture in Horace's poetic career that he escaped from routine and artificiality and recovered strength and freshness by turning his eyes away from the imaginary scenery of some literary convention towards the piece of solid ground on which he was standing himself. Why should he persist in making invented characters dispute far-fetched or irrelevant themes when his own life and his intercourse with his fellow men provided him with plenty of genuine matter, sometimes mere trifles, sometimes serious difficulties and conflicts, but always matter arising from real situations, in the lives of real persons, and always the kind of matter that lends itself naturally to the form of communication which we call a letter? With his propensity for philosophical contemplation Horace would not isolate the case in hand, but would widen the issue so that it might become a common concern of his readers; moreover, he would set it against the background of recognized principles so that it should attain the dignity of evident truth.

And so there came into being the collection of twenty epistles, the most harmonious of Horace's books. Philosophical problems had been discussed in letters before, and letters in verse had occasionally been written before, but nothing comparable to Horace's *Epistles* had ever existed in Greek or Roman literature.[1]

---

[1] For the novelty of Horace's *Epistles* see Wilamowitz, *S.u.S.* 323, and Heinze, *Vom Geist des Römertums*, 237 and 246.

2. EPISTLE XIV

Horace's *Epistles* are an organic continuation of his *Satires*. They show many characteristic features of those *sermones*, both in form and in matter. But at the same time they appear as genuine letters. We all know that many letters, in life as well as in literature, are in fact soliloquies, some of them human documents of very great interest. But as a rule we shall find those letters most attractive in which not only the writer but also the person addressed, though not in a position to speak directly, is present, so that we think we see him before us or at any rate catch some glimpses of his character and of the world in which he is moving. The degree to which the other man is taken into account varies a great deal in almost any correspondence, and so it does in Horace's *Epistles*. When in a letter to Maecenas (i. 19) he vents his anger at the reception with which his odes have met, his mind, very understandably, is filled with a single emotion; he could speak of nothing else. But not even here is the addressee irrelevant: by opening his heart to Maecenas Horace makes it clear that he trusts him absolutely and also shows himself confident that Maecenas understands the value of the new poems, whatever the majority of the Roman public may think of them.[1] However, in most of the epistles the person to whom Horace is writing has an even more important role.[2] Several instances will be discussed later on. Meanwhile I wish to exemplify the point by a brief examination of an epistle (XIV) in which, if we accept a widely held opinion,[3] the figure of the addressee should be regarded as a poetical fiction, the letter itself being a conventional sermon.[4]

An unprejudiced reader may be surprised that it should have been possible to miss so completely the nature of this epistle. About the very real *vilicus* and Horace's very real relations to him something will be said presently. But in addition there is in the epistle a detail which

---

[1] Cf. p. 339 below.

[2] 'Voilà le caractère propre des *Épîtres*; tout y est direct, vivant, particulier; rien de général ou d'abstrait. Une lettre à Celsus ou Florus n'est pas faite pour Iccius ou Bullatius. . . . Et voilà . . . ce qui distingue l'œuvre d'Horace des traités antérieurs, presque impersonnels sous leur forme épistolaire. L'épître reste avec lui, une lettre personnelle' (E. Courbaud, *Horace . . . à l'époque des épîtres*, Paris 1914, 29).

[3] This opinion, as far as I can see, goes back to Orelli–Baiter's introductory note, accepted by, for example, Wilkins, Kiessling, Wickham, Lejay, and now W. Wili, *Horaz*, 1948, 288 ('In ihr [*Epist.* i. 14] ist das Briefhafte auf den fiktiven Empfänger, den eigenen Gutsverwalter, zusammengeschrumpft'). When Heinze in his introduction to the epistle speaks of 'fiktiver Adressat', that is a relic of Kiessling's commentary; Heinze's own view comes out in the following sentence and, more decidedly, *Vom Geist des Römertums*, 242. But it was especially Courbaud, op. cit. 29 and 159 f., who dealt the death-blow to the idea of the fictitious addressee.

[4] 'Under cover of a comparison between his own tastes and the bailiff's, he . . . preaches his habitual sermon against restlessness and the desire of change' (Wickham).

clearly shows that this is not a 'sermon' hung up on some arbitrarily chosen peg, but a true letter, spontaneously written in circumstances which are still recognizable. The second sentence (6 ff.) runs:

> me quamvis Lamiae pietas et cura moratur
> fratrem maerentis, rapto de fratre dolentis
> insolabiliter, tamen istuc mens animusque
> fert et avet[1] spatiis obstantia rumpere claustra.

These lines bear the stamp of reality. Horace's sympathy for Lamia has prevented him for the time being from returning to his Sabine farm. Otherwise he would not have written this letter but would have talked things over with the bailiff. After a playful introduction (1–5) he first says what it is that is keeping him back in Rome. Such an explanation is natural at the beginning of a letter of this kind. Then he turns to the man's complaints. It appears that the bailiff, either in a letter or through a third person, had let Horace know once more how utterly he disliked the life he was compelled to lead in the country and that he wanted to change back to a place in his master's town house. Horace deals gently with him. He seems to be really fond of the slave who has long been connected with him and who now represents to the ageing poet a part of the wild but lovely days of his youth and brings back to him that Horace (32–34)

> quem tenues decuere togae nitidique capilli,
> quem scis immunem Cinarae placuisse rapaci,
> quem bibulum liquidi media de luce Falerni.

These lines with their emphatic repetition of the initial *quem*—hammering in, as it were, the identity—serve here primarily as a foil to what follows: they emphasize the completeness of the change that has taken place in Horace's conduct of life; from the safe position of his present sobriety he might be tempted to say ἔφυγον κακόν, ηὗρον ἄμεινον. But the emotion that vibrates in these three *quem* clauses is perhaps not one of unmixed satisfaction. Wherever Cinara appears in a Horatian poem there is always a strong nostalgic note. But to return to Horace's treatment of his *vilicus*: although he is convinced that what the man wants is foolish, he refrains from using severe language, not only because he likes his servant, but also because it has become part of his philosophical self-education to view human affairs in true perspective. In a manner both kindly and wise he begins by including himself among the many who are guilty of μεμψιμοιρία (10–13). Nothing could be fairer than the phrase (12) *stultus uterque*, which refers, it is true, to representatives of a general type but also to the two

---

[1] It is sad that the edition of Horace which in Bentley's country is commonly used has no room, even in the apparatus, for Bentley's *avet*.

individuals from whom the discussion started, the *vilicus* and Horace. The way in which in this section a general reflection on a human weakness is connected with the discussion of a special instance of that weakness is typical of the *Epistles*. It is instructive to compare the beginning of the first satire of Book I, where the theme is precisely the same, μεμψιμοιρία:

> Qui fit, Maecenas, ut nemo, quam sibi sortem
> seu ratio dederit seu fors obiecerit, illa
> contentus vivat, laudet diversa sequentis?
> 'o fortunati mercatores' gravis annis
> miles ait multo iam fractus membra labore.
> contra mercator . . ..

Here, as in the Hellenistic diatribes that are among the roots of such a satire, there comes first a general proposition, subsequently illustrated by a series of examples. The epistle proceeds in the reverse order: the discussion begins with an issue which actually concerns Horace and the man to whom he is writing, and only by ascending from this special issue to a higher plane is a point reached from which the general aspects of the problem become visible. This approach from the angle of a practical question—typical of the Roman attitude to moral philosophy—is a distinctive feature of Horace's epistles. It is this approach, above all, that makes them real letters: in the foreground there is, not a thesis, but a human situation, a personal problem, arising out of another man's circumstances, or Horace's own, or both.

We noticed already how gently Horace is conversing with his bailiff. Indeed the whole letter shows that the master, without condescension and without betraying his own different views, looks sympathetically on the slave's desires and crude tastes. His trivial pleasures are depicted with gusto. In his present position the poor fellow has to do without even the most modest fun: in the neighbourhood of that wretched place in the valley of the Digentia there is not even a rustic inn[1] to provide him with a drink and a flute-girl so that after the day's labours he might dance with heavy tread to her tune. We remember from the *Iter Brundisinum* the good-humoured amusement with which Horace watches the entertainments of the lower classes. Needless to say, accomplished little pictures like the one at which we have just been looking (24–26) are designed to please Maecenas and other sophisticated men. Horace's epistles are never mere private documents but are always written also for the reader of the book.

Throughout the letter Horace, instead of lecturing the slave or

---

[1] A 'Fuhrmannsschenke' as Wilamowitz, *Hell. Dichtung*, ii. 312, calls the *caupona* of the *Copa Syrisca* (referred to in Orelli–Baiter's note on 25).

talking down to him, is bent upon entering properly into his sphere
of life and way of thinking. Hence the pleasant beginning with the
challenge to a match, *certemus* (4), and, as part of it, the picturesque
detail taken from the bailiff's daily work, *spinas animone ego fortius an tu
evellas agro*.[1] Every now and then Horace seems to adjust his own
language to that of the *vilicus*. That is probably the case when he is
using *tesqua* (19), an old and rare word, which in Horace's day might
well have given the impression that *nostri sic rure loquuntur*;[2] the *vilicus*
has by now lived long enough in the country to have adopted some
elements of the local jargon.

Horace, no doubt, genuinely cares for the slave and tries to prevent
him from taking a false step. But the letter reaches its greatest intensity
in the passage where the poet tells us how he himself, after sowing his
wild oats, has at last won equanimity and a simple, but unshakeable,
happiness (32–39), *nec lusisse pudet, sed non. incidere ludum*. More than
anything else it is this outlook on life, long growing in Horace's mind,[3]
but only recently brought to full realization, that makes him dislike
living in busy Rome and long for the peaceful days and the healthy
toil (39) at his farm. Much though he cherishes his *villa rustica* for its
own sake, its main value to him now appears to lie in the fact that it
enables him, unhampered by silly conventions and tiresome obligations, to live a life such as befits a thoughtful man, ὁμολογουμένως τῇ
φύσει ζῆν. The praise of independence and simplicity in which the letter
culminates will strongly appeal even to those readers who take little
interest in the fickleness of Horace's bailiff and in the poet's relations
with him. And so we are once more reminded of the double nature of a
Horatian epistle. The letter, as will have become evident, was written
for the *vilicus*,[4] but it is also written for us, the readers of the book.
Most of Horace's epistles are *Gelegenheitsgedichte* in the sense in which
Goethe used the term, poems suggested by a given occasion and written
for some immediate practical purpose, to accompany a present, to convey congratulations, to bring comfort in distress, and so forth. But a
Gelegenheitsgedicht deserves to be included in a published book only if it
is self-contained, that is to say if its meaning is made as clear to the
general reader as it will have been to the person for whom it was
originally conceived, and, no less important, if it conveys something

[1] For the use of *evellere herbas* and the like in the farmers' language see *Thes. l. Lat.* v. 2.
1009. 67 ff.

[2] Kiessling observed on *tesqua* 'in der Bauernsprache haften geblieben'; see further E.
Norden, *Aus altröm. Priesterbüchern*, 20 f., and E. Vetter, *Handbuch der italischen Dialekte*, i.
376.

[3] See, for instance, *Sat.* 2. 6. 60–76.

[4] The sense in which this is to be understood has been admirably formulated by Courbaud, op. cit. 29: 'quant au *vilicus* . . ., qu'il doive lire ou non les admonestations de son
maître, Horace lui écrit comme s'il devait les lire.'

that is not the narrow concern of a particular individual in a particular situation but is capable of impressing many kinds of men. The best *Gelegenheitsgedichte*, ancient as well as modern, satisfy these demands. One ancient example, near to Horace's time, may serve as an illustration. If there was ever a true *Gelegenheitsgedicht*, it is Catullus' fiftieth poem. No one can doubt that the gay verse-competition between Calvus and Catullus did actually take place on the day before the night, or the early morning, when the hendecasyllables were written and straight away dispatched to Calvus (14–17). Hardly more than twelve hours can have elapsed between the little private entertainment and Calvus' reading of the poem in which it is described. And yet Catullus finds it necessary to give this minute account:

> Hesterno, Licini, die otiosi
> multum lusimus in meis tabellis,
> ut convenerat esse delicatos.
> scribens versiculos uterque nostrum
> ludebat numero modo hoc modo illoc,
> reddens mutua per iocum atque vinum.

It would be absurd to assume that Catullus thought Calvus needed so extensive a reminder of what the two friends had been doing the evening before. The poet's real intention is obvious: he is thinking of the reader as much as of Calvus; the reader has to be made acquainted with the whole background of the poem if he is to share in its life and enjoy it as much as Catullus trusts that Calvus will. Horace's letter to the *vilicus*, too, is a self-contained poem, complete in itself, differing thereby from a document of actual life, which as such remains fragmentary. It tells the reader all he needs to know about the man's position, his long connexion with Horace, and his present mood. And, moreover, it shows a deliberate regard for the reader, any reader, in that it views a special and momentary issue—the bailiff's wish for a change in his situation—as a typical instance of an error that at one time or another endangers the true happiness of most men: *cui placet alterius, sua nimirum est odio sors*. By taking this turn towards our common human experience the epistle makes a direct appeal to the reader: *tua res agitur*.

3. EPISTLES II AND XVIII

In the book of the *Epistles* Horace's young friend Lollius Maximus is treated in a most remarkable manner. Apart from Maecenas, Lollius is the only person to whom more than one epistle is addressed.[1]

---

[1] Cf. Courbaud, op. cit. 207.

And to make the distinction still more conspicuous, one of the two letters to Lollius, II, is placed immediately after the first epistle, by which the book is dedicated to Maecenas, and the other, XVIII, immediately before the last letter, XIX, which is again addressed to Maecenas (XX is not a letter but the epilogue of the book). About the family of Lollius nothing is known; the widely accepted hypothesis that he was a son of M. Lollius, consul in 21 B.C.,[1] is unprovable.[2] What does, however, emerge from the evidence before us is that Horace must have been very fond of the young man whom he honoured in his book in such a singular way.

It has been said that in the epistle *Troiani belli scriptorem* the character of a letter is maintained only at the beginning and at the end.[3] That seems to me, to say the least, an exaggeration. The situation of Lollius influences the tone of the whole letter. It is unlikely that Horace in an epistle, even an early epistle,[4] should have permitted himself to lecture so freely if he were not writing to a very young man and to one prepared to follow his guidance. The admonition at the end (67 ff.), *nunc adbibe puro | pectore verba, puer, nunc te melioribus offer. | quo semel est imbuta recens servabit odorem | testa diu*, takes up the image at 54, *sincerum est nisi vas, quodcumque infundis acescit*, and the whole didactic finale is in keeping with the general tendency of the letter. Warnings such as those given at 33 ff., *ut te ipsum serves non expergisceris? . . . et ni | posces ante diem librum cum lumine, si non | intendes animum studiis et rebus honestis, | invidia vel amore vigil torquebere*, may be very useful also to middle-aged men, but they are particularly appropriate for undergraduates, who as a rule are not early risers.

The much older and more experienced friend does not hesitate to speak as a mentor and speak in unmistakable terms, but he will not rub in his superiority. He takes the sting out of his moralizing by including himself in the number of the many who are at fault. Ulysses

---

[1] Cf. p. 425 below.

[2] The old identification (Ps.-Acro) of the Lollius of *Epist.* i. 2 with the consul of 21 B.C., adhered to as late as Dacier and Baxter, was refuted for good by J. M. Gesner; he took the addressee of the two letters to be a son of the consul of 21 B.C. (however, Gesner saw, which is to his credit, the difficulty of assuming the cognomen *Maximus* for a member of the noble *gens* of the Lollii; he therefore took *maxime* as = *natu maxime*, which is, of course, most unlikely). The identification with the son of the consul of 21 was accepted as certain by Orelli–Baiter and as probable by Wilkins, Kiessling, Heinze, and many others; L. Müller rejected it on partly arbitrary grounds. Courbaud, op. cit. 206 ff., wrote two pages to shake Müller's position and made some good points, but he did not succeed in proving that the Lollius of the letters was the son of the consul of 21 B.C. It seems to me necessary to accept the judgement of Dessau, *Prosop. Imp. Rom.* ii. 295, and Groag, *RE* xiii. 1387: the former denies implicitly any connexion between the Lollius of the *Epistles* and the consul of 21, the latter explicitly.

[3] 'Den Briefcharakter wahrt nur Eingang und Schluß; im übrigen hält der Dichter eine allgemeingültige Mahnrede', etc. (Heinze).

[4] See the end of Kiessling's introduction, which was slightly modified by Heinze.

proves a paragon of wise and steadfast ἀρετή (17–26),[1] but we others (27), *nos numerus sumus.*[2]

It is not difficult to reconstruct the reasons which induced Horace to place this letter immediately after the dedicatory epistle. For one thing he wanted, as we have seen, to pay a handsome compliment to his young friend. But it is probable that he also considered the contents of this letter to Lollius most suitable to emphasize a prominent strain of the *Epistles. Troiani belli scriptorem,* in certain respects reminiscent of some of the later satires, is rather dogmatic, more so than any óther piece of the book. It therefore exemplifies very clearly, though perhaps in a one-sided manner, the poet's concern with certain serious problems. In the programmatic first epistle Horace declares (10 f.):

> nunc itaque et versus et cetera ludicra pono:
> quid verum atque decens, curo et rogo et omnis in hoc sum.

The beginning of the second epistle, following an interpretation of Homer that had long become common, proclaims that Homer (3 f.)

> quid sit pulcrum, quid turpe, quid utile, quid non,
> planius ac melius Chrysippo et Crantore dicit.

The close relation of this passage to the passage quoted from the first epistle is unmistakable, for the *verum atque decens* there, the πρέπον as applied to ethics,[3] is not substantially different from the *pulcrum* here, the opposite of *turpe. Epist.* i. 2, while maintaining the character of a true letter, deals thoroughly with one of the central themes announced in i. 1. We have to infer that Horace regarded this letter to Lollius as an effective demonstration of his departure from the *ludicra* and his insistence on the values that matter most. If the letter might seem rather strongly didactic, there were many others to follow in which there would be no lack of lighter tones.

It has long been seen[4] that the second letter to Lollius, XVIII, was written in 20 B.C.; its date is therefore about two years later than that of the other, II.

The epistle begins in an easy colloquial manner, *Si bene te novi.*[5] The

---

[1] In the clause (22) *adversis rerum immersabilis undis* the adjective *immersabilis* is ἅπαξ λεγόμενον. For its use in this context, and also for the phrasing at *Odes* 4. 4. 65 *merses profundo, pulcrior evenit* (notice the sense), Horace was probably indebted to Catullus 68. 13 *accipe, quis merser fortunae fluctibus ipse.*

[2] The 'testimonium', NOS NVMERVS s[, on a vase from the neighbourhood of Mainz, *CIL* xiii, no. 10017. 53 (*Carm. Lat. epigr.* iii. 156), is absent from the editions of Keller and Klingner.

[3] Cf. Heinze on *Epist.* 1. 1. 10 and Pohlenz, *Nachr. Gött. Ges.* 1933, 60 and 86 ff.

[4] See Bentley's note on 56.

[5] The phrase belongs obviously to the 'Umgangssprache'; in the extant Republican literature it is not very often found. Cicero, who admits it into one of his earliest speeches

semi-serious *liberrime Lolli*[1] maintains the informal note. Horace, who has been a friend to Lollius for several years (54–64), knows his enthusiasm for liberty and senses the danger that he might be imposed upon by the ostentatiousness and the offensive bad manners of certain champions of extreme independence (5–8). That would be regrettable at all times, but fatal in the present circumstances, when Lollius, as emerges from this letter, is about to join the retinue of one of the great.[2] Having to deal with a young man of strong convictions, the mentor's task is delicate; so Horace tackles it with remarkable caution. He remains gentle throughout, but after a somewhat playful start he soon becomes serious. The arrangement of the introductory section is characteristic of the *Epistles.* The discussion starts from the type of the *scurra*, abhorred by Lollius, then proceeds to a picture of the opposite extreme, the man who poses as *virtutis verae custos rigidusque satelles,* and finally puts these *vitia* in perspective by setting them against the general background of the Aristotelian[3] definition of ἀρετή, 9 *virtus est medium vitiorum et utrimque reductum.* The reverse procedure will be found, for instance, at *Sat.* 1. 2. 24 ff.: there the beginning is made by a general maxim, *dum vitant stulti vitia, in contraria currunt,* which is then illustrated by a series of *exempla* (25 ff.), *Maltinus tunicis demissis ambulat,* and so forth. Our letter, like others,[4] takes its cue from a definite situation in actual life and ascends from there to a comprehensive view of the complex of kindred issues.

After his slightly stiff sketch of a lecture on the essence of *virtus* Horace unbends. The two contrasting types, the cringing *scurra* and the intransigent unsociable dogmatizer,[5] are shown in

(S. Rosc. 57 *sed, si ego hos bene novi, litteram illam . . . ad caput adfigent*), never uses it in a letter (a playful variation occurs at *Att.* 5. 21. 13 *hoc quid intersit, si tuos digitos novi, certe habes subductum*), but Balbus does (ap. Cic. *Att.* 9. 7 B. 2 *praestabo, si Caesarem bene novi, eum . . .*). As for the following instances of *si bene te novi,* Ovid, *Am.* 2. 18. 39, *Ars Am.* 3. 51, *Pont.* 1. 6. 4, 2. 3. 49, Martial 3. 68. 11, I am inclined to derive them directly from the living usage, although an influence of Horace's epistle cannot be excluded. Cf. also Sen. *Epist.* 16. 7 *iam ab initio, si bene te novi, circumspicies . . .* (quoted by Orelli–Baiter). Hor. *Sat.* 1. 9. 22, *si bene me novi,* a clumsy witticism of the bore, based on the same formula, has been compared by the commentators.

[1] For its implications see Kiessling–Heinze, ad loc., and add Heinze's note on 8 *dum volt libertas . . ..*

[2] 'Le nom du protecteur demeure impossible à déterminer' (Courbaud, op. cit. 256 n. 2).   [3] Recognized in antiquity: ἀρετὴ μετριότης (Porph. on 9).

[4] Cf. on *Epist.* 1. 14. 10 f., pp. 311 f. above.

[5] There seems to be a good deal to be said in favour of Bentley's insertion of *et* at the end of 15: it removes the harsh asyndeton to which the interpolator (cf. p. 100 above) responsible for the reading *rixatus* in the Bland. vet. took exception. Wilkins calls Bentley's correction clumsy; I do not know why. In the *Epistles,* as elsewhere in Horace, *et* at the end of a line is common; at 1. 7. 27 it is in *synaloepha* with a word of the same metrical value as *caprina.* In cases of such elisions the survival of *et* at the end of the verse was precarious; it vanished from the παράδοσις, for instance, at *Odes* 3. 1. 39 and 4. 9. 41 (here *et,* which Klingner ascribes to Heinze, was added in the Renaissance: see, for example, Lambinus'

some lively scenes (10–20) 'd'un comique excellent et d'un art savoureux'.[1]

A new section, again in a more serious tone, begins with a formidable catalogue of the sins that are at all costs to be avoided by one who wishes to be the companion of a rich and powerful man (21–24). The five symmetrical *quem* clauses seem to hammer in the commandments 'that and that and that thou shalt beware of'. A short speech of the patron, whose seeming concern for the welfare of his protégé scarcely conceals his lack of human sympathy (26–31), is followed by the story of Eutrapelus (31–36), taken, like so many *exempla* in the *Satires*, from the social life of that generation in Rome that immediately preceded Horace's own.[2] This story is in the following section balanced, again in the manner familiar from the *Satires*, by a story taken from Greek tragedy (41–44).

Lollius, in his new position, will have to put up with a great deal of inconvenience and annoyance, but one sacrifice which he must be prepared to make will be, Horace knows, far more irksome to him than all the rest. What he has most at heart is to write poetry,[3] and that he will seldom be free to do, involved as he will be in his patron's sports (40 ff.). In this section (down to 66) it is especially obvious—but it holds good for the whole letter—that Horace's advice springs by no means merely from utilitarian considerations. A young man who has a part to play in Roman society must learn to adapt himself to other people's way of life and not pamper his solitary self-indulgence. Besides, Lollius is of a healthy constitution and has been an excellent soldier; it will be good for him to take energetic exercise and keep his body fit (47–57). Nor should an occasional simple pastime be uncongenial to him: Horace, who is familiar with Lollius' home, reminds him in a few delightful sentences of the sea-battle of Actium which he, his brother, and the boys of the neighbourhood used to perform on a lake or pond of the paternal *villa* (59–64).

From these pleasant recollections Lollius and we, the readers, are roused by some rather stern notes, reminiscent of public ordinances, *videto*, . . . *fugito* (68 f.); playfulness has once more given place to serious admonition.[4] Horace seems slightly embarrassed (67) that

---

text and the end of Bentley's note). At *Odes* 3. 8. 27 f. the asyndeton seems to be intentional (cf. Leo, *Plaut. Forsch.*, 2nd ed. 358 n. 2).   [1] Courbaud, op. cit. 259.

[2] Ritter's unfortunate idea of letting the rich patron, after *certare* (31), continue his speech with the account about Eutrapelus (to the end of 36) was accepted by Kiessling, Mewes, Heinze, and Klingner. L. Müller rightly observes on 31–36 'Beispiel für *odit et horret* in V. 25'. Besides, the formal symmetry with the Amphion παράδειγμα as well as Horace's general practice of interspersing *exempla* shows Ritter's arrangement to be wrong.

[3] See Heinze's helpful note on 40.

[4] At the end of 67 Kiessling (followed by Heinze and Klingner) put the comma before, instead of after, *tu*; I find this intolerably artificial.

he should have to mention rules of common decency to a man like Lollius.

At l. 76 a new section begins with *qualem commendes*. The reader who, perhaps with Book XIII of Cicero's letters *Ad familiares* fresh in his memory, considers what a plague the recommendation-hunters must have been in those days will not be surprised by the solemn warnings (*etiam atque etiam aspice*) which Horace feels bound to give on this head. 'Do not obstinately protect the man who, after being recommended by you, shows that he did not deserve it (78 f.), but cling faithfully to a proved friend and defend him against slanderous talk: his danger may soon become your own danger (80–85);[1] your position in the great man's favour is altogether unsafe (86–88),[2] and, whatever your temperament and your inclinations, there will always be some class of persons to whom you must be the object of annoyance and envy (89–93).'[3] Finally, Horace repeats his warning (6) against *asperitas agrestis et inconcinna gravisque* with a slight modification (94), *deme supercilio nubem*, do not parade the *triste supercilium* of the rigid champion of virtue.

In the following section (96–103) the poet lifts our hearts by one of his unforgettable sayings:

> inter cuncta leges et percontabere doctos,
> qua ratione queas traducere leniter aevum . . ..

Inter cuncta he says, concisely and discreetly; no need to detail any longer the various types of unpleasantness which besiege us as soon as we enter into the life of society, only to learn that *perditur haec inter misero lux*. From all those distractions there is always an escape open to a sensible man: he should read the works of the philosophers, consult them again and again, and make their thoughts his own. By doing so he will not only acquire absolute values, but will also become capable of dealing in an intelligent and dignified manner with the difficulties that inevitably arise when we have to live with others.[4] Here Horace, without disregarding his friend's special needs, raises his advice to the level of what to him is universal truth. The long series of moral problems, formulated in seven interrogative propositions (97–103), culminates in a reassertion of the poet's Epicurean creed, λάθε βιώσας,

---

[1] Comparing the end of 84, *proximus ardet*, with Virg. *Aen.* 2. 311 f., *iam proximus ardet | Ucalegon*, I think it possible that both poets echo the ending of a verse of Ennius.

[2] It is a pleasure to see that Lambinus recognized in 86, *dulcis inexpertis . . .*, an adaptation of Pindar's words, *fr.* 110, γλυκὺ δὲ πόλεμος ἀπείροισιν κτλ.

[3] At 91 f. the words *bibuli media de nocte Falerni oderunt* are interpolated (Meineke); see now Jachmann, *Studi in onore di U. E. Paoli*, 1955, 403 ff.

[4] This second profit which may be gained by the study of philosophy is not directly stated in Horace's words, but is clearly implied: see Courbaud's excellent analysis (262) of this passage.

secretum iter et fallentis semita vitae.[1] This leads the writer quite naturally to speak briefly of his own present position, a practical fulfilment of the ideal of λάθε βιώσας. The transition is effortless also because in a fairly long letter, after concerning yourself all the time with the situation of the person you are writing to, you will be expected to add at least a few remarks about yourself.

In this concluding sketch of Horace's own βίος (104–12), the consummation of an accomplished epistle, there is not the faintest trace of complacency, only profound happiness and gratitude. The simple and affectionate description of his surroundings,

> me quotiens reficit gelidus Digentia rivus,
> quem Mandela bibit, rugosus frigore pagus,

is full of implications: what a difference between the refreshing coolness of this quiet place in the hills with its hardy inhabitants and the climate, the physical and the moral climate, of hot, dusty, noisy Rome!

Horace regarded a prayer as an adequate and as a perfectly sincere expression of his happiness and gratitude.[2] The letter to Lollius concludes with a special type of prayer, a prayer which does not ask for further and greater blessings but for the preservation and the wise enjoyment of all that has already been granted to the speaker. This type of prayer, an old one, is very dear to Horace,[3] and anyone who knows something about him will understand why that is so.

The prayer is followed by a brief epilogue (111 f.), which ends with the words *aequum mi animum ipse parabo*. This cheerful acknowledgement of man's own responsibility is derived not from popular religion but probably from the same Greek doctrine to which a little earlier (103) *secretum iter et fallentis semita vitae* referred.[4]

We may have a feeling of relief when at the end of this worldly-minded letter a voice that carries conviction speaks of the ideal which we know to be Horace's own and one with which we are in natural sympathy ourselves. But it would be a mistake to regard all else in this epistle as a dark foil to a shining finale. The advice that Horace gives to Lollius is not insincere nor is it a betrayal of the poet's own convictions. The principle of λάθε βιώσας is not a key that opens every gate; life is not as simple as that. There is a time for complying with the rules of society and a time for withdrawing into one's own self. Horace himself had long been practising what he now advises Lollius to do.

---

[1] On *Epist.* 1. 17. 10, where the same verb, *fefellit*, is used, the scholia comment by quoting λάθε βιώσας.

[2] Cf. p. 141 above.   [3] Cf. pp. 138 f. above.

[4] Heinze quotes Epicurus, *fr.* 65, μάταιόν ἐστι παρὰ θεῶν αἰτεῖσθαι ἅ τις ἑαυτῷ χορηγῆσαι ἱκανός ἐστι. Cf. also (quoted by Courbaud, 263 n. 5) Sen. *Epist.* 41. 1 *facis rem optimam . . . si . . . perseveras ire ad bonam mentem, quam stultum est optare, cum possis a te impetrare.*

But even apart from the special circumstances of Lollius' case—for this epistle like the others is meant for any reader as well as for its addressee —the inconveniences that must be endured, the sacrifices that must be made if a life with our fellow men is to be possible at all, they all are necessary to complete our self-education. If these irritations were absent, we might be lost in effeminate inaction, incapable of achieving anything for ourselves or for others. What is important, however, is, in the midst of all these distractions, never to lose sight of our true goal, but to train ourselves to such independence that we shall be able, if need be, to say *cuncta resigno*, to walk out of the busy life and take the *secretum iter*.

4. EPISTLE XVII

Here we may in passing glance at Epistle XVII, *Quamvis, Scaeva, satis per te tibi consulis*. The two letters, XVIII and XVII, for all their difference, have a good deal in common, so that the error of some ancient commentators, who thought both were addressed to the same person,[1] if a stupid error, is at least understandable.

Nothing else is known of Scaeva. From this epistle it appears that Horace did not greatly care for him. The ironical opening[2] is of a piece with the rest of the letter. The older man lets Scaeva have his advice for what it is worth; he may take it or leave it. Horace has no intention of spending much energy in an attempt to improve the morals of a conceited (1 f.) young careerist. There is nothing here of the fine sense of responsibility that guided the poet's pen when he was writing the carefully balanced letter to Lollius. But Horace is not being dishonest either. The ideal of λάθε βιώσας appears in this letter (10) as well as in the letter to Lollius, but here it is almost obscured by an atmosphere of shrewd expediency and general scepticism. If Scaeva cannot detect what Horace really believes in, so much the worse for him.

Horace had announced that he was going to instruct Scaeva *quo tandem pacto deceat maioribus uti*. But he soon shifts his ground: the main theme of the letter seems to be the question whether or not it is justifiable to attach oneself to one of the great and to become a *scurra* (19).[3] The issue is brilliantly illustrated by the dialogue between Aristippus and Diogenes (13–22) delivered in the succinct and witty manner

---

[1] Ps.-Acro in the heading of XVII: *Praecepta vitae ad Lollium Scaevam*, etc. But it seems probable that Porphyrio, in whose text the beginning of the heading of XVII is mutilated, gave the same information, for at the beginning of XVIII he says *Aliud praeceptum, quo monet*, etc.

[2] Cf. F. Jacoby, 'Theognis', *Sitz. Berlin*, Phil.-hist. Kl. 1931, 126 n. 1.

[3] Courbaud, 247 f., makes some excellent observations on this shifting of the argument.

familiar from the *Satires*.[1] Here, and throughout the letter, the pros and cons on either side are presented with frightening impartiality. Horace seems to judge the behaviour of the champion of self-contained *virtus* no less severely than that of the *scurra*. The end of the epistle, from 43 on, fulfils to a certain degree the promise given at the beginning: for the benefit of an apprentice in the *ars scurrandi* some rules are laid down to show him how to exploit his patron without annoying him. This conclusion is somewhat upsetting,[2] and so is the whole epistle.

Why did Horace write such an extraordinary letter, something that has seemed to many critics unworthy of him? Scaeva had apparently informed him rather complacently of his intention of attaching himself to some great man, and this letter is Horace's reply. But, owing to the way in which his mind worked, he could not and would not keep his thoughts within the narrow compass of a special case. Scaeva's base ambition appeared to him as a typical instance of a moral disease of which he had seen much in the society of his day. Vividly recalling the humiliation to which men's greed often subjects them he grew angry, and his anger was not tempered by any regard for Scaeva. Nor in considering the other extreme, the merely theoretical display of moral intransigence and financial independence, did he recover a more benevolent mood. Hence the acidity of the epistle.[3]

What has been said will, I hope, provide an answer to the question which, considering the many points of contact between epistles XVII and XVIII, may not unnaturally be asked: did Horace, in writing the letter to Scaeva, already think of writing the following letter to Lollius?[4] The letter to Scaeva clearly stands in its own right. The fact that a good deal of its matter is also found in the letter to Lollius is not due to any comprehensive planning but rather to Horace's long experience of, and deep concern with, the social phenomena and the moral problems which were once more brought to his mind by the present circumstances of Scaeva and Lollius. It was presumably only when the poet had to settle the final arrangement of his book that he decided to place the letter to Scaeva in front of the letter to Lollius. The two epistles, he must have felt, were linked together by the similarity of their general background and also by the light they threw on certain ethical conflicts. But, above all, they complemented one another

---

[1] 'Un de ces dialogues familiers au poète, aussi brusquement introduits que vivement menés, où les opinions s'entrechoquent comme des lames d'épée' (Courbaud, 250).

[2] 'Toute cette fin de l'épître, très vive, très amusante, . . . ne laisse pas d'être déconcertante' (ibid. 255).

[3] Kiessling and Heinze, in their introduction to this epistle, have not convinced me that Horace here is bent upon rejecting some envious criticism of his relations to Maecenas.

[4] Courbaud, 253, asks this very question and gives the right answer, 'c'est assez peu vraisemblable'.

in the most desirable fashion.[1] Horace saw no reason why he should tone down the letter to Scaeva, but once this letter was followed by the letter to Lollius, the effect of its cynicism would be mitigated by the impression which the mellow wisdom of the next epistle was bound to make upon the reader.

5. EPISTLE IV

The short letter to Tibullus,[2] i. 4, shows some of the most characteristic and most engaging qualities of Horace's epistles. It is graceful, warm-hearted, and rich in stylistic shades, and, though brief, full of mellow, unobtrusive wisdom. This epistle is typical also in that it maintains the manner of a real letter. The background, a simple one, can be reconstructed with a fair degree of certainty from indications in the letter. Since Tibullus left Rome for the *villeggiatura* at his place *in regione Pedana*,[3] at the foot of the Sabine hills, Horace has not heard from him. He therefore asks him to let him know in what way he is spending his time in the country. He also invites him to come and see for himself how flourishing his friend Horace is (15 f.).[4] The letter was presumably written from Horace's Sabine farm; it would have been very easy for Tibullus to make the short trip from the neighbourhood of Zagarolo or Gallicano to Tivoli and from there to the valley of the Licenza.

Since Horace is writing to a fellow poet, and one considerably younger than himself, he at once asks in what kind of poetic work his friend is at present engaged; in the circumstances it would be surprising if this question were not asked.[5] It is in keeping with the conciseness of this letter that the topic of writing poetry is but slightly touched upon and that of possible types of poetry only one is alluded to, in a manner perfectly intelligible to Tibullus and the contemporary reader but not to us,

scribere quod Cassi Parmensis opuscula vincat.[6]

[1] 'When the two Epistles are taken together they deal pretty fully with the subject' (Wickham).

[2] Attempts have of course been made to deny that *Epist.* i. 4 and *Odes* i. 33 are addressed to the poet Tibullus.

[3] Cf. Mommsen, *Hermes* xvii, 1882, 46 n. 5 (*Ges. Schriften*, v. 73 n. 4); T. Ashby, *The Roman Campagna in Classical Times*, 137.

[4] Zeune, in his re-edition of Baxter's *Horace*, drew the right conclusion, 'videtur Tibullum ad sese invitasse Horatius'. The letter is not, of course, a formal invitation for a particular day but rather a standing offer in a manner customary between near friends.

[5] Compare in the letter to Florus, i. 3, the questions at 20 f., *ipse quid audes? quae circumvolitas agilis thyma?* and the whole preceding section (from 6 on).

[6] Kiessling remarks 'Porphyrio kennt ihn [Cassius Parmensis] als fruchtbaren Tragiker: sonst ist von seiner litterarischen Thätigkeit nichts Sicheres uns überliefert [i.e. Ps.-Acro must be left out of account], sodaß wir nicht wissen, was für von Tibull geplante *opuscula*

To complete his inquiries Horace adds the question which to men like himself, to Virgil and many of their friends would appear as an obvious one, 'or are you perhaps leaving poetry aside for a while and profiting from the healthy stillness of your retreat to ponder on the problems that matter most?',

> an tacitum silvas inter reptare salubris
> curantem quidquid dignum sapiente bonoque est?

What follows is perhaps the gentlest of the many gentle transitions in Horace's writings and certainly the one in which his quiet kindliness and his capacity for sharing another's difficulties show themselves most distinctly. From the assumption that Tibullus may now be devoting himself to philosophical meditations Horace does not pass on straight to the lesson, *inter spem curamque* ... (12 ff.), which Tibullus should derive from such meditations. Interrupting apparently the course of his thought, he holds, as it were, a mirror up to his friend and tells him in the most encouraging terms how easy it is for him with his physical and mental gifts and his wealth to be happy and how little reason he has to torment himself:

> non tu corpus eras sine pectore: di tibi formam,
> di tibi divitias dederunt artemque fruendi.

The words *non tu corpus eras sine pectore* prove to be an ingenious adaptation of a very old saying. Odysseus, provoked by the behaviour of Antinous, cries out:[1]

> ὦ πόποι, οὐκ ἄρα σοί γ' ἐπὶ εἴδεϊ καὶ φρένες ἦσαν.

This sentence, with its one negative (οὐκ), is a severe condemnation; by the addition of a second negative (*non ... sine ...*) it becomes a compliment. The Latin corresponds fairly closely to the Greek: *pectus* is a perfect rendering of φρένες[2] and εἶδος differs from *corpus* only in that it connotes the positive quality which Horace makes explicit by means of the following *formam*. The similarity of the two passages extends even to the tense—anything but common in Latin—of the verb, *eras*.[3]

... hier gemeint sind' (cf. also F. Jacoby, *Rh. Mus.* lx, 1905, 69); this cautious comment seems to me better founded than the inferences of F. Skutsch, *RE* iii. 1743, Heinze, and others. Nor do I think it significant ('bezeichnend') that Horace 'den Caesarmörder und Erzfeind des Augustus Cassius von Parma als sein [Tibullus'] Vorbild [!] nennt' (F. Marx, *RE* i. 1320).

[1] p 454.

[2] In addition to the commentaries (as early as Lambinus *sine pectore* was rendered by ἄφρων) see Housman on Manilius 4. 529 and compare especially Ovid, *Trist.* 3. 7. 43 f., *nil non mortale tenemus pectoris exceptis ingeniique bonis*, which inspired Goethe's deeper version ('Dauer im Wechsel'), 'Danke, daß die Gunst der Musen Unvergängliches verheißt: Den Gehalt in deinem Busen Und die Form in deinem Geist.'

[3] The grammar books are silent on this use of the imperfect, and the expedient accepted

In the list of the blessings bestowed on Tibullus there appears one by which Horace always sets great store, the *ars fruendi* (7).[1] The following description of the man privileged by Fortune's most valuable gifts (9 f.),

> qui sapere et fari possit quae sentiat et cui
> gratia fama valetudo contingat abunde,

is distinguished by great intensity, but the next line,

> et mundus victus non deficiente crumina,

returns to the level of slightly playful everyday talk.[2] Immediately after, the tone changes again: the three lines

> inter spem curamque, timores inter et iras
> omnem crede diem tibi diluxisse supremum:
> grata superveniet quae non sperabitur hora—

although they do not contain an original or unfamiliar thought, are so full of vigour and deep feeling and worded with such perfect harmony that they sink into our memory for good. *Sed iam satis est philosophatum*, as the Plautine slave says; two more lines, implying an invitation, conclude the letter on a note of graceful self-mockery.

We now return to what I called the apparent interruption at 6, *non tu corpus eras . . ..* In his introduction to this epistle Wickham says 'A

by many commentaries (e.g., Orelli–Baiter, 'semper, ex quo inter nos versari coepisti egoque te cognovi', and Heinze, 'wie ich im Zusammensein mit dir erfahren habe: und natürlich gilt das Gleiche auch noch für die Gegenwart') is far from convincing, to say nothing of such excuses as 'the time [of *eras*] is explained by the emphasis laid in v. 2 on "nunc" ' (Wickham). Arthur Palmer, in A. S. Wilkins's annotated edition of the *Epistles*, is more helpful: he compares Prop. 1. 13. 34, *non alio limine dignus eras* (where Rothstein produces idle talk and Butler and Barber say nothing), on which he remarks '*eras = es* but stronger, "you are not and never were" ' [?], and adds 'I think the idiom is the same as in [*Odes* 1. 27. 19] *quanta laborabas Charybdi*'. About this last passage one may feel doubts, but it is very probable that the use of *eras* in Propertius is the same as in our epistle. I have long regarded these two instances of *eras* as borrowings from Greek syntax (for such borrowings and their limitations see especially F. Leo, *Plautin. Forsch.*, 2nd. ed. 103 f.; Wackernagel, *Vorles. üb. Syntax*, i. 10 f.; Löfstedt, *Syntactica*, i. and ii, *passim*; Sachindex, s.v. 'Gräzismen'); recently I found Dacier's note, 'assurément il a mis, à la maniere des Grecs, *eras* pour *es, vous estiez* pour *vous estes*'. It is not only the Greek imperfect in the common connexion with ἄρα (as in οὐκ ἄρα μοῦνον ἔην Ἐρίδων γένος) but also the plain imperfect (in statements) that ought to be compared, as, for example, A. *Cho.* 243 πιστὸς δ' ἀδελφὸς ἦσθ' ἐμοὶ σέβας φέρων. Cf. also the very ordinary question τουτὶ τί ἦν; (e.g. Ar. *Ach.* 157).

[1] Cf. pp. 138 f. above.
[2] The word *crumina* (*Thes. l. L.* iv. 1241), in what is left of Latin literature, is common only in Plautus. The jurist Labeo, in his commentary on the XII Tables, uses it, apparently as an archaism, in a passage (Gellius 20. 1. 13) in which the ἅπαξ λεγόμενον *depalmare* also occurs. In Apuleius (*Met.*, once) it is clearly an archaism. Juv. 11. 38, *deficiente crumina* (end of the verse) is an echo of this passage of Horace. Horace may have borrowed it from an early writer (Lucilius? it does not occur in the fragments), but it seems more likely that he should have heard it in the language of the common people.

comparison with Od. 1. 33, which is also addressed to the poet Tibullus, suggests that the enumeration of his advantages and the exhortation
to imitate Horace's philosophy of life have a definite personal purpose.'
The fallacy that underlies this statement is widespread. Even that
most sympathetic, cautious, and penetrating interpreter of Horace's
Epistles, E. Courbaud, says:[1] 'L'épître 4 ne saurait être considérée à
part de l'ode I, 33'. If that were so, if we really depended for our
understanding of the epistle on information derived from the ode, then
Albi, nostrorum sermonum candide iudex, might be called an unsatisfactory
letter and would certainly be a bad poem. In fact, however, the epistle is
self-contained: it tells the reader—for it is meant for the reader as well
as for Tibullus—all that he needs to know if he wants to understand the
epistle and to appreciate it as it deserves. Provided, that is, that the
reader is *emunctae naris*, that he has a flair for subtle transitions and
delicate implications.

The first thing that will strike an attentive reader is the peculiar
sequence of thought which we have already noticed: from the idea
that Tibullus is possibly engaged in philosophical studies (4 f.) Horace
does not proceed to its obvious application, the moral support which he
might gain from these studies (12 ff.), but he suddenly breaks into an
assessment of his friend's personality and his situation in the world (6
ff.). Secondly, the praise which Horace here pours out, or at any rate
part of it (*di tibi formam . . . dederunt, . . . cui gratia, fama . . . contingat
abunde*), would seem, coming from so tactful a writer, surprisingly
fulsome unless it was inspired by some definite intention. The intention
emerges from the very manner in which Horace recalls circumstances
so well known to his correspondent. There must recently have been
moments in the life of Tibullus when all his advantages were of no avail
to him and when the last thing he was able to practise was the
ars fruendi. Horace is careful not to indicate how he has received
the information about his friend's state of mind, and he is far too
experienced to say in so many words that Tibullus has been suffering from serious depressions. But he knows what is the matter with
him, and this knowledge is at the root of the whole letter. In what
he writes there is no shade of criticism, no word to the effect that
Tibullus ought to be grateful for what the gods have given him.
Horace does not raise his voice: soothingly, as one would talk to a sick
child—the pretty illustration from the nursery (8) is not out of place—
he tries to show to his friend that by giving way to melancholy thoughts
he is doing an injustice to himself. 'Just look at what you are and in
what position you are placed, possessed of everything that should make
a man happy.' Only after this gentle and fortifying preparation does

---

[1] *Horace . . . à l'époque des épîtres*, 83.

he strike a note of serious admonition, *inter spem curamque* . . ., thereby
implying how foolish we are when we persist in spoiling this short and
precarious life by self-inflicted torments. Horace, himself anything but
a melancholy character, shows wonderful sympathy with the sufferings
of his Tibullus: to try to help him is his sole concern.[1] In the same
manner he, the freethinker, endeavoured to meet his friend Maecenas
in the maze of his superstitions and thus to deliver him from his gloom.[2]
Horace's epistle to Tibullus leaves us convinced that the *humanitas* of the
man is a match for the *urbanitas* of the letter-writer.

6. EPISTLE VII

The famous letter to Maecenas, i. 7, begins with a frank admission:
Horace, by not keeping his promise, has badly disappointed Maecenas,
who has been waiting many weeks for his friend's return:

> Quinque dies tibi pollicitus me rure futurum
> Sextilem totum mendax desideror.

It is possible that this is a reply to a complaint made by Maecenas,[3]
and equally possible that Horace volunteers this apology.[4] After saying
'I am to blame', he continues 'and yet,[5] Maecenas, grant me your
indulgence, not only when I am ill, but also when I am afraid of
becoming ill', . . . *dabis aegrotare timenti, Maecenas,[6] veniam.* Horace, on
the whole, enjoyed excellent health. Therefore Maecenas will not have

---

[1] '. . . simple billet de seize vers, mais billet charmant par la vivacité de l'affection, je
dirai: presque touchant par la peine que prend Horace pour mettre un peu de gaieté dans
une âme malade' (Courbaud, op. cit. 89).

[2] Cf. pp. 218 f. above.

[3] So Wieland, followed by many commentators: 'Der ganze Ton dieses . . . Briefes, und
besonders einige Stellen desselben, scheinen voraus zu setzen, dass ihm Maecenas ent-
weder selbst in einem Briefe, worauf dieser die Antwort ist, oder vielleicht durch einen
gemeinschaftlichen Freund etwas insinuiert habe, das einem Vorwurf von Undank-
barkeit ähnlich sah.'

[4] So Orelli–Baiter on 2, *mendax desideror.*

[5] At the end of 2 there is about equally good manuscript authority for either *atque* or
atqui. Since the confusion of the two words is very common, it is the sense that must decide.
Kiessling (whose note was retained by Heinze) was wrong in vindicating *atque* by translating it 'und obendrein'; an adversative sense is required by the context. Klingner's second
edition (1950) rightly accepts *atqui.* Leo, who successfully defended the Plautine adversative *atque* against alterations (*Nachr. Gött. Ges.*, Phil.-hist. Kl. 1895, 422 ff.), also (424)
pointed to the far more extensive use of *atqui* in Terence, and to Cicero's predilection for
atqui. Klotz, *Thes. l. L.* ii. 1077. 16, observes that after Plautus almost always not a bare
atque but *atque . . . tamen* or *ac tamen* is used when the sense is adversative. Therefore *atque*
cannot be considered here.

[6] Readers familiar with Horace's ways will appreciate the delicate touch in the position
of the vocative *Maecenas*, which, instead of coming earlier in the letter, is placed so as to
form part of the urgent request *dabis aegrotare timenti veniam.* For an analogous function of
the vocative *Maecenas* see above, p. 215.

taken the excuse too seriously, as little as Augustus did, who had offered Horace a post as his private secretary—which would have brought the poet into close and permanent connexion (*convictor*) with him—and, when Horace declined the honour, wrote back to him '. . . *quoniam id usus mihi tecum esse volui, si per valetudinem tuam fieri possit*'. That it is with his tongue in his cheek that Horace says *aegrotare timenti* is shown by the manner in which he elaborates the notion of the risk through four and a half lines, *dum ficus prima . . . testamenta resignat*. There was some danger of contracting malaria in Rome during the late summer months, whereas in a hilly region one would be safe,[1] but the comic exaggeration with which Horace paints a series of lugubrious scenes makes it difficult to believe that he could have been wholly in earnest. The picturesque detail at l. 6, *dissignatorem decorat lictoribus atris*,[2] is in the best parodic style of the *sermones*, and the heavy clause at the end of the period, *et testamenta resignat*, rounds off the description on a sinister note. The lines 8 f., *officiosaque sedulitas et opella forensis adducit febris . . .* fulfil a perfectly good function here, but they also seem to recall *Sat.* 2. 6. 18 ff., where Horace, speaking of the peaceful life at his Sabine farm, says

> nec mala me ambitio perdit nec plumbeus auster
> autumnusque gravis, Libitinae quaestus acerbae.

I do not know whether the similarity is intentional, but it is conceivable that Horace at the beginning of this letter, which was hard for him to write because, whatever he might say, Maecenas would be disappointed, meant to remind his friend of that other *sermo* in which, many years ago, he had described in a mood of perfect happiness what Maecenas' friendship meant to him and how profoundly grateful he was for the gift of the Sabine farm.

If the opening nine lines, the hard core of which was the request *dabis aegrotare timenti . . . veniam, dum ficus prima calorque . . .*, held out no hope for Maecenas so far as the immediate future was concerned, his worst disappointment was still to come. The beginning of the next period,

> quodsi bruma nives Albanis inlinet agris,

sounds promising enough, for its natural continuation would be 'then

---

[1] This the ancients had learnt from long experience although they did not know that the carrier of the infection is the anopheles mosquito that breeds in the stagnating waters of the plain.

[2] Cf. Mommsen, *Staatsrecht*, i.[3] 375 n. 3. On *matercula* (7) the commentators observe 'misella mater' (Baxter), 'die zärtliche Mutter', and the like, and some such connotation may well be intended, but we should also remember that W. Schulze, *Zur Geschichte lateinischer Eigennamen*, 136 n. 4, has shown the fixed pattern (not confined to Greek and Latin) in pairs such as *puer* and *puella*, *adulescens* and *adulescentula*, *sacerdos* and *sacerdotula*, παῖς and παιδίσκη. To this list *pater et matercula* might be added.

I shall return to town'. By that time the unhealthy season would definitely be over;[1] the explicit mention of *bruma* and of snow on the Alban hills puts it beyond doubt that there can no longer be any reasonable ground for *aegrotare timere*. But, alas, what does follow is the very reverse of what Maecenas was entitled to expect:

> ad mare descendet vates tuus et sibi parcet
> contractusque leget.

The next sentence, in which Horace at last commits himself to an approximate date for his return, *te, dulcis amice, reviset cum Zephyris* and so forth, begins on a deeply affectionate note; but will his being called *dulcis amicus*, and the polite *si concedes* which follows, suffice to sweeten for Maecenas the bitterness of the interminable delay? By now it has become abundantly clear that, whatever may be thought of Horace appearing as *aegrotare timens*, the true reason for his prolonged absence is a different and far more serious one.

To bring this reason home to Maecenas Horace makes a fresh start, introducing an αἶνος in the somewhat abrupt manner familiar to us from his satires, *non quo more piris vesci Calaber iubet hospes . . ..*[2] Here, where every word is carefully weighed and every implication considered, it is of the greatest importance that the sentence begins with an emphatic *non*. Horace is entirely sincere in rejecting the idea that Maecenas has made his gifts to him in the spirit in which the Calabrian peasant offered his pears to his guest. Nor is there the slightest suggestion that the value of the Sabine farm, even from the point of view of the donor, might be compared with the value of those pears. The story of the Calabrian, in all probability a reminiscence from Horace's boyhood,[3] is amusing, but its primary *raison d'être* in this context is that it leads up to the general maxim which concludes it as a kind of ἐπιμύθιον (20–23):

> prodigus et stultus donat quae spernit et odit:
> haec seges ingratos tulit et feret omnibus annis.
> vir bonus et sapiens dignis ait esse paratus,
> nec tamen ignorat quid distent aera lupinis.

These four sentences, each of which fills a whole line, are arranged in the strictest possible symmetry. Two distichs correspond to one another, headed by their subjects which are indicated in clauses of equal length

---

[1] It is September that is regarded as the most critical period; cf. (after a detailed description of the Sabine farm) *Epist.* I. 16. 15 f. *hae latebrae dulces . . . incolumem tibi me praestant Septembribus horis.*

[2] Wieland deserves praise for clearly separating (by a blank) this section from the preceding one.

[3] So Kiessling and E. Courbaud, op. cit. 286.

and metrical value, but antithetic in sense, *prodigus et stultus* and *vir bonus et sapiens*. In the first distich the subject is followed by a characterization of the value of the gifts, *quae spernit et odit*, and the second line describes the moral type to which the persons belong who are given such presents. In the second distich, there comes after the subject first a word classifying the persons who receive the gifts, *dignis*, and in the second line the emphasis lies on the assessment of the relative values of the gifts, *quid distent aera lupinis*. In other words, the parallelism of the two distichs is stressed by the fact that in both of them the first halfline (hemiepes) belongs to the grammatical subject, but in the rest of the distichs the arrangement is varied in accordance with the not uncommon pattern *A B B A*.

From these remarks it will be seen that at l. 23 I take *aera* and *lupina* to refer, not to the deserts of the persons to whom gifts are made,[1] but to the value of the gifts. This interpretation, which, considering the use that in everyday life is made of *aera* and *lupina*, seems the obvious one, is supported by the arrangement of 20–23 as analysed above. It is further strengthened by the fact that in the current doctrines of Hellenistic ethics, on which Horace always depended for reflections of this kind, it was considered essential not only that men who obtained benefactions should be deserving persons, but also that the benefactions should be of real value. Aristotle[2] deals with this aspect of munificence[3] in a section headed by the words ὁ δὲ μεγαλοπρεπὴς ἐπιστήμονι ἔοικεν. He says αἱ δὴ τοῦ μεγαλοπρεποῦς δαπάναι μεγάλαι καὶ πρέπουσαι . . . and[4] ἀναγκαῖον δὴ καὶ ἐλευθέριον τὸν μεγαλοπρεπῆ εἶναι· καὶ γὰρ ὁ ἐλευθέριος δαπανήσει ἃ δεῖ καὶ ὡς δεῖ, and at the end of this section[5] he provides us with a good illustration of *quid distent aera*

---

[1] This explanation, found in one branch of the scholia (*quae sit differentia inter bonos et malos*), has been accepted by many commentators, e.g., Orelli–Baiter, L. Müller, Heinze, but not, for example, by Lambinus, Dacier, Kiessling, Wickham, Lejay, Villeneuve (note on his translation of 23 [Collection Budé]), nor by Courbaud, op. cit. 288, who sums up the argument thus: 'cette monnaie . . . désigne les véritables bienfaits d'une part, et, de l'autre, les bienfaits apparents, ceux qui n'ont pas plus de valeur que l'*aurum comicum*.' I should have thought it unnecessary to write my article, 'Der siebente Brief des Horaz', *250 Jahre Weidmannsche Buchhandlung*, Beilage zu Heft 4 der Monatsschrift für höhere Schulen, Berlin 1930, 13 ff., if at that time I had known Courbaud's book, the most tactful and, on the whole, most adequate book on Horace which I have seen. I am very much to blame for neglecting it so long. As for Epistle VII, I cannot, of course, subscribe to every word in Courbaud's discussion, but I agree entirely with his approach to the letter and with the gist of his analysis and appreciation of it. The articles by K. Büchner, 'Der siebente Brief des Horaz', *Hermes*, lxxv, 1940, 64 ff., and by Gunning, 'Der 7. Brief des Horaz und sein Verhältnis zu Maecenas', *Mnemos.*, S. III, 10, 1942, 303 ff., do not indicate whether Courbaud's book was known to their authors.

[2] *Eth. Nic.* 4. 1122ᵇ2 ff.

[3] Lambinus in his note on 20, *prodigus et stultus*, refers to Book IV of *Eth. Nic.* The contact with Horace goes beyond the few passages I quote.

[4] 1122ᵇ10.   [5] 1123ᵃ10.

lupinis: καὶ ἐπεὶ τῶν δαπανημάτων ἕκαστον μέγα ἐν τῷ γένει, καὶ μεγαλο-
πρεπέστατον . . . τὸ ἐν μεγάλῳ μέγα, . . . καὶ διαφέρει τὸ ἐν τῷ ἔργῳ
μέγα τοῦ ἐν τῷ δαπανήματι (σφαῖρα μὲν γὰρ ἢ λήκυθος ἡ καλλίστη μεγαλο-
πρέπειαν ἔχει παιδικοῦ δώρου, ἡ δὲ τούτου τιμὴ μικρὸν καὶ ἀνελεύθερον)·
διὰ τοῦτό ἐστιν τοῦ μεγαλοπρεποῦς, ἐν ᾧ ἂν ποιῇ γένει, μεγαλοπρεπῶς
ποιεῖν . . . καὶ ἔχον κατ' ἀξίαν τοῦ δαπανήματος. Aristotle's doctrine of
the type of benefaction that should result from ἐλευθεριότης and
μεγαλοπρέπεια and of the obligations it entails was developed further by
the Stoics[1] and above all by Panaetius, whose detailed discussion of
these problems—starting from Aristotle—forms the groundwork of the
relevant sections in Cicero's *De officiis*.[2] Here we find not only the
equivalent of the antithesis of *prodigus et stultus* and *vir bonus et sapiens*,[3]
but also the distinction between those *beneficia* which are of real value
and those which are not.[4] Whether or not a gift can be regarded as a
beneficium depends upon the spirit in which it is given and on the motives
that actuate the donor. Cicero, adapting a topic of the Stoics, says *nec
enim cum tua causa cui commodes, beneficium illud habendum est, sed feneratio*.[5]
Seneca more than once sharply defines what constitutes a genuine
beneficium, for instance *Benef.* 1. 6. 1 *non quid fiat aut quid detur refert, sed
qua mente, quia beneficium non in eo quod fit aut datur consistit, sed in ipso
dantis aut facientis animo . . .*, and 3. 8. 2 *donavit aliquis magnam pecuniam
sed dives, sed non sensurus impendium; donavit alius, sed toto patrimonio
cessurus; summa eadem est, beneficium idem non est*. We need not trace the
ramifications of this discussion; from what has been quoted it emerges
that, according to the current doctrine, a gift loses a great deal of its
value and does not deserve to be called a *beneficium* if either the donor
expects from it a profit for himself (*feneratio*), or if he gives something
away *non sensurus impendium*. The latter is clearly the case of the *Calaber
hospes*; he is one who *donat quae spernit et odit*. But the twofold general
maxim, 20–23, is not only the ἐπιμύθιον of the preceding αἶνος, it also
points forward to what follows, to the settling of the relations between
Maecenas and Horace. The mention of the *prodigus et stultus* has no
reference whatsoever to Maecenas nor is he to be thought of as one
who *donat quae spernit et odit*; but the *vir bonus et sapiens* points clearly to

---

[1] We find in the catalogue of the writings of Cleanthes the title περὶ χάριτος, but very
little is known about its contents (*Stoic. Vet. Fragm.* i, *frs.* 578–80).
[2] See especially Pohlenz, 'Antikes Führertum', *Neue Wege zur Antike*, ii. 3, 1934, 34 ff.
[3] Cf. *De off.* 2. 55 *Omnino duo sunt genera largorum, quorum alteri prodigi, alteri liberales . . ..*
[4] Ibid. 1. 49 *quae beneficia* [viz. those which are conferred without care] *aeque magna non
sunt habenda atque ea quae iudicio considerate constanterque delata sunt*.
[5] That this epigrammatic turn belongs to the old stock-in-trade of Stoic ethics is shown
by Sen. *Benef.* 6. 12. 2 *multum . . . interest utrum aliquis beneficium nobis det sua causa an et sua.
. . . multum, ut ait Cleanthes, a beneficio distat negotiatio*. Seneca himself, like Cicero, calls the
use of a *beneficium* for selfish purposes *feneratio*: (*Benef.* 1. 2. 3) *turpis feneratio est beneficium
expensum ferre*. Cf. also (in its context) Cic. *Lael.* 31 *neque enim beneficium feneramur*.

him, and the assertion *nec tamen ignorat quid distent aera lupinis* must also
be applicable to him. A *vir bonus et sapiens*, and so Maecenas, puts his
benefactions at the disposal of persons who are worthy of them, *dignis
ait esse paratus*,[1] and at the same time[2] he knows very well the difference
between real coins and sham coins, between true benefactions and
gifts that merely look like benefactions. Such a man will endow only
those of whose gratitude he can be sure, but—this is clearly implied by
the whole context—he will not exploit the gratitude of his friends so as
to present them with gifts of doubtful value. From the general maxims
Horace returns to the present issue by adding (24)

> dignum praestabo me etiam[3] pro laude merentis.[4]

We have seen that *nec tamen ignorat quid distant aera lupinis* must be
applicable to Maecenas. Now it is clear that Horace could never dream
of imputing to Maecenas an act by which, while giving away valueless
things, he would wish to parade as a benefactor. What, then, is the
implication of possible *lupina* so far as Maecenas is concerned? To this
puzzle there is no clue in the part of the letter which we have been
examining up till now. But the following period (25 ff.) begins at once
with a conditional clause which makes the reader hold his breath,

> quodsi me noles usquam discedere, ...

This clause, after what immediately preceded, appears to be of a startling directness. It indicates the possibility that Maecenas, after what
he had done for Horace, might claim the right to tie the poet permanently to his, Maecenas', company, forgetful of the warning *nec enim
cum tua causa cui commodes, beneficium illud habendum est, sed feneratio*. In the
present circumstances the conditional clause which begins with *quodsi*,
'and so if', seems to demand as its principal clause either something

---

[1] This requirement, too, has its established place in the traditional theory of true benefactions, see, for example, Cic. *Off.* 1. 45 *tertium est propositum ut in beneficentia dilectus esset
dignitatis*; Sen. *Benef.* 1. 1. 2 *id* [viz. the frequency of ingratitude] *evenire ex causis pluribus
video. prima illa est quod non eligimus dignos quibus tribuamus.*

[2] This English phrase renders *et tamen* or *nec tamen non* perfectly; so does *cependant*
(Lejay paraphrases 'il sait cependant distinguer entre un présent sans valeur et un
bienfait important'). I ought not to have criticized Heinze's paraphrase, 'er weiß jedoch
auch sehr wohl...'. Wackernagel immediately wrote to me '*tamen* ist natürlich adversativ,
könnte aber kaum, ohne daß der Sinn litte, durch eine andere Adversativ-Partikel
ersetzt werden; man braucht so viel ich sehe die Bedeutung "zugleich aber, ebenso sehr"'.
For this idiomatic use of *et tamen* see, for example, Madvig on Cic. *Fin.* 2. 84; Munro on
Lucr. 5. 1177; Reid on Cic. *Acad.* 2. 109.

[3] 'Not only because I, as one who receives your gifts, belong to the class of *digni* (22),
but also ...'.

[4] 'Le complément [*pro*] se rapporte à l'ensemble de l'expression *dignum me praestabo*'
(Lejay). As regards the connotations of *laude merentis* in this context, it is helpful to compare
Epist. 2. 1. 246 f. *munera quae multa dantis cum laude tulerunt dilecti tibi Vergilius Variusque
poetae* (quoted by Orelli–Baiter).

to the effect of 'then you will be turning your gift into an obligation', or the announcement *cuncta resigno* (34). But in the place of such a grim apodosis there follows, to the reader's surprise and relief, a gentle remark in which Maecenas could not possibly find the faintest sting,

> reddes
> forte latus, nigros angusta fronte capillos,
> reddes dulce loqui, reddes ridere decorum et
> inter vina fugam Cinarae maerere protervae.

'If you never want me to leave you, then give me back . . .'—there follows a list of things which it would not be in the power of Maecenas or of anyone to give back to him. To Maecenas this accumulation of ἀδύνατα can only mean 'to expect me to stay with you always and everywhere is as impossible as that I should once more become a young man'. But as Horace puts it he seems to say 'how glad I should be if I could do what you expect of me, could be strong enough for it and be young once more!' Instead of arguing he appeals to his friend's sympathetic indulgence. But, like many of the finest passages in Horace's letters, the long sentence *reddes . . . fugam Cinarae maerere protervae*, if primarily meant for the person to whom the letter is written, reveals at the same time something of the inner life of the writer. There is under the smiling surface a note of nostalgic longing for the bygone days of his youth. A subdued emotion reveals itself in the *reddes* placed symmetrically at the beginning of each of the three clauses[1]—here, as almost always in Horace, the use of anaphora indicates strong feeling— and, most significant of all, at the end of the period the shade of Cinara is conjured up.[2] This detail seems to forecast the regretful words in one of Horace's latest odes (4. 1. 3 f.), *non sum qualis eram bonae sub regno Cinarae*. It is in fact more than a detail: the sadness of the ageing poet which finds its expression in some passages of the fourth book of his *carmina* appears also in the *reddes* clauses of the letter, but only as an undertone. Here melancholic thoughts are not allowed to linger.

It is on an entirely different note that the next section begins, abruptly:[3]

> forte per angustam tenuis volpecula rimam
> repserat in cumeram frumenti . . . .

---

[1] William Lamb in his free version of this passage (see Lord David Cecil, *The Young Melbourne*, 1939, 201) was careful to keep the effect of the repeated initial *reddes*: 'Then give me back the scorn of scare Which spirits light in health allow; And give me back the dark brown hair . . . And give me back the sportive jest . . . And give me back the fervid soul . . . .' I cannot say whether it is purely accidental that the poet's words in Goethe's *Vorspiel auf dem Theater*, 'So gieb mir auch die Zeiten wieder, Da ich noch selbst im Werden war . . . Gieb ungebändigt jene Triebe . . . Gieb meine Jugend mir zurück!' recall the Horatian passage.   [2] Cf. p. 311 above and p. 411 below.

[3] 'The transition is made abrupt by the familiar Horatian inversion which places an

Apparently nothing could be slighter, nothing farther removed from the thoughts concerned with a possible tension in the relationship of two friends than such a homely Αἰσώπειος λόγος, delivered in the plain style that throughout the ages has belonged to this genre. But in its present context the old fable proves by no means so playful as it sounds at first: it serves a very serious purpose.[1] Volpecula's sad fate contains a warning which Horace is determined to heed, even at the risk of having to give up his most cherished possession. He applies the moral of the fable to himself in absolutely unambiguous terms (34). Let no one think that when he says *cuncta resigno* he is carried away by a theoretical enthusiasm for poverty or is making a false pretence like those *qui Curios simulant et Bacchanalia vivunt*; he is entirely sincere and fully aware of the consequences of his determination:

> nec somnum plebis laudo satur altilium nec
> otia divitiis Arabum liberrima muto.

Complete freedom from external obligations is what he values more highly than anything in the world: *otia liberrima* is a very strong expression. It cannot be proved, but it is not improbable, that in his profession *nec otia divitiis Arabum liberrima muto* there is also an echo of the words of Lucilius,

> publicanus vero ut Asiae fiam, ut scripturarius,
> pro Lucilio, id ego nolo, et uno hoc non muto omnia.

The uncompromising *cuncta resigno* may have made Maecenas wince, but it could hardly surprise him. Horace 'a de longue date préparé Mécène à cette éventualité. Il lui a écrit jadis dans une ode [3. 29. 49 ff.]: "Si la fortune m'est fidèle, tant mieux; mais si elle commence d'agiter ses ailes pour me fuir, je lui restitue aussitôt les présents qu'elle m'a faits, je m'enveloppe de ma vertu et j'épouse sans dot une honnête pauvreté." *Resigno quae dedit*, c'est déjà le *cuncta resigno* de notre épître.'[2]

After the firm declaration ending with *nec otia . . . liberrima muto* once

---

illustration or a comparison before that which it is meant to illustrate, and gives it independent form, as if a thing adduced for its own sake' (Hendrickson, *Am. Journ. Phil.* xxi, 1900, 126).

[1] 'Seinem mächtigen, gütigen Beschützer Maecenas, dem Freunde, der ohne seinen Horaz nicht leben kann: ihm zu sagen, daß auch Horaz selber seine Freiheit nötig habe, daß Maecenas auf seine Gesellschaft mindestens zeitweise nicht Anspruch machen dürfe: diese schmerzliche Wahrheit mit jenem edlen Freimut und mit jener liebevollen Schonung vor ihm auszusprechen, die noch Spätern in ähnlicher Lage den Mut gab das gleiche zu tun: dafür ist dem Horaz auch die Fabel nicht zu gering' (K. Meuli, 'Herkunft und Wesen der Fabel', *Schweizerisches Archiv für Volkskunde*, l, 1954, 65 ff. [24 of the offprint]).

[2] Courbaud, op. cit. 282.

more a fresh start is made and once more the tone changes. In a single
sentence of moving intensity Maecenas is reminded of the true nature
of their long friendship and of Horace's unfaltering devotion to him:

> saepe verecundum laudasti, rexque paterque
> audisti coram, nec verbo parcius absens.

This solemn declaration should make it impossible for Maecenas to
nourish any doubt about his friend's loyalty and gratitude. But however profound Horace's regard is for the feelings of Maecenas, he remains firm in his decision not to sacrifice any part of his personal
independence. Rather than do that he would gladly return to his
benefactor everything he has received from him:

> inspice si possum donata reponere laetus.

The warning given shortly before, *cuncta resigno*, is here repeated in such
a manner as to put its seriousness beyond doubt. But that is enough.
Horace can be confident that Maecenas will have fully understood not
only the words of the letter but also all their implications. Therefore
there is no need for him to return to this painful point and to mention
once more the consequences which he would be prepared to face
should Maecenas insist on his request. In the rest of the letter he relaxes
very noticeably.

The episode of Telemachus and Menelaus (40–43) does not imply
any reflection on the generosity of the benefactor. The horses and
chariot that Menelaus offers to his young guest are a magnificent present, but unfortunately Telemachus has no use for it since he has to live
in Ithaca, ἐν δ᾽ Ἰθάκῃ οὔτ᾽ ἄρ δρόμοι εὐρέες οὔτε τι λειμών. The moral of
the story is

> parvum parva decent: mihi iam non regia Roma,
> sed vacuum Tibur placet aut imbelle Tarentum.

What Maecenas has been offering to the poet, the opportunity of
living permanently in the company of his powerful friend, is in itself
of great value—like the horses of Menelaus—but Horace is prevented
from accepting it by circumstances beyond his control. Emphatically
he says *parvum parva decent*. When Horace is resorting to his habitual
expedient of semi-serious εἰρωνεία, *dissimulatio opis propriae*, he readily
uses the word *parvus*. The instance that first comes to mind is *Odes*
4. 2. 31 f., *operosa parvus carmina fingo*; it goes closely together with
Odes 4. 15. 1 ff., *Phoebus . . . me . . . increpuit lyra, ne parva Tyrrhenum per
aequor vela darem*, and with a passage in the letter to Augustus,[1] *neque
parvum carmen maiestas recipit tua nec meus audet rem temptare pudor quam*

---

[1] *Epist.* 2. 1. 257 ff.

vires ferre recusent. In those cases it is the writing of lofty poetry to which Horace's *parvitas* is alleged to be an insurmountable hindrance; in the case of the letter to Maecenas it is life on a grand scale. There is still another reason for Horace's unwillingness to yield to his friend's solicitations: when he says *mihi iam non regia Roma . . . placet*, the important *iam* must not be disregarded.[1] This *iam* clearly implies 'now I am too old for that kind of life',[2] and so the thought harks back to 25–28. Without in any way recanting what he had said Horace explains and somehow excuses his conduct. There is no longer any hint at the possibility of an irreparable decision. It is in this balanced mood that the letter persists to the end. Its crowning piece, the tale of Philippus and Mena, is the most accomplished of all the paradigmatic stories in Horace's *sermones* and altogether one of the happiest products of his pen. It must not, however, be isolated but must be viewed in connexion with the other αἶνοι of this letter.

No other Horatian satire or epistle contains within so small a compass such variety of αἶνοι as does *Epist.* i. 7.[3] An anecdote which the poet presumably heard when he was a small boy (14–19) is followed by an Aesopic fable (29–33); next comes the sketch of a scene from the *Odyssey* (40–43), and the rear is brought up by the long story which occupies more than half of the whole epistle (46–95) and seems so dominating that some readers could hold it to be an independent poem.[4] The story is taken from everyday life in Rome; the persons who play a part in it had long been dead at the time of Horace's writing.

Looking at this masterpiece, it seems impossible to say what we admire most, the carefully planned structure, the precision and vivacity in the execution of every detail, or the *humanitas* that permeates the whole. The tempo of the narrative is *molto allegro*: a few well-chosen indications outline the action and suggest the atmosphere within which it takes place; and yet the reader is not given the feeling of being rushed. Matters of subordinate importance are dealt with rapidly (72 f.):

> ut ventum ad cenam est, dicenda tacenda locutus
> tandem dormitum dimittitur,

or (81 ff.)

> persuadet uti mercetur agellum.
> mercatur. ne te longis ambagibus ultra
> quam satis est morer: ex nitido fit rusticus.

---

[1] Few commentators say anything about it; H. Schütz makes the odd remark '*iam*, weil H. vorher in Rom gewesen ist'.

[2] So rightly L. Müller.

[3] For the sophisticated variation of αἶνοι in the mammoth satire ii. 3 see p. 143 n. 1 above.

[4] On the branch of our MSS in which a new epistle begins at 46 see, besides the critical editions, v. Christ, 'Horatiana', *Sitz. Bayer. Akad.* 1893, 99.

But the poet has plenty of time to spare whenever he wants to add a significant trait to his picture. So he pauses in his perfunctory account of the dinner to let us listen to the uncontrolled chatter (*dicenda tacenda locutus*) of the excited and overawed guest. The enviable and blissful leisure of the Roman *popolano*, who, after the morning's strenuous work, in the hot hour after lunch-time, is loitering in the shade of a barber's shop and, since the instrument happens to be at hand, is manicuring himself into a *signore*, emerges from this unhurried description (49 ff.):

> conspexit, ut aiunt,
> adrasum quendam vacua tonsoris in umbra
> cultello proprios purgantem leniter unguis.

In the sequence of varied events it is perhaps the most touching moment when Mena, who, like so many of his social class, has never been outside the walls of stuffy Rome, is allowed, on one of the rare holidays, the *feriae Latinae*,[1] to breathe for the first time the air of the countryside (76 f.):

> impositus mannis arvum caelumque Sabinum
> non cessat laudare.

The little drama—for such it is—of the changes in Mena's life, from its happy, modest, and uneventful beginnings to his sudden rise, to the catastrophe, and finally to his repentance and return to his former state, unfolds, broadly speaking, in five scenes. The first two, on two consecutive days, take place in the centre of Rome, the next (72 f.) at the house of Philippus on the slope of the Esquiline hill, the next (77 f.) during an excursion to the *villa rustica*, and the final one (86–95) again at the town house of Philippus.

In his treatment of Philippus and Mena Horace is strictly impartial. Philippus appears as the distinguished public figure that he was and as a real gentleman. He is not unkind; the words (79) *et sibi dum requiem, dum risus undique quaerit* must not be thought to suggest that he is merely exploiting Mena for his own amusement: he means no harm, but he is not familiar enough with the life and the true needs of such a man nor has he sufficient imagination to anticipate what is bound to happen. The portrait of Mena is perfect and most engaging. We cannot forget it, as little as we can forget the features of the many humble

---

[1] On an ordinary working day Mena could not possibly leave his business, nor would L. Marcius Philippus (on his attractive personality see Münzer, *RE* xiv. 1567 f.), *strenuus et fortis causisque* . . . *agendis clarus*, free himself for a trip to his Sabine estate. The late hour, judging by Roman standards, to which Philippus, despite his age, protracts his activities in the Forum points perhaps to special industriousness; see Constans's note (*Cicéron, Corresp.*, ed. by Constans and Bayet, iv. 246 top) on Cic. *Fam.* 8. 9. 1 *agit causas liberalis, sed raro post meridiem.*

Romans of the late Republic and the early Empire whose clear eyes above a sharp-cut mouth look at us, with a firm but not unfriendly expression, from the moulded frame of their tombstones as if through a window.

Mena's language, too, characterizes him admirably. Taken aback by the aristocrat's extraordinary civility, he pours out excuses for his rude behaviour (66 ff.), *ille Philippo excusare laborem et mercennaria vincla, quod non mane domum venisset, denique quod non providisset eum*, but a moment later, highly embarrassed by the invitation to dinner, he replies curtly (70) *ut libet*.[1] Finally, when failure after failure has driven him to despair, the poor man's language rises to pathetic eloquence (92 ff.):

> 'pol me miserum, patrone, vocares,
> si velles' inquit 'verum mihi ponere nomen.
> quod te per genium dextramque deosque penatis
> obsecro et obtestor, vitae me redde priori.'

Mena makes his living as an auctioneer, more accurately a *praeco*. The position of the *praeco* in the auctioneering business was perhaps slightly inferior to that of the *coactor argentarius*,[2] but that their social status cannot have been very different seems to follow from what Horace himself says where he speaks of his father.[3] The father was a *coactor*; so Horace was well acquainted with that walk of life. There is no reason to assume a close likeness of Mena to Horace's father, but it is not improbable that the warm sympathy with which the figure of Mena is worked out results, at any rate in part, from Horace's devotion to his father and from his lasting respect for the moral qualities often found among the humble class of men to which he belonged.

The story of Philippus and Mena could not fail to delight Maecenas as much as it delights us. Maecenas will have smiled when he was reading the second half of the letter at the beginning of which he may have frowned in angry disappointment. But the story fulfils still another function. What it exemplifies is summed up in the last line of the epistle,

> metiri se quemque suo modulo ac pede verum est.

This sentence varies in a more general and authoritative form the thought of the earlier maxim (44) *parvum parva decent*. It contains a final

---

[1] Kiessling's note, taken over by Heinze, 'höfliche Zusage, anders gefärbt wie 19', is wrong. The phrase *ut libet* is no more polite here than at Ter. *Haut.* 738, 934, and elsewhere.

[2] See Mommsen, *Hermes* xii, 1877, 97 n. 5 (*Ges. Schriften*, iii. 231 n. 1); Heinze on *Sat.* 1. 6. 85; see, however, for a slightly different view, Lejay on *Sat.* 1. 6. 86. For the functions of the (auctioneering) *praeco* in general see *RE* xxii. 1198 f.

[3] *Sat.* 1. 6. 85 ff. *nec timuit, sibi ne vitio quis verteret, olim si praeco parvas aut, ut fuit ipse, coactor mercedes sequerer.*

injunction, meant not for his generous benefactor, but for Horace himself. Should he be brought into a position for which he is not suited, he
would have only himself to blame. He knows the limitations of his
nature and knows what is indispensable to him; he therefore must act
accordingly. In this final statement there is no longer a note of wary
self-defence nor any hidden warning. Horace has succeeded in making
Maecenas understand him, and now he serenely formulates a piece
of time-honoured wisdom,[1] a maxim that has proved its value in the
recent crisis through which the two friends have passed.

That the letter which was addressed to Maecenas was published in
its present form and included in the book of the epistles, which is
dedicated to Maecenas, is to the credit not only of Horace but of
Maecenas as well. Nothing could show more clearly that Horace's
sincere and courageous message left no sting in his friend's heart.
We know that Maecenas had many weaknesses, but lack of *magnani-
mitas*, μεγαλοψυχία, was not among them. Nor did Horace ever waver
in his profound attachment to him. The still fashionable talk about a
cooling of their friendship in their later years is contradicted by the
evidence. A reader familiar with Horace's manner of expressing himself
needs only to point to *Odes* 4. 11. 13–20.[2] And as regards Maecenas, it
will suffice to recall the clause in his will:[3] '*Horati Flacci ut mei esto
memor*'.

7. EPISTLE XIX

usque ego postera
crescam laude recens, dum Capitolium
scandet cum tacita virgine pontifex.

The high expectations with which Horace, in 23 B.C., issued his three
books of *carmina* have been fulfilled. But the immediate effect of their
publication was very different. The reception that the majority of the
Roman public, and in particular Horace's fellow poets, gave to the new
lyrics was deeply disappointing. Horace vented his annoyance in a
letter to Maecenas (i. 19). He would not have done so had he not been
sure that Maecenas was one of the few who did understand and appreciate his friend's daring achievement.

Prisco si credis, Maecenas docte, Cratino,

---

[1] The expression in l. 98 also seems to be traditional in this context. Cf. Sen. *Benef.* 2. 16.
1 *Urbem cuidam Alexander donabat . . . .. Cum ille cui donabatur* se ipse mensus *tanti muneris
invidiam refugisset dicens non convenire fortunae suae*, '*Non quaero*' inquit '*quid te accipere deceat,
sed quid me dare*'. Against which Seneca argues *nihil enim per se quemquam decet* (cf. Horace's
parvum parva decent).

[2] See pp. 416 ff. below.   [3] See p. 16 above.

nulla placere diu nec vivere carmina possunt
quae scribuntur aquae potoribus.

This manner of beginning with a commonplace maxim reminds us of some of the *Satires*.[1] That is perhaps no mere accident. The finest judge of Horace's *Epistles* says of this letter that it is conceived 'sur un ton d'ironie satirique et d'apologie personnelle, qui permet de la rapprocher des satires 4 et 10 du livre I et 1 du livre II'.[2] The reference to the wise saying of old Cratinus that as a water-drinker you cannot produce good poetry, ὕδωρ δὲ πίνων χρηστὸν οὐδὲν ἂν τέκοις,[3] recalls a view on the nature of inspired poetry which by the time of Horace had been widely accepted.[4] Horace, while professing his agreement with the well-known doctrine, treats it with mocking exaggeration as befits the style of his *sermo*.[5] Within the letter the reference to ὕδωρ δὲ πίνων κτλ. serves an obvious purpose: it prepares the way for Horace's repudiation of the silly behaviour of his *imitatores*, from 8 (*forum putealque Libonis*)[6] to the culmination in the outburst of 19–20. But the maxim fulfils perhaps an additional function and is more intimately connected with the primary concern of the letter than would appear at first sight. There seems to be here, as an undercurrent, the idea that Horace's *carmina*, the fate of which is the central theme of the epistle, do not belong to those poems that *non placere diu nec vivere possunt* and *quae scribuntur aquae potoribus*. Horace has said of his poetry, and still believes, that it is an achievement *quod non imber edax, non aquilo impotens possit diruere aut innumerabilis annorum series et fuga temporum*. He has also said, and still believes, that he, the poet inspired by Dionysus, *Bacchi plenus*, must sing what the mighty god bids him: *dulce periculum est, o Lenaee, sequi deum*.[7] Sentences such as *vina fere dulces oluerunt mane Camenae* and *non cessavere poetae nocturno certare mero, putere diurno* make it abundantly clear what Horace thinks of the rant of drunken poetasters,

---

[1] i. 1, i. 3, and ii. 2. Compare, however, also *Epist.* i. 6, *Nil admirari*.

[2] Courbaud, op. cit. 318.

[3] This is in all probability the genuine form of the line; cf. Körte, *RE* xi. 1651. Horace was justified in adding *carmina* to his paraphrase, since the context in the Πυτίνη made it clear that the issue in question was the begetting of poetry.

[4] See especially Hans Lewy, 'Sobria ebrietas', *Beihefte zur Zeitschrift für die neutestamentl. Wissensch.* 9, 1929, 45 ff.

[5] See Heinze's note on the expressions (5–7) *oluerunt vina, vinosus*, and *potus*. In a recent book a scholar who is greatly interested in Horace alleges that 'Horaz sich zu den "Wassertrinkern" (*aquae potores*) bekennt'.

[6] It seems strange that Courbaud, 319 n. 1, should recommend the badly attested reading *edixit* at 10. It has often been observed (see, for example, Orelli–Baiter) that the futures at 9, *mandabo, adimam*, echo the traditional formulas in the edicts of the magistrates. But above all, if the first person of the singular were not used at 10 in *edixi*, there would be no link with the thought of 17 f., *quodsi pallerem casu . . ..*

[7] I had long connected the beginning of *Epist.* i. 19 with *Odes* iii. 25 when I discovered that Dacier (note on *Epist.* 1. 19. 3 f.) had done the same.

but on the other hand he has no sympathy whatever for the 'water-drinkers' and will never go back on his own 'edict', *adimam cantare severis.*

From his scornful dismissal of the writers who ape him slavishly and ignorantly[1] Horace proceeds to a positive assessment of his own work. A proud and emphatic sentence (21 f.),

> libera per vacuum posui vestigia princeps,
> non aliena meo pressi pede,[2]

opens the central section of the epistle. This section shows once more an arrangement typical of Horace's *sermones*. He has a definite progress of thought very clearly in mind, but, as if he were afraid of appearing stiff and pedantic, he conceals his plan and gives the impression of gliding casually from one topic to the next. Consequently he seems in the end to arrive by mere chance at the point at which he had in fact been aiming from the outset. In the present instance Horace begins (23 ff.) by asserting that he had been the first to Latinize Archilochus[3] and to adopt, not indeed his subject-matter and his expressions, but his metres and his violent moods. Such borrowing from a great model—Horace goes on—need not lower the value of a poet's work: Sappho modified Archilochean metres, and so did Alcaeus. In this passage the function of Sappho is subordinate, and preparatory, to that of Alcaeus:[4] it is on the poetry of Alcaeus that Horace dwells (29–31) in order to demonstrate that, though indebted to Archilochus for the metrical form of his poems, he still preserves his independence in every other respect. Only at this point does the discussion reach its primary object (32 f.): *hunc* (i.e. Alcaeus)[5] *ego, non alio dictum prius ore, Latinus volgavi*

---

[1] Heinze (on 19) justly observes 'Wen und welche Art von Nachahmung H. dabei im Auge hat, wissen wir nicht'. But in one case we catch at least a glimpse of the kind of imitation that followed in the wake of Horace's *carmina*. After the *Odes* had been published, young Titius plunged boldly into experiments of Pindarizing lyrics (see *Epist.* 1. 3. 9 ff. and cf. Wilamowitz, *S.u.S.* 316 f.). Horace, it is true, does not speak unkindly of Titius, but it is not difficult to guess what he thought of the juvenile amateur *Pindarici fontis qui non expalluit haustus.*

[2] Lucretius, 1. 925 ff., was compared by Orelli–Baiter, Callim. *fr.* 1. 25 ff. Pf. by Heinze. It seems worth while to recall a note of the earlier commentators (e.g. Lambinus, Baxter, Orelli–Baiter, and more recently also Lejay) on *per vacuum*, for here *vacuum* has obviously a tinge of its juridical meaning (*Vocab. Iurispr. Rom.* v. 1183 'non occupatus, sine possessore') and so forms a nice contrast to the subsequent *aliena.*

[3] There was hardly a risk that the words *Parios ego primus iambos ostendi Latio* could by an educated and fair-minded reader be taken as an idle boast on the ground that Archilochus had been known before to many Roman writers and readers. See on this point Heinze's note on 23 (which silently corrects Kiessling's view). Horace's claim is as justified as was his earlier claim (*Odes* 3. 30. 10–14), *dicar ... princeps Aeolium carmen ad Italos deduxisse modos* (emphatically repeated in this epistle, 32 f.), despite the fact that Lesbian stanzas in Latin did exist before him.

[4] The same design is used on a larger scale and in a loftier style in *Odes* 2. 13. 24–32.

[5] That *hunc* can only refer to Alcaeus was irrefutably shown by Bentley.

fidicen. In other words, when we follow the gradual movement of Horace's thought we may be tempted to think that he is bent upon demonstrating the originality—despite their Archilochean elements—of his *iambi*, and that Alcaeus is brought in merely to strengthen the preceding self-defence (*ne me foliis . . . carminis artem*), since the indebtedness of Alcaeus to Archilochus is not substantially different from Horace's own indebtedness to the Parian poet. Only after coming to 32 ff. do we realize that the principal issue in this epistle is not the vindication of the *Epodes*, published many years ago, but the vindication of the *Odes*, which quite recently had suffered unfair treatment at the hands of the general public. What Horace says about his *iambi* and their relation to the work of Archilochus is no doubt important, and he still takes a pride in his early achievement; nevertheless it is obvious that the discussion about the *Epodes* is here subservient to the discussion about the *Odes*.

Horace emphasizes very strongly the analogy of his own relation to Archilochus with the relation of Alcaeus to Archilochus: of himself he says (24 f.) *numeros . . . secutus Archilochi, non res et agentia verba Lycamben*, and of Alcaeus *temperat Archilochi musam pede . . . sed rebus . . . dispar, nec socerum* (i.e. Lycambes) *quaerit quem versibus oblinat atris . . ..* The repetition is doubtless deliberate; otherwise Horace would not have again spoken of *res* nor would he have referred twice to the invectives against Lycambes although he was familiar with many other poems showing the ψογερὸς Ἀρχίλοχος in a characteristic vein.[1] The parallelism is not, however, carried to the point of pedantic exactitude. It is indeed an important element of Horace's assertion that he claims to have followed not only *numeros Archilochi* but *animos* as well (24 f.), namely the Parian poet's general disposition and also his characteristic θυμός, his angry temperament; but once this point has been made, it is abandoned. The common factor in the comparison of Horace's relation to Archilochus with Alcaeus' relation to Archilochus is the dependence of the two later poets on the metre of Archilochus. That is the constant note in this whole section. It is the formal aspect first announced in *numeros* that is then expressed in (27) *modos et carminis artem* and finally in (28) *temperat musam pede*. At this point we are face to face with one of the most controversial passages in Latin poetry. We have to take the bull by the horns: τρεῖν μ' οὐκ ἐᾷ Παλλὰς Ἀθήνη.

Bentley disposed of a misunderstanding which from the scholia had found its way into the printed commentaries.[2] According to that exegesis *Sappho* and *Alcaeus* (28 f.) referred to Horace's Sapphic and Alcaic poems. But while killing one gross error, Bentley fathered two

---

[1] That ancient poets and writers who had but a slight acquaintance with Archilochus usually, when they mention him, harp on Lycambes is a different matter.

[2] e.g. Lambinus, Dacier.

others, which—such was the power of his persuasion—were to have
miraculously long spells of life. This is Bentley's paraphrase : 'Ne mireris,
inquit, aut queraris, quod numeros Archilochi non mutaverim; scias
et Sapphonem et Alcaeum (quos poetas!) *musam suam illius pede tem-*
perare; scias utrumque Archilocheos numeros suis Lyricis immiscere.'
Here it is assumed, first, that at l. 28 *Archilochi* does not go with *musam*
but with *pede*, and, secondly, that *temperare* is more or less synonymous
with *miscere* or *immiscere*. As regards the first point, Bentley's view is still
the prevalent one;[1] as for his interpretation of *temperat*, the idea that
'the metaphor suggested is of mixing a cup',[2] though often criticized,
has by no means disappeared altogether. We must examine the two
points separately. Bentley's interpretation of *temperat Archilochi musam*
pede m. S. was expressly accepted by Lucian Müller, who, however,
added the remark that he did not know any instance of the word-
order supposed by Bentley, viz. *temperat Archilochi musam pede* meaning
'temperat musam (suam) Archilochi pede'.[3] He therefore, after considering various possibilities of transposing the words,[4] left the text of
the line as it stands in the manuscripts and daggered it. Subsequent
commentators might have paid some attention to Müller's observation.[5]
I have examined all the satires and epistles of Horace and have found
no case in which a genitive is governed not by the noun that immediately
follows it but by another noun that follows later in the sentence.[6] The
situation is of course different when the governing noun is separated

[1] See, for example, the notes by Lejay and Heinze, and Villeneuve's translation, 'la
mâle Sappho règle le pas de sa muse sur la marche d'Archiloque'.

[2] Wickham.

[3] It is worth noticing that Bentley's conscience seems to have been far from easy about
the word-order he was forced to assume. Instead of producing a parallel, as was his habit,
he 'talks big': 'Ceterum hanc vocum ordinationem lege versus et collocationis norma
flagitari, nemo, uti credo, praeter Poetas aut in Poetis versatissimos agnoscet.'

[4] Müller's objection to the transposition *pede musam m. S.*, 'doch dürfte Manchen miß-
behagen der Klang in *musam mascula* wegen der gehäuften *m*', is without substance, cf.
Ars P. 286 *minimum meruère* and the like. I, too, have played with the idea of reading *pede*
musam. It does happen that copyists introduce the familiar bucolic diaeresis against the
word-order of the παράδοσις. So—to confine myself to Horace—*Sat.* 1. 3. 117 (Porph. and
some MSS), *Epist.* 1. 6. 56 (Schol. Pers. 4. 17), 1. 16. 56 (Flor. Nostr.), and, in stray
medieval MSS (see Keller's edition of 1925) *Sat.* 2. 4. 47 and *Epist.* 1. 10. 41. It is possible
that the same thing happened at *Sat.* 1. 2. 78 (so Vollmer and Heinze, whereas Lejay and
Klingner regard *sectarier* as the original reading), but there the decision is difficult.
However, I now think (see my subsequent remarks) that the transposition would produce
an entirely wrong sense.

[5] Wilamowitz, 'Geschichte der Philologie', in Gercke u. Norden, *Einleit. i. d. Alter-*
tumsw. i, 3rd ed. 64, says 'Unter Haupts Augen hat Lucian Müller sein wertvolles Buch
De re metrica poetarum Latinorum verfaßt, nach dem man viel von ihm erwarten durfte.
Aber er hat sein Talent durch seinen Character zerstört. Aus der häßlichen Polemik
seiner zahlreichen Schriften wird man nur mit Widerstreben einzelne gute Einfälle
heraussuchen.' But, as Wilamowitz implies, it is necessary to overcome our reluctance and
to remember that L. Müller's knowledge of Latin was considerable.

[6] Cf. also p. 251 n. 6 above.

from the preceding genitive by a group consisting of noun plus verb, *si Democriti pecus edit agellos cultaque*.[1] We must therefore take *Archilochi musam* together. And that is precisely what is required by the sense of this particular sentence and also by the context of the whole passage. But before we go on, a word must be said about the meaning of *temperat*. For our present purpose we need not concern ourselves with the use of *temperare* in general,[2] but have only to try to find out what meaning Horace was likely to connect with the verb when he was using the construction *temperare aliquid aliqua re*. The evidence from Horace's poems is unambiguous:[3] *Odes* 2. 16. 26 f. *amara lento temperet risu*, 3. 19. 6 *quis aquam temperet ignibus*. The use of the verb is the same, for instance, at Virg. *Georg.* 1. 110 *(unda) scatebris arentia temperat arva* and Ovid, *Pont.* 3. 6. 24 *iustitia vires temperat ille suas*. Nor is this use unknown in prose.[4] The meaning of *temperare* in these and similar passages corresponds exactly to that of the English 'to moderate' in the sense given at the beginning of the article in the *Shorter Oxford English Dictionary*, 'to render less violent, intense, rigorous, or burdensome'. In the words *temperat Archilochi musam pede* . . . this meaning was rightly recognized, for instance, by Dacier (who, however, missed the sense of the passage) and Baxter.[5]

---

[1] *Epistle* 1. 12. 12 f. Cf. my note on A. *Ag.* 1434 and Appendix F, iii. 827 f. Detailed work (not just statistics) on word-order is badly needed.

[2] M. B. Ogle, in his courageous and useful paper on ll. 28 f., *Am. Journ. Phil.* xliii, 1922, 55 ff., goes much too far in denying the meaning 'miscere' altogether; consequently he is driven to artificialities in the case of *Epod.* 17. 80, where, as he admits himself (57), 'the meaning "mix" seems to be necessary'. When he says (58) 'Nor in the prose of the Republican period have I found any passages in which temperare is a simple miscere, but always is there present, as in poetry, the underlying idea of restraint, moderation', he is clearly wrong. It will be sufficient to look at Cic. *Off.* 3. 119 *nec vero finis bonorum et malorum, qui simplex esse debet, ex dissimillimis rebus misceri et temperari potest*, or *Tim.* 22 *ea cum tria sumpsisset in unam speciem temperavit* (translating 35 a τρία λαβὼν αὐτὰ ὄντα συνεκέρασατο εἰς μίαν πάντα ἰδέαν). A helpful guide to the understanding of this meaning of the verb is given at the beginning of the article in Ernout and Meillet, *Dict. Etym. lat.*, 'trans. correspond au grec κεράννυμι "mélanger, mêler", en particulier "mêler de l'eau au vin ou à un liquide pour l'adoucir, couper" '. The latter connotation (perhaps originally the primary notion) is often implied, but not always. Cf. also Benveniste, *Mélanges Ernout*, 1940, 12, who reaches this conclusion: 'Le sens propre est donc "doser convenablement un mélange".'

[3] We are here dealing only with passages in which the verb has the notion of mixing qualified by the connotation of moderating, softening, and the like. At *Odes* 1. 8. 6 f., *Gallica nec lupatis temperet ora frenis*, that notion is not to be found at all; the meaning, simply 'moderari', as often elsewhere, is quite clear.

[4] See, for example, Cic. *Att.* 4. 6. 1 *virum bonum . . . in summa magnitudine animi multa humanitate temperatum*, *Nat. D.* 2. 131 *. . . ventos etesias; quorum flatu nimii temperantur calores*, *Tusc.* 1. 2 *rem . . . publicam nostri maiores certe melioribus temperaverunt et institutis et legibus*.

[5] Kiessling has this note: '*temperat* = *moderatur* od. IV 3, 18'; he was followed by L. Müller, Lejay ('*temperat* signifie "régler" '), and Heinze (see also his article 'Die lyrischen Verse des Horaz', *Ber. Sächs. Ges. d. Wiss.*, Phil.-hist. Kl. lxx, 1918, 4. Heft, 25 n. 3, 'ordnend beherrschen'). It will be seen that this rendering is less adequate than 'leniora reddere' (Baxter).

'Sappho moderates (softens, tones down, and the like) by her metre the poetry of Archilochus.' It follows from the usage of the verb that the object of *temperat* cannot be *suam (Sapphus) musam* but only *Archilochi musam*. In establishing a relation between the form, metre, style of Archilochus and the form, metre, style of the Lesbian poets it would be absurd to say that the form and manner of the Lesbians undergo a process of softening by being blended with formal elements derived from Archilochus. The statement must be made the other way round, since it is obvious that the poetry of Archilochus, as compared with that of the Lesbians, or ἴαμβος (in the widest sense) as compared with lyrics proper, stands for greater harshness and rigidity. The process of *temperare* takes place when something Archilochean is turned into something Sapphic or Alcaic. *Archilochi musam*, though a general expression, refers in this context unmistakably to the form, and especially the metrical form, of the poems of Archilochus. The closely-knit texture of the whole passage excludes any ambiguity:

> ac ne me foliis ideo brevioribus ornes
> quod timui mutare modos et carminis artem,
> temperat Archilochi musam pede mascula Sappho,
> temperat Alcaeus.

The logic of this demonstration would be faulty and the whole argument go to pieces if the statement about the Lesbian poets did not strictly correspond to the statement Horace has just made about himself. In other words, what Horace says about Sappho (and Alcaeus), however he expresses it, must mean 'timui mutare modos et carminis artem'. *Archilochi musam*, then, is not substantially different from 'Archilochi carminis modos et artem'. Moreover, as we have seen, *modos et carminis (Archilochei) artem* harks back to 24 f. *numeros Archilochi*.[1] At 28 Horace, continuing the previous argument, does not crudely say 'Sappho borrowed the form of Archilochus' or 'she did not alter the form of Archilochus', but says instead *temperat musam Archilochi pede (suo)*, a statement in which it is clearly implied that Sappho took over the *musa Archilochi*, for otherwise she could not have made that poetic form an object of her *temperare*. A reader who desires a mechanical repetition of the same phrases must turn to other writers than Horace.

The interpretation here advocated[2] is almost identical with the one that two and a half centuries ago was laid down by the much despised

---

[1] The strict correspondence between the three clauses (a) *numeros secutus Archilochi*, (b) *mutare modos et artem carminis (Archilochei)*, and (c) *temperat Archilochi musam . . .* should alone be sufficient to show that the object in the clause is *Archilochi musam*; to understand *musam suam* would destroy the parallelism.

[2] This interpretation seems to shine through a sentence of Wilamowitz (*Griech. Verskunst*, 149): 'ut Sappho peregrinos numeros sua arte temperaret'.

Baxter in a brief note, 'Sappho atque Alcaeus ante me Archilochi Metra, immistis aliis pedibus, leniora reddiderant.' If I had to give a translation of 28, it would be something like this: 'Sappho of the man-like spirit softens the poetry (the form of the poetry) of Archilochus by the way in which she treats the metre.' Scholars have more than once tried to let *pede* go with *mascula*,[1] but that cannot be done: the consistency of the whole discussion—its real interest, it will be remembered, is not in Sappho but in Alcaeus—moreover, the sense of *temperat*, and finally the contrast in the following clause (*sed rebus et ordine dispar*) require that *pede* should also belong to *temperat Alcaeus*. The epithet *mascula* applied to Sappho has been exposed—inevitably, one may say—to a perverse interpretation ever since antiquity.[2] That anything of that sort could have been in Horace's mind will not, I hope, seem probable to a reader who remembers *Odes* 2. 13. 23–25 and 4. 9. 10–12.[3] The word *mascula* is not dragged in from the *chronique scandaleuse*: it is essential to the thought of the passage. It is, Horace suggests, extraordinary for a woman to walk in the footsteps of that most virile poet Archilochus, but Sappho, θαυμαστόν τι χρῆμα, could do so, for the power of her poetry was as great as any man's.

It has long been seen[4] what lies behind Horace's assertion that Sappho and Alcaeus have adopted—and transformed—the metrical form of Archilochus. Horace's readers were familiar with a theory according to which the various types of Greek verse are composed of certain simple elements, which can be arranged in different order and also admit *adiectio* and *detractio*.[5] To show how on that theory the Lesbian metres could be derived from elements contained in the verses of Archilochus I will, for simplicity's sake, adduce only two examples.

---

[1] So, for instance, Welcker, *Kl. Schriften*, ii. 115 (but see his recantation, ibid. i. 139f.). One of the latest to hold this view was presumably Pasquali, *Or. lir.* 109 n. 2, 'Saffo è, secondo me, detta *pede mascula*, appunto perchè ha attinto ad Archiloco ritmi tutt' altro che femminili'.

[2] Porph., ad loc., *vel quia in poetico studio . . . vel quia tribas diffamatur fuisse.*

[3] When Philipp Buttmann knew that he was soon to die, he felt it heavy on his conscience that he had done a grave injustice both to Sappho and to Horace by reading, with many others, the vulgar slander into *mascula*. He therefore prefixed to the second volume of his *Mythologus* a special note, at the end of which he says 'meine wirkliche Schuld gegen beide [Sappho and Horace] gut zu machen, halte ich für eine meiner heiligsten Pflichten, ehe ich aus diesem Kreise der redenden Menschengeschlechter scheide; welche ich hiemit erfülle'. The note is dated 'February 1829'. He died four months later.

[4] W. Christ, 'Die Verskunst des Horaz im Lichte der alten Überlieferung', *Sitz. Bayer. Akad.* 1868, i. 1 ff. As regards the passage in the epistle, I prefer Kiessling's interpretation (on 28) to the more elaborate one attempted by Heinze (28 f. of the article quoted p. 344 n. 5). Against Heinze's view that Horace's treatment of the Aeolic metres shows him 'mitten im Entwicklungsgange der hellenistisch-römischen Verskunst stehend' (op. cit. 31 f.), see Wilamowitz, *Griech. Verskunst*, 128.

[5] Caesius Bassus, *Gramm. Lat.* vi. 271. 5 *cum omnia metra varientur aut adiectione aut detractione aut concinnatione aut permutatione.* Caesius reproduces in the main Varro's view. Cf. Leo, *Hermes*, xxiv, 1889, 281, and *Saturn. Vers* 8.

Caesius Bassus,[1] discussing the κῶλον *stet nive candidum* (*edite regibus*)—
the first part of the verse, *vides ut alta*, is of course the same as πάτερ
Λυκάμβα—says: *ex hemistichio pentametri heroi delibata syllaba compositum
est: reddita enim syllaba fit tale, 'stet nive candidulum'*. In other words: from
ἀχνυμένη σκυτάλη we may obtain τῶν ἀνέμων στάσιν by the *detractio*
of one syllable. And a little farther down[2] Caesius applies the same
method to the line *silvae laborantes geluque* and shows (with ruthless disregard for the necessity of a caesura) that it is an iambic trimeter, *silvae
laborantes geluque frigido*, minus its concluding cretic. We need not
assume that Horace took this theory quite seriously. For him it was
enough that it provided him with an argument to prop his self-defence
since it showed the Lesbians to be dependent on the metres of
Archilochus.[3]

At 29 *ordine*, often misunderstood, was rightly taken by Heinze[4] to
mean the οἰκονομία, *dispositio*, the arrangement of the subject-matter in
the poems.

When Horace, after so careful a preparation, comes to the principal
issue of this epistle (31 ff.), his voice has the ring of genuine pride:

> hunc ego, non alio dictum prius ore, Latinus
> volgavi fidicen. iuvat immemorata ferentem
> ingenuis oculisque legi manibusque teneri.

In the bold claim *non alio dictum prius ore* expressions are echoed which
he had used at the entrance into his most majestic edifice of Alcaic
stanzas (3. 1. 2 f.), *carmina non prius audita*, and in the poem that is to be
regarded as a forerunner of the great cycle of the Roman Odes,[5] *adhuc
indictum ore alio* (3. 25. 7 f.). In the following line he expresses the same
thought in a different way, *immemorata ferentem*, daringly using a compound which he presumably coined for this passage.[6] The phrase
Latinus fidicen, too, is highly significant: it forms a link with words in
the ode in which Horace's enthusiasm for the task of renewing the
lyrics of Alcaeus in Latin found an early expression (1. 32. 3 f.), *age dic
Latinum, barbite, carmen*, and with the late poem in which, at the height
of his success, he rejoices at what he has achieved as *Romanae fidicen
lyrae* (4. 3. 23). In the last line of this proud section the connotations of

---

[1] *Gramm. Lat.* vi. 268. 14. [2] p. 269. 1 ff.

[3] Heinze, op. cit. 28, 'Etwas wie eine Erschleichung muß bei dieser Argumentation
vorliegen—darum kommen wir bei keiner Deutung herum'.

[4] Op. cit. 30: 'Neben den *res*, der πραγματεία, kann *ordo*, meine ich, nur in dem Sinne
stehen, in dem es die antike Rhetorik und Poetik so oft jenem Begriff zugesellt: im Sinne
von τάξις, οἰκονομία, *dispositio*: so z. B. Dionys. de imit. 2 von Panyasis: πραγματείᾳ καὶ τῇ
κατ' αὐτὸν οἰκονομίᾳ διήνεγκεν, und Horaz selbst: *cui lecta potenter erit* res, *nec facundia
deseret hunc nec lucidus ordo* a. p. 40.'

[5] Cf. p. 259 above.

[6] In our Latin texts it recurs only in Ausonius.

ingenuis are more easily felt than paraphrased; they include a liberal education and the behaviour that results from it, physical and moral cleanliness,[1] everything noble as opposed to everything base and vulgar. Horace's *carmina* are meant *ingenuis oculisque legi manibusque teneri*; a book, a *liber*, that has come down in the world must expect *contrectatus manibus sordescere volgi*.[2]

With a sharp movement Horace turns from the ideal reader of his poems to the unfortunately much more common type, the *ingratus lector* (35). In this last section of the epistle he vents without restraint his anger at the general reaction to the publication of his *opuscula*, his odes. His indignation is mingled with a strong, almost haughty, consciousness of his own superiority:

> non ego ventosae plebis suffragia venor
> impensis cenarum et tritae munere vestis;
> non ego, nobilium scriptorum auditor et ultor,
> grammaticas ambire tribus et pulpita dignor.

Each of the two parallel couplets is ushered in by an impassioned *non ego*.[3] Here, as generally in Horace, the use of anaphora indicates strong emotion. 'Not I, Horace—let other people descend to what base bribery they like.' At 39 there is a famous 'crux interpretum', *nobilium scriptorum*. I do not want to dwell on the story of the long and, as it seems to me, undeserved sufferings of this phrase.[4] In my attempt to understand the passage I take as my guide the trend of thought in this epistle. In the centre of the letter are the great old poets whose follower Horace had become and whose form and spirit he endeavoured to renew in a different tongue (*Parios ego primus iambos ostendi Latio, numeros animosque secutus Archilochi*, and *hunc ego . . . Latinus volgavi fidicen*). It is, I think, to them and to poets like them that *nobilium*

---

[1] L. Müller's reference to *Odes* 3. 1. 4 *virginibus puerisque canto* points in the right direction.

[2] *Epist.* 1. 20. 11.

[3] Compare *Sat.* 1. 10. 76 and notice the somewhat similar context.

[4] Kiessling (the body of his long note was not altered by Heinze) and Reitzenstein, *Hermes*, lix, 1924, 18, returned to the view, held by Lambinus, Bentley, and others, that the *nobiles scriptores* are bad contemporary writers, to whose recitations Horace is obliged to listen, '*et ultor*: et qui eis vicissim mea recito. sic enim eos ulciscor: vel qui castigo, et corrigo' (Lambinus). Neither of these two interpretations of *ultor* (Bentley, Kiessling, and Reitzenstein accept the former) has a sufficient foundation in the context. But far worse is the ensuing neglect—or distortion—of *nobilium*. Kiessling's dismay is remarkable: 'Es bleibt nichts Anderes übrig als *non ego nobilium scriptorum auditor et ultor* sarkastisch zu nehmen ['irony the last resource of commentators']', etc. Another widely accepted interpretation, 'auditeur des vers de mes amis et leur vengeur contre les attaques des écoles opposées' (Lejay), is less objectionable in itself, but its consequence is that attention is diverted to something completely outside the scope of this highly condensed letter. Its supporters point to *Sat.* i. 10 (see also Courbaud, 329), but there both the situation and the theme are different.

scriptorum refers. For the particular connotation of *nobilium* we may
compare *Odes* 3. 13. 13, *fies nobilium tu quoque fontium*, where the *fons
Bandusiae*, until now unknown, is promised lasting fame together with
Castalia, Hippocrene, and all the other fountains immortalized long
ago by Greek poets.[1] It may also be remembered that Horace[2] calls
himself one whom the waters of Tibur *et spissae nemorum comae fingent
Aeolio carmine nobilem.* But we are not yet out of the wood: *auditor* and
ultor have still to be accounted for. It is well known that *auditor* appears
often as synonymous with *discipulus*, relating to the schools of rhetoricians, philosophers, and others.[3] The reason why Horace here chose this
particular word is not far to seek: he wanted to emphasize as strongly
as possible the contrast to *grammaticas ambire tribus et pulpita.* Had he
joined those gatherings of the *grammatica tribus*, he would have been an
auditor in the primary sense of the word. He insists, negatively, on his
not belonging to any clique or school and, positively, on his regarding
the old poets as his masters and teachers.[4] Nothing could be more to
the point than that in this connexion he also claims to be their *ultor.*
Alcaeus and the other lyric poets of the classical period—that at any
rate is Horace's thought—were buried in oblivion until he resuscitated
their songs in his own odes. Cicero says[5] *ut laudem eorum* [i.e. *summorum
oratorum*] *iam prope senescentem . . . ab oblivione hominum atque a silentio
vindicarem.* The verb *vindicare* comes from the same sphere as *ultor*, with
which it has a close affinity.

The following words, *hinc illae lacrimae*, besides being a quotation
from Terence, had for the ancient reader the further attraction of a
modest metrical trick. An iambic hemiepes could in some cases scan
also as a dactylic hemiepes. So Callimachus[6] borrows half a line from
the *Bacchae* of Euripides and makes it the beginning of a pentameter,
"ἱερὸς ὁ πλόκαμος", τοὐμὸν ὄνειαρ ἐμοί. Similarly Horace in the present
passage takes over a hemiepes, and at *Sat.* 2. 3. 264, *exclusit, revocat.
redeam?*, more than a hemiepes, from Terence.

The mood of resentment does not soften in the brief dialogue that
enlivens the last section of the epistle (41–47). The cold irony of the
other speaker is most offensive:

> fidis enim manare poetica mella
> te solum, tibi pulcher.[7]

---

[1] Cf. p. 203 above.   [2] *Odes* 4. 3. 10–12.
[3] Cf. *Thes. l. Lat.* ii. 1294.
[4] When young Walther, in the course of the mastersingers' scrutiny, is called upon to
name his master, he boldly replies 'Herr Walther von der Vogelweid, der ist mein
Meister gewesen', whereupon Hans Sachs observes 'Ein guter Meister!', but Beckmesser
'Doch lang schon tot'. (I know that now I shall be charged with romanticizing Horace.)
[5] *De orat.* 2. 7.   [6] *Epigr.* 48. 6.
[7] The mockery is made still more noticeable by the pompous style. The construction

Nor is the poet's reply very polite. The concluding maxim, a hackneyed one, about the evil consequences of anger (48 f.) does nothing to lessen the tension. It is without a smile that we are dismissed at the end of this letter, the only thoroughly bitter document that we have from Horace's pen.

8. EPISTLE XIII

When dispatching a message of particular delicacy, we may wish to impress upon our messenger the need for using all possible discretion in delivering it; sometimes our anxiety to see the errand done properly may lead us to become somewhat 'fussy' in our admonitions. Such behaviour is dictated by human nature and therefore common in all ages. In the spring of the year 43 B.C. Cicero wrote to Decimus Brutus, who at that time was already in a very critical position,[1] to ask him to support L. Aelius Lamia's candidature for the praetorship. Before he comes to the point, he finds it necessary to make precautionary remarks of a noticeable prolixity:[2] *Permagni interest, quo tibi haec tempore epistola reddita sit, utrum cum sollicitudinis[3] aliquid haberes an cum ab omni molestia vacuus esses. itaque ei praecepi quem ad te misi ut tempus observaret epistolae tibi reddendae. nam quem ad modum coram qui ad nos intempestive adeunt molesti saepe sunt, sic epistolae offendunt non loco redditae; si autem, ut spero, nihil te perturbat, nihil impedit,[4] et ille cui mandavi satis scite et commode tempus ad te cepit adeundi, confido me quod velim facile a te impetraturum.*

manare aliquid, here used for the first time and altogether rare (*Thes. l. Lat.* viii. 322 f.), is likely to originate in elevated language; in *poetica mella* the parody is unmistakable. The δίκωλον *te solum, tibi pulcher* has an almost hymnic ring. Its form is doubtless Horatian, but it is possible that a Greek model contributed to its making. It would not be surprising if Horace, who knew Pindar so well, should have attempted to reproduce, by means of a different *figura sermonis*, the strong effect of the jeer καλός τοι πίθων παρὰ παισίν, αἰεὶ καλός (*Pyth.* 2. 72 f.).

[1] Cf. Münzer, *RE*, Suppl. v. 383.

[2] *Fam.* 11. 16. 1.

[3] Horace writes to Augustus, *Epist.* 2. 1. 219 ff., *multa quidem nobis facimus mala saepe poetae . . . cum tibi librum sollicito damus aut fesso.*

[4] This is one of those formulas of politeness which found their way, not so much, I think, from Greek literature into Latin literature as from Greek society into Roman society, at least as early as the third century B.C. Cf. Plato *Prot.* 310a εἰ μή σέ τι κωλύει. . . ., Men. *Epitr.* 10 (51 Körte) εἰ δή σε μηδὲν κωλύει, διάλυσον ἡμᾶς; letter of the middle of the third century B.C., *Pap. Petr.* 2. 11. 1 (*Epist. priv.* ed. Witkowski, no. 3). 3, καὶ νῦν δέ, εἰ δυνατόν ἐστιν καὶ μηθέν σε τῶν ἔργων κωλύει, πειράθητι ἐλθεῖν κτλ.; Cic. *Quinct.* 82 *si te nihil impediret*; Hor. *Epist.* 1. 2. 5 *cur ita crediderim, nisi quid te detinet, audi.* The same formula of politeness occurs in a slightly different form at, for example, Ar. *Lys.* 412 f. σὺ δ' ἦν σχολάσῃς, . . . ἐνάρμοσον; Plat. *Phaed.* 58d ταῦτα . . . προθυμήθητι . . . ἀπαγγεῖλαι, εἰ μή τίς σοι ἀσχολία τυγχάνει οὖσα; *Phaedr.* 227b εἴ σοι σχολὴ προϊόντι ἀκούειν; Plaut. *Aul.* 771 *tecum . . ., si otium est, cupio loqui*, *Merc.* 286 *dicam, si videam tibi esse operam aut otium*, *Most.* 1008 f. *nisi quid magis es occupatus, operam mihi da*; Hor. *Epist.* 2. 2. 95 *mox etiam, si forte vacas, sequere et procul audi.* The same effect is obtained if the conditional clause runs *nisi molestum est* and the like. For Plautine instances see Lodge, *Lex Plaut.* ii. 81, right-hand column, top, and

In Horace's thirteenth epistle we see that his concern for the safe transport of his parcel, the *signata volumina*, and his alarm at the idea that, in handing it over to Augustus, the messenger might be lacking in reserve are so intense that the whole letter—a short one—looks like a torrent of anxious warnings, one tumbling over the other. The writer's apprehension seems to anticipate every conceivable possibility of blunders on the part of the messenger or of unfortunate accidents.

The order to deliver the books to Augustus is not given as an absolute command but made dependent on three momentous ifs, arranged according to that very common pattern of spontaneous, pre-rhetorical rhetoric, the 'tricolon crescendo',[1]

si validus, si laetus erit, si denique poscet.

When sending a messenger on an errand in some matter that we have particularly at heart, we are naturally afraid lest he should spoil everything by being over-zealous in the service of his master. So Deianira tells Lichas[2]

ἀλλ' ἕρπε, καὶ φύλασσε πρῶτα μὲν νόμον,
τὸ μὴ 'πιθυμεῖν πομπὸς ὢν περισσὰ δρᾶν,

and Horace writes to Vinnius

ne studio nostri pecces odiumque libellis
sedulus importes opera vehemente minister.

The following section (6–10) is enlivened by jokes to which Vinnius' *cognomen*, Asina, gives rise.

It is easy to see that the man for whom this letter was really written is not its insignificant addressee but Augustus. We may safely assume

compare, for example, Ter. *Ad.* 806, Cic. *Fin.* 2. 5, *Fam.* (from Book XIII only) 2; 23. 2; 56. 1; 67. 2; 70. Another variation appears in the form *hoc si tibi commodum est* (Plaut. *Cist.* 486) or *nisi tibi est incommodum* (*Most.* 807); for similar expressions cf. Cic. *Att.* 4. 4a. 2; 4. 8a. 1; 12. 7. 1, *Fam.* 13. 69. 2.

[1] Many Latin sentences built in accordance with the 'Gesetz der wachsenden Glieder' (Behaghel), i.e. so that B is longer than A, and C longer than B, are examined by E. Lindholm, *Stilistische Studien zur Erweiterung der Satzglieder im Lateinischen*, Lund 1931. This device, very much favoured by, for example, Tacitus, Macaulay, and Sir Winston Churchill, is as old as European literature and probably much older. It is sometimes operative even in the arrangement of a triad of proper names, as, for instance, at Homer A 145 ἢ Αἴας ἢ Ἰδομενεὺς ἢ δῖος Ὀδυσσεύς, or Υ 232 Ἶλός τ' Ἀσσάρακός τε καὶ ἀντίθεος Γανυμήδης. Si clauses arranged in this way are fairly common, e.g. (tricolon as in the Horatian line under examination) Cic. *Fam.* 5. 2. 10 *si acerbe, si crudeliter, si sine causa sum a tuis oppugnatus*; Caelius ap. Cic. *Fam.* 8. 10. 5 *si tempus, si senatus coget, si honeste a nobis recusari non poterit*; for a kindred, if somewhat different, arrangement see, for example, Ennius, *Ann.* 431 *si luci, si nox, si mox, si iam data sit frux*; Cic. *Quint.* 82 *si te nihil impediret, si voluntas eadem maneret, si valeres* [cf. Horace's *si validus*], *denique si* [cf. Horace's *si denique*] *viveres*. A tricolon (not crescendo) with anaphora of *ubi* shows once more how stereotyped were the forms of these expressions of politeness, Ter. *Eun.* 484 f. *verum ubi molestum non erit, ubi tu voles, ubi tempus tibi erit, sat habet si tum recipitur.*

[2] S. *Trach.* 616 f.

that a copy of the letter accompanied the parcel of the *signata volumina*. The position which the name of the Princeps occupies in the epistle is illuminating. Its first line, *Ut proficiscentem docui te saepe diuque*, is merely an introductory reminder, and the last few clauses, from 18 *oratus multa prece* on, consisting of a modestly elaborated farewell, form a kind of epilogue. The main body of the letter, then, which contains the instructions for the messenger, begins at l. 2 with *Augusto* and ends at l. 18 with *Caesaris*.

The *carmina* (17) contained in the *signata volumina* are, as was stated by Lachmann,[1] the three books of the *Odes*. They were published after the middle of the year 23 B.C. The present letter was written either in the second half of 23 or in 22 before the autumn, when Augustus, who on the first of September was still in Rome, left Italy for Sicily.[2]

The intricacy of the circumstances under which the letter was written pained Wickham, and he exclaimed: 'Are we to imagine, then, that Horace's Odes were unknown to him [Augustus] for some months after their publication? or are we to look upon this as a formal presentation of a book which the poet already knew to be approved of?' Neglecting the 'or', I should think that to both these questions there can be but one answer, a firm 'of course we are'. Otherwise—to continue the discussion in the same style—are we to imagine that Horace told his publishers, the Sosii, to send a presentation copy of his *Carmina* to Augustus on the very day of the publication (or perhaps an 'advance-copy' such as may have been sent to Maecenas)? In the months following the publication of the *Odes* Augustus had many more urgent matters to think of than the most recent poetical productions; moreover, he had only recently recovered from an illness thought to be fatal. And to Horace's way of thinking it would have been extremely tactless, not to say impertinent, if he had volunteered to send his books to the Princeps unless the Princeps had made it known that he would like to be given them. Even now the poet is picking his steps with remarkable caution. The happy disguise by which he is addressing not Augustus but the messenger enables him to guard himself in a series of nicely varied expressions against the charge of wishing to importune Augustus at the wrong moment or of overrating the value of his gift (16 ff. *ne volgo narres te sudavisse ferendo carmina quae possint oculos aurisque morari Caesaris*). The letter is brief, light, and witty, and at the same time it expresses Horace's deep respect for the Princeps, of whose heavy

---

[1] *Kl. Schriften*, ii. 155.

[2] Mommsen's error in dating the letter too early (he left *Odes* iii. 14 out of account) was corrected by Kiessling, 'Zu augusteischen Dichtern', *Philol. Unters.* ii. 49; see also Courbaud, 312. It is possible that Augustus, at the time when Horace sent the books to him, was in southern Italy, but, as Villeneuve observes (*Horace, Épîtres*, Notice, 27), it is equally possible that he was in Rome and Horace somewhere *in villeggiatura*.

responsibilities he is fully aware. If we want to appreciate the importance of this document, we have to remember the history of Horace's
relations with Augustus.

In the two epodes I and IX, written the one shortly before, the other
immediately after the battle of Actium,[1] Caesar figures as the man with
whose fate the fate of Maecenas is indissolubly linked[2] and as the man
on whose victory the safety and freedom of Rome depend;[3] Horace and
Maecenas, in feeling *curam metumque Caesaris rerum*, feel what in other
ages would be called patriotic anxieties. The same feeling underlies
the Cleopatra ode, i. 37, written in the autumn of 30 B.C. About the
same time, or possibly a little later, Horace wrote his dialogue with
Trebatius,[4] in which he had to decline a suggestion which, in the course
of time, was to be repeated more than once, *aude Caesaris invicti res
dicere*. He does decline, firmly if very modestly, but he also manages, in
an indirect way, to give very full praise to Caesar's personality and
achievements.[5] However, he is determined not, or at any rate not·yet,
to trouble Caesar with a product of his pen (17 ff.):

> haud mihi dero
> cum res ipsa feret: nisi dextro tempore Flacci
> verba per attentam non ibunt Caesaris aurem;
> cui male si palpere, recalcitrat undique tutus.

If you endeavour to interest Caesar in a work of literature at all, it
should be done in the most considerate manner. This is a conviction
that remains fixed in Horace's mind: it underlies the whole letter to
Vinnius Asina and finds a strong expression in the late epistle to Augustus, where he says[6] *multa quidem nobis facimus mala saepe poetae . . . cum
speramus eo rem venturam ut, simul atque carmina rescieris nos fingere, commodus ultro arcessas et egere vetes et scribere cogas*. But in the Trebatius satire
it also serves as an excuse for evading the uncongenial task of writing
laudes Caesaris in epic form.

As regards Horace's attitude to Augustus in Books I to III of the
Odes, I need not repeat what I have tried to show in discussing the
relevant poems; it will be sufficient to recall some major points. In
the early ode i. 2, *Iam satis terris*, Horace, while respecting the customary proprieties of Roman religion and also the aversion of the Princeps
to ruler worship in Rome, still allowed himself, though only in an
unmistakable flight of poetic imagination, to touch upon certain conceptions current in the Hellenistic world. This daring venture he never
repeated. In the great Pindarizing ode, i. 12, *Quem virum aut heroa*,

---

[1] Cf. pp. 69 ff. above.
[2] See *Epod.* 1. 3 f. *paratus omne Caesaris periculum subire, Maecenas, tuo.*
[3] See Epod. ix.   [4] *Sat.* ii. 1.
[5] See pp. 148 ff. above.   [6] 2. 1. 219 ff.

written several years later, Augustus was given a place only in the concluding prayer to Jupiter: there he appears, a purely human figure,
as one who, under the supreme god, holds a *minor potestas* (49 ff.) :

> gentis humanae pater atque custos,
> orte Saturno, tibi cura magni
> Caesaris fatis data: tu secundo
> Caesare regnes,

and in the last stanza:

> te minor latum reget aequus orbem.

The conception which we found in the two Actium epodes and the
Cleopatra ode, that Caesar's cause is the cause of Rome and that her
welfare depends on his victory, remains fundamental to Horace's
patriotic lyrics in general; it gains in substance and colour as the poet's
art matures. We hear a nobly condensed version of it in an ode which
belongs to the late pieces of the first collection :[1]

> ego nec tumultum
> nec mori per vim metuam tenente
> Caesare terras.

This personal confession has to be taken seriously. It may be called un-
heroic, and some may even be inclined to give it still harsher names.
But it undoubtedly expresses what Horace and many honest men
throughout Italy most intensely felt.[2] Only too fresh were the memories
of the days when

> fas versum atque nefas: tot bella per orbem,
> tam multae scelerum facies.

Freedom from fear had at last been granted to the people of Italy.
But to men such as Virgil and Horace the rule of Augustus did not
merely mean material security. They saw in it a manifestation of order
overcoming chaos, of reason replacing brutal force. Viewed in this
light, the new régime acquired a more than temporal dignity. Inspired
by this idea Horace, freely elaborating a Pindaric conception, composed
the central hymn of the Roman Odes, iii. 4, *Descende caelo*.[3] The writing
of that poem and of other odes in a similar strain was to Horace not a
matter of expediency, but something that filled him with genuine
enthusiasm: this, at any rate, is the conclusion to which we came after

---

[1] 3. 14. 14 ff.
[2] In the latest and finest of his odes concerned with Augustus Horace, speaking for the
common people, says (4. 5. 25 ff.) *quis Parthum paveat, quis gelidum Scythen* . . . *incolumi
Caesare?* . . . *condit quisque diem collibus in suis* . . ..
[3] See pp. 281 ff. above.

weighing carefully the evidence of *Quo me, Bacche, rapis.*[1] Any critic of Horace should at least admit that the poet himself believed in the ideas and the hopes which he made the themes of his patriotic odes, believed that it was Augustus who had saved the Roman world from utter ruin. The only alternative Horace could see to the rule of the Princeps was endless chaos. Would it have been nobler for a man who had fought against Octavian on the side of Brutus and Cassius to die with the dying Republic? It seems doubtful whether any such thought ever entered Horace's mind. He wanted the Roman State to survive and he wanted to live in it himself. Being perfectly sincere, he had no taste for what Tacitus calls *inanis iactatio libertatis.*

In all those odes of Books I to III in which Augustus figures he is treated with unambiguous and convincing respect, admiration, and gratitude, but nowhere is there any indication of personal intimacy. It is indeed unlikely that at that time any such intimacy should have existed.[2] The letters of Augustus to Horace excerpts of which are preserved in Suetonius cannot be dated, but in all probability none of them was written before the publication of the first collection of the odes. All the known facts point in the same direction: that it was the publication of the three books of *carmina* that altered the relationship of Horace and Augustus. Perhaps it was Maecenas who, not long after the books had been issued, interested Augustus in these poems the like of which Rome had never seen. Consequently Augustus let the poet know that he would welcome a copy, and Horace sent him the papyrus rolls and the letter which was ostensibly addressed to Vinnius Asina. This letter shows how much the approval of the Princeps and the encouragement coming from him meant to Horace. His respect for Augustus and his considerate regard for his heavy burden remained unaltered, but there is in the letter a light touch, a happy mood, and a quiet confidence that make the reader feel that Horace is at ease not only with Vinnius but also with Augustus. As far as we can see it was in the following years that the two men drew together more closely and the correspondence began of which we catch at least some occasional glimpses. The decision in 17 B.C.—primarily, if not solely, the decision of Augustus—that the *Carmen Saeculare* should be composed by Horace after his own individual fashion[3] had an immense influence on the

---

[1] *Odes* iii. 25. See pp. 259 f. above.

[2] I have considered this problem again and again and have always reached the same conclusion as Wilamowitz, *S.u.S.* 313 n. 1, 'Daß der patriotische Libertinensohn sich in seinem Urteil [that there was a pressing need for moral redintegration] mit dem Caesar zusammenfand, ist für beide ehrenvoll; eine auch nur mittelbare [this is perhaps putting it too strongly] Beziehung zwischen beiden vor dem Jahre 23 ist weder erweislich noch wahrscheinlich.'

[3] Cf. pp. 380 ff. below.

poet's life and work; with all it entailed it could only enhance Horace's devotion to the man who, in the midst of his cares, showed true insight into the nature of the bold new lyrics and, moreover, translated his appreciation into a most gratifying action.

The more the poet's attachment to Augustus deepened and the more a real friendship—something beyond what was commonly called *amicitia*—bound the two men together, the more difficult Horace found it to eulogize the Princeps in poetry. In the relations of grown-up men not given to shallow sentimentality there exists sometimes a delicacy of feeling that might seem fit for a shy adolescent. When we come to *Odes* iv. 2, *Pindarum quisquis studet aemulari*, and iv. 5, *Divis orte bonis*, we shall see that Horace rejected, though with inimitable grace and warmth of feeling, the suggestion of praising Augustus in a Pindarizing epinikion and that, considerably later, he did praise him, but in a manner not at all reminiscent of Pindar, a manner entirely his own. We shall also see that Horace's latest epistle, ii. 1, *Cum tot sustineas*, is a monument to Augustus such as no one but Horace would have been able to erect.

9. EPISTLE XX

It might not be a bad pastime to consider the various ways in which poetry as well as common sayings has profited from the accident of grammatical gender. Instances in ancient literature are plentiful, from ἄλλοτε μητρυιὴ πέλει ἡμέρη, ἄλλοτε μήτηρ to νόμος ὁ πάντων βασιλεὺς θνατῶν τε καὶ ἀθανάτων and χρόνος ὁ πάντων πατήρ, to ἡ πόλις γὰρ δυστοκεῖ, to *ut mater iuvenem . . . votis ominibusque et precibus vocat . . . sic desideriis icta fidelibus quaerit patria Caesarem*, and so forth. Seafaring nations look on a ship not as a thing but rather as a living being; it was therefore natural for Greek and Roman poets to speak of a ναῦς, a *navis*, in such a manner that at the same time a woman was to be thought of, and this habit suggested to Horace a piece of elaborate imagery.[1] It is upon a less common idea that the happy invention of the twentieth epistle is based. Here Horace takes advantage of the fact that, unlike βυβλίον or τεῦχος,[2] the Latin word for a book is masculine. From the very beginning of the epistle the reader is led to take as the addressee not only the book, the papyrus roll, but also, inseparable from it, a young person:

> Vortumnum Ianumque, liber, spectare videris,
> scilicet ut prostes Sosiorum pumice mundus.

[1] See pp. 157 f. above.

[2] The modest entry in Liddell and Scott, τεῦχος IV, 'τ. = *volumen, Gloss.*', with 'Addenda', p. 2107, could be enriched from W. Schubart, *Das Buch bei den Griechen und Römern*, 2nd ed., 1921, 176.

The first line in itself is harmless enough: why should not the
book—and the young household slave—be on the look-out for the
tabernae in the forum and for the world beyond? But the following
explanation, *scilicet ut prostes Sosiorum pumice mundus*, sounds far less
innocent. The connotations of *prostare* as applied to the boy are definitely
unpleasant, and whereas a papyrus roll, in order to be saleable, has to
be *arida pumice expolitum*, a boy who is on show and appears *pumice
mundus* has forfeited any claim to respectability.[1] Up till now the *liber*,
in its double capacity as an unpublished book and a young slave, has
had no experience whatever of the outside world. *Qua* book it has been
kept under lock and seal by its author (3 *odisti clavis et . . . sigilla*), for it
still belonged to the class of *rudes curae*, 'quas novit unus scrinioque signatas
custodit ipse virginis pater chartae'.[2] *Qua* slave it has been brought up (5
nutritus) in the master's house and educated and trained in the same
manner as, for instance, those *pueri litteratissimi, anagnostae optimi et
plurimi librarii* in the household of Atticus, of whom we are told that
neque . . . horum quemquam nisi domi natum domique factum habuit.[3] So the
young slave with whom the new book is here identified represents
a well-known type; he is, in the words of another Horatian epistle
(2. 2. 6 ff.),

> verna ministeriis ad nutus aptus erilis,
> litterulis Graecis imbutus, idoneus arti
> cuilibet.

If we want to form an idea of what the master might feel for such a
well-bred and able young servant, we have only to remember the
moving passage in one of Cicero's letters,[4] *mehercule eram in scribendo*

---

[1] Wickham's commentary has its merits, but it always clings to the proprieties established in the Victorian age. Consequently his notes on 2 do not contain the slightest hint
at a possible ambiguity. And in the introduction to this epistle he says that the book 'is
addressed in terms borrowed in part from the image of a favourite slave. . . . The figure is
lightly handled, not pressed (as by some commentators) into tasteless detail.' The question whether the idea of the slave as well as the book is maintained throughout the epistle
has been discussed for centuries, and it is precisely on l. 2 that the interpretations clash
most fiercely. Against Baxter's note, 'Prostes, Dilogωs posuit: nam prostant et libri et
meretricii. Signate igitur subjecit *pumice*: nam hujusmodi pueri erant *pumice leves*, quod
ait Juvenalis [9. 95; for fuller references see *RE* iii. 474]', J. M. Gesner protested angrily:
'Pueri natura leves non indigent pumice. Simpliciter ad cultum voluminum respicit.
Tota haec Dilogia mihi non placet.' Baxter is clearly right. The implications of the adjective in the phrase *pumice mundus* would not be lost on a Roman reader; cf. Sen. *Nat. quaest.*
7. 31. 2 *lēvitate et politura corporum muliebres* munditias *antecessimus*. The objection in Gesner's
first sentence misses the point. A dark-haired Mediterranean boy, even before reaching
maturity, will not have a white skin. Once he finds himself on that slippery road (*prostes*),
he will pluck the hair from his body, and then, to smooth his skin, proceed to κισηρίζειν,
pumicare.

[2] Martial 1. 66. 6 f., quoted by Orelli–Baiter.

[3] Nepos, *Att.* 13. 3 f.

[4] *Att.* 1. 12. 4.

conturbatior. nam puer festivus anagnostes noster Sositheus decesserat meque plus quam servi mors debere videbatur commoverat.

So long as the *liber* (the book, the boy) is sheltered in Horace's house, all is well: only the poet himself and certain intimate friends will be acquainted with the contents of the book; no stranger will be tempted to make advances to the handsome boy.[1] But once the wish for publicity (4 *paucis ostendi gemis et communia laudas*) has been fulfilled, there is no escape from degradation. Belated complaints will be of no avail; *liber* ought to have known better.[2] After his preliminary warnings, Horace proceeds to a regular prophecy, which he introduces (9) by a reservation of a type customary in prophecies, *quodsi non . . . desipit augur.*[3] The young creature that at the beginning of its career belonged to one lover only (the man who first purchased it) will, *cum plenus languet amator*, sink even lower: for a while the favourite of several well-to-do people in Rome (10), it will soon be degraded to a common *prostibulum* (11 *contrectatus*[4] *. . . manibus . . . volgi*). By that time it will be reduced to misery; shabbiness will have wasted its appearance that had once been so attractive.[5] The detail in 13, *aut fugies Uticam aut vinctus mitteris Ilerdam*, requires no comment so far as the slave is con-

---

[1] There was always the danger of this happening. Horace finds it necessary to give the following advice to a young man (*Epist.* 1. 18. 72 f.) : *non ancilla tuum iecur ulceret ulla puerve intra marmoreum venerandi limen amici.*

[2] Elsewhere ('Kolon und Satz I', *Nachr. Gött. Ges.*, Phil.-hist. Kl. 1932, 211) I have shown that at 7 in *et scis* the particle has its adversative force (cf. also Leo, *Nachr. Gött. Ges.* 1895, 423, and Hofmann, *Thes. l. Lat.* v. 2. 893), 'and yet you know (for I have told you again and again)'; cf. A. *Prom.* 1076 ff. εἰδυῖαι γὰρ . . . εἰς ἀπέραντον δίκτυον ἄτης ἐμπλεχθήσεσθ' ὑπ' ἀνοίας. As for the application of the phrase (8) *in breve cogi* to a human being, the military term at Ter. *Haut.* 669 (quoted by Dacier and others) is hardly relevant; but Prop. 4. 1. 128, *in tenues cogeris ipse lares* (quoted by Orelli–Baiter), points to the idiom on which Horace bases his secondary meaning (the primary one refers to the papyrus roll).

[3] Cf. Soph. *El.* 472 f. εἰ μὴ 'γὼ παράφρων μάντις ἔφυν καὶ γνώμας λειπομένα σοφᾶς (cf. also *OT* 1086 f. εἴπερ ἐγὼ μάντις εἰμὶ καὶ κατὰ γνώμαν ἴδρις) ; Hor. *Odes* 3. 17. 12 f. *aquae nisi fallit augur annosa cornix*; Virg. *Aen.* 3. 433 f. *si qua est Heleno prudentia, vati si qua fides, animum si veris implet Apollo*; Shakespeare, *Cymbeline*, 4. 2. 352 (Soothsayer) 'which portends—unless my sins abuse my divination . . .'.

[4] What becomes of a book which has had to suffer from *contrectari* at the hands of the many is obvious. But *contrectare* is also almost a technical term in the erotic sphere: see *Thes. l. Lat.* iv. 774. 47 ff.

[5] The commentators confine their observations on the phrase at 12, *tineas pasces taciturnus inertis*, to its reference to the book, although from *taciturnus* it ought to be sufficiently clear that here, as throughout the letter, the slave also must be taken into account. What prevented scholars from grasping Horace's implication was probably their belief that *tineae* meant generally 'moths' and here exclusively the kind of vermin that would infest papyrus. A passage in which *tineae* can mean only the lice on a man's head, Claudian 18. 113 f., *miserabile turpes exedere caput tineae*, is quoted in all dictionaries. Ernout and Meillet, *Dict. Étym. lat.*, say correctly 'tinea désigne toute espèce de vers ou de mites, . . . pou, vermine', etc. The sense 'louse', besides 'moth', etc., was indubitably current in Horace's time as well as in that of Claudian. Nothing could show more clearly the misery which is in store for Horace's poor slave than that he will be so destitute that he can no longer afford to keep his hair tidy. That is about the last thing a southerner would be prepared to give up. In this connexion the proverbial saying (cf. Plaut. *Pseud.* 219 f.) to which Catullus, 10.

cerned, but it is true to life also in regard to the book.[1] The anticipation of the terrible downfall of the obstinate creature is accompanied by an outburst of ἐπιχαιρεκακία, 'Schadenfreude'; a diminutive αἶνος, after the fashion of the *Satires*, provides a pretty ornament (14–16). The prophecy concludes with the announcement of this ultimate humiliation:

> hoc quoque te manet, ut pueros elementa docentem
> occupet extremis in vicis balba senectus.

It was part of the routine of elementary school teaching that the children had to learn to read from texts of poetry;[2] owing to the high price of papyrus any otherwise useless book of verse would do for that purpose if no copy of a classic happened to be at hand. And again the slave—by now grown very old—comes into the picture. Many educated men, poets and scholars among them, had to be content if in their old age they could make a living from the humblest kind of schoolmastering. One instance from the Hellenistic world and one from Rome will suffice here. A well-known epigram by Aratus of Soli runs:[3]

> αἰάζω Διότιμον ὃς ἐν πέτρῃσι κάθηται
> Γαργαρέων παισὶν βῆτα καὶ ἄλφα λέγων.

The jeer is directed against the poet Diotimos of Adramytteion.[4] The sad end of the career of another learned man, an older contemporary of Horace, said to have been a slave, *verum ob ingenium atque doctrinam gratis manumissus*, is reported by Suetonius:[5] *Lenaeus, Magni Pompei libertus et paene omnium expeditionum comes, defuncto eo filiisque eius schola se sustentavit in Carinis ad Telluris, in qua regione Pompeiorum domus fuerat.*

But Horace, though in a severe mood, is not being cruel. The future that awaits the would-be runaway is indeed dark, but there appears some sunshine at the end. On a fine afternoon, life, outdoor life of course, can never be wholly unbearable in a southern country. The prophet proceeds thus:

> cum tibi sol tepidus[6] pluris admoverit auris . . ..

The hour is towards sunset, and the scene is, either somewhere in

---

11, alludes (*nihil neque ipsis . . . esse nec cohorti, cur quisquam caput unctius referret*) is instructive. Cf. also Hor. *Sat.* 2. 3. 125 f.

[1] Cf. W. Schubart, op. cit. 160, 'Jedenfalls waren die Provinzen des römischen Reiches z. T. von der römischen und wohl auch alexandrinischen Ausfuhr abhängig; in den kleineren und entlegenen Provinzstädten konnte der hauptstädtische Buchhändler seine übrig gebliebenen Exemplare, seine Ladenhüter, noch an den Mann bringen.'

[2] Cf., for example, Quintilian, *Inst.* 1. 8. 5 *optime institutum est ut ab Homero atque Vergilio lectio inciperet, quamquam ad intellegendas eorum virtutes firmiore iudicio opus est.*

[3] Steph. Byz. s.v. Γάργαρα, Macrob. *Sat.* 5. 20. 8, *Anth. Pal.* 11. 437.

[4] Cf. Wilamowitz, *Eur. Her.* i.[2] 67 n. 123, *Hellenist. Dichtung*, i. 143.

[5] *Gram.* 15.   [6] That is, the sun *quo vespertina tepet regio* (*Sat.* 1. 4. 29 f.).

Africa or Spain or in a Roman suburb, in front of the old man's hovel. There he will bask in the mild sunshine, and soon a little crowd of neighbours and their children will gather around him. 'Là viendront les villageois Dire alors . . . "Par des récits d'autrefois . . .".' The lonely old man will gladly yield to their entreaties. Encouraged by the friendly atmosphere he will plunge into his recollections and will not mind boasting a little of his glorious past.[1] 'My master, you know, many years ago, he was a fine man and also a great poet. He came from a very humble family, and yet—would you believe it?—the best people of Rome used to invite him to dinner, Maecenas quite often, and sometimes even the Emperor Caesar Augustus . . .', and so forth. In this manner the old man's listeners will hear from him—and the readers of the book will read in its last column—the brief tale with which the epistle concludes.

This sketch of an autobiography begins with (20) *me libertino natum patre*: Horace still lays as much stress on this fact as he did more than fifteen years ago.[2] And the pride that he takes in having been able *in tenui re maiores pinnas nido extendisse* is as strongly expressed in this epilogue of the *Epistles* as it was in the epilogues of the second (2. 20. 5 *pauperum sanguis parentum*) and the third (3. 30. 12 *ex humili potens*) books of the *Odes*. The appended argument, (22) *ut quantum generi demas virtutibus addas*, formulates most concisely the *iustus titulus* of a Roman self-made man. Thus the great prototype of the *homo novus*, Marius, says[3] *alii si deliquere, vetus nobilitas, maiorum fortia facta, cognatorum et affinium opes, multae clientelae, omnia haec praesidio adsunt; mihi spes omnes in memet sitae, quas necesse est virtute et innocentia tutari; nam alia infirma sunt.* We shall do less than justice to the meaning of the next line, *me primis urbis belli placuisse domique*, unless we realize that in the context of this brief summary nothing obliged Horace to mention *belli*; he indulges in this unmistakable allusion to the campaign which ended at Philippi because he wants to make it absolutely clear that he has remained faithful to the memory of Brutus, Cassius, and the other leaders of the defeated party.[4] There follows a precise and unflattering description of the poet's physique (24)[5] and his moral character (25), and at the end the year and month in which he was born are indicated.

---

[1] That is all very natural and would happen in Rome as well as anywhere else. Suetonius in his Life of Virgil (*Vita Donati* 34) reports *Erotem librarium et libertum eius exactae iam senectutis tradunt referre solitum . . .*; there follows a fanciful story, the authenticity of which is supposed to be guaranteed by the important part which Eros himself played in it (*statimque sibi imperasse ut utrumque volumini ascriberet*).

[2] *Sat.* 1. 6. 6 and 45 ff.   [3] Sall. *Iug.* 85. 4.

[4] Cf. pp. 12 f. above.

[5] 'So wie er es jetzt tat, hat kein Grieche von sich geredet; geht er doch so weit, seine Leiblichkeit zu schildern, und wir erkennen einen Typus, den man in Süditalien häufig antrifft' (Wilamowitz, *Süddeutsche Monatshefte*, 28. Jahrgang, Oktober 1930, 44).

The thought of 25, *irasci celerem, tamen ut placabilis essem*, is in itself intelligible enough, but its connotations come into full relief only when we remember the educational background of the society to which Horace belonged. The cultural atmosphere at that time was saturated with doctrines and principles of Hellenistic ethics, which were to such a degree common property and, as it were, floating in the air that they need not be traced to any particular source. Since, however, Aristotle's influence was strong, he may be used to represent a widely held view. He[1] describes the typical behaviour of irascible persons thus: οἱ μὲν οὖν ὀργίλοι ταχέως μὲν ὀργίζονται (cf. *irasci celerem*) καὶ οἷς οὐ δεῖ καὶ ἐφ' οἷς οὐ δεῖ καὶ μᾶλλον ἢ δεῖ, παύονται δὲ ταχέως (cf. *tamen ut placabilis essem*)· ὃ καὶ βέλτιστον ἔχουσιν. The philosopher knows that short-tempered men, who on the slightest provocation fly into a rage but will soon calm down, are morally superior to those men who first conceal their anger, keep it for years in cold reserve, and then take a late vengeance on those who have offended them, men such as the Tacitean figures of Domitian and Tiberius.[2] In the Hellenistic period and after, many educated men, if they happened to be good men, allowed current ethical doctrines to exert a strong influence on their behaviour in the difficulties and conflicts of everyday life. Cicero was justly annoyed at the manner in which his brother Quintus, when *pro praetore* in Asia, proved incapable of controlling himself and kept on bullying the provincials. In order to be patient with the shortcomings of Quintus, Marcus resorted to the literature περὶ ὀργῆς and reminded himself and his brother of its principles,[3] and in a letter to Atticus, Quintus' brother-in-law, he pleaded for Quintus by referring in general terms to the passage of Aristotle's *Ethics* which has been quoted above.[4] Horace had long known that his irascibility was far from laudable[5] and he now singles it out as a prominent feature of his character. But he also knows that he belongs to those who παύονται ταχέως, and he probably finds some comfort in what he does not say but implies, ὃ καὶ βέλτιστον ἔχουσιν.

Only if one of the listeners carries his curiosity to the point of inquiring about the poet's age is the old slave advised to say anything about it:

> forte meum si quis te percontabitur aevum . . ..

---

[1] *Eth. Nic.* 4. 11. 1126ᵃ13 ff.

[2] Cf. also (I owe this reference to a marginal note by F. Leo) a trait in Plutarch's forbidding portrait—as forbidding as the bronze bust from Volubilis—of the younger Cato, 1. 5, πρὸς ὀργὴν οὐ ταχὺς οὐδ' ὀλισθηρός, ὀργισθεὶς δὲ δυσπαραίτητος.

[3] *Ad Quint. fr.* 1. 1. 37 *quae de iracundia dici solent a doctissimis hominibus.*

[4] *Ad Att.* 1. 17. 4 (quoted by Orelli–Baiter) *si ita statueris et irritabiles animos esse optimorum* (cf. ὃ καὶ βέλτιστον ἔχουσιν) *saepe hominum et eosdem placabiles* . . .. It is no mere accident that he, like Horace, uses in this context the word *placabilis*.

[5] *Sat.* 2. 3. 323 (in Damasippus' catalogue of Horace's vices) *non dico horrendam rabiem.*

The semblance of spontaneity is not confined to this detail, but is essential to the pretty invention as a whole. Horace has been careful not to give the impression that, out of the blue or following some literary convention, he is springing a short autobiography upon the reader. It is not he, Horace, who volunteers these pieces of information, but an old servant, talkative by nature (*liber*!), to whom prolonged *taciturnitas* (12) would be pain and grief.

The last section of the epistle, 20–28, is graceful and apparently simple. But when we try to analyse it, we find that various literary traditions have contributed to it. In dealing with such a delicate subject we must not mechanize the working of the poet's mind nor must we treat a little masterpiece, which is *sui generis*, as if it were a direct continuation of other forms of literature. Rather should we attempt to find out what models, in a subsidiary function, are likely to have induced Horace to give this particular shape to the conclusion of his book of *Epistles*.

It is probable that, when Horace decided to place a brief account of his origin and his person at the end of his book, he was, amongst other things, influenced by the fact that a σφραγίς, a seal, was found at the end of various Hellenistic books of poetry.[1] For our purpose it will be sufficient to quote the last two lines of Nicander's *Theriaca*,

καί κεν ʽΟμηρείοιο καὶ εἰσέτι Νικάνδροιο
μνῆστιν ἔχοις, τὸν ἔθρεψε Κλάρου νιφόεσσα πολίχνη,

and to recall the most magnificent σφραγίς of Augustan poetry, the last eight lines of Virgil's *Georgics*.[2] There is no need here to penetrate into the earlier history of the σφραγίς and kindred forms of the self-presentation of a poet.[3] Lines 20–28 of Horace's epistle have this in common with a typical σφραγίς that at the end of a book of poetry the reader is given some information about the person of the poet. But at the same time it is clear that the conclusion of the epistle cannot properly be called a σφραγίς. The primary purpose of 'sealing' a book is to establish its author's 'copyright' and to prevent strangers from stealing it; therefore it is necessary that the σφραγίς should contain the poet's name.

---

[1] See especially Wilamowitz, *Sitz. Berl. Akad.* 1912, 116 ff. (*S.u.S.* 296 ff.), who amplified and corrected Leo's discussion of the problem (*Nachr. Gött. Ges., Phil.-hist. Kl.* 1898, 470 ff., cf. also his *Griech.-röm. Biographie*, 324). Cf. also Wilamowitz, *Hellenist. Dichtung*, ii. 124. Wilamowitz's main conclusion is not impaired by the fact that he includes in his list a few extraneous examples. For instance, the epigram by Nossis, *Anth. Pal.* 7. 718 (*S.u.S.* 299, cf. Maas, *RE* xvii. 1054), is clearly an ἐπιτύμβιον and not a 'Schlußgedicht' (*Hellenist. Dichtung*, i. 135).

[2] For the manner in which Virgil's marvellous 'seal' evolved from a modest Hellenistic type see my remarks in *Das Problem des Klassischen und die Antike*, ed. by W. Jaeger, 1931, 51 f., and in *Maia*, i, 1948, 249 f.

[3] The best introduction to this very complex problem is provided by F. Jacoby, 'Theognis', *Sitz. Berl. Akad.* 1931, 112–23. Cf. also Wilamowitz, *Timotheos, Die Perser*, 1903, 99 f.

Since the name—or a substitute for it—is conspicuously absent from these lines, they are not intended to serve as a σφραγίς; we must content ourselves with the assumption that Horace, stimulated by the custom of poetical σφραγῖδες, produced, not indeed a σφραγίς, but a σφραγίς-like tail-end of his own invention.

Leo,[1] if he could not make a good case for deriving the end of Horace's epistle from—insufficiently attested—succinct biographies, γένη, appended to the editions of poetic texts by the Alexandrian scholars and their successors, was certainly right in recognizing here certain elements belonging to the stock-in-trade of Hellenistic biography. These elements are, first, a statement about the man's origin (20 f.), secondly a description of his physique (24), and thirdly an account of his moral character (25).[2]

It appears, then, that Horace has put a very much reduced autobiography in that place of his book where the reader might look for a σφραγίς, and that, moreover, he has described himself on the lines of a typical biography. That the book can talk about its author at all is due to the established custom of the σφραγίς, but that it can talk about him in such an unobtrusive and engaging manner is due to the happy conception out of which the *liber* and the young slave were born as one and the same living being.

[1] See p. 362 n. 1.
[2] For φύσις and τρόπος as regular items in the biographies see Leo, *Griech.-röm. Biogr.*, *passim.* Cf. also (Leo, 3) Suet. *Iul.* 44. 3 *ea quae ad formam* [τὴν φύσιν] *et habitum et cultum et mores* [τὸν τρόπον] . . . *pertineant.*

VII

CARMEN SAECULARE

SUETONIUS, in his *Life of Horace*, speaking of Augustus' attitude to the poet, says: *scripta quidem eius usque adeo probavit mansuraque [perpetua]*[1] *opinatus est, ut non modo saeculare carmen componendum ⟨ei⟩*[2] *iniunxerit sed et Vindelicam victoriam Tiberii Drusique privignorum suorum ⟨illustrandam⟩,*[3] *eumque coegerit propter hoc tribus carminum libris ex longo intervallo quartum addere.* This account is on the whole accurate. That Horace was chosen to write the *Carmen Saeculare*, and afterwards the two poems in praise of the victories of Drusus and Tiberius, is rightly adduced as evidence of the high esteem in which his odes were held by Augustus: Augustus thought that they were not only good poetry but *mansura*, that they would last when tastes had changed;[4] he therefore wanted Horace to immortalize the great festival of the new era and also the military successes of the two young commanders, the stepsons of the Princeps. It is also true that when Horace, after a long interval, returned to the writing of lyrics and eventually decided to add a fourth book of *carmina* to the former three, the active encouragement given him by Augustus was an important factor in bringing about this decision. In one factual detail, however, Suetonius is obviously wrong. The two epinikia for Drusus and Tiberius cannot be regarded as the starting-point of Book IV of the *Odes*, for by the time when those epinikia were being written, the production of a new group of *carmina* was already well advanced. Nor is it likely that in the action of Augustus there should have been an element of compulsion such as the biographer alleges from the point of view of a later age (*ut . . . eum coegerit propter hoc tribus carminum libris . . . quartum addere*). The story of the

---

[1] Several early editors have changed *perpetua* to *perpetuo*, which Reifferscheid accepted. Since I do not think that the very special expression Cic. *Leg.* 2. 22, *sacra privata perpetua manento*, is sufficient to support the MS reading, I prefer to regard *perpetua* as a gloss of *mansura*, which in this sense is common, cf. *Thes. l. L.* viii. 292 f. (where, however, Ovid, *Am.* 3. 15. 20 must be cancelled, for there *mansurum superstes* go together). On Virg. *Aen.* 3. 86, *mansuram urbem*, Servius comments *duo petit, et urbem et perpetuitatem* (cf. *Corp. Gloss. Lat.* iv. 451. 40 *mansuram perpetuam urbem futuram*).

[2] *ei*, which I have added, is required by the sense. For *iniungere* with a dative in Suetonius cf. *Tib.* 24. 2; *Cal.* 18. 1; *Claud.* 24. 2.

[3] My supplement (*exempli gratia*). Cf. Porphyrio on *Odes* 4. 1. 1 *post . . . tres carminum libros maximo intervallo hunc quartum scribere compulsus esse dicitur ab Augusto, ut Neronis privigni eius victoriam de Raetis Vindelicis quaesitam inlustraret.*

[4] The implications of *mansura* are well illustrated by Horace's own words, *ne forte credas interitura quae longe sonantem natus ad Aufidum . . . verba loquor.*

gradual growth of the fourth book and of the motives which induced the poet to write it is to be learnt, fortunately, not from Suetonius, but from Horace's own book. But at present we are only concerned with the *Carmen Saeculare*.

Horace's annoyance at the cool reception which the three books of his *carmina* met with after their publication in 23 B.C. proved to be more than a transitory mood. Although the anger which he vented in the nineteenth epistle, *Prisco si credis, Maecenas docte, Cratino*, gave place, as time went on, to a milder resignation, he resolved to accept the failure of his proud venture as final and never to write lyrics again. He solemnly announced this resolution in the overture of his book of *Epistles* (1. 1. 10 ff.), and re-announced it in no less unequivocal terms when, a few years later, he wrote the letter to the sons of Piso.[1] Six years passed by after the publication of Books I–III, and no lyrics came forth from Horace's pen. It seems likely that he would to the end of his life have persisted in his resolution had it not been for the extraordinary task to which he was called in connexion with the celebrations of the *ludi saeculares* in 17 B.C.

About these celebrations we are uncommonly well informed.[2] In addition to Horace's *Carmen Saeculare*, there exists a summary of the ceremonies in Zosimus 2. 5,[3] and, moreover, we possess the full text of the oracle which the Sibyl was kind enough to produce precisely at the moment when such a manifestation was required by Augustus and his learned advisers.[4] The oracle is preserved not only in Zosimus, but in excerpts from a much earlier source, Phlegon's (time of the Emperor Hadrian) book Περὶ μακροβίων.[5] This body of evidence (Horace's ode, Phlegon, Zosimus), to which may be added the general report on *saeculum* and *ludi saeculares* provided by Censorinus, *De die natali* 17,

---

[1] *Ars P.* 304–6.

[2] The best introduction to the problems connected with the *ludi saeculares* is Nilsson's article, *RE* i A. 1696 ff. Since he wrote, important new fragments of the records of the secular games celebrated in A.D. 204 (for those known before see *CIL* vi. 4. 2, nos. 32326 ff.) have come to light; cf. Hülsen, *Rh. Mus.* lxxxi, 1932, 366 ff. (with the text), and the publications reviewed by Weinstock in *Gnomon*, xii, 1936, 657 ff. However, these new documents, including the hexametric *carmen*, are only remotely relevant to the problems of Horace's *Carmen Saeculare*.

[3] pp. 60 f. Mendelssohn; critical edition of this section also in H. Diels, *Sibyllinische Blätter*, 131 ff. The chapter (5) in Zosimus, τοιοῦτος δέ τις ὁ τρόπος ἀναγέγραπται τῆς ἑορτῆς κτλ., does not pretend to be a description of the particular festival of 17 B.C., but rather of the customary celebrations of *ludi saeculares*. But its account can be safely applied to the Augustan festival, especially since we now see from the records of the games celebrated under Septimius Severus that no essential changes were made in the ritual.

[4] Diels has shown that the oracle was written *ad hoc*; this view was reaffirmed, against Mommsen (who was followed by Karl Meister, *Lateinisch-griechische Eigennamen*, 1916, 64 ff.) in Nilsson's sound argumentation, op. cit. 1712 and 1717; cf. also F. Altheim, *A History of Roman Religion*, 397.

[5] Best text now in *F Gr Hist* 257 F 37.

and some scattered pieces of information,[1] had long been known. From
it a good deal could be learnt about the background of the Augustan
festival.[2] It was clear that, whatever legends were current about
secular games celebrated as early as the beginning of the Roman
Republic, the first ascertained occasion was the year 249 B.C., in the
First Punic War, when *prodigia* were frightening the people and
the *Xviri* (later *XVviri*) *sacris faciundis* were directed to consult the
Sibylline books, through which they received the order *uti Diti patri et
Proserpinae ludi Tarentini in campo Martio fierent tribus noctibus et hostiae
furvae immolarentur utique ludi centesimo quoque anno fierent.*[3] In 146 B.C.
ludi saeculares were celebrated for the second time, but afterwards no repetition proved feasible, until Augustus, after repeated procrastination,
decided in the spring of 17 B.C. that the ancient ritual should be revived in a new spirit and that the sacrifices, lasting three nights and
three days, should begin on the evening of the 31st of May of that year.
This was to be the opening of a new series of *saecula*, each consisting of
110 years.[4] No one then living had ever seen or could hope ever to see
again a similar festival.[5] Its long and exacting programme was worked
out to the minutest detail. The exegesis of the ordinance laid down in
the words of the Sibyl was entrusted to the famous jurist Ateius Capito,
the greatest expert in what would later have been called canon law.[6]
It goes without saying that the leading *magister* of the *XVviri*, Augustus,
took a personal interest in the preparations.

But despite all this valuable evidence, it is now clear that the true
nature of Augustus' innovation, and, what primarily concerns us here,
the function allotted to Horace's poem within the framework of the
whole ceremony, would be insufficiently understood if, late in the last
century, a flood of fresh light had not been spread by an extraordinary
discovery made at Rome. In September 1890, in the course of work on

---

[1] The most important of them is Augustus' own testimony, *Res gestae* 22, *Pro conlegio
XVvirorum magister conlegii, collega M. Agrippa, ludos saeclares C. Furnio C. Silano cos. feci.* The
names of the other four men who, together with Augustus, were *magistri* of the collegium in
17 B.C. are recorded in the appendix at the end of the *Fasti cos. Capitolini, CIL* i. 1.² 29 (this
entry was made under the reign of Augustus, see Mommsen, *Röm. Forsch.* ii. 61 f.). For the
names of the *quindecimviri sacris faciundis* present during certain parts of the *ludi saeculares*
held in 17 B.C. see Martha W. Hoffman Lewis, 'The Official Priests of Rome under the
Julio-Claudians', *Papers Amer. Acad. in Rome*, xvi, 1955, 87 ff.

[2] See especially Mommsen, *Röm. Chronologie*, 2nd ed. 180 ff.

[3] Varro, quoted by Censorinus, *D.N.* 17. 8.

[4] Reitzenstein, *Nachr. Gött. Ges.* 1904, 324, suggested that the change from a *saeculum*
of 100 years to one of 110 years was due to Oriental influences.

[5] Zosimus 2. 5 (beginning), περιόντες οἱ κήρυκες εἰς τὴν ἑορτὴν συνιέναι πάντας ἐκέλευον
ἐπὶ θέαν, ἣν οὔτε πρότερον εἶδον οὔτε μετὰ ταῦτα θεάσονται.

[6] Zosimus 2. 4. 2 τὸν θεσμὸν Ἀτηίου Καπίτωνος ἐξηγησαμένου. On the intrusion of the
clause which in the MS precedes, ὑπάτων ὄντων κτλ., see Mommsen, *Ephem. epigr.* viii
1891, 239 n. 2 (*Ges. Schriften* viii. 582 n. 3).

the embankment of the Tiber between the church of S. Giovanni dei
Fiorentini and the modern Ponte Vittorio Emanuele (this piece of the
river bank formed part of the ancient *Tarentum*), there was pulled down
a ramshackle wall of late date, and out of it came large fragments of a
huge block of white marble[1] bearing an inscription which was at once
recognized as the official records, the 'Acta', of the secular games
celebrated in 17 B.C. The visitor to Rome, when he is enjoying in the
Museo delle Terme the green loveliness of the Great Cloister, should
find time to look at the place on its north-west wall where the famous
inscription is now to be seen; his eye will be caught by the one line
containing only the momentous words *carmen composuit Q. Horatius
Flaccus*.[2]

The Italian authorities showed themselves worthy of Fortune's great
gift: the government at once arranged systematic excavations, and the
Accademia dei Lincei confided the publication and explanation of the
invaluable document to the man whom Providence seemed to have
made for the task, Mommsen, then 73 years old. He, in his own words,
'mandato ut honorificentissimo ita gravissimo ut debui posthabitis
negotiis aliis omnibus illico obtemperavi'. But he was not content to
expound, with his unrivalled learning and precision, the new text for
the benefit of his fellow savants.[3] He wanted also to give an idea of the
importance of the recent discovery to 'the numerous older and the few
younger men who from their schooldays preserve a friendly re-
membrance of old Horace';[4] he therefore delivered in the same year a
lecture at a public meeting of the Archaeological Society at Berlin on
'Die Akten zu dem Säkulargedicht des Horaz' and published it in a
weekly meant to provide the general reader with political, economic,
and literary information.[5]

In the first part of his lecture Mommsen deals with the character
of the secular games of 17 B.C., not by giving a detailed description of
the ritual as it had become known through the new document, but
by emphasizing its principal features and trying to elucidate the

---

[1] One fragment of it had in the sixteenth century been found at the same place.

[2] A good photograph of the part of the inscription related to Horace's *carmen* is reproduced in R. Paribeni, *L'Italia Imperiale*, 1938, p. 100.

[3] *Mon. Ant.* i, 1891, 617 ff., repeated, without substantial changes, in *Ephem. epigr.* viii,
1891, 225 ff. (*Ges. Schriften*, viii. 567 ff.).

[4] When Mommsen and Wilamowitz travelled in southern Italy in the summer of 1873,
Mommsen startled his young companion by his verdict on the poets (in the German sense
of the word) of the Empire. 'He really cared only for Horace and, of course, Petronius'
(Wilamowitz, *Erinnerungen*, 2nd ed. 161). For the harshness of Mommsen's sweeping
condemnation, who in this respect as in others reminds us of Scaliger, cf. his *Röm. Geschichte*, v. 655 (written in 1884), where he calls the whole volume of Roman literature
under the Empire 'ein überhaupt wenig erfreuliches Buch'. But from the fire of this
criticism Horace emerged unscathed.

[5] Reprinted in Mommsen's *Reden und Aufsätze*, 351 ff.

fundamental ideas which it was meant to express.[1] He points out[2] that 'here as everywhere else the new monarchy started from the great conception of abolishing the order of the Republic by rejuvenating it'. The new *ludi saeculares*, like the earlier ones, were based on Greek prophecies, were performed *Achivo ritu*,[3] and 'moved entirely within the sphere of the Hellenic gods'. The priesthood in charge of the celebrations was the same which had been in charge of the secular games under the Republic. And, during the new festival as before, expiation rites were performed on three consecutive nights down at the *Tarentum* on the bank of the Tiber.[4] But the new ritual differed from the older one in that it was no longer the King and Queen of the nether world, *Dis pater* (Pluto) and Proserpina, to whom sacrifices were made,[5] but the Moerae, on whom men's fate and prosperity depend, the Ilithyiae, goddesses of childbirth, and Mother Earth. The most momentous innovation, however, was the addition of the three great ceremonies performed by day, each of which now followed one of the celebrations at night, whereas the former *ludi saeculares* had been a night festival only. This innovation entailed sacrifices and prayers to Iuppiter optimus maximus and Iuno regina, and to Apollo and Diana; and so the entire religious character of the festival was changed.[6]

After giving his penetrating analysis of the ritual as reported in the inscription Mommsen turns to the poem of Horace. He begins with the censorious remark that, since we had now a much better knowledge of the task to which the poet was put, we must admit that he discharged it with but moderate success. And at this point Mommsen lets go.

> Noch einmal sattelt mir den Hippogryphen, ihr Musen,
> Zum Ritt in's alte romantische Land!

[1] The reader of the following pages may find it helpful to have at hand a text of the section of the 'Acta' which has a direct bearing on Horace's *carmen*. It can be read, apart, of course, from *CIL* vi. 32323, in Dessau, *Inscr. Lat. sel.* ii. 282 ff. (no. 5050) and in Heinze's commentary, a portion of it also in R. H. Barrow, *A Selection of Latin Inscriptions*, 1934, 63 f. (no. 107) and in Ussani's commentary; the tiny extract printed in V. Ehrenberg and A. H. M. Jones, *Documents*, etc. 60 (no. 32), is insufficient.

[2] In what follows I partly translate and partly paraphrase Mommsen's sentences, *Reden und Aufsätze*, 353 f.

[3] The term is used at l. 91 of the inscription in regard of the sacrifices to the Moerae, but allows of a wider application.

[4] Cf. the account of the ritual for the celebrations in 249 B.C., *uti Diti patri et Proserpinae ludi Tarentini in campo Martio fierent tribus noctibus*, etc. (p. 366 above).

[5] Mommsen, *Ges. Schriften* viii. 581 n. 1, rightly maintained his decision on this point, despite the protest of Wilamowitz (Mommsen und Wilamowitz, *Briefwechsel*, 366).

[6] Here Mommsen indulges in a symbolic interpretation of the new ritual, which I must quote, since his criticism of Horace's *carmen* is its direct outcome: 'Der Gegensatz der ernsten und mächtigen, aber auch harten und finsteren republikanischen Weltanschauung und der freieren, reicheren, anmutigeren des verjüngten Großstaats tritt vielleicht nirgends mit so berechneter Absichtlichkeit uns entgegen, wie wenn wir den Götterkreis uns vergegenwärtigen, zu welchem die alten Bürgermeister, und den, zu dem die neuen Souveräne am Beginn des neuen Jahrhunderts gebetet haben.'

He boldly outlines the kind of song which Horace would have written if only he had known how to produce the right poem for the occasion. He would have used the two series of gods which determined the arrangement of the celebrations, the celestial deities, Jupiter, Juno, and Apollo with his sister, and the deities of the nether world, the Moerae, the Ilithyiae, and Mother Earth—he would have used these two series, in a double sequence of mighty images, to make man, as he walks the soil of earth between the welkin and the womb of the depth, behold both the glory and the limitations of his fate. This was *not* done by Horace, 'das hat Horaz nicht getan'. He names and praises all those deities, but he marshals them in a loose array, instead of doing 'what a true poet would have done' and connecting them so as to bring out the ideas which obviously bind them together. Mommsen added several other charges, some of them grave; and the upshot was that on this occasion Horace fell short of what he might have been expected to achieve. So the wonderful old scholar, by the manner in which he criticized the poet, revealed his own self and showed that after all his gigantic rational exertions he remained at heart what he had always been, a disciple of the Romantic School. His love for Horace seemed lost in a much deeper passion. But even so the true appreciation of the *Carmen Saeculare* was ultimately to gain from Mommsen's enormous misapprehension.

A little less than a year after Mommsen had delivered his impetuous lecture, J. Vahlen, professor of classics in the University of Berlin, read to the Academy, whose dominant member was Mommsen, a meticulously meditated paper, 'Über das Säculargedicht des Horatius',[1] a paper which still, after more than sixty years, is the most important single contribution to the understanding of one of the major poems of Horace.[2] After paying a sincere tribute to the work done by Mommsen not only in expounding the inscription but also in pointing out some startling discrepancies between Horace's *carmen* and the actual ceremonies, Vahlen states the difference of his own approach from that of Mommsen: his, Vahlen's, way 'will not lead from the document to the

[1] Published in *Sitz. Berlin*, 1892, 1005 ff., reprinted in Vahlen's *Gesamm. Philol. Schriften*, ii. 369 ff. There is some interest in the fact that Mommsen always said 'Horaz', whereas Geheimrat Vahlen liked to speak, though not consistently, of 'Horatius'. Scholars who, whether in Germany or in Britain, propagate such artificialities as 'Horatius', 'Akhilleus', 'Arkhilokhos' are guilty of widening the gulf between their countrymen and the classics.

[2] In 1910 Warde Fowler published a long paper on the *Carm. Saec., CQ* iv. 145 ff. (reprinted in his *Roman Essays*, 111 ff.), and said, 149 n. 7, '[Wissowa] quoting Vahlen, whose paper I have not been able to see'. A copy of the volume of the *Sitzungsberichte* had been for eighteen years in the Bodleian Library, two minutes from the college in which Warde Fowler was living all the time. In 1933 Deubner published in *Philol.* lxxxviii, 1933, 469 ff., an article 'Zum Aufbau des Carmen saeculare', and completely ignored, to his cost, Vahlen's paper, the main theme of which was the 'Aufbau'.

poem but, in the opposite direction, from the analysis of the poem to the new information furnished by the document'.[1] Vahlen quotes the passage in which Mommsen outlined the poem which Horace, had he been a true poet and grasped his opportunity, would have written, and he adds this comment: 'Who would deny that, on the lines here suggested, a gifted poet would have been able to produce a fine song for the festival? I am, however of the opinion . . . that Horace, too, invented a plan which was not ill fitted for the Roman poet and the Roman national festival and would not be a disgrace to him.' In detail, Vahlen at several points replaces Mommsen's censure by a cautious and convincing exegesis. But what gives his article its decisive value is the analysis of the poem as a whole and the elucidation of its general design.[2]

On one fundamental point Vahlen is in complete agreement with his great antagonist. Mommsen had proved[3] that the period beginning at l. 37 with *Roma si vestrum est opus* must not be taken together with the preceding prayer to Apollo and Diana, but opens a new section and refers, at any rate primarily, to the Capitoline deities, since the sacrifice mentioned at ll. 49 f. (*bobus albis*), as is shown by the 'Acta', can belong only to them.[4] I call this point fundamental, for it is on its recognition that the understanding of the structure of the poem depends to a large extent. Between l. 36 and l. 37 there runs an incision which divides the song into two halves, A (1–36) and B (37–72); the whole is rounded off by a brief epilogue (73–76). Each of the two halves

---

[1] The study of literary history (and not in the ancient world only—a widespread type of 'Goethephilologie' comes at once to mind) would have been spared a great deal of harm if Vahlen's approach had oftener been preferred to the opposite one. It must, however, be admitted that this road requires an experienced traveller whereas the other καὶ ἰλαδὸν ἔστιν ἐλέσθαι ῥηιδίως· λείη μὲν ὁδός, μάλα δ' ἐγγύθι ναίει. As regards the *Carmen Saeculare*, the wisdom of Friedrich Leo (*Hermes*, xxxviii, 1903, 3) may be recalled: 'Es ist nicht richtig, daß Horazens Säcularlied erst verstanden werden kann, seit wir lesen *eodemque modo in Capitolio*: man hätte die in der Vereinigung der beiden Cultstätten liegende poetische Einheitlichkeit erkennen sollen, ehe die Inschrift lehrte, daß das Gedicht für den Vortrag sowohl auf dem Palatin als auf dem Capitol bestimmt war. Die historische Notiz ist gut die Einzelheiten zu erläutern; wenn sie für das Verständnis des Ganzen nötig ist, so ist es kein Gedicht.'

[2] In the following sketch I shall largely draw on Vahlen but shall also take into account the triadic arrangement, which was observed by E. Menozzi, *Stud. Ital.* xiii, 1905, 67 ff., and by E. Redslob, *Krit. Bemerkungen zu Horaz*, 1912, 65 f. (I have not seen the book), whom Heinze followed. Like Menozzi I connect the triadic structure of the *Carmen Saeculare* with that of *Odes* i. 12 and recognize in both a Pindarizing trait. Heinze was right in taking full advantage of Vahlen's article; his commentary on the *Carmen Saeculare* is on the whole so good that I can leave most of the detail aside and, with a few exceptions, confine myself to making some general observations.

[3] *Ephem. epigr.* viii. 257 (*Ges. Schriften*, viii. 602) and *Reden und Aufsätze*, 357 f.

[4] The importance of this point as settled by Mommsen was stressed also by W. v. Christ, *Sitz. Bayer. Akad.* 1893, 141. Wickham did not accept Mommsen's conclusion (Vahlen's article was apparently unknown to him), and the colon which he, like earlier editors, placed after l. 36 is still found in the revised Oxford text.

is composed of three triads:[1] A, I (1–12), II (13–24), III (25–36), and
B, I (37–48), II (49–60), III (61–72).

The song begins with a prayer to Apollo and Diana, which after the
invocation of the two deities emphasizes the occasion of the present
festival and the reason for it.[2] There follows one of the most glorious
passages in ancient poetry (9–12):

> alme Sol, curru nitido diem qui
> promis et celas aliusque et idem
> nasceris, possis nihil urbe Roma
> visere maius.[3]

Much has been written on the manner in which the Sun is brought into
this context and on the function which his invocation fulfils. Vahlen,
not unmindful of the Sibyl's words (16 f.), καὶ Φοῖβος Ἀπόλλων, ὅστε
καὶ Ἥλιος κικλήσκεται, nevertheless maintained that Horace did not
take into account the identity of Helios and Apollo and did not want
his audience to be conscious of it. The prayer (or rather wish)[4] addressed to Sol is, according to Vahlen, not closely attached to the
opening lines of the poem but independent. In these statements (with
which Heinze in the main agrees)[5] there is an element of truth, but
they go too far. It is true that a crude identification of Apollo and
Helios would, everything else apart,[6] be absurd in a poem where
Apollo is thought of as the lord of the temple on the Palatine (65).[7]
But it is a mistake to draw a rigid line and to separate in cold logic
what the poet has obviously attempted to merge. Fortunately we need
not build our argument on the slippery ground of Hellenistic-Roman
theology. The consequences of the view which severs Sol completely
from Apollo come out in Heinze's note on the first two lines of the
poem. Since ancient times[8] most—though not, of course, all—
commentators have referred *lucidum caeli decus* to both Phoebus and
Diana. If this interpretation is accepted, it follows that Pheobus is not
indeed identified with, but brought into a certain relation to, the Sun.

---

[1] For the modified (non-metrical) sense in which I use the term 'triad' see my discussion of *Odes* i. 12, pp. 291 ff. above.

[2] At l. 6 *lectas* seems to belong to the language of religious ritual; the passage should be
taken together with the observations of Donatus to which G. Rohde, 'Die Kultsatzungen
der röm. Pontifices', *RGVV*, xxv, 1936, 166 (add Serv. *Aen.* 8. 179), has drawn attention.

[3] For the expression *promis et celas* see p. 445 n. 3 below.

[4] Cf. Heinze on l. 9.

[5] Cf. also the remark in his lecture of 1928, posthumously published in *Gnomon*, viii,
1932, 499.

[6] In this connexion it is worth while re-reading Wilamowitz, *Glaube d. Hell.* i. 256.

[7] It is far too simple to say 'Sole e Apollo sono per Orazio tutt' uno' (Pasquali, *Or. lir.*
736 n. 2).

[8] Cf. Porph.: 'Lucidum caeli decus. *Hoc ad ambos refertur: ad Phoebum, quia idem sol est, et
Dianam, quia eadem luna est.*'

For if *lucidum caeli decus* is put in apposition to both Apollo and Diana, it can only mean that we are to think of them also as having control, the one over the sun, the other over the moon. To avoid this consequence Heinze resorts to a desperate expedient.[1] He takes *lucidum caeli decus*, though not without qualms,[2] to relate to *Diana* alone. I cannot believe that Horace, at this most conspicuous place, could have so completely upset the balance of his twofold invocation, even if he had thought it possible to disregard the position allotted to Apollo in the religious policy of Augustus, in the ritual of the secular games, and in this very *carmen*. It is Apollo, and not his sister, who remains the leading partner throughout. It must, then, be admitted that *lucidum caeli decus* applies also to Apollo, and so we are faced with the apparent contradiction that, although Apollo is in this poem kept distinct from Sol, the manner in which he is invoked in the initial sentence points to his being somehow connected with the sun.

The solution of this dilemma was indicated by F. Altheim.[3] He accepted Vahlen's and Heinze's view that Horace does not identify Apollo and Helios, but avoided exaggerating the consequences. 'We must not begin', he says, 'with any expectation of a single explanation for the age of Horace. For that age, too, it is true that the mutual attraction of the two gods runs through different stages. A single example will make this clear. Whereas the Sibylline oracle identified Apollo and Helios, and the same path was trodden by learned speculation and even in rarer cases by cult, Propertius, in his description of the Palatine temple [II, 31] speaks, it is true, of the chariot of the sun-god having stood on its roof, but has nothing to say of his identity with the owner of the shrine'.[4] Farther on Altheim says: 'Sun and Apollo [in 1–12 of the *Carm. Saec.*] are not one and the same, but the god appears as his master and thus as director of the fate of the world. . . . On the one side stands the god, on the other the star of heaven that is subject to his will.' This more subtle interpretation gets rid of the unsatisfactory assumption that the third stanza is independent of the beginning of the poem; we now see that the first triad is a closely knit whole. We may add another, still more important, observation. The *carmen* was first sung in front of the temple of Apollo on the Palatine, the sanctuary which more than any other was a manifestation of the personal religious

---

[1] Mitscherlich and Ussani likewise refer *lucidum caeli decus* to Diana only, though apparently for different reasons. Protests against this way of taking the clause are at least as old as Dacier.

[2] He remarks '*Phoebe* steht somit, ganz gegen den Stil der hellenistischen hieratischen Poesie, hier ohne jedes Epitheton'. Never mind Hellenistic poetry, but what about the style of Horace?

[3] *A History of Roman Religion*, 396 ff.

[4] The elegy of Propertius had already been taken into account by Heinze (on 9).

tendencies of the régime of Augustus. If Horace had been a slave of the ritual which had been worked out for the celebrations, he would doubtless have made an allusion to the temple right at the beginning of his poem. In fact, however, he not only refrains from any such allusion until the last triad (65), but he eliminates at the beginning any idea of a particular place of worship. Phoebus is first invoked as *lucidum caeli decus*, and connected with this invocation is a wish regarding the sun (9 ff.). In other words, Apollo is here conceived not so much as Apollo Palatinus, but rather as a universal or, as some of our contemporaries would probably prefer to say, a cosmic power. The opening part of the song indeed takes the celebrations on the Palatine into account; otherwise it would not begin with Apollo and Diana. But as little as the whole song is this opening part meant to be a direct reproduction of the ceremonies. However impressive the sacrifices and prayers which had taken place at the altar in front of the magnificent new temple, the poet, being a poet, starts from something wider and greater, from the powers—she who is *silvarum potens* is one of them—that control man's life everywhere and at all times, ἔστ' ἂν ὕδωρ τε ῥέῃ καὶ δένδρεα μακρὰ τεθήλῃ.

The middle stanza (17–20) of the second triad has often been subjected to scorn.[1] I do not feel competent to define what in all circumstances is poetic and what in all circumstances is 'prosy'. But I may be permitted to ask the reader to pause for a moment before he indulges in judgements of hazardous subjectivity. The incriminated stanza runs:

> diva, producas subolem, patrumque
> prosperes decreta super iugandis
> feminis prolisque novae feraci
> lege marita.

It is commonly assumed that anything connected with legislation and the sphere of life to which it belongs must be incompatible with all that the children—or the great-grandchildren—of a Romantic Age are in the habit of calling genuine poetry. Now this stanza alludes in unambiguous

---

[1] See, for instance, Peerlkamp, who obelized the stanza and commented on it: 'Quattuor versus Horatio plane indigni ... diserta mentio legum et decretorum hominem prodit, nescientem quid gravitas et decor poeticus ferant', etc., or, less excusably, Warde Fowler, *CQ* iv, 1910, 148 (*Roman Essays*, 115), 'the impression it [the *Carmen Saeculare*] always gives me is that Augustus wrote out in prose what he wanted put into it, and that his laureate did this with consummate skill and *concinnitas*; but the result, for me at least, is that it is as flat as such compositions usually have been. Nay, it is occasionally prosy, as e.g. in the fifth and sixth stanzas.' The narrowness of Warde Fowler's view on the *Carmen Saeculare* is firmly, if respectfully, exposed by Alfred Noyes, *Horace: A Portrait*, New York 1947, 245 f. His judgement on the patriotic lyrics of Horace in general is much sounder than that of many professional scholars.

terms to a definite piece of Augustan legislation.[1] Therefore it seems to be doomed beyond redemption. And since we are at it, let us not be half-hearted but go ahead and condemn as unpoetic whatever smells of a law or some element of political life. A suitable first victim offers itself in Athena's speech[2] beginning with κλύοιτ' ἂν ἤδη θεσμὸν Ἀττικὸς λεὼς πρώτας δίκας κρίνοντες αἵματος χυτοῦ, another in the speech of Theseus,[3] where he slightly varies the formula actually used in the Athenian assembly, τίς θέλει πόλει χρηστόν τι βούλευμ' ἐς μέσον φέρειν ἔχων;—and soon the quarry will be more plentiful than we can cope with. But, seriously, without idealizing the past, should we not try to understand that not everything that to us sounds dry or technical or downright prosaic must necessarily have sounded so to an Athenian or a Roman? Could we not consider the possibility that a subject which we shy at when when we meet it in the daily paper may, to many contemporaries of Augustus, despite all their sophistication, still have seemed dignified enough for serious poetry? But even if we keep to our own primary reaction, unaffected by any thought of historical relativity, even then we ought to find it easy to respond to the feeling in this particular stanza. For the legislation which is the theme of these lines is not concerned with technicalities of private or public law but goes straight to the roots of the life of human society. I, for one, am not ashamed to confess that I am moved when I picture these handsome children, who represent Rome's finest youth, singing to the goddess *diva, producas subolem, patrumque prosperes decreta* . . .. Here they are, radiant, grateful for the unique distinction that has come to them, and aware that, while they are singing and praying, the eyes and ears of the men and women of Rome and of thousands of boys and girls are upon them, and that they are singing and praying for them all. Will they not wish that in a future *saeculum* there will again be Roman children, many Roman children, to be as happy as they and the others are now, and is it not fitting for them to implore Heaven's favour for the decrees of the Fathers (what a blessing for a poet if the constitutional life of his nation knows such a term)? If the race should die out, there would be no more secular games. So the children pray *patrum prosperes decreta*, not because they are worried about the birth-rate, but

> certus undenos deciens per annos
> orbis ut cantus referatque ludos
> ter die claro totiensque grata
> nocte frequentis.

Let us admit that this is a lovely climax and that, whatever *raison*

---

[1] For the detail see Hugh Last, *Camb. Anc. Hist.* x. 441 ff.
[2] A. *Eum.* 681 ff.
[3] Eur. *Suppl.* 426 ff.

d'état lay behind this part of the ceremonies (the sacrifices to the Ilithyiae), the whole triad is excellent poetry. In stating this we should not neglect the character of the language: its solemnity ennobles especially the middle stanza, *diva, producas subolem*, etc.[1]

The following triad (25–36) combines in its first two stanzas prayers to separate deities, to the Moerae[2] and to Terra Mater, the first of whom received their sacrifices on the first night of the festival, whereas Mother Earth received hers on the third night. The third stanza with its prayer to Apollo and Diana harks back to the beginning of the song and so rounds off its first half.

The second part of the poem, as Mommsen and Vahlen have shown,[3] begins at 37 *Roma si vestrum est opus.* The object of the prayers, as follows from the nature of the festival, is, broadly speaking, very similar in the two parts: it is the prosperity and the continuance of Rome and her State. But the point of view is different. The first part is mainly concerned with the physical conditions of Rome's welfare; the second part with the moral and political elements on which the prosperity and the reputation of the State are based.[4] It is significant that the first sentence of the second part with *Iliae turmae* enters at once the sphere of Roman history. It is equally significant that the influence of the *Aeneid*, published not long before the preparations for the secular games began, is in this part strongly marked. The *Carmen Saeculare* is in fact the first great milestone on the road over which the *Aeneid* was to travel through the centuries; the next two are the fourth book of Propertius' elegies and the fourth book of Horace's odes.

The beginning of the second triad (49 ff.) brings the poem to its summit:

> quaeque vos bobus veneratur albis
> clarus Anchisae Venerisque sanguis,

[1] For the restricted use of *suboles* and *proles* (both archaic and later, as solemn words, poetic) see Cic. *De orat.* 3. 153 (for *proles* cf. also Norden on Virg. *Aen.* 6. 784); for the solemn character of *prosperare* cf. Marx on Lucilius 656; *super iugandis feminis* seems to be the earliest instance of *super* with the gerundive (Schmalz–Hofmann, *Lat. Gramm.*, 5th ed. 540)—the fact that the construction occurs in Tacitus (*Ann.* 15. 5 and 15. 24) points, perhaps, to its origin in archaic literature. The particle *-que*, which is twice used in this stanza, is altogether much commoner in the *Carmen Saeculare* than in the rest of Horace. Löfstedt, *Syntactica*, ii. 342 n. 2, who (following Flinck) mentions this, remarks: 'Die Ursache wird wohl darin liegen, dass *-que* schon damals weniger volkstümlich als literarisch war und daher für den feierlichen, gehobenen Ton des Carm. saec. ganz besonders gut paßte.'

[2] The conception of *veraces cecinisse, Parcae*, etc., is presumably a direct outcome of Catullus LXIV. Even if it were certain that in the finale of Aristophanes' *Birds* (1734 ff.) the Μοῖραι are supposed to sing the hymenaeus themselves, that would be very different from their prophesying the future in song. In the main Wilamowitz, *Hellenist. Dichtung*, ii. 303, is right. The relative clause *quod semel dictum est*, etc., is object to *cecinisse*: see p. 172 n. 3 above.

[3] Cf. p. 370 above.

[4] Here I have followed Vahlen, *Sitz. Berlin*, 1892, 1015, very closely.

> impetret, bellante prior, iacentem
> lenis in hostem.

This is the only passage in the *carmen* which conveys a visual idea of a detail of one of the great ceremonies. This restriction is doubtless deliberate, for here 'the ruler, presented in a clearly perceptible and suggestive picture, is prominent as the shining centre of the whole'.[1] The fine antithesis at the end of the stanza, *bellante prior, iacentem lenis in hostem*, inevitably reminds every reader, ancient[2] or modern, of *parcere subiectis et debellare superbos*. But Horace in all probability is not borrowing from the *Aeneid*: the maxim can be traced back to a much earlier period, to the time when the leading men of Rome, whom the hard-earned experience of their own people had taught to behave reasonably and whose minds had mellowed through the adaptation of Greek thought, came to develop ideas of fairness and *humanitas*.[3] The other two stanzas (53–60) of this triad turn from prayers for blessings to come to praise of those blessings which Rome and her Empire already enjoy. First comes the subjection of the enemies at the frontiers,[4] then the restoration of peace, order, and decency at home:

> iam Fides et Pax et Honos Pudorque
> priscus et neglecta redire Virtus
> audet adparetque beata pleno
> Copia cornu.

Now is being fulfilled what the generation suffering from the dissolution of the old political system and from the misery of civil war had been longing for. In 46 B.C. Cicero said:[5] *omnia sunt excitanda tibi, C. Caesar, uni, quae iacere sentis belli ipsius impetu . . . perculsa atque prostrata: constituenda iudicia, revocanda fides, comprimendae libidines, propaganda suboles,*[6]

---

[1] Vahlen, op. cit. 1016.

[2] See the scholia.

[3] Cf. E. Norden on Virg. *Aen.* 6. 847 ff. (p. 336 of the 3rd ed.) and, for the general background, R. Harder, *Die Antike*, v, 1929, 301 f. Norden does not mention Cic. *S. Rosc.* 154, *populum Romanum, qui quondam in hostis lenissimus existimabatur*, nor Cic. *Marcell.* 8 (about Caesar), *victo temperare, adversarium . . . non modo extollere iacentem* (Horace uses the same word), *sed etiam amplificare eius pristinam dignitatem*, etc.

[4] On l. 55, *responsa petunt*, Kiessling (whose note Heinze retained) comments 'wie von göttlichem Munde'. But is it not, perhaps, implied that Rome is being asked to give *responsa* in the same sense in which first the *pontifices* and later the Republican jurists were asked to do so (cf. P. Jörs, *Röm. Rechtswissenschaft zur Zeit der Republik*, 83 f.; F. Schulz, *History of Roman Legal Science*, 17 and 61), viz. to tell those who consulted them what was law and what was not, what was right and what was wrong? At *Odes* 4. 14. 7 the Vindelici are called *legis expertes Latinae*, and at 4. 15. 21 f. *non qui profundum Danuvium bibunt edicta rumpent Iulia* (Virg. *Georg.* 4. 561 f., *victorque volentis per populos dat iura* has a different sense, cf. *Aen.* 8. 670).

[5] *Marcell.* 23.

[6] Cicero's own evidence (cf. p. 375 n. 1 above) makes it clear that he is here rising to the level of poetic style.

omnia, quae dilapsa iam diffluxerunt, severis legibus vincienda sunt.[1] There can
be no doubt that some points of this programme of reform had in the
meantime become what nowadays would be called slogans,[2] but neither
can there be any doubt that good men were still capable of feeling the
true value of all that Fides and Pax and their companions had to give
and of being profoundly grateful for their return.

In the last triad (61–72) certain characteristic forms of prayer are
maintained,[3] but it is no longer a prayer:[4] it is an expression of trust in
the benevolence of the gods, who are protecting and will further protect Rome, Latium,[5] and all that belongs to the *res Romana*, and therefore will grant the prayers devised by the *quindecimviri* and sung by the
boys and girls.[6]

The concluding stanza, placed outside the triads and thereby marked
as the epilogue of the whole song, provides again an instance of the
happy transformation of a traditional element of prayers. For in the
clause *haec Iovem sentire deosque cunctos* we hear an echo of the 'generalis
invocatio' with which, after the invocation of several particular gods,
Roman prayers used to conclude, *more pontificum, quoniam[7] ritu veteri in
omnibus sacris post speciales deos, quos ad ipsum sacrum quod fiebat necesse erat
invocari, generaliter omnia numina invocabantur.*[8] A slight playfulness may be
intended in the expression *haec sentire*: 'Jupiter and all the other Senators of Heaven, are, I am sure, of the same opinion as Apollo and
Diana'—the *sententia* of these two can safely be inferred from what they
are doing, *prorogat, curat, adplicat auris*—'and will give their vote
accordingly, and so the decree will be unanimous'.[9]

[1] H. Strasburger, *Histor. Z.* clxxv, 1953, 253 f., has shown that the whole section to
which this passage belongs must not be taken as a mere eulogy, since it contains, though
couched in guarded language, a serious criticism, reminding Caesar of what he ought to
have done but has not yet done.

[2] Velleius, in his survey of the reign of Augustus, says (2. 126. 2): *revocata in forum fides,
summota e foro seditio . . . sepultaeque ac situ obsitae iustitia, aequitas, industria civitati redditae,*
and so forth.

[3] Notice especially the 'relative predications' at ll. 63 f. and 69 and the *si* clause at 65.

[4] Similarly, at the end of *Odes* i. 21 (cf. p. 210 above) the typical form of a prayer is used
to forecast its fulfilment.

[5] In Heinze's note on l. 66, *Latium*, the reference to the 'Acta', l. 93, has to be cancelled,
for the new fragments of the 'Acta' of the secular games of Septimius Severus, published
after Heinze's death, show that the formula was *utique semper Latinus optemperassit* (see
Hülsen, *Rh. Mus.* lxxxi, 1932, 376). Norden, *Aus altrömischen Priesterbüchern*, 105, took
Mommsen's supplement to be the text of the inscription.

[6] That at l. 68 and l. 71 f. the indicatives *prorogat, curat, adplicat* are correct has been
admirably shown by Bentley, who also saw that only so does the last stanza receive its proper
connexion. To his argument may be added the fact that in Horace's *Odes* no instance of a
prayer in the third person is found (the stanza 1. 30. 5 ff. enumerates mere companions
of the goddess to whom the prayer is addressed). The wrong subjunctives still linger in the
editions of Page, Bennett (Loeb Library), and Tescari.   [7] *quos* trad.

[8] Serv. Dan. *Georg.* 1. 21. Some literature on the topic can be found in my note on A.
Ag. 513 (ii. 262).

[9] On *sentire* Kiessling observes 'als *sententia* des Götterrates, welcher über Roms Zukunft

It is a delightful touch that only in the last stanza, which is, as it were, *extra argumentum*, the choir of boys and girls speaks in its own name. Before, in the solemnity of the prayers, they said distantly and magnificently *virgines lectas puerosque castos*, but now, when all is happily over and they are about to go home, they say 'I', *spem . . . domum reporto*, and, thinking of all the trouble during the rehearsals in learning their part,[1] they add:

> doctus et Phoebi chorus et Dianae
> dicere laudes.

Mommsen concluded from the 'Acta' that the *Carmen Saeculare* was performed as a procession song. This hypothesis, which was soon queried by Vahlen[2] and subsequently by other scholars,[3] seems now to have been generally abandoned,[4] and there the matter should rest.[5] No compromise should be considered.[6] The sense of Horace's poem is completely lost as soon as we attempt to tie it down to any particular stage in the course of the ceremonies of the three nights and the three days. So far from forming a part of them, the *carmen* is deliberately placed outside them. The text of the 'Acta' is unambiguous (147 f.): *Sacrificioque perfecto* [i.e. the sacrifice on the last day] *pueri XXVII . . . et puellae totidem carmen cecinerunt; eodemque modo in Capitolio.* The *carmen* did not accompany any of the sacrifices and prayers; on the contrary, it was sung when the elaborate ceremonies had all been completed. Therefore it keeps at a distance from the many details of the cult as we now know them, and, instead, surveys in retrospect the whole of the past celebrations, connecting and condensing the ideas which the great festival was meant to symbolize. All this has been admirably demonstrated by Vahlen. It only remains to add a general observation and then to draw a conclusion which may help us to understand the

entscheidet', and Ussani 'quasi *in hanc sententiam ire*, che era la formula tecnica ad indicare il voto favorevole dei senatori'.

[1] Cf. on *Odes* 4. 6. 35 f., below, pp. 405 f.

[2] *Sitz. Berlin*, 1892, 1019. In 1894 Wissowa (see his *Gesammelte Abh.* 206 n. 1) made an unsuccessful attempt to back Mommsen's view.

[3] See, for example, Warde Fowler, *CQ* iv, 1910, 147 f. (*Roman Essays*, 113 f.); Pasquali, *Or. lir.* 736 n. 2.

[4] Cf. Weinstock, *Gnomon*, xii, 1936, 659.

[5] It may, of course, be safely prophesied that the procession song will from time to time find a new champion.

[6] Wilamowitz, *S.u.S.* 316 n. 1, after an excellent general remark, continues: 'es [the *Carmen Saeculare*] ist eben als Prosodion [cf. 320, 'als er selbst ein Processionslied verfassen sollte'] auf dem Palatin, auf dem Zuge, auf dem Capitol gesungen, wie man solche Lieder singt; die Procession nimmt an der Wiederholung keinen Anstoß'. The underlying error comes out in the phrase 'solche Lieder'. There were in Rome no such songs when Horace wrote: what he was asked to do and did do was something quite new.

implications of an event which proved decisive not only for Horace personally but also for the final development of his lyrics.

The performance of a song in connexion with a religious festival, but after the completion of the ceremonies proper, was without precedent in ancient sacred poetry and might well have been called revolutionary. So long as cult poetry in Greek lands had a real life, it was not treated as ornamental to the primary acts of worship but as an indispensable part of them.[1] Every religious song had from the outset the time and place of its performance fixed by the nature of the ritual itself; there was no possibility of a change of order, to say nothing of the song becoming a mere appendix or epilogue. Even a procession song, though obviously less static than other hymns, was arranged in such a way that its sections maintained a close connexion with definite stages of the performance of the ritual and with a definite locality. The choir would move from one shrine to another, halt in front of each shrine, and there sing either the whole προσόδιον (or paean or whatever it might be called) or an appropriate section of it.[2] As for Rome, there exists fortunately a piece of evidence which shows the manner in which procession songs were performed on the rare occasions when they were used, *Graeco ritu*,[3] in Republican Rome. It has often been regretted that Livy, or his annalistic source, has, from stylistic fastidiousness,[4] deprived us of the text of the procession song composed in 207 B.C. by Livius Andronicus. But the historian has at least preserved an accurate description of the ceremony of which the song formed a part; his account goes ultimately back to the records of the *decemviri sacris faciundis* who, in consequence of a series of *prodigia*, had ordered the performance of expiatory rites to propitiate Iuno regina and who themselves took part in the procession. *Decrevere . . . pontifices ut virgines ter novenae per urbem euntes carmen canerent . . . conditum ab Livio poeta carmen.*[5] The procession started from the temple of Apollo outside porta Carmentalis:[6] *ab aede Apollinis boves feminae albae duae porta Carmentali in*

---

[1] See the general remarks pp. 38 ff. above.

[2] See Wilamowitz's interpretation, *S.u.S.* 246 ff. (especially 247 and 252), of Pindar's paean (II) for Abdera, and also his article on the inscription of the μολποί of Miletus, *Sitz. Berlin*, 1904, 628 f.: the παιωνίζεσθαι at various places is mentioned in the document. Cf., moreover, E. Vetter, *Handbuch der italischen Dialekte*, i, 1953, 106, on the meaning of *statif* in the ritual of the 'tabula Agnonensis': 'statif besagt daß die Festprozessionen an ihren [i.e. of the fifteen gods mentioned] Altären Halt machten und opferten'.

[3] It is obvious that Livius Andronicus must have depended to a large extent on Hellenistic cult-songs. See O. Crusius, *Die delphischen Hymnen*, 141, and what Leo quotes, *Gesch. d. röm. Lit.* 58 n. 1.

[4] Livy 27. 37. 13 *tum septem et viginti virgines, longam indutae vestem, carmen in Iunonem reginam canentes ibant, illa tempestate forsitan laudabile rudibus ingeniis, nunc abhorrens et inconditum si referatur.* Nothing is known of the metre of the song; there is no sufficient reason for assuming (with Diels, *Sibyll. Blätter*, 90) that it was Saturnian.

[5] Livy 27. 37. 7.   [6] Cf. Platner and Ashby, *Topogr. Dict. of Ancient Rome*, 15.

urbem ductae; post eas duo signa cupressea Iunonis reginae portabantur; tum septem et viginti virgines, longam indutae vestem, carmen in Iunonem reginam canentes ibant . . . ; virginum ordinem sequebantur decemviri coronati laurea praetextatique. a porta Iugario vico in forum venere; in foro pompa constitit, et per manus reste data virgines sonum vocis pulsu pedum modulantes incesserunt. inde vico Tusco Velabroque per bovarium forum in clivum Publicium atque aedem Iunonis reginae[1] perrectum. ibi duae hostiae ab decemviris immolatae et simulacra cupressea in aedem inlata.[2] It is unmistakable that both the procession and the song are an organic part of the act of worship and are necessary to its functioning: performed in the presence of the two sacred images (obviously two old and venerable ξόανα) and adorned by a solemn dance with relics of magic implements and gestures (the holding of the rope), they serve to lead the victims, the two white cows, to their destination, to propitiate the goddess by stages and to render her amenable to the sacrifice which, as the crowning piece of the long and elaborate ceremony, is to take place at Juno's own house. The success of the whole function will to a large extent depend on the meticulous execution of this procession and of the song that belongs to it. Nothing could be more different than the place and purpose assigned to Horace's *Carmen Saeculare*, performed after the completion of all the sacrifices. The ceremony arranged by the *decemviri* in 207 B.C. would have been of no avail without the *pompa* and the *carmen* of Livius Andronicus; the ceremony arranged by the *quindecimviri* in 17 B.C. would, from the religious point of view, have been exactly the same if no *carmen* whatever had been performed after its conclusion. And what is true of the hymn of Livius Andronicus is true of all conceivable precedents of the *Carmen Saeculare*. They all had their being inside some cult and were indissolubly linked to that cult by their subservience to particular acts of worship. Horace's song had its being solely in the sphere of poetry, and the only links which connected it with the cult were links of thought. If the song greatly enhanced the impression made by the celebrations, it did so from without. To plan and execute such a thing was indeed a bold innovation.[3]

---

[1] On the Aventine; the temple had been struck by lightning (27. 37. 7).

[2] Livy 27. 37. 11–15.

[3] If the quotation of the 'commentator Cruquianus' (introd. to *Carmen Saeculare*) from Verrius Flaccus (*Verrius . . . Flaccus refert carmen saeculare et sacrificium institutum . . . Diti et Proserpinae*, viz. at the secular games of 249 B.C.) is trustworthy also in regard to the detail of the performance of a *carmen saeculare*, it is very likely that the song was recited by *virgines* only. For the choir of twenty-seven maidens which performed the procession song of Livius Andronicus in 207 B.C. see the text above. Livy's report, 22. 1. 17 ff., on the expiatory rites of 217 B.C. is to be supplemented from Macrobius *Sat.* 1. 6. 13 f. *Laelius augur* (cf. Münzer, *RE* xii. 413) . . . *bello Punico secundo decemviros* [*duumviros* codd.: corr. Diels, *Sibyll. Blätter*, 85 n. 1] *dicit ex senatus consulto propter multa prodigia libros Sibyllinos adisse . . . acta igitur obsecratio est pueris ingenuis itemque libertinis, sed et virginibus patrimis matrimisque pronuntiantibus carmen*. Here it is clear that the boys said the

What lay behind this plan? Since in the order of the celebrations the place assigned to the performance of the *carmen* was at the end of the prayers and sacrifices, it follows that Horace must have been asked to compose it for that place. So we are forced to ask another question: What induced the body in charge of the festival to make an arrangement so strangely deviating from the conventions of sacred poetry? The obvious thing, so it might seem, would have been to follow the known precedents and ask the poet to write a hymn which could be incorporated into some part of the ceremonies. This, however, was not done. At the time of the festival three books of *carmina* written by Horace had been known for about six years. To any intelligent reader of these books it must have been clear that a Horatian ode would not claim, like an early Greek poem, or like most Hellenistic cult songs, to have a function within the reality of practical life. A Horatian ode, resigning any direct connexion with what actually happened in a cult or in some other sphere of human activity, would be content with reflecting life in the mirror of poetry. These new lyrics were self-contained. Their complete emancipation was essential. However, when the possibility of a performance of a hymn at the secular games was first considered, there may have been a strong temptation to compromise between a Horatian ode and a traditional sacred song. The very occasion of the celebrations and, moreover, the fact that the voice of the festival song was to come, not from the columns of a roll of papyrus, but from the lips of boys and girls, seemed to call for a relaxing of the poet's rigid limitations, for something less remote from the customary form of choric songs. Nothing is known about the consultations which preceded the final settlement of the programme. But it would not be surprising if Augustus, and whoever else played a leading part in the preparations, had at some stage suggested to Horace that he should compose a hymn after the fashion of Livius Andronicus and other ancient poets. If such a suggestion was made, it was turned down. It seems to me highly probable that Horace himself was consulted before anything was decided. He, no doubt, would have made it clear that it was not for him to write a conventional hymn, but only to write a Horatian ode. However, whether the decisive suggestion came from Horace or from somebody else, it met with the agreement of the Princeps. And, once accepted, this plan proved to be the greatest

prayers but that the song was performed by the girls only. On the expiatory rites of 200 B.C. Livy, 31. 12. 9 (ultimate source again the records of the Xviri), says *carmen praeterea ab ter novenis virginibus cani per urbem iusserunt* [scil. *Xviri*] *donumque Iunoni reginae ferri . . . . carmen, sicut patrum memoria Livius, ita tum condidit P. Licinius Tegula.* It seems therefore probable that it was an innovation when in 17 B.C. a choir of twenty-seven boys was added to the customary choir of twenty-seven girls. For Greek choirs of boys and girls in the Hellenistic period and under the Empire see Wilamowitz's note in Norden, *Agnostos Theos*, 392.

triumph of Horace's achievement as a lyric poet. Whatever the taste of the average Roman reader might be, Augustus and those nearest to him had now demonstrated that they not only appreciated the merits of Horace's odes but also approved of the bold and individual character of these *carmina non prius audita*. For in the face of all precedents, they asked him to write a poem such as no other man could have written, a typical Horatian ode, not meant to be part of the religious ceremonies but to be an ideal image of them, and therefore to be performed after the completion of all the sacrifices. By making this arrangement Augustus and his advisers showed that they respected the limits which Horace himself had set to his art. They encouraged him to persist in his own manner because they understood the meaning and aims of his poetry. This complete recognition stirred Horace profoundly. Disappointment and resignation gave way to fresh impulses, and the dammed-up stream of his lyrics began to flow again. And so Augustus, who, two years before, had saved the *Aeneid* from destruction, was now instrumental in bringing Horace back to his true life and his true task.

VIII

THE LETTER TO AUGUSTUS

SUETONIUS, it will be remembered,[1] reports that Augustus had so high an opinion of the lasting merits of Horace's work that he induced him to write the *Carmen Saeculare* and afterwards the two odes on the Alpine victories of Drusus and Tiberius. The biographer continues (*ut* . . .) *post sermones vero quosdam lectos nullam sui mentionem habitam*[2] *ita sit questus: 'irasci me tibi scito, quod non in plerisque eiusmodi scriptis mecum potissimum loquaris. an vereris ne apud posteros infame tibi sit quod videaris familiaris nobis esse?' expressitque eclogam ad se, cuius initium est 'Cum tot sustineas . . . tua tempora, Caesar.'*[3] It is obvious that in this context *sermones quosdam* cannot refer to the epistles of the first book but only to the letters *ad Pisones* and *ad Florum*.[4] When Suetonius says that Augustus *expressit* the epistle *Cum tot sustineas*, he judges the relationship between Augustus and Horace from his own standpoint and from the conditions prevailing at the Hadrianic court.[5] Horace was probably very much gratified by the wish which Augustus uttered in such an engaging manner and by the interest which he took not only in Horace's writings in general but also in his discussions of problems concerning Roman poetry. The letter in which he responds to the request (*Epist.* ii. 1) shows him perfectly at ease.

The four opening lines of the epistle are distinguished by their conciseness and by the tactful manner in which the Princeps is approached:

> Cum tot sustineas et tanta negotia solus,
> res Italas armis tuteris, moribus ornes,
> legibus emendes, in publica commoda peccem,
> si longo sermone morer tua tempora, Caesar.

In a situation like this it is natural for a writer to remind himself that he is trespassing upon the time of a man whose obligations are so

---

[1] See p. 364 above.

[2] No conjectures should be considered; cf. *Thes. l. L.* viii. 775. 52 ff.

[3] It is this passage that provides direct evidence for the Suetonian origin of the *Vita*: see p. 1 above.

[4] See, for example, Kiessling's introduction to *Epist.* ii. 1; Schanz–Hosius, *Gesch. d. röm. Lit.* ii. 133; A. Rostagni, *Suetonio De poetis*, 117.

[5] The same is true of the expressions *iniunxerit* and *coegerit* which Suetonius uses when speaking of the stimulus given by Augustus to the writing of the *Carmen Saeculare* and of Book IV of the *Odes*; see p. 364 above.

numerous and great.[1] Horace gives a fine turn to the common topic: if he took up Caesar's time with a lengthy discussion, he would be interfering not so much with the convenience of Caesar himself as with the *publica commoda*, for the personal interest of Caesar coincides with what Lucilius called *commoda patriai*. The nature of Augustus' régime is outlined in three pithy clauses, *res Italas*[2] *armis tuteris, moribus ornes,*[3] *legibus emendes;*[4] this description is to be completed by a passage in the last section[5] of the epistle. The short preface concludes effectively with *Caesar*.

More than once in this epistle a reader who wants to grasp the trend of thought could blame the editors for not using indentation to guide him. Why do they not mark in print the break after l. 4, which is as sharp as can be?[6] After the end of the preliminary sentence we come to the main body of the letter. The new section, *Romulus et Liber pater . . .*, begins with an asyndetic sentence, at the head of which the grammatical subject is placed; exactly the same form is employed for the same purpose at the beginning of 50 and of 139; we also notice that in each of the three passages special stress is laid on the subject (at 5 on the series of subjects). No overt connexion exists between the thought of the first four lines of the epistle and the thought that Romulus, Dionysus, the Dioscuri, and other heroes obtained only after their death the recognition that was due to them. Under the surface, however, there is something that links together the two sections, something that would not escape a contemporary reader. When, immediately after Caesar, there appear *Romulus et Liber pater et cum Castore Pollux*, followed by Hercules (10 ff.), it strikes a familiar note. To quote only two out of several similar instances, in the third and fourth stanzas of *Odes* iii. 3

---

[1] Cf., for instance, Cic. *Att.* 9. 11. A. 3 (to Caesar) *a te peto vel potius omnibus te precibus oro et obtestor, ut in tuis maximis curis aliquid impertias temporis huic quoque cogitationi . . .*. Horace's first line recalls what Cicero, *S. Rosc.* 22, says of Sulla, *cum et pacis constituendae rationem et belli gerendi potestatem* solus *habeat, . . . cum* tot tantisque negotiis *distentus sit,* etc.

[2] For the background against which this conception of *res Italae* should be viewed see R. Syme, *The Roman Revolution*, 285 ff., 359 f., 363 ff.

[3] Kiessling had a helpful note, '*ornare* ist = *instruere*, nicht "schmücken", sondern "ausstatten" ' (instances of the meaning 'equip' can be found in the dictionaries, notice especially Virg. *Aen.* 12. 344; see also Sonnenschein on Plaut. *Rud.* 187; Levens on Cic. *Verr.* 5. 44 [p. 98]); Heinze cancelled it and wrote instead '*ornare*, denn *boni mores* sind die schönste Zier eines Volkes'.

[4] On the reference of the last two clauses to Augustus' *morum legumque regimen* (Suet. *Aug.* 27. 5) see Mommsen, *Staatsrecht*, ii.[3] 706 n. 2. The commentators compare *Odes* 3. 24. 35 f. *quid leges sine moribus vanae proficiunt*. But in this connexion it should also be noticed that the differentiation of νόμος and ἔθος plays a role in Greek theory from the fourth century B.C.; see R. Hirzel, *ΑΓΡΑΦΟΣ ΝΟΜΟΣ, Abh. Sächs. Ges. d. Wiss.*, phil.-hist. Cl. xx. 1. 1900, 49 n. 3.

[5] I use, for convenience's sake, the term 'section', but the qualification made on p. 393 below should be borne in mind.

[6] Wieland's translation, Lejay's little edition (Hachette), and the Loeb text are laudable exceptions to the general indifference.

we find all those saviour-heroes assembled, *quos inter Augustus recumbens purpureo bibet ore nectar*, and in an ode written about the same time as our epistle, Augustus is addressed thus (4. 5. 33 ff.):

> te multa prece, te prosequitur mero
> defuso pateris, et Laribus tuum
> miscet numen, uti Graecia Castoris
> et magni memor Herculis.

So in high poetry Augustus could be more or less directly included in the number of those benefactors of mankind who, sons of a god and a mortal mother, had earned heaven by their deeds and whom men had worshipped ever since, *ollos quos endo caelo merita*[1] *locaverint, Herculem, Liberum, Aesculapium, Castorem, Pollucem, Quirinum.*[2] But here, in a *sermo* delivered in the sphere of social intercourse, any such explicit inclusion would be utterly out of place. The sentence *Romulus et Liber pater . . .*, as we have seen, is clearly separated from the first lines addressing Augustus. There is—and there must always have been felt there—a full stop after *Caesar*, marking a strong incision; anyone who recites the poem will have to pause here for a moment. Moreover, what happened to Romulus and the other heroes serves in this context not as a parallel to the fate of Augustus but as a contrast (15 ff.). And yet, full stop or no full stop, the Roman reader who saw *Caesar* directly followed by *Romulus et Liber pater . . .* was bound somehow to connect him with them, in other words to find it implied that Caesar Augustus, too, was to be looked upon as one of the δαίμονες ἁγνοὶ ἐπιχθόνιοι . . . ἐσθλοὶ ἀλεξίκακοι, φύλακες θνητῶν ἀνθρώπων. That this was in fact Horace's intention is put beyond doubt by a detail. The *ingentia facta* of the heroes are summed up in the following clauses (7 f.)

> dum terras hominumque colunt genus, aspera bella
> componunt, agros adsignant, oppida condunt.

The other achievements, including *oppida condunt*,[3] can be properly ascribed to those mythical persons, but *agros adsignant* cannot: it proves that the whole circle of heroes (5–12) is conceived in such a way that we have to imagine as its central figure the one not mentioned in this section but before (1–4) and after (15 ff.), Augustus. Hercules is separated from the others (10 ff.); this avoids a monotonous enumeration and

[1] Cf. in the epistle *meritis* (10).

[2] Cic. *Leg.* 2. 19. Pliny, *H.N.* 7. 95, says of Pompeius Magnus *aequato non modo Alexandri Magni rerum fulgore, sed etiam Herculis prope ac Liberi patris*. This could possibly derive from some *laudes Pompei* written in Pompey's own time.

[3] A. D. Nock, *JHS* xlviii, 1928, 27, observes (with special regard to Dionysus) 'to found cities was a typical act of the culture-hero in Hellenistic theorising'. Cf. also Cic. *Rep.* 1. 12 *neque enim est ulla res, in qua propius ad deorum numen virtus accedat humana quam civitates aut condere novas aut conservare iam conditas.*

also brings into relief the bravest of the heroes, the great sufferer to whose adventures Horace had once likened those of Augustus.[1] His fate exemplifies most clearly *invidiam supremo fine domari* and so leads naturally to the general maxim (13 f.) *urit enim fulgore suo . . . exstinctus amabitur idem.*[2] In contrast to the meanness and envy from which those benefactors had to suffer there shines the grateful recognition which Augustus has been able to win in his lifetime. The magnificent period in which this thought is expressed[3] ends with the resounding clause

> nil oriturum alias, nil ortum tale fatentes.

When we compare this line with the stanza written a year or two earlier,[4]

> quo nihil maius meliusve terris
> fata donavere bonique divi
> nec dabunt, quamvis redeant in aurum
> tempora priscum,

and bear in mind that this stanza contains a topic for a Pindarizing ἐπινίκιον suggested to Iullus Antonius, we shall learn something about what Horace considered the stylistic requirements of a *sermo* as distinct from high lyrics. In substance the praise of Augustus is no less strong in the epistle than in the ode, but the toning down of the style is considerable. Even so, the verse *nil oriturum alias . . .* is kept high above the average stylistic level of the epistles.

It appears, then, that the first seventeen lines contain certain elements of *laudes Caesaris*, first fairly directly expressed in the proem (1–4), then partly disguised (5–12), partly overt (15–17). It seems likely that Horace was reluctant to engage Augustus straight away in a discussion on poetry as he might have done with anyone else. Such *disinvoltura* might have been taken as a lack of modesty. While avoiding any fulsome flattery, he is anxious to show his awareness of the very special situation in which he finds himself. Besides, it is a rule of common politeness not to assail your correspondent directly with a display of your personal concerns, but first to entertain him with something that

---

[1] Odes 3. 14. 1–4. At 10 *contudit*, with the object *hydram*, is of course the *mot juste*, but the verb is also commonly used to denote the inflicting of a shattering defeat, cf. *Thes. l. L.* iv. 806; so it is used by Horace at *Odes* 3. 6. 10; 4. 3. 8.

[2] These topics had long become commonplace, cf., for example, Thuc. 2. 45. 1 (Pericles) φθόνος γὰρ τοῖς ζῶσι πρὸς τὸ ἀντίπαλον, τὸ δὲ μὴ ἐμποδὼν ἀνανταγωνίστῳ εὐνοίᾳ τετίμηται; Demosth. 18. 315; [Sall.] *Ep. Caes. sen.* 2. 13. 7 *nam vivos interdum fortuna, saepe invidia fatigat: ubi anima naturae cessit, demptis optrectatoribus, ipsa se virtus magis magisque extollit.*

[3] As regards 16, *iurandasque tuum per numen* (cf. Weinstock, *JRS* xxxix, 1949, 167) *ponimus aras*, I have found no comment grammatically satisfactory. I take it that the sense must be 'altars *at* which we swear by your godhead', and I am inclined to believe that Horace has here allowed himself a bold, highly poetical construction, in harmony with the tone of the following line.

[4] *Odes* 4. 2. 37 ff.

is nearer to his own interests. The epistle gives the impression of spontaneity as though it owed its existence entirely to Horace's initiative; it would have been impossibly tactless to hint at the fact that Augustus had actually asked for it.

When Horace turns from the praise of Augustus[1] to the charge against the Roman public, who are enthusiastic about the oddest pieces of ancient writing but despise and hate all modern poetry (18–27), the reader feels that now he has come to the real theme of the epistle. The section that begins at 18 and ends at 92 is in the main a good-natured demonstration[2] of the absurdity of the opinion according to which a Latin poem can be of any value only if it happens to be an old poem. The general demonstration (up to 49 *miraturque nihil nisi quod Libitina sacravit*) is subsequently illustrated by a series of characteristic instances of the manner in which both the professional experts (51 *critici*)[3] and the common people (60 ff.) extol the early Latin poets, deliberately shutting their eyes to their shortcomings (50–92). As for the reactionaries and the literary snobs, who pretend profound admiration for the crudest and most unintelligible relics of archaic Latin,[4]

---

[1] At 18 the apparatus of the Oxford text is to blame for still mentioning Bentley's conjecture *hoc*; at the end of the line *uno* goes with *te* (Klingner in his article 'Horazens Brief an Augustus', *Sitz. Bayer. Akad.*, Phil.-hist. Kl. 1950, Heft 5 [I shall quote it as 'Brief'], 9, has deleted the comma which in his edition he put at the end of 18).

[2] This demonstration is deliberately presented in terms of hackneyed school logic (cf. Orelli–Baiter on 28–33); its *pièce de résistance* is the enthymeme of 31, where the whole point is lost if we reject Bentley's emendation *olea* (*oleam* trad.). For the very common ἀπὸ κοινοῦ of a preposition see Bentley on *Odes* 3. 25. 2; Wilamowitz on E. *Her.* 237; Marx on Lucilius 390 and 1239 f.; F. Leo, *Anal. Plaut.* i, 1896, 43, where the present passage is duly registered.

[3] The manner in which the thought proceeds in the new section beginning at 50 is well illustrated by Vahlen, *Ges. philol. Schriften*, i. 467: 'Damit man nicht denke, ich übertreibe und schiebe denen, die ich bekämpfe, Unwahres unter, so höre man doch, was für Beurteilungen der alten Dichter Roms heutzutage im Schwange sind.' The judgements on Ennius and Naevius are parallel to one another; each of them is self-contained; at 52 the expressions *promissa* and *somnia Pythagorea*, as Lambinus and Kiessling saw, refer solely to Ennius' future fame and have nothing to do with Naevius. Heinze's misinterpretation is rejected by Klingner, 'Brief', 11 n. 13, to whom I cannot, however, concede that laudatory epithets like *sapiens et fortis* 'können nur noch komisch wirken': Horace is angry at such wrongheadedness. I also fail to see that 62, *ad nostrum tempus Livi scriptoris ab aevo*, 'mit seiner Komik und Übertreibung dem Faß den Boden ausschlägt' (Klingner, 12). The principal point of the passage on Naevius (53 f.) was illustrated by Kiessling: 'Aber es kommt noch besser: ist nicht selbst des noch älteren Naevius . . . Heldengedicht vom ersten punischen Krieg in Aller Händen?'

[4] Kiessling (on 50) and Leo conjectured with probability that it was Varro, or rather the *Varroniani* (Leo, *Gesch. d. röm. Lit.* 399 n. 2), whom Horace had in mind; see also Dahlmann, 'Varros Schrift "de poematis" ', *Abh. Akad. Mainz*, Geistes- und sozialwiss. Kl., 1953, Nr. 3, 147, 'mehr noch [than against Varro himself] gegen die Lehren der von seiner Autorität abhängigen zeitgenössischen Literarkritiker'. The same view was held by H. Nettleship, *Lectures and Essays*, second series, 52, who adds the pretty conjecture that 'in these verses Horace is probably firing his parting shot at the criticisms he was made to swallow in his boyhood'.

their real motive is not love for the ancient but envious hatred of contemporary poetry (86–89):

> ingeniis non ille favet plauditque sepultis,
> nostra sed impugnat, nos nostraque lividus odit.

A reactionary attitude of this kind, based upon spiteful contempt for modern poets and writers, incensed the great eighteenth-century scholar David Ruhnken so much that he determined to rouse the proud and old-fashioned University of Leyden, which had made him Professor of History and Eloquence, by his inaugural oration *De doctore umbratico*, a masterpiece as fresh and refreshing today as when it was delivered two centuries ago.

Horace is not primarily concerned with refuting the wrong judgements on the early Roman poets. What is, however, vital for him, since the success of his life's work depends on it, is to overcome the dull opposition to any fresh production and the common incapacity to recognize any higher stylistic standards. It is significant that in the comments made by that section of the public with which Horace declares himself in agreement[1] (66–68) there appear precisely the same criticisms which he had once made in his polemic against Lucilius, *dure* (cf. *Sat.* 1. 4. 8) and *ignave* (cf. *Sat.* 1. 4. 12 *piger scribendi ferre laborem*), to which we must add the charge of *nimis antique*, which coincides in substance with what he said, by way of exculpation, about Lucilius in *Sat.* 1. 10. 67 ff. In the late epistle to Augustus as in the early satires the sharp criticism of the older poets is not an end in itself but an inevitable first step: only when the prejudices of the reactionary critics and the general reader have been cleared away, will it be possible to show what the new poetry of the Augustan age was already achieving and could be expected to achieve in the future. In this epistle it is Horace's primary object to outline the character and scope of that new poetry and to allot to it its proper place in the body politic. This central theme he approaches, after the preparation which we have examined, from a different angle in the section that, with a fresh start,[2] begins at 93.

It was the firm conviction of Virgil and Horace, and, for that matter, of any educated Roman at least from the middle of the third century B.C., that, like any other artistic and intellectual activity, writing poetry was possible only if one continued and modified the Greek tradition. It could not occur to Horace to go back on the advice he had given to the young sons of Piso, *vos exemplaria Graeca nocturna*

---

[1] The final clause, 68, *et Iove iudicat aequo*, should not be taken as an allusion to Augustus; I agree with Klingner, 'Brief', 13 n. 14, as against Kiessling and Heinze.

[2] The fresh start at 93 is unmistakable, but, in a manner characteristic of Horace in general and of this epistle in particular, there is also a transition from *Graecis* at 90 to *Graecia* at 93; cf. Klingner, 'Brief', 15.

versate manu, versate diurna. Still, his somewhat condescending attitude in the section of the letter to Augustus which is put under the heading *Graecia* (93) is at first sight puzzling. Without denying the perfection of the works of Greek art, music, and poetry, he treats them as the play-things of little children,[1] who in their fickleness eagerly seize any new toy, only to tire of it very soon and run after another one. The section opens significantly with *nugari* (93) and continues with the even less complimentary phrase *in vitium labier*.[2] The whole description makes it clear that the amusements of those Greeks would be utterly unworthy of any serious adult, let alone a Roman. The contrast here implied becomes explicit in the next section, which is marked by its initial word *Romae* (103) as the antithetic sequence to 93 ff.: ἡ μὲν Ἑλλὰς κτλ., ἐν δὲ τῇ Ῥώμῃ . . ..[3] The brief account in the section 103–7 is strictly con-fined to the working day, particularly its early hours, of a *pater familias* as it took its customary course in old times. It is a fine picture—Mommsen justly praised it[4]—but since it here serves as a foil to the following description of the thorough change that afterwards took place in the life of Rome, it is a somewhat simplified and one-sided picture. Those Romans of the past are portrayed as hard-working, honest men, given to strict husbandry, reliable in their business relations, respectful to their elders, and ready to advise younger men and assist those who depend on them. They appear devoid of any interest in higher culture, but there is in this description nothing of the bitterness with which in the epistle to the sons of Piso the money-mindedness of the Romans and the educational system that fostered it were made responsible for the insensibility of the people to poetry.[5]

It appears, then, that in this σύγκρισις of the ways of life in Greece and in primitive Rome each side is described with some exaggeration. The reason is not far to seek. In this context Horace is not interested in producing an objective sketch of the βίος τῆς Ἑλλάδος and the βίος τῆς Ῥώμης: what he wants to provide and does provide is a pair of sharply

---

[1] On 99 *puella* Kiessling comments '*puella*, weil *Graecia* voraufgeht'. I prefer to think of common experience and of Homer Π 7 ff. (referring to Patroclus!).

[2] For the underlying theory according to which prolonged peace and freedom from fear were apt to lead to *luxuria* and moral decline see pp. 212 f. above. There is, of course, an intentional parallelism between 93 f., *positis nugari Graecia bellis coepit*, etc., and 162 f., (the Roman) *post Punica bella quietus quaerere coepit quid Sophocles*, etc., where Horace found it convenient to adopt the fantastic chronology of Accius rather than the documentary evidence about which Atticus and Cicero had learned from Varro.

[3] A very similar antithesis begins in the same abrupt manner at *Epist.* 1. 18. 49 *Romanis sollemne viris opus* . . . (preceded by the idea of the Greek Muses), and an exactly analogous arrangement occurs at *Ars P.* 323–5, *Grais* . . . *Grais* . . ., then, after a full stop, *Romani pueri*.

[4] *Röm. Forschungen*, i. 373 n. 36.

[5] *Ars P.* 325 ff.

contrasted pictures, which, as he goes on, are to merge into a harmonious complex. Horace was certainly aware of the painful narrowness in the outlook of the early Romans, and no less aware of the very serious part—anything but *sub nutrice puella velut si luderet infans*—played by poetry in the great days of Greece. It was not unknown to him that the Greeks had long discovered and recognized that τοῖς μὲν γὰρ παιδαρίοισιν ἐστὶ διδάσκαλος ὅστις φράζει, τοῖσιν δ' ἡβῶσι ποηταί, but he wished to reserve for the climax of his letter the conception of the poet as teacher and educator of his people. However, this artistic design is, perhaps, not the only reason why Horace here looks down on the Greeks' infatuation about agonistic games, the decorative arts, music, and poetry. It may be permissible to detect here a trace of a certain ambiguity in the mental attitude of many highly educated Romans. The Philhellenism of most of Rome's leading men was sincere: they admitted ungrudgingly the superiority of the Greeks not only in the arts but in most of the activities that make life rich and interesting. There is, however, always the possibility of a sudden change of front, when a sharp line will be drawn between one's own incomparable nation and the rest of the world, and the foreigners will either be blamed for their un-Roman behaviour or, more often, smiled at with condescension, for they, poor things, know no better and must not be taken too seriously. It can always happen that those who shortly before have been treated as revered masters, will, without warning, be put in their place and become mere *Graeculi*. But we must return to the epistle.

In Horace's simplifying account the Greeks appear as extremely gifted at art and poetry, but immature and unreliable; children rather than men. The Romans, on the other hand, the Romans of former days, are described as men of high moral standards, excellent householders and loyal citizens, but shut out from any access to the world of poetry. However, that state of affairs in Rome is now a thing of the past. *Mutavit mentem populus levis et calet uno scribendi studio* (108 f.).[1] A fever for writing poetry has seized young and old, nor is this passion confined to the professionals: *scribimus indocti doctique poemata passim* (117). From what we have heard so far, this would seem to be a change

---

[1] C. G. Schütz (editors of Horace ought to give him his initials, to avoid confusion with Hermann Schütz, the commentator of Horace), whose *ingenium* was by no means *lentum*, rightly deleted (*Opusc.* 247) 101, 'nihil enim affert nisi ieiunum locum communem, qui pulcrum orationis filum misere interrumpit, nec satis convenit poetae proposito'. Nowadays most editors seem to be quite happy with 'der spielend hingeworfenen Verbesserung' (Vahlen, *Philol. Schriften* i. 480) by Lachmann (commentary on Lucretius, p. 37), who sandwiched the line between 107 and 108, where it disrupts the sharp antithesis and deprives the asyndetic fresh start, *mutavit mentem populus*, of its force. Besides, what business has *odio est* in this context?

for the worse. But Horace does not leave it there, for he continues
(118 f.)

> hic error tamen et levis haec insania quantas
> virtutes habeat, sic collige.

A poet is not a greedy person: all he cares for is poetry. He is aloof
from the worries that make other men's lives miserable (119–21); so
simple are his needs that he would not think of dishonest transactions,[1]
and though, like Horace himself, he is but a poor soldier,[2] he can, in a
modest way, be useful to the community. Thus passing from the private
life of the poet to the work he produces, Horace first points to the
assistance that poetry might give in the education of the young,[3] and
then suggests some of its main functions as an illuminating and con-
soling force in the lives of all men (130 f.). By now the slightly playful
tone which was noticeable at the beginning of this section (119 ff.) has
completely faded out. When Horace says (130 f.) *recte facta refert,
orientia tempora notis instruit exemplis*, he may have in mind, above all, the
Aeneid. The following sentences, to the end of the section (138), allude
unmistakably to the performance of the *Carmen Saeculare* a few years
earlier.[4] The excitement that the poet felt on that great occasion still
vibrates here. However, Horace appears to be thinking not merely of
his own hymn. There are also allusions (135–8) to the kind of artless
carmina that at many places in ancient Italy accompanied acts of
worship or served as spells. The blending of homely native elements
with Greek ideas and artistic forms suited the tastes of Horace and
Virgil no less than it agreed with the general inclinations of Augustus.

The style of this passage leaves behind the modest manner of the *sermo*
and soars upwards until it reaches the height of the magnificent line

> carmine di superi placantur, carmine Manes.[5]

We may assume that this glorification of Roman poetry (132–8),
which Horace has placed exactly in the centre, was regarded by him as
the crown of his epistle.

[1] The combination of two especially important classes of legal relationship which we
find at 122 f., *non fraudem socio puerove incogitat ullam pupillo*, is typical; cf., for instance, Cic.
Rosc. com. 16, *Si qua enim sunt privata iudicia summae existimationis et paene dicam capitis, tria haec
sunt, fiduciae, tutelae, societatis. aeque enim perfidiosum et nefarium est fidem frangere quae continet
vitam, et pupillum fraudare qui in tutelam pervenit, et socium fallere qui se in negotio coniunxit.*

[2] Kiessling's note, taken over by Heinze, on (124) *militiae* is unfortunate; *militiae* is, of
course, genitive, here as well as at Tac. *Ann.* 3. 48. 1. For the construction cf. Schmalz–
Hofmann, (405 c).

[3] The thought in 129, *asperitatis et invidiae corrector et irae*, is well illustrated by *Epist.* i. 2 as
a whole and by Horace's account of his reading of the *Iliad* at school, *Epist.* 2. 2. 42.

[4] The reference was understood by the ancient commentators (Ps.-Acro on 133). With
137 *locupletem frugibus annum* compare the echo of the *Carmen Saeculare* at *Odes* 4. 6. 39 f.

[5] The use of anaphora in Horace is almost always a sign of serious emphasis. Cf.
p. 206 and p. 311 above.

Before we go on it may help if we briefly sum up what has been established so far. Greek poetry, Horace has asserted, with all its perfection, was the product and outcome of an unmanly, morally inferior kind of life. Early Roman life, on the other hand, sound, virile, and full of a sense of responsibility, was averse to poetry. Yet it is possible to have the best of both these worlds and to combine the moral and political virtues of a Roman with the best gifts of the Greek Muse. A poet, a Roman poet, can become his fellow citizens' guide and teacher, can instruct, comfort, and elevate their minds without pampering and enfeebling them. That is his noblest task; that is what had been recently achieved by men whom Augustus encouraged and honoured with his confidence. Poetry conceived in this way, so far from being a plaything for idle hours, is eminently πολιτικόν, *utile urbi*. Therefore contemporary poetry is entitled to the attention of the first citizen of Rome, to whom *res Italas moribus ornare* is one of his foremost duties. He may even be expected to give some thought to the difficulties with which the poetry of the new era has still to struggle.

These difficulties are twofold, for the existence of a dignified Roman poetry is endangered from within by the lack of a firm stylistic standard and from without by the lack of real sympathy and understanding on the part of the public. The first point, the danger of deficiency, is discussed from 139–76. Despite the refinement which Latin poetry has achieved through the efforts of conscientious writers trained in the school of the Greeks, there still remains in it far too much rusticity. The barbarous Saturnian is gone, polite manners have driven away the old untidiness (159 f.),

> sed in longum tamen aevum
> manserunt hodieque manent vestigia ruris.

This is the keynote of the whole section, which significantly begins with *agricolae* (139).[1] There follows at 146 the phrase *opprobria rustica* and at 157 *agresti Latio*. Since Roman poetry has grown on such a soil, it has always been and still is difficult for it to adjust itself to the requirements of *urbanitas*. The *vestigia ruris* are most conspicuous in the dislike of the average Latin poet for painstaking polish: *turpem putat inscite metuitque lituram* (167). It is the slapdash writing of Plautus that makes Horace criticize him so severely at the end of the section (170–6); Plautus stands for all those Roman poets whose technique, in Horace's opinion, is careless and who are therefore considered deficient, whatever their other merits. It is because Horace is engaged in an embittered struggle for his own and his friends' artistic ideals, and not because

[1] Cf. also Klingner, 'Brief', 22.

he wants to give an account of a period of literary history, that he embarks on the long discussion from 139 on.[1]

But we have not yet done full justice to the beginning of this section. From what has been said it will have become clear that a fresh trend of thought sets in with 139, *agricolae prisci*. But this fresh start will at first be hidden to the reader who comes from the preceding section: he must, on the contrary, have the impression that the former thoughts are being carried on and merely given a new turn. The subject-matter after 139 seems to be very much the same as before: the homely verses as an element of the peasants' cults (139–48) apparently belong to the type of poetry outlined in 134–8. But the connexion is superficial, for from 139 the point of view changes completely. This subtle manner of disguising the transition to a new 'section'—there are not, or ought not to be, any sections in the talk of educated men of good manners—is characteristic of Horace's *sermones*, satires as well as epistles. It is one of the devices by which the writer, apparently yielding to spontaneous incentives and gliding from idea to idea, avoids any semblance of a rigid systematic procedure. Another instance of this type of disguised fresh start meets us when we now return to the point up to which we had pursued our reading of the epistle.

In the section beginning at 177, the keyword of which is *scaenam*, Horace, who has just been censuring the manner in which Plautus dashes across the *pulpita*, seems to continue his critical survey of the performances on the Roman stage. But it soon becomes clear that he is no longer concerned with the playwrights and their slovenliness, but with another obstacle to a free development of noble dramatic poetry in Rome.[2] This second difficulty arises from the craving of the public for stronger and ever stronger visual attractions, gigantic displays on the stage and massive side-shows, which dazzle the eye of the spectator and divert his mind from the word and thought of the poet. It is the sort of thing which had made it impossible for Cicero, a sincere lover of dramatic poetry, to enjoy performances in the contemporary theatre. The worst of it, Horace says (187 f.), is that the tyranny of these vulgar instincts is by no means confined to the rabble,

> verum equitis quoque iam migravit ab aure voluptas
> omnis ad incertos oculos et gaudia vana.[3]

---

[1] On this point I agree entirely with Klingner, 'Brief', 22 f.

[2] 'Die Verse 177 ff. sind . . . obwohl in der Form durch das zuletzt vom Plautus Ausgesagte einigermaßen bestimmt, von der Charakteristik dieses Dichters zu trennen und als der Anfang einer neuen Gedankenreihe zu betrachten' (Vahlen, *Philol. Schriften*, i. 489).

[3] Hearing is here, from the poet's point of view, considered more valuable than seeing. That is at variance with the general opinion (alluded to by Horace, *Ars P.* 180 ff.) according to which ὀφθαλμοί . . . ὤτων ἀκριβέστεροι μάρτυρες (Heraclit. *fr.* 101A D.) and

Lest Horace's severe condemnation of the abuses which have become common in theatrical performances might give the impression that he is hostile to drama as such, he takes pains at the end of this section to make it clear that he fully appreciates the potential value of tragedy. 'The true tragic poet', he says (210–13), 'appears to me as a man able to achieve the impossible, a magician who fills my mind with imaginary sensations and passions and transports me to wherever the action of the play takes place.'

At 214, *verum age et his*, there begins a new section. It is linked up with the preceding section by a simple thought, 'not only drama but also the other genres of poetry deserve attention'. Here again a smooth formula of transition conceals a considerable change in the writer's point of view. Up till now the development of Roman poetry, its virtues and its shortcomings, its potentialities and its handicaps, have been discussed in a manner suitable for any reader who might be expected to take an interest in these problems. But from 214 to the end of the epistle the principal theme is 'Roman poetry and Augustus'. This theme is treated under two aspects, first 'Augustus as a reader of contemporary poetry', and, secondly, 'Augustus and his rule as a subject of poetry'. The new theme is approached with characteristic elegance and discretion. The transition from addressing the general reader to addressing the one reader, Augustus, is almost imperceptible. The smoothness of the movement may be best appreciated when we examine a number of corresponding passages in which, by means of an imperative or some analogous verbal expression, the attention of the reader is directed to a certain point, or he is given a warning, or some intention of his is anticipated. The imperative at 170, *aspice*, is directed to any reader, and so at 208 is the warning *ac ne forte putes* . . . . After reading these expressions we are bound to take the subsequent imperative (214 ff.) *verum age et his . . . curam redde brevem* in the same sense, at any rate at first. But as soon as we reach the continuation (216 ff.) *si munus Apolline dignum | vis complere libris et vatibus addere calcar, | ut studio maiore petant Helicona virentem*, we cannot escape the conclusion that the person here addressed is in fact Augustus. Such gliding transitions, it need hardly be repeated, are not uncommon in Horace. In this epistle there is, however, a special intention behind the arrangement by which the

---

pluris est oculatus testis unus quam auriti decem (Plaut. *Truc.* 489). Cf. Pfeiffer on Callim. *fr.* 282 (i. 264 f.) and add Sen. *Epist.* 6. 5 and Dio Chrys. 12. 71 (i. 175 v. Arnim). When Callimachus, loc. cit. (ὀκκόσον ὀφθαλμοὶ γὰρ ἀπευθέες, ὅσσον ἀκουὴ εἰδυλίς), disagrees with the popular view, he may be influenced by the doctrine of Aristotle, *De sensu* 437ᵃ 3–17, who says that πρὸς μὲν τὰ ἀναγκαῖα κρείττων ἡ ὄψις καθ' αὑτήν, πρὸς δὲ νοῦν κατὰ συμβεβηκὸς ἡ ἀκοή κτλ. (cf. Sir David Ross's commentary, 185, bottom) and reaches the conclusion that φρονιμώτεροι τῶν ἐκ γενετῆς ἐστερημένων εἰσὶν ἑκατέρας τῆς αἰσθήσεως οἱ τυφλοὶ τῶν ἐνεῶν καὶ κωφῶν.

figure of the Princeps detaches itself gently and gradually from the figure of the general reader. The purpose of this arrangement is still more clearly revealed in the passage 219–28. Under the heading

> multa quidem nobis facimus mala saepe poetae

the *multa mala* which the poets in their wrongheadedness bring upon themselves are arranged in five strictly parallel *cum* clauses. The first of these clauses, *cum tibi librum sollicito damus aut fesso*, can be nicely illustrated by the anxious warnings which Horace impresses on the messenger whom he asks to deliver to Augustus a copy of his *carmina*.[1] This first clause and the last in the series, *cum speramus eo rem venturam ut, simul atque | carmina rescieris nos fingere, commodus ultro | arcessas et egere vetes et scribere cogas* (226–8), refer solely to Augustus, whereas the three middle clauses (from 221 *cum laedimur* to 225 *tenui deducta poemata filo*) are unmistakably concerned with the ways in which the recitation or the publication of a new book of poetry will be received, not by Augustus in particular, but by any reader or by the reading public in general. We may even go so far as to say that in the situation suggested by the second *cum* clause, *cum laedimur, unum si quis amicorum est ausus reprehendere versum*, there is hardly any room at all for Augustus. What inference have we to draw from these observations? The passage which we have been examining is most carefully designed. Therefore the apparent inconsistency in referring at one moment to one reader and at the next to another one must be intentional. With *verum age et his . . . curam redde brevem* (214 ff.) Horace is indeed turning to Augustus; he also makes it plain that for the purposes of his present discussion it is Augustus' reaction to poetry that matters most. But at the same time he is exceedingly careful not to isolate the Princeps from the rest of the reading public by placing him on a pedestal of his own. Augustus is to appear as one, though the most distinguished, of the educated Romans interested in poetry. Horace, at this stage, understood Augustus and his intentions as few men did, and he was able to express this understanding better than anyone else. It might not be wholly unprofitable if some of our hard-working historians turned for a moment away from their epigraphic and numismatic studies and paid some attention to the figure of the Princeps as it is reflected in Horace's mature work. They may also ask themselves whether a letter such as this could possibly have been written, let us say, to Louis XIV, great prince though he was.

It is of a piece with Horace's dignified freedom in conversing with the first man of Rome that he is not afraid of going counter now and then to some predilection of Augustus. The comments made in this

---

[1] *Epist.* i. 13. Cf. p. 351 above.

epistle on early Roman comedy are anything but kind. And yet Horace must have known, for all Rome knew it, that Augustus took a particular pleasure in those ancient plays and saw to it that they were often performed in public.[1] Augustus will not have been annoyed when his own judgement on works of literature was contradicted; besides, he will have been quick to see that his friend Horace, in assailing Plautus, had an axe to grind.

The passage that begins at 219 and ends at 228 is formed as a digression; its conclusion is marked by *tamen* at 229, which corresponds to *quidem* at 219. Horace now returns to the point he had raised in 214 ff. But again an almost imperceptible shift takes place. The sentence *sed tamen . . . indigno non committenda poetae* (229–31) looks as if it were merely subservient to the theme of 214 ff.; there is nothing surprising in the assumption that *virtus belli spectata domique* is the foremost topic of dignified poetry. But as the reader goes on he discovers that *virtus*, which was apparently used in a general sense, here refers also, and in fact primarily, to the *virtus* of the one man who in the present time excels all others *belli domique*. Thus, without a sharp break, we have passed from Augustus the reader to Augustus the subject of poetry.

The next section, headed by the name of Alexander the Great (232) culminates in the thought (245 ff.) that Augustus, the sympathetic patron of Virgil and Varius, was happier than Alexander in the choice of the poets whom he favoured. This thought leads up to a general maxim (248–50),

> nec magis expressi voltus per aenea signa
> quam per vatis opus mores animique virorum
> clarorum apparent.

This idea, for which the commentators compare the late ode to Censorinus (iv. 8), seems to have belonged to the stock-in-trade of writers of eulogies. We find it, for instance, used by Isocrates,[2] but it is certainly older; similar sentences in choric lyrics are well known. Horace's expression *mores animique virorum clarorum*, like *belli spectata domique virtus* at 230 f., ostensibly refers to illustrious men in general, but in this context, immediately after Virgil and Varius have been

---

[1] Suet. *Aug.* 89. 1 *delectabatur etiam comoedia veteri et saepe eam exhibuit spectaculis publicis.* This can only refer to the *fabula palliata*, as was pointed out in 1863 by Madvig, *Kl. philolog. Schriften*, 476. There will have been other points as well on which Augustus and Horace did not see eye to eye. 'In dem schönen Briefe an Augustus hat er sich auch nicht gescheut Ansichten über die Poesie vorzutragen, die denen des Kaisers schwerlich entsprachen' (Wilamowitz, *Süddeutsche Monatshefte*, 28. Jahrgang, Oktober 1930, 44).

[2] Isocr. 9 (*Euag.*), 73 ἐγὼ δὲ . . . ἡγοῦμαι μὲν εἶναι καλὰ μνημεῖα καὶ τὰς τῶν σωμάτων εἰκόνας, πολὺ μέντοι πλείονος ἀξίας τὰς τῶν πράξεων καὶ τῆς διανοίας, ἃς ἐν τοῖς λόγοις ἄν τις μόνον τοῖς τεχνικῶς ἔχουσιν θεωρήσειεν. Cf. also 2 (*Nicocl.*), 36 βούλου τὰς εἰκόνας τῆς ἀρετῆς ὑπόμνημα μᾶλλον ἢ τοῦ σώματος καταλιπεῖν.

mentioned as heralds of the greatness of Augustus, it is above all Augustus who must be thought of when we hear of *viri clari* whose personality is to be portrayed in poetry.

In stating that *per vatis opus mores animique virorum clarorum adparent* Horace felt he was touching a delicate spot. He had never fulfilled the hope cherished by his friends that he would write a great poem, preferably an epic, in praise of Augustus. In passing, it is true, he had more than once honoured the Princeps, and lately he had extolled him or at any rate planned to extol him in some of his odes, but all that did not fully come up to the expectations of those contemporaries who wanted him *Caesaris invicti res dicere*. In these circumstances to discuss the need for a lasting poetic monument of *mores animique virorum clarorum* and especially those of Augustus, to contend that it was one of the most important tasks of Rome's poets to produce such a monument, and yet to ignore the fact that in the opinion of judicious men no one was better qualified to undertake that task than Horace himself—that would have been both insincere and cowardly. As far as Augustus' own feelings were concerned, such behaviour was bound to strike him almost as a deliberate insult. That was the last thing Horace would have wished. So he does not dodge the issue but makes a bold move (250 ff.) :

> nec sermones ego mallem
> repentis per humum quam res componere gestas,
> terrarumque situs et flumina dicere . . ..

But even at this point he still maintains for a moment the pretence of having in mind κλέα ἀνδρῶν in general. He does not immediately say by whom the *res gestae* have been achieved and of what particular campaigns in foreign lands he is speaking, and only after a series of allusive sentences is the veil definitely lifted with the expression (253 f.) *tuis . . . auspiciis*.

The pattern of this *recusatio* (for such it is) is very much the same as in the introductory satire of the second book, written fifteen or sixteen years before this epistle. There Trebatius had advised the poet to cease annoying people with his satires and instead to praise Caesar's successes ; and Horace had replied

> cupidum, pater optime, vires
> deficiunt.

Now he tells Augustus that he would gladly become the herald of his deeds

> si quantum cuperem possem quoque ; sed neque parvum
> carmen maiestas recipit tua, nec meus audet
> rem temptare pudor quam vires ferre recusent.

Of him, Horace, nothing, alas, but a *parvum carmen* could be expected. In the same vein he had, a year or two before, said of himself
operosa parvus carmina fingo.[1] He is obliged to follow his maxim *parvum
parva decent*.[2] But a *parvum carmen* would be entirely unsuitable for the
maiestas of Augustus (258). The word *maiestas*, transferred from the
maiestas populi Romani or *imperi* to the Princeps, is here chosen with purpose, for the reader will be conscious of its connexion with *maius esse* as
opposed to *minus esse*.[3] However, if Horace cannot shoulder so heavy a
burden,[4] if he cannot write a great patriotic poem, he can at least use
to the best advantage his familiar expedient, the *recusatio*, and can in
passing outline the theme which he declines to elaborate. Within the
compass of a few lines he manages to draw a magnificent picture.
With a brief allusion, 252 f. *arces montibus impositas*, an echo of his
epinikion for Tiberius,[5] he touches upon the recent Alpine conquests of
the stepsons of Augustus, proceeds to glorify the successful conclusion
of the wars all over the world and the closing of the temple of Janus,
and rounds his survey off with the line (256)

> et formidatam Parthis te principe Romam,

in which the choice of the words, their arrangement, and the heavy
rhythm all seem to suggest the *gravitas* and power of Rome and of her
leader. This passage is solely concerned with the military achievements of the régime; it is obviously intended to supplement the succinct
laudes Caesaris in the proem of the epistle. There, though *armis tutari* was
mentioned, the emphasis was on the internal policy and the social and
moral reforms. Taken together, the two passages give a condensed, but
by no means inadequate account of the rule of Augustus.

The next sentence (260), *sedulitas autem stulte quem diligit urguet*, again
recalls a thought of the *recusatio* in the dialogue with Trebatius,[6] *cui male
si palpere, recalcitrat undique tutus*. The epistle concludes with a deftly
balanced period (from 264 on). We shall grasp the real objective of the
two *neque . . . nec* clauses (264–6) when we notice that this is an instance
of the fairly common form of *comparatio paratactica*,[7] where, according to
our way of thinking, we should subordinate the first parallel clause to
the second, like this: 'as little as I should care to have a bad portrait of
me made by a sculptor, so little should I wish to have myself celebrated
in a bad poem'. So we are still in the same context into which we
entered at 232. Alexander the Great, we were reminded there, had

---

[1] *Odes* 4. 2. 31 f. [2] *Epist.* 1. 7. 44.
[3] See also A. Dihle, *Stud. It.* N.S. xxvi, 1952, 173 n. 3.
[4] The expression at 259 *rem . . . quam vires ferre recusent* recalls the advice given to the
sons of Piso, *versate diu, quid ferre recusent, quid valeant umeri* (*Ars P.* 39 f.).
[5] *Odes* 4. 14. 11 f. *arces Alpibus impositas tremendis*.
[6] *Sat.* 2. 1. 20. [7] See p. 220 n. 5 above.

himself portrayed by the painter Apelles and the sculptor Lysippus, but the poem that praised him was written by the incompetent Choerilus; Augustus, on the other hand, put his confidence in poets who showed themselves worthy of it. At the end of the epistle, too, what really matters is the quality of portraits and eulogies, not of someone chosen at random, but of Augustus. But here Horace disguises the obvious reference to the Princeps by speaking in the first person (264–6), *nil moror . . . nec prave factis decorari versibus opto*; in other words he gives the impression of making a statement that might be applied to himself and to anybody who wants to be portrayed in a work of decorative art or in a poem. In this manner Horace tones down what he has to say of Augustus. The demand that the person and the achievements of the Princeps should be represented in a worthy manner is nothing special, not a consequence of his elevated position, but something that any ordinary citizen would have the right to insist upon. Here as before Horace, the *fidus interpres* of the intentions of Augustus, refuses to fix a gulf between the ruler and the rest of mankind.

It is a serious matter with which Horace has been dealing in this epistle, and he does want Augustus to take it seriously. But he is writing a letter, and, moreover, is writing to the man who has to discharge his heavy obligations under a greater strain than anyone else. The society to which Horace belongs respects a strict code of *urbanitas*, and Horace himself is most sensitive to the commands of tact. Not for the world would he wish on this occasion to look like an importunate sermonizer. Throughout the letter he has been careful to avoid the rigidity of a systematic argumentation. The easy grace of educated men talking to one another has been happily maintained. Only every now and then has it been necessary to treat certain momentous points in a somewhat emphatic manner. Therefore the poet is the more anxious that at the end a lighter tone should prevail. From the *maiestas* at 258 the finale runs down in a steady diminuendo until the reader, after a glimpse of a picturesque detail in the life of the *vicus Tuscus*, is quickly dismissed with a parting smile.

IX

ODES, BOOK IV

I. ODE VI

THE singular honour which the Roman authorities conferred upon Horace by choosing him as the poet of the *Carmen Saeculare* and, moreover, the insight into the nature of his odes which they showed in asking him to write a hymn of an entirely unconventional, a Horatian, type—these were the main factors in resuscitating his lyric poetry. But with them there combined a happy incident to intensify the new impulse. Here we possess the best possible information, since the two odes iv. 6 and iv. 3 reflect the poet's frame of mind at the time of the rehearsals and the final performance of the *Carmen Saeculare* and during the period that immediately followed.

There is perhaps no better example than *Odes* iv. 6, *Dive, quem proles Niobaea*,[1] to illustrate the manner in which Horace had to approach the theme of a lyric poem, even when its essence sprang from a very personal experience. If a modern poet felt as exhilarated as Horace felt during the rehearsals of the *Carmen Saeculare*, he would be free to express his feelings directly. Horace, on the other hand, once he had determined to write lyrics proper, poems which could be classed with the songs of the *lyrici vates*, was no longer at liberty to start from any point he pleased, as he might have done if he had contented himself with *iambi*, hendecasyllables, or any of the minor genres of poetry. Within the more exacting genre which he had chosen he had to construct his poems according to one of the recognized prototypes to be found in the works of *Pindarus novemque lyrici*. A modern reader may be tempted to think that the first six stanzas of the ode iv. 6, fine though they are in themselves, have little to do with the concluding part in which the poet's individual experience is directly and forcefully expressed.[2] To Horace, however, it must have seemed unquestionable that he should start from the neutral ground of a traditional conception and then gradually work his way to his own personal concern.

---

[1] For the spelling *Niobaea* see Housman, *Journ. Phil.* xxxiii, 1914, 72.

[2] The extremity of the nineteenth-century reaction to this ode comes out alike in the endeavours of the χωρίζοντες (Peerlkamp obelized ll. 29–44, whereas Bücheler, *Rh. Mus.* xiv, 1859, 158 ff. [*Kl. Schriften*, i. 166 ff.] took these lines to be a second poem) and in Verrall's criticism (*Studies . . . in the Odes of Horace*, 76 ff.). These scholars, and others with them, all started from the same misunderstanding.

Like many Horatian odes, iv. 6 borrows its form from the religious songs of classical Greek poetry. It is in the main a solemn hymn and prayer to Apollo. In praising the god prominence is given to what he did for the Trojans by slaying Achilles and so postponing the capture of the city. For this topic Horace is indebted to Pindar's sixth paean, written for the θεοξένια at Delphi. There, 81 ff. (59 ff. Turyn), it is said of Apollo: Ἰλίῳ δὲ θῆκεν ἄφαρ ὀψιτέραν ἅλωσιν, κυανοπλόκοιο παῖδα ποντίας Θέτιος βιατάν, πιστὸν ἕρκος Ἀχαιῶν, θρασεῖ φόνῳ πεδάσαις.[1] Moreover there are signs of Pindar's influence in the whole structure of Horace's ode. The relative clause which, as is customary in hymns and prayers, amplifies the initial vocative, deals with some of the deeds of the god; it is not until l. 25 that the vocative *dive* is taken up by *doctor argutae fidicen Thaliae, Phoebe*. Such an insertion of extensive pieces of epic tales is familiar from many passages in Pindar, as also in other lyric poets. Another Pindaric feature in the structure of this ode is far less common and deserves special attention. From the middle of the eighth stanza (31 ff.) Horace is no longer addressing Apollo, but the choir of boys and girls who are to perform the *Carmen Saeculare*. The apparent harshness of this transition, which has been used as an argument for assuming that ode iv. 6 is not one poem but two,[2] can now be properly understood. An abrupt transition of a similar kind was used by Pindar in the very poem which suggested to Horace one of the main topics of this ode. Pindar's sixth paean begins with an address to Pytho, but at l. 121 (90 Turyn) the poet turns to the young men of whom the chorus consists: ἰὴ ἰῆτε νῦν, μέτρα παιηόνων ἰῆτε, νέοι.[3] This Pindaric motif, if it did not actually inspire the transition from the invocation of the god to the appeal to *virginum primae puerique claris patribus orti*, at any rate provided an illustrious precedent and may have encouraged the Roman poet to do what he did.

We have seen that for Horace, within the genre of poetry he had chosen, it would have been impossible to begin at once with the matter which was his immediate concern. This does not mean, however, that the hymn to Apollo which occupies the greater part of the ode was to

[1] Attention was drawn to this Pindaric trait in *Odes* iv. 6 by R. Heinze in the 5th edition (1908) of Kiessling's commentary, immediately after the publication in 1908 of the fragment of the paean, *Pap. Oxy.* v. 40 ff.

[2] Bücheler, loc. cit.: 'wie ist es möglich, daß der Dichter, welcher den ganzen Hymnus hindurch, wo er des Gottes Erwähnung tut (V. 1 *Diue* ... V. 28 *leuis Agyieu*), ihn selbst anredet, unmittelbar nach dieser letzten Anrede fortfährt: *Spiritum Phoebus mihi* ... *nomenque dedit poetae* und ohne weiteres sich an die Mädchen und Knaben wendet?'

[3] This is the end of the second triad. At the beginning of the next triad we find an even greater harshness: all of a sudden Aegina is being addressed. For a possible explanation see Wilamowitz, *Pindaros*, 134 f. ('eine sinnreiche Vermutung' according to O. Schroeder, *Pindars Pythien*, 1922, 68). What Farnell, *The Works of Pindar*, ii. 408, puts in its place, viz. the assumption 'that it is an apologetic postscript', etc., does not seem to fit in with the conditions of the production of a paean.

Horace merely a requirement of literary convention. The true artist
reveals himself by being able to make a virtue of necessity. In Horace's
hymn the majesty of the avenging god is presented with great force,
and the tale of Achilles and Troy, compressed into a few stanzas,
maintains the dignity of the theme.

Up to the end of the fifth stanza the ode moves entirely within the
sphere of Greek mythology. Then there comes one of those gentle
transitions in which Horace excels. While still working out the story
of the capture of Ilion, he inserts one detail which carries us from Troy
to Italy and the beginnings of Roman history: *ni . . . pater adnuisset
rebus Aeneae potiore ductos alite muros.*[1] This movement in space and time
prepares our minds for a change in the approach to Apollo. When the
vocative of the first line is taken up at l. 25, the god is no longer invoked as the slayer of the Niobids, Tityus, and Achilles, but as *doctor
argutae fidicen Thaliae*, κιθαρῳδός[2] and χοροδιδάσκαλος. It is the poet's
divine patron to whom Horace is now praying. But still he withholds
any explicit mention of himself. Using what appears to be a general
expression he asks the god *Dauniae defende decus Camenae.* This disguise,
however, is transparent. Even if Horace had not already brought his
native land, the kingdom of Daunus, into close connexion with his own
lyrics,[3] the meaning of the phrase *Dauniae decus Camenae* would be
obvious. After this preparation the poet at last steps forward in his own
person: *spiritum Phoebus mihi, Phoebus artem carminis nomenque dedit poetae.*
The form of this sentence indicates the exalted mood in which he is
speaking. Horace is not given to using anaphora idly; where he does
use it, it conveys a strong emphasis and is, as a rule, reserved for
thoughts of special dignity. It is worth noticing that we find in two other
odes the same stylistic pattern emphasizing the same idea that Horace
as a poet enjoys divine patronage for himself and his work: 1. 17. 13 f.
di me tuentur, dis pietas mea et musa cordi est, and 3. 4. 21 f. *vester, Camenae,
vester in arduos tollor Sabinos.* In the present passage, *spiritum Phoebus mihi*,
etc., we should be careful not to deprive *spiritum* of its full value. This
word has been degraded in the course of its long history, but here it
still contains the notion of πνεῦμα θεοῦ[4] and so conveys the idea that the
poet's work is brought about by divine inspiration.

Thus the circle narrows steadily: from a theme on the periphery,

---

[1] This transition from the Greek to the Roman sphere is very much like the transition
at *Odes* 3. 30. 7; see p. 302 above. For the significance of the mention of Aeneas see
p. 375 above.

[2] It will be remembered that one of the two performances of the *Carmen Saeculare* took
place in front of the temple of Apollo Palatinus. The cult-statue of that temple was the
Apollo κιθαρῳδός (Propertius ii. 31) of Scopas (Pliny, *Nat. hist.* 36. 25).

[3] *Odes* 3. 30. 11 f.

[4] See R. Reitzenstein, *Die hellenistischen Mysterienreligionen*, 3rd ed. 321.

Apollo the wrathful god of the old stories, we move to Apollo the master of the lyre and leader of the Muses, and then from the Greek Muses to the *Daunia Camena* and Horace's inspired poetry. One further step, an easy one, takes us to the centre of the circle. In the circumstances that gave rise to this ode it would have been unnatural for Horace to speak of his poetry merely in general terms and not to touch on the great task in hand, the *Carmen Saeculare*, for the performance of which the preparations were now well advanced. So when at this point, after bringing his own person and work into the poem, he goes on to address the young singers of the festival hymn (31 ff.), there is nothing artificial or violent in this fresh turn. When Pindar in his paean (6. 121 f.) suddenly turned to the νέοι of his chorus, there was no need for him to prepare the audience for it: they, at the celebration at Delphi, saw the young men in front of them. Horace, on the other hand, writing for an audience to whom he might recite the poem and for the readers of his book, is at pains to lead them step by step towards the central point, and only when their thoughts are close to it does he venture the uncommon apostrophe *virginum primae puerique claris patribus orti*.

The next stanza, still addressed to the maidens and boys, contains something which strongly appeals to the modern reader's imagination: *Lesbium servate pedem meique pollicis ictum*. It is tempting to wring from these words a reference to a picturesque detail of actual life by assuming that *mei pollicis* means 'the thumb of the poet beating time in his capacity as χοροδιδάσκαλος'.[1] We may be much attracted by this picture of the short and plump figure of Horace in such unfamiliar surroundings, his sunburnt face beaming encouragingly at the young singers who, excited and awed by the presence of the famous poet, are waiting for the moment when he will raise, not indeed his baton, but, almost as good, his fat thumb.[2] Unfortunately this picture is but a fantasy. To say nothing of the idea that in Greece or Rome there existed a 'conductor' who, by the movements of his hands, guided the singing of the choir,[3] it is altogether unlikely that Horace, a

---

[1] So Wickham, ad loc., with Verrall, *Studies in the Odes of Horace*, 76, and many others.

[2] 'Senza dubbio si deve trattare di un battere che si vede e si segue con lo sguardo, non altrimenti che la bacchetta di un direttore di orchestra' (Tescari, ad loc.).

[3] From the passages quoted by Reisch, *RE* iii. 2382. 28 ff., it must be inferred that the κορυφαῖοι or ἡγεμόνες, whom Dio Chrysostom, 56. 4, calls τοὺς σημαίνοντας τοῖς ᾄδουσι καὶ μέλος ἐνδιδόντας, did the σημαίνειν or ἐνδιδόναι (cf. ἐνδόσιμον) not with their hands, but with their voices: the ἡγεμών started singing, then the others joined in (cf. Arist. *Probl.* 19. 22. 919ᵃ 37). It seems that sometimes a short prelude was played by the instrument or instruments and that then the singers joined in. This instrumental prelude, too, could be called ἐνδόσιμον (Hesychius, ἐνδόσιμον· τὸ πρὸ τῆς ᾠδῆς κιθάρισμα, Suidas [s.v. ἐνδόσιμον] ὁ δὲ ψαλμὸς οἷος ἐνδόσιμος εἶναι τῇ ᾠδῇ); see, for example, Schol. Pind. *Pyth.* 1. 4 a προκατάρχονται γὰρ αἱ ᾠδαὶ παρὰ τῆς κιθάρας, εἶθ' οὕτως ἕπεται ὁ τῶν χορευτῶν ῥυθμός; *Ol.* 2. 1 a πρότερον γὰρ ἐνδίδωσι τὸ μέλος ὁ κιθαριστής, ἔπειτα ἡ ᾠδὴ λέγεται; 1 c πρῶτον γὰρ ἔκρουον, εἶτα ἐπῇδον. For the ambiguity of προοίμια at the beginning of *Pyth.* 1 see

non-musician, should have undertaken the arduous task of rehearsing and conducting the performance of a choir of amateurs,[1] and only an absolutely unambiguous piece of evidence could induce us to believe that such a thing did happen in the year 17 B.C. The phrase *mei pollicis ictum* is certainly not sufficient for us to build upon it so bold an assumption. Scholars have compared Quintilian, *Inst.* 9. 4. 51 *ubi tempora etiam manu mota metiuntur et pedum et digitorum ictu*, but there the reference is to someone singing or reciting verses, who beats time with his fingers or his foot to assist himself in keeping the rhythm. Such gestures, inevitably not very conspicuous, would be of little use to a choir. The natural way of taking *mei pollicis ictum* is indicated by the scholiast: *modulationem lyrici carminis, veluti ipse lyram percutiat.*[2] A scrutiny of all the passages in which Horace uses the words *cithara, barbitos, lyra* puts it beyond doubt that wherever he speaks of himself as playing an instrument he means nothing more than that he is composing lyric poetry; 'the picture of Horace playing the lyre must be regarded as a fiction'.[3] The detail which we find here, the plucking of the strings with the thumb (of the left hand),[4] forms part of the same metaphor. With *pollicis ictum* Ovid's line[5] *reddidit icta suos pollice chorda sonos* has been rightly compared. What Horace is asking the young singers to do is to keep the rhythm of his hymn as he has fixed it.

The conclusion at which we have arrived is relevant also to the general character of Horace's lyrics. We have seen[6] that a Horatian ode has no place in the sphere of any actual events, such as for instance the celebration of a religious ceremony, but serves rather as an ideal screen on to which certain ideas and emotions arising out of, or connected with, some actual events may be projected. It follows that if we want to do justice to this kind of poetry, we should not fall in with

Schroeder's German commentary on l. 4. For ἐνδόσιμον cf. Cope and Sandys on Arist. *Rhet.* 3. 14. 1. 1414^b 24 (iii. 163).

[1] Cf. the last sentence of Heinze's introduction (in the 7th edition of his commentary) to *Odes* iv. 6.

[2] This interpretation was followed by Dacier and many other commentators, including Heinze. G. L. Hendrickson, *Class. Philol.* xlviii, 1953, 73 ff., still takes it for granted that Horace functioned 'as director of the chorus of boys and girls'; the poet 'by the use of "*mei* pollicis" implies that he would himself be director of the public performance' (p. 79).

[3] So R. Heinze, *Neue Jahrb.* li, 1923, 166 f. (reprinted in *Vom Geist des Römertums*, 1938, 208 f.); cf. also T. Birt, *Horaz' Lieder, Studien zur Kritik und Auslegung*, [1926] 157 f. (he is, however, wrong in his interpretation, 158 ff., of *Odes* 4. 6. 35 f.). On the other hand, E. Bickel, *Geschichte der röm. Literatur*, 1937, 561 f., without paying attention to Heinze's arguments, takes *Romanae fidicen lyrae* and the like literally and concludes that Horace's odes were 'von vornherein zum Singen bestimmt'. Wilamowitz's brief observation, *Textgesch. der griech. Bukoliker*, 140, 'er [Horace] sang seine Verse nicht, er rezitierte sie', hits the mark.

[4] Cf. Ps.-Asconius on Cic. *Verr.* ii. 1. 53 (237. 3 Stangl).

[5] *Fasti* 2. 108.

[6] Cf. p. 381 above.

the modern tendency to use a piece of poetry to obtain an almost photographic picture of what happened on such and such a day at such and such a place. Instead of trying by violent means to push a whole poem into the external world, from which some of its elements are derived, we ought to respect its ideal character. In the case before us commentators ought not to transplant the ode *Dive quem proles* into some Roman hall or courtyard or temple in which something arbitrarily spun out of the poem might be enacted,[1] but they ought to read the hymn as a Horatian hymn. Then they will have no difficulty in perceiving how the prayer to Apollo moves from a remote starting-point gradually to the poet's immediate concern, until the Homeric god has become the patron of Horace's own poetry so that finally the address to the choir of maidens and boys springs forth with apparent spontaneity.

If we have to reject the interpretation which regards the ode iv. 6 as a faithful description of what Horace was doing and saying when, according to the wide-spread assumption, he was acting as χορο-διδάσκαλος, it does not follow that there does not exist a very close connexion between this ode and the rehearsals of the *Carmen Saeculare*. Although Horace did not in person rehearse the festival hymn or conduct the choir, he was bound to take a keen interest in the preparations and could not escape being drawn into the general excitement. We may be sure that he attended more than one rehearsal and also that this experience must have meant a great deal to him. Many years before he had in a flight of bold imagination professed to sing his noble poetry *virginibus puerisque*; now they were facing him, the sons and daughters of Rome's greatest families, good-looking, well-mannered, and eager to do their best. Horace was always susceptible to the charm of healthy youth; how much must he have enjoyed conversing with those fine young people at a time when he found it often very hard to accept the melancholy fact that he was growing old![2] He was there not as a mere onlooker; his was the work they were performing with enthusiastic zeal. Lovely voices they had and a musical ear; but when it came to keeping time, they would every now and then falter as happens to choirs of amateurs all over the world. Remembering such unfortunate

---

[1] 'Der Chor der Mädchen und Knaben . . . ist versammelt; der Dichter und Chormeister Horaz tritt vor seine Schar, um sie die Weise zu lehren, und weiht die gemeinsame Arbeit durch ein Gebet an Apoll und eine feierliche Mahnung an die jugendlichen Sänger', etc. These sentences in Heinze's introduction to the ode (7th edition) were taken over from his sixth edition; he would probably have changed them if he had lived to see the later part of his book through the press, for they are contradicted by the end of his introduction in its last form, where he expressly denies that Horace functioned as χορο-διδάσκαλος. I nevertheless quote the passage because it gives precisely the picture of 'the situation' which is fancied by many modern readers.

[2] See pp. 414 ff. below.

little accidents the poet says imploringly *Lesbium servate pedem meique pollicis ictum.*

We have no means of finding out in what manner Horace communicated this ode to the young singers. But it is not an improbable guess that he either had the text of it sent to them or, perhaps, recited it himself during an interval at one of the rehearsals. In one way or another they will, before the final performance of the *Carmen Saeculare*, have become acquainted with this ode, which was obviously designed to please and encourage them.

If Horace expects the greatest attention from his young singers, he can also assure them that their efforts will not be without their reward. In the last stanza he turns from the ensemble of the double choir to one of the girls, who here may represent all of them:

> nupta iam dices 'ego dis amicum,
> saeculo festas referente luces,
> reddidi carmen docilis modorum
>   vatis Horati'.

This is a graceful and chivalrous gesture; it would not be quite the same if he addressed the boys instead. Horace may also know that the young women are likely to form a more reliable link with posterity than their male companions. The poet is thinking ahead, 'quand vous serez bien vieille'. In years to come some of the girls will tell their children, and, perhaps, their grandchildren, all about the great festival of which their young listeners have heard so much and a repetition of which few, if any, of them will have a chance of seeing themselves. The *matrona*, as she then will be, may also indulge in a harmless piece of boasting: 'and, you know, that choir of the girls consisted entirely of picked singers, twenty-seven in all, and I—well I was one of them. And the hymn we had to sing was specially written for the occasion by the poet Horace.' The name is an essential element of her proud memories, and the poet might say 'il nome mio, che di necessità qui si registra'. His name has in this context a more than private dignity: *carmen composuit Q. Horatius Flaccus* was the result of a carefully considered decision of the highest authorities. So it came to pass that once, and once only, Horace allowed his name to appear in one of his odes. The severe standards of these lyrics excluded the possibility of the poet's name being mentioned in a casual way as was suitable for minor genres such as Catullus' *choliambs* and hendecasyllables or Horace's own *iambi*; elegy, too, owing to its history and character, was in this respect completely free. When Horace here for once waived his self-imposed restriction, he did not lay himself open to the charge of vanity, for in the anticipated situation of the last stanza it is not from his own lips that his name comes. Nor should we forget that this ode, for all its flexibility, remains to the end a hymn to Apollo. *Spiritum Phoebus mihi, Phoebus artem carminis nomenque dedit poetae*; in this context the *vates Horatius* is to be regarded as the god's mouthpiece.

One further observation must be made on this apparently small detail. It is probably no accident that Horace's name was in his lyrics heard only at the end of an ode intimately connected with the performance of the *Carmen Saeculare*. Not until he had been recognized as Rome's *vates* and placed on an equal footing with the Greek lyric poets did he venture, though under a subtle disguise, to renew the ancient custom of concluding a song with the poet's σφραγίς.[1]

2. ODE III

The other ode to which the production of the *Carmen Saeculare* gave rise, iv. 3, is in a lighter vein than the Pindarizing hymn to Apollo. This time the beginning,

> Quem tu, Melpomene, semel
> nascentem placido lumine videris,

echoes a passage from the first poem in Callimachus' Αἴτια,[2]

> Μοῦσαι γὰρ ὅσους ἴδον ὄθματι παῖδας
> μὴ λοξῷ, πολιοὺς οὐκ ἀπέθεντο φίλους,[3]

where the Alexandrian poet in his turn is indebted to Hesiod.[4] In Horace's adaptation the place of 'the Muses' is taken by Melpomene alone because in the epilogue of the first collection of his odes (3. 30. 16) he had made her the divine patroness of his new lyrics.[5]

The invocation of the Muse culminates in the thanksgiving for the favours she has bestowed on the poet (21-24). This climax is reached through a gradual ascent. In the manner which is derived from early Greek poetry—it is well known also from the first ode in Horace's first book—the different ambitions of men are passed in review so as to form a foil to the goal that is placed at the end, the poet's own ideal. First comes the victory in one of the great Panhellenic games, then, introduced by *res bellica*, the triumph of the conqueror, where the name

---

[1] The playful transformation of Hellenistic σφραγῖδες in the epilogue of the book of *Epistles* (cf. pp. 362 f. above) is no precedent to *vatis Horati*; it belongs to a different genre.

[2] *Fr.* 1. 37 f. Pf., cf. *Epigr.* 21. 5 f.

[3] This couplet was in the *Αἴτια* separated by only a few lines from the passage which suggested the beginning of the last ode in Horace's fourth book, cf. p. 449 below.

[4] *Theog.* 81 ff. Both Hesiod and Callimachus are adduced in Dacier's commentary.

[5] This reference to iii. 30 is similar to his calling his Muse *Daunia* in 4. 6. 27 (cf. 3. 30. 11).

of the Capitol at the beginning of the third stanza strikes a powerful
Roman note after the Hellenizing ideas and expressions of the beginning.
Now we are on the soil of Latium and are thus prepared for the scenery
of Tibur pictured in the next line. The device by which Horace here
paves the way for his use of the pronoun of the first person (15 *me*) is
very similar to that which he employs for the same purpose in iv. 6.[1]
When in ll. 10 ff. he speaks of someone whom the waterfalls and groves
of Tivoli inspire to write Aeolic lyrics, the form of the sentence still
continues to suggest a type of man, but in fact one man only can be
meant, Horace:

> sed quae Tibur aquae fertile praefluunt
> et spissae nemorum comae[2]
> fingent Aeolio carmine nobilem.

Aeolium carmen comprises the whole of Horace's lyrics, but when he was
writing this ode, it was one such *carmen*, the great secular hymn, that
was uppermost in his mind; the recollection of it brings back the
performance itself and all it meant to the poet. So his pride and delight
burst forth:

> Romae principis urbium
> dignatur suboles inter amabilis
> vatum ponere me choros,
> et iam dente minus mordeor invido.

The *iuventus Romana*, represented by the section that had to sing the
hymn on the great festival, *docilis modorum vatis Horati*, are proud of
their poet, who, they say, is to them what in past ages Simonides and
Pindar were to their choirs. By their loving admiration they place him
among the ranks of the bards who were and are men's delight. Horace
had once expressed to Maecenas his bold hope *quodsi me lyricis vatibus
inseres, sublimi feriam sidera vertice*. That hope had been fulfilled, and the
favourable judgement of Maecenas was shared by Augustus and other
eminent men. But was that a reason for Horace not to prize the spontaneous enthusiasm of Rome's youth and express his gratification as
strongly as he felt it?[3]

---

[1] See p. 402 above.

[2] Cf. i. 1. 30. For the parallelisms of thought and expression between the two odes see
Wickham's introduction to iv. 3.

[3] See, however, Bücheler, *Kl. Schriften*, ii. 324, 'me non perspicere fateor cur ad natorum
potius quam ad parentum iudicium Horatius provocarit, tamquam pueris romanis
placere maius et honorificentius fuerit quam Censorino et Maecenati et Augusto'. Of
Bücheler's conjecture at 15 *vatem* (it does not matter that another scholar had made it
before) Wilamowitz said in 1913 (*Sappho u. Simonides*, 319 n. 2) 'Büchelers Emendation
vatem verschmähen heisst eingestehen, dass man das Gedicht nicht versteht'; and in 1917
Heinze put *vatem* into his text and retained it in his last edition. Bücheler's whole argumentation seems to me wrong. His paraphrase of the passage as he reads it is 'pueri ac
puellae suis choris me interponunt sacrorum artisque divinae magistrum qui carmina

At the beginning of the last stanza but one (17) the invocation of the Muse is taken up with fresh intensity: *o testudinis aureae*....¹ The two concluding stanzas, which form a single deftly balanced period, move in a steady crescendo up to the end of the ode. In the first half of this conclusion, beginning with a 'relative predication' after the fashion of κλητικοὶ ὕμνοι, the ἀρεταί of the goddess are praised in a general way; in the second half the poet thanks her for what she has done for himself:

> quod monstror digito praetereuntium
> Romanae fidicen lyrae;
> quod spiro et placeo, si placeo, tuumst.

Horace is always perfectly sincere with himself as with others; he does not mind voicing the pleasure, a healthy man's unsophisticated pleasure, which his newly won fame gives him. Of shyness his nature knows nothing. The wide difference in the constitution and temperament of the two friends Virgil and Horace is well illustrated by the fact that the one *si quando Romae, quo rarissime commeabat, viseretur in publico, sectantis demonstrantisque se subterfugeret in proximum tectum*, and the other rejoiced *quod monstror digito praetereuntium*. Fame has not come to him through some lucky chance; he has earned it by sustained efforts and his devotion to a high ideal. At an early stage of his work on the new lyrics he had besought the Greek *barbitos* to become the instrument of a Latin song (1. 32. 3 f. *age dic Latinum, barbite, carmen*); now when the inhabitants of the *princeps urbium* show him to one another, they know that he is *Romanae fidicen lyrae*, a κιθαρῳδός, but a κιθαρῳδός of the Roman lyre, something not to be dreamt of until Horace had written his odes. His pride is untainted by arrogance: despite all the applause he has not forgotten how precarious the readers' approval is; so the

---

praeeam, modos doceam, adspirem canentibus. choros cogita qualis carmen saeculare cantavit, qualem exerceri a poeta videmus in IV 6.' This is based on the erroneous assumption that Horace functioned as χοροδιδάσκαλος and that a reference to this is contained in iv. 6 (see p. 404 above). Moreover, Bücheler destroys the connexion between *inter . . . vatum ponere me choros* and 1. 1. 35 *quodsi me lyricis vatibus inseres*, although it has long been seen that the references to the proem of the first three books are essential to iv. 3 (see especially 3–12). Besides, if something like *Horatium inter choros puerorum ac puellarum ponere* was to be thought of at all, such an arrangement would be the business, not of the young singers, but of the *XViri sacris faciundis*. The attribute *amabiles* is very suitable for the famous lyric poets. The adjective occurs in Horace, apart from this passage, six times; two of the passages are concerned with poetry: in *Odes* 3. 4. 5 f. the poet's own θεία μανία is called *amabilis insania* and in *Epist.* 1. 3. 24 he says *amabile carmen*. The adverb *amabiliter* is in Horace found only in *Epist.* 2. 1. 148, where *libertas . . . lusit amabiliter* refers to the *versus Fescennini*. On one detail Bücheler is right: according to the general usage one might expect to hear of *vatum chorus* instead of *vatum chori*. Horace had probably a good reason for using the plural, but unfortunately we cannot make it out. Did he perhaps think of one choir of Greek poets and another of *Romani vates* (*Epist.* 2. 2. 94)?

¹ For the solemn ring of *o* in such invocations see p. 169 n. 2 above.

final *si placeo* is as sincere as the rest. Nor does he forget the true source of his poetry, the gift from heaven, πνεῦμα θεοῦ.[1]

3. ODE I

It has become clear why it was necessary to qualify the statement of Suetonius about the origin of the last book of Horace's *carmina*.[2] The two odes on the victories of Drusus and Tiberius cannot be regarded as the starting-point of this book, for it was obviously the production of the *Carmen Saeculare* and the circumstances connected with it which induced Horace to give up his resigned attitude and to return to the writing of poetry proper, lyrics. The first fruits of this change of mind, the odes iv. 6 and iv. 3, were produced more than two years before Drusus and Tiberius won their victories in the Alps. Once the flow of poetry had started again, it did not cease, though it was far less rapid than in Horace's younger days. Remembering the literary habits of the time we can hardly doubt that the poet, as soon as he could be sure of the strength of his renewed productivity, must have considered the plan of adding another book of odes to his former publication.

In the Augustan period a book composed of a number of poems was as a rule intended to be taken as an artistic unity. There are, however, considerable differences in degree. It seems to me that of the extant poetic works of that period no other book shows so refined an arrangement as the last book of Horace's odes. This will, I hope, become evident in the course of our survey. For the moment it may be best to concentrate on the opening poem, by which Horace means to attune our minds to what we are to find on the subsequent pages.

Like many odes of Horace, iv. 1 is couched in the traditional form of a prayer. But this time it is not, as in most cases, a prayer for the appearance of a deity, a κλητικὸς ὕμνος, but the reverse, a kind of ἀποπομπή.[3] This type of prayer is based on a widespread and very ancient belief. If a daemon or god is bent upon harming you—and in the early days, before the gods became humanized, that seems to have been their favourite occupation—it will do you little good if you just

---

[1] The parallelism between 4. 6. 29 f. *spiritum Phoebus mihi . . . dedit* and 4. 3. 24 *quod spiro . . . tuum est* is unmistakable.

[2] See p. 364 above.

[3] Cf. Lucian, *Philops.* 9, τῶν . . . πυρετῶν τὰς ἀποπομπὰς καὶ τῶν ἑρπετῶν τὰς καταθέλξεις. The prayers by which it is hoped to get rid of a god or daemon are of course entirely different from the ἀποπεμπτικοὶ ὕμνοι described by Menander, *Rhet. Graec.* iii. 336 Spengel, viz. farewell prayers addressed to benevolent deities (cf. Wilamowitz, *Pindaros*, 330). For the type of ἀποπομπή with which we are here concerned see in general O. Weinreich, 'Gebet und Wunder', *Tübinger Beiträge zur Altertumswissenschaft*, Heft 5, 1929, 175 ff., and, on some special points, my commentary on A. *Ag.* 1573.

cry out 'spare me' (φείδου, *parce*).[1] You have to do that as a matter of form, but if you are wise you will add some more effective bait. If you are able to point to a really attractive substitute, then, perhaps, you may succeed in diverting the god from his original object, from you and yours. An obvious candidate for such a substitute is an enemy, either your country's[2] or a personal one; but if you do not want to be so specific, you may be content with asking the daemon to prey on 'others'. Of the latter variety we possess a classic example in a rhyme still to be heard in Austria and southern Germany.[3] There the saint whose special concern is arson is invoked thus:

> O heiliger Sankt Florian,
> verschon dies Haus, zünd andre an!

The idea of turning the harmful one away from ourselves to 'others' (on condition of 'leaving this house') recurs, for instance, in the covenant which Clytemnestra is prepared to make with the daemon of the Pleisthenids,[4] ἰόντ' ἐκ τῶνδε δόμων ἄλλην γενεὰν τρίβειν θανάτοις αὐθέν-ταισιν, and in Catullus' prayer to Cybele,[5] *procul a mea tuos sit furor omnis, era, domo: alios age incitatos, alios age rabidos.*

In *Odes* iv. 1 the ἀποπομπή is worked out with great care in its positive part as well as in the opening negative part. Horace, whom Venus after a prolonged truce is now assailing once more, declares himself to be an unsuitable target for her attack: at his time of life, *circa lustra decem*, he is, or at any rate pretends to be, past amorous adventures. It is not, however, with unmixed satisfaction that he speaks of his being at last safe; the simple words *non sum qualis eram bonae sub regno Cinarae*, where the epithet *bonae* is full of feeling, breathe true regret.[6] Cinara, whom Horace mentions only in poems of his later period when she had long been dead,[7] is different from the many girls who swiftly pass through his songs; she seems to be more real than any of them. To recall her means recalling the bygone days of his youth.[8] Now age and experience have hardened him against any tender emotions (6 f.); he is no longer

---

[1] See E. Norden on Virg. *Aen.* 6. 63, and add, for example, Homer π 185, where Telemachus implores his father, whom he believes to be a god, φείδεο δ' ἡμέων; the prayer to Apollo in the inscription from Erythrai (fourth century B.C.), published by Wilamowitz, 'Nordionische Steine', *Abhdl. Preuß. Akad.* 1909, 41, ὦ ἄναξ Ἄπολλον, φείδεο κούρων, φείδεο . . .; Hor. *Odes* 2. 19. 7 f. and 4. 1. 2; Juvenal 6. 172 *parce precor, Paean.*

[2] A very common turn. Horace himself furnishes a pretty instance, *Odes* 1. 21 13 ff. (where the fulfilment is anticipated, but the form of the prayer can still be recognized); cf. also 3. 27. 21 ff. (p. 192 above).   [3] Cf. Weinreich, op. cit. 191 f.

[4] A. *Ag.* 1571 ff.   [5] 63. 92 f.

[6] 'Jadis, j'aurais dit: C'est Lisette. Hélas! hélas! j'ai cinquante ans' (Béranger).

[7] Heinze, in the first part of his note on *Odes* 4. 1. 3, has some good remarks on this point. The assumptions of Bücheler, *Rh. Mus.* lxi, 1906, 625 f. (*Kl. Schriften*, iii. 341), do not seem to me sufficiently well founded.

[8] See especially *Epist.* 1. 7. 25 ff.

fit for the ἔργα Ἀφροδίτης. So he endeavours to send the goddess away
(*abi*), but not merely to 'other people' or to an enemy; on the contrary,
it is a good friend of his whom he asks her to visit. At this point we have
reached the positive part of the argument in Horace's ἀποπεμπτικὸς
ὕμνος; it occupies the five central stanzas, half of the whole ode.

The young man whom the poet recommends to Venus as a prospective victim, Paullus Fabius Maximus, belongs to Rome's oldest and
highest nobility.[1] Moreover, he is wealthy and possessed of all the
qualities of body and mind which should make him attractive to
Venus (*centum puer artium*). From him the goddess may expect, not
some modest offering such as Horace could give her, but a marble
statue to be worshipped in the costly shrine which Maximus will erect
for her in the grounds of his villa at the most enchanting spot in the
vicinity of Rome, on that ridge of the Alban hills which overlooks the
Lago di Albano on the one side and the Lago di Nemi on the other.
There Venus will be surrounded by the gay company which Maximus
is in the habit of entertaining by day and night with rich feasts and
hilarious dancing to the tunes of a full orchestra. As far as Horace himself is concerned, he can but repeat what he has said at the beginning:
the time is past when love-making and drinking and revelling could
tempt him (29–32).

Persuasive though the entreaties of the ageing poet seem to be, they
are of no avail. Venus refuses to break off her attack, οὐ γάρ τ᾽ αἶψα
θεῶν τρέπεται νόος αἰὲν ἐόντων. When Horace's prayer is over, he finds
himself precisely where he was before:

> sed cur, heu, Ligurine, cur
>   manat rara meas lacrima per genas?
> cur facunda parum decoro
>   inter verba cadit lingua silentio?
>
> nocturnis ego somniis
>   iam captum teneo, iam volucrem sequor
> te per gramina Martii
>   campi, te per aquas, dure, volubilis.

So far we have confined ourselves to reading the ode as we should
read it if it had come down to us as an isolated poem. But that is not
the case. We find the ode placed at the beginning of a book the publication of which must have caused a considerable stir in the literary
circles of Rome; therefore the place which this poem occupies must be
taken into account if we want to understand its implications.[2] During

---

[1] See F. Münzer, *Römische Adelsparteien und Adelsfamilien*, 1920, 98 ff.

[2] The task of approaching a poem in two different ways is very much the same here as—
on a minor scale—in the case of the concluding ode of Book I (see p. 298 above).

many years Horace had written no lyrics and had said more than once that he would never write lyrics again. And here he was back with another book of odes. In these circumstances no reader could possibly miss the double meaning of the beginning

> Intermissa, Venus, diu
> rursus bella moves?

To say 'I am engaged in Love's warfare' was, according to a common literary convention, equivalent to saying 'I am writing erotic poems'.[1] Thus it is made clear from the outset that, in addition to what this ode means in itself, it is also to be taken as an introduction to the whole book. It is in fact an overture. Like the overture of many a classical opera it introduces the main themes of the subsequent work and merges them into an organic whole.[2] After what he has heard in this opening piece the reader is entitled to expect some love poems and in particular an ode on Horace's unsuccessful courting of Ligurinus. An integral part of this theme is the feeling of growing old and the resignation it entails; this motif, too, will recur in other odes of the book. But these themes, important in themselves, have in the introductory poem still another function: they surround as a kind of frame the eulogy of a Roman nobleman. By this arrangement Horace has made it clear that he proposes to treat, along with familiar subjects of lyric poetry, something novel, the praise of select contemporaries, not in occasional remarks, but as the predominant theme of entire poems. The significance of this new element is indicated by the conspicuous place assigned to the *laudes Maximi* in iv. 1. The portrait of Paullus Fabius Maximus is to be the first in a series of similar ones, and this gallery of portraits is the most distinctive element of the fourth book. Looking at the eulogy of Maximus from this point of view we shall be able to appreciate the importance of a strange detail.

Almost all the pleasant things which Horace says about his young friend and his way of life are well suited to win the favour of Venus. There is, however, one noticeable exception, *pro sollicitis non tacitus reis* (14). Certainly an activity worthy of a good Roman,[3] but οὐδὲν πρὸς τὴν Ἀφροδίτην. However, we have only to pause for a moment to

---

[1] The first stanza of *Odes* iii. 26 is quoted as a particularly clear instance; notice especially *defunctum bello barbiton*.

[2] Unless the function of an overture in this sense is taken into account, full justice cannot be done to Tibullus i. 1 or to Hor. *Epist.* i. 1. In Propertius' elegy iv. 1 the first half (1–70) is intended to prepare us for the novelty of the Roman Αἴτια, whereas ll. 135 ff. make it clear that this book, like the former ones, will contain some erotic elegies, though few in proportion to the rest.

[3] Scipio Aemilianus says to Polybius (Polyb. 31. 23. 11) δοκῶ γὰρ εἶναι πᾶσιν ἡσύχιός τις καὶ νωθρός, ὡς ἀκούω, καὶ πολὺ κεχωρισμένος τῆς Ῥωμαϊκῆς αἱρέσεως καὶ πράξεως, ὅτι κρίσεις οὐχ αἱροῦμαι λέγειν.

realize why Horace found it necessary to insert here such a heterogeneous thought. If his chief purpose had been to confess in a prayer to
Venus his hopeless struggle against love and to enliven this prayer by
means of an ἀποπομπή, it would have been quite enough to heap upon
Maximus a quantity of ἐπαφρόδιτα such as would ingratiate him to the
goddess. But since the eulogy of Maximus was to be the first of a series
in which some of the most eminent contemporaries were to be praised,
the situation became different. It would not have been proper to make
one of Rome's most distinguished aristocrats, a young man on the
threshold of a brilliant career, appear as a very charming person, but,
in the main, a ladies' man. Somehow his real position in life and also
the Roman standard of values had to be taken into account. True, the
words *et pro sollicitis non tacitus reis* are not in keeping with their continuation *et centum puer artium late signa feret militiae tuae*, but some concession had to be made if the poet wanted to mingle the figures of
Homeric gods and goddesses with the ambitions and ideals of Roman
society at the time of Augustus.

4. ODES X AND XIII

The promise made implicitly in the last two stanzas of the first ode is
fulfilled in the Ligurinus poem (iv. 10). It has long been seen that not
only the general theme of this ode but some of its detail as well derives
from a group of Hellenistic epigrams in which either a παῖς καλός is
being warned that the time of his power will soon be over, or a young
man, a short while ago at the height of his beauty, is being scorned by
his former lover, to whom he has been so cruel. The undeniable fact
that Horace owes something to these topics has blinded some critics to
the true character of his ode.[1] The real theme of Horace's poem is not,
as at first may seem, disappointment in the pursuit of παιδικὸς ἔρως, but
something more simple and touching, regret for the bygone days of
youth. If the reader is sensitive to the tone of the concluding sentence,

'heu' . . .
'quae mens est hodie, cur eadem non puero fuit,
vel cur his animis incolumes non redeunt genae?',[2]

he will hear in it not only the anticipated complaint of Ligurinus but

---

[1] Mitscherlich, followed by, for example, W. E. Weber and T. Obbarius, saw in this
ode a mere *lusus poeticus* adhering closely to Greek models. Pasquali, *Or. lir.* 461, says
'Forse in nessun altro carme egli segue così servilmente i suoi modelli; in nessun carme si
comporta, oseremo dire, più passivamente rispetto all' ispirazione'; he then goes on to
speak of 'la mancanza di originalità' in this ode.

[2] It will be remembered that Horace, from the period of the epodes, was fond of concluding a poem with a direct speech.

also the voice of a man who cannot help looking back on the time when
he was young himself.[1] In this connexion we should also notice that in
the poem it is Horace who utters the words which he knows Ligurinus
will utter in years to come. This device suggests to the reader that what
is put in the mouth of Ligurinus comes in fact from an experience
through which the poet has gone himself. Ligurinus will say *quae mens
est hodie, cur eadem non puero fuit?*; it is probably more than a verbal coincidence that Horace, when speaking of his own *senectus*, which makes
him unfit to continue writing poetry, says *non eadem est aetas, non mens*.[2]

The ode iv. 13 may in some respects be regarded as a counterpart to
iv. 10. What links the two poems together is not so much the nature of
the Hellenistic motifs that underlie each of them as the particular turn
which Horace has given them. In epigrams, to leave aside other genres
of Greek poetry, the theme of the ageing courtesan was not uncommon.[3]
Its crudest elements were brought out, as was required by the χαρακτὴρ
Ἀρχιλόχειος, in two epodes of Horace (VIII and XII). In two odes (i.
25 and iii. 15) the same theme is handled in a different mood and style.
But none of these earlier poems, whether Hellenistic or Horatian,
matches the ode iv. 13 in intensity of feeling and expression, and none
contains, embedded in the treatment of a rather repulsive subject,
such gems of pure poetry. Here the requirements of this particular
literary τόπος are by no means neglected, and the end of the ode returns
to the taunt with which it began. But what gets hold of the reader's
mind and, I venture to suggest, induced Horace to take up once more
the old theme, is something quite different.

The fate of the person who is directly addressed serves in iv. 13 as
in so many Horatian odes as a mirror in which a wider picture can be
seen. The jubilant note of the beginning (*Audivere, Lyce, di mea vota, di
audivere, Lyce*) is not maintained: in the next sentence (2–6) the pathetic
element in the behaviour of the old *amoureuse* is predominant. And the
words of the fourth stanza make it all but impossible to refer them
exclusively, or even primarily, to Lyce, for what is described here is

---

[1] In Petrarch's epistle 'De brevitate vitae' (*Famil. Rer.* 24. 1) the theme is illustrated by
a series of quotations from Roman poets, headed by the Ligurinus ode. Goethe, who felt
strongly the privations imposed by the approach of old age and who only after bitter
struggles attained the wisdom of resignation, began at the age of 55 the short story 'Der
Mann von funfzig Jahren' (*circa lustra decem*), which he later inserted into *Wilhelm Meisters
Wanderjahre*. The 'man of fifty' applies to himself the words of Ligurinus (*heu! quae mens . . .
genae?*) but deepens their meaning: Goethe's free variation in rhymed verse ('Wie ist heut
mir doch zu Muthe') includes his own experience in recalling his troubled, and yet so
enviable, boyhood.

[2] *Epist.* 1. 1. 4. Cf. Cicero, *ad Att.* 9. 10. 3 (written when he was 57 years old) *alia res
nunc tota est, alia mens mea.*

[3] Cf., for example, *Anth. Pal.* 5. 204 (Meleager), and, for later adaptations of the old
type, 5. 21 (Rufinus), and 5. 273 (Agathias).

our common lot: no treasures can bring back *tempora quae semel notis condita fastis inclusit volucris dies*. Though the poet has his share in this common lot, up to this point nothing has been said that would oblige us to think of him in the first place. But when in the subsequent sentences the feeling is deepening and the language becomes impassioned—

> quo fugit venus, heu, quove color? decens
> quo motus? quid habes illius, illius
>   quae spirabat amores
>   quae me surpuerat mihi,

> felix post Cinaram . . .?—

then the scorn and its wretched victim are almost forgotten, and all that seems to matter is the regret for the lost land of youth, the poet's youth, and, if the reader happens to be old enough, his own youth as well. Horace, who at first seemed to rejoice in hurting Lyce, is now himself smarting under an old wound:

> sed Cinarae brevis
> annos fata dederunt.

If at the end he returns to ridiculing the old woman in a lighter vein, he does so to round off the poem and also, perhaps, to draw a veil over what he has let us see.

5. ODES XI AND XII

The mood of the ageing man, *circa lustra decem*, perceptible alike in the ode on Lyce and in that on Ligurinus, colours still more intensely *Odes* iv. 11 and makes it different from all other love poems of Horace. The themes of those two odes, the prophecy of what is in store for the boy who spurns his lover and the jeering at a decaying courtesan, offered less scope for the direct expression of the poet's present experience than the theme which iv. 11 has in common with many odes, invitation to a banquet.

The party at this banquet is to be very small; it looks as if there will be no one present except Horace and the young woman whom he is inviting to his house. And yet elaborate preparations are being made (1–12), for it is a great occasion, the birthday of Maecenas (14–20). This is the only mention of Maecenas in Book IV. It has been assumed that in the later period of Horace's life his friendship with Maecenas had been cooling. And yet the tone of this passage[1] and especially the

---

[1] It is characteristic of Horace's sincerity that he is content with saying *sanctiorque paene natali proprio* in contrast to the usual exaggerations (*quasi fieri ullo modo possit, quod in amatorio sermone dici solet, ut quisquam plus alterum diligat quam se*, as Cicero, *Tusc.* 3. 72, dryly remarks).

expression *Maecenas meus*, which Horace uses nowhere else, ought to be sufficient to disprove any such assumption. In this connexion we have also to pay attention to certain structural and stylistic devices which tend to emphasize the importance of the lines in which his friend's birthday is mentioned. To begin with, the name of Maecenas is placed in the fifth stanza of this ode composed of nine stanzas, in other words precisely in the centre. That Horace reserves this position for the most important thought, or one of the most important thoughts, of a poem is not without parallel.[1] Secondly, the topic 'birthday of Maecenas' is brought into full relief by the magnificent period stretching from 13 *ut tamen noris* to 20 *ordinat annos*, with its marked contrast to the long series of asyndetic parallel clauses in the preceding three stanzas, where, with the one exception of the short relative clause in 5 (*qua crinis religata fulges*), not a single subordination is found.[2]

Horace had often enough voiced the loyalty and gratitude he felt for Maecenas; so there was no need now to write a special poem in his praise. But since in the book which was to contain a number of eulogies of his friends and of certain eminent members of Rome's society he did not want to omit Maecenas altogether, he used the idea of an intimate celebration of his friend's birthday to say in a few affectionate lines what he felt for him. In this manner the ode to Phyllis, where Venus receives her full share, is also linked up with those poems of the book which are monuments of praiseworthy men.

After Maecenas, it is Phyllis' turn. She is a *psaltria*, but this time she is not being asked to entertain others, but to be Horace's guest in her own right. The poet does all he can to make his invitation attractive. It is as if he said in a quiet voice: 'My dear child, I am an old man, really no company for a pretty girl like yourself, though I do care a great deal for you. You need not pretend to be in love with me; I know all about your affair with Telephus and how it came to an end. What a pity! But you remember what happened to men and women in the old stories when they overreached themselves, and you know the saying of Pittacus, ὡς τὸ κηδεῦσαι καθ' ἑαυτὸν ἀριστεύει μακρῷ, καὶ μήτε τῶν πλούτῳ διαθρυπτομένων μήτε τῶν γέννᾳ μεγαλυνομένων ὄντα χερνήταν ἐραστεῦσαι γάμων.[3] But let us not moralize. You are a fine musician,

---

[1] See on i. 17, p. 206 above, and cf., for example, the position of the vocative *Vergili* in the tenth line of i. 24 (consisting of twenty lines).

[2] In the third stanza, *cuncta festinat manus*, etc., the asyndeta contribute to the impression of breathless bustle produced by the verbs (*festinat, cursitant, trepidant, rotantes*) and the phrase *huc et illuc*. In the first stanza, on the other hand, the threefold recurrence of the emphatic *est* at the beginning of each clause suggests the idea of plenty; the effect is similar to that in Alcaeus, *fr.* 54 D., 357 L. and P. πὰρ δὲ Χαλκίδικαι σπάθαι, πὰρ δὲ ζώματα πόλλα καὶ κυπάσσιδες.

[3] A. *Prom.* 890 ff. Cf. also Callimachus, *Epigr.* 1. Horace's *te digna* (*dignum* belongs to *decet*) is a perfect rendering of τὰ κατὰ σαυτόν.

and I think I know something about music myself. Here I have a new tune; I should very much like to hear you sing it with your lovely voice. Shall we try and practise it and, perhaps, forget our worries for a while?'

It is all gentleness and mellow resignation. When the poem is over, we still hear one deep note, *meorum finis amorum*—*non enim posthac alia calebo femina*. Horace could not have said more in so few words, nor could he have spoken with greater simplicity.

The ode iv. 11 is followed by another invitation to a banquet, addressed to a certain Vergilius of whom otherwise nothing is known.[1] This ode, *Iam veris comites*, is not distinguished by depth of feeling or novelty of detail, and yet it is one of Horace's truly felicitous poems. Several traditional topics merge into a graceful whole.[2] The tone throughout is one of easy playfulness. We should not make too much of line 26, *nigrorumque memor dum licet ignium*, for this thought was common in this context at least from Alcaeus on; the expression reminds us of 2. 3. 15 f. (in the same context) *dum res et aetas et sororum fila trium patiuntur atra*.

What gives this poem its special charm is the perfect choice of words, the swift change of pictures, and, above all, the lightness of its rhythm.

> Iam veris comites, quae mare temperant,
> impellunt animae lintea Thraciae,
> iam nec prata rigent . . ..

The lines seem to dance.

A considerable skill has been at work to produce this effect of effortless perfection. The impression of lightness is possibly increased by the neat separation of each stanza from the subsequent one.[3] The stanza in

---

[1] It has not escaped my notice that from time to time somebody attempts once more to show that the addressee of this ode is the author of the *Aeneid*. Even if we disregard for a moment the improbability of a much earlier poem being included in the fourth book—fancy Horace addressing the poet Virgil of all men as *iuvenum nobilium cliens* and ascribing to him *studium lucri*, and then publishing the poem after his friend's death! A minimum of common human feeling should save us from the sense of humour that turns Horace, the most tactful of poets, into a monster of callousness. C. Franke, *Fasti Horatiani*, 1839, 222 f., has in a few sentences said all that has to be said on this point.

[2] For the first two stanzas Kiessling has compared the epigrams of Leonidas and his imitators from the beginning of Book X of the *Anthologia Palatina*. Horace is indebted to them not only for his general pattern but also for certain points of detail; in his treatment of the story of the swallow (stanza 2) he is also influenced by old Greek lyrics. The chief motif of the second half of the ode, as Lambinus saw, recalls Catullus 13 *Cenabis bene, mi Fabulle, apud me*; there the position is the reverse: Fabullus was to bring his *cena* with him and his host will provide him with a precious *unguentum*. Behind both poems lies perhaps a traditional τόπος of sympotic poetry.

[3] There are few odes in Horace which, like iv. 12, exhibit a full stop at the end of each

the centre of the ode, the fourth, serves a purpose similar to that assigned
to the central stanza in the preceding ode: it contains the name of the
man whom Horace is honouring by addressing him here. Vergilius was
probably no very distinguished person; Horace does not even attempt
to extol him. But to be given a place in this book at all must have been
most gratifying to the man who, as far as can be guessed from his friend's
hints, seems to have been a very pleasant companion.

6. ODE VII

The odes iv. 11 and iv. 12 are instances of the manner in which
Horace sometimes places in the centre of a poem a thought whose
significance he wishes to accentuate. An analogous device is used in the
arrangement of the fourth book as a whole. But before turning to the
ode which occupies the middle of this book, iv. 8, it will be useful to say
something about iv. 7, since, among other things, it is meant to serve as
a preparation for iv. 8.

No reader of iv. 7, *Diffugere nives*, can fail to notice the close parallelism between this ode and i. 4, *Solvitur acris hiems*. The similarity is not
confined to the basic theme and the general pattern, but comes out in
several points of detail as well. It is, moreover, intensified by the
metrical form. There are in the *Odes* no more than four instances of
epodic structure, i. 4, i. 7, i. 28, and iv. 7. Now if out of these four odes
two, i. 4 and iv. 7, have a common theme, it is clear that the epodic
form of the later poem, in conjunction with its subject, is meant to recall the earlier poem. Horace used various devices to link up his new
book with the former collection of his odes and thus to stress the consistency of his lyric *œuvre*. His wish to achieve this end was probably the
stronger since some of the most conspicuous features of Book IV seem
to separate it from the earlier books rather than connect it with them.

Diffugere nives, the only ode which A. E. Housman was tempted to
translate, is certainly an accomplished poem, but we should not use its
perfection to slight its lovely forerunner, *Solvitur acris hiems*. Rather
should a comparison with the earlier ode help us to find out what
aspects are peculiar to the later poem. Both odes, like many songs in
many lands, begin with the thought 'winter is over, spring has come'.
But in the ode to Sestius this thought appears in its simplest form:
besides spring, only one season is mentioned, winter, which provides

stanza. Leaving on one side the special case of the ἀμοιβαῖον iii. 9, *Donec gratus eram tibi*,
and the three very short odes i. 30, i. 38 (of two stanzas each) and i. 23 (three stanzas), we
find this structure confined to three odes in one particular metre (*glyc.* + *asclep.* twice
repeated in each stanza), viz. i. 13, i. 19, and iii. 28. As for asclepiadic stanzas of the type
of iv. 12, this ode provides the only example of a full stop after each stanza.

some comforts indeed but only indoors (3), and, for the rest, hems in and locks up everything. Now it is gone; so let us enjoy the many pleasures of open-air life. This motif of the seasons is considerably widened in *Diffugere nives*. Here the contrast of winter and spring gives rise to a γνώμη (7 f.), *immortalia ne speres monet annus et almum quae rapit hora diem*, and with this idea in mind the seasons are viewed again, not only winter and spring, but all four of them. Now it is not, as before, their contrast that matters, but rather their ceaseless change (a thought delicately forecast in line 3, *mutat terra vices*) and the perishing of one when the next arrives and conquers it.

> damna tamen celeres reparant[1] caelestia lunae:
>   nos ubi decidimus[2]
> quo pater Aeneas, quo dives Tullus et Ancus,
>   pulvis et umbra sumus.

Thus, in an almost imperceptible movement, we have been gliding from the antithesis of winter and spring to the idea of the merciless mutability of all things in the world, and from that idea to the notion of the perishable nature of man. The thought seems to be darkening more and more until the cheerfulness of the beginning has all faded away. The last stanza but one, *cum semel occideris*, offers no consolation, and in the concluding stanza we are told that neither the protection of a goddess nor a hero's friendship could rescue those who had to go down to Hades in the prime of their youth.[3] Death, not Spring, seems now to be the poem's chief theme. Death, it is true, plays its part in the ode to Sestius as well, but how different is its function there! It appears most naturally as Spring's dark foil, and all it has to do in that gay poem is to urge Sestius to make the most of the happy season and of this short life of ours. It is perhaps only a slight exaggeration to say that in i. 4 the thought of death is in the background of the poem but in iv. 7 in its centre.

The difference in weight between the two odes will be most easily recognized if we consider for a moment the manner in which the analogous temporal clauses, 1. 4. 17 *quo simul mearis* and 4. 7. 21 *cum semel occideris*, are continued. In the former poem the principal clause runs *nec regna vini sortiere talis nec tenerum Lycidan mirabere*, in the latter *non, Torquate, genus, non te facundia, non te restituet pietas*. One could hardly find a more significant illustration of the wide difference between the

---

[1] 'They recover their losses', see D. Daube, 'On the use of the term *damnum*', *Studi in onore di Siro Solazzi*, Naples 1948, p. 40 of the offprint.

[2] I have no doubt that this is a deliberate variation of Catullus 5. 4 f. *soles occidere et redire possunt: nobis cum semel occidit brevis lux*, etc., and that Horace's line 21, *cum semel occideris*, is an echo of Catullus' *cum semel occidit*.

[3] The affectionate last two lines recall the end of iii. 4.

Grecian παίζειν with its elaborate regulations for the συμπόσιον and its devotion to παιδικὸς ἔρως on the one hand and on the other the full *gravitas* of the *res Romana* as embodied in the traditions of the nobility. The lighter mood is not completely absent from the later ode either, but here it appears only in a passing remark (19 f. *cuncta manus avidas fugient heredis, amico quae dederis animo*), which in its context sounds rather conventional; one does not believe that the poet's heart is in it. In the sentence in which Torquatus is addressed by name the sternness of the final judgement is magnificently emphasized by the threefold *non*,[1] which recalls to a modern ear the voices of the Furies in Gluck's Orpheus. At the same time this sentence has the effect that Torquatus receives his full share of that praise of distinguished men which is one of the main themes in this book. True, he is given no direct eulogy, but in the form of a negative statement ('once thou hast died, *non, Torquate, genus, non te facundia, non te restituet pietas*') threefold excellence is ascribed to him. Still, all this glory is transitory and will soon perish with the rest of earthly life.

In l. 15 the simple thought (*nos ubi decidimus*) 'quo plures abierunt' is expressed in a remarkable way: *quo pater Aeneas*, etc. A detail such as this shows once more how strong the influence of Virgil's poem was at that time.[2]

7. ODE VIII

I have said that iv. 7 serves as a preparation for iv. 8, and I have now to demonstrate it. iv. 8 culminates in the idea that it is through a poet's praise alone that anyone born of a mortal mother, whether his father be a man or a god, can be granted immortality. iv. 7 is dominated by the thought that death brings with it the complete annihilation of all we are and all we care for. In the poem itself no redeeming feature appears; its keynote is *pulvis et umbra sumus*. But when we pass on to the following ode we learn better: there exists in fact an escape from oblivion, though one escape only. Each of these poems is self-contained, but the latter is also meant to supplement the former. Given the existence of encomiastic poetry and its fixed conceptions, the connexion of the main theme of *Diffugere nives* with that of *Donarem pateras* would seem natural. The progress from the one theme to the other, implied by the order in which the two poems are placed in the centre of this book, is plainly and concisely expressed in an epinikion of Bacchylides,[3] βαθὺς μὲν αἰθὴρ ἀμίαντος· ὕδωρ δὲ πόντου οὐ σάπεται· εὐφροσύνα δ' ὁ

---

[1] In Catullus' description of the despondent Ariadne (64. 63–65) three lines begin with *non*.

[2] Cf. p. 375 above.   [3] 3. 85 ff.

χρυσός· ἀνδρὶ δ' οὐ θέμις, πολιὸν παρέντα γῆρας, θάλειαν αὖτις ἀγκομίσσαι
ἥβαν. ἀρετᾶς γε μὲν οὐ μινύθει βροτῶν ἅμα σώματι φέγγος, ἀλλὰ Μοῦσά
νιν τρέφει.

It has been well observed that, in contrast to the solemn tone of its
second half, *Donarem pateras* begins on a note of playfulness (1-12). This
may be partly due to the personal character of Censorinus and the
nature of his relations with Horace. But probably a more general factor
has also to be taken into account. The idea that a lyric poem could
secure lasting fame, though familiar to the classical age of Greece, had
no roots in the life of Roman poetry as known to Horace's contemporaries.[1] To make so high a claim was, in a sceptical world, extremely
hazardous; the poet who ventured to do so was apt to expose himself
to the scorn of his readers. Horace's cautious introduction ('songs are
but a substitute for what I would give if only I were rich') forestalls any
possible charge of presumption. Once more he shows himself a master
of εἰρωνεία in its original sense, προσποίησις ἐπὶ τὸ ἔλαττον.

The playful tone is maintained to the end of the first part, *carmina
possumus donare, et pretium dicere muneri*. No well-mannered person would
seriously insist upon the value of the present he is making to a friend.
But at this point the playfulness comes to an end, and after reaching
the goal of the whole prelude, the idea of *carmina* (11), the poet speaks
without restraint and without false modesty of the immortalizing
power of poetry.

Censorinus is clearly included in the number of those whom the
poet's songs are to rescue from oblivion, but what is said in this poem
applies in fact to the whole group of similar odes in Book IV. In the
magnificent second part of this ode Horace reveals the *raison d'être*
not so much of this particular poem as of the whole group to which it
belongs. That the principles laid down in *Donarem pateras* have a
bearing on the fourth book as such, or at all events on its most representative elements, the eulogies, can be seen from the metre of
this central poem. The commentators have observed that Horace did
not use the metre of iv. 8 except in i. 1 and iii. 30, that is to say in the
proem and the epilogue of the first collection of his odes, and they have
rightly concluded that the echo here is deliberate.[2] By alluding to his
former programmatic utterances Horace seems to imply that he still
believes in a long after-life for his poetry—*usque ego postera crescam laude
recens, dum Capitolium scandet cum tacita virgine pontifex*—, but also to

[1] What the elder Cato reported on certain *carmina . . . multis saeculis ante suam aetatem in
epulis . . . cantitata a singulis convivis de clarorum virorum laudibus* (Cic. *Brut.* 75, cf. *Tusc.* 1. 3
and 4. 3) was based on very dim information (we cannot say whether it was more than a
learned reconstruction suggested by Greek customs); by Horace's time such traditions
might engage the interest of some antiquarians, but were certainly not a living force.

[2] Cf. on iii. 30, p. 302 above.

point to the fact that what he now claims as his highest privilege is a conception not to be found in his earlier lyrics.

The idea that lyric poetry can immortalize men's achievements is completely absent from the first three books of the *Odes*. This is a remarkable fact. For Horace, at the period of his earlier *carmina*, was thoroughly familiar with the works of Simonides, Pindar, and Bacchylides, and could not fail to see what an important part that idea played there.[1] And yet he refrained from using it himself, at any rate so far as men's fame was concerned. He did, however, apply it, though only once, to a more modest subject. The last stanza of *Odes* iii. 13, *O fons Bandusiae*, runs:

> fies nobilium tu quoque fontium
> me dicente cavis impositam ilicem
> saxis, unde loquaces
> lymphae desiliunt tuae.

In the case of the lovely Bandusian spring Horace did not consider it presumptuous to prophesy that it would live for ever in his song and thus join the company of the 'honoured founts' praised by the old Greek poets, Castalia, Hippocrene, Pirene, and all the rest of them. But to make a similar prediction about a fellow-man—that he was not prepared to do, not yet. The reasons for this restraint are not difficult to understand. In Rome a man's claim to lasting fame was primarily based on what he had achieved in public life. By the time when Ennius wrote his *Annals* it was also admitted that epic poetry might be a means of keeping alive the memory of a great soldier or an eminent statesman. But serious Latin lyrics, lyrics of a dignity comparable to the dignity of the work of a Simonides or a Pindar, were unknown until Horace attempted to fill the gap with his *carmina*. His instinct warned him not to rush at once into a venture which was bound to upset the Roman conception of genuine *gloria*. Only when, several years after the publication of the three books of odes, he had been asked to undertake what once a Pindar might have undertaken, to write the hymn for the great national festival, and was thereby recognized as *Romanae fidicen lyrae*, only then did he feel entitled to follow those ancient poets in promising to his friends that through his songs they would gain immortality.

8. ODE IX

Unlike the Censorinus ode, which in a gentle climb works its way up to the summit, the next ode soars from the start into the ether and maintains its high level to the end.

---

[1] The idea is not, of course, confined to choric lyrics. Cf., for example, Sappho *fr.* 58 D., 55 L. and P., κατθάνοισα δὲ κείσῃ κτλ.

> Ne forte credas interitura quae
> longe sonantem natus ad Aufidum
> non ante volgatas per artis
> verba loquor socianda chordis . . ..

Horace had regained, and strengthened, the proud confidence that inspired the epilogue of his earlier lyrics, *Exegi monumentum aere perennius*.

The ode *Ne forte credas* is complete in itself, but it is also linked up with *Donarem pateras*. The fundamental theme of the Censorinus ode (*neque si chartae sileant quod bene feceris, mercedem tuleris*) is worked out and exemplified in the subsequent poem.

> vixere fortes ante Agamemnona
> multi: sed omnes inlacrimabiles
> urgentur ignotique longa
> nocte, carent quia vate sacro.

The progress in thought from iv. 8 to iv. 9 is similar to the transition which we observed within one and the same poem in iv. 6 and iv. 3, where it is only after speaking of poetry, or a poet, in apparently general terms that Horace proceeds to introduce his own person. Whereas in iv. 8 the theme is poetry (including epic) and poets in general,[1] iv. 9 begins with the poetry of one individual, Horace from Venusia. But important though his personal claim is, even more important in this ode is the dignity of the particular poetic genre which he has chosen for his work, lyrics. 'Homer admittedly holds the first place, but', so Horace argues, 'that does not mean that the works of the great lyric poets are dead and forgotten.' The great lyric poets—but Horace does not speak of them in such general terms: he makes them pass, one by one, in solemn procession, headed by the most illustrious of them, Pindar. Within the framework of this ode Horace had to confine himself to a selection. Seven lyric poets are named or alluded to (the island of Ceos representing both Simonides and Bacchylides), but only one, the last in the series, receives more than a brief word and is described in such a way and with such affection that the reader is given at least some idea of the true nature of her poetry:

> spirat adhuc amor
> vivuntque commissi calores
> Aeoliae fidibus puellae.

---

[1] It is, perhaps, significant that in iv. 8 the only poet specially mentioned is Ennius (20 *Calabrae Pierides*) and that immediately after there follows a theme from his *Annals* (22 ff. *quid foret Iliae . . . Romuli*). Epic poetry had the privilege, even in Rome, of immortalizing men. iv. 9 makes Horace's new claim explicit: not only epic poetry can be a lasting monument, but lyrics as well.

οἴη πέπνυται, τοὶ δὲ σκιαὶ ἀίσσουσιν. It is invaluable to have this direct testimony of the deep admiration which Horace felt for Sappho.

Once it has been convincingly shown that the most eminent lyric poets of the past are no less alive than Homer, it follows that a eulogy in lyrics can be as reliable a pledge of enduring fame as the glorification in epic to which Hector, Agamemnon, and many others owe all we know about them. Now the way is free for the poet who wants to assure his reader that he, Horace, also can bestow immortality:

> non ego te meis
> chartis inornatum silebo
> totve tuos patiar labores
>
> impune, Lolli, carpere lividas
> obliviones.

There was no need to say in so many words that the classical poets' privilege of immortalizing those men whom they praised belonged by right to Horace as well; at this stage of his career he could take it for granted that he himself was on an equal footing with the *lyrici vates* into whose circle he had been admitted.

Up to line 30 we may well have the impression that it is the reader to whom the poet is speaking. As it turns out, this is a delusion, but one that has been encouraged through more than seven stanzas. There can be no doubt that in this long programmatic section Horace wants to convince his readers that he is fully justified in undertaking something that had never been attempted before in Latin lyrics. He therefore takes advantage of an ambiguous 'thou', *ne forte credas*. Only when nearly two-thirds of the poem are over does it become clear that here, as in most Horatian odes, an individual person, Lollius, is being addressed. This man is known even to those modern readers who are no specialists in Roman prosopography. In that grim chapter near the beginning of Tacitus' *Annals* (i. 10) in which the shortcomings and disasters of the reign of Augustus are passed in review the *Lolliana clades* is conspicuous.[1] What induced Horace to dedicate an ode to Lollius we do not know.[2] However, he performed his delicate task with admirable tact and gathered ungrudgingly all that could possibly be said in favour of him.[3] If, nevertheless, the eulogy sounds somewhat laboured, this is

---

[1] The Tacitean defamers of Augustus exaggerate the seriousness of the affair: the situation on the Rhine frontier was soon under control (see p. 433 below).

[2] No hypotheses should be based on *Epist.* i. 2 and 18; see p. 315 above.

[3] Attention has often been drawn to the contrast between Horace's words ll. 37 f. *abstinens ducentis ad se cuncta pecuniae*, and the verdict of Velleius, 2. 97. 1, *M. Lollio, homine in omnia pecuniae quam recte faciendi cupidiore*. On this point see the balanced judgement of Groag, *RE* xiii. 1383 f., which is at any rate in keeping with what we know about Horace; for a different view see R. Syme, *The Roman Revolution*, 429.

clearly not the poet's fault. He did what he could, but the fact remained that to him *laudes Lollii* did not prove a congenial topic.[1] So he
allotted to it a decent minimum of space in an extensive poem. It may
be doubted whether Lollius was greatly pleased in reading the ode in
which it takes the poet so very long to come to his addressee. He may
have hoped that at least the concluding part of the poem would be
solely concerned with himself and his *virtutes*. But if he cherished any
such hope, disappointment awaited him. The last two stanzas are
entirely filled with general moral maxims, fine maxims indeed, but
not particularly relevant to Lollius. But whatever the reactions of
Lollius may have been, Horace's reader has good reason to be grateful
for the difficult position in which the poet found himself and which he
overcame by adorning a poor theme with his survey of the immortal
songs of the Greek poets. It is impossible to say whether Horace, as
soon as he decided to round off his ode to Lollius in such a way,
wanted it to follow, and to supplement, the ode *Donarem pateras*, or
whether this arrangement was the result of later consideration. At
all events, within the plan of the whole book *Ne forte credas* is no less
fundamental than *Donarem pateras*, to which *Diffugere nives* forms a
significant prelude. This central triad, firmly linked together, is kept
separate both from the poems which precede it and from those that
follow it.

9. ODES IV AND XIV

The ode (iv. 4) on the Alpine victories of Augustus' stepson Drusus,
taken as a whole, is a poem of great beauty, but it also shows a few
signs of being a *tour de force*. Its adaptations of certain Pindaric patterns,
though less formal than those in i. 12, *Quem virum aut heroa*, and less
profound than those in iii. 4, *Descende caelo*, are the most daring ones
in Horace.[2] It is the more remarkable that in this ἐπινίκιον he did not
attempt, as he had done in i. 12 and in the *Carmen Saeculare*, to reproduce in his own way the triadic arrangement characteristic of
Pindar's major odes. We cannot say whether Horace at any stage
contemplated for his ode on Drusus a quasi-triadic structure, but

---

[1] I cannot follow E. Courbaud, *Horace, sa vie et sa pensée à l'époque des épîtres*, 207 f., who
infers from this ode that Horace was a devoted friend of Lollius.

[2] Many commentators have been alive to the strong Pindaric strain in this ode. Scaliger
(see Lambinus on 18 *quibus mos unde deductus*) compared Pind. *Nem.* 5. 16 ff. for the manner
in which the poet at 21 f. declines to answer the question he had raised. Dacier remarked
'Il n'y en [of the odes] a peutestre point où il ait tant approché du tour et de la majesté
de Pindare'. Making allowance for the inevitable limitations of a seventeenth-century view
on Pindar, Dacier's observation must be considered very pertinent.

supposing he did, it is easy to see what induced him to give it up. It was above all the effect of grandeur which he wanted to produce in this poem, and in order to achieve this he constructed the exordium in a manner incompatible with a break at the end of the third and the sixth stanzas. *Monte decurrens velut amnis*, the beginning of the ode rolls along in a mighty period of full twenty-eight lines[1] until at last it comes to a stop with the momentous name of *Nerones*.[2] Within this period another device is used to intensify its majestic character: the first simile (1–12) is followed by a parallel one, *qualemve laetis caprea pascuis*, etc. Here we are not concerned with the question whether or not such a sequence is to the liking of modern critics; we have simply to state that the duplicating of similes in parallel sentences or clauses was employed by several Augustan poets as a means of stressing the importance of a passage by adding to its stylistic weight. So Horace himself concludes the ode iii. 20 with the neat comparison *qualis aut Nireus fuit aut aquosa raptus ab Ida*, and—a slightly remoter parallel—at 4. 11. 25 ff. he introduces two mythological παραδείγματα, *terret ambustus Phaethon avaras spes et exemplum grave praebet ales Pegasus*, etc. Virgil's Dido is haunted in her dreams by terrible visions,[3]

> Eumenidum veluti demens videt agmina Pentheus
> et solem geminum et duplicis se ostendere Thebas,
> aut Agamemnonius scaenis agitatus Orestes
> armatam facibus matrem et serpentibus atris
> cum fugit, ultricesque sedent in limine Dirae.

Still nearer to the double simile in the ode to Drusus is the passage in the *Georgics* (3. 89 ff.), where the description of the noble horse culminates in this bunch of mythological comparisons:

> talis Amyclaei domitus Pollucis habenis
> Cyllarus et, quorum Grai meminere poetae,
> Martis equi biiuges, et magni currus Achillei.
> talis et ipse iubam cervice effundit equina
> coniugis adventu pernix Saturnus, et altum
> Pelion hinnitu fugiens implevit acuto.

As to the special form of Horace's opening stanzas, *Qualem ministrum ... qualemve ... leonem ...*, it recalls the majestic beginning of Propertius' elegy i. 3, whose form may be traced as far back as the Hesiodic

---

[1] The triumphal ode i. 37, *Nunc est bibendum*, apart from the introductory stanza, consists of a single period of twenty-eight lines.

[2] A similar effect is produced by the beginning of the proem of the *Aeneid*, where a highly elaborate period reaches its end (7) in naming the τέλος of the whole tale, *altae moenia Romae* (echoed, and supplemented, in the conclusion of the proem, l. 33, *Romanam condere gentem*).

[3] *Aen.* 4. 469 ff.

Catalogues with their repeated ἤ οἴη ... ἤ οἴη ...,

> Qualis Thesea iacuit cedente carina
> languida desertis Cnosia litoribus,
> qualis et accubuit primo Cepheia somno
> libera iam duris cotibus Andromede,
> nec minus assiduis Edonis fessa choreis
> qualis in herboso concidit Apidano:
> · talis visa mihi . . ..

The ode *Qualem ministrum* is divided into two parts of nearly equal length,[1] of which the first (1–36) celebrates the recent victories of Drusus and the second (37–76) the victory won by his ancestor near the river Metaurus in 207 B.C. In an aristocratic society it is natural that a recent victory should recall the achievements of the conqueror's ancestors; consequently such a connexion of the present with the past plays a great part in Pindar's (and not only Pindar's) epinikia and gives rise to some fine pieces of narrative. Horace's artistic tact and his understanding of Roman traditions show themselves in his choice of an episode of Rome's most famous war.

In the first part of the ode there is one detail by which many lovers of Horace have been offended, the far-fetched parenthesis 18–22. It

---

[1] The symmetry of the two parts would be complete if Heinze were right, who in the last, 7th, edition (1930) of his commentary, p. 403, says 'zwei gesonderte Teile zu je neun Strophen werden durch eine gemeinsame Schlußstrophe zusammengehalten'. But this statement depends on Heinze's view of the last stanza of the ode. Recanting his former opinion, he asserted that Hannibal's speech ends with l. 72 and that the last four lines contain the poet's own comment. This has been the opinion of many readers, from the scholiasts to Klingner's edition. In defence of the opposite view Vahlen, *Opusc. acad.* ii. 518 ff., pointed out that the last stanza fits in exceedingly well with Hannibal's speech, but neither he nor R. Helm, *Philol.* xc, 1935, 356 ff., who followed his lead, nor, so far as I know, anyone else has mentioned what seems to me the decisive argument. The commentators talk as if mere considerations of content must determine who is the speaker of the last stanza, and as if in the form of the sentence there were nothing to decide the issue. This seems to me wrong. If a change of speaker took place after 72, how was the reader to realize it at a time when there existed no quotation marks and the like? Did the poet perhaps rely on the off-chance that some clever individual might hit on the right solution? In Horace essential things are made clear without any ambiguity. He—and for that matter any ancient poet who mastered his craft—was perfectly capable of marking the end of a speech unmistakably. In the only two instances where, after a speech of another person, the end of an ode contains an utterance of the poet himself, iii. 3 and iii. 5, there can be not the faintest doubt that the words of Juno come to an end at 3. 3. 68 and the words of Regulus at 3. 5. 40, since what follows (*non hoc iocosae conveniet lyrae* and *fertur* . . .) cannot possibly be taken as a continuation of the speeches. It is, on the other hand, fairly common for an epode or ode to conclude with the end of a speech; see Epodes V, XII, and XIII, and *Odes* i. 7, i. 15, iii. 11, and iii. 27 (the dialogues, Epode XVII, and *Odes* iii. 9, are left aside). It is to this larger group that iv. 4 belongs, as the transition from 72 to 73 shows. As regards the reading at 73, I am not sure that the majority of the editors is right in preferring the *perficiunt* of the Blandinius to *perficient* (for the need of caution in following the Blandinius see pp. 100 f. and p. 317 n. 5 above).

was obelized by Guyet,[1] but even at that time this crude treatment, which was to find many admirers in the nineteenth century, had really no longer a claim to be considered, for it had been refuted in advance by Scaliger,[2] who for the poet's attitude in this passage had pointed to an analogy in Pindar. Pindar's influence on the form of this parenthesis has meanwhile been generally recognized,[3] but important though this influence is, another factor should not be entirely neglected. Hellenistic, and consequently Roman, historians, when dealing with a campaign in a foreign country, were in the habit of introducing their narrative with a description of that country, its chief peculiarities, and the origin and customs of its inhabitants.[4] The material which they had to use for this purpose often contained traditions of a mythical or doubtful or highly controversial nature. In such a case they followed as a rule the principle formulated in Lucian, μῦθος εἴ τις παρεμπέσοι, λεκτέος μέν, οὐ μὴν πιστωτέος πάντως, ἀλλ᾽ ἐν μέσῳ θετέος τοῖς ὅπως ἂν ἐθέλωσιν εἰκάσουσι περὶ αὐτοῦ.[5] Thus we read in Sallust's *Bell. Iug.* 17. 2 at the beginning of the χωρογραφία of Africa *sed quae loca et nationes ob calorem aut asperitatem, item solitudines minus frequentata sunt, de iis haud facile compertum narraverim*; in Tacitus' description of Britain[6] *naturam Oceani atque aestus neque quaerere huius operis est* (cf. Horace's *quaerere distuli*) *ac multi rettulere* and *Britanniam qui mortales initio coluerint, indigenae an advecti, ut inter barbaros, parum compertum*, and at the end of the *Germania* (46. 6) *cetera iam fabulosa . . . quod ego ut incompertum in medio relinquam*. This particular feature, together with the whole system of such descriptions of countries and nations, seems to have found its way from historiography into the poetic glorifications of victorious campaigns. The nature of the subject made it all but inevitable that a

[1] Peerlkamp says of the parenthesis, *quibus mos . . . est omnia*, 'iam Lambinus non probabat'; Keller and Holder in the *editio maior* (cf. also O. Keller, *Epilegomena*, 309), and, among the most recent editors, Lenchantin de Gubernatis (1945) and A. Y. Campbell (1945) allege that Lambinus deleted the passage. But Lambinus (I am using his 2nd edition, Paris 1568) not only quotes Scaliger's comparison of the ἀπορία in Horace with a similar one in Pindar, but on 22 f. *sed diu*, etc., gives a wholly adequate explanation of the form of this parenthesis. In the text of the ode the brackets before *quibus* and after *omnia* are, as Lambinus explicitly says, 'interpositionis nota'; it is not his fault that they were mistaken for ὀβελοί. [2] See p. 426 n. 2 above.

[3] Macaulay seems to have reached the right solution quite independently. In the letter from Calcutta which I have already quoted (p. 276 n. 4 above) he writes: 'The most obscure passage—at least the strangest passage—in all Horace may be explained by supposing that he was misled by Pindar's example: I mean that odd parenthesis in the "Qualem ministrum": *quibus mos unde deductus per omne*—. This passage, taken by itself, always struck me as the harshest, queerest, and most preposterous digression in the world. But there are several things in Pindar very like it.'

[4] There is no need to quote the vast literature on the subject. The first chapter of E. Norden's book *Die germanische Urgeschichte in Tacitus Germania* gives a good idea of the problems involved.

[5] *Hist. Conscr.* 60. For this principle and its application, which is not confined to χωρογραφία, see Latte, *Philol.* lxxxvii, 1932, 265 f. [6] *Agr.* 10. 7 and 11. 1.

poem of that kind should not lack its χωρογραφία. Horace himself
furnishes a welcome testimony: on one of the occasions where he
declines to celebrate in verse the military achievements of Augustus he
says[1] *nec sermones ego mallem | repentis per humum quam res componere gestas |*
terrarumque situs et flumina dicere et arces | montibus impositas et barbara regna,
etc. But what especially concerns us here is the way in which the
authors of those descriptions first refer to a much-vexed problem (a
ζήτημα, a *quaestio*) and then decline to give a solution. This topic
appears also in Tibullus, who, in the elegy (i. 7) written to celebrate
the triumph of Messalla over the Aquitanians, touches upon his
patron's activities in the East and says (23 f.)

> Nile pater, quanam possim te dicere causa
> aut quibus in terris occuluisse caput?

Horace, then, in the passage which has scandalized so many critics,

> quibus
> mos unde deductus per omne
> tempus Amazonia securi
>
> dextras obarmet, quaerere distuli,
> nec scire fas est omnia,

seems to have blended a Pindaric type of parenthesis and a Pindaric
turn of thought with a topic derived from the poetic eulogies of
illustrious warriors fashionable in his own time. It is well known that
anything even remotely reminiscent of a panegyric was utterly dis-
tasteful to Horace.[2] I would not put it past him to have taken advantage of the Πινδαρικὸς χαρακτήρ of his parenthesis to poke fun, in
passing, at the silly pedantries of certain panegyrists, especially if he
could be sure that Drusus would take the point and appreciate the
indirect compliment paid to his own good taste.

In the concluding speech of Hannibal, Horace preserves complete
freedom and does not seem to be in the least afraid lest the ideas which
he puts into the mouth of the Carthaginian commander might prove
unsuitable for him. That can perhaps best be seen from the last stanza
with its affectionate praise of the Claudii, but it is also noticeable in the
reminiscences from the *Aeneid* in 53 ff. and in the wealth of Greek
μυθολογήματα at 61–64, which nicely balance the piece of Italic landscape inserted into the Pindaric simile of the preceding stanza (57 ff.).[3]

---

[1] *Epist.* 2. 1. 250 ff.   [2] See the scornful parody *Epist.* 1. 16. 27 ff.

[3] Even if iv. 4 were not the thoroughly Pindarizing poem which it is, I should not for a
moment doubt that the stanza 57 ff., *duris ut ilex tonsa bipennibus,* etc., was inspired by
what is perhaps Pindar's finest simile, *Pyth.* 4. 263 ff. It seems strange that this point should
have escaped most of the commentators of Horace (Tescari, however, quotes the Pindar
passage), whereas Heyne and Boeckh in their notes on *Pyth.* 4 recall Horace. Elsbeth
Harms, *Horaz in seinen Beziehungen zu Pindar* (Diss. Marburg 1936), who on p. 51 paraphrases ll. 57–60, fails to notice the Pindaric model.

Incidentally, this juxtaposition of Roman and Greek imagery, so very characteristic of Horace, should alone have sufficed to protect 61–64 from wanton deletion.[1]

The epinikion for Drusus, placed before an ode addressed to Augustus, has its counterpart in the epinikion for Tiberius (iv. 14), again followed by an ode to the Princeps. As iv. 4 is not addressed to Drusus[2] so iv. 14 is not addressed to Tiberius. But unlike the former ode, the latter has a definite addressee, Augustus. His name in the vocative appears in the first stanza, and the subsequent stanzas affirm in the most unambiguous terms that he, Augustus, is in fact the conqueror; his is the victory as are the armies: *quem . . . Vindelici didicere nuper quid Marte posses: milite nam tuo Drusus Genaunos . . . Breunosque . . . deiecit . . ., maior Neronum . . . Raetos auspiciis pepulit secundis.* If we want to appreciate the precision of these expressions, it will be well to remember their constitutional background. The legal situation of a general who was *de facto* commander-in-chief of an army was under the principate very different from what it had been before. The change is apparent when we compare the legitimate claim of an imperator under the Republic, *ductu auspicio imperioque eius Achaia capta, Corinto deleto*, etc.,[3] with the account of Tacitus[4] *ob recepta signa . . . ductu Germanici, auspiciis Tiberii.* Under the new régime it was the Princeps to whom the *auspicia* belonged[5] and who had the supreme command of all troops in the Empire;[6] he alone, with a few exceptions in special cases, was entitled to the triumph.[7] This state of affairs is perfectly reflected, in general, in the fact that Horace's triumphal ode for Drusus has no addressee and the ode for Tiberius is addressed to Augustus, and, in particular, in the

---

[1] Meineke, after others (cf. Orelli–Baiter–Hirschfelder, 'Excursus III' to iv. 4, pp. 533 f.), obelized the stanza; he was followed, among others, by Lehrs, who (p. cxxviii of his edition of Horace) feels sure that 'diese Anhäufung mythologischer Gelehrsamkeit in Hannibals Munde ist gewiß absurd'.

[2] It is not addressed to anyone. In one group of our manuscripts the poem has indeed the heading *ad urbem Romanam*. But this is due to the normalizing influence of the same 'Systemzwang' which induced Heinze to say in his introduction to the ode 'H. wendet sich nicht, wie es Pindar zu tun pflegt, mit seinem Lied an den Sieger selbst, sondern an *Roma*, und das Lied gibt sich somit . . . als Mahnung an das römische Volk', etc., and in his essay 'Die horazische Ode', *Neue Jahrb.* 1923, 153 (*Vom Geist des Römertums* 186), 'es kommt auch vor daß . . . das ganze Volk (*o Roma* IV 4, *o plebs* III 14) angeredet wird'. The latter statement, correct in regard to iii. 14, is inadequate in regard to iv. 4. A later passage in Heinze's essay (p. 168, *Vom Geist des Römert.* 211), 'Aber die Anrede *quid debeas o Roma Neronibus* (4. 37), mitten in den Panegyrikus auf Drusus gestellt, scheint wirklich nur stilistische Form', is nearer the mark. The simple truth was seen by Dacier, who also makes a sound observation on the spontaneous character of the apostrophe at 37.

[3] *CIL* i.[2] 626. Cf. Hor. *Odes* 1. 7. 27 *Teucro duce et auspice.*

[4] *Ann.* 2. 41. 1.

[5] See Mommsen, *Staatsrecht*, i.[3] 94.

[6] Ibid. ii.[3] 260, 848.

[7] Ibid. i.[3] 135 f.

expressions 14. 9 *milite . . . tuo* and 14. 33 f. *te copias, te consilium et tuos praebente divos*. The weaving of a thread of Roman constitutional law into the tissue of a Pindarizing ode might at first sight look like one of the jokes which the Muse of poetry is apt to indulge in in her less responsible moods; but on closer inspection we shall be inclined to see in it rather a symptom of the complexity inherent in almost all the poetry of the Augustan age.

By writing the epinikion for Drusus in his grandest style Horace had made it exceedingly difficult for himself to produce a poem to match this ode when he was soon afterwards called upon to celebrate the victories won by Tiberius in the course of the same campaign in which his younger brother had distinguished himself. However, he did his utmost not to allow the latter ode to fall short of the former. Throughout the poem he uses both the general structure of sacred hymns and several of their typical turns,[1] embroidering them with Pindaric motifs.[2] The splendour of the language is heightened by rare words[3] and bold new coinages. Like iv. 4, iv. 14 opens with one long unbroken period; this time it consists not of seven but of six stanzas, since the whole ode is shorter.

The most conspicuous ornament of the ode for Drusus is the pair of elaborate similes that fills its first four stanzas. This piece has its equivalent, though naturally on a smaller scale, in the poem for Tiberius: he is first compared to the irresistible stormwind and then to the mighty river in Horace's home country. The first of these two similes is introduced (20) by *qualis*, an echo of the beginning of iv. 4, the second is made independent (25 *sic tauriformis volvitur Aufidus*).

10. ODE II

For reasons which will soon become clear I have delayed what I have to say on the ode iv. 2, *Pindarum quisquis studet aemulari*,[4] a poem written earlier, though not much earlier, than the odes for the victories of

---

[1] See E. Norden, *Agnostos Theos*, 152 f.

[2] Norden, loc. cit., rightly says that the beginning with a question is in the style of Pindar; more specially it is by beginning with a bipartite question (*Quae cura patrum quaeve Quiritium*) that Horace has adapted typical Pindaric openings: cf. *Ol.* 2. 1 (tripartite); *Isthm.* 7. 1 ff., *fr.* 29 Schroeder (9 Bowra, 19 Turyn), 1 ff. (in these two cases a long series of questions at the beginning).

[3] For the extremely rare verb *aeternare* (5) and its connotations see, besides Heinze, Instinsky, *Hermes*, lxxvii, 1942, 325 n. 5. The word was to have a great future; Dante says to Brunetto Latini (*Inf.* 15. 85) *m'insegnavate come l'uom s'eterna* (χρὴ ἐφ' ὅσον ἐνδέχεται ἀθανατίζειν).

[4] For a more extensive interpretation of this ode see my paper 'Das Pindargedicht des Horaz', *Sitz. Heidelberger Akad.*, 1932–3, 2. Abh., details of which are here corrected.

Drusus and Tiberius.[1] In 17 or 16 B.C.[2] the Germanic tribes of the
Usipetes, Tencteri, and Sugambri crossed the Rhine and inflicted a
serious defeat on Lollius;[3] the danger seemed so great that Augustus
found it necessary to go to Gaul himself and safeguard the threatened
frontier. He left Rome in midsummer 16. But before he arrived on the
scene of the trouble, the Germans had withdrawn across the Rhine, and
the situation was soon under control. It was probably at an early stage
of Augustus' long absence from Rome, in the second half of the year
16, 'when the first favourable messages had arrived from the Rhine',[4]
that the Senate began preparations for an elaborate reception of the
emperor on his return to Rome. In connexion with these plans Iullus
Antonius seems to have suggested to Horace that for the occasion of
Augustus' expected triumph an epinikion after the fashion of Pindar
should be written by him, Horace.[5] That young nobleman, the younger
son of the triumvir Antonius and of Fulvia, was brought up in the
house of his stepmother Octavia, who was devoted to him; it seems to
have been for his sister's sake that Augustus treated Iullus with a
favour second only to that shown towards Agrippa and his own stepsons Tiberius and Drusus.[6] A man in such a position, even making
allowance for the sometimes slightly indiscreet zeal of youth, is not
likely to have suggested anything which he could not expect to be
welcome to the Princeps. Nor would contemporaries have thought it a
far-fetched idea that the triumph of Augustus should be celebrated in
an epinikion written by Horace in a modified Pindaric style. Not much
more than a year before Horace had proved what he could do when
called upon to compose a great patriotic hymn of an exacting type; the
quasi-pindaric structure of the *Carmen Saeculare* will not have escaped

---

[1] The wrong view that iv. 2 was written in 13 B.C. is still maintained in some editions, e.g.
those of Plessis (1924) and Tescari (1936); Villeneuve (1927), too, assumes (p. xli and
p. 151) that iv. 2 was written after iv. 4 and iv. 14. The correct date, 16 (or, perhaps, early
in 15), was made out by Dacier, who, rejecting the later date, stressed the significance of
ll. 34–36. That only the earlier date is consistent with the explicit words of the ode as well
as with its implications was extensively shown in C. Franke's careful argumentation, *Fasti
Horatiani*, 1839, 207–10. For some more recent discussions of the date see *Das Pindargedicht*,
22 n. 3.

[2] For the chronology see Groag, *RE* xiii. 1381 ff.; Schönfeld, ibid. iv. A. 660; Syme,
Cambr. Anc. Hist. x. 360 n. 1.

[3] Cf. p. 425 above.

[4] F. Bücheler, *Rh. Mus.* xliv, 1889, 319 (*Kl. Schriften*, iii. 163).

[5] This has been said by many commentators (cf. also J. Vahlen, *Monatsber. Berl. Akad.*
1878, 691 [*Gesammelte philol. Schriften*, ii. 48]), and it is in fact what appears to emerge from
Horace's ode in its entirety. It is also obvious that, if we assume that the idea of writing a
Pindaric poem was suggested by Iullus, the manner in which the vocative *Iulle* is placed
in the opening sentence is particularly appropriate, cf. p. 206 n. 1.

[6] See Plutarch, *Ant.* 87. 2. For the facts of Iullus' life (his later career and downfall
do not concern us here) cf. Groebe, *RE* i. 2584 f., and Groag, *Prosopogr. Imp. Rom.* i.[2]

the attention of competent judges. There must also have been many who remembered that about 25 B.C., after a long and hazardous campaign in the west, Horace had written, not indeed an epinikion, but a majestic Pindarizing ode in honour of Augustus and his house (i. 12, *Quem virum aut heroa*). Besides, there were in Horace's work other unmistakable signs of his thorough study of Pindar and of his genius for recasting the Theban poet's motifs and applying them to new and different purposes. What better opportunity could be found for using that splendid instrument than the celebrations planned by the Senate and people of Rome for the return of their victorious ruler? So everything conspired to make Iullus' suggestion plausible and a refusal on Horace's part exceedingly difficult. But he did refuse.

The reasons for this refusal are not immediately obvious. It may therefore be best to return to this point when we have seen what kind of substitute Horace offers. Whatever his motives were, if he decided not to fulfil the expectations of Iullus Antonius and, probably, of many other friends, and perhaps even to disappoint Augustus himself, this decision must have been the result of long and careful consideration. Whenever something uncongenial was proposed to him, such as the writing of an epic panegyric, Horace would not hesitate to turn the proposal down. But it was very different when a person intimately acquainted with the wishes of Augustus suggested a task for which Horace was singularly suited and of which he knew that if he undertook it he would give the Princeps the greatest possible satisfaction. Such a matter had to be taken very seriously. Horace did not want to hurt the feelings of the well-meaning Iullus and even less those of Augustus. As he was determined not to write a poem on the lines suggested to him, he had to make an extremely strong case for not doing so, and, moreover, to produce something that, though different from the hoped-for epinikion, might be considered no less gratifying.

In declining similar suggestions Horace had in the past resorted to an all but unassailable excuse by pleading incapacity for doing what his friends wanted him to do: when asked to extol *Caesaris invicti res* he replied[1] *cupidum . . . vires deficiunt*; to the suggestion that he might praise the warlike exploits of Augustus and Agrippa his answer was[2] *nos, Agrippa, neque haec dicere nec . . . conamur, tenues grandia*; and the whole of the ode ii. 12, *Nolis longa ferae bella Numantiae*, hinges on a *recusatio* of the same type. Such reasons were to Horace no mere excuse: he, if anyone, was by nature and self-education an εἴρων and enjoyed minimizing his own potentialities. It is also possible that he was sometimes perfectly sincere in pleading incompetence. He may have felt that his production was slow and that, if he was to say something worth

---

[1] *Sat.* 2. 1. 12 f.

[2] *Odes* 1. 6. 5 ff.

saying, he had to make a sustained effort. It is significant that a note very similar to *operosa parvus carmina fingo* had already been struck in one of his earliest works, *Sat.* 1. 4. 17 f., *di bene fecerunt inopis me quodque pusilli finxerunt animi, raro et perpauca loquentis.*

The element of exaggeration inherent in any act of εἰρωνεία is increased to almost fantastic dimensions in Horace's reply to Iullus. He magnifies the peril arising from an attempt to write after Pindar's fashion as greatly as he minimizes his own ability.[1] To make the difference between Pindar and himself impressive, he begins by outlining the scope and character of Pindar's poetry and thus produces one of the finest passages in his odes; the picture which he gives here was to determine for centuries the western world's conception of the 'Dircaean swan'.[2] Fully acquainted with Pindar's work as it lay spread out in the seventeen books of the Alexandrian edition, Horace, without going into irrelevant detail, conveys a general idea of its main themes[3] and also of those qualities of its style which seemed to him most significant. *Monte decurrens velut amnis, imbres quem super notas aluere ripas* the hymn on the power of Pindar's song rushes in an unbroken period through five full stanzas, as though the Roman poet were carried away by his admiration of a phenomenon in which there seems to act a force of nature rather than the mind of a man.[4] It is conceivable that Horace was himself aware of the one-sidedness of this picture, in which neither the artistic devices shaped in the course of a long tradition nor Pindar's own craftsmanship and painstaking care are considered; however, for Horace's immediate purpose it was all-important to widen as much as possible the gulf by which ὁ πολλὰ εἰδὼς φυᾷ is separated from the μαθόντες. It is for the same purpose that he enormously over-emphasizes the deadly risks of the task he has been asked to undertake. He seems to have forgotten his own conviction that the production of any creative work may become a matter of life and death to its creator. Addressing Asinius Pollio, who was engaged in writing the history of the civil war, he had said[5] *periculosae plenum opus aleae tractas et incedis per ignis suppositos cineri doloso*: at any step you are in danger of having your feet burned by the fire hidden under the thin layer of ashes.[6] Even greater is the boldness required of the real tragedian:[7] *ille per extentum*

---

[1] In the self-characterization, 27 ff., a fine detail, *apis . . . more modoque grata carpentis thyma per laborem plurimum*, is inspired by Simonides, as Wilamowitz observed, *Sitz. Berlin*, 1908, 340 n. 1; cf. also H. Fränkel, *Gnomon*, xxv, 1953, 388.

[2] Cf. Wilamowitz, *Pindaros*, 4.

[3] In doing so he uses a poet's freedom. For instance, what he (21) 'über Pindars θρῆνοι aussagt, ist ganz römisch gefärbt' (P. Maas, *RE* vi A. 596).

[4] For the comparison *monte decurrens velut amnis*, etc., see p. 224 n. 2 above.

[5] *Odes* 2. 1. 6 ff.

[6] The idea conveyed by *incedis* is as suitable for the prose work, the πεζὸς λόγος, of Asinius Pollio as the Icarian flight is for the Pindarizing song.   [7] *Epist.* 2. 1. 210 ff.

funem mihi posse videtur ire poeta meum qui pectus inaniter angit, inritat, mulcet, falsis terroribus implet, ut magus, et modo me Thebis, modo ponit Athenis. Most significant of all is Horace's vision of his own vocation:[1] the enthusiasm that urges him to compose his new patriotic lyrics appears to him like the spell under which the Maenad is forced to follow her powerful god across the snowy mountains in the far north; she rushes along, not heeding the dangers that menace her in the pathless wilderness; she has no choice, nor has the inspired poet: *dulce periculum est, o Lenaee, sequi deum*. And yet Horace pretends that, to deter him from any thought of Pindarizing,[2] it will be sufficient to remember that a poet who would venture on such a flight would almost certainly meet with the fate of Icarus and crash into the sea.[3] No trace here of the almost fanatical courage which Horace pictures in the Bacchus ode; now his only concern seems to be a desire for safety.

It would not have been possible for Horace to answer Iullus' request merely by declaring that he was unable to write a poem such as Iullus had suggested. Some kind of positive contribution was required, and the way of producing it was indicated by one of the common features of a *recusatio*:[4] *Scriberis Vario fortis et hostium victor . . ., nos, Agrippa, neque haec dicere nec . . . conamur, tenues grandia*, 'Varius will write the poem in your praise which you are expecting from me;

---

[1] *Odes* iii. 25; cf. pp. 257 ff. above.

[2] It now seems to me that, in the ambiguous situation in which Horace found himself, he chose deliberately the comprehensive and somewhat vague term *Pindarum aemulari*. Hence we should not try to narrow its meaning unduly. Peerlkamp's sagacious note on the difference between *aemulatio* and *imitatio* has strongly influenced the later commentators, and, if only indirectly, Pasquali, *Or. lir.* 119 f., but its contention is not borne out by the material available in *Thes. l. Lat.* i. 970–80. *aemulari* may mean μιμεῖσθαι as well as ζηλοῦν (and also φθονεῖν). From the article in the *Thesaurus* it will also be seen that T. E. Page's attempt (on *Odes* 4. 2. 1) to differentiate, '*aemulari* with the acc. is used of an honest and noble rivalry, with the dative of mean and ignoble envy', is arbitrary.

[3] Some modern commentators insist unduly on the foolishness or even insanity of Icarus' endeavour, see, for example, Heinze 'schmählich scheitern müßte jeder Versuch es ihm [Pindar] gleichzutun', and, worse, Tescari 'il suo tentativo fallirà ed egli ne avrà il danno e le beffe'. Of 'Schmach' or 'beffe' Horace says nothing; what he does say is *vitreo daturus nomina ponto*. On the importance of the idea of eternal *gloria* that accrued to Icarus see my *Pindargedicht*, 16 f. It was this aspect of the Horatian thought which, to the exclusion of everything else, inspired the Renaissance poet Sannazaro. His sonnet (63) on Icarus, the knowledge of which I owe to a letter from Professor J. H. Whitfield to the *Sunday Times* (25 Jan. 1949), ends thus:

> Ben può di sua ruina esser contento,
> s' al ciel volando a guisa di colomba
> per troppo ardir fu essanimato e spento.

> Ed hor del nome suo tutto rimbomba
> un mar si spatioso, un elemento:
> chi hebbe al mondo mai si larga tomba?

[4] Cf. p. 434 above.

I myself, Agrippa, a man of limited abilities, shall not try my hand at such a mighty task'. In the present instance Horace had no need to look round for a potential writer of the desired poem, for in the person of the young man from whom the suggestion came a most suitable candidate seemed to be at hand. Like many members of Rome's polite society, Iullus Antonius was known to be an amateur poet; from the fact that in the one scrap of evidence which tells us something about his literary activities only an epic poem is mentioned it must not, of course, be inferred that he did not dabble in lyrics as well. Not even attempts at πινδαρίζειν were beyond the ambition of some of those dilettantes: Horace, inquiring after the occupations of a young man in the suite of Tiberius, asks[1] *quid Titius . . . Pindarici fontis qui non expalluit haustus, fastidire lacus et rivos ausus apertos?* It is Iullus, then, the πατὴρ τοῦ λόγου, to whom Horace now turns as the prospective writer of a lyric[2] epinikion for Augustus' triumph:

> concines maiore poeta plectro
> Caesarem, quandoque trahet ferocis
> per sacrum clivum merita decorus
>   fronde Sygambros.

Horace does not say 'you will sing Caesar in Pindaric style', but merely 'in a style grander than I could use'; but that he contemplates, or at any rate pretends to contemplate, the possibility that Iullus might in his poem for Caesar lean on Pindar's ἐπινίκια is suggested by the two stanzas preceding the lines just quoted: *multa Dircaeum levat aura cycnum, tendit, Antoni, quotiens in altos nubium tractus: ego apis Matinae more modoque . . . operosa parvus carmina fingo.* Here the contrast between the poetry of Pindar and that of Horace himself finds its sharpest expression, and the vocative *Antoni*, adroitly embedded in the sentence which describes the power of Pindar's poetry, leads on to the subsequent *concines*. At the end of the ode the contrast between the *maius plectrum* to be used by Antonius and the smallness of Horace's own poetry is symbolized in the antithesis of the young nobleman's excessive sacrifice, *decem tauri totidemque vaccae*, and the poet's offering, a modest thing in itself, but very dear to him, and described with all the loving care which Horace, *operosa carmina fingens*, bestows on such a subject.

It is not likely that Horace really believed that Iullus would write the poem he was suggesting to him. But this is an irrelevant question. The real purpose of *concines maiore poeta plectro*, etc., is not to elicit a

---

[1] *Epist.* 1. 3. 9 ff.

[2] On this point, i.e. the impossibility of referring *concines maiore poeta plectro*, etc., to anything but a *lyric* epinikion, I have nothing to add to what I have said in my *Pindargedicht.*

poem from Iullus, but rather to fortify Horace's self-defence. More-over, the anticipation of the young man's epinikion provides a splendid opportunity for saying briefly but solemnly what Horace thinks should be said in praise of the recent victories of Augustus and of his rule in general,

> quo nihil maius meliusve terris
> fata donavere bonique divi
> nec dabunt, quamvis redeant in aurum
> tempora priscum.

By professing so strongly the loyalty, the affection, and the admiration which he felt for the Princeps Horace made it all but impossible to assume that it was any lack of sympathy with the suggested theme which prevented him from writing the triumphal song that Iullus had asked him to write. Though apparently in passing, he did pay a glorious tribute to Augustus.

Thus far the ode has appeared to us as in the main a variation, enlivened indeed by intense feeling and adorned in an uncommonly rich manner, but still a variation of the *recusatio* used more than once for similar purposes by Horace as well as by his fellow poets, containing the usual topics, 'I am not fit' (or 'not yet ready') 'for what you want me to write', or 'our friend so-and-so could do it to perfection'. Such an excuse would serve well enough so long as the poet did not feel himself under any personal obligation. But now Horace's situation was different. After the publication of the three books of his *carmina* his attitude to Augustus had changed. To the loyalty and admiration for Rome's leader which he had long felt there was now added a strong element of personal affection, for, as time went on, there grew between the Princeps and the poet a genuine friendship based on mutual under-standing, sympathy, and confidence. Being the sincere man he was, Horace could not be content with making Iullus the mouthpiece of the patriotic enthusiasm which he himself shared; he had to speak in his own person. So, after outlining in three magnificent stanzas the con-tent of the triumphal song to be composed by Iullus, he most un-expectedly starts afresh:

> tum meae, si quid loquar audiendum,
> vocis accedet bona pars et 'o sol
> pulcher, o laudande' canam recepto
> Caesare felix.
>
> teque,[1] dum procedis, io Triumphe,
> non semel dicemus, io Triumphe,
> civitas omnis dabimusque divis
> tura benignis.

---

[1] For the reading see my summary of the discussion, *Pindargedicht*, 11 n. 2.

This is an extraordinary turn. Iullus Antonius had suggested that the home-coming of the victorious ruler should be celebrated in a Pindarizing ode by the poet whom a short while ago the judgement of the most authoritative men had chosen to glorify Rome's greatest festival and so to become the Latin resuscitator of classical Greek lyrics, *Romanae fidicen lyrae*. Horace declines and steps aside, only to reappear after a moment, not in the role of a Pindarizing bard or any bard at all, but indistinguishable from any ordinary citizen. It is not without point that in his words the singular of the first person, *meae vocis*, is immediately taken up by its plural, *non semel dicemus . . . civitas omnis, dabimusque*. His imagination pictures to him the day of the expected triumph, when the majestic procession will slowly move along the Sacra via, down from the Velia, across the Forum towards the Capitol. Thousands and thousands of excited people will be lining the road on both sides and thronging in the wake of the procession, and one amidst the shouting crowd, no more conspicuous than all the others, will be Horace.[1] No Pindaric ode now, no elaborate poetry at all; the medium through which he voices his enthusiasm is the homely *versus quadratus*, 'which the Roman soldier used to sing presumably as early as the triumph of Camillus'.[2] The form is simple, almost rustic, but what a depth of affection is expressed in the words *o sol pulcher, o laudande*!

By following the movement of the poem we have found the answer to our initial question: how was it possible that Horace, who was devoted to Augustus, yet refused to write the epinikion suggested by Iullus? He had not become averse to that borrowing from Pindar to which some of his former odes owed so much not only in detail but also in their general structure. Nor is it likely that he meant from now on to forsake any kind of Pindarizing; in fact he wrote soon afterwards the two highly Pindarizing poems in honour of the Emperor's stepsons. But he did not want to eulogize Augustus himself in that manner. What he had come to feel for him, gratitude, admiration, and finally affection, was not fit to be clad in the purple of a magnificent artistic convention. It was not the bard's voice that should pay homage to the man who had been saving and was still saving Rome, Italy, and the civilized world from chaos. Just as devotion to Augustus was not the privilege of any individual, but was felt by thousands of ordinary citizens, so the language in which that devotion was voiced should be

[1] The concluding line of Propertius' elegy iii. 4, *me sat erit Sacra plaudere posse Via*, is not really similar, for there the role of the poet is put in contrast with that of the warrior.

[2] The words are Niebuhr's, more fully quoted in my article 'Die Vorgeschichte des versus quadratus', *Hermes*, lxii, 1927, 364 n. 1. That *o sol pulcher, o laudande* corresponds, not only metrically but also stylistically, to the first half of a typical *versus quadratus* was seen by R. Heinze.

one that seemed to come from the heart of the common man. 'O sol pulcher, o laudande', that is how the poet echoes the grateful rejoicing of the mass of the people. He was perfectly able to Pindarize if he chose to do so. But while studying the different styles of many masters, he had not lost the capacity for expressing great things with perfect simplicity. At the final stage of his career he could afford to leave the *vates* behind and to appear as *quivis unus ex populo*.

II. ODE V

Although after the *clades Lolliana* order on the Rhine frontier was soon restored,[1] Augustus was detained in Gaul and Spain far longer than had been expected. Not until the summer of 13 B.C. did he return to Rome. While he was still absent, Horace wrote the ode (and in all probability sent a copy of it to Augustus) which he later on placed in the book after the epinikion for Drusus. He, like many others, felt deep anxiety for the safe return of the Princeps, and whereas some time ago he had declined to write a solemn triumphal song, he now, unasked and unprompted, endeavoured to express his own feelings and those of his fellow citizens and so produced one of his most perfect poems.

The ode iv. 5 begins with a lofty, prayer-like invocation: *Divis orte bonis, optume Romulae custos gentis*, 'thou who hast come into being by the favour of the helping gods, best guardian of the race of Romulus'. On *divis bonis*[2] a word must be said. To the modern reader it seems natural, and indeed self-evident, that a god should be good. But this conception is due to the influence of Christianity. A Greek god (speaking of the pre-philosophic period), to prove himself a god, has to be powerful and superior, κρείσσων, but goodness is no primary concern of his, nor of a Roman god either. The testimony of the language is unambiguous.

---

[1] See p. 433 above.

[2] Dacier explained '*divis* ne dépend point du mot *orte*, c'est un ablatif absolu, les Grecs auroient dit θεῶν εὐμενῶν ὄντων' and compared 4. 2. 37 f. *quo nihil maius meliusve terris fata donavere bonique divi*. Most commentators have accepted this view. A few, however, e.g. Mitscherlich, Kiessling, and, following him, Heinze explain 'divis orte bonis als *Veneris sanguis* Carm. saec. 50'. I cannot believe that this is right. 4. 2. 37 f. (cf. *Epist*. 2. 1. 17) seems to show that *boni divi* are mentioned here not as the ancestors of Augustus, but as those through whose grace he came into the world to save mankind. For the point of syntax *Sat*. 2. 3. 8 *iratis natus ... dis* (cf. also *Sat*. 2. 7. 14 *Vertumnis ... natus iniquis*, 1. 5. 97 f. *Gnatia Lymphis iratis exstructa*) has often been compared. What at the beginning of the ode to Augustus matters most is not his pedigree, but rather the thought that his existence is due to an act of Providence. T. E. Page attempts a compromise: 'perhaps Horace purposely uses a phrase which suggests both ideas: Augustus is at once a proof of heaven's favour and himself of heavenly race'. This is subtle and possibly right, although it seems to imply a vagueness which would be less strange in Virgil than in a poem of Horace's maturest period.

The expression *deus bonus* in the singular is exceedingly rare,[1] and the plural, *di boni*, so far from being common, is in the main confined to one particular use, the exclamation *di boni*.[2] This exclamation clearly originated as a cry for help: a person suddenly faced with some horrible sight or anything threatening him invokes instinctively the help and protection of the gods. A Roman Catholic will cry out 'Jesus Maria', an ancient Greek Ἄπολλον ἀποτρόπαιε.[3] Naturally the formula *di boni*, like many similar ones, lost in course of time a good deal of its original force and often served merely to denote surprise, amazement, admiration, indignation, and so forth.[4] A few instances may illustrate the kind of context in which the phrase is found.[5] Caecilius *com.* 280, *di boni, quid hoc?*; Terence, *Heaut.* 254, *di boni, quid turbaest!*; *Eun.* 225, *di boni, quid hoc morbist?*; Cicero, *ad Att.* 1. 16. 5, *o, di boni, rem perditam!*; 15. 29. 1, *di boni, quanta* ἀμηχανία*!*; Sen. *Dial.* 6. 16. 2, *in qua istud urbe, di boni, loquimur?* The phrase in Sallust, *Or. Phil.* 3, *pro di boni, qui hanc urbem . . . adhuc tegitis*, shows a fine feeling for the original force of the invocation of the protecting gods, the θεοὶ ἀλεξίκακοι.[6] It follows that, when Horace said (4. 2. 37 f.) *quo nihil maius meliusve terris fata donavere bonique divi*, he meant that, together with the Μοῖραι, it was the protecting deities, the immortal guardians of Rome's welfare and her helpers in any emergency, whose munificence had given Augustus to the *orbis terrarum*. The same idea, slightly varied, is expressed in the opening words of the ode iv. 5, *Divis orte bonis* (a bad or misshapen man would be *dis iratis natus*). The next clause specifies the thought of the first: *optume Romulae custos gentis*. It has been rightly observed that these words echo the passage in the *Annals* of Ennius where, after the death

---

[1] There is no need here to discuss the *Bona Dea*, an Italic goddess whose old figure was subsequently transformed by various Greek influences (cf. Wissowa, *Religion und Kultus*, 2nd ed., 216 ff.; F. Altheim, 'Terra Mater', *Religionsgesch. Versuche und Vorarbeiten*, xxii. 2, 1931, 94 ff.; A. Greifenhagen, *Röm. Mitt.* lii, 1937, 236 ff.). It is sufficient to say that people who invoked one particular goddess as *Bona Dea* are not likely to have regarded *bonitas* as a typical quality of the gods. I suspect that *Bona Dea* was meant in the same sense, the 'Helpful One', which we find in the exclamation *di boni*.

[2] I leave aside, of course, Cic. *Nat. deor.* 3. 84 (speaking of sanctuaries in Greece) *mensas argenteas . . . in quibus quod more veteris Graeciae inscriptum esset 'bonorum deorum'*, which refers to Ἀγαθοὶ δαίμονες.

[3] An idiomatic, if somewhat free, rendering of Ἄπολλον ἀποτρόπαιε, τοῦ χασμήματος would be *di boni, quantus ille rictus!*

[4] Cf. my remarks on *si dis placet*, *Stud. It.* xxvii–xxviii, 1956, 123 f., where I might have referred also to Ellis, *Commentary on Catullus*, on 56. 6.

[5] For further evidence see *Thes. l. Lat.* ii. 2086, v. 1. 892, 905 (ibid. 1651. 70, no instances of *boni divi* are quoted except Hor. *Odes* 4. 2. 38 and 4. 5. 1).

[6] With regard to the use of *di boni* it is worth noticing that in the earliest passage in which θεοὶ ἀλεξίκακοι occur they are given the epithet ἐσθλοί: Hesiod, *Erga* 122 f. τοὶ μὲν δαίμονες ἁγνοὶ ἐπιχθόνιοι καλέονται ἐσθλοὶ ἀλεξίκακοι, φύλακες θνητῶν ἀνθρώπων (for the text, the genuine form of which is preserved in Plato, see F. Leo, *Hesiodea* [Index schol. Göttingen 1894] 17, and Wilamowitz, ad loc.). The Dioscuri, ἀλεξίκακοι *par excellence*, are invoked as ἀγαθοί (Ar. *Lys.* 1301, cf. Eur. *El.* 990).

of Romulus, the longing of the people for its ruler finds moving expression:

> o Romule, Romule die,
> qualem te patriae custodem di genuerunt![1]

But it should also be remembered that the idea of the ruler as *custos* of his people, a very old and wide-spread conception, was in the age of Augustus renewed and intensified, a process in which Hellenistic ideologies may have played a part.[2]

After the solemn invocation there follows, in a very different tone, *abes iam nimium diu*.[3] Nothing can be simpler than these words; they are the kind of language, direct, sad, and with a faint tinge of reproach, which a mother would use in addressing a son for whom she is longing. In the following sentence the initial noun, *reditum*, is at the end taken up by *redi*. Thus the main theme of the whole poem is emphatically expressed in the first stanza: *abes iam nimium diu . . . redi*. The concluding *redi* is varied and intensified in the first line of the next stanza:

> lucem redde tuae, dux bone, patriae:
> instar veris enim voltus ubi tuus
> adfulsit populo, gratior it dies
> et soles melius nitent.

The stanza is radiant with light (*lucem, adfulsit, soles . . . nitent*) and with happiness at spring's return. In pre-Hellenistic and Hellenistic eulogies of kings the comparison of the appearance of a ruler to that of the sun outshining the stars had become a hackneyed topic.[4] Horace's tact makes it natural for him to avoid such gross flattery: in a kindred but far more delicate simile[5] he conveys the idea of the blessings ensuing from Augustus' presence among his people.

But Augustus is still far away and anxiety prevails. The imploring words *lucem redde tuae . . . patriae* give rise to a new picture: as a mother with vows, omens, and prayers calls her son who has for more than a year been kept away from home across the sea, so the *patria* (how fortunate is the Latin language to have this feminine) asks Caesar:

> ut mater iuvenem, quem notus invido
> flatu Carpathii trans maris aequora

---

[1] Another Ennian phrase, *sancto . . . senatu* (*Ann.* 238) was quoted by Orelli–Baiter, note on ll. 3 f., *patrum sancto concilio* (parallels from Cicero and Virgil in Mitscherlich's note). A full list of the instances of *sanctus senatus* and the like is given by G. Forni, ʿἹερὰ ε θεὸς σύγκλητοςʾ, *Memorie dei Lincei, Classe di scienze morali*, vol. v, serie 8, 1953, 70 n. 1.

[2] Cf. my remark on *Odes* 1. 12. 49, p. 296 above.

[3] Cf. Cicero, *Att.* 2. 1. 4. *nimis abes diu*.

[4] See, besides the commentators on Horace, Housman on Manilius 4. 765.

[5] Cf. Heinze, ad loc., and Pasquali, *Or. lir.* 195. The idea of *voltus . . . tuus adfulsit populo* is based on an old and widespread religious conception; see Meuli, *Mus. Helv.* xii, 1955, 207 f.

cunctantem spatio longius annuo
dulci distinet a domo,

votis ominibusque et precibus vocat,
curvo nec faciem litore dimovet,
sic desideriis icta fidelibus
quaerit patria Caesarem.

The cumulative effect of the various words for distance, remoteness, separation, and length of time is very strong, but even more than in the words the endless longing is pictured in the unbroken period[1] that seems to extend like the curve of the sea-shore on which the loving mother's eyes are fixed. The stylistic contrast between these two stanzas and the two that follow them (17–24) is extreme: after the legato of the one long period with its subordinate clauses we hear the staccato of eight short primary sentences. There is in Horace's lyrics nothing really comparable[2] to this long series of strictly parallel asyndetic sentences, each of them filling a line, without a single enjambement to vary the uniformity of the structure and soften the rigidity of the rhythm.[3] The effect of this peculiar form is complex: it is as if we were listening to a summary, where the state of affairs in the different spheres of economic, social, and moral life is registered and each point dealt with under a separate heading;[4] but we also receive the impression of something very compact and solid, rammed together by the monotonous strokes of a big hammer. And, finally, there is in the straightness of these clauses and in their avoidance of even the slightest subordination an element of the archaic and, perhaps, the rustic, something that recalls the *vetera carmina* recited in the old days of the *patria*, whose safety and prosperity under the present rule are here extolled.[5] Now the land is free from roaming hordes (16), the sea from pirates

---

[1] Whenever I read this my favourite ode aloud, I have to take a very deep breath before plunging into the third and fourth stanzas, within which not even a slight pause is permissible.

[2] The fine Horatian scholar A. Palmer said of the ode iv. 5 (*Hermathena*, lx, 1942, 107) 'there are several things in this Ode which make me suspect that it was not written by Horace'. Such an observation should stimulate an intensive study of the uncommon features rather than lead to violent textual criticism.

[3] It is instructive to compare with these asyndetic clauses those in 4. 11. 6–12. A forerunner to 4. 5. 17–24, though in a more flexible style, may perhaps be seen in *Odes* 3. 18. 9–16, where the theme, too, is kindred: there the various blessings of the *pax dei*, here those of the *pax Augusti*.

[4] It is in keeping with the matter-of-fact character of this list that it is introduced (17) by *etenim*, a definitely 'unpoetical' word, which many poets avoid altogether. Horace uses it five times in the *Satires*, but nowhere else in his lyrics. Cf. B. Axelson, 'Unpoetische Wörter', *Publications of the New Society of Letters at Lund*, xxix, 1945, 123 n. 15.

[5] By what has here been said about the stylistic character of the lines 17–24 any attempt to interfere with *rura* at 18 is implicitly rejected: the exceptional harshness of the repetition of this word is in keeping with the exceptionally harsh structure of the two stanzas.

(19); reliability and honesty are again established (20). Turning to the moral improvements which the new régime has brought about, the renewal of the purity of married life (21) and, closely connected with it, the encouragement given to the propagation of legitimate offspring (23)[1] are singled out for special praise, obviously in agreement with the general tendencies of the social policy of Augustus and in particular with the recently enacted *Lex Iulia de adulteriis*.[2]

From the homeland and the prosperous state of its internal life the poet's mind naturally turns to the frontiers of the Empire, which, a short time ago, were exposed to the inroads of the barbarians and to sudden upheavals; no such dangers need be feared *incolumi Caesare*. Here again the sentence structure demands our attention:

> quis Parthum paveat, quis gelidum Scythen,
> quis Germania quos horrida parturit
> fetus incolumi Caesare? quis ferae
> bellum curet Hiberiae?

The four *quis* clauses, following in breathless succession, recall the anxieties of the past age when, now from one frontier and now from another, the hosts of their enemies threatened the very existence of the Romans, who no longer knew which way to look first. In contrast to the excited rush of this stanza the next stanza moves in a calm and harmonious flow, expressive of the happiness of peace:

> condit quisque diem collibus in suis
> et vitem viduas ducit ad arbores;
> hinc ad vina redit laetus et alteris
> te mensis adhibet deum.

Here the farmer, whose tilling of the soil was placed at the head of the former survey (17 f.), is shown once more, this time working in his vineyard. Horace, when he is thinking of the people of Italy, sees with his inner eye, not the hundreds of thousands that push themselves through

---

[1] The commentators, from Lambinus on, compare l. 23, *laudantur simili prole puerperae*, with Hesiod, *Erga* 235, τίκτουσιν δὲ γυναῖκες ἐοικότα τέκνα γονεῦσιν, quite properly. It should, however, be remembered that Hesiod (as was pointed out by, for example, Mazon and Wilamowitz, ad loc.), unlike Theocritus, 17. 44, and Horace, who both use his expression, did not think of adultery. What Hesiod did have in mind is best illustrated by a set formula used in many oaths, for example, in the oath sworn by the Athenians before the battle of Plataea, preserved on a stele from Acharnai (cf. L. Robert, *Études épigraphiques et philologiques*, 1938, 307 ff.), ll. 43 f. καὶ γυναῖκες τίκτοιεν ἐοικότα γονεῦσιν, εἰ δὲ μή, τέρατα; in the oath quoted by Aeschines 3 (*Ctesiph.*). 111 καὶ ἐπεύχεται αὐτοῖς μήτε γῆν καρποὺς φέρειν, μήτε γυναῖκας τέκνα τίκτειν γονεῦσιν ἐοικότα, ἀλλὰ τέρατα; the oath of Dreros (Dittenberger, *Syll.*³ 527), ll. 85 ff. καὶ μήτε μοι γᾶν καρπὸν φέρειν μήτε γυναῖκας τίκτειν κατὰ φύσιν; the oath of Hierapytna (Schwyzer, *Exempla* 198), ll. 24 ff. καὶ μήτε γᾶν μήτε δένδρεα καρπὸς φέρεν μήτε γυναῖκας τίκτεν κατὰ φύσιν.

[2] Cf. Last, *Cambr. Anc. Hist.* x. 441.

the narrow and noisy streets of Rome, but the hard-working peasants and farmers all over the peninsula. Such a vision is not surprising in a poet of Horace's taste and convictions, but it must not be forgotten that what had been a romantic idealization even at the time of the elder Cato (*De agric.* praef. 2 *maiores nostri . . . virum bonum quom laudabant, ita laudabant, bonum agricolam bonumque colonum*) was far more so in the Augustan age, when, under a highly capitalistic system, the number of landowners whose farm was their home had been, and was still, rapidly decreasing, while the greater part of the land was in the hands of wealthy people residing in the cities.[1] However, considerations like these need not impair our delight in Horace's picture. Although what he says about each man working in his own[2] vineyard and then returning to his own home must not be unduly pressed, there still remained on the Italian country-side some farmsteads to which his words would apply. Above all, a poet should not be forbidden to do what Pindar calls τὰ καλὰ τρέψαι ἔξω.

In the concluding section of his poem Horace's thought leaves behind the toils of the hot day and dwells instead on the late afternoon's work[3] and the hours of rest that follow it; *hinc ad vina redit laetus* . . .. The hints in the ode convey the atmosphere of the homely pleasures which Horace once fully described,[4]

> o noctes cenaeque deum, quibus ipse meique
> ante Larem proprium vescor vernasque procacis
> pasco libatis dapibus. prout cuique libido est

---

[1] Cf. Rostovtzeff, *Social and Economic History of the Roman Empire*, 61 ff.; Oertel, *Cambr. Anc. Hist.* x. 386; and especially Last, ibid. 435 f.; notice also Tibiletti's balanced assessment, *X. Congresso di Scienze Storiche, Relazioni*, ii, Florence 1955, 291 f. In Virgil's first eclogue the owner both of the land which Tityrus cultivates and of Tityrus himself (before his manumission) lives in Rome (cf. Leo, *Hermes*, xxxviii, 1903, 8 n. 2). An excellent account of Horace's views on the question of the *latifundia* is given by J. F. D'Alton, *Horace and his Age*, 160 f.

[2] The possessive *suis*, as has been rightly observed, does not stress the legal ownership, but the fact that now the vineyards (and the farms as a whole) are no longer threatened by violent occupation.

[3] As regards the phrase 29 *condit diem*, much harm has been done by Dacier's compromising note, '*condere diem* . . . c'est proprement *enterrer le jour*, c'est-à-dire, le finir [up to this point he is correct], le passer tout entier' and his translation 'chacun passe sans alarme les journées entieres'. So also, among others, Heinze, Plessis, Villeneuve, and Tescari ('trascorre', in support of which he wrongly quotes Lucretius 3. 1090, where the right interpretation is given by Heinze and Bailey). A different, but not less erroneous, meaning was ascribed to *condit diem* by Kiessling. The expression is in fact unambiguous: 'conditur dies cum sol occidit, aut certe paullo post solis occasum' (Lambinus); 'sees the sun down' (Wickham). Virgil's (*Ecl.* 9. 52) *condere soles*, a free adaptation of Callim. *Epigr.* 2. 3, has long been compared. A kindred idea is found in *Carm. Saec.* 9 f. *alme Sol . . . diem qui promis et celas*: the Sun is, as it were, the *condus promus* (Plaut. *Pseud.* 608; cf. also Horace's own expression, *Epist.* 1. 1. 12, *condo et compono quae mox depromere possim*), i.e. *is qui promit et condit diem*; we may regard *celare* as a choice variant of *condere*.

[4] *Sat.* 2. 6. 65 ff.

siccat inaequalis calices conviva solutus
legibus insanis, seu quis capit acria fortis
pocula seu modicis uvescit laetius. ergo
sermo oritur . . ..

After the meal the protecting gods are in the customary manner
honoured with prayers and libations. And at this point, without any
effort or artificiality, the language rises to a higher level, and the tone
becomes full and solemn. The repeated 'thee . . . thee . . . thee . . . thy
. . .' is reminiscent of sacred hymns, and at the end, when the great
σωτῆρες of Greek religion are called in, the stanza concludes in sonorous grandeur:

> et alteris
> te mensis adhibet deum:

> te multa prece, te prosequitur mero
> defuso pateris, et Laribus tuum
> miscet numen, uti Graecia Castoris
> et magni memor Herculis.

Of all the delicate transitions in Horace the present one is perhaps the
most delicate and the most convincing. The worship of Augustus in the
modest form in which it here appears is not dragged in by a turn of
flattery: it comes perfectly naturally, forming an essential part of the
simple ceremonies which are observed every evening at the hearth of
the ordinary Italian peasant. Nor should our desire to pile up evidence
for the 'ruler-cult' tempt us to misrepresent Horace's statement. We
are not justified in seeing, with Mommsen,[1] in the words *Laribus tuum
miscet numen* an allusion to the new regulation according to which at the
compita altars were erected *Laribus Augustis et Genio Caesaris*. It is more to
the point to compare the report in Dio Cassius,[2] who, speaking of the
honours conferred upon the Princeps after the final victory in the east
in 30 B.C., says καὶ ἐν τοῖς συσσιτίοις οὐχ ὅτι τοῖς κοινοῖς ἀλλὰ καὶ τοῖς
ἰδίοις πάντας αὐτῷ σπένδειν ἐκέλευσαν,[3] although I think it possible that
even the private banquets to which, together with the public ones, the
decree of the Senate refers, were somewhat more formal than the meals
of a modest household which Horace has in mind. To understand the
simple ideas underlying the last three stanzas of the ode we need not

---

[1] *Hermes*, xv, 1880, 109 f. (*Gesammelte Schriften*, vii. 181 f.). Mommsen was followed by
Kiessling, ad loc., and by Wissowa, *Rel. u. Kultus*, 2nd ed. 172 n. 4; Boehm, *RE* xii. 811;
and Frazer on Ovid, *Fasti* 5. 146. But Heinze, ad loc., rightly rejected that view since it
would not be consistent with the private domestic celebrations which form the background
of these stanzas.

[2] 51. 19. 7.

[3] Dio's passage was adduced by Dacier to illustrate Horace, *Odes* 4. 5. 31 ff.

think of any legalized form of worship, for such ideas arise in the ancient
world spontaneously whenever thankfulness for salvation from great
peril leads men to believe that he who has rescued them must have
been endowed with more than human powers. When Marius had
defeated the Cimbri at Vercellae, οἱ πολλοὶ κτίστην τε ῾Ρώμης τρίτον
ἐκεῖνον ἀνηγόρευον, ὡς οὐχ ἥττονα τοῦ Κελτικοῦ τοῦτον ἀπεωσμένον τὸν
κίνδυνον, εὐθυμούμενοί τε μετὰ παίδων καὶ γυναικῶν[1] ἕκαστοι κατ᾽ οἶκον
ἅμα τοῖς θεοῖς καὶ Μαρίῳ δείπνου καὶ λοιβῆς ἀπήρχοντο.[2]
The sentence that began with *condit quisque diem* ends:

> et Laribus tuum
> miscet numen, uti Graecia Castoris
> et magni memor Herculis.

This is a good instance of the harmonious blending of Roman and
Greek elements which delights us so often in Horace. In the Augustan
age as in the preceding period it was the opinion of some eminent
antiquarians that the Lares were the transfigured and deified souls of
dead men.[3] If this theory was known to Horace, it may have stimulated him to stress the analogy between the cult of Augustus as associated with the Lares and that of the deified Greek heroes, the Dioscuri
and Herakles. But it is not necessary to assume any special incentive,
for it was a natural conception—and a conception dear to Horace on
account of its poetical value—to list Augustus (and Romulus) with those
Greek heroes who had struggled on earth to protect mankind from
monsters and all sorts of dangers and were afterwards admitted into
heaven to be for ever δαίμονες ἁγνοὶ . . . ἐσθλοὶ ἀλεξίκακοι, φύλακες
θνητῶν ἀνθρώπων.[4]
The setting remains unchanged in the last stanza:

> 'longas o utinam, dux bone, ferias
> praestes Hesperiae' dicimus integro

---

[1] Compare *Odes* 4. 15. 27 f. *cum prole matronisque nostris rite deos prius adprecati* and notice
the context there.

[2] Plutarch, *Marius* 27. 9.

[3] Arnobius 3. 41 (p. 139. 6 Reifferscheid, p. 198. 6 Marchesi) *Varro* (cf. R. Agahd,
'M. Terenti Varronis antiqu. rer. divin.', etc., *Fleckeisens Jahrb.*, Suppl. xxiv, 1898, 189) . . .
haesitans nunc esse illos [i.e. the Lares] *Manes . . . nunc aerios rursus deos et heroas pronuntiat
appellari, nunc antiquorum sententias sequens Larvas esse dicit Lares, quasi quosdam genios et func-
torum animas mortuorum* (for the vindication of the MS reading at the end of the sentence
see Marchesi's critical apparatus and H. Hagendahl, *La Prose métrique d'Arnobe*, 1937, 40).
Cf. Paulus Festi s.v. *Laneae* (p. 121 M., 108 Lindsay) *Lares . . . animae putabantur esse hominum
redactae in numerum deorum.* For the extensive modern discussion to which these statements
have given rise see E. Tabeling, 'Mater Larum', *Frankfurter Studien z. Relig. u. Kultur der
Antike*, i, 1932, 1 ff.; K. Meuli, *Mus. Helv.* xii, 1955, 217 f.

[4] Cf. *Odes* 3. 3. 9–16 (Pollux, Hercules, Augustus, Dionysus, Romulus), *Epist.* 2. 1. 5–17
(Romulus, Dionysus, Castor and Pollux, Hercules, Augustus). For a Stoic view according
to which Herakles, the Dioscuri, and Dionysus were worshipped after their death because
they had in their lifetime been benefactors of mankind see Pohlenz, *Die Stoa*, ii. 141.

sicci mane die, dicimus uvidi
cum sol Oceano subest.

Here the tone becomes still warmer. No longer are we given a mere
description of what the farmer and his *familia* are doing after the day's
work; we are actually listening to their voices, and in their prayers
there joins now another person, the poet himself. And not he alone.
In the *dicimus* of this stanza, as in the analogous *dicemus* of the Pindar
ode (4. 2. 50), it is through the addition of 'we' that the range of the
poem is greatly widened. The *dicemus* in the ode to Iullus carried our
thoughts from the two poets and their different performances to the rejoicing of the *civitas omnis*; here, in the ode to Augustus, the farmers,
engaged in their simple celebrations, are joined by Horace and, in fact,
by the whole population of Italy, for no one who listens to the last
stanza can doubt that the prayer *longas o utinam, dux bone, ferias praestes
Hesperiae* is meant to express the wishes of all who live in the land of
Hesperia. And again, as in the Pindar ode, it is not in the role of
Romanae fidicen lyrae that Horace greets and praises the Princeps, but as
one of the people. To be so simple was possible for him only when he
had reached his full maturity. Not until then was he ready to sing of
Augustus in this sincere, modest, and moving manner.

The rare and momentous vocative *dux bone*[1] points from the end of
the ode to its beginning (5): the two invocations match and supplement each other, and the echo of the former prayer rounds off the
whole poem. In the last line, *cum sol Oceano subest*, both thought and
sound produce a fine diminuendo.

Perhaps the best means of assessing the degree of perfection which
Horace reached in *Divis orte bonis* is to compare it with a very good
poem of his earlier period, iii. 14, *Herculis ritu*. It would not be true to
say that in that ode the final topic, Horace's modest banquet, is not
linked up with the main theme, the public celebrations in honour of
Augustus.[2] But, much though we admire the poet's skill in connecting
heterogeneous elements, *Herculis ritu* seems to be moving on two different planes. In *Divis orte bonis*, on the other hand, every thought,
every picture is an organic part of a living whole, and from the first
word to the last the poem runs in an unhampered flow, as if it had its
origin in a single effortless inspiration. The difference between the
earlier and the later poem cannot be accounted for merely by the

---

[1] Heinze, on *Odes* 4. 5. 5, is right (against Kiessling) in rejecting the interpretation which
refers *dux bone* to the military leader. For the usual connotations of *dux* see, for example,
R. Syme, *The Roman Revolution*, 311; the term was much discussed in the fascist era. The
reader may do well to look up the article *dux* in *Thes. l. Lat.* For the rarity of *dux bonus*
(Hor. *Odes* 4. 8. 14 f. is different) see J. Vogt, *Hermes*, lxviii, 1933, 91 n. 4.
[2] See above, pp. 290 f.

improvement of poetic technique: the man's mind had steadily grown so that he could reach a level where consummate art became an instrument of Nature herself.

12. ODE XV

The poem which is placed at the end of Book IV is the latest of Horace's datable odes, and possibly the latest of all his poems. It was written soon after Augustus' return from the West[1] in the summer of 13 B.C.[2] Its main theme may be summed up thus: the time of war and disorder is over and the Empire will again enjoy peace and prosperity.

The ode starts with a motif ultimately derived from the exordium of Callimachus' Αἴτια,[3] the same exordium which provided the 'motto' for iv. 3, *Quem tu Melpomene*.[4] But Horace's words,

> Phoebus volentem proelia me loqui
> victas et urbis increpuit lyra,

with their stress on *proelia*, of which there is nothing in the passage of Callimachus, show clearly that he depends, not directly on Callimachus, but on Virgil's adaptation,[5]

> cum canerem reges et proelia, Cynthius aurem
> vellit et admonuit.

In the lines of Horace the old topic is given a new turn. Like Callimachus, Virgil, and Propertius,[6] Horace makes Apollo warn the poet not to embark on a subject too big for him (3 f. *ne parva Tyrrhenum per aequor vela darem*), but this warning, given in a brief clause, is followed by the much weightier argument which, beginning at the end of the first stanza, fills the three following stanzas: now that peace and order have been restored, a poet has better things to do than *proelia loqui*. The

---

[1] This *terminus post quem* has been established in an impressive demonstration by C. Franke, *Fasti Horatiani*, 223 ff.

[2] The Fasti of Amiternum have against the 4th July an entry to the effect that on that day in 13 B.C. the erection of the Ara Pacis Augustae was decreed by the Senate (*CIL* i.[2] 320; *Res gestae divi Augusti*, ed. J. Gagé, 174). It is generally considered a probable inference that the 4th July of 13 B.C. was the day of Augustus' return to Rome (cf., for example, *RE* x. 357; Gagé, op. cit. 94).

[3] *Fr.* 1. 21 ff. Pf. καὶ γὰρ ὅτε πρώτιστον ἐμοῖς ἐπὶ δέλτον ἔθηκα γούνασιν, Ἀπόλλων εἶπεν ὅ μοι Λύκιος κτλ.

[4] Cf. above, p. 407.

[5] *Ecl.* 6. 3 f.

[6] 3. 3. 13 ff.

long period in which the blessings of the *aetas Caesaris* are reviewed requires our close attention:

> tua, Caesar, aetas
>
> fruges et agris rettulit uberes
> et signa nostro restituit Iovi
>   derepta Parthorum superbis
>   postibus et vacuum duellis
>
> Ianum Quirini clausit et ordinem
> rectum evaganti frena licentiae
>   iniecit emovitque culpas
>   et veteres revocavit artis,
>
> per quas Latinum nomen et Italae
> crevere vires famaque et imperi
>   porrecta maiestas ad ortus
>   solis ab Hesperio cubili.

The first thing that strikes our ear is the vast πολυσύνδετον (... *et* ... *et* ... *et* ... *et* ... *-que* ... *et* ...), which is continued in the relative sentence of the fourth stanza (... *et* ... *-que et* ...). This structure suggests an almost unlimited sequence of beneficial achievements.[1] Another noticeable feature in this series is the use made of the prefix *re-* (*rettulit* ... *restituit* ... *revocavit*). Such a repetition when used by a stylist so careful in the variation of his phrases must be intentional. The accumulation of *re-* compounds points to a fundamental ideology underlying the régime of Augustus. So far from admitting that what had happened was a 'Roman Revolution', the Princeps took great pains to make the new system appear as the restoration of the true *res publica* and all it stood for.[2] He says himself[3] *legibus novis me auctore latis multa exempla maiorum exolescentia iam ex nostro saeculo reduxi.*[4] In Velleius

---

[1] It is perhaps more than a coincidence that in the epistle to Augustus (ii. 1), written at about the same time as *Odes* iv. 15, Horace sketches (251–6) a eulogy of the military achievements of the Princeps in a large πολυσύνδετον (four times *et*, three times *-que*). Demetrius, *Eloc.* 63, in discussing the force of the πολυσύνδετον, says ἡ γὰρ τοῦ αὐτοῦ συνδέσμου θέσις ἐμφαίνει τι ἄπειρον πλῆθος. It is worth remembering that in *Odes* 4. 5. 17–24 a very similar effect is produced by the opposite stylistic device. 'The truth of the matter is that a great chain or series is of its essence impressive, whether connectives are inserted or omitted. Whether asyndeton or polysyndeton is the more impressive in a particular place, depends on the nature of the context' (Denniston, *The Greek Particles*, xlv).

[2] 'Augustus in re publica restituenda ante omnia hoc sive secutus est sive certe prae se tulit corruptum aevum revocandum esse ad antiquos mores' (Mommsen, *Res gestae divi Augusti*, 2nd edition, 40).

[3] *Res gestae* 8. 5.

[4] Mommsen's supplement *reduxi* has been confirmed by the copy of Antiochia, where RED is preserved.

Paterculus[1] we find a passage which sounds almost like an echo of Horace's stanzas, but in all probability represents a current glorification of the rule of Augustus: *finita vicesimo anno bella civilia, sepulta externa, revocata pax . . . restituta vis legibus . . . imperium magistratuum ad pristinum redactum modum . . . prisca illa et antiqua rei publicae forma revocata; rediìt cultus agris* etc. About a special class of reforms Suetonius,[2] says: *in re militari . . . etiam ad antiquum morem nonnulla revocavit.* The suggestive verb *revocare*, which occurs more than once in these texts and is used with special emphasis in Horace's ode (12), had served patriots of the preceding generation to describe the reforms which they deemed necessary if the commonwealth was to recover from the injuries of the civil war.[3]

In the resounding conclusion of the long sentence which extols the prosperity of the present age we notice a claim in which from time immemorial the masters of one great empire after another seem to have rejoiced and which never lost the mark of its origin in Oriental grandiloquence, *porrecta . . . ad ortus solis ab Hesperio cubili.*[4] The next two stanzas (17–24) celebrate Augustus as the preserver of internal and external peace and the protector of the frontiers; the six clauses of this section are linked together by the *non* which emphatically opens each

---

[1] 2. 89. 3 f.   [2] *Aug.* 24. 1.

[3] Cic. *Marcell.* 23 *constituenda iudicia, revocanda fides*, etc.

[4] In the inscriptions on vases which Lugal-zaggisi, who conquered Sumer early in the third millennium B.C. (see S. H. Langdon in *Cambr. Anc. Hist.* i. 402), dedicated to the god Enlil in Nippur, he gives Enlil credit for having subjected the land 'from sunrise to sunset' (text in F. Thureau-Dangin, *Die Sumerischen und Akkadischen Königsinschriften*, 1907, 155). Cf. Hdt. 7. 8. 1 (speech of Xerxes) εἰ τούτους . . . καταστρεψόμεθα . . . γῆν τὴν Περσίδα ἀποδέξομεν τῷ Διὸς αἰθέρι ὁμουρέουσαν. οὐ γὰρ δὴ χώρην γε οὐδεμίαν κατόψεται ἥλιος ὁμουρέουσαν τῇ ἡμετέρῃ κτλ., Aeschines 3. 132 ὁ τῶν Περσῶν βασιλεύς, . . . ὁ τολμῶν ἐν ταῖς ἐπιστολαῖς γράφειν ὅτι δεσπότης ἐστὶν ἁπάντων ἀνθρώπων ἀφ' ἡλίου ἀνιόντος μέχρι δυομένου, Aristides Rhetor εἰς Ῥώμην 10 (ii. 94 Keil) ὅπερ γάρ τις ἔφη τῶν λογοποιῶν (i.e. Aeschines Socraticus, see Keil's note) περὶ τῆς Ἀσίας, λέγων ὅσην ὁ ἥλιος πορεύεται, ταύτης πάσης ἄρχειν ἄνδρα ἕνα κτλ. (cf. ibid. 16), Rhet. Her. 4. 33. 44 *imperii magnitudinem solis ortu atque occasu metiemur*, Cic. *Catil.* 4. 21 *Pompeius cuius res gestae atque virtutes isdem quibus solis cursus regionibus ac terminis continentur*, Sest. 67 Cn. *Pompeius . . . qui . . . imperium populi Romani orbis terrarum terminis definisset*, Sall. *Catil.* 36. 4 *imperium populi Romani . . . quoi quom ad occasum ab ortu solis omnia domita armis parerent*, etc., Crinagoras (49 Rub.), *Anth. Pal.* 16. 61, on Tiberius (cf. Cichorius, *Röm. Studien* 313 f.), Ἥλιος Ἀρμενίην ἀνιὼν ὑπὸ χερσὶ δαμεῖσαν κείνου, Γερμανίην δ' εἶδε κατερχόμενος, Claudian 21 (*De consul. Stilich. liber I*). 160 f., *ductor Stilicho tot gentibus unus, quot vel progrediens vel conspicit occiduus sol*, Menander Protector *fr.* 43 (*Fragm. Hist. Graec.* ed. C. Müller, iv. 246), speech of the Turk leader Turxanthos to the ambassador of the Byzantine emperor (cf. Gibbon, *Decline and Fall*, ch. xlii, vol. iv, p. 357 Bury), ἐμοὶ . . . ὑποκέκλιται πᾶσα ἡ γῆ, ἀρχομένη μὲν ἐκ τῶν τοῦ ἡλίου πρώτων ἀκτίνων, καταλήγουσα δὲ ἐς τὰ πέρατα τῆς ἑσπέρας. I have confined myself to passages which I noticed by chance; for a fuller collection of part of the evidence and especially for the occurrence of this motif in certain encomia on Alexander the Great see F. Christ, 'Die röm. Weltherrschaft in der antiken Dichtung', *Tübinger Beitr. z. Altertumsw.* 31. Heft, 1938, 53 ff., who does not, however, go far enough into the early history of the topic. For the kindred idea of the ocean as the boundary of the Roman world see W. Theiler, 'Das Musengedicht des Horaz', *Schriften der Königsberger Gel. Ges.* 12, 1935, 262 n. 5.

of them: it is the absence of the old evils that is stressed. The common heading of all these clauses is given in the words *custode rerum Caesare*. The idea of Caesar as *custos* is familiar,[1] but *custos rerum* (as Rome is called *caput rerum* in Livy 1. 45. 3 and elsewhere) is a bold superlative.[2]

In much the same way as in the final section of *Divis orte bonis* (4. 5. 29) the end of the last ode (25 ff.) turns from the theme of the defence of the frontiers to the pleasures and celebrations in the ordinary citizen's home. And again Horace, who began this ode, as a skilled poet, the pupil of Apollo, with an Alexandrian motif, at the end includes himself in the number of all those who in joy and gratitude remember the great warriors of the past and Anchises and his descendants, including the man who now is Rome's guardian: *nos . . . canemus*. The splendour which is spread over the last two stanzas makes them a worthy finale of this poem and of the whole book. Here, as in the *Carmen Saeculare* and several times in the late odes, an echo of the *Aeneid* enhances the dignity of the poem. But it is above all the warmth of feeling that moves the reader. The simple loveliness of this scene, *cum prole matronisque nostris . . . virtute functos more patrum duces . . . Troiamque et Anchisen et almae progeniem Veneris canemus*, calls to mind the description which Italy's greatest poet gave of the domestic life in the old days of his city, when many a woman

> favoleggiava con la sua famiglia
> de' Troiani, di Fiesole e di Roma.

Dicemus, io Triumphe, civitas omnis dabimusque divis tura benignis; . . . '*longas o utinam, dux bone, ferias praestes Hesperiae*' *dicimus* . . .; *nos . . . canemus*. It is in this manner, not as the proud poet whom *gelidum nemus Nympharumque . . . chori secernunt populo*, but by saying 'we', that Horace at long last came to praise and thank Augustus. He had to go a long way before he was able to speak like that. In some of his early epodes he did not hesitate to pretend that he, a Roman Archilochus, was addressing an assembly of the people of Rome and was speaking as their representative (*iuremus in haec, . . . eamus omnis . . . civitas, . . . nos manet Oceanus circumvagus: arva beata petamus*). Similar notes are heard in one of his earliest and most daring political odes (*tandem venias precamur . . . neve te nostris vitiis iniquum ocior aura tollat*). But this manner he gave up as soon as he realized the limits within which he had to keep if

---

[1] Cf. p. 296 above.

[2] It is equally bold when Virgil (*Georg.* 1. 26), after the model of *cura annonae, cura viarum*, etc., suggests to Octavian the possibility of his taking over the *cura terrarum*. Cf. p. 297 n. 1 above.

he wanted to be a sincere poet. It is worth noticing that no such use of the pronoun 'we' is to be found in the mass of his work between those early poems and his latest odes.[1] The *nos* of his most mellow lyrics is entirely different from the *nos* which he had formerly used. What once had been a sign of rash imitation had become the true expression of a new personal experience. Instead of usurping a place that did not belong to him Horace could now claim a right which he had earned by subjecting himself to a long and severe discipline and by listening all the time to the voice of his own true self.

[1] For the evidence see my remarks on *Odes* i. 2, pp. 250 f. above.

GENERAL INDEX

Acta ludorum saecularium, 367 ff.

Active used when a person has something done by somebody else, 215 n. 2.

Addressee, odes without, 240 n. 2.

Aeneid, its early influence, 375, 402 n. 1, 421, 430, 452.

aequabilitas, 86.

Ageing, pains of, 414 ff.

αἶνοι, *see* Fable.

— 95, 112 f., 119, 143, 336, 359.

— beginning of, 83.

Alfenus, 89 f.

Alpinus, poet, 130 n. 1.

Anacreon and Horace, 68, 179 ff.

Ἀνάγκη and Τύχη, 252 n. 1.

Anaphora, use of, in Horace, 206, 311, 333, 391 n. 5, 402.

Animals, domestic, in the *Odes*, 203.

Announcement *ABC* followed by *CBA* in the execution, 292 n. 2.

ἀπὸ κοινοῦ of preposition, 387 n. 2.

Apollo patron of Augustus, 248.

Apophthegms, Greek, transferred to Romans, 83.

Aratus, epigram by, 359.

Archilochus, 48, 60, 342 ff.

Artificialities in scholarship ('Akhilleus', 'Horatius'), 369 n. 1.

Asclepiades, epigrams of, 66, 182 n. 4.

Assembly of the people in Rome, 44 f.

Astrology, 218 f.

Attributive use of *saepe* and the like, 78 n. 1.

Auction, Roman, 5, 338.

Audire est operae pretium and kindred formulas, 81 f.

Aufidus, 3.

Augustan poetry, complexity of, 432.

Augustus, amazing letter-writer, 17 f.

— fond of early Roman comedy, 396 n. 1.

— and Horace, 17 ff., 148 ff., 353 ff., 438 ff.

— in Horace's *Odes*, 239 ff.

— portrayed by Horace, 395, 399.

Auspicia of the Princeps, 431 f.

Authenticity of works of literature questioned by ancient critics, 22 n. 1.

avaritia, danger of, 96 f., 240, 262.

Bacchylides, 66 n. 6, 189 f., 192.

Bagehot on Horace's *Satires*, 113 n. 3.

Banquet, Greek, and poetry, 36 f., 39.

Banquet, invitation to, 204, 227, 289.

— preparation for, 298.

Barrus, 102 n. 7.

'Bathos', Horatian or Victorian?, 299 f.

Bentley, 44 n. 4, 171 f., and *passim*.

Bion of Borysthenes, 6 f., 92 f.

Birth of unnatural (deformed) children, 444 n. 1.

birthday, 23.

Blandinius vetustissimus, 97–101, 317 n. 5, 428 n. 1.

Bona Dea, 441 n. 1.

Book of poems, in the Augustan period, a unity, 410.

Bringing up to date of a poem thought unnecessary, 75, 287 f.

Brutus at Athens, 9 f.

Buttmann, Philipp, 63 n. 1, 208, 346 n. 3.

Caecuban wine, different brands of, 73 n. 3.

Caesaris laudes, 148 ff., 386, 398.

Canidia, 62 ff., 69, 123, 148, 208 n. 1.

Capitol, present and past, 303 f.

Cassius Parmensis, 323 n. 6.

Castoris aedes, 65 n. 1.

Cato Uticensis, 236, 295 n. 3.

Catullus, reminiscences from, in Horace, 65 n. 1, 209 ff., 420 n. 2.

χωρογραφία in Hellenistic historiography, 429 f.

Cicero and Trebatius, 145 f.

Cinara, 311, 333, 411, 416.

clamor and *concursus* in descriptions of battle-scenes, 118.

Clough, 106, 276 n. 2.

coactor, 4 f.

columna symbolizing solid support, 252 n. 2.

Comparatio paratactica, 220, 398.

Concilium deorum, 267.

Conversion of Horace?, 254 ff.

Courbaud, Edmond, 310 n. 2, 326, 330 n. 1, and *passim*.

Cumae, 279.

Curses, ἴδοιμι τὸν δεῖνα τοιαῦτα παθόντα and the like, 29 n. 1.

— in oaths, 441 n. 1.

'Curses', type of Hellenistic poetry, 34 f.

custos, said of a ruler, *see* φύλαξ.

———— 452.

Dacier, 5 n. 6, 35 n. 4, 79 n. 4, 168 n. 1, 168 n. 6, and *passim*.

Daemons or gods intending to harm men, 204 n. 4, 410.
Dante, 432 n. 3, 452.
— his *Ulisse*, 270 f.
Dead or insignificant persons ridiculed, 88 f.
Dedication repeated at the beginning of the second half of a book, 101.
Diaeresis, bucolic, introduced by copyists, 343 n. 4.
Difficulties not to be glossed over, 274 f.
Dionysiac ecstasy, 199, 258 f.
Dirae, 34.
Double simile in Augustan poetry, 427 f., 432.

Early Roman poetry and Horace, 388.
εἰ μή σέ τι κωλύει, and the like, 350 n. 4.
εἰρωνεία, Horace's, 14, 335, 422, 434 f.
Elegiac and iambic poems in the archaic period, 36 ff.
Ennius, 124, 424 n. 1, 442 n. 1.
Epicurus, 254 ff., 319 f.
Epigrams, Greek, and Horace, 59.
— Hellenistic, transformed by Horace, 182 n. 4, 197 f., 201 ff.
— relating the history of a dedicated object, 121 f.
ἐπινίκια, 40 f., 277, 426 ff.
Epistles, Horace's, character of, 309 f., 312 ff., 393, and *passim*.
et at the end of a line, 317 n. 5.
Ethics, Hellenistic, and Horace, 232, 330 ff., 361.
Eulogies more lasting than portraits, 396.
Europa, story of, in decorative art, 194 n. 4.
Evocatio, 237 ff.

Fable, 334.
Faked works of Virgil and Horace, 21 f.
Fortuna, 226, 253 f., 256.
'From sunrise to sunset', claim of empires, 451 n. 4.
Full stop at the end of each stanza, 418 n. 3.
Furius (L. Furius Philus?), 237 f.
Future, concessive use of, 216 n. 1, 219 f.
Future used in invitation, 214 n. 2.

Gatherings of Greek citizens addressed by poets, 37 f.
Gelegenheitsgedicht, 216, 246 n. 4 (end), 313 f.
Gemination, emphatic, 217 n. 5.
Generalis invocatio of gods, 377.
Gigantomachy in decorative art, 282 f.
Goethe, 62 n. 3, 152 f., 333 n. 1, 415 n. 1.
Goodness not quality of ancient gods, 440 f.
Gracchus, Gaius, 238 f.

Grammatical gender exploited in poetry, 356.
Greek sphere and Roman sphere in the Roman mind, 265 ff.
— spoken by educated Romans, 19.

Headings (*ad Tyndaridem* and the like) not essential to ancient poems, 208 f.
Hearing more valuable than seeing, 393 n. 3.
Helios and Apollo, 371 f.
Hellenistic, *see* Epigrams, Ethics.
— poetry treating gods in a playful spirit, 194 f.
Herald, poet functioning as, 181, 289.
Herder, 254 n. 4.
Heredia, 122 n. 3.
Heroes founders of cities, 385 n. 3.
—, Greek and Roman, 294 f., 447.
Hexameters consisting of three words, 76.
Hiero of Syracuse, 277 ff.
Hipponax not author of the Strasbourg epodes, 31 n. 2.
ἱστορίη, Ionian, 270.
Horace, biography, 1 ff.
—, bolder after the *Carmen Saeculare*, 423.
— a courtier?, 293, 395.
— 'director of a chorus'?, 403 ff., 408 n. 3.
— early study of Greek lyrics, 9.
— education at school and at the university, 7 ff., 282.
— external life, after his youth, uneventful, 168.
— his father, 5 f., 103.
— love for his home country, 3 f.
— loyalty to the heroes of his youth, 12 f., 360.
— moralizer?, 270 n. 1.
— never lies, 260, 298.
— personal experience and influence of literary models, 106 f., 400.
— his philosophy, 255, and *passim*.
— problems of poetics discussed for practical purposes, 125, 388.
— 'the real H.', as opposed to the writer of patriotic lyrics?, 232 n. 1, 240.
— his religion, 140 f., 164 f., 198 f., 200 f., 255, 296, 307.
Horace's *De arte poetica* miscalled, 125 n. 3.
— *Odes* recited, not sung, 404.
Humanitas, Roman, roots of, 160, 376.
Hyperbaton, 152 n. 1, 241 n. 1.
— *magis . . ., minus . . .*, and the like, 84 f.
Hypercriticism preparatory to true understanding, 217 f., 428 ff., 443 n. 2.

Iambic hemiepes turned into dactyls, 349.

Icarus, 436 n. 3.
illuc unde abii redeo and similar formulas, 97 ff.
Imperfect in cases like *non eras* (οὐκ ἄρ' ἦσθα), 324 n. 6.
Indices lectionum sometimes written in a hurry, 71 n. 3.
Irascibility, 361.
'Irony' last expedient of despairing commentators, 46 n. 2, 254 n. 4, 348 n. 4.
Isocrates, 396.
Iullus Antonius, 433 ff.

Juno, the Carthaginian, 237 ff.
Juvenal, 113, 129, 144 f.

καὶ γάρ introducing a παράδειγμα, 185 f.
κῶμος, 40.

Landino, Cristoforo, 188 n. 2.
Landowners, 445.
Landscape, pictures of, in Augustan poetry, 110.
Lares, 446 f.
λάθε βιώσας, 319 f.
Latifundia, 445.
Latinus, pater, 133.
leges and *mores*, 384 n. 4.
Leo, Friedrich, 25 n. 4, 67, 370 n. 1, and *passim*.
Leopardi, 257 n. 1.
Livius Andronicus, 379 f.
Local patriotism in ancient Italy, 305.
Lollius, consul of 21 B.C., 425 f., 433.
Lollius Maximus, 314 f.
Lucilius, 131 f., 150 ff.
— and Horace, 79 f., 105, 107 ff., 127 f.
Lucretilis, 205 n. 4.
Ludi saeculares, 365 f., 380 n. 3.
Lyric metres, theory deriving them from basic elements, 346 f.
— poets, Greek, and Horace, 9, 424 f.
Lyrical form of topics which occur also in *sermones*, 228, 386.
Lyrics of earlier poets used in fifth-century Athens, 41.

Macaulay, 276 n. 4, 429 n. 3.
Maecenas, author of a historical work?, 221 n. 2.
— and Horace, 123, 142 f., 300, 339, 416 f.
— Horace's manner of addressing him, 69 n. 1, 217 n. 2.
— odes addressed to, 214 ff.
— present at Actium?, 71 ff.
— as writer, 16 f.
Magnanimity towards defeated enemy, 160 f., 376.

mala carmina, 149 n. 1.
Malaria, 109, 328.
Maxims, traditional, derived from both old poetry and popular philosophy, 223.
Melpomene, 306 n. 2.
μεμψιμοιρία, 90 ff., 311 f.
Mena, 336 ff.
mens nova and ἀνακαίνωσις τοῦ νοός, 257 n. 3.
Mercury and Augustus, 247 ff.
— and Horace, 163 f.
Military expeditions and explorations, 271 f.
Mommsen, 240 n. 1, 367 ff.
— at Venosa, 3 n. 4.
Motto borrowed from Greek poem, 159, 177, 291, 407.
Müller, Lucian, 343 n. 5.
Muses, one or several: number irrelevant, 281 n. 1.
Mythological themes, reproduced in lofty style, 196 f.
— — treated mockingly, 218.
Mythology, Greek, balancing Roman history, 266 f.

Name of the person addressed carefully placed, 206 n. 1, 215 n. 5, 236 n. 2, 327 n. 6, 433 n. 5.
namque introducing an *exemplum*, 185 f., 256.
Niebuhr on Horace, 2 n. 3.
nota censoria, metaphor applied to Old Comedy, 126 n. 2.
Novalis, 258 f.

Oaths, Greek, 444 n. 1.
ὀνομαστὶ κωμῳδεῖν in passing, 85 f.
Onysius?, 20 n. 2.
Overture, 230, 413.

p-alliteration, 104 n. 2.
Panegyrics, 430.
Papyrus, price of, 20 n. 5.
παράδειγμα, 213.
παράδειγμα from mythology or history, 185 f.
Parcae, singing, 375 n. 2.
parvum carmen, 398.
parvus in Horace's understatements, 335 f.
Passive, apparently impersonal, as in *ventum erat*, 115 n. 1.
patria personified, 442 f.
Pedana regio, 323 n. 3.
Peerlkamp, 289 n. 1, 302 n. 1, 400 n. 2.
Philhellenism combined with contempt for Greeks, 390.
Philosophy, moral, Roman attitude to, 312, 319.

φύλαξ (*custos*) said of a king, 296 n. 2.
Pindaric influence on Horace, 426 ff.
— themes recast by Horace, 283 ff., 293, 426 ff.
Pindar's work, Horace's survey of, 435.
Pirithous, 285.
Platonic dialogues, introductions of, used by Horace, 136 f.
Plautus in Horace's judgement, 392 f., 396.
Poems, understanding of, not dependent on outside information, 26, 208 f., 370 n. 1.
Poet protected by the gods, 187, 281.
Poetics, problems of, discussed by Latin poets, 124 f.
Poetry, Greek, once an integral part of 'real life', 36 ff.
Politeness, formulas of, Greek and Latin, 350 n. 4.
Politics read into poetry, 267 ff., 273.
Polybius, 302 f.
Polysyndeton, 224, 235, 450.
Pompey, 385 n. 2.
Pomptine Marshes, 109 f.
Poplicola cognomen of *Pedius*, 135.
Poseidippus, epigrammatist, 197 f.
Poseidonius, 212 f.
Potsherds as writing material, 20.
Prayers addressed to several gods, 247 n. 1, 293 n. 1.
— ἀποπομπή, 192, 210, 410 f.
— for the enjoyment of present blessings, 138 f., 320.
— expressing Horace's feelings, 141, 320.
— formulas of, 173, 198 n. 2, 204 n. 3, 210, 306 n. 1, 377, 410 f., 446.
Prayers and prayerlike hymns, their influence on Horace's poetry, 168.
Priamel, 230 f.
Priapea, 122 f.
Procession songs, 378 f.
Propaganda?, 240, 260, 268 n. 5, 373 n. 1.
Propempticon, 35.
Propertius and Horace, 221 n. 3.
— his relations to Maecenas, 225 n. 2.
Prophecies introduced by reservations, 358 n. 3.
— with warnings such as φύλαξαι, *vites*, *caveto*, 117 f.
Prosiness?, 373 f.
Pseudonyms of women in erotic poetry, 62.
pumicare, practice of, 357 n. 1.
pupillum fraudare, 391 n. 1.

Quaeret aliquis fortasse and the like in speeches, 54 f.
quam neque ... valuerunt perdere Marsi ...

nec ... nec ..., (*hanc*) *perdemus*: a traditional pattern, 50 n. 3.
Quasi-triads in the *Odes*, 291 f., 370 f.

r-sounds, 25, 81 n. 1.
Reader's curiosity at fault, 63 n. 1, 215 n. 1.
Recommendation-hunters, 319.
Recusatio, 219 ff., 234, 397 f., 434 f., 436 ff.
Regulus, legend of, 272 n. 5.
Reitzenstein, Richard, 27, 201 n. 3, and *passim*.
Relative clauses placed before the clauses to which they relate, 172.
Religious poetry in archaic Greece, 39 f.
Repudiating questions, 99 f.
Restoration, by Augustus, of the *res publica*, 450 f.
rex in relation to *parasitus*, 18.
Rex, puns on the cognomen, 120 n. 1.
Riddles, propounding of, no purpose of Horace's poems, 73 f., 157, 188, 208.
River, simile used of poetry, 224 n. 2.
'Roman Odes', 260 ff.
Romantic School, German, 258, 368 f.
Rome not the birthplace of Latin poets and writers, 4.
— city of, *see* Capitol, *Sacra via*.
— — —, 104 f., 115 f., 142, 303 f., 337.
— Esquiline, 123.
— Monte Testaccio, 20.
— Museo delle Terme, 367.
Ruler-cult, 247 ff., 446.
Ruhnken, 388.

Sabine farm, Horace's, 15, 141, 320.
Sacra via, 115, 439.
salsamentarius, topic in biographies, 6.
Sannazaro, 436 n. 3.
Sappho and Horace, 167, 424 f.
— *mascula*, 346.
Saviour-heroes, 384 f.
Scholiasts' tyranny, 133 f., 236, 254, 299, 304, 428 n. 1.
Schoolmastering at the end of a career, 359.
Scipio Aemilianus, 238 f., 303.
scribae quaestorii, 14 f.
Sea-gods prophesying, 189 n. 3.
Self-made man, 360.
Self-portraiture, Horace's, not meant to be a 'confession', 152 f.
Sertorius, 49.
Ship representing the State, 154 f.
Ships represented as women, 157 f.
Solon, 83, 271.
Speech at the end of a poem, 66, 428 n. 1.
σφραγίς, 362 f., 407.

Spontaneity, semblance of, 79, 166, 193, 256.
Stage directions embodied in a poem, 181 f.
Stesichorus, 209.
Stylistic differences of ancient literary genres, 159 f., 386, 406.
Suetonius, chief of the Imperial Chancery, 17.
— not a gossip-monger, 6 n. 2.
— Vita Horati, 1 ff.
Suicide of women, 194 n. 2.
Sulcius or Sulgius?, 127 n. 3.
συνάφεια, break of, in Sapphic and Alcaic stanzas, 184 n. 2.
Syntax, Greek, influencing Latin, 324 n. 3.
Systemzwang, 188, 227 n. 1., 431 n. 2.

Tarquinius, 295 n. 2.
Tempestates, 35.
Ten poems making up a book of Augustan poetry, 112.
-τερος and -τατος confused, 20 n. 4.
Terracina, 110.
testamentum, 23.
θεοὶ ἀλεξίκακοι, 441, 447.
θεωρίη, 271 f.
Tiber, inundations of, 246 n. 4.
Tibullus, 323 ff.
Tigellius Hermogenes different from Sardus Tigellius, 86 n. 2.
Tityrus, Virgil's, 445 n. 1.
Tmesis, 104 n. 3.
Transfer of the capital considered by Augustus?, 267 ff.

Transitions disguised, 275, 384, 393 f., 402.
Trebatius, 145 ff.
Triads, see Quasi-triads.
Tricolon crescendo, 351 n. 1.

u-sounds, 25 n. 3.
Unpoetical words, 240 n. 2, 443 n. 4.
urbanitas to be maintained in conversation, 129, 399.

Vahlen, 369 ff.
Varro's disciples, 387 n. 4.
Vaticanus mons, 215 n. 5.
Venusia, 2 ff.
Versus quadratus, 439.
Virgil, see Aeneid and Tityrus.
— fourth eclogue, 50 ff.
— Georgics, sections written at different times, 287 f.
Virgil's shyness, 409.
virtus, technical sense, as in comica virtus, 128 n. 3.
Vocative preceded by descriptive phrase in apposition to it, 222, 225 n. 1.

'We' = 'we, the Roman people', in the Odes, 250 f., 452 f.
Wickham, E. C., 357 n. 1.
Wieland, 140.
Wilamowitz, 65 n. 3, 172 n. 3, 200 n. 2, and passim.
Word-order, see Hyperbaton.
— 251 n. 6, 297 n. 4, 343 f.
— involved, 53 f., 111 n. 2.

POEMS AND PASSAGES DISCUSSED

AESCHINES
  3. 111: 444 n. 1.
  3. 132: 451 n. 4.
AESCHYLUS
  Pers. 659 f.: 204 n. 4.
  Prom. 890 ff.: 417 n. 3.
  1076 ff.: 358 n. 2.
ALCAEUS
  fr. 10 L. and P.: 178.
  77 L. and P.: 50 n. 2.
ANACREON, *fr.* 43 D.: 179,
  180 n. 2, 183.
ANTIPATER SIDONIUS, *Anth.*
  Pal. 9. 58. 6: 225
  n. 3.
Append. Verg., *Dirae* 37–
  39: 34.
ARCHILOCHUS, *fr.* 79 Diehl:
  27 ff., 31 f.
ARISTOPHANES
  Ach. 672 ff.: 198 n. 2.
  Birds 1734 ff.: 375 n. 2.
  Frogs 330 f.: 204 n. 4.
  Knights 624 ff.: 81 n. 4.
  Lys. 1301: 441 n. 6.
ARNOBIUS 3. 41: 447 n. 3.
AUGUSTUS, *Res gestae* 8.5:
  450.

BACCHYLIDES, *Pap. Oxy.*
  2364, *Addendum*: 66
  n. 6.
BALBUS ap. Cic. *Att.* 9. 7
  B. 2: 316 n. 5.

CAELIUS ap. Cic. *Fam.* 8.
  15. 2: 82 n. 4.
CALLIMACHUS
  fr. 1. 21 ff. Pf.: 449 n. 3.
  282 Pf.: 393 n. 3.
Carm. popul. Graec. 30 Diehl:
  186.
CATULLUS
  1. 8–10: 232.
  iv: 122.
  x: 114 f.
  xiii: 418 n. 2.
  xxxv: 68 n. 1.
  xlii: 182.
  l: 314.
  51. 13–16: 211 ff.
  liii: 120.

CATULLUS (*cont.*)
  61. 9 f.: 204 n. 4.
  64. 26: 217 n. 2.
  64. 63–65: 421 n. 1.
  68. 70 f.: 204 n. 4.
CICERO
  Att. 1. 12. 4: 357 f.
  2. 1. 4: 442 n. 3.
  9. 10. 3: 415 n. 2.
  Caecin. 75: 84 n. 2.
  Fam.: *see* Caelius.
  vii. 17: 145 n. 3.
  11. 16. 1: 350.
  Marcell. 18: 287.
  23: 376 f.
  Phil. 2. 68: 50 n. 3.
  13. 49: 49 n. 3.
  Pis. 10: 50 n. 3.
  Planc. 19–23: 305.
CORNELIUS NEPOS, *Atticus*
  19. 4 ff.: 18.

[DIO CHRYS.] 64. 8: 254
  n. 2.

ENNIUS, *Ann.* 465 f. Vahlen:
  81 f.
EURIPIDES
  Suppl. 184 f.: 55.
  fr. 911 N.²: 301 n. 1.

HERODOTUS, 7. 8. 1: 451
  n. 4.
HESIOD
  Erga 122 f.: 441 n. 6.
  235: 444 n. 1.
Hist. Aug., LAMPR., *Comm.*
  10. 9: 19 n. 6.
HORACE
  Ars. P. 409 f.: 299.
  Carm. Saec.: 364 ff.
  9 f.: 445 n. 3.
  25 ff.: 172 n. 3.
  Epist. 1. 1. 4: 415.
  1. 1. 13 ff.: 255.
  1. 1. 56: 3 n. 2.
  i. 2: 315 ff.
  1. 2. 27: 316 n. 2.
  1. 3. 9 f.: 341 n. 1, 437.
  i. 4: 323 ff.
  1. 4. 6: 324.
  i. 7: 327 ff.

HORACE *Epist.* (*cont.*)
  1. 7. 20–23: 329 ff.
  i. 13: 350 ff.
  i. 14: 310 ff.
  1. 14. 9: 311 n. 1.
  i. 17: 321 ff.
  1. 17. 43: 18 n. 4.
  i. 18: 316 ff.
  1. 18. 15: 317 n. 5.
  1. 18. 31–36: 318 n. 2.
  1. 18. 67: 318 n. 4.
  1. 18. 91 f.: 319 n. 3.
  i. 19: 339 ff.
  1. 19. 10: 340 n. 6.
  1. 19. 28: 342 ff.
  1. 19. 39: 348 f.
  i. 20: 356 ff.
  ii. 1: 383 ff.
  2. 1. 12–14: 242.
  2. 1. 16: 386 n. 3.
  2. 1. 18: 387 n. 1.
  2. 1. 31: 387 n. 2.
  2. 1. 101: 390 n. 1.
  2. 1. 124: 391 n. 2.
  2. 1. 210 ff.: 435 f.
  2. 1. 252 f.: 398.
  2. 2. 41–52: 7 ff.,
  13 f.
  2. 2. 58 ff.: 6 f.
  2. 2. 197 f.: 3 n. 3.
  Epodes i: 69 ff., 287.
  ii: 59 ff.
  iii: 68 f.
  iv: 57 f.
  v: 64.
  vi: 56 f.
  vii: 55 f.
  viii: 58 f.
  ix: 71 ff.
  9. 33 f.: 73.
  x: 24 ff.
  10. 21 f.: 32 f.
  xi: 67.
  11. 9 f.: 182 n. 4.
  xii: 58 f.
  xiii: 65 f.
  xiv: 67 f.
  xv: 67.
  15. 7 ff.: 67.
  xvi: 42 ff.
  16. 15 f.: 53 ff.
  16. 39: 48 n. 2.

HORACE (cont.)

Epodes (cont.)

xvii: 64 f.

17. 42–44: 209 n. 2.

Odes i. 1: 230 ff.

1. 1. 30 ff.: 174, 200
n. 4.

i. 2: 242 ff.

i. 4: 419 ff.

i. 6: 233 f.

1. 7. 1 ff.: 231.

i. 9: 176 f.

i. 10: 161 ff.

i. 12: 291 ff.

1. 12. 17 f.: 293.

i. 14: 154 ff.

i. 15: 188 ff.

i. 16: 207 ff.

i. 17: 204 ff.

i. 18: 177 f.

i. 19: 198 n. 1.

1. 19. 16: 204 n. 4.

i. 20: 214 ff.

1. 20. 10: 216 n. 1.

i. 21: 209 f.

1. 21. 13 ff.: 411 n. 2.

i. 22: 184 ff.

i. 23: 183 f.

1. 24. 2 ff.: 306 n. 2.

i. 27: 179 ff.

1. 27. 19: 324 n. 3.

i. 28: 74 n. 1.

i. 30: 197 ff.

i. 32: 168 ff.

1. 32. 1–4: 171 ff.

1. 32. 15 f.: 169 ff.

i. 34: 253 ff.

i. 35: 251 ff.

1. 35. 5 f.: 251 n. 6.

i. 37: 158 ff.

i. 38: 297 ff.

ii. 1: 234 ff.

2. 1. 21: 236.

2. 7. 9–14: 164.

2. 7. 10: 11 f.

ii. 12: 219 ff.

2. 12. 1–9: 266 f.

2. 12. 9: 219 f.

ii. 13: 166 ff.

ii. 16: 211 ff.

ii. 17: 217 ff.

ii. 19: 199 ff.

ii. 20: 299 ff.

iii. 1: 261 ff.

iii. 3: 267 ff.

3. 3. 53–56: 270 ff.

iii. 4: 273 ff.

HORACE Odes (cont.)

3. 4. 9–16: 274.

3. 4. 37–40: 273 n. 3.

iii. 5: 272 f.

iii. 6: 261, 285 ff.

iii. 8: 222 f.

3. 8. 27 f.: 317 n. 5.

iii. 11: 196 f.

iii. 12: 178.

iii. 13: 202 ff.

iii. 14: 288 ff.

iii. 16: 229 f.

3. 16. 20: 215 n. 5.

3. 17. 12 f.: 358 n. 3.

iii. 18: 204 n. 4, 205
n. 2.

3. 18. 11 f.: 206 n. 3.

iii. 22: 201 f.

iii. 24: 240 ff.

3. 24. 25 ff.: 242.

iii. 25: 257 ff.

3. 25. 9: 257 n. 4.

iii. 27: 192 ff.

3. 27. 58 ff.: 194 n. 2.

iii. 29: 223 ff.

3. 29. 6–8: 227 n. 1.

3. 29. 10: 225 n. 3.

iii. 30: 302 ff.

3. 30. 10 ff.: 304 f.

iv. 1: 410 ff.

iv. 2: 432 ff.

4. 2. 49: 438 n. 1.

iv. 3: 407 ff.

4. 3. 15: 408 n. 3.

iv. 4: 426 ff.

4. 4. 18–22: 428 ff.

4. 4. 57 ff.: 430 n. 3.

4. 4. 73–76: 428 n. 1.

iv. 5: 440 ff.

4. 5. 2: 442 n. 3.

4. 5. 17–24: 443.

4. 5. 18: 443 n. 5.

iv. 6: 400 ff.

4. 6. 44: 406 f.

Book IV, the central
odes (vii–ix): 426.

iv. 7: 419 ff.

4. 7. 15–29: 266.

iv. 8: 421 ff.

iv. 9: 423 ff.

4. 9. 41: 317 n. 5.

iv. 10: 414 f.

iv. 11: 416 ff.

iv. 12: 418 f.

iv. 13: 415 f.

iv. 14: 431 f.

iv. 15: 449 ff.

HORACE (cont.)

Sat. i. 1: 90 ff.

1. 1. 108: 94 f., 97 ff.

1. 1. 114 f.: 96 n. 1.

i. 2: 76 ff.

1. 2. 13: 77 n. 2.

1. 2. 31–35: 83.

1. 2. 81: 84 f.

i. 3: 86 ff.

1. 3. 65: 88 n. 1.

i. 4: 124 ff.

i. 5: 105 ff.

1. 5. 15: 109 n. 1.

1. 5. 39–44: 112.

1. 5. 51–53: 111 n. 1.

1. 5. 72: 111 n. 2.

1. 5. 77 ff.: 108 f.

1. 5. 86: 111 n. 3.

1. 5. 101 ff.: 254 n. 3.

i. 6: 101 ff.

1. 6. 56–61: 103 f.

1. 6. 71 ff.: 2 f.

1. 6. 89: 5.

i. 7: 118 ff.

1. 7. 33 f.: 119 n. 5.

i. 8: 121 ff.

1. 8. 10 f.: 123 n. 5.

1. 8. 15: 123 n. 5.

i. 9: 112 ff.

1. 9. 31–34: 117.

1. 9. 48–52: 116.

1. 9. 62 f.: 117 n. 1.

i. 10: 128 ff.

1. 10. 7–15: 128.

1. 10. 27–30: 133 ff.

1. 10. 31 ff.: 130.

1. 10. 43: 130 n. 5.

1. 10. 66: 131 n. 3.

1. 10. 84: 132 n. 2.

ii. 1: 145 ff.

2. 1. 30 ff.: 150 ff.

2. 1. 34 f.: 146.

2. 1. 34 ff.: 2.

2. 2. 2: 136.

ii. 3: 143 n. 1.

2. 3. 77: 82 n. 1.

2. 3. 264: 349.

2. 4. 1 ff.: 136.

ii. 5: 144 f.

2. 5. 62: 245 n. 3.

ii. 6: 138 ff.

2. 6. 3: 138 n. 2.

2. 6. 8 f.: 242 n. 1.

2. 6. 17: 139 f.

2. 6. 23 ff.: 141.

2. 7. 111–15: 228 n. 1.

2. 8. 4 ff.: 137.

LABEO (on the XII Tables)
ap. Gellium 20. 1.
13: 325 n. 2.
LABERIUS, 101 ff. Ribb.:
50 n. 3.
Lampoon of the Caesarian
period, p. 93 Morel:
58.
LEONIDAS, *Anth. Pal.* 7. 408.
3: 57 n. 2.
LIVY
1. 24. 7: 289 n. 1.
1. 32. 6: 289 n. 1.
v. 51–54: 268 n. 1.
xxvii. 37: 379 f.
31. 12. 9: 380 n. 3.
LUCILIUS
110 ff.: 108.
117: 108 n. 1.
620 f.: 150.
1138–41: 112 n. 2.
LUCRETIUS 5. 780 ff.: 98 f.

MACROBIUS, *Sat.* 3. 9. 6–8:
237 f.
MOSCHUS, *Europa*: 194 ff.
135: 195 n. 2.

PINDAR
Isthm. 7. 1 ff.: 293 n. 1.
Paean vi: 401.
Pyth. i: 276 ff.
1. 13: 278 n. 1.
1. 72: 279 n. 3.

PINDAR (*cont.*)
fr. 29 Schr. (9 Bowra):
293 n. 1.
PLAUTUS
Capt. 244–6: 117 n. 2.
Persa 315: 215 n. 2.
PLUTARCH, *Marius* 27. 9:
447.
POLLUX 9. 20: 225 n. 3.
PROPERTIUS
1. 3. 1–6: 427 f.
1. 13. 34: 324 n. 3.
ii. 1: 221 n. 3.
iv. 1: 413 n. 2.

SALLUST, *Or. Phil.* 3: 441.
SAPPHO, *fr.* 16 L. and P.:
231.
SENECA, *Dial.* 9. 11. 2–5:
226 n. 1.
SERVIUS on *Aen.* 12. 841:
237 f.
SIMIAS, *Anth. Pal.* 6. 113: 121.
SOPHOCLES
Ant. 1144: 204 n. 4.
El. 472 f.: 358 n. 3.
SUETONIUS
Aug. 58. 2: 139.
Vita Horati: 1 ff., 364,
383.
TACITUS
Ann. 2. 26. 2: 243 n. 2.
Dial. 2: 136 n. 1.
TERENCE, *Haut.* 93 ff.: 194
n. 1.

VARRO, *Sat. Men.* 1: 253
n. 4.
VELLEIUS PATERCULUS 2.
88. 1: 71 n. 6.
2. 89. 3 f.: 451.
VIRGIL
Aeneid 1. 1–33: 427 n. 2.
2. 311 f.: 319 n. 1.
4. 89: 225 n. 3.
4. 469 ff.: 427.
6. 817: 295 n. 2.
6. 853: 376 n. 3.
8. 98 ff.: 225 n. 3.
12. 259: 138 n. 1.
12. 828: 268.
Ecl. 1. 42: 245.
1. 82 f.: 25 n. 3.
9. 2 ff.: 241 n. 1.
10. 4 f.: 135.
Georg. 1. 26: 297 n. 1,
452 n. 2.
1. 328 f.: 244.
1. 498 ff.: 243.
2. 35: 242 n. 1.
2. 156 f.: 110.
3. 1 f.: 265.
3. 14 f.: 110.
3. 17–20: 265 f.
3. 89 ff.: 427.
3. 202–4: 265.
4. 559–66: 362 n. 2.

ZENO, *Stoic. Vet. Fragm.* i.
62 f.: 87 n. 6.

WORDS

LATIN

a, interjection, 181 n. 1,
  217 n. 3.
ad arma, ad arma, 252 n. 3.
adlaborare, 297 n. 4.
aemulari, 436 n. 2.
aeternare, 432 n. 3.
amabilis, 408 n. 3.
asellus iucundissimus, 19 n. 6.
atque and *atqui*, 327 n. 5.

boni divi, 440 f.

civicus, 235 n. 4.
columen, 217 n. 2.
condere diem, 445 n. 3.
condus promus, 445 n. 3.
conterraneus, 146 n. 5.
contundere, 386 n. 1.
crumina, 325 n. 2.
cumque, 170 f.
custos rerum, 452.

damnum, 420 n. 1.
denique = praeterea, porro, 87
  n. 1.
di boni, 441.
dux bone, 448.

et = καίτοι, 358 n. 2.
evellere herbas, 313 n. 1.

fortis regarding style, 130
  n. 5.

generare, 293 n. 3.
gestire, 272 n. 1.

hosticus, 117 n. 2.

immersabilis, 316 n. 1.
imperitare, 191 n. 5.
infans, 'speechless', 104 n. 1.

ingenuus, 348.
insinuatus, 15 n. 9.
intermiscere, 134 f.
irritat amnes, 224 n. 1.

laganum, 104 n. 4.
lasanum, 104 n. 4.
lectus (participle), 371 n. 2.
lentus, 211 n. 1.
lex regarding works of literature, 148 n. 2.
ludere, 172, 174 f.

matercula, 328 n. 2.
Megilla or *Megylla?*, 180
  n. 3.
Mevius, not *Maevius*, 26 n. 2.
monstrum, 160.
motus rei publicae, 235 n. 4.

-ne ut (or *utne*), 99 f.
nervi used of style, 147 n. 4.
nihil curo and the like, 297
  n. 4.
nobilis, 348 n. 4.
nolis in independent clauses,
  220 n. 2.

o with imperative or optative subjunctive, 242 n. 1.
o plebs, 289 n. 1.
odisse, odium, 263.
ordo, 347 n. 4.
ornare, 384 n. 3.
otium, 212 f.

paenitet me, 5 n. 6.
pectus = φρένες, 324 n. 2.
penis, 19 n. 4.
plena deo, 199 n. 1.
procedit impersonal, 82 n. 2.
prognatus, 82 n. 4.

proles, 375 n. 1.
prosperare, 375 n. 1.

-que, 375 n. 1.
-que, somewhat adversa-
  tive?, 219 n. 4.
quo = ad quem, 102 n. 2.
quodsi, concluding, 24, 332.

recantare, 209.
responsa, 376 n. 4.

salve mihi, 169 f.
sanctus senatus, 442 n. 1.
satis iam, 243 f.
si bene te novi, 316 n. 5.
sic introducing a para-
  deigma, 193 n. 1.
spernere (*aspernari*), coupled
  with *odisse*, 263.
spiritus = πνεῦμα θεοῦ, 402,
  410.
suboles, 375 n. 1.
sudor, 191.
sume tibi aliquid and the like,
  18 n. 6.

tamen in the phrases *et
  tamen, nec tamen*, 332 n. 2.
temperare, 344.
tesqua, 313 n. 2.
tinea, 358 n. 5.

unde = a quo, 102 n. 2.
ut libet, 338 n. 1.
utcumque, 217 n. 5.

vacuus, 341 n. 2.
vitalis, 147 n. 2.
vocare, 299 f.
volens, 306 n. 1.

GREEK

βίος, 151 n. 1.
ἔχειν κατ' οἶκον (*κατὰ χώραν*), 279 n. 3.
ὀροθύνειν, 224 n. 1.
παλινῳδία, 209.

προελθών introducing quotation, 179 n. 2.
σύμφωνος, 280.
σχολάζειν, 212.
τεῦχος = volumen, 356 n. 2.

τρυφή, 212 f.
ὑπερηφανεῖν, 19 n. 3.
φείδεο in prayers, 411
  n. 1.
χαῖρέ μοι, 169.